A PRACTICAL APPROACH TO

# LOCAL GOVERNMENT LAW

# A PRACTICAL APPROACH TO

# LOCAL GOVERNMENT LAW

## SECOND EDITION

John Sharland

PARTNER, SHARPE PRITCHARD

OXFORD

UNIVERSITY PRESS

# OXFORD
## UNIVERSITY PRESS

Great Clarendon Street, Oxford OX2 6DP

Oxford University Press is a department of the University of Oxford.
It furthers the University's objective of excellence in research, scholarship,
and education by publishing worldwide in

Oxford New York

Auckland Cape Town Dar es Salaam Hong Kong Karachi
Kuala Lumpur Madrid Melbourne Mexico City Nairobi
New Delhi Shanghai Taipei Toronto

With offices in

Argentina Austria Brazil Chile Czech Republic France Greece
Guatemala Hungary Italy Japan South Korea Poland Portugal
Singapore Switzerland Thailand Turkey Ukraine Vietnam

Published in the United States
by Oxford University Press Inc., New York

© John Sharland 2006

British Library Cataloguing in Publication Data

Data available

Library of Congress Cataloging in Publication Data

Data available

Typeset by RefineCatch Limited, Bungay, Suffolk
Printed in Great Britain
on acid-free paper by
Antony Rowe Ltd, Chippenham

ISBN 0–19–928347–8   978–0–19–928347–7

1 3 5 7 9 10 8 6 4 2

# PREFACE

Inevitably, after the text of this book was completed, there were further developments in this area of law. Three of these are of some importance.

In the field of negligence, the outcome of the appeal to the House of Lords in *D v East Berkshire Community Health NHS Trust* [2005] 2 WLR 993 needs to be mentioned, though it leaves the law unchanged. The approach adopted by the Court of Appeal, i.e. that in a child abuse investigation, parents are not owed a duty of care by those carrying out those investigations, was endorsed by the House of Lords. (There was a strong dissenting speech by Lord Bingham.) They decided that the appropriate level of protection for a parent in these circumstances was that clinical and other investigations must be conducted in good faith. This afforded parents a similar level of protection to those suspected of crimes generally.

Unsurprisingly the House of Lords rejected an invitation to jettison the whole concept of the duty of care. The alternative approach suggested was that the court should look back over everything that happened and decide whether the end result was acceptable. In doing so, it was proposed, the court would be guided by 'more flexible notions' than the common law standard of reasonableness and freed from the requirement to consider whether a duty of care was owed. In effect, the court would make its own value judgment. This idea was rejected by the House of Lords, as it had been by the Court of Appeal, because it was considered that, without an alternative control mechanism, this would be likely to lead to a prolonged period of uncertainty.

In the field of competition law, the extent to which a public body needs to be considered as an undertaking for and consequently subject to the competition rules, remains in doubt. The *FENIN* case (*Federación Nacional de Empresas de Instrumentación Científica, Médica, Técnica y Dental v Commission of the European Communities* [2003] 5 CMLR 1) is subject to an appeal to the European Court of Justice. The Advocate General's opinion was delivered on 10 November 2005. His recommendation is that the appeal should be allowed and the case referred back to the Court of First Instance. This is because the question of whether, in the circumstances of this case, the provision of free health services could be classified as a non-economic activity depended on whether public and private health sectors co-existed or whether the provision of public health care predominated in Spain. There was no information about this in the judgment of the Court of First Instance. Hence the Advocate General's recommendation for the case to be referred back to that court for the necessary fact finding to take place. The essential point is: where a state body is acting in what is referred to as the 'political sphere', it is not subject to competition law. However, if the state, or a part of the state, participates in a market, it must follow the same rules as everybody else.

Finally, the important human rights decision *R v Governors of Denbigh High School* [2005] 1 WLR 3372 needs to be mentioned. The claimant is a Muslim school girl who attended school dressed in the *jilbab*, a form of dress which concealed the shape of her arms and legs. This was considered by some to indicate a stricter adherence to the Muslim faith than the wearing an alternative form of dress that was permitted by the school; this was the *shalwar kameeze* which consisted of a smock and loose trousers. The claimant was not allowed at school wearing the *jilbab* and she lost almost two years' schooling before she was able to attend another school which permitted her to wear the *jilbab*.

The Court of Appeal, reversing the decision of the judge at first instance, held that the claimant had been unlawfully excluded from school, had been denied her right to manifest her religion, contrary to Article 9 of the Convention and had been denied access to suitable and appropriate education, contrary to Article 2 of the First Protocol.

The court distinguished the decision in *Sahin v Turkey* 41 EHRR 109 in which the European Court of Human Rights had upheld the right to ban female students from wearing Islamic headscarves at university on the ground that this was an interference with Article 9 rights, which was necessary in a democratic society. The court in that case was much influenced by the fact that the headscarf was seen as having political significance and that a secular state was entitled to take a stance against what they saw as symbols of extremist political movements.

The Court of Appeal noted that the UK, unlike Turkey, was not a secular state. Indeed, express provision was made for the teaching of religion in schools. The school itself also permitted certain types of Islamic dress including headscarves. The issue was therefore whether this particular restriction on uniform was justified as being necessary in a democratic society. Brooke LJ held that the school's decision-making should have been along the following lines:

(1) Has the claimant established that she has a relevant Convention right that qualifies for protection under Article 9(1)?
(2) Subject to any justification that is established under Article 9(2) has the Convention right been violated?
(3) Was the interference with her Convention right prescribed by law in the Convention sense of that expression?
(4) Did the interference have a legitimate aim?
(5) What are the considerations that need to be balanced against each other when determining whether the interference was necessary in a democratic society for the purpose of achieving that aim?
(6) Was the interference justified under Article 9(2)?

The school had not considered that the claimant had a right under English law and that the onus lay on them to justify interference with that right. Instead, they started from the premise that its school uniform policy was there to be obeyed. They had approached the issue in completely the wrong way and the appeal was allowed.

The Court of Appeal also expressed the hope that schools would receive guidance on human rights issues. However, guidance is difficult to provide when the law is in a state of uncertainty. The decision-making process outlined above requires teachers and governors to grapple with a set of fearsomely difficult concepts about which judges and lawyers hold divergent views. This case is going to be considered by the House of Lords. In view of the number of potential human rights issues affecting schools, they are likely to need, not only guidance, but specific legal advice on issues which could give rise to claims.

John Sharland
November 2005

# CONTENTS SUMMARY

# CONTENTS

# TABLE OF CASES

# TABLE OF STATUTES

# TABLE OF STATUTORY INSTRUMENTS

# TABLE OF EUROPEAN LEGISLATION

# 1

# ORIGINS AND BACKGROUND

## A   THE ORIGINS OF LOCAL GOVERNMENT IN BRITAIN

The modern system of local government derives from a variety of arrangements which **1.01**
were developed on an ad hoc basis throughout history. Some have obscure origins dating
back to medieval times. Others are much more recent. The process is, of course, continuing
to this day. In general, the pattern has been that a particular need for some form of
government has given rise to a response from those within the community who considered it to be their duty to rise to the challenge. The most important developments in
local government took place in the nineteenth century. This was in some ways the great
era in local government with figures such as Joseph Chamberlain becoming a political
figure of national importance as Mayor of Birmingham before becoming a Member of
Parliament. The three most important components from which the system was developed
in the nineteenth century were the parishes, the justices of the peace, and the municipal
corporations.

The origins of the parishes lay in the variety of arrangements which citizens made in the **1.02**
time when some form of self-government was the only possible form of effective government for isolated communities. Justices of the peace began to be appointed in the thirteenth
century. Their purpose was to ensure the maintenance of law and order. However, in the
fifteenth century they were also given responsibility for roads and bridges. Municipal
corporations arose from the right of urban communities to purchase their right to self-
government from the Crown. The important responsibility for the collection and distribution of poor relief, the origin of the modern social security system, was given to the overseers
of the parishes in 1601. Their entitlement to raise money from the occupiers and tenants
within their parishes was the origin of the rating system.

Throughout history it could be said that there was a loose hierarchy in local administration. **1.03**

For instance, a sheriff of a county ranked higher than a justice of the peace who in turn ranked higher than an overseer of a parish. There was, however, no real system. During the eighteenth century the business of local administration began to get complicated. There was a rapidly growing population and advances in science, technology and engineering. The industrial revolution which began towards the end of the eighteenth century brought about a radically different type of society in which the urban population was increasingly important. As new requirements for administration arose, new bodies were established to answer these needs.

**1.04**  By the early nineteenth century there was a clear need for major structural reform. The task fell to the reforming Whig administration of the 1830s which set about creating a streamlined system of local government in the wake of the passing of the 1832 Great Reform Act, which abolished rotten boroughs and established a more democratic system of parliamentary representation. The Poor Law Act 1834 broke down the parishes and set up local Poor Law Unions to replace them. The Municipal Corporations Act of the following year removed the powers of the old corporations and transferred them to elected bodies. It is these bodies, with their elected membership served by salaried officers, which form the basis of the modern system.

**1.05**  The next important change was brought about by the Local Government Act 1888. This set up a dual system. In the larger towns there were county boroughs which had responsibility for all aspects of local government. In the shire counties, responsibilities were divided between the county councils and rural or urban district councils. During the twentieth century, the history of local government was one of power being taken away from local authorities and responsibilities for important functions transferred to central government. Local authorities lost responsibility for social security, for health and, to a large extent, education. In the meantime the role of the state extended into other areas and local authorities were charged with overseeing some of the most important activities: social housing, children's welfare, and town and country planning.

**1.06**  There was no real reason why the arrangements made in 1888 should not have lasted until the present day. However, from the 1960s onwards, the system fell victim to political tinkering. In 1965 the London County Council was abolished and the Greater London Council was established bringing in a two-tier system of local government in London which included the outer London Boroughs. Then in 1972 there was a rearrangement of counties and the introduction of the two-tier system to the other large conurbations with the creation of metropolitan counties. The restructuring imposed by the Local Government Act 1972 was partly, but not wholly, based on the Redcliffe-Maud report which had been commissioned by the Wilson government which did not have time to implement the recommendations before losing the 1970 election.

**1.07**  In 1985 the GLC was abolished along with the metropolitan counties. London and the other large cities reverted to a unitary system again. In 1988, the Inner London Education Authority, which had been responsible for education functions in Inner London, was abolished and the London boroughs became education authorities. By 1992 it was decided that local government would benefit from another shake-up. The two-tier system of regions and districts in Scotland and counties and districts in Wales was replaced by a system of unitary authorities. In England, instead of legislating for any system, arrangements were made for a Commission to be established to make recommendations for each area of the country.

The result of this reorganisation was the creation of a number of new unitary authorities  **1.08**
such as Milton Keynes, York, Isle of Wight, and Bath and North East Somerset, which like the city councils have responsibility for all local authority functions within their area. In addition the old two tier (county and district) system was retained in most areas. Further changes have taken place since the election of the Labour government in 1997. Following successful referenda, the Scottish Parliament and the National Assembly for Wales were established. These created a large measure of self-government. A new tier of local government was created for London by the Greater London Authority Act 1999. The office of the Mayor of London was established together with a new London Assembly. A wide range of transport powers, those of the highway authority in respect of trunk roads, responsibility for buses and, after the part privatisation of the underground system had reached the point of no return, the tube network, were given to a new body, Transport for London.

Another attempt to create a new layer of local government has probably proved abortive.  **1.09**
The Regional Assemblies Act 1998 provided for the setting up of elected bodies based on regions. The establishment of an assembly for a region required a successful referendum first. The first such referendum, which sought a view on the proposal for an assembly for the North-East, resulted in a decisive rejection of the idea.

## B    THE FUNCTIONS OF LOCAL AUTHORITIES

In general, county councils are responsible for social services, education, transport, high-  **1.10**
ways, and some planning functions particularly in connection with minerals and waste. District councils are responsible for housing, environmental health and trading standards, and most planning issues. Unitary authorities have responsibility for all these functions. In London, the Mayor and Greater London Authority have a strategic overview role with the power to give policy direction and veto individual planning decisions. Parish and community councils have the most local functions of all, with powers over allotments, leisure grounds and the like within their area.

## C    LOCAL GOVERNMENT FINANCE

The council tax has continued to attract controversy but it shows no sign of going away.  **1.11**
However, it contributes only a small proportion of local government income. The largest component of local authority revenue expenditure is still financed by central government in the form of grants. Authorities also receive a share of commercial rates, which are now set nationally (the national non-domestic rate). The remainder is financed by council tax, essentially a property tax dependent on the value of the property occupied by the tax payers. The government has the power to determine the maximum level of council tax an authority can

levy. Other authorities, such as county councils and the GLA, are precepting authorities i.e. they receive their local share of revenue finance in the form of a precept collected by authorities responsible for levying council tax. Fire and police authorities are also financed in this way.

**1.12** There have been various proposals for the reform of the council tax. There have been protests about the levels of council tax in some areas. The tax is a disproportionate burden on those with low incomes but properties with a relatively high value, typically the elderly. The Liberal Democrats have proposed replacing it with a local income tax. The Government has set up an inquiry into local taxation, led by Sir Michael Lyons, which is due to report late in 2005.

**1.13** Capital expenditure is normally financed by borrowing, though an increasing number of large capital projects are financed by way of a private finance initiative in which a private sector body finances and builds a new facility and then operates it for a lengthy period, usually twenty-five years.

Traditionally central government has exercised tight control over local authority capital expenditure. There has recently been a relaxation in the rules over capital expenditure with 'prudential borrowing' allowing local authorities a greater say in determining how much capital they need to borrow and spend.

## D   THE STRUCTURE OF LOCAL AUTHORITIES

**1.14** There have been significant changes to the internal structure of local authorities in recent years. These were imposed on authorities by the Local Government Act 2000. The traditional structure of a series of committees covering the main service areas has been replaced. Authorities were given a choice of possible replacement structures. The idea of elected mayors, which was at one time thought to be a means of raising the profile of local government, has not caught on. Most authorities have chosen a form of cabinet government. This means that there is a cabinet consisting of councillors each with responsibility for a key area of the authority's functions. However, there are still meetings of full Council, presided over by the mayor or chairman, which all members of the authority attend. Some vestiges of the old arrangements still survive, particularly planning committees.

**1.15** In most local authorities councillors are elected largely on the basis of which political party they represent. Particularly in larger authorities, the political groups will be well organised. They will determine their policies at meetings of the group and vote in accordance with these policies in council meetings. In some of the smaller districts independent members may still play an important role. Only one major authority is non-party political: the Corporation of London, where members do not stand for election on the basis of party political affiliations. Because of the tendency of the electorate to become disenchanted with governments, the party which has been in opposition nationally has tended to perform well in local elections. Another feature of local government has been the number of councils where there has been no overall control and which rely on power-sharing arrangements made between two of the three main political parties.

Traditionally, in local government the Conservative party were associated with policies of **1.16** low local taxation, disposing of assets, particularly council accommodation (an example of a national policy which originated in local government), and externalisation of services. The Labour party used to be associated with maintaining services, regeneration, economic development, and equal opportunities initiatives. The Liberal Democrats were associated with environmental improvements and initiatives to bring services closer to the communities for which they are provided. This traditional pattern of political association has broken down from the early 1990s. Authorities have, whatever their political complexion, shown an increasing willingness to enter into arrangements with the private sector to ensure that their projects go ahead. There has also been an increased tendency for services to be externalised in response to the need to ensure greater capital investment.

In the new structures of local authorities, there is still normally a close association between **1.17** the officer hierarchy and the political structure. Though there are no longer committee chairs, chief officers usually have a single member to whom they are accountable. There are a few appointments which a local authority must make. These include a head of paid service, normally called the Chief Executive. There is also an obligation to appoint an officer to be responsible for the financial affairs of the authority and a monitoring officer. Other statutory posts include a director of education and a person to be responsible for children's services. Local authorities are still largely divided into departments, normally each headed by an officer called a director. These departments will normally reflect the main functions of that authority. For instance, it is to be expected that in a large metropolitan authority there will be a director of housing, a director of education, and so on.

---

# E THE FUTURE OF LOCAL GOVERNMENT

In the last few years, the centralising tendencies of successive governments have to some **1.18** extent been reversed. The tendency to move powers away from local authorities has not completely disappeared. Education, in particular, has increasingly been the subject of direct control by government, at the same time as powers have been removed from authorities and given to schools themselves. When it is felt by government that a local authority will not be able to deliver, another solution is found. For instance, responsibility for planning in key areas where ensuring rapid development is seen as a political imperative, is given to English Partnerships, a quango, rather than left with the responsible local authority. It is difficult to escape the conclusion that in certain circles within government there is a lack of faith in the ability of local authorities to deliver.

On the other hand, some of the more restrictive controls over local authorities have been **1.19** removed. In addition, local authorities have been given new powers, the effects of which could be very far-reaching. The prescriptive compulsory competitive tendering requirements of the Local Government Act 1988 were repealed by the 1999 Act and replaced by the best value regime. The requirements to review local authority services have been changed since the original legislation to give local authorities the power to decide which services to review and when. The introduction of the well-being power in the LGA 2000 represents a huge increase in local authority powers, effectively allowing them to take such action as they see fit if they consider that it will be of benefit to their area. The LGA 2003 gives authorities, in certain circumstances, the power to trade with the private sector. This all represents a considerable degree of confidence in local government. The challenge though for local authorities is to make use of these powers.

# 2

# COUNCILLORS

## A   ELIGIBILITY

### Eligibility requirements—general

**2.01**   There are four broad requirements for eligibility to serve as a councillor. They concern citizenship, age, residence, and the absence of disqualification. Candidates must be British subjects, citizens of the Republic of Ireland, or citizens of the European Union who do not fall into either of those two categories: Local Government Act (LGA) 1972, s. 79(1). The expression 'British subject' is defined for this purpose by the British Nationality Act 1981, s. 51(1)(b) as 'a person who has the status of a Commonwealth citizen under this Act'. Therefore citizens of the countries listed in Schedule 3 to that Act are entitled to stand for elected office in local government. They must have attained the age of 21 years on what is referred to as the 'relevant day'. This, confusingly, is two dates in elections requiring nomination: the date of nomination and the date of the election. In the case of all other elections, it is the date of the poll: LGA 1972, s. 79(2).

### Residence requirements

**2.02**   The residence requirements are more complex. The candidate must:

(a)   be a local government elector for that area on the 'relevant day' and continue to be thereafter; or

(b)   have occupied as owner or tenant any land or other premises in that area for 12 months preceding that day; or

(c)   have had his or her principal or only place of work for the preceding 12 months in that area; or

(d)   have resided in the area for the preceding 12 months; or

(e)   in the case of parish or community councils, have resided in the area of the parish or community or within three miles of it for the preceding 12 months.

The word 'land' is defined in s. 270 of the LGA 1972 as including 'any interest in land and any easement or right in, to or over land'. This is a very wide definition. It is curious to reflect that possession of an easement or other obscure interest in land is thought to be a sufficient interest in an area for a person to be allowed to stand for public office. Given this wide definition, it is questionable whether the word 'premises' was needed as well. This word is not defined in the Act but modern case law gives it a wide meaning. See, for instance, *Gardiner v Sevenoaks RDC* [1950] 2 All ER 84, in which it was held to include man-made enclosed caves, and *Bracey v Read* [1962] 3 All ER 472, in which it was decided that the word should encompass 'gallops' on open downland.

**2.03**   The word 'work' was considered in the Court of Appeal in *Parker v Yeo* (1992) 90 LGR 645. In this case Mr Yeo had been a city councillor since 1983 and based his qualification on the fact that he was employed within the city council's area. In 1990, the business for which he worked ceased trading and he retired. He continued to sit as a councillor and in May 1992 he was re-elected. He based his qualification on the ground that his duties as a city councillor which he undertook mainly at the civic centre constituted 'work' within the meaning of

LGA 1972, s. 79(1)(c). He had attended and sat on various committees and working groups, served as deputy leader of the Conservative group, and no doubt dealt with correspondence and performed numerous other tasks. His election was challenged by the unsuccessful candidate. The petition succeeded in the Divisional Court, but this was overturned by the Court of Appeal. It was held that the word 'work' should be given its ordinary and natural meaning, that the duties Mr Yeo undertook at the civic centre would normally be described as work, and that there was much to be said on policy grounds for allowing those who used their time and energy in serving a particular area to be able to use this service as a reason for continuing to represent that area. It was suggested that voluntary work or the work of a candidate in 'shadowing' a councillor could also constitute work for the purposes of this section.

The issue of residence was considered in *Fox v Stirk and Bristol Registration Officer* [1970] 2 QB **2.04** 463, in which the Court of Appeal held that students in a hall of residence were entitled to be registered as electors for the area in which the hall was situated. The students occupied their rooms for at least 29 weeks of the year, sometimes longer, but they had to vacate them for at least six weeks each year. Lord Denning said there were three general principles to be considered:

(a)  A person may have more than one residence.
(b)  Temporary presence at an address does not make a person resident at that address.
(c)  Temporary absence does not lead to loss of residence.

The word has no technical or special meaning but ordinarily implies a degree of permanence.

The case of *Hipperson v Electoral Registration Officer for Newbury District* [1985] QB 1060 con- **2.05** cerned the eligibility to stand for the local authority of the women encamped at Greenham Common. Their names were included in the electoral register, then removed by the electoral registration officer as a result of an objection. Their exclusion was based on the illegality of their residence. Their appeal to the county court was allowed on the ground that, while they had always been in breach of s. 137 of the Highways Act 1980, the illegality of their residence did not affect their qualification for voting. An appeal by the objector to the Court of Appeal was dismissed. The Court held that the standard of accommodation was irrelevant: there was no need for people to live in a permanent building in order to be able to vote. The fact that their residence there was precarious, in the sense that they might well soon have to leave, was also irrelevant. As Donaldson MR remarked: 'In practice [the camp] seems to have a marked degree of continuity.' It is surprising that this argument was put forward. The notion of disqualification on the basis of precariousness seems alarming as well as extremely difficult to implement. Would those in danger of eviction because of rent or mortgage arrears be disqualified? This would be placing quite a burden on the shoulders of the electoral registration officer. It was also pointed out that disqualification on the basis of illegality would also have very wide consequences, disqualifying a whole range of citizens. However, a distinction was drawn between breach of a statute and breach of a court order: 'If a court has ordered a citizen to cease to reside at a particular address, he cannot rely on his continued presence at that address as a qualification for the franchise.'

## B   DISQUALIFICATIONS

**2.06**   In addition to holding the above qualifications, a candidate for membership of a local authority must not be disqualified. The disqualifications set out in s. 80 of the 1972 Act are as follows:

(a)   holding any office or employment, appointments to which are or may be made or confirmed by the local authority;

(b)   being bankrupt or having made a composition or arrangement with creditors;

(c)   having been sentenced within the previous five years to a term of imprisonment (whether suspended or not) of not less than three months;

(d)   being disqualified under Part III of the Representation of the People Act 1983 or under the Audit Commission Act 1998.

A further disqualification was added by the Local Government and Housing Act 1989, in that holders of 'politically restricted' posts in a local authority cannot stand for election in any local authority. Politically restricted posts are dealt with in the next chapter.

## C   RIGHTS TO INFORMATION

### Statutory rights

**2.07**   Councillors have more rights to information than do members of the public. The public's rights are considered in chapter 15. The rights of councillors have fuelled a considerable amount of litigation. They derive from common law and statute. The statutory rights are contained in s. 100F(1) of the LGA 1972:

> any document which is in the possession or under the control of a principal council and contains material relating to any business to be transacted at a meeting of the council or a committee or sub-committee of the council shall, subject to subsection (2) below, be open to inspection by any member of the council.

**2.08**   Subsection (2) allows documents not to be disclosed if they contain exempt information falling within paragraphs 1 to 6, 9, 11, 12, and 14 of Part I of Schedule 12A to the Act. Schedule 12A is set out in Appendix 1 below. It sets out the categories of information which a local authority may deem too sensitive for the general public. Section 100F(2) in effect designates some of the categories as super-sensitive, too confidential even for the eyes of elected members. The reasoning behind the choice of paragraphs is not entirely clear. Personal information is obviously regarded as highly confidential, unless the identity of informants can be regarded as personal; commercial information is seen as rather less sensitive.

**2.09**   There are two other important limitations contained within s. 100F(1). First, the information must be 'in the possession or under the control of' the council. Some information could be available on council premises but fall outside this description, such as information relating to the activities of a trade union or a political party. Secondly, the information must relate to business being transacted at a council meeting, or a committee or sub-committee meeting. Information about matters which have not come to the attention of one of these bodies is excluded altogether from the section. Section 100F(5) provides that 'the rights conferred by this section on a member of a principal council are in addition to any other rights he may have apart from this section'. Thus it is clear that the common law rights of councillors to information are preserved.

## The 'need to know' test

The extent of these rights was considered by the House of Lords in *R v Birmingham City*   **2.10**
*Council, ex parte O* [1983] 1 AC 578. This concerned a councillor, who was not a member of the social services committee but who had information which led her to have some anxiety about a family who had been approved by the city council as prospective adopters. She sought access to the social services files and, on the advice of the Council's legal adviser, the council resolved to disclose them. This decision was challenged by the family who were the subject of the enquiry. However, as the courts perceived, the real conflict was between the city council and its social workers. The House of Lords reviewed the case law and con-cluded that there was no right to a 'roving commission', that simply being a councillor did not entitle a person to trawl through every filing cabinet in the Town Hall in the hope of finding something interesting and that 'mere curiosity' was not in itself a good enough reason for granting access. They concluded too that committee members had the right to all information relating to the business of that committee. Then Lord Brightman, giving the leading judgment, continued (p. 594):

> In the case of a committee of which the councillor is not a member, different considerations must apply. The outside councillor, as I will call him, has no automatic right of access to documentary material. Of him, it cannot be said that he necessarily has good reason, and is necessarily entitled, to inspect all written material in the possession of the council and every committee and the officers thereof. What Donaldson LJ described as a 'need to know' must be demonstrated.

Whether a councillor does have a 'need to know' is of course a question to which there may be scope for considerable disagreement. It is a question for the council to decide. Provided that this decision is not challengeable on any of the administrative law grounds the courts will not interfere. In this case the House of Lords declined to interfere with the decision to grant disclosure.

## Rights of committee members to information

For committee members, the House of Lords was prepared to grant very wide access indeed   **2.11**
(p. 594):

> In the case of a committee of which he is a member, a councillor as a general rule will *ex hypothesi* have good reason for access to all written material of such committee. So I do not doubt that each member of the social services committee is entitled by virtue of his office to see all the papers which have come into the possession of a social worker in the course of his duties as an employee of the council. There is no room for secrecy as between a social worker and a member of the social services committee.

The words 'as a general rule' might still allow for exceptions. In spite of the fact that the above passage indicates that a member of the social services committee does in fact have a 'roving commission' it is still possible that a council should decline access to committee members if it was considered that a councillor was seeking the information for improper motives.

**2.12**  The *Birmingham* case established that a councillor's 'need to know' can override confidentiality. The documents in that case were highly confidential, and the councillor was under a duty, once they were disclosed to her, to respect that confidentiality. However, once a need to know is established, then it is no answer for the council to plead confidentiality as a ground of non-disclosure. Nor is it an answer for the council to say that there are other means of obtaining the same information.

**2.13**  In *R v Hackney LBC, ex parte Gamper* [1985] 1 WLR 1229, the applicant David Gamper was leader of the opposition Liberal Group on Hackney Council. The council had, after the Local Government, Planning and Land Act 1980 came into force, set up a public services committee to oversee the operations of the direct labour organisations (DLOs). It also established three sub-committees to deal with policy and operational matters. One of these was responsible for the building works DLO. Mr Gamper was a member of the public services committee and also chaired the Shoreditch district housing committee. In that capacity, and also in his capacity as an individual councillor, he received complaints from the council's tenants about the DLO's performance, especially about the length of time it took to undertake repairs and the time properties remained empty awaiting renovation. He was therefore concerned about the efficiency of the DLO and requested copies of the documents from the sub-committee responsible for it. He also tried to attend one of the sub-committee's meetings. However, shortly afterwards, Standing Orders were changed so that only appointed members could attend certain sub-committees, including those responsible for the DLOs.

**2.14**  In its letter refusing copies of the documents and access to the sub-committee meetings, the council said that its view was that 'certain sub-committees should be held in private because of the confidential nature of their business' and concluded by saying:

> I do hope you will recognise the special circumstances that apply here and whilst in no way wishing to impugn the integrity of Councillor David Gamper, the utmost need to preserve confidentiality for the direct labour organisations who are competing on a commercial basis for contracts and thereby maintaining the jobs of the workforce.

This was a weak argument and does not appear to have been put forward as a defence when Mr Gamper sought judicial review of the above decision. Instead, the council appears to have relied on the argument that he could obtain the information he required in other ways, such as by raising questions at council meetings. The court described this answer as 'unconvincing': the applicant had a 'general concern for the efficiency of the DLO operation as a whole'. He was a member of the parent committee which had 'a residual responsibility for the activities of the delegate and an obligation, in certain circumstances, to exercise some degree of control' (Donaldson LJ in the Court of Appeal decision of *R v Birmingham City Council, ex parte O* [1982] 1 WLR 679 at p. 691, quoted on p. 1238). On this ground alone he had established a need to know.

**2.15**  The court then had to decide whether it should intervene and quash the decision. Following the *Birmingham* ruling that the decision was a matter for the council and open to review by the courts only on the basis of *Wednesbury* unreasonableness, the court concluded that the council had failed to take into account a relevant factor, namely whether the applicant had established a need to know. Lloyd LJ also concluded that in imposing a blanket denial the council had acted in a way that no reasonable council could act if properly directed. He declined, however, to draw the conclusion that the council was motivated by an improper purpose, namely to protect the DLO at all costs.

The court finally had to consider the issue of attendance at meetings, as the existence of such a right had not been considered in the *Birmingham* case, or in any other decided cases. Lloyd LJ's conclusion was that there was no logical distinction between the two. The question was: did the councillor need to attend in order to perform his duties properly? The right to attend does not carry with it a right to participate or a right to vote. The question of whether a 'more urgent need to know' was required to justify attendance at meetings than receipt of documents was left open. It has not been considered in any subsequent case. However, there is no sensible reason for believing that a more stringent test should be required.

---

## D   DUTIES OF COUNCILLORS

Councillors have a duty to consider the issues on which they are called upon to vote. They **2.16** cannot fetter their discretion by agreeing in advance to vote in accordance with party policy in all circumstances or the dictates of some other body so as to deprive themselves of all real choice. If they do so, then their decision is liable to be quashed. However, party policy and party loyalty are relevant considerations and can be taken into account provided they do not exclude all other considerations. The issue of the extent to which councillors could take these factors into account was considered by the Court of Appeal in *R v Waltham Forest LBC-ex parte Baxter* (1998) 86 LGR 254. The London Borough of Waltham Forest had decided to impose a very large rate increase—62 per cent in the case of domestic rates—leading to some disgruntlement among many of those called upon to pay. Some of the more determined among the disgruntled ratepayers sought judicial review of the council's decision. Although the basis of their complaint was originally unclear, the case resolved itself into a dispute about whether some members of the council had fettered their discretion by voting in accordance with the Labour group policy instead of being guided solely by their own convictions.

In the Divisional Court it was also suggested that the councillors voted as they did because **2.17** they were following the instructions of a Labour party body known as the Local Government Group; this allegation was not made out on the facts. The Court of Appeal said that if it had been, this would have been a ground for quashing the decision. Instead, the argument centred on the decision of the Labour group in council: some members who had argued and voted against the rate increase at the group meeting, voted for it in council. If they had not done so, the increase would not have been agreed. Four of the councillors concerned gave evidence at the hearing before the Divisional Court who dismissed the application.

The applicants appealed. Lord Donaldson MR held first that no inference could be drawn **2.18** from the fact that the way the councillors voted on the issue in council was contrary to their earlier expressed views. Apart from anything else, it was open to them to change their opinion at any time. The evidence of the four councillors was re-examined with some care. One felt that it would be preferable to remain in the group and continue to argue his case to his colleagues from within. He would have felt obliged to resign from the group if he had voted against its policy in council. The others essentially set great store by party unity and felt that to defy group policy would lead to less effective local government. Lord Donaldson MR summed up in the following passage what a councillor's duty was:

> It is to make up his own mind on how to vote, giving such weight as he thinks appropriate to the views of other councillors and to the policy of the group of which he is a member. It is only if he abdicates his personal responsibility that questions can arise as to the validity of his vote. The distinction between giving great weight to the views of colleagues and to party policy, on the one hand, and voting blindly in support of party policy may on occasion be a fine one, but it is nevertheless very real.

If the above decision had been decided otherwise, it would have been a major blow to the way in which political parties operate within local government. The Court of Appeal judgment makes it very difficult indeed to impugn local authority decisions on the basis that councillors have fettered their discretion by following the views of their political group.

## E STANDARDS OF CONDUCT

### Background

**2.19** There used to be three separate regimes for ensuring that councillors maintained an appropriate standard of conduct when carrying out their public duties:

1. The provisions in the Local Government Finance Acts allowing them to be surcharged and/or disqualified if they incurred unlawful expenditure.
2. The requirements relating to disclosure of pecuniary interests in the Local Government Act 1972.
3. The National Code of Local Government Conduct adopted pursuant to s. 31 of the Local Government and Housing Act 1989.

The effects of surcharge could obviously be drastic. If the sums involved were large, councillors could face personal bankruptcy. These provisions were abolished by the Audit Commission Act 1998.

**2.20** A failure to observe the rules relating to pecuniary interests was a criminal offence, for which a councillor could potentially be imprisoned. However, a breach of the Code of Conduct was unlikely to result in any effective sanction. If there was an Ombudsman investigation and the breach of the Code was considered to be maladministration, the councillor could be named in the report. It was also possible for political parties to take action against their members. This could involve suspension from the applicable group or removal from a particular committee. If a councillor was found to be in breach of the Code this could be made public knowledge.

**2.21** There were thus two regimes which could be draconian and one which was almost useless.

There was felt to be a need to draw a clearer distinction between corrupt behaviour (which needed to be punished under the criminal law) and failure to declare interests (which did not need to be criminal behaviour but did need to be subject to some effective sanctions). There was also a lack of logic about some aspects of the Code of Conduct. For instance, it required personal interests to be treated in the same way as pecuniary interests. This was remarked on by the report of the Widdicombe Committee in 1986. The Widdicombe report did not result in any changes to the Code of Conduct or the laws relating to pecuniary interests, although the Code was for the first time placed on a statutory footing.

The issue of such conflicts was considered in detail by the Nolan Committee on standards in public life which in its third report which considered local government concluded:  **2.22**

> Potential conflicts of interest are likely to occur frequently, and public interest requires that a sensible balance should be struck between avoiding impropriety, and enabling councillors to fulfil the role for which they were elected.

This is really the essence of the problem. Councillors should be part of the communities which elect them. Thus events in their area are likely to affect their homes and businesses. A very strict approach to pecuniary interests of this nature would therefore be an attack on one of the positive aspects of local decision-making, which is that people are able to have an influence on what happens in their area. On the other hand, if elected representatives are seen to act from personal interests, as opposed to representing the interests of their communities, then this will soon undermine public confidence in the decision-making process. Following the Nolan report, the issue of members' conduct was considered by the Government and its conclusions were contained in the White Paper 'Modern Local Government— In Touch with the People'. This proposed a mandatory code and a new National Standards Board to supervise enforcement.

## Principles governing the conduct of members

These recommendations were enacted in the LGA 2000. Part III of the Act deals with the conduct of members and employees. The Secretary of State has power both to set out the principles which are to govern the conduct of members and to prescribe a model code. Section 49 gives power to the Secretary of State to specify the principles which are to govern the conduct of members of authorities in England. This also applies to co-opted members. These powers are given to the National Assembly for Wales to determine the principles which should apply to Welsh authorities.  **2.23**

The principles are set out in the Relevant Authorities (General Principles) Order 2001. (SI No. 2001/1401) and the Conduct of Members (Principles) (Wales) Order (SI No. 2001/2276 (W.166)). The set of principles is the same in both orders:  **2.24**

1. **Selflessness.** Members should serve only the public interest and should never improperly confer an advantage or disadvantage on any person.
2. **Honesty and Integrity.** Members should not place themselves in situations where their honesty and integrity may be questioned, should not behave improperly and should on all occasions avoid the appearance of such behaviour.

3. **Objectivity.** Members should make decisions on merit, including when making appointments, awarding or recommending individuals for rewards or benefits.
4. **Accountability.** Members should be accountable to the public for their actions and the manner in which they carry out their responsibilities, and should co-operate fully and honestly with any scrutiny appropriate to their office.
5. **Openness.** Members should be as open as possible about their actions and those of their authority, and should be prepared to give reasons for those actions.
6. **Personal judgement.** Members may take account of the view of others, including their political groups, but should reach their own conclusions on the issues before them and act in accordance with those conclusions.
7. **Respect for others.** Members should promote equality by not discriminating unlawfully against any person, and by treating people with respect, regardless of their race, age, religion, gender, sexual orientation, or disability. They should respect the impartiality and integrity of the authority's statutory officers, and its other employees.
8. **Duty to uphold the law.** Members should uphold the law and, on all occasions, act in accordance with the trust that the public is entitled to place in them.
9. **Stewardship.** Members should do whatever they are able to do to ensure that their authorities use their resources prudently and in accordance with the law.
10. **Leadership.** Members should promote and support these principles by leadership, and by example, and should act in a way that secures or preserves public confidence.

**2.25**  It is difficult to see what purpose is served by setting out this bland uncontroversial list of objectives. It is not specific enough to have any value as a framework for what local government is intended to achieve. Some of the principles are also open to more than one interpretation. For instance, 'accountability' could refer to accountability to the authority of which he is a member, the members of the public in his area, the ward he represents, or to the political party which selected him as their candidate. It might also be argued that some of these principles run counter to the way in which authorities are run now that they have new and more streamlined structures in place. The cabinet or mayoral style of government is likely to mean less openness. There are fewer opportunities to attend meetings at the Town Hall than there once were.

## Codes of conduct

**2.26**  The Secretary of State and the National Assembly for Wales have power under s. 10 of the 2003 Act to draw up model codes of conduct. The Secretary of State has power to invite another body to draw up a proposed model code, or revisions to a model code and to consult with specified persons about the proposed code.

Authorities are under a duty to adopt a code of conduct (s. 51). Their code:

(a)  must incorporate any mandatory provisions of the model code which apply to that authority;
(b)  may incorporate optional provisions from the model code;
(c)  may include other provisions which are consistent with the code.

**2.27**  Whenever an authority adopts or revises a code under these provisions they must:

(a)  ensure that copies are available at an office of the authority during office hours;

(b)  advertise the adoption/revision in a local newspaper;

(c)  send a copy to the Standards Board (if in England) or the Commissioner for Local Administration (if in Wales).

When the code was adopted for each authority the existing councillors had to provide a written undertaking to observe the code. New councillors and new co-opted members must undertake to comply with the code before they are allowed to carry out their functions as members.

## The Code of Conduct—general

There have been various model codes drawn up. There is a code for England set out in The **2.28** Local Authorities (Model Code of Conduct) (England) Order 2001 SI No. 3575. There is also a separate code for parish councils: Parish Councils (Model Code of Conduct) Order 2001 SI No. 3576. Prior to the adoption of these codes, the Government undertook a lengthy consultation exercise. They first invited the Local Government Association to draw up a suggested draft code for England. They then issued a draft code for consultation before finally adopting the model code.

Paragraph 1 of the code provides that a member must observe the authority's code of **2.29** conduct whenever he:

(a)  conducts the business of the authority;

(b)  conducts the business of the office to which he has been elected or appointed;

(c)  acts as a representative of the authority.

Paragraph 1(2) provides that the code is not (apart from paragraphs 4 and 5(a)) to have effect in relation to a members' activities undertaken in anything other than an official capacity. Sometimes the distinction between official and private business is not easy to draw. Is a councillor attending a meeting of the local political party which selected him as a candidate acting as a representative of the authority? If he was a member of the party in the ward he represents, he might be attending the meeting in a personal capacity even if he was not a councillor. If though his position as a councillor creates an expectation that he will report back on events in the Council it could be argued that this meant he was conducting the business of the authority. What if the Leader of the Council or Mayor is attending a social event e.g. with the local Chamber of Commerce? Does the fact that they would probably not be invited if it was not for the office they hold mean that they are attending in an official capacity?

Paragraphs 2 to 6 of the model code set out the general obligations to which a member is **2.30** subject. These are an interesting mixture of airy principles and practical guidance. Under paragraph 2 a member must—

(a)  promote equality by not discriminating unlawfully against any person;

(b)  treat others with respect;

(c)  not do anything which compromises or which is likely to compromise the impartiality of those who work for, or on behalf of, the authority.

Thus it would be a breach of the code to commit an act of unlawful discrimination, such as

racial discrimination, but it would not be a breach to discriminate on grounds where discrimination was legal. The second of the above principles must be seen as an attempt to
elevate the level of debate within authorities. It is too vague to be useful advice. The third
principle would be more helpful if it was accompanied by practical guidance about what it
meant. It could mean, for instance, that putting pressure on officers to provide advice which
was politically expedient, as opposed to impartial but inconvenient, would constitute a
breach of the code.

**2.31**  Paragraph 3 deals with confidential information. A member must not—

(a)  disclose information given to him in confidence by anyone, or information acquired
     which he believes is of a confidential nature, without the consent of the person
     authorised to give it, or unless he is required by law to do so; nor

(b)  prevent another person from giving access to information to which that person is
     entitled by law.

Whether information is given in confidence will be a question of fact to be judged by the
circumstances. It does not need to be expressly stated to be confidential at the time it is
given. For instance, personal information told to a councillor at an advice surgery is likely to
be regarded as confidential even when not explicitly stated to be so.

**2.32**  Paragraph 4 is another vague exhortation:

> A member must not in his official capacity, or any other circumstances, conduct himself in a
> manner which could reasonably be regarded as bringing his office or authority into disrepute.

This is one of the exceptions to the rule that the code is concerned with official conduct
only. There is little guidance though on what sort of conduct will be considered as bringing
the authority into disrepute. Presumably any criminal offence, other than a minor motoring
offence, will come into this category. Short of this, it is difficult to see why elected representatives should be expected to observe different standards of conduct in their personal lives
than other citizens.

**2.33**  Paragraph 5 both states the need for probity and also attempts to define the dividing line
between the functions of an authority and political purposes. A member—

(a)  must not in his official capacity, or in any other circumstances, use his position
     as a member improperly to confer on or secure for himself or any other person, an
     advantage or disadvantage; and

(b)  must, when using or authorising the use by others of the resources of the authority:
     (i)   act in accordance with the authority's requirements, and
     (ii)  ensure that such resources are not used for political purposes, unless that use could
           reasonably be regarded as likely to facilitate, or be conducive to, the discharge of
           the functions of the authority or of the office to which the member has been
           elected or appointed.

Councillors will often be involved in activities which could be deemed political but which are
also relevant to their position as councillors. No doubt many councillors would see a benefit
to the authority in activities which would be regarded by others as political infighting.

**2.34**  Paragraph 6 is a reminder of the importance of taking into account officers' advice. A member must when reaching decisions have regard to any relevant advice provided to him by

(i)   the authority's chief finance officer acting in pursuance of his duties under s. 114 of the Local Government Finance Act 1988, and

(ii)  the authority's monitoring officer acting in pursuance of his duties under s. 5(2) of the Local Government and Housing Act 1989; and

give the reasons for those decisions in accordance with the authority's and any statutory requirements in relation to the taking of an executive decision. (See para 2.36 below.)

Under paragraph 7 members are under an obligation, if they become aware of a breach of their authority's code of conduct, to report this to the Standards Board.

## The Code of Conduct—personal interests

For the purposes of the code, there are two levels of interests:                              **2.35**

(a)  personal interests—which must be disclosed but which do not prevent a member being involved in making decisions which affect such interests;

(b)  prejudicial interests—which require a member to abstain from involvement in any decision which relates to that interest.

A personal interest is defined by paragraph 8:

> A member must regard himself as having a personal interest in any matter if the matter relates to an interest in respect of which notification must be given under paragraphs 14 and 15 below, or if a decision upon it might reasonably be regarded as affecting to a greater extent than other council tax payers, ratepayers or inhabitants of the authority's area, the well-being or financial position of himself, a relative or a friend or—
>
> (a)   any employment or business carried on by such persons;
>
> (b)   any person who employs or has appointed such persons, any firm in which they are a partner, or any company of which they are directors;
>
> (c)   any corporate body in which such persons have a beneficial interest in a class of securities exceeding the nominal value of £5,000; or
>
> (d)   any body listed in sub-paragraphs (a) to (e) of paragraph 15 below in which such persons hold a position of general control or management.

The word 'relative' is defined as meaning 'a spouse, partner [meaning a member of a couple who live together], parent, parent-in-law, son, daughter, step-son, step-daughter, child of a partner, brother, sister, grandparent, grandchild, uncle, aunt, nephew, niece, or the spouse or partner of any of the preceding persons'.

Paragraphs 14 and 15, referred to in the above paragraph, deal with the registration of   **2.36**
financial and other interests (Paragraph 14 deals with financial interests. Paragraph 15 deals with other interests.):

> **14.** Within 28 days of the provisions of an authority's code of conduct being adopted or applied to that authority or within 28 days of his election or appointment to office (if that is later), a member must register his financial interests in the authority's register maintained under section 81(1) of the Local Government Act 2000 by providing written notification to the authority's monitoring officer of—

(a)    any employment or business carried on by him;

(b)    the name of the person who employs or has appointed him, the name of any firm in which he is a partner, and the name of any company for which he is a remunerated director;

(c)    the name of any person, other than a relevant authority, who has made a payment to him in respect of his election or any expenses incurred by him in carrying out his duties;

(d)    the name of any corporate body which has a place of business or land in the authority's area, and in which the member has a beneficial interest in a class of securities of that body that exceeds the nominal value of £25,000 or one hundredth of the total issued share capital of that body;

(e)    a description of any contract for goods, services or works made between the authority and himself or a firm in which he is a partner, a company of which he is a remunerated director, or a body of the description specified in sub-paragraph (d) above;

(f)    the address or other description (sufficient to identify the location) of any land in which he has a beneficial interest and which is in the area of the authority;

(g)    the address or other description (sufficient to identify the location) of any land where the landlord is the authority and the tenant is a firm in which he is a partner, a company of which he is a remunerated director, or a body of the description specified in sub-paragraph (d) above; and

(h)    the address or other description (sufficient to identify the location) of any land in the authority's area in which he has a licence (alone or jointly with others) to occupy for 28 days or longer.

**15.** Within 28 days of the provisions of the authority's code of conduct being adopted or applied to that authority or within 28 days of his election or appointment to office (if that is later), a member must register his other interests in the authority's register maintained under section 81(1) of the Local Government Act 2000 by providing written notification to the authority's monitoring officer of his membership of or position of general control or management in any—

(a)    body to which he has been appointed or nominated by the authority as its representative;

(b)    public authority or body exercising functions of a public nature;

(c)    company, industrial and provident society, charity, or body directed to charitable purposes;

(d)    body whose principal purposes include the influence of public opinion or policy; and

(e)    trade union or professional association.

A member who has a personal interest in a matter who attends a meeting of the authority at which that matter is considered must disclose to that meeting the existence and nature of that interest at the commencement of that consideration, or when the interest becomes apparent. The interest therefore does not need to be disclosed at the beginning of the meeting, but when the item in which the member has an interest is reached. If a member participates in an 'executive decision' (an 'executive decision' means a decision made or to be made by a decision-maker in connection with a function which is the responsibility of the executive of a local authority: Regulation 2 Local Authorities (Executive Arrangements) (Access to Information) (England) Regulations 2000 SI No. 2000/3272) in which he has an interest, he must ensure that any 'written statement' of that decision records the existence and nature of that interest. There is therefore a duty on a member to ensure that any minute of the relevant meeting is correct in this respect.

## The Code of Conduct—prejudicial interests

A 'prejudicial interest' is defined by paragraph 10 which provides that a personal interest in a   **2.37**
matter becomes a prejudicial interest 'if the interest is one which a member of the public
with knowledge of the relevant facts would reasonably regard as so significant that it is likely
to prejudice the member's judgement of the public interest'. There are a series of exceptions
set out in paragraph 10(2) broadly corresponding to the dispensations which were issued
under the old rules relating to pecuniary interests:

> A member may regard himself as not having a prejudicial interest in a matter if that matter
> relates to—
>
> (a)  another relevant authority of which he is a member;
> (b)  another public authority in which he holds a position of general control or management;
> (c)  a body to which he has been appointed or nominated by the authority as its representative;
> (d)  the housing functions of the authority where the member holds a tenancy or lease with a
>       relevant authority, provided that he does not have arrears of rent with that relevant
>       authority of more than two months, and provided that those functions do not relate
>       particularly to the member's tenancy or lease;
> (e)  the functions of the authority in respect of school meals, transport and travelling
>       expenses, where the member is a guardian or parent of a child in full time education,
>       unless it relates particularly to the school which the child attends;
> (f)  the functions of the authority in respect of statutory sick pay under Part XI of the Social
>       Security Contributions and Benefits Act 1992, where the member is in receipt of, or is
>       entitled to the receipt of such pay from a relevant authority; and
> (g)  any functions of the authority in respect of an allowance or payment made under sections
>       173 to 176 of the Local Government Act 1972 or section 18 of the Local Government and
>       Housing Act 1989.

Under paragraph 12 of the code, a member with a prejudicial interest in any matter must—   **2.38**

(a)  withdraw from the room or chamber where a meeting is being held whenever it
      becomes apparent that the matter is being considered at that meeting, unless he has
      obtained a dispensation from the authority's standards committee;
(b)  not exercise executive functions in relation to that matter; and
(c)  not seek improperly to influence a decision about that matter.

The meaning of paragraph 12 was considered by the Court of Appeal in the following case.

### R v North Yorkshire County Council, ex parte Richardson

The first major case arising from the operation of the new code of conduct was *R v North*   **2.39**
*Yorkshire County Council, ex parte Richardson* [2004] 1 WLR 1920. (The case was partly
concerned with the interpretation of the Environmental Impact Assessment Regulations.
This aspect lies outside the scope of this book.)

**The facts.**  Paul Richardson was a member of the North Yorkshire County Council. He lived   **2.40**
in the village of Littlethorpe and also represented his village on the County Council. The
operators of a local quarry applied for an extension of their permission to quarry sand
and gravel. This extension would have allowed them to carry on operations very close to
Littlethorpe, and Mr Richardson's house would have been among those most affected.

Mr Richardson was therefore faced with the type of conflict typical of the genuinely local councillor. Since he was the sole representative of the electoral division which included Littlethorpe, he saw himself as the voice on the Council of his constituents, who were strongly opposed to the extension of the quarry. However, he also had a strong personal interest as the extension would mean that quarrying would be permitted within 250 yards of his house.

2.41  The application for planning permission was due for consideration at the Council's Planning and Regulatory Functions Committee on 11 June 2002. Mr Richardson was not a member of this committee but was intending to attend it to make representations on behalf of his constituents. On 5 June he was informed that he had a prejudicial interest within the meaning of the Code and he would therefore not be allowed to attend or speak at the 11 June meeting. He attended at the outset and made a statement to the effect that the rights of representation of the Littlethorpe community had been denied by Government legislation. He then withdrew from the room. He subsequently challenged the decision to require him to withdraw arguing that he did not have a prejudicial interest and that, even if he had, there was no obligation on him to withdraw. His application was rejected by Richards J. He appealed to the Court of Appeal.

2.42  **The decision.**   Lord Justice Simon Brown indicated that four questions arose on this part of the case:

(a)  Which 'member[s]', assuming that they have a prejudicial interest in a matter, are required by paragraph 12(1) of the Code to 'withdraw from the room or chamber where a meeting is being held when . . . the matter is being considered at that meeting'? Is this requirement imposed on all members of the authority or only on those who are members of the committee holding the relevant meeting?

(b)  Whatever the answer to the first question, is a member, paragraph 12 notwithstanding, entitled to attend such a meeting in his personal capacity as opposed to his representative capacity?

(c)  Was Mr Richardson properly to be regarded as having a 'prejudicial interest' in the matter of this planning application?

(d)  Did Mr Richardson indicate that, even were he not permitted to attend the June meeting in his representative capacity, he wished to attend in his personal capacity?

He dealt with them in the order of their importance, since the first were of general importance and application, the third touched upon the correct approach to determining what amounts to a prejudicial interest, and the fourth was a question turning on the individual facts of this case.

## The meaning of the word 'member' in paragraph 12

2.43  The conclusion of Richards J had been that there was no justification for treating the word 'member' in paragraph 12 as meaning simply a member of the committee. Throughout the Code the word 'member' denotes a member of the Council. Where the Code refers to a member of a particular committee, it does so specifically as in paragraph 11 where there is a reference to committees 'of which he may also be a member'. Richards J also considered that the background material (i.e. the Widdicombe report, the Nolan report, and the consultation paper which preceded the legislation) showed that a restrictive approach was intended.

Lord Justice Simon Brown quoted from the judgment of Richards J where he dealt with the **2.44** submission that to construe the word 'member' in paragraph 12 as meaning a member of the Council would impose an unnecessary and disproportionate restriction on members' abilities to represent their constituents such as to make it unlawful to have promulgated a code in these terms. Richards J considered that:

1.  The relevant test was rationality rather than proportionality. The judge was not convinced that the concept of proportionality had replaced rationality as the correct test in domestic law.
2.  It was clearly rational for the Secretary of State to adopt a code which required a councillor to withdraw from a meeting of a committee where a matter in which he had a prejudicial interest was being considered. (The judge remarked that he considered that the test of proportionality would also have been satisfied.)
3.  The code reflected the outcome of a complex balancing exercise following extensive consultation and deliberation. The Secretary of State placed particular weight on the importance of maintaining public trust and confidence in the operation of the system. He was entitled to do so.
4.  A councillor who is not a member of the relevant committee may still exert influence by virtue of his position as a councillor, and in such a situation there is still a real risk that public trust in the decision-making process could be impaired.
5.  The highest standards in public life are properly viewed as promoting rather than offending the principles of local democracy. There is moreover no particular require-ment that any particular councillor attends a particular meeting. The nature of commit-tees is that they take decisions on behalf of the Council without every councillor being in attendance. Nor is the attendance of a particular councillor the only way in which the relevant community can be represented.

These conclusions were challenged in the Court of Appeal. It was argued that the judge had failed to give sufficient weight to the decision of the Court of Appeal in *R v Flintshire County Council, ex parte Armstrong-Braun* [2001] LGR 344 in which the court had struck down a standing order which would have prejudiced the rights of individual members. This was a weak argument, really amounting to no more than an assertion of the importance of local democracy. Simon Brown LJ could see no inconsistency between the two decisions. There was also an argument that in paragraph 11 of the code it was clear that the word 'member' was used in the more limited sense of a member of a committee. However, in the rest of the code, the word 'member' was used to describe a member of the council. In paragraph 11 the distinction was made clear by the language used. It referred to committees 'of which he may also be a member'.

## The entitlement of a member to remain at a meeting in his personal capacity

Richards J at first instance said that this did not arise on the facts, since no such request was **2.45** made. However, he expressed the view that the Code would not prevent this, since a councillor attending a meeting as a private citizen would not be undertaking activities in an official capacity. Simon Brown LJ considered that in reaching this conclusion, Richards J had erred in his approach:

> A member of the authority attending a council meeting cannot in my judgment, simply by declaring that he attends in his private capacity, thereby divest himself of his official capacity as a councillor. He is still to be regarded as conducting the business of his office. Only by resigning can he shed that role.

### Whether Mr Richardson's interest was properly to be regarded as prejudicial

**2.46**  The argument that Mr Richardson did not have a prejudicial interest relied on a passage from paragraph 118 of the Nolan report to the effect that:

> If one hundred households are affected by a Council decision, then most people would agree that a councillor similarly affected has no special interest which might debar him or her from speaking or voting, providing the interest is declared.

A local petition against the development attracted 400 signatures. This was put forward as an argument that Mr Richardson had the same interest as his constituents, albeit to a greater degree than most. As Richards J pointed out though, the next sentence of the Nolan report went on to say 'if in a different decision ten households are affected, then in most circumstances a councillor might feel that taking part in a decision was inappropriate'. However, the test to be applied was that set out in the Code. Richards J stated that in his judgment 'a member of the public with knowledge of the relevant facts would reasonably have regarded Mr Richardson's interest as so significant that it was likely to prejudice his judgment of the public interest'. He also considered whether, if Mr Richardson had been a member of the committee and had participated in a decision to refuse planning permission the developer would have had good grounds for objecting that Mr Richardson's participation gave rise to the appearance of bias. He concluded that in these circumstances a fair minded observer would have concluded that there was a real possibility of bias.

**2.47**  The Court of Appeal upheld the judge's decision on this point, Simon Brown LJ describing it as 'self-evidently correct'. On the basis that he had concluded that Mr Richardson was unable to attend in a personal capacity, the final question did not arise. However, had it been an issue, Simon Brown LJ considered that it should have been resolved in favour of Mr Richardson on the basis that his statement at the outset of the meeting indicated that he considered himself as barred from the meeting in a personal role.

**2.48**  This case provides helpful guidance on what advice should be given about how to approach the issue of prejudicial interests.

1.  It is clear that a fairly restrictive approach is required. When considering whether or not a personal interest is prejudicial, it is safer to assume that something is a prejudicial interest. Unless the group affected is very wide, the argument that a councillor is only one of a number of people affected by a particular decision will not remove the subject matter of that decision from the category of prejudicial interests.

2.  It is for individual councillors to decide whether an interest is prejudicial or not. Although the issue was not considered in the case, it would seem inappropriate for the Council to issue instructions to individual councillors about what they can and cannot do. They can be given strong advice (as Mr Richardson was) and the consequences of

failing to heed that advice can and should be spelt out to them, but ultimately the decision is a matter for them.

3. Councillors cannot attend a meeting while an item in which they have a prejudicial interest is being considered, whether or not they are a member of the relevant committee. Nor are they are able to attend in a personal capacity.

The test of what constitutes a personal or prejudicial interest is objective. In *Scrivens v Ethical Standards Office* [2005] EWHC 529 it was argued that a councillor was not failing to comply with the code if he reasonably but mistakenly concluded that he did not have a personal or prejudicial interest. This argument was rejected. The purpose of these rules was to maintain high standards in public life. Only the application of an objective test would be consistent with that object.

## Ensuring compliance with the code

Along with the new Code of Conduct the LGA 2000 also introduced a new system for **2.49** maintaining standards of conduct in local government. This includes both local and national elements. Locally, each local authority must have its own standards committee, independent of the executive, which is charged with ensuring the maintenance of high standards of conduct within that authority. Nationally, there is a standards board which gives guidance about standards of conduct to local authorities. Complaints can be made to the standards board about the conduct of individual members. These may be investigated by ethical standards officers. If they consider the matter serious enough following investigation, they can refer the matter to an adjudication panel. This panel then has the ability to impose sanctions including the suspension of the councillor from his authority.

## Standards committees

Under s. 3 of the LGA 2000, each relevant authority (i.e. each county council, district **2.50** council, London borough, or (in Wales) county borough; (the position is slightly different for parish and community councils)) must establish a standards committee. (See below paragraphs 2.55 to 2.57.) Subject to the requirements of any Regulations each authority must fix for itself the number of members of their standards committee and their term of office.

The standards committee of each relevant authority in England (and each police authority **2.51** in Wales) must include at least two members of the authority and at least one person who is not a member, or officer of that or any other relevant authority. If the authority is operating executive arrangements (i.e. an elected mayor or a form of cabinet government: see chapter 4) then the standards committee must not include the elected mayor, the executive leader, or any member of the executive. This is to ensure that, the standards committee, while forming part of the authority, has a degree of independence from those who run it.

Regulations may be made by the Secretary of State (the National Assembly in Wales) **2.52** governing the size and composition of committees, public access to meetings, publicity and administrative arrangements. The Relevant Authorities (Standards Committees) Regulations 2001 SI No. 2812 provide as follows:

An authority must ensure that:

(a) if the committee has more than three members, at least 25 per cent of its membership must be made up of independent members
(b) if the authority is operating executive arrangements under Part III of the Act, no more than one member of the Standards Committee is a member of the executive.

If it is a responsible authority (i.e. it has responsibility for parish councils) then the committee must include a member of one of the parish councils for which it is responsible but this person must not also be a member of the responsible authority.

## Functions of standards committees

**2.53** Standards committees of relevant authorities have the following general functions:

(a) promoting and maintaining high standards of conduct by the members and co-opted members of the authority, and
(b) assisting members and co-opted members of the authority to observe the authority's code of conduct.

They also have the following specific functions:

(a) advising the authority on the adoption or revision of a code of conduct;
(b) monitoring the operation of the authority's code of conduct; and
(c) advising, training or arranging to train members and co-opted members of the authority on matters relating to the authority's code of conduct.

**2.54** There are powers for the Secretary of State to make regulations and issue guidance on the exercise of functions by standards committees of relevant authorities in England and police authorities in Wales. The National Assembly for Wales has the same powers in relation to standards committees for relevant authorities in Wales.

## Arrangements for parish councils

**2.55** Parish councils (and community councils in Wales) do not have their own standards committees, forming part of their own structure. Instead, they are monitored by standards committees of the responsible district or unitary county council (county borough or county councils in Wales). In England the arrangements are as follows (the same provisions also apply to community councils in Wales with the appropriate county or county borough councils exercising responsibility for the community councils within their area):

The standards committee of the responsible district or unitary county council has the same functions in relation to the parish council and its members as it has for the district or county council and its members. It may set up a sub-committee for the purposes of dealing with the parish council matters. The parish council must be consulted before any decision is made about whether the functions are to be discharged by the committee or a sub-committee. The district or unitary authority must also consult the parish council about the number of members and term of office of any standards committee or sub-committee responsible for such parish council's standards.

If the standards committee itself decides to assume responsibility for parish council **2.56**
standards then it:

(a)  must include at least one member of any of the parish councils for which it is the
     responsible authority, and
(b)  must ensure that at least one person falling within paragraph (a) above is present at any
     meeting where matters relating to those parish councils, or the members of those parish
     councils are being considered.

If a sub-committee is established by the relevant district or county to oversee parish council
standards then it must include:

(a)  at least one person who is not a member or an officer of that (i.e. the responsible district
     council) or any other relevant authority, and
(b)  at least one member of any of the parish councils for which that district or county
     council is responsible.

A district or unitary council is responsible for a parish council for the purposes of these
provisions if that parish is situated wholly within its area. If it is what is called a common
parish council i.e. it includes electors from the area of more than one district, then it is the
responsibility of the district council within the area of which the largest number of that
parish's electorate resides.

Although these arrangements give local authorities responsibility for ensuring that standards **2.57**
of conduct within their area are maintained, and give standards committees responsibility
for training and advising members, they do not set up a system whereby breaches of the code
of conduct can be investigated locally and for the local imposition of sanctions against those
who breach its provisions. Instead, a new national body was created for this purpose.

## The Standards Board for England

The board is established by s. 57 of the LGA 2000. Its membership, which must number at **2.58**
least three, is appointed by the Secretary of State. When exercising its functions it 'must have
regard to the need to promote and maintain high standards of conduct by members and
co-opted members of relevant authorities in England'. The board has the following
functions:

(a)  it must appoint ethical standards officers,
(b)  it may issue guidance to relevant authorities in England and police authorities in Wales
     on matters relating to the conduct of members and co-opted members of such
     authorities,
(c)  it may issue guidance to relevant authorities in England and police authorities in Wales
     in relation to the qualifications or experience which monitoring officers should possess,
(d)  it may arrange for any such guidance to be made public.

Anybody can report a member to the Standards Board for breach of the Code of Conduct.
The allegation must be made in writing. If the Standards Board considers that an allegation
should be investigated, it must refer the matter to one of its ethical standards officers for
investigation. If it considers that it should not be investigated, then it must write to the

person who made the allegation, notifying that person of its decision and giving the reasons for it.

**2.59**  The Standards Board has since its creation in 2001 received a substantial number of trivial allegations, often by political opponents. It has taken the view that investigating these is a waste of its resources. It is now committed to focusing on allegations concerning serious misbehaviour with the potential to damage the reputation of local government. There are published criteria which need to be satisfied before an allegation will be referred for investigation. It must satisfy one of the following criteria:

- it is serious enough, if proven, to justify the range of sanctions available to the Adjudication Panel for England or local standards committee,
- it is part of a continuing pattern of less serious misconduct which is unreasonably disrupting the business of the authority and there is no other avenue left to deal with it short of investigation.

**2.60**  The Board has advised that an allegation within one of the following categories is unlikely to be referred for investigation:

- it is believed to be malicious, relatively minor, or tit for tat,
- the same, or substantially similar, complaint has already been the subject of an investigation or inquiry and there is nothing further to be gained by seeking the sanctions available to the Adjudication Panel for England or the local standards committee,
- the complaint concerns acts carried out in the member's private life which are unlikely to affect his or her fitness for public office,
- it appears that the grievance is really about dissatisfaction with a council decision,
- there is insufficient information currently available to justify a decision to refer the matter for investigation.

### Investigations by ethical standards officers

**2.61**  If the complaint has overcome these hurdles, it will be investigated by an ethical standards officer. There are currently four such officers. The total complement of staff engaged on investigations is thirty. The functions of ethical standards officers are set out in s. 59 of the LGA 2000. They are to investigate:

(a)  cases referred to them by the Standards Board, and

(b)  other cases in which such officer considers that a member or co-opted member (or former member or co-opted member) of a relevant authority in England has failed, or may have failed, to comply with their authority's code of conduct and which have come to the attention of any such officer as a result of an investigation under paragraph (a).

An ethical standards officer cannot initiate an investigation without having been asked to do so by the Board. However, the effect of paragraph (b) above is that, if he uncovers further alleged misconduct during the course of an investigation, he can pursue an investigation into that further misconduct without having to go back to the Standards Board for authority.

**2.62**  An investigation has to result in one of four findings:

(a) that there is no evidence of any failure to comply with the code of conduct of the relevant authority concerned,

(b) that no action needs to be taken in respect of the matters which are the subject of the investigation,

(c) that the matters which are the subject of the investigation should be referred to the monitoring officer of the relevant authority concerned, or

(d) that the matters which are the subject of the investigation should be referred to the president of the Adjudication Panel for England for adjudication by a tribunal falling within section 76(1).

Ethical standards officers can cease an investigation at any stage or refer it to the authority's monitoring officer: s. 60(2).

There are provisions designed to ensure that ethical standards officers cannot be accused of bias or conflicts of interest. An ethical standards officer may not conduct an investigation into a member or co-opted member of an authority if he has within the previous five years been a member or an officer of that authority or member of a committee or sub-committee (including joint committees or sub-committees) of that authority. If an ethical standards officer has a direct or indirect interest in any matter which is, or is likely to be, the subject of an investigation, he must disclose that interest to the Board and take no part in the investigation. A breach of any of these provisions does not affect the validity of acts done by an ethical standards officer. **2.63**

Ethical standards officers can adopt such procedures for carrying out investigations as they consider appropriate. However, they must give any person who is the subject of an investigation an opportunity to comment on any allegation that he has failed or may have failed to comply with the relevant authority's code of conduct. (It is likely that, even if this statutory requirement did not exist, the outcome of an investigation which failed to observe this requirement could be the subject of legal challenge.) An investigation is not to affect: **2.64**

(a) any action taken by the relevant authority concerned, or

(b) any power or duty of the relevant authority concerned to take further action with respect to any matters which are the subject of the investigation.

For instance, it will not affect any legal proceedings in which the authority may be involved or any disciplinary action which they might take arising from the circumstances which gave rise to the investigation.

Under s. 62 ethical standards officers are given considerable powers to ensure that they are able to carry out their duties effectively. They can obtain all the documents they need. They have a right of access to every document relating to a relevant authority which appears to them necessary for the purposes of conducting the investigation. For this purpose 'documents' includes information held by a computer or in any other electronic form. They can compel witnesses to provide them with information and attend before them to answer questions. An ethical standards officer, or a person authorised by such an officer may: **2.65**

(a) make such inquiries of any person as he thinks necessary,

(b) require any person to give him such information or explanation as he thinks necessary, and

(c)   if he thinks necessary, require any person to attend before him in person for the purpose of making inquiries of that person or to require that person to give any information or explanation.

**2.66**   There is a general duty on local authorities to provide assistance to ethical standards officers. A relevant authority 'must provide an ethical standards officer, or a person authorised by such an officer with every facility and all information which he may reasonably require for the purposes of conducting an investigation under s. 59 in relation to a member or co-opted member (or former member or co-opted member) of the authority'.

**2.67**   There are additional powers to obtain documents and information under s. 62(4). Under this provision, an ethical standards officer, or a person authorised by him may require any person:

(a)   to furnish information concerning communications between the authority concerned and any government department, or

(b)   to produce any correspondence or other documents forming part of any such communications.

In relation to such information, no obligation in respect of secrecy imposed on 'persons in Her Majesty's service imposed by any rule of law or enactment shall apply'. Nor is the Crown entitled to claim privilege in relation to such documents. However, apart from these exceptions, which essentially appear to be designed to prevent non-disclosure of potentially embarrassing documents with blanket claims of official secrecy or privilege, there is a rule that 'no person may be compelled for the purposes of an investigation under s. 59 to give any evidence or produce any document which he could not be compelled to give or produce in civil proceedings before the High Court'. Failure to comply with the above requirements without reasonable excuse is a criminal offence, punishable by a sentence of up to six months imprisonment on summary conviction or up to two years' imprisonment on conviction on indictment.

**2.68**   In addition to his powers to compel witnesses and order disclosure of documents and information, an ethical standards officer may obtain advice from any suitably qualified person and pay that person such fees and allowances as he may determine with the approval of the Secretary of State. This means that during the course of an investigation, the officers have access to independent legal advice and technical advice if they require it.

**2.69**   The extensive powers to obtain documents and information under sections 61 and 62 are subject to strict rules about the circumstances in which such information can be disclosed. This is allowed only if one of five conditions is satisfied:

(a)   the disclosure is made for the purposes of enabling the Standards Board for England, an ethical standards officer, the Commission for Local Administration in Wales, a Local Commissioner in Wales or the president, deputy president, or any tribunal of either of the Adjudication Panels to perform their functions under Part III of the LGA 2000,

(b)   the person to whom the information relates has consented to its disclosure,

(c)   the information has previously been disclosed to the public with lawful authority,

(d)   the disclosure is for the purposes of criminal proceedings in any part of the United Kingdom and the information in question was not obtained under section 62(2) (see above),

(e)  the disclosure is made to the Audit Commission for the purposes of any functions of the Audit Commission or an auditor under the Audit Commission Act 1998.

The above provisions also apply to standards committees and appeal tribunals in the **2.70** performance of any of their functions under the Local Authorities (Code of Conduct) (Local Determination) Regulations 2003 but for these bodies there are two other situations in which information may be disclosed:

(a)  for the purpose of enabling a standards committee or standards sub-committee to perform any of its statutory functions under Part III LGA 2000 in connection with the investigation and consideration of an allegation of a breach of an authority's code of conduct,

(b)  for the purposes of enabling a tribunal drawn from members of the Adjudication Panel to consider any appeal from a finding of such a standards committee or sub-committee in connection with an allegation of a breach of an authority's code of conduct.

There is in addition power for the Secretary of State or a relevant authority (which includes all local authorities) to give a notice in writing to an ethical standards officer that disclosure of a specified document or information would be contrary to the public interest. If such a notice is served, then the ethical standards officer may not disclose the specified document or information. It is difficult to envisage the circumstances in which it is thought likely that this power would need to be used.

Once an ethical standards officer has carried out an investigation and decided which of the **2.71** findings he is required to arrive at is appropriate, then depending on the outcome of the investigation, he may either have the option of producing a report or be under an obligation to produce a report. If the ethical standards officer decides that there is no evidence of failure to comply with the code or that no action should be taken, then he may, but does not have to, produce a report. If he does produce a report, then he must send a copy to the monitoring officer and may send a summary to any local newspapers. If he does not produce a report then he must notify the monitoring officer of the authority concerned of the outcome of the investigation.

If, during the course of his investigation, an ethical standards officer concludes that the **2.72** matters he is investigating relate partly to a matter which could be subject to an investigation by the local government ombudsman, he can consult the appropriate ombudsman, and, if he considers it necessary, inform the person who made the original allegation of the steps necessary to make a complaint to the Local Government Ombudsman. There is the same power for the local government ombudsman, when carrying out an investigation, to consult with the Standards Board and, if he considers it necessary, inform the complainant of the steps necessary to make an allegation to the Board.

An ethical standards officer may decide, as a result of his investigation, to refer the matter to **2.73** a monitoring officer. If so, he must produce a report on the outcome of his investigation and send a copy of this to the monitoring officer and the standards committee of the relevant authority. The final, and most serious potential result is to refer the matter to an Adjudication Panel. If he determines that the matter should be sent to an Adjudication Panel, he must produce a report on the outcome of his investigation and send a copy both to the monitoring officer of the authority concerned and to the president of the Adjudication Panel.

**2.74** If a member who was subject to an investigation has ceased to be a member of the authority where the allegations arose but is a member of an authority when the investigation is concluded, the reports must also go to the monitoring officer of the new authority. In addition, the ethical standards officer must:

(a) inform any person who was the subject of an investigation, and

(b) take reasonable steps to inform any person who made any allegation which gave rise to the investigation,

of the outcome of the investigation.

**2.75** There is also power for an ethical standards officer to produce an interim report. If the prima facie evidence leads the ethical standards officer to conclude that:

(a) the person who is the subject of the report has failed to comply with the code of conduct,

(b) the nature of that failure is such that disqualification is likely to result, and

(c) that it is in the public interest to suspend or partially suspend that person immediately,

then the interim report can include a recommendation for such suspension. The period may not exceed six months or the remainder of the member's term of office, if shorter. If such a recommendation is made, it must be referred to the president of the Adjudication Panel so that the issue can be decided by a tribunal.

### Investigations referred to monitoring officers

**2.76** Under s. 66 LGA 2000 there is power for the Secretary of State to make regulations as to how investigations referred to monitoring officers should be dealt with. These are the Local Authorities (Code of Conduct) (Local Determination) Regulations 2003. They set out the procedure for dealing with hearings before standards committees and appeals from the decisions of these committees. When a matter has been referred to a monitoring officer he must send a copy of the report to the member concerned and arrange for the standards committee to meet to consider it. The standards committee must then arrange a hearing. The hearing must take place within three months of the receipt of the report by the monitoring officer. A period of at least fourteen days must elapse between receipt of the report and the hearing unless the member concerned agrees to this period being shortened.

**2.77** There are provisions designed to ensure that the hearing complies with the rules of natural justice. The member must be given an opportunity to present evidence in support of his case, to call witnesses, and to make representations either orally, either himself or through a representative or, if he chooses, in writing. The representative can be counsel, a solicitor or, if the committee agrees, any person he chooses to represent him. The standards committee may itself arrange for the attendance of witnesses. Following a hearing, the standards committee must make one of the following findings:

(a) that the member had not failed to comply with the code of conduct;

(b) that the member had failed to comply with the code of conduct but that no action needs to be taken;

(c) that the member had failed to comply with the code of conduct and that a sanction should be imposed.

If the person is no longer a member of an authority the committee must censure him. If the    **2.78**
person is a member then one of the following sanctions can be imposed:

(a) censure of that member;

(b) restriction for a maximum period of three months of that member's access to the premises of the authority and that member's use of the resources of the authority (but this must be a reasonable and proportionate restriction to the nature of the breach and must not unduly restrict the member's ability to perform his functions and duties as a member);

(c) partial suspension for a maximum period of three months;

(d) partial suspension for a maximum period of three months or until such time as he submits a written apology or undertakes any training or conciliation specified by the standards committee;

(e) suspension for a maximum period of three months;

(f) suspension for a maximum period of three months or until such time as he submits a written apology or undertakes any training or conciliation specified by the standards committee.

Partial suspension means that a member is prevented from exercising particular functions or having particular responsibilities: s. 83(7). The standards committee have to produce a written notice of their finding and, unless it was a finding that it was no breach and the member requests that it is not published, they must arrange for it to be published in a local newspaper.

There is a right to apply for permission to appeal to an Adjudication Panel. The application    **2.79**
must be made to the president of the Adjudication Panel within 21 days of receipt of the finding of the standards committee. In deciding whether to grant the member the right of appeal the president has to have regard to whether there is a reasonable prospect of the appeal being successful (either in whole or in part). If the right to appeal is granted the matter is sent to an appeals tribunal appointed by the president of the Adjudication Panel from members of the Adjudication Panel. If the member consents, the appeal may be dealt with by way of written representations. The appeals tribunal may uphold or reverse the finding of the standards committee. If they uphold the finding, in whole or in part, they may confirm the sanction imposed or impose a different sanction.

## Hearings by case tribunals

An allegation is only considered by a case tribunal if an ethical standards officer considers    **2.80**
that it should, following an investigation, be referred to the Adjudication Panel. There are two Adjudication Panels, one for England and one for Wales. The members of the Adjudication Panel for England are appointed by the Lord Chancellor. The members of the Adjudication Panel for Wales are appointed by the National Assembly for Wales. Case tribunals are selected by the president of the relevant Adjudication Panel. They must consist of at least three members. If a tribunal is convened to consider an interim report then it is known as an interim case tribunal.

There are rules to ensure compliance with the rules of natural justice and guard against    **2.81**
allegations of bias. A member of an Adjudication Panel who has sat as a member of an

interim tribunal cannot sit as a member of a case tribunal considering the same allegations. A member of an Adjudication Panel cannot sit on any case tribunal if he has within the previous five years been a member or officer (or a member of any committee, sub-committee, joint committee; or joint sub-committee) of the authority which the allegations concern. If a member of the Adjudication Panel is directly or indirectly interested in a matter which is to be referred to a case tribunal, he must disclose the nature of his interest to the president or deputy president of the Panel and cannot sit on any case tribunal or interim case tribunal carrying out an adjudication in respect of that matter.

**2.82**   A person who is the subject of an adjudication conducted by a tribunal or interim case tribunal may appear before that tribunal in person or be represented by counsel or a solicitor or any other person he wishes to represent him. Adjudications must be carried out in accordance with any regulations made by the Secretary of State or the National Assembly for Wales. No regulations have been made for England though the Adjudication Panel has published procedures. Regulations for Wales were made by the Adjudications by Case Tribunals and Interim Case Tribunals (Wales) Regulations 2001 (SI No. 2001/2288). The presidents of the Adjudication Panels also have power to give directions as to the practice and procedure to be followed by case tribunals and interim case tribunals.

**2.83**   An interim case tribunal can decide to suspend or partially suspend a member for a period of up to six months or (if shorter) the remainder of that person's term of office. There is a right of appeal to the High Court against the suspension or partial suspension or against the length of the suspension or partial suspension.

A case tribunal can suspend or partially suspend a person from being a member of the relevant authority. It can also disqualify a person from being a member of that or any other authority. The suspension may be for a maximum period of one year, or the remainder of that member's term of office, if shorter. The disqualification is for a maximum period of five years. There is a right of appeal to the High Court.

**2.84**   A case tribunal which decides that a member has failed to comply with the code of conduct must produce a notice to that effect. It must specify the details of the failure and any sanction imposed. It must be sent to the standards committee of the authority concerned and a copy sent to the Standards Board for England if the authority concerned is in England or the Commission for Local Administration in Wales if the authority concerned is in Wales. A copy must also be given to any person who is the subject of a decision to which the notice relates. It must also be published in a newspaper local to the authority concerned.

**2.85**   Case tribunals which have carried out an adjudication can make recommendations to the relevant authority about any matters relating to:

(a)   the exercise of the authority's functions,
(b)   the authority's code of conduct, or
(c)   the authority's standards committee.

**2.86**   An authority which receives recommendations must prepare a report within three months giving details of what action the authority has taken or are proposing to take as a result of the recommendations. The report must be sent to the Standards Board for England or the Local

Commissioner for Wales as applicable. If the Board or Commissioner is not satisfied with the report they can require the authority to publish a statement giving details of the case tribunal's recommendations and the authority's reasons for not fully implementing them.

The following two cases give an indication of the way in which the courts will approach **2.87** appeals against decisions of case tribunals.

In *Murphy v Ethical Standards Officer* [2004] EWHC 2377 (Admin) a councillor had spoken at a council meeting about an ombudsman report which had criticised him. He had been advised that he should declare an interest and withdraw from the meeting for that item. A case tribunal found that he had failed to comply with the provisions of the authority's code of conduct and suspended him from acting as a councillor for one year. The court considered that the suspension of one year was disproportionate. Councillor Murphy's interest in the report was known to everyone and he had received conflicting and confusing advice. A four month suspension was substituted.

In *Hathaway v Ethical Standards Officer* LTL 13/5/2004 the court declined to interfere with a one year suspension following a conviction for assault even though the effect of the suspension was that, since he would be unable to stand at the next election, he would be debarred from acting as a councillor for at least three years.

---

## KEY DOCUMENTS

Relevant Authorities (Standards Committees) Regulations 2001 (SI No. 2001/2812)

Local Authorities (Model Code of Conduct) (England) Order 2001 (SI No. 2001/3575)

Parish Councils (Model Code of Conduct) Order 2001 (SI No. 2001/3576)

Local Authorities (Code of Conduct) (Local Determination) Regulations 2003
  (SI No. 2004/2617)

Adjudications by Case Tribunals and Interim Case Tribunals (Wales) Regulations 2001
  (SI No. 2001/2288)

Guidance on the code of conduct and standards for councillors can be found on the
  Standards Board website: <http://www.standardsboard.gov.uk>

The adjudication panel has its own website: <http://www.adjudicationpanel.co.uk>

# 3

## OFFICERS

## A   INTRODUCTION

**3.01**   Local authorities are major employers. Being a local government officer, though, can no longer be considered a job for life with a pension at the end. Compulsory redundancies are no longer uncommon and functions are frequently outsourced to the private sector with employees being transferred under the Transfer of Undertakings (Protection of Employment) Regulations. For senior posts it is possible for member/officer relations to become strained and the turnover in such posts is often high. In certain fields, such as finance, there are often recruitment difficulties.

### Power to appoint staff

**3.02**   Local authorities have a wide discretion to appoint such staff as they think necessary for discharging their functions: LGA 1972, s. 112. Local government officers are appointed on such terms and conditions, including conditions as to remuneration, as the authority appointing them thinks fit: s. 112(2). In practice, wage rates are negotiated nationally. This practice does not override the discretion. Local authorities are at liberty to reach locally agreed settlements. Payments in excess of the nationally agreed scales may lawfully be made provided that they are reasonable: *Carr v District Auditor for No. 1 District Alston-with-Garrigill* (1952) 50 LGR 538. Indeed, particularly in areas where staff are hard to recruit, it may be necessary for authorities to offer additional incentives.

**3.03**   Like every discretion, it must be exercised lawfully. The power to pay wages must not be used for an improper purpose. The council is under a duty to have regard to the factors which would influence an ordinary employer and cannot fix them on an arbitrary basis. In *Roberts v Hopwood* [1925] AC 578, the House of Lords held that the council had exercised its powers to pay wages to staff for the ulterior and improper purpose of giving gifts or gratuities. However, there is no rule that making pay settlements which are considerably larger than existing norms is in itself unlawful: *Pickwell v Camden London Borough Council* [1983] 1 All ER 602. The payment of retrospective wages for extra duties is unlawful as is the giving of gratuities to officers: *Re Magrath* [1934] 2 KB 415. This needs to be remembered especially when negotiating terms of severance with officers. It may in these circumstances be claimed that extra duties were carried out which were not recognised and additional remuneration should now be paid for these. Payments of this nature are very unlikely to be justifiable and carry a strong risk of illegality.

**3.04**   There is a duty to appoint staff only on merit: Local Government and Housing Act 1989 (LGHA 1989) s. 7(1). Appointments made on the ground of nepotism or political favouritism, for example, would therefore be automatically unlawful. This provision does not mean that authorities necessarily have to establish procedures which would provide for a completely objective examination. There is room for considerable differences of opinion about merit and about the matters which can be taken into account when assessing it. However, authorities do have to be careful that their procedures do not give rise to discrimination. In addition there are specific duties to appoint a chief finance officer (LGA 1972 s. 151), a head of paid service (LGHA 1989 s. 4), and a monitoring officer (LGHA 1989 s. 5). The functions of these officers are considered below.

# B POLITICALLY RESTRICTED POSTS

Members of local authorities cannot be appointed as officers of those authorities. If they **3.05** cease to be members, they cannot be appointed as officers for twelve months: LGA 1972 s. 116. The LGHA 1989 introduced restrictions on the extent to which certain categories of local government officers could engage in political activity. This was to put an end to the practice known as 'twin-tracking' whereby officers in one authority also pursued political careers in another authority.

The officers to whom these restrictions apply are as follows: **3.06**

(a) the head of paid service;
(b) the statutory chief officers;
(c) non-statutory chief officers (who report directly to the head of paid service);
(d) deputy chief officers (who report to a chief officer);
(e) the monitoring officer;
(f) political advisers;
(g) officers to whom statutory powers are delegated;
(h) officers paid more than a certain amount fixed by regulations (currently linked to spinal column point 44 on the pay scale published by the National Joint Council);
(i) officers who regularly give advice to the authority, or one of its committees or sub-committees, or a joint committee on which it is represented;
(j) officers who regularly speak on behalf of the authority to journalists or broadcasters.

Those who simply provide secretarial, clerical, or other services are not treated as deputy chief officers or non-statutory chief officers. Teachers, including head teachers and staff employed in higher and further education, are excluded from these provisions.

Those included on the list can apply for exemption to the adjudicator appointed by the **3.07** Secretary of State. The adjudicator may also, on the application of any person or otherwise, direct a local authority to include a post on the list. If satisfied that the post does not fall within the list set out above, the adjudicator must give a direction that, while the direction has effect, the post is not to be regarded as politically restricted and must therefore be excluded from the authority's list of politically restricted posts. The adjudicator must give priority to applicants who wish to contest a forthcoming election.

The local authority is under a duty to provide the adjudicator with information reasonably **3.08** required to carry out his functions. It must also comply with the adjudicator's directions and inform any holder of a post which is subject to a direction of the terms of that direction. The adjudicator also has a duty to give general advice about how to determine questions about whether a post should be regarded as politically restricted. Before giving such advice the adjudicator must consult such representatives of local government and of employees in local government as he considers appropriate.

Officers in politically restricted posts may not do any of the following (LGHA 1989 s. 1): **3.09**

(a) be or remain a member of a local authority or a Member of Parliament;
(b) announce the intention of standing as a candidate for Parliament, the European Parliament, or a local authority without resigning first;

(c)   act as an election agent;

(d)   act as an officer, or participate in the management of any political party or any branch of it;

(e)   canvass on behalf of a political party in an election;

(f)   speak in public, or publish any written or artistic work with the apparent intention of affecting public support for any political party.

**3.10**   The restriction referred to in (f) above does not apply to political advisers unless the circumstances are likely to create the impression that the adviser is speaking as an authorised party representative or that publication is authorised by a political party. The restrictions contained in (b) to (f) above are made conditions of the officer's contract of employment. The only sanction for breach of these, therefore, is the possibility of disciplinary action by the employing authority.

## C   DISCIPLINE AND DISMISSAL

**3.11**   The power to appoint staff on such terms as the authority thinks fit includes provisions about disciplinary action and grounds for dismissal. Local authority officers have the benefit of employment protection legislation. There is not usually any public law element to the dismissal or disciplining of a local government officer and such decisions will not therefore usually be susceptible to challenge on administrative law grounds. However, this is subject to certain exceptions. In *R v Liverpool City Council, ex parte Ferguson* [1985] *The Times* 20 November, the Council resolved to dismiss a whole category of staff (teachers) on which it depended to carry out one of its statutory duties. This action was the direct consequence of the council's failure to set a lawful rate which would have enabled it to balance its budget. In these circumstances, the court granted an order of mandamus to quash the decision.

**3.12**   Similarly, administrative law remedies are available to employees affected by an authority's decision to adopt an employment policy which is in itself unlawful. In *R v Hammersmith and Fulham London Borough Council, ex parte NALGO* [1991] COD 397 the authority had adopted a policy that set out various criteria by which staff would be selected for redundancy. NALGO considered that these criteria would be likely to discriminate against individuals on the grounds of race and would therefore be contrary to the Race Relations Act 1976. The council argued that leave to take judicial review proceedings should be refused on the basis that this remedy was not available for resolving what was essentially an employment dispute. This argument was rejected. The applicants would not have been able to obtain the remedies they were seeking from an employment tribunal. Not all employment issues which affected all staff would be justiciable, but if a local authority adopted a policy which contravened the Race Relations Act 1976 or the Sex Discrimination Act 1975, judicial review would be available to quash it. On the facts before the court, the local authority had not done this: the most the applicants could argue was that the legislative provisions could be breached depending on how the policy was applied in individual cases. If this happened, redress could be obtained through an employment tribunal claim. In these circumstances, it was not an appropriate case for judicial review.

## D   CHIEF OFFICERS AND HEADS OF PAID SERVICE

There is power under s. 8 LGHA 1989 for the Secretary of State to make standing orders as to **3.13** staff and to include in these such provisions as the regulations may prescribe. Such standing orders have been made to regulate the appointment of chief officers and disciplinary action taken against heads of paid service: Local Authorities (Standing Orders) Regulations (SI No. 2001/3384).

### Appointment of chief officers

Where a local authority proposes to appoint a chief officer, and it is not proposed that the **3.14** appointment should be made exclusively from among existing officers, it must:

(a)   draw up a statement specifying—
  (i)   the duties of the officer concerned, and
  (ii)  any qualifications or qualities to be sought in the person to be appointed;
(b)   make arrangements for the post to be advertised in such a way as is likely to bring it to the attention of persons who are qualified to apply for it; and
(c)   make arrangements for a copy of the statement mentioned in (a) to be sent to any person on request.

Where a post has been advertised in accordance with the above procedure the authority must: **3.15**

(a)   interview all qualified applicants for the post; or
(b)   select a short list of such qualified applicants and interview those included on the short list.

If no qualified person has applied, the authority must go through the advertising process again.

It is hard to believe that the above is anything other than normal practice for local authority **3.16** chief officer posts. Appointments of non-statutory chief officers (see above) can be excluded from these provisions as may the appointments of assistants for political groups.

### Protection for chief executives

These standing orders also provide a degree of protection for Chief Executives against **3.17** undeserved disciplinary action. If it appears to an authority that misconduct by its head of paid service needs to be investigated, it must appoint a 'designated independent person'. This appointment has to be agreed between the head of paid service and the authority or, in default of agreement, made by the Secretary of State. The authority may suspend the head of paid service while the investigation is taking place, but any such suspension must be on full pay and must not exceed two months.

The designated independent person: **3.18**

(a)   may direct—
  (i)   that the authority terminate any suspension of the officer,
  (ii)  that any such suspension shall continue after the two month period or any previously extended period,

(iii) that the terms on which any suspension has taken place shall be varied in accordance with the direction,

(iv) that no steps towards disciplinary action or further disciplinary action other than steps taken in the presence of or with the agreement of the designated independent person, are to be taken before a report is made under (d) below;

(b) may inspect any documents relating to the conduct of the relevant officer which are in the possession of the authority, or which the authority has power to authorise him to inspect;

(c) may require any officer of the authority to answer questions concerning the conduct of the relevant officer;

(d) shall make a report to the authority—

(i) stating his opinion as to whether (and if so the extent to which) the evidence he has obtained supports any allegation of misconduct, and

(ii) recommending any disciplinary action which he considers to be appropriate;

(e) shall at the same time send a copy of the report to the officer.

## E  TRANSFER AND SECONDMENT

**3.19**  Under the LGA 1972 s. 113 there is specific power to enter into an agreement with another local authority to put officers at the disposal of that other authority on terms set out in the agreement. Officers moved to another authority by the agreement must be consulted before the agreement is entered into, but there is no requirement that they consent. There is similar power to put local authority staff at the disposal of health authorities and NHS trusts, again subject to prior consultation with the officers concerned. Secondment has also been used by local authorities in strategic partnerships with the private sector.

## F  THE TRANSFER OF UNDERTAKINGS REGULATIONS (TUPE)

### The application of TUPE to contracting

**3.20**  Because of the extent to which local authority activities have been transferred to the private sector the Transfer of Undertakings (Protection of Employment) Regulations 1981 (TUPE) have been particularly important in protecting the employment of those who work on these contracts. TUPE is a subject which lawyers advising on local government contracts will need to be familiar with. The Regulations gave effect to the Acquired Rights Directive (originally Council Directive EEC/77/187 now Council Directive 2001/23/EC). The purpose of the Directive was to provide for employees working for a business not to lose their jobs when the running or ownership of the business was transferred. Before the Directive was transposed into UK law, on the transfer of a business employees would have their contracts of employment terminated.

**3.21**  The applicability of these regulations to the public sector was not appreciated until the early 1990s. There was originally a restriction to the effect that the regulations applied only to commercial undertakings. This was considered to be wrong and the regulations were amended in 1994. The ECJ paved the way to this change with the case of *Dr Sophie Redmond Stichting v Bartol* [1992] IRLR 366. In this case a Dutch local authority had terminated grant funding for one body providing a service to drug addicts and awarded the grant instead to a different foundation. The ECJ concluded that this gave rise to a transfer of employment under the Acquired Rights Directive.

This approach was followed in the UK in the cases of *Wren v Eastbourne Borough Council*   **3.22**
[1993] IRLR 425 and *Dines v Initial Healthcare Services* [1994] IRLR 336. In the first of these cases the local authority had obtained competitive tenders under the CCT regime for its refuse collection service. The in-house bid was unsuccessful and the employees were dismissed by the local authority. Some, but not all, of the employees were re-employed by the new contractor. The employees who lost their jobs took proceedings for unfair dismissal. They were unsuccessful at the industrial tribunal but their appeal to the Employment Appeals Tribunal (EAT) was allowed. It was held that a transfer of services without any transfer of assets could constitute the transfer of an undertaking.

The Court of Appeal confirmed the correctness of this approach in *Dines v Initial Healthcare*   **3.23**
*Services*. This case concerned the transfer of a hospital cleaning contract. The contract for this work was let following a process of competitive tendering. The cleaning company which had been carrying out the work was unsuccessful so the contract was awarded to a new contractor. The new cleaning company took over most of the staff but at lower wages and there were some dismissals. The employees claimed that there had been a transfer of their employment to the new cleaning contractor. They failed both before the industrial tribunal and the EAT but their appeal to the Court of Appeal was successful. The Court of Appeal took the view that because the employees were doing essentially the same job in the same place for the same people, this was a transfer for the purposes of the regulations. It did not matter that there were no assets transferred.

The ECJ's approach to the application of the Directive to contracting out situations does not   **3.24**
appear to have been entirely consistent. In *Schmidt v Spar-und Leihkasse Der Früheren Ämter Bordesholm, Kiel und Cronshagen* [1994] IRLR 302 the ECJ held that the duties of a single part-time employee were capable of constituting an undertaking which transferred when her cleaning duties were assigned to a company which had been carrying out cleaning at other branches of her employer. However, in *Süzen v Zehnacker Gebäudereigigung GmbH Krankenhausservice* [1997] IRLR 255 the ECJ indicated that not all contracting out situations would give rise to a TUPE transfer. This case concerned a cleaner employed under a school cleaning contract who was dismissed when the contract was taken over by a different company. She sought a declaration that she was employed by the new company. The ECJ made the following pronouncements:

> ... the mere fact that the service provided by the old and the new awardees of the contract is similar does not therefore support the conclusion that an economic entity has been transferred. An entity cannot be reduced to the activity entrusted to it. Its identity also emerges from other factors, such as its workforce, its management staff, the way in which its work is organised, its operating methods or indeed, where appropriate, the operational resources available to it.
>
> The mere loss of a service contract to a competitor cannot, therefore, by itself, indicate the existence of a transfer within the meaning of the Directive. In those circumstances, the service

undertaking previously entrusted with the contract does not, on losing a customer, thereby cease fully to exist, and the business or part of a business belonging to it cannot be considered to have been transferred to the new awardee of the contract.

**3.25** The above statements are typical of the somewhat Delphic nature of the ECJ's judgments. They are not particularly helpful as practical guidance as to how to approach the application of TUPE to a given set of circumstances. The *Süzen* decision has meant that courts since then have been more cautious (and to some extent less predictable) about the circumstances in which they will apply TUPE to contracting out situations. For instance in *Betts v Brintel Helicopters Ltd* [1997] IRLR 361 when Shell decided to award one of its helicopter contracts to a new contractor, no assets or equipment were transferred and the centre of operations moved from Beccles to Norwich. The new contractor did not take over any of the existing staff who had been working on the contract. The Court of Appeal held that TUPE did not apply. The implication of the Court of Appeal judgment was that in labour intensive industries such as cleaning, if the same or a substantial proportion of the same staff transfer the undertaking will retain its identity and TUPE will apply. However, in industries where the situation is more complex, a more wide-ranging enquiry will be needed.

**3.26** If employers who wished to avoid the application of TUPE considered that all they needed to do was refuse to take on the workforce, then the case of *ECM (Vehicle Delivery Service) Ltd v Cox* [1998] IRLR 416 corrected this misapprehension. A contract for a vehicle delivery service was awarded to a different company which refused to take on any of the employees responsible for delivering vehicles under the old contract. The employees' claim of unfair dismissal was successful in the employment tribunal and their decision was upheld by the EAT and the Court of Appeal. The employers' argument that all that was being transferred was an activity was rejected by the EAT and Court of Appeal on the basis that the employees' continued employment was dependent on the existence of the contract. (Although the same could be said of the employees in *Betts* where a different conclusion was reached.) The courts were also unimpressed that the employees had been dismissed specifically to avoid the application of TUPE. As Morison P said in the EAT, it 'would not be proper for a transferee to be able to control the extent of his obligations by refusing to comply with them in the first place'.

**3.27** The approach taken above in the *ECM* case, that in a contracting out case the motive for the decision not to take on the workforce could be important has subsequently been endorsed by the EAT in *RCO Support Services and Aintree Hospital Trust v Unison* [2000] IRLR 624, in which a change of contractor in hospital cleaning and catering contracts was held to constitute a TUPE transfer, and by a majority of the Court of Appeal in *ADI (UK) Ltd v Willer* [2001] IRLR 542, which concerned a contract for security services. The new contractor did not employ any of the employees who had been working on the old contract. The Court of Appeal remitted the case back to the employment tribunal for them to investigate the reason why the employees had not been taken on.

### Identifying a TUPE transfer

**3.28** In identifying whether in a given situation a TUPE transfer has taken place, or, a more common problem for local authority solicitors, whether it will take place, it is necessary to approach the issue by identifying the answers to two questions:

1. Is there an undertaking which is capable of being transferred?
2. Is there a transfer to which TUPE applies?

In *Cheesman v R Brewer Contracts Ltd* [2001] IRLR 144 the EAT set out guidance on how to **3.29**
approach both of these questions. As to whether there is an undertaking the following
factors need to be considered:

1. There needs to be a stable economic entity whose activity is not limited to performing
   one specific works contract. It needs to be an organised grouping of persons and of
   assets enabling (or facilitating) the exercise of an economic activity which pursues a
   specific objective. (This is a conclusion drawn from ECJ case law such as *Rygaard v Strø
   Mølle Akustik A/S* [1996] IRLR 51 in which an employee who was working on a short-
   term one-off building contract was held not to constitute a 'stable economic entity'
   capable of transferring pursuant to the Directive.)
2. The undertaking must be sufficiently structured and autonomous but need not
   necessarily have significant assets, tangible or intangible.
3. In some sectors such as cleaning and security the activity is essentially based on man-
   power. (The conclusion being that in these sectors the question of whether there are
   assets capable of being transferred is irrelevant.)
4. An organised grouping of wage-earners who are specifically and permanently assigned
   to a common task may amount to an economic entity.
5. An activity of itself is not an entity; the identity of an entity emerges from other
   factors, such as its workforce, management style, the way in which its work is
   organised, its operating methods and, where appropriate, the operational resources
   available to it.

As regards the issue of whether there was a transfer, the ECJ case of *Spijkers v Gebroeders* **3.30**
*Benedik Abattoir CV* [1986] CMLR 296 had already established a list of the factors to be taken
into account, which has been applied subsequently in the ECJ and the UK courts. It is
necessary to look at all these factors, not consider one in isolation. The ECJ emphasised that
what is needed is an overall appraisal which is a matter for the national courts determining
these questions. The list is as follows:

1. The type of undertaking.
2. Whether or not its tangible assets are transferred.
3. The value of its intangible assets at the time of transfer.
4. Whether or not the majority of its employees are taken over by the new company.
5. Whether or not its customers are transferred.
6. The degree of similarity between the activities carried on before and after the transfer.
7. The period, if any, for which they are suspended.

This list was referred to by the EAT in *Cheesman* who made the following additional points: **3.31**

1. The decisive question is whether the entity in question retains its identity. Is its
   operation actually continued or resumed?
2. There is a need to take into account the type of business or undertaking being considered. The degree of importance to be given to the criteria used to establish whether
   a transfer of an undertaking takes place will vary according to the nature of the
   activity.

3.  If an economic entity can function without significant assets, the maintenance of its identity after a transfer cannot logically depend on the transfer of such assets.
4.  There can still be a TUPE transfer if no assets are transferred.
5.  The absence of a contractual link between the transferor and transferee may be evidence that there has not been a TUPE transfer but it is not conclusive.
6.  If no employees are transferred the reasons for this can be relevant in assessing whether there was a transfer. (See para 3.26 above.)

## Part of an undertaking

**3.32**  The TUPE regulations also apply when part of an undertaking is transferred. This part must be 'transferred as a business'. Thus the transfer of either assets or employees will not of itself constitute a transfer under TUPE without some type of business transfer of an identifiable part of the transferring entity. The test applied by the EAT in *Green v Wavertree Heating and Plumbing Co Ltd* [1978] ICR 928 was that there was no need for the part of the business being transferred to be a separate and self contained business in itself. It was enough that it was a recognisable and identifiable part of the business as a whole.

## Which employees belong to the undertaking

**3.33**  This is another question which frequently presents itself in transfers involving local authorities. The principle was established in *Botzen v Rotterdamsche Droogdok Maatschappij BV* [1986] 2 CMLR 50. The ECJ in that case decided that the question of whether an employee belonged to the undertaking or part of undertaking which was being transferred was to be determined by whether he was assigned to that part of the undertaking from a managerial point of view. The test is less easy to apply in practice. The solution proposed by the Advocate General in that case, namely that the individual must be wholly employed in the unit which is being transferred subject only to minimal duties elsewhere has not been adopted in practice. However, the fact that an employee spends more than 50 per cent of his time on work for a particular part of an organisation is not sufficient to conclude that he is assigned to this part if there is a TUPE transfer. It may also mean that some jobs which are entirely dependent on a particular economic unit may not form part of that unit for the purposes of TUPE. For instance a personnel officer who spends all his or her time on work for an ICT department might have no job if that department's work is outsourced but the personnel officer would not form part of the unit transferred for the purposes of TUPE. The fact that an employee's contract of employment includes a mobility clause will not override the factual situation if they are in practice employed at a particular location: *Securicor Guarding Ltd v Fraser Security Services Ltd* [1996] IRLR 552.

**3.34**  The EAT decision in *Duncan Web Offset (Maidstone) Ltd v Cooper* [1995] IRLR 633 contained guidance as to the factors which should be considered in deciding the issue of assignment:

(a)  the amount of time spent on one part of the business or the other;
(b)  the amount of value given to each part by the employee;
(c)  the terms of the contract of employment showing what the employee could be required to do;

(d) how the cost to the employer of the employee's services were allocated between different parts of the business.

## Dismissals for TUPE and changes in terms and conditions

Dismissal for a reason connected with the transfer is automatically unfair unless it is for **3.35** an economic, technical, or organisational reason entailing changes in the workforce. In addition it is forbidden to contract out of the application of the regulations. What then is the position of employees who are dismissed but taken on with new terms and conditions or who agree to a variation in their terms and conditions? The first situation arose in the House of Lords' case of *Wilson v St Helen's Borough Council* [1998] 3 WLR 1070. This concerned a home which trustees wished to transfer to the local borough council. The council agreed to take it over on condition that there were changes in the terms and conditions of employment of the staff. The staff were dismissed at the time of transfer and some of them were offered employment by the council on new terms and conditions (which did not include an allowance which they had been paid previously). Over a year later the staff brought proceedings in the industrial tribunal claiming that the failure to pay them the allowance they had previously received constituted an unlawful deduction under the Wages Act 1986. The issue was eventually considered by the House of Lords. The court considered that the dismissals had been effective to terminate the contracts of employment of the employees. It was therefore open to the new employer to agree new terms and conditions of employment which were binding on the employees. It is unlawful to vary the terms and conditions as a result of the transfer. But this does not mean that terms and conditions can never be varied:

> I do not accept the argument that the variation is invalid only if it is agreed on as a part of the transfer itself. The variation may still be due to the transfer and for no other reason even if it comes later. However, it seems that there must, or at least may, come a time when the link with the transfer is broken or can be treated as no longer effective.

If an employee is not dismissed, then it is not open to him to agree changes to his terms and **3.36** conditions of employment as a result of the transfer: *Crédit Suisse First Boston (Europe) Ltd v Lister* [1998] IRLR 700.

## Information and consultation requirements

The transferor and transferee must both provide information in respect of any employee **3.37** affected by a TUPE transfer. The duty is to provide the information to the appropriate representatives. In a local government context this will normally be the trade unions but may be other representatives elected by the employees concerned. The obligation is to provide information in respect of affected employees. Thus if employees are affected by the transfer even if they are not actually transferred, then the information must be provided to their representatives. The information to be provided is as follows:

(a) the fact that the transfer is to take place, when, approximately, it is to take place, and the reasons for it;
(b) the legal, economic and social implications of the transfer for the affected employee;
(c) whether or not it is intended to take measures in respect of the affected employees and, if so, what measures.

**3.38**  If the transferee employer intends to take measures in respect of transferring employees he must provide details of these to the transferor who must pass the information to the recognised trade unions for the transferring employees. In addition, if the transferee envisages that he will take measures in respect of any transferring employees, there is a duty on both the transferor and transferee employers to consult with appropriate representatives with a view to reaching agreement as to the measures to be taken.

**3.39**  There has only been one decided case which has provided significant guidance on the information and consultation requirements: *Institute of Professional Civil Servants v Secretary of State for Defence* [1987] IRLR 373. The conclusions drawn by the High Court in that case were:

(a)  Information must be provided in good time to enable consultations to take place. Even if there is no need to consult (because no measures are envisaged) the information must be provided in time to allow for voluntary consultations.

(b)  There is no requirement on the employer to produce information in any particular form, in particular the representatives do not have the right to insist on the production of original documents.

(c)  The word 'measures' is of the widest import and includes any action, step, or arrangement.

(d)  The word 'envisages' means visualises or foresees but it does not require consultation about mere possibilities. The duty to consult only arises when there is a definite plan or proposal.

## Local government reorganisation

**3.40**  The ECJ has decided that the Directive does not apply on a transfer of administrative functions from one local government organisation to another: *Henke v Gemeinde Schierke* [1996] IRLR 701. Frau Henke lost her job as secretary to the Mayor of Schierke as a result of a process of local government reorganisation. The ECJ held that administrative functions were not an economic activity and that therefore this type of reorganisation did not give rise to a transfer in accordance with the Directive. The effect of this decision is limited in the UK because of the effect of s. 38 of the Employment Relations Act 1999 which allows the Secretary of State to apply TUPE to situations where it would not otherwise apply.

## Policy on local authority contracting

**3.41**  In January 2000 the Government published guidance on the application of TUPE to public sector contracting in the form of the Cabinet Office Statement of Practice. This set out a framework which the Government expected to be followed by all public sector organisations including local authorities. The policy behind the guidance was based on the following principles:

1.  Contracting-out exercises with the private sector or voluntary organisations and transfers between different parts of the public sector should be conducted on the basis that TUPE will apply unless there are genuinely exceptional reasons why it should not do so.

2.  This includes second and subsequent rounds of contracting and situations where a function is brought back into the control of the public sector having previously been outsourced.
3.  In circumstances where TUPE does not apply in strict legal terms, the principles of TUPE should be followed so that staff are treated no less favourably than they would have been if TUPE had applied.
4.  There should be appropriate arrangements to protect occupational pensions, redundancy, and severance terms for transferred staff.

The statement goes on to advise that public authorities engaged on a tendering exercise **3.42** should take the following steps:

1.  At the earliest appropriate stage in the contracting exercise it should state that staff are to transfer and this should normally have the effect of causing TUPE to apply. (This is a strange piece of advice. First, it is an exaggeration to say that stating in advance that staff will transfer will normally have the effect of causing TUPE to apply. It will make it more likely, but it is simply one factor. Second, it appears to cut across the duty of a best value authority in that the price of ensuring that TUPE applies in situations where it normally would not could mean a more expensive service.)
2.  At the earliest appropriate stage staff and recognised unions (or, if none, other independent staff representatives) are informed in writing of the intention that staff will transfer and that TUPE should apply.
3.  When potential bidders are invited to tender they are told that it is intended that staff will transfer and that TUPE should apply. They should also be told that they can if they wish submit bids where staff do not transfer and TUPE will not apply but these will only be accepted if they fall within the genuinely exceptional circumstances. (This appears to be over-simplifying the position. Whether there is a TUPE transfer or not will depend on a variety of circumstances. There could be types of outsourcing of services which do not involve TUPE transfers but which do not fall within the list of exceptions set out below.)
4.  The contracting exercise is operated on the basis that the intention is that staff will transfer and TUPE should apply. The authority should consider all bids received. However, if the bid falls outside the exceptional circumstances then the authority reserves the right not to accept the tender. (It would be wise to consider all the circumstances, with particular reference to the guidance given in the case law referred to above before coming to a firm view about whether TUPE would apply.)
5.  In a very few cases bids made on the basis that TUPE will not apply will fall within the exceptional circumstances and should be accepted, though the costs of redundancy and/or redeployment need to be taken into account. (The notion that these will be a very few cases may not be correct. The local authority is likely to have a clear view before the contract is let as to whether TUPE is likely to apply or not. There are likely to be circumstances where it is clear that there will not be a transfer of staff and TUPE will have no application.)
6.  Where there is then a contractual requirement that staff should transfer, the requirements of TUPE should be scrupulously followed by the local authority which should also ensure that the bidders' proposals meet the requirements of TUPE. (Again, this

appears to simplify the position. The issue of whether TUPE applies is not determined by whether there is a contractual requirement to this effect.)

**3.43**   The Statement also advises that the re-tendering of contracts where staff originally from the public sector have transferred to an external contractor should also give rise to a TUPE transfer. The re-tendering exercise should take place in the same way described above The same principles also apply to transfers of staff back to the public sector from an external organisation.

**3.44**   The Statement advises that there are a small number of cases where the policy set out above may not be followed and TUPE may not apply. The circumstances that may qualify for such exceptions are broadly:

- where a contract is for the provision of both goods and services, but the provision of services is ancillary in purpose to the provision of the goods; or
- where the activity for which the public sector organisation is contracting is essentially new or a one-off project; or
- where services or goods are essentially a commodity bought 'off the shelf' and no grouping of staff specifically and permanently assigned to a common task; or
- where the features of the service or function subject to the contracting exercise are significantly different from the features of the function previously performed within the public sector, or by an existing contractor e.g. a function to be delivered electronically and in such a way that it requires radically different skills, experience, and equipment.

**3.45**   There are obviously circumstances in which TUPE will not apply which do not figure on the above list. These will include situations where, for instance, what is being transferred is not an identifiable and recognisable part of an existing 'business'. Or the operation could be transferred elsewhere without taking on any of the existing staff or assets, as in the *Brintel* case referred to above. There is no clear advice in the Statement as to how local authorities should respond in these circumstances. The authority will still have to form its own judgement as to whether TUPE will apply. The Statement was accompanied by an annex entitled A Fair Deal for Staff Pensions. This provided that when staff are transferred from the public to the private sector, there need to be arrangements in place to ensure that they benefit from a broadly comparable pension scheme. This can be achieved by considering the new employer's existing or proposed pension arrangements and having an actuary certify that these are broadly comparable. (The Government Actuary's Department will provide advice on this.) It can also be achieved by the provider being admitted to the local government pension scheme.

**3.46**   The Government issued a Code of Practice on Workforce Matters in Local Authority Service Contracts as Annex D of the Best Value Circular 03/2003. This reiterates support for the principles set out in the Cabinet Office Statement in the following terms:

> In its contracting-out of services, the local authority will apply the principles set out in the Cabinet Office Statement of Practice on Staff Transfers in the Public Sector and the annex to it, A Fair Deal for Staff Pensions. The service provider will be required to demonstrate its support for these principles and its willingness to work with the local authority fully to implement them.

**3.47**   In addition the Code provides that the same principles should be extended to new employees joining an outsourced workforce. It provides that the service provider should offer employment on fair and reasonable terms and conditions which are, overall, no less favourable than those of transferred employees. The effect of TUPE will therefore not only be that the terms and conditions of employment of transferred staff will need to be maintained but the same terms and conditions will need to be applied to those joining the workforce from outside.

The Code also deals with monitoring and enforcement. The service provider should be **3.48** under an obligation to the authority to provide information which will enable the authority to judge whether these obligations are being complied with. There is also said to be an obligation on local authorities to enforce the provisions of the Code. This means that if a local authority is not satisfied that the contractor is fulfilling its obligations, the authority should if need be, take action by seeking to enforce the contract. (It does not appear to be suggested that employees should be given the right to enforce the contract itself under the Contracts (Rights of Third Parties) Act 1999.) It also advises that there should be an ADR mechanism which is suitable for resolving disputes over these issues.

## Revised Acquired Rights Directive

Negotiations began about a revised version of the Acquired Rights Directive as long ago as **3.49** 1994. The process was very slow and a new Directive was not adopted until 1998. A consolidated version of the Directive was adopted in 2001. For the first time there is a definition explaining what is meant by a transfer of an undertaking:

(a)  This Directive shall apply to any transfer of an undertaking, business or part of an undertaking or business to another employer as a result of a legal transfer or merger.

(b)  Subject to subparagraph (a) and the following provisions of this Article, there is a transfer within the meaning of this Directive where there is a transfer of an economic entity which retains its identity, meaning an organised grouping of resources which has the objective of pursuing an economic activity, whether or not that activity is central or ancillary.

(c)  This Directive shall apply to public and private undertakings engaged in economic activities whether or not they are operating for gain. An administrative reorganisation of public administrative authorities, or the transfer of administrative functions between public administrative authorities, is not a transfer within the meaning of this Directive.

It can be seen that this definition adds nothing new. It is simply a reflection of the legal position arrived at after many individual cases were considered by the ECJ.

This Directive needs to be transposed into the domestic law of Member States. In September **3.50** 2001 the Government published a detailed background paper on its proposals for reform of the TUPE regulations. Its intentions can be summarised as follows:

1.  That TUPE or an equivalent means of protecting employment should apply to transfers within public sector administration.

2.  That it would be made clear that TUPE applied to changes in service provision.

3.  That the employee's occupational pension rights would transfer under TUPE.

4.  That there would be an obligation on the transferor to give the transferee written notification of all the rights and obligations in relation to employees that are to be transferred.

5.    It would be clarified that TUPE does not preclude transfer-related changes to terms and conditions made for an economic, technical, or organisational reason entailing changes in the workforce.

## Revised TUPE regulations

**3.51**   A revised set of draft regulations were circulated by the DTI for public consultation in March 2005. These would spell out that TUPE applies to a service provision change. This is defined as a situation in which:

1.    activities cease to be carried out by a person ('a client') on his own behalf and are carried out instead by another person on the client's behalf ('a contractor'),
2.    activities cease to be carried out by a contractor on a client's behalf (whether or not those activities had previously been carried out by the client on his own behalf) and are carried out instead by another person ('a subsequent contractor') on the client's behalf, or
3.    activities cease to be carried out by a contractor or a subsequent contractor on a client's behalf (whether or not those activities had previously been carried out by the client on his own behalf) and are carried out instead by the client on his own behalf.

This can be summarised as contracting out, reletting, and bringing services in-house.

**3.52**   In addition effect is given to the case law on the definition of an undertaking by providing that before the service provision change:

1.    there must be an organised grouping of employees situated immediately before the change in the United Kingdom which has as its principal purpose the carrying out of the activities concerned on behalf of the client,
2.    the client intends that the activities will, following the service provision change, be carried out by the transferee other than in connection with a single specific event or task.

The activities must not consist wholly or mainly of the procurement or supply of goods for the client's use. There is also consideration being given to a general exclusion for the provision of professional services.

## G   DUTIES OF PARTICULAR LOCAL AUTHORITY OFFICERS

**3.53**   In certain circumstances, local authority officers can be under a duty to challenge the decisions of the authorities who employ them. This slightly bizarre requirement was imposed, first, by the Local Government Finance Act 1988 on those responsible for the financial affairs of local authorities and then extended to other officers by the LGHA 1989.

## Duties of the officer responsible for financial affairs

**3.54**   It has, since 1972, been an obligation of local authorities to appoint an officer to have responsibility for their financial affairs. This officer will normally these days be called the

Director of Finance. The holder of this post did not, before 1988, need to have any particular qualifications, although in practice a background, if not a formal qualification, in account-ancy was likely to be necessary. The Local Government Finance Act 1988 now means that any new appointments must only be to those with a formal accountancy qualification. This requirement went hand in hand with the powerful statutory responsibilities placed on the Director of Finance.

This officer has a duty to make a report (under s. 114 LGFA 1988) where the local authority or **3.55** one of its committees, or a joint committee on which it is represented:

(a)   has made or is about to make a decision that involves or would involve the authority incurring expenditure that is unlawful; or

(b)   has taken or is about to take a course of action which, if pursued to its conclusion, would be unlawful and likely to cause a loss or deficiency on the part of the authority; or

(c)   is about to enter an item of account the entry of which is unlawful.

There is also a duty to make a report if it appears to the officer that the expenditure of the authority incurred (including proposed expenditure) in a financial year is likely to exceed the resources (including borrowing) available to meet that expenditure.

When preparing a report the officer is under duty to consult with the head of paid service **3.56** and the monitoring officer. This duty was added later. These offices did not exist until the enactment of the LGHA 1989. Once the report is prepared, a copy must be served on the auditor and every member of the local authority. Once this has been done, the local author-ity has to convene a meeting of the full council within 21 days, to decide whether it agrees or disagrees with the views contained in the report and what action (if any) it proposes to take in consequence of it. This decision cannot be delegated; it must be taken by the full council itself. Between the report being sent and the council meeting, the council must desist from doing whatever the officer considered to be illegal or, if the report was served on the basis that expenditure was exceeding income, must desist from entering into any new agreement that involves expenditure being incurred.

These curious provisions are inexplicable without some knowledge of the conflict between **3.57** the Government and some local authorities over local government expenditure during the 1980s. It might be thought that the job of advising on whether a particular course of action or expenditure was illegal or not was that of a lawyer rather than an accountant. The second duty is in some ways even more surprising. If the local authority is running out of money, the Director of Finance could reasonably be expected to mention this important fact without a statutory duty. The fact that these new duties were in practice already undertaken by officers was pointed out when these provisions were being considered in Parliament. The provisions were introduced in the wake of resistance by some authorities during the 1980s to the Government's restrictions on local authority expenditure. This resulted in a number of authorities having recourse to creative means of borrowing, incurring future liabilities, in order to arrive at a balanced budget, avoiding both the increases in rates and the expenditure cuts that would otherwise have been necessary. These devices were forbidden by legislation. Some authorities tried to put extra pressure on the Government by delaying the making of a rate. This culminated, in Lambeth and Liverpool, in councillors being surcharged and disqualified for this delay. In the cases of both authorities, though, clear advice had been given about the illegality of the proposed course of action. This advice was disregarded by the councillors concerned.

**3.58**  The chief finance officer's duty as regards illegal conduct or proposed illegal conduct obviously overlaps to a very large extent with the duty of the chief monitoring officer, considered below. If there is illegal conduct involving expenditure of money, it may be that a report from both is required.

**3.59**  In general, on a practical level, it is unlikely that a report on the basis that expenditure above resources was being incurred would be made without prior reports and discussions with members to ensure that corrective action was taken. However, if no corrective action was taken, or this proved ineffective, then it would be the duty of the chief financial officer to serve a report. Similarly, it is improbable that a report on the basis of illegal expenditure would be made unless there had been some prior warning. This may not be possible where there is a discovery that illegal action has been taking place, or where action thought to be legal has been discovered to be illegal, as was the case with the London Borough of Hammersmith and Fulham swap transactions.

**3.60**  It was predicted at the time of enactment that these provisions would be rarely, if ever, used, in that they would be unlikely to be necessary unless there was a complete breakdown of trust between the local authority and its chief financial officer. In fact relations between members and finance officers have been rather more robust than these forebodings suggest. These provisions have been used on a number of occasions, in some cases by officers who continued to enjoy the confidence of their authority.

### Duties of the head of paid service

**3.61**  The reporting duty on the head of paid service is rather less contentious. This is simply to report 'when he considers it appropriate to do so' on any proposals concerning:

(a)  the manner in which the discharge by the authority of its different functions is co-ordinated;

(b)  the number and grades of staff required by the authority for the discharge of its functions;

(c)  the organisation of the authority's staff; and

(d)  the appointment and proper management of the authority's staff.

**3.62**  As soon as practicable after preparing such a report, a copy must be sent to each member of the council. It must be debated by the full council at a meeting held not less than three months after the delivery of the report. The duty of considering the report cannot be delegated. It is interesting to note the lack of urgency when compared with the 21-day deadline for considering reports of the chief financial officer and monitoring officer. It is quite surprising that it was thought necessary to impose a duty to report about matters of this nature. Any person appointed as head of paid service would have to consider and make recommendations about how the authority goes about fulfilling its functions, its structure, management, and staffing.

## Duties of the chief monitoring officer

More substantial duties fall on the chief monitoring officer. The local authority has to **3.63** appoint one of its officers to undertake this role, the duties of which are set out in s. 5 of the LGHA 1989. Although the duties are essentially of a legal nature, there is no requirement for this officer to have any legal qualifications. There is nothing to stop a local authority appointing the same person as chief monitoring officer and as head of paid service, and in many authorities the Chief Executive is responsible for the monitoring officer's functions.

The duty of the monitoring officer is to report:     **3.64**

> . . . if it at any time appears to him that any proposal, decision or omission by the authority, by any committee, sub-committee or officer of the authority or by any joint committee on which the authority are represented, constitutes, has given rise to or is likely to or would give rise to—
>
> (a)  a contravention . . . of any enactment or rule of law or of any code of practice made or approved by or under any enactment; or
> (b)  any such maladministration or injustice as is mentioned in Part III of the Local Government Act 1974 (Local Commissioners) or Part II of the Local Government (Scotland) Act 1975. (LGHA 1989, s. 5(2))

The monitoring officer is under a further duty to consult with the head of paid service and the chief finance officer when preparing a report under this section.

Once the report is ready, it must be served on every member of the local authority. They **3.65** must then consider it at a full council meeting held within 21 days of the report being sent. Once again, this responsibility cannot be delegated. As with the chief finance officer's reports, there is a prohibition period between the sending of the report and the holding of the meeting. During this time the authority must ensure that no step is taken that gives effect to the proposal or decision that is the subject of the report.

The performance of these duties is hardly calculated to enhance officer-member relations. In **3.66** fact, though, before the enactment of these provisions, whenever obvious illegality has been contemplated, this has been pointed out to the councillors concerned in explicit terms. The 1989 Act does not make any distinction between different types of illegality. When there is a breach of some enactment then this will be clear and there will be no room for doubt about the advice to be given. However, for a local authority to vote in favour of defying a statutory provision is an unlikely scenario. It is more likely to turn on whether the council acted outside its powers, or whether the decision was vitiated by one of the other possible grounds for judicial review. These concepts are complex, and there will always be room for more than one view on whether a particular course of action is illegal. In these circumstances, an officer's opinion can turn a decision that might be of debatable legality into an obviously illegal decision. Obviously, monitoring officers will not issue reports lightly. Attempts will be made to avoid the necessity of preparing a report and these will normally be successful. It is also likely that before a report is actually prepared, independent advice in the form of counsel's opinion will normally be sought.

There is also a need for common sense about the application of these provisions. An **3.67** organisation as large as some local authorities is likely to fall foul of the law in a number of ways. As a landlord, it may fail to keep all its tenanted properties in repair; as a provider of

transport services, it may fail to keep its vehicles in repair. Yet it cannot seriously be suggested that all these matters, however trivial, should be the subject of the cumbersome
LGHA 1989, s. 5 procedure requiring a full council meeting to be convened. The requirement
to report on maladministration is still more problematic. What constitutes maladministration may be highly subjective. Also, by its very nature, it is unlikely to come to the monitoring officer's attention until it is too late for intervention to be of any use. It would seem
improbable that the duty relating to reporting of maladministration can ever be used
effectively.

## H   DUTIES OF ALL OFFICERS

**3.68**   Like councillors, officers have duties to prevent conflict between their private financial
interests and the interests of the authority. If it comes to the notice of an officer that the
authority has entered into, or is proposing to enter into, a contract in which that officer has a
pecuniary interest, whether direct or indirect, there is a duty to give notice in writing to the
authority of this fact (LGA 1972 s. 117). An officer is to be treated as having an indirect
pecuniary interest in the same circumstances that a member would be under the old rules in
ss 94 to 97 of the LGA 1972, now repealed.

**3.69**   It is also a criminal offence for any officer 'under colour of his office or employment' to
accept 'any fee or reward whatsoever other than his proper remuneration'. This will include
legal costs paid to an officer in respect of legal proceedings taken by a third party: *R v
Ramsgate Corporation* (1889) 23 QBD 66. However, if a council officer has become involved in
legal proceedings only because of the performance of his or her duties, then the legal
costs could properly be paid by the local authority as part of the officer's conditions of
employment under LGA 1972 s. 112.

## I   MISCONDUCT IN A PUBLIC OFFICE

**3.70**   In the leading case of *R v Bembridge* (1783) 3 Doug 327, 99 ER 679, Lord Mansfield laid down
the general principle (332, 681):

> a man accepting an office of trust concerning the public, especially if attended with profit, is
> answerable criminally to the King for misbehaviour in his office; this is true, by whomever and
> in whatever way the officer is appointed.

**3.71**   In *R v Bowden* [1995] 4 All ER 505 it was argued unsuccessfully that the offence applied only
to servants of the Crown. It was held that the general principle stated above, derived from *R v
Bembridge*, applied to all public officers. There had been no case which limited the principle
to servants of the Crown. An argument that the post Mr Bowden held was too lowly to
fall within the scope of the offence was also rejected. The court pointed out that he was
responsible for the receipt and disbursement of public money and that his salary was paid
from public funds. He was therefore a 'public officer' as defined in the authorities. The court
also considered this argument to be reinforced by the definition of public office in the Public

Bodies Corrupt Practices Act 1889 s. 7, namely 'any office or employment of a person as a member, officer or servant of such a public body' which was itself defined as 'any council of a county . . . of a city or a town, any council of a municipal borough'.

The elements of the offence of misconduct in a public office have recently been defined in   **3.72**
*Attorney-General's reference (No. 3 of 2003)* [2004] EWCA Crim 868. The elements of the offence were summarised as:

(i)    a public officer acting as such,
(ii)   wilfully neglected to perform his duty and/or wilfully misconducted himself,
(iii)  to such a degree as to amount to an abuse of the public's trust in the officeholder,
(iv)  without reasonable excuse or justification.

## J   CORRUPTION

The criminal laws against corruption are contained in the Prevention of Corruption Acts   **3.73**
1889 to 1916. The maximum penalty for breach of these provisions is seven years' imprisonment.

Under the Public Bodies Corrupt Practices Act 1889, it is an offence for any member, officer   **3.74**
or servant of a public body, or anybody acting on their behalf, corruptly to solicit, receive or agree to receive any gift, loan, fee reward, or advantage for doing or forbearing to do anything in connection with the public body concerned. Giving or agreeing to give any such gift, loan, fee, reward or advantage is similarly an offence. Under the Prevention of Corruption Act 1906, all those acting as agents are forbidden from taking rewards from those who do not employ them.

## KEY DOCUMENTS

Cabinet Office Statement of Practice January 2000
Code of Practice on Workforce Matters in Local Authority Service Contracts (Annex D of Best
    Value Circular 03/2003)

# 4

# THE STRUCTURE OF LOCAL GOVERNMENT

## A  BACKGROUND

The 1998 White Paper Modern Local Government—In Touch with the People identified   **4.01**
new structures for local authorities as being crucial in ensuring that local authorities are
answerable to the communities which elect them. It stated that the main problems were:

- many decisions were taken behind closed doors by a select group of councillors;
- councillors spent too much of their time at committee meetings which were
  unproductive;
- there was little clear political leadership;
- people did not know who was taking the decisions.

The White Paper praised the efforts being made by some local authorities to streamline their   **4.02**
decision-making processes. It proposed that one of the key steps towards the implementation of healthy local democracy would be the separation of the executive and backbench
roles of councillors. The advantages of this were said to be threefold:

- Efficiency. A small executive can act quickly, responsively and accurately.
- Transparency. It will be clear to the public who is making the decisions.
- Accountability. The executive will be judged by whether it has implemented the policies
  on which it was elected.

It proposed three types of new model for structures of local authorities:   **4.03**

- a directly elected mayor with a cabinet;
- a cabinet with a leader; and

- a directly elected mayor and council manager.

It would be for local authorities to choose which structure suited them best. If they proposed an elected mayor, this would need to be ratified by a local referendum.

**4.04**  More detailed proposals for the new arrangements were set out in the 1999 consultation paper Local Leadership Local Choice which also contained a draft bill. It proposed the same three models as the 1998 White Paper, though recognised that there was scope for alternative structures. It indicated councils would be required to draw up a detailed proposal for the new form of governance it was proposing to adopt. The new executive would:

- not normally reflect the political balance of the authority but be formed by the majority party or a coalition;
- usually give specific portfolios to individual members of the executive; and
- take decisions either as a whole cabinet, in sub-groups, as individuals, or combinations of these.

**4.05**  The leadership role of the new executive was described in the consultation paper in the following terms. It would

- lead the community planning process;
- lead the preparation of plans and strategies;
- consult on and draw up the annual budget, including capital plans, for submission to the full council;
- lead the search for best value;
- take in-year decisions on resources and priorities to deliver the strategies and budget approved by the full council, consulting with other councillors and stakeholders in the local community as necessary; and
- be the focus for forming partnerships with other agencies and the business and voluntary sectors locally to address local needs.

**4.06**  The consultation paper also proposed that all councils would have to set up overview and scrutiny committees. These would have to reflect the political balance of the Council and would have the following functions. It would:

- consider and investigate broad policy issues and make reports and recommendations to the executive or council as appropriate;
- consider the budget plans, proposed policy framework and other plans of the executive, and make reports and recommendations, including recommendations proposing amendments, to the executive or council as appropriate;
- provide advice to the executive on major issues before final decisions are made; and
- review decisions taken by the executive and how it is implementing council policy and make reports and recommendations, including proposals for changes to policies or practices, to the executive or council as appropriate.

## B  NEW STRUCTURES—EXECUTIVE ARRANGEMENTS

These proposals were enacted in the LGA 2000. Under s. 11 local authorities must adopt one **4.07**
of the new forms of structure described as executive arrangements. The section specifies
three types of executive and specifies that regulations may be made allowing other forms.
The three specified types of arrangements are for executives consisting of:

(a)  an elected mayor and other members of an executive appointed by the mayor;
(b)  a leader elected by the executive and other members either appointed by the leader or
      elected by the authority;
(c)  a mayor and a chief officer appointed by the authority.

The second of these options 'the leader and the cabinet executive' has come to be seen as **4.08**
the normal arrangement. At the time of writing 316 authorities have a leader and a cabinet,
10 have a mayor and cabinet, and only one has a mayor and a council manager. 59 have
alternative arrangements.

A local authority may propose a different form of executive to the Secretary of State provided **4.09**
that they consider that it satisfies the following conditions:

(a)  that it would be an improvement on the arrangements which the authority have in
      place at the time the proposal is made;
(b)  that it would be likely to ensure that decisions of the authority are taken in an efficient,
      transparent and accountable way;
(c)  that it would be an appropriate form of executive for all local authorities, or for any
      particular description of local authority, to consider.

Such a proposal must: **4.10**

(a)  describe the form of executive which the authority is asking for;
(b)  describe what provision it is asking for to be made for discharge of its functions by the
      executive;
(c)  describe how it considers the conditions set out at (a) to (c) in paragraph 4.09 above
      are satisfied.

Regulations made prescribing a different form of executive under s. 11(5) of the Act may **4.11**
provide for:

(a)  a form of executive some or all of the members of which are elected by the local
      government electors in the area to a specified post in the executive associated with the
      discharge of particular functions;
(b)  a form of executive some or all of the members of which are elected by those elected but
      not to a specified post of the type referred to in (a) above;
(c)  the system of voting that will be used for elections under paragraph (a) or (b).

When deciding whether to make regulations under s. 11(5) prescribing a particular form of **4.12**
executive and what functions should be discharged by it, the Secretary of State must have
regard to:

(a)  any proposals made to him for a different form of executive;

(b)  the extent to which he considers that the operation by a local authority of executive arrangements involving that form of executive would be likely to ensure that decisions of the authority are likely to be taken in an effective, transparent, and accountable way;

(c)  the extent to which that form of executive differs from the forms of executive permitted by or under section 11 (i.e. those listed in paragraph 4.07 above);

(d)  the number and description of authorities for which he considers that form of executive would be an appropriate form of executive to consider.

It is of course open to local authorities to apply for permission to move to a new type of executive of their own devising at any time.

## C   OPERATION OF EXECUTIVE ARRANGEMENTS

**4.13**   Every authority was required to draw up proposals for the operation of executive arrangements and send a copy of these to the Secretary of State. When sending the proposals to the Secretary of State they were required to submit details of the consultation process which they had undertaken and the outcome of this. In drawing up proposals, local authorities must also consider the extent to which the proposals, if implemented, are likely to assist in securing continuous improvement in the way in which the authority's functions are exercised, having regard to a combination of economy, efficiency, and effectiveness. A local authority proposing a form of executive with a mayor and cabinet or a mayor and council manager was required to hold a referendum.

**4.14**   There are powers given to the Secretary of State to make a direction that an authority should hold a referendum and allowing the electors of a local authority area to petition for a referendum. The electors can only petition for a form of executive which involves an elected mayor. Such a petition must be supported by at least 5 per cent of the electors within the authority's area. There cannot be more than one referendum every five years. Following the introduction of the LGA 2000, all local authorities took the above steps. However, there is power for local authorities to change their executive arrangements. If they do so, then they need to go through the whole process again. This will include holding a referendum if they are proposing a type of executive for which a referendum is required.

## D   CONSTITUTION

**4.15**   Every local authority operating executive arrangements is required to have a constitution: s. 37. The constitution must contain:

(a)  such information as the Secretary of State may direct;

(b)  a copy of the authority's standing orders;

(c)  a copy of the authority's code of conduct;

(d)  such other information (if any) as the authority considers appropriate.

The authority must ensure that copies of its constitution are available at its principal office for inspection by members of the public at all reasonable hours. It must also supply a copy of the constitution to anybody who requests it. It may charge a reasonable fee for this.

---

## E   FUNCTIONS OF THE EXECUTIVE

The introduction of executive arrangements does not fit in with the rule under s. 101 LGA **4.16** 1972 allowing the discharge of functions by a committee, sub-committee, or officer. Provision needed to be made as to which functions are the responsibility of the executive. This is set out in regulations made under s. 13. Under s. 13(3) the Secretary of State is empowered to make provision for any function of a local authority specified in the regulations:

(a) to be a function which is not to be the responsibility of an executive of the authority under executive arrangements (i.e. the executive is excluded from discharging these functions),

(b) to be a function which may be the responsibility of such an executive under such arrangements (i.e. the authority can decide whether the executive should discharge this function or not), or

(c) to be a function which
   (i) to the extent provided by the regulations is to be the responsibility of such an executive under such arrangements, and
   (ii) to the extent provided by the regulations is not to be the responsibility of such an executive under such arrangements (i.e. the regulations set out the extent to which the function is to be exercised by the executive).

Under s. 13(9): **4.17**

Any function which is the responsibility of an executive of a local authority under executive arrangements—

(a) is to be regarded as exercisable by the executive on behalf of the authority, and

(b) may be discharged only in accordance with any provisions made by or under this Part which apply to the discharge of any such function by that form of executive.

In other words, a function which is, under the applicable regulations, the responsibility of the executive can only be exercised by the executive. The executive will also have to obey any rules relating to the discharge of functions set out in either the Act itself or any secondary legislation made under it.

The applicable regulations for this purpose are the Local Authorities (Functions and **4.18** Responsibilities) (England) Regulations 2000: (SI No. 2000/2853). (For Wales they are the Local Authorities (Functions and Responsibilities) (Wales) Regulations 2001 (SI No. 2001/ 2291 (W.179)).) These regulations divide functions into three categories:

(a) Functions which are not to be the responsibility of an authority's executive (i.e. functions which the executive cannot exercise). These are set out in Schedule 1 to the regulations.

(b) Functions which may be the responsibility of an authority's executive (i.e. functions which can, but do not need to be exercised by it). These are set out in Schedule 2.

(c) Functions which are not to be the sole responsibility of an authority's executive (i.e. functions which may be exercised by the executive subject to the limitations set out in the regulations). These are set out in Schedule 3.

The schedules to the regulations, showing which functions fall into which category are set out in Appendix 1. It needs to be remembered though that any function which is not specified in the regulations (which are the majority of functions) are the responsibility of the executive: s. 13(2).

**4.19** The first set of functions referred to in the regulations (those which cannot be exercised by the executive) are excluded because they are either subject to a separate and specialised statutory regime (such as planning) or they require an evaluation (which may be quasi-judicial) of the merits of an application (as in licensing) or are functions which are exercised by the full council or would otherwise be constitutionally unsuitable for exercise by the executive. They fall into the following categories:

(a) functions relating to town and country planning and development control;
(b) licensing and registration functions;
(c) functions relating to health and safety at work;
(d) functions relating to elections, parishes, and parish councils;
(e) functions relating to name and status of areas and individuals (i.e. name changes and conferring honorary titles);
(f) powers to make, amend, revoke or re-enact by-laws;
(g) power to promote or oppose local or personal Bills;
(h) functions relating to pensions of local government employees or members of fire brigades;
(i) miscellaneous functions including appointment of staff, making standing orders, and various functions relating to highways and footways.

**4.20** Regulation 2 also sets out some other functions, which are also not to be exercised by the authority's executive, which can be summarised as follows:

(a) various consequential functions, such as imposing conditions or limits on licences granted in exercise of one the functions specified in (a) to (i) above;
(b) making arrangements for the discharge of functions by a committee or officer (under s. 101 of the LGA 1972);
(c) making appointments to committees under s. 102 LGA 1972;
(d) any other function which, under any enactment, can only be discharged by an authority (i.e. which can only be discharged by the full council).

The functions set out in Schedule 2 (which may be the functions of an executive but do not have to be) are a miscellaneous set of functions which relate to education, police, best value, and the environment. What they all have in common is that they are viewed by the government as being the types of matter in respect of which a local authority could reasonably wish to make subject to arrangements other than the executive. It might be appropriate for these to be exercised by a committee with a degree of specialist expertise or by an officer. If it was not for Schedule 2, then these functions would have to be exercised by the executive.

The functions set out in Schedule 3 are not to be the sole responsibility of an authority's **4.21** executive. These are the various plans and strategies which authorities now have to produce. Under regulation 4 certain actions in respect of these plans or strategies are excluded from being the responsibility of the executive. This applies to:

(a) formulating or preparing the plans or strategies listed in Schedule 3;
(b) formulating plans or strategies for the control of the authority's borrowing or capital expenditure;
(c) formulating or preparing any other plan or strategy whose adoption or approval is, by virtue of regulation 5(1) to be determined by the authority.

The last of these is a reference to Schedule 4 which contains another list of functions which would normally be the responsibility of the executive and provides that in the circumstances listed in the right column of that schedule these functions must be exercised by the authority itself and not the executive.

The actions excluded from being the responsibility of the executive are as follows: **4.22**

(a) the giving of instructions requiring the executive to reconsider any draft plan or strategy submitted by the executive for the authority's consideration;
(b) the amendment of any draft plan or strategy submitted by the executive for the authority's consideration;
(c) the approval, for the purpose of its submission to the Secretary of State or any Minister of the Crown for his approval, of any plan or strategy (whether or not in the form of a draft) of which any part is required to be so submitted; and
(d) the adoption (with or without modification) of the plan or strategy.

Two things about this provision are worth noting. One is that, although it prevents the executive having sole responsibility for these plans, the way in which responsibility is shared between the executive and the authority is very much going to be a matter for each individual authority. There could be a process whereby, once the detailed plan was formulated by the executive, it was accepted by the authority with a minimum of scrutiny. On the other hand, it would be open to the authority to set up a system which involves detailed examination and amendment where necessary of every aspect of the plan. The other issue to note is that s. 101 does not apply to the functions which an authority has to assume as a consequence of this regulation. In other words, the authority cannot delegate the responsibility of discharging these functions to a committee, a sub-committee, or an officer. Scrutiny by full council is unavoidably a cumbersome process. The possibility of delegation might have enabled a more focused and detailed review of a draft plan to take place.

An executive will have the responsibility of amending, modifying, varying, or revoking a **4.23** plan of the type referred to in paragraph 4.22 above where this is:

(a) required for giving effect to requirements of the Secretary of State or a Minister of the Crown in relation to a plan or strategy submitted for his approval, or to any part so submitted; or
(b) authorised by a determination of the authority when approving or adopting the plan or strategy, as the case may be.

The effect of this is that the executive will be responsible for changing a plan to comply with a Minister's requirements or if specifically authorised by the authority to do so, when approving or adopting the plan. Slightly more obscurely, the function of applying for permission to dispose of housing land under the Housing Act 1985 or the Leasehold Reform, Housing and Urban Development Act 1993 is a function of the executive but the function of authorising the making of the application is not.

**4.24**  Some actions relating to the calculations required for setting an authority's council tax or issuing a precept are the responsibility of the executive:

(a)  the preparation, for submission to the authority for their consideration, of—

   (i)   estimates of the amounts to be aggregated in making the calculation or of other amounts to be used for the purposes of the calculation and estimates of the calculation; or

   (ii)  the amounts required to be stated in the precept;

(b)  the reconsideration of those estimates and amounts in accordance with the authority's requirements;

(c)  the submission for the authority's consideration of revised estimates and amounts.

**4.25**  As has been noted above, Schedule 4 to the regulations contains a list of functions which in the circumstances listed in the right hand column are to be exercised by the authority itself rather than the executive. However, under regulation 5(2) the function can be exercised by the executive (or in accordance with the arrangements made by the executive) if there is a need for urgency. There are two conditions:

(a)  the circumstances which render necessary the making of the determination may reasonably be regarded as urgent; and

(b)  the individual or body by whom the determination is to be made has obtained from the chairman of a relevant overview and scrutiny committee or, if there is no such person, or if the chairman of every relevant overview and scrutiny committee is unable to act, from the chairman of the authority or, in his absence, from the vice-chairman, a statement in writing that the determination needs to be made as a matter of urgency.

**4.26**  A person or body who does make a decision in these circumstances, must make a report to the authority as soon as practicable afterwards setting out:

(a)  the determination (i.e. the decision made by that person or body);

(b)  the emergency or other circumstances in which it was made (i.e. the reasons why it was urgent); and

(c)  the reasons for the determination (i.e. the reasons for the decision itself).

The Act provides a regulation making power to allow executives to make arrangements for their functions to be exercised by area committees, other local authorities, or joint committees. Some authorities, particularly in the field of planning, delegated some of their functions to more locally based committees, to enable these decisions to be taken by those with a greater knowledge of the neighbourhood which would be affected by the decision. The purpose was to bring some aspects of local government closer to the communities which it affected.

Under s. 18 the Secretary of State can make regulations to allow for discharge of functions **4.27** which would normally be exercisable by the executive to be discharged instead by an area committee. An area committee is defined as a 'committee or sub-committee of the authority' which satisfies the following conditions:

(a) the committee or sub-committee is established to discharge functions in respect of part of the area of the authority,
(b) the members of the committee or sub-committee who are members of the authority are elected for electoral divisions or wards which fall wholly or partly within that part, and
(c) either or both of the conditions in subsection (5) are satisfied in relation to that part.

The conditions referred to in (c) above are:

(a) that the area of that part does not exceed two-fifths of the total area of the authority,
(b) that the population of that part, as estimated by the authority, does not exceed two-fifths of the total population of the area of the authority as so estimated.

An area committee could therefore be set up to take decisions which affected a very small area; a committee for a single ward would fall within the requirements of the section. However, an authority which wanted to delegate certain decisions to a committee representing approximately half its area would be unable to do so because of the two-fifths requirement referred to above.

Under s. 19 regulations can be made allowing for arrangements whereby the functions of an **4.28** executive can be exercised by another authority or the executive of that authority or a committee or member of that executive. Under the Local Authorities (Arrangements for the Discharge of Functions)(England) Regulations (SI No. 2000/2851) authorities can make arrangements:

(a) for the discharge of an executive's functions by an area committee (regulation 6);
(b) for the discharge of an executive's functions by another local authority or another executive (regulation 7);
(c) for the discharge of its functions (which are not functions of its executive) by the executive of another local authority (regulation 8). (This power can only be exercised if the function is also a function of that other local authority and is the responsibility of the executive of that authority.)

The same powers exist in Wales by virtue of the Local Authorities (Discharge of Functions) (Wales) Regulations 2001 (SI No. 2001/2287 (W. 175)). Section 20 gives the Secretary of State power to make regulations for functions of executives to be made the subject of joint arrangements under s. 101(5) of the LGA 1972. This allows local authorities to set up joint committees for the discharge of their functions. The effect of this is that the functions of local authority executives could be discharged by joint committees. There is also the possibility of joint area committees being set up.

## F  OVERVIEW AND SCRUTINY COMMITTEES

**4.29**  The Government's proposals for modernising local authorities included a separation of the executive and backbench roles of councillors. It is envisaged that the majority of decisions of local authorities will be taken by the executive or by individuals or members of sub-committees to whom the executive has delegated its power. However, part of the role of the backbench councillor is to provide a check on the role of the executive. One of the means of ensuring that an executive is held to account is the requirement to have an overview and scrutiny committee which must be independent of the executive and has power to enable decisions of the executive to be discussed and reviewed at a public meeting by the members of the committee.

**4.30**  The powers which must be given to overview and scrutiny committees are as follows:

(a)  to review or scrutinise decisions made, or other action taken, in connection with the discharge of any functions which are the responsibility of the executive,

(b)  to make reports or recommendations to the authority or the executive with respect to the discharge of any functions which are the responsibility of the executive,

(c)  to review or scrutinise decisions made, or other action taken, in connection with the discharge of any functions which are not the responsibility of the executive,

(d)  to make reports or recommendations to the authority or the executive with respect to the discharge of any functions which are not the responsibility of the executive,

(e)  to make reports or recommendations to the authority or the executive on matters which affect the authority's area or the inhabitants of that area,

(f)  in the case of the overview and scrutiny committee or committees of an authority to which s. 7 of the Health and Social Care Act 2001 applies, to review and scrutinise, in accordance with regulations made under this section, matters relating to the health service (within the meaning of that section) in the authority's area, and to make reports and recommendations on such matters in accordance with the regulations.

It can be seen from the above that the overview and scrutiny committee has a dual role. It can require the authority to think again about action taken or decisions made by the authority's executive or otherwise by the authority. It also has a role in providing advice and recommendations to the authority.

**4.31**  In order to ensure its independence from the executive, an overview and scrutiny committee cannot include any member of the executive. In order to ensure that it remains focused on its primary purpose, an overview and scrutiny committee cannot exercise any functions other than those that are allocated to it under s. 21 of the Act. The only exception to this is the function of carrying out a best value review under s. 5 of the LGA 1999. If the carrying out of such a review is not the responsibility of the executive, the authority can arrange for it to be carried out by its overview and scrutiny committee.

**4.32**  The ability to review or scrutinise a decision which has been made but not implemented could be an important check on the powers of an executive. It includes power:

(a)  to recommend that the decision be reconsidered by the person who made it, or

(b)   to arrange for its function under subsection (2)(a) (i.e. the power to review or scrutinise the decision) to be exercised by the authority.

It must be noted that even if the decision is reviewed by the authority itself in a full council meeting, it cannot simply be overturned. The authority can only recommend that the executive should reconsider it. However, it is likely that, in this situation, the executive would give great weight to the views of the authority.

An overview and scrutiny committee can appoint sub-committees and may delegate any **4.33** of its functions to any such sub-committee. Such a sub-committee cannot exercise any functions apart from such functions as it is given by the overview and scrutiny committee. As with the overview and scrutiny committee itself, such a sub-committee cannot include any member of the authority's executive. Both the overview and scrutiny committee itself and any sub-committee can include members who are not members of the authority but any such co-opted members do not have voting rights. The exception to this is where co-opted parent and church governors are considering issues relating to education.

There need to be arrangements in place to ensure that members of the overview and **4.34** scrutiny committee are notified of issues which are relevant to the functions of that committee so they have an opportunity of placing these issues on their agenda. Section 21 (8) provides that executive arrangements by a local authority must include a provision which enables:

(a)   any member of an overview and scrutiny committee of the authority to ensure that any matter which is relevant to the functions of the committee is included in the agenda for, and is discussed at, a meeting of the committee, and

(b)   any member of a sub-committee of such a committee to ensure that any matter which is relevant to the functions of the sub-committee is included in the agenda for, and is discussed at, a meeting of the sub-committee.

Meetings of the overview and scrutiny committee and its sub-committees must, unlike **4.35** meetings of the executive, be open to the public unless exempt information is being discussed. The requirements as to access to information set out in Part VA of the LGA 1972 apply to them. The committee and its sub-committees also have power to summon members and officers before it and to invite others to attend. Under s. 21 (13) it may:

(a)   require members of the executive, and officers of the authority, to attend before it to answer questions, and

(b)   may invite other persons to attend meetings of the committee.

The power to require attendance extends to all officers but only extends to members if they are members of the executive. It is the duty of any member or officer summoned by the committee to attend it. However, the Act is silent on what the consequences could be for failure to attend. Presumably it could be a disciplinary matter for an officer and potentially a breach of the code of conduct for a member. The Act provides that such a member or officer is not obliged to answer any question which he would be entitled to refuse to answer in or for the purposes of proceedings in a court in England and Wales.

## KEY DOCUMENTS

Modern Local Government—In Touch with the People (White Paper) Cm 4014

Local Leadership Local Choice (Consultation Paper)

Local Authorities (Functions and Responsibilities) Regulations 2000 (SI No. 2000/2853)

Local Authorities (Functions and Responsibilities) (Wales) Regulations 2001 (SI No. 2001/2291 (W.179)

Local Authorities (Arrangements for the Discharge of Functions) (England) Regulations 2000 (SI No. 2000/2851)

Local Authorities (Executive Arrangements) (Discharge of Functions) (Wales) Regulations 2001 (SI No. 2001/2287 (W.175)

Local Authorities (Arrangements for the Discharge of Functions) (England) (Amendment) Regulations 2001 (SI No. 2001/3961)

Local Authorities (Executive Arrangements) (Discharge of Functions) (Wales) Regulations 2002 (SI No. 2002/802 (W.87))

# 5

# MEETINGS

## A INTRODUCTION

Since the nineteenth century local authorities have operated by delegating much of their **5.01** business to committees so that a smaller number of people could consider matters in greater detail than would be possible in a full meeting of the council. Committees spawned sub-committees. For most members of local authorities, attending meetings took up a large part of their lives. Many of these meetings did not provide a genuine forum for debate. The decisions supposedly made in committee were in reality taken beforehand in meetings of the majority group.

There was a widespread feeling that the cumbersome structure and endlessly repetitive meet- **5.02** ings cycle was neither the best way of regulating local democracy nor the best way for elected members to spend their time. Authorities have had to adopt new structures to give effect to executive arrangements. For this reason most authorities have fewer formal meetings of councillors than they used to. Not all of these are open to the public. An authority's overview and scrutiny committee will always be open to the public. Under s. 21(11)(a) LGA 2000 an overview and scrutiny committee is treated in the same way as meetings of any other committee of the authority. Part VA of the LGA 1972 applies to such meetings. Meetings of a local authority's executive need not be open to the public. This is dealt with under E below.

## B   RIGHTS OF ATTENDANCE

**5.03**   Prior to the reforms in the LGA 2003 the law progressively widened the rights of the public
and press to witness at first hand the workings of local democracy. The rights of the press to
attend council meetings were first enshrined in statute by the Local Authorities (Admission
of the Press to Meetings) Act 1908. There was still plenty of scope for preventing reporters
hearing the type of news which might be of genuine interest. A council could exclude the
press at any time on the grounds of the 'special nature of the business' or, if there was no
plausible argument for saying that the business was anything other than utterly routine, it
could simply reconstitute itself as a committee and throw the reporters out on the grounds
that they had no right of access to committee meetings.

**5.04**   The rights of the press and public to attend council meetings were put on a proper footing by
the Public Bodies (Admission to Meetings) Act 1960. In practice, by this time, many authorities were happy to allow any members of the press or public who wished to attend council
meetings to do so. The attendance rights were extended to committees by the Local Government Act 1972 and to sub-committees by the Local Government (Access to Information)
Act 1985.

**5.05**   There is a detailed statutory framework setting out not only rights to attend meetings but
also access to agendas, reports, minutes, and other documents. This is contained in ss. 100A–K
of the Local Government Act 1972. These provisions do not regulate how meetings are
conducted; this is a matter for the council's standing orders. Where these are silent, the
common law comes into play.

## C   EXCLUSION OF THE PRESS AND PUBLIC

**5.06**   Section 100A of the 1972 Act provides that all meetings of principal councils are to be open
to the public. There are exceptions to this:

(a)   There is an obligation to exclude the public when 'confidential information' is likely to
be discussed.

(b)   There is a power to exclude when 'exempt information' is being discussed.

(c)   There is power to exclude individuals to suppress or prevent disorderly behaviour.

In addition, there is no obligation, except in certain circumstances, considered below, for a
local authority executive or one of its committees to meet in public.

### Confidential information

**5.07**   Confidential information is narrowly defined. It extends only to information furnished to
the council by a government department on terms that it should remain confidential and
information which the council is forbidden to disclose by statute or a court order. Why
the first category of confidential information extends only to what has been communicated
by a government department and not to information provided by other statutory bodies

(e.g. the police or a health authority), other local authorities, or indeed individuals, is unclear. The information provided by individuals and bodies other than government departments might be highly sensitive. If this is provided to the council on terms that it should remain confidential, it would normally be anticipated that this agreement should be respected. Yet even in the case of informants of criminal offences, there is no obligation to ensure that their identity is protected, only a power.

## Exempt information

The categories of exempt information are set out in a list in LGA 1972, Schedule 12A which is   **5.08**
set out at Appendix 1 below. In order to exclude the public on the basis that exempt information is likely to be discussed, the meeting needs to pass a resolution to this effect. The fact
that no exempt information is in the event discussed is irrelevant. Provided that at the time
the resolution was passed, it looked likely that there would be such discussion, the local
authority will have been within its rights in passing the resolution. As usual, the courts will
not interfere with the decision simply because it was wrong: it needs to be irrational before it
can be successfully challenged. It can be seen that the scope for challenging a resolution to
exclude the press and public on this ground is very limited.

The resolution excluding the public must:   **5.09**

(a)   identify the proceedings, or the part of the proceedings, to which it applies; and
(b)   state the description, in terms of Schedule 12A of the LGA 1972, of the exempt
      information giving rise to the exclusion of the public.

The first part is straightforward enough. It will normally be the rest of the meeting or, in the
event of a meeting being convened simply to deal with exempt business, the whole meeting.
The second part implies that the precise paragraph in Schedule 12A must be specified.

## Effect of breach

It is not entirely clear what the effect of a breach of this provision would be. In a case which   **5.10**
considered a similar provision under the Public Bodies (Admission to Meetings) Act 1960,
which required 'special reasons' for excluding the public to be stated in the resolution, the
Divisional Court held that the provision was directory only, so that a breach of it did not
vitiate the decision-making process: *R v Liverpool Taxi Fleet Operators' Association* [1975] 1
WLR 701. Section 100A is worded in mandatory terms, using the word 'shall'. The normal
rule is that a decision taken in breach of a mandatory decision is void. However, whether the
courts would quash a decision for breach of this formality is open to question.

## Power to prevent disorderly conduct

The final exception to the right of attendance is preserved by s. 100A(8) of the LGA 1972.   **5.11**
Section 100A is stated to be without prejudice to any power of exclusion to suppress or
prevent disorderly conduct or other misbehaviour at a meeting. The use of the word 'any',
implying that such a power may or may not exist, shows extreme caution on the part of the
draftsman. It is well established that there is a common law power possessed by the chair of
any public meeting to exclude members of the public on the ground of disruptive behaviour:

see, for instance, *Doyle v Falconer* (1866) LR 1 PC 328. The extent to which other types of misbehaviour can be used as a ground of exclusion will probably be governed by the extent to which they impede the committee from getting on with the business. Threatening gestures, waving placards, and causing distractions could all come into this category, even if such behaviour falls short of constituting the offence of threatening behaviour. It is worth noting that this power belongs to the chair. There is no need for the committee to resolve that the people causing the disruption should be excluded. Indeed, the members of the committee may disagree on this. Once the chairman has decided to exercise this power, and the people excluded do not leave, then it is lawful for police officers to use reasonable force to exclude them. The committee could also resolve in advance to exclude members from a subsequent meeting if it appeared that this was necessary to ensure that the business could be transacted: *R v Brent Health Authority, ex parte Francis* [1985] 1 All ER 74.

**5.12**   An interesting case on the issue of exclusion is *R v Brent London Borough Council, ex parte Assegai* (1987) *The Independent* 12 June. The applicant was an exuberant man, associated with some members of the (at that time) ruling Labour group. He was in the habit of visiting the Town Hall, attending meetings, giving his opinions and generally contributing to local democracy in North West London. He did not intend to be intimidating but some councillors and officers may have felt intimidated. The council resolved to exclude him from all council premises. His challenge to this decision was upheld. Before excluding him in this way, the council should have given him the opportunity of making representations and taken these into account before making a final decision. The same principle does not necessarily apply when dealing with a gang of obstreperous hecklers in a crowded room. It is unrealistic in these circumstances for the chair to invite representations and to consider them before throwing the offenders out. This is very different from taking the drastic step of excluding somebody from council premises altogether.

## D   PROCEDURE AT MEETINGS

**5.13**   The calling of meetings and the procedure to be followed during meetings are regulated by a local authority's standing orders. There is power to adopt procedural standing orders under s. 107 of the LGA 1972. There is no duty to adopt them, except in the case of those prescribed under regulations made under s. 20 of the LGHA 1989. In practice all local authorities will have quite detailed procedural standing orders which will usually follow a similar pattern.

The power to prescribe procedural standing orders is general: the Secretary of State may lay down what rules he thinks fit. However, there is specific mention of the rights of minority members, the rights of individual members to requisition meetings and to ensure that particular items of business are referred to the full council and set out how votes should be dealt with. These are all covered in the Local Authorities (Standing Orders) Regulations 2001 (SI No. 2001/3384).

**5.14**   In *R v Flintshire County Council, ex parte Armstrong-Braun* (2001) LGR 344 a resolution was presented to the council recommending a change in standing orders so that all resolutions required both a proposer and a seconder. The report said that the changes were being put forward 'in an effort to clarify and tidy up the existing Standing Orders'. The applicant was an individual local councillor and not a member of a political group. He challenged the decision to adopt the new standing order. He failed in the Divisional Court but was successful in the Court of Appeal. Schiemann LJ concluded that '.... this Council did not consider the full democratic implications of the alterations which they were proposing'. The Council should have been advised of the advantages of enabling a single councillor to raise issues. Powerful considerations were needed to justify a standing order such as this. These should have been put before the Council and the decision should be recorded in the minutes in a way which showed the relevant issues had been considered by the Council.

## Procedure for voting

Voting is by a simple majority of those present and voting: LGA 1972, Schedule 12. Paragraph 39 provides that 'all questions coming or arising before a local authority shall be decided by a majority of the members of the authority present and voting thereon'. In *R v Highbury Corner Magistrates Court, ex parte Ewing* [1991] 3 All ER 192 it was argued that the vote of Islington Council to reset their community charge was invalid because there was no actual show of hands or counting of votes. The motion was put and the members of the council remained silent, allowing the resolution to be passed. The High Court held that this was a valid means of voting to approve a resolution. **5.15**

In the event of a tie, the chairman (or, in the case of a full council meeting the mayor) has a second or casting vote. This can be very important. Councils where no political party has overall control are quite common, and some active and controversial local authority administrations have been kept in power by a mayor's casting vote. **5.16**

There is no implied rule that the mayor or chairman exercising a casting vote is under an obligation to leave party political considerations out of account. Neither is there any legitimate expectation on the part of a person affected by a decision taken in this way that a vote should be exercised in a non-party political manner. In *R v Bradford Metropolitan City Council- ex parte Corris* [1990] 2 QB 363 the Court of Appeal considered the exercise of the Mayor's casting vote. The Lord Mayor was elected annually and there was a convention that the post was rotated among the three main political parties. At the meeting when the Mayor was chosen, the Conservative candidate, Councillor Smith Midgley was elected unopposed. At the meeting a SLD councillor (Social and Liberal Democrat, now the Liberal Democrats) said that he would support Councillor Smith Midgley's election on the understanding that he 'would not act politically'. At a time when the Council was hung with 45 Conservative councillors and 45 others, the Mayor used his casting vote to carry a series of controversial resolutions including an increase in council rents. The decision to use the Mayor's casting vote in this way was challenged by way of judicial review. The Divisional Court dismissed this application and the Court of Appeal dismissed an appeal. There was no duty to exercise a second or casting vote impartially or in order to maintain the status quo. Neither the convention of rotating the position of Mayor nor the circumstances of Councillor Smith Midgley's election imposed any fetter on his right to exercise his vote honestly and in accordance with what he believed to be in the best interests of those who might be affected by that vote. **5.17**

When a meeting is called, at least three clear days' notice must be given: LGA 1972, s. 100A(6)(a). This excludes both the day on which it is given and the day on which the **5.18** meeting is held, as well as Saturdays and Sundays: *R v Swansea City Council, ex parte Elitestone Ltd* (1990) 90 LGR 604. The notice must be displayed publicly at the council's premises and sent to each member. The only exception to this is if there is urgent business. In this event the chairman must consider that the business is urgent and the reason for considering it urgent must be specified in the minutes.

**5.19**   There is an obligation to keep records in the form of minutes of all decisions made: LGA 1972, Schedule 12 para. 41. These will be contained in a minute book, which will normally be looseleaf. The minutes must be signed as a true record by the chairman at the next meeting of the council or committee.

---

### E   MEETINGS OF THE EXECUTIVE

**5.20**   A meeting of a local authority's executive or a committee of an executive may be open to the public or may be held in private: s. 22(1) LGA 2000. Subject to any regulations about meetings of executives, it is a matter for each individual local authority to decide which meetings should be open to the public and which should be held in private: s. 22(2).

**5.21**   Access to information about decisions of a local authority executive are governed by the Local Authorities (Executive Arrangements) (Access to Information) (England) Regulations 2000 (SI No. 2000/3272). This provides that after any meeting of a decision-making body (executives, their committees, or joint committees of executives), whether public or private, at which an executive decision is made, a statement must be produced in respect of such decision. This must include:

(a)   a record of the decision;

(b)   a record of the reasons for the decision;

(c)   details of any alternative options considered and rejected by the decision-making body at the meeting at which the decision was made;

(d)   a record of any conflict of interest in relation to the matter decided which is declared by any member of the decision-making body which made the decision; and

(e)   in respect of any declared conflict of interest, a note of any dispensation granted by the local authority's standards committee.

An 'executive decision' means a decision in connection with the discharge of a function which is the responsibility of the executive of a local authority.

**5.22**   If the leader or the person who is likely to preside at a meeting of a decision-making body reasonably believes that a key decision will be made, then the meeting or the relevant part of it, must be open to the public. A key decision means an executive decision which is likely—

(a)   to result in the local authority incurring expenditure which is, or the making of savings which are, significant having regard to the local authority's budget for the service or function to which the decision relates; or

(b)   to be significant in terms of its effects on communities living or working in an area comprising two or more wards or electoral divisions in the area of the local authority.

Local authorities with executive arrangements must also prepare forward plans setting out **5.23**
the matters likely to be the subject of key decisions over the following four months. These
plans should be prepared on a monthly basis. They should contain, in respect of each matter
which is likely to be the subject of a key decision as many of the following particulars as are
available when the plan is produced:

(a) the matter in respect of which the decision is to be made;
(b) where the decision-maker is an individual, his name, his title if any, and, where the
    decision-maker is a decision-making body, its name and a list of its members;
(c) the date on which, or the period within which, the decision is to be made;
(d) the identity of the principal groups or organisations whom the decision-maker proposes
    to consult before making the decision;
(e) the means by which any such consultation is proposed to be undertaken;
(f) the steps that may be taken by any person who wishes to make representations to the
    local authority executive or to the decision-maker about the matter in respect of which
    the decision is to be made, and the date by which those steps are to be taken; and
(g) a list of the documents, submitted to the decision-maker for consideration in relation to
    the matter in respect of which the decision is to be made.

## KEY DOCUMENTS

Local Authorities (Executive Arrangements) (Access to Information) (England) Regulations
   (SI No. 2000/3272)
Local Authorities (Standing Orders) (England) Regulations 2001 (SI No. 2001/3384)

# 6

# POWERS OF LOCAL AUTHORITIES

## A  THE *ULTRA VIRES* DOCTRINE

### The development of the *ultra vires* rule and s. 111 of the Local Government Act 1972

Local authorities owe their existence to statute. It follows from this that they owe their **6.01**
powers to statute as well. They are not sovereign bodies. This means that they can do nothing outside the powers given to them by legislation. This is known as the doctrine of
*ultra vires*. The doctrine developed during the course of the nineteenth century in connection with railway companies. Its meaning was considered by the House of Lords in *Attorney-
General v Great Eastern Railway Co* (1880) 5 App. Cas 473, and was explained succinctly by
Lord Blackburn at p. 481:

> ... where there is an Act of Parliament creating a corporation for a particular purpose, and

giving it powers for that particular purpose, what it does not expressly or impliedly authorise is to be taken to be prohibited . . .

**6.02**   It is worth noting the word 'impliedly'. From the beginning of the development of the rule, the courts have understood that in a large and complex organisation the inflexible application of the doctrine would lead to absurd results. Thus Lord Selborne LC (at p. 478) said that the rule

> . . . ought to be reasonably, and not unreasonably, understood and applied, and that whatever may fairly be regarded as incidental to, or consequential upon, those things which the Legislature has authorised, ought not (unless expressly prohibited) to be held, by judicial construction, to be *ultra vires*.

**6.03**   The judicial interpretation of the doctrine has, as far as local authorities are concerned, been given statutory effect by s. 111(1) of the LA 1972 which provides that:

> Without prejudice to any powers exercisable apart from this section but subject to the provisions of this Act . . . a local authority shall have power to do anything (whether or not involving expenditure, borrowing or lending of money or the acquisition or disposal of any property or rights) which is calculated to facilitate, or is conducive or incidental to, the discharge of any of their functions.

**6.04**   The word 'functions' has been defined widely by the House of Lords as meaning 'all the duties and powers of a local authority: the sum total of the activities Parliament has entrusted to it' (Lord Templeman in *Hazell v Hammersmith and Fulham London Borough Council* [1991] 1 All ER 545 at p. 554, adopting the definition used by the Court of Appeal in that case: [1990] 3 All ER 33 at p. 83). However, this definition still leaves some issues unresolved. What of activities which are themselves incidental? Can s. 111(1) be taken to authorise activities which are incidental to these as well, so that provided there is a statutory power or duty being supported, a whole range of subsidiary activities can be regarded as lawful? And what of activities which are expressly authorised by statute but which support other local authority functions rather than being powers or duties in themselves?

**6.05**   For instance, the collection of domestic refuse is a duty of a local authority; the provision of a swimming pool is a power. There is no express power to buy refuse collection vehicles or wave machines. It was precisely to avoid the need for such impossibly specific legislation that the principle now enacted in s. 111 of the 1972 Act was developed. So a local authority can, relying on s. 111, buy a refuse collection vehicle to assist in fulfilling its duty to collect domestic refuse, or a wave machine on the basis that it is incidental to its power to provide a swimming pool. But what if it enters into a subsidiary transaction in order to finance the provision of the equipment? It might, for example, find it advantageous to buy the equipment from an intermediary, which purchased it and then leased it to the Council, with a loan which was guaranteed by the Council. Could arrangements like this come within s. 111? Could activities which are incidental to borrowing be considered lawful under the section? Borrowing is subject to a separate legislative code, but a local authority does not borrow money just for the sake of it: it borrows in order to fulfil some purpose.

**6.06**   The scope of s. 111 was during the 1990s the subject of detailed consideration in a number of important cases. These have provided answers to the questions posed in the above paragraph and the legal principles derived from them are summarised below. It is still important to look at each transaction or proposal on a case by case basis, and analyse the statutory powers. Each case will depend to some extent on its own facts. This is particularly important now local authorities are increasingly entering into transactions where the risk is shared with or transferred to the private sector. The approach to the *ultra vires* rule and s. 111 which emerged from these cases remains good law. However, its effect has been modified by the powers of local authorities to certify that contracts are legal under the Local Government (Contracts) Act 1997 and the creation of a new wide-ranging power, the well-being power under s. 2 of the LGA 2000.

## *Hazell v Hammersmith and Fulham London Borough Council*: interest rate swaps

**The facts.** Towards the end of 1990 the House of Lords had to consider the power of local **6.07** authorities to enter into interest rate swaps. The expression 'interest rate swaps' includes several types of transaction, which are explained in the Appendix to the judgment of the Divisional Court: [1990] 3 All ER 33 at p. 63. The simplest form, a swap contract, is an agreement by which each party agrees to pay the other on fixed dates over a given period amounts calculated by reference to different rates of interest on the same notional principal sum. In a typical transaction one rate of interest will be fixed and the other will be variable, calculated in accordance with a widely used commercial rate.

The case arose out of the activities of the London Borough of Hammersmith and Fulham in **6.08** the swaps market. It had established a capital market fund to conduct transactions to take advantage of interest rate movements in 1983. In 1987 and 1988, the number and type of these transactions had increased dramatically. By 31 March 1989, the Council had entered into 592 swap transactions, the total principal sum underlying these transactions being £6,052m. In 1988, the Council's activities gave concern to the auditor, who in July 1988 advised the Council that its capital market activities were unlawful in that they were simply speculative trading for profit. From July 1988, in the light of this advice, the Council changed direction and embarked on a process which it referred to as the interim strategy, which was designed to minimise its exposure to losses and gradually withdraw from the swaps market.

In February 1989 the auditor applied for a declaration that the items appearing in the capital **6.09** market fund were contrary to law and should be rectified. By this time interest rates, which had been falling, were now rising. The Council's transactions were of such a nature that this meant that, instead of continuing to profit, it was now facing catastrophic losses. A number of banks, which clearly had commercial interests in the outcome of the proceedings, were joined as respondents and given the opportunity to argue the legality of the transactions. The local authority supported the auditor's application as it stood to lose if the transactions were held to be lawful.

**The decision.** The Divisional Court held that the transactions were all unlawful. It did so **6.10** on a number of grounds, principally that the capital market activities were in the nature of speculative trading and fell outside the type of activity which could be undertaken under s. 111(1). The Court of Appeal allowed the banks' appeal in part, holding that swaps for the purpose of speculation were unlawful, as they were tainted with the improper purpose of trading, but that the interim strategy was lawful since it was for the lawful purpose of mitigating loss to the ratepayers. The difference of approach between the Divisional Court and the Court of Appeal can be seen as a difference of emphasis: whether the issue of *ultra vires* is seen as a question of power or purpose. The Court of Appeal saw it as a question of purpose, whereas the Divisional Court and the House of Lords held that it is a question of power. It is clear that activities which would otherwise be lawful can be rendered unlawful because of the purpose for which they are entered into. However, the first question must always be whether the authority has power to enter into the transaction in the first place.

**6.11**   In his speech in the House of Lords ([1991] 1 All ER 545) Lord Templeman said that there were three reasons why a local authority might want to enter into a swap transaction: speculation, replacing, and reprofiling. The first is straightforward: a local authority predicts which way interest rates are going and enters into a swap transaction in order to profit from the trend. The second relates to an individual loan. If a local authority has taken out a loan at a fixed rate of interest and believes interest rates are falling, then it might wish to enter into an interest rate swap transaction in order to replace the fixed-rate interest payments with variable payments. In these circumstances the notional principal in the swap transaction would be the same as or less than the amount originally borrowed. The swap transaction here would be called the parallel contract. But this is not in any sense a variation of the original contract for borrowing: it is an indirect way of replacing one form of interest repayment with another. The third reason, reprofiling, involves a local authority increasing the proportion of variable interest which it pays. This has to be related to existing borrowing obligations, otherwise it is simply speculation. Reprofiling is therefore replacing which involves more than one transaction. The banks argued that reprofiling and replacing were lawful under s. 111. This argument was accepted by the Court of Appeal, and it was on this basis that they found the Council's interim strategy to be lawful.

**6.12**   In the House of Lords the banks argued that the Court of Appeal's decision should be upheld on the grounds that entering into interest rate swaps was 'calculated to facilitate, or conducive or incidental to' one of the local authority's functions. This of course raises two questions: What is meant by a function of a local authority? Which function could the swaps be related to? As stated above, it was accepted that the word 'functions' meant 'all the duties and powers of a local authority: the sum total of the activities Parliament has entrusted to it': [1990] 3 All ER 33 at p. 83.

**6.13**   The difficulty for the banks was then to find a function which the swaps could be said to support. There were four arguments, two of which could be related only to the swaps undertaken during the interim strategy period. The functions suggested were as follows:

(a)   Borrowing.
(b)   Debt management.
(c)   A general duty to take reasonable steps to protect ratepayers from the consequences of an earlier act.
(d)   The duty of a council to make arrangements for the proper administration of its financial affairs.

Borrowing is obviously a function of a local authority since councils are given specific statutory powers to borrow. Lord Templeman went on to examine whether swaps were 'calculated to facilitate or conducive or incidental to' this function.

The arguments to this effect foundered on the speculative nature of swap transactions. The **6.14** prospect of being able to reduce the interest payable might encourage an authority to enter into a swap transaction. However, any authority which borrowed because of the possibility of using swaps in this way would be failing in its duty to its ratepayers to act prudently. It needed to balance the cost of borrowing against the resources available to it for payment of these costs. If it borrowed in reliance on successful swap operations then it could not be acting prudently because it was impossible to predict future interest rate movements.

One objection to the argument that swaps are 'incidental to' borrowing was that they were **6.15** separate transactions and often carried out some time after the loan in respect of which the interest rates were being exchanged. The other was the general proposition established by the case law that, if an incidental power is claimed, it is necessary to consider and construe the provisions of the statute which confer and limit the function itself. A power could not be said to be incidental simply because it was desirable or convenient. Lord Templeman then considered the contents of Schedule 13 to the 1972 Act and concluded that they formed a comprehensive code defining and limiting local authorities' powers of borrowing. In these circumstances, any incidental power to enter into swap transactions would be inconsistent with the existence of a comprehensive code covering the same subject matter.

The Court of Appeal had accepted the argument that swap transactions were incidental to **6.16** the function of debt management, but Lord Templeman held that debt management was not a function: it was just a phrase and it could be used to describe the kind of activities that a prudent local authority would undertake when considering its borrowings, such as whether one type of loan should be substituted for another, whether a loan should be taken out on the basis of payment of fixed or variable interest, and so on. Formulated in this way, the objection to swap transactions becomes obvious: if they are legal, they have to be considered as part of the authority's process of debt management. If they were illegal, they could not be. So the legality needs to be established first.

The third and fourth arguments were doomed for the same reason. The Court of Appeal had **6.17** acceded to them for pragmatic reasons:

> . . . it is sometimes necessary to accept that 'what's done is done' and, even if it should not
> have been done, the law should lean in favour of such solution as enables the situation to be
> so far as possible rectified with minimum loss and inconvenience to all involved.
> [1990] 3 All ER 33 at p. 90.

However, by the time they reached this conclusion, the Court of Appeal had also held that parallel swap contracts could be lawful. Once they were held to be unlawful, the argument lost all force. Clearly, the court could not sanction an unlawful act simply because it was expedient.

The only other substantive speech in the House of Lords was that of Lord Ackner. He did not **6.18** go through the arguments in the same detail as Lord Templeman, but again pointed to the existence of a detailed statutory code regulating borrowing as a sign that an express statutory power would be necessary for local authorities to undertake interest rate swap transactions.

He also reached the same conclusions about the third and fourth arguments referred to above. He was not persuaded that the duty of a local authority to exercise care and prudence when holding and preserving ratepayers' funds could be described as a 'function' of a local authority. Neither was he convinced that the duty of a local authority under s. 151 of the LGA 1972 to 'make arrangements for the proper administration of their financial affairs' was a 'function' for the purposes of s. 111 either. However, even if this hurdle was overcome, it would be necessary for the activity to be lawful for this section to be relied on.

**6.19**   A number of conclusions may be drawn from this important case:

(a)   The word 'functions' means 'all the powers and duties of a local authority: the sum total of activities which Parliament has entrusted to it'. However, this definition needs to be treated with some caution. A function can be a specific power or duty, such as refuse collection (a duty) or the provision of leisure facilities (a power), or it can be an activity for which statutory power is given but which exists in order to enable other activities to be carried out. Examples of this latter type of function are borrowing and the appointment of staff. However, not everything that could fall within the category of powers and duties constitutes a 'function'. Thus powers and duties of a general nature, such as the duty to behave prudently when dealing with ratepayers' money or the duty to act fairly, are not functions. Nor are duties of an essentially administrative nature.

(b)   In order for an activity to be lawful on the grounds that it is 'calculated to facilitate, conducive to or incidental to' the local authority's functions it is necessary to show that there is a function, which must be both lawful and identifiable. If no function can be identified, or if it is unlawful, the activity will be unlawful.

(c)   In deciding whether an activity is incidental to a function, it is necessary to consider and take into account the provisions of the statutory measures conferring and limiting the functions.

(d)   An activity cannot be regarded as incidental to a function simply because it is desirable or convenient.

(e)   The existence of a detailed statutory code governing the way in which a power or duty is to be exercised is a strong indication that it would be inconsistent to imply an additional incidental power outside the statutory code.

(f)   The powers of local authorities are constrained by statute: their legal personalities cannot be divided in such a way as to provide them with additional powers outside the statutory framework.

**6.20**   The aftermath of this case has important implications for the consequences of *ultra vires* actions. These are considered further below. The principles by which a local authority's subsidiary powers under s. 111 of the 1972 Act are to be interpreted were developed further in the House of Lords' decision in *R v Richmond upon Thames London Borough Council, ex parte McCarthy & Stone (Developments) Ltd* [1992] 2 AC 48 and the Court of Appeal judgments in *Crédit Suisse v Allerdale Borough Council* [1996] 4 All ER 129 and *Crédit Suisse v Waltham Forest London Borough Council* [1996] 4 All ER 176.

### *R v Richmond upon Thames London Borough Council, ex parte McCarthy & Stone (Developments) Ltd*

**6.21**   This case concerned Richmond's policy of charging for pre-planning consultations. It was often found to be helpful to developers to have consultations with planning officers prior to making a formal planning application. From 1985 the Council adopted a policy of charging for these consultations. This was done selectively and the amount was £25. After paying under protest for two such consultations, McCarthy & Stone made representations to the council to request it to change its policy. When the Council refused to do so, the developers sought judicial review of that refusal. The High Court and the Court of Appeal both upheld the legality of the charge but the developers appealed to the House of Lords. Their appeal was allowed, unanimously.

It was common ground that there was no specific power to charge for such consultations. In   **6.22**
these circumstances, it was necessary for the authority to identify a further statutory author-
ity and it sought to rely on s. 111 of the LGA 1972. It was said that statutory authority to charge was necessary because of the principle derived from *Attorney-General v Wilts United Dairies Ltd* (1921) 37 TLR 884 (CA), (1922) 38 TLR 781 (HL). This was to the effect that if an officer of the Crown seeks to impose a charge, it is necessary to show that this has been authorised by Parliament. It was conceded that the principle also applied to local authorities. Even without such a principle, it is highly unlikely that the courts would have been prepared to imply a general power to charge for local authority services.

Lord Lowry confirmed his agreement to the definition of the word 'functions' given in the   **6.23**
Court of Appeal and the House of Lords in the *Hazell* case (see above). He also quoted the words of Lord Ackner: 'I accept that the word "functions" in section 111 covers the powers and duties of the local authority *under the various provisions of the Act.*' Emphasising the last words enabled Lord Lowry to draw the conclusion that only functions which were expressly authorised by the legislation constituted 'functions' for the purposes of s. 111. This is placing a somewhat strict interpretation on Lord Ackner's words. The expression 'under the various provisions of the Act' could be taken to mean both express and implied powers under the Act. Nonetheless, this interpretation was the basis for rejection of the local authority's argument (p. 70):

> It is accordingly clear that the consideration and determining of planning applications is a function of the council, but the giving of pre-application advice, although it facilitates, and is conducive and incidental to, the function of determining planning applications, is not itself a function of the council.

A distinction was therefore drawn between considering and determining planning appli-   **6.24**
cations, which was a function, and the giving of pre-planning application advice, which was not. Thus it became a question of whether an activity which was incidental to (or conducive to or calculated to facilitate) something which was itself only incidental to (or conducive to or calculated to facilitate) a function, could be justified under s. 111 (p. 70):

> The council presented its case on the basis that charging for the service facilitates, or is con-
> ducive or incidental to, the giving of the pre-application advice but, even assuming that to be a fact, this way of presenting the case would simply amount to saying that imposing a charge facilitates, or is conducive or incidental to, a service which in its turn facilitates, or is conducive or incidental to, the council's planning function.

Local authorities have now been given power to charge for discretionary services under s. 93 of the LGA 2003. The above decision though remains good law on the interpretation of s. 111.

### *Crèdit Suisse v Allerdale Borough Council*

**6.25**  **The facts.** The facts of the *Allerdale* case are quite complex. Allerdale Council is in the Lake District and was being urged by the Keswick Town Council to consider the provision of a swimming pool. The site of the disused Keswick railway station was identified for this purpose and all that was lacking was the funds. A scheme was devised so that, as it was candidly put in the instructions to counsel to advise on the legality of the proposed arrangements, the council could 'have a leisure pool built for the inhabitants of the area and tourists at no cost'. It was proposed that, in addition to a swimming pool, there should be a time-share development. A company would be set up to buy the land and develop the leisure pool complex and time-share accommodation. The scheme would be financed by a loan from a bank. The loan would be repaid from the proceeds of sale of the time-share units. In addition, the loan was to be guaranteed by the council. The board of directors of the company was to consist of members of the council and one council officer.

**6.26**  The company was established in April 1986. In May, it took out a loan from Crèdit Suisse consisting of a maximum of £4,500,000 in principal and £1,500,000 by way of interest. The council guaranteed this loan. In August of that year the company agreed to buy the station site and an adjoining field. The development began. In 1987 the first stage of the time-share development and the leisure pool were completed. However, in 1988 problems surfaced on two fronts. The sales of the time-share units were slower than anticipated, which was a problem as repayments were due to begin in March 1989. In addition, the council's auditor expressed the provisional view that in setting up the company and guaranteeing the loan the council had acted outside its powers. In 1989 the company was unable to meet the repayments which it owed the bank from the sale of time-share units. It went into voluntary liquidation. The council, because of the advice which it had received, declined to honour the obligations which it had entered into under the contract of guarantee. The bank took legal action to recover the outstanding payments from the local authority. After a lengthy trial, Colman J found that the provision of the guarantee was *ultra vires*. The bank appealed.

**6.27**  **The appeal and decision.** The bank argued that the council had power to enter into the arrangement under s. 19 of the Local Government (Miscellaneous Provisions) Act 1976. This allows a local authority to provide 'such recreational facilities as it thinks fit'. It specifically includes 'without prejudice to the generality of the foregoing' both indoor and outdoor swimming pools and also allowed the council to provide 'assistance of any kind'.

**6.28**  Three arguments arising from this were dealt with quite shortly by the Court of Appeal. The first was that the council, by setting up the company and other arrangements, was providing the facilities under s. 19(1). The Court pointed out that the whole purpose of the arrangements was for the company to be separate from the council. It could not be acting simply as the agent of the council, because if it was then the borrowing would be unlawful. It was the company rather than the council that was providing the facilities. The second argument, which met with quick rejection, was that the provision of time-share accommodation could be a recreational facility. The Court accepted Colman J's analysis that staying in a time-share unit was not in itself a recreational activity in the same way that, say, camping was. Neither could the time-share accommodation be described as 'assistance of any kind'. Reading those words in context, they referred to those making use of the recreational facilities. They could not mean assistance to those providing the facilities.

The main issue was whether the provision of the guarantee and the establishment of the **6.29** company were lawful under s. 111 of the LGA 1972. It was argued that the arrangements were calculated to facilitate or were conducive or incidental to the discharge of the council's functions under s. 19 of the 1976 Act, referred to above, and their functions under s. 2 of the Local Authorities (Land) Act 1963, which allows authorities to erect buildings and construct or carry out works on land for the benefit or improvement of their area. Referring to the *Hazell* and *Richmond* cases, Neill LJ said that it was first necessary when considering the implied powers under s. 111 to identify the relevant statutory functions. In this case these were the powers in s. 19 of the 1976 Act and s. 2 of the 1963 Act. It was also necessary to examine the context in which the implied powers were to be exercised. The context, in the judgment of Neill LJ, included the following relevant circumstances:

(a)   Local authority finances are conducted on an annual basis. Income and expenditure must be attributed to the year in which the income arises or expenditure is incurred.
(b)   The scheme necessarily involved incurring substantial financial obligations. It could not possibly have been undertaken out of the council's ordinary income.
(c)   The council's expenditure and power to borrow are subject to statutory control.
(d)   The means by which the council can carry out its statutory functions in s. 19 and s. 2 are provided for in the 1972 Act. Parliament intended that the council should discharge these functions by means of its power to borrow. There is a comprehensive code defining and limiting the powers of a local authority to borrow.

The only way in which the arrangements were 'calculated to facilitate or conducive or **6.30** incidental to' the statutory functions was by enabling the council to obtain the use of borrowed money outside the statutory scheme. Analysed in this way, the question boiled down to whether s. 111 of the 1972 Act could be used thus. Neill LJ found that it could not:

> The implied powers in section 111 do not provide an escape route from the statutory controls. In my view that is clear not only as a matter of principle but also on the construction of section 111 itself. Section 111 (3) ensures that the powers exercisable under section 111 (1) have to be used in conformity with the other statutory provisions.

Gibson LJ and Hobhouse LJ also agreed that the scheme was *ultra vires*, but had another reason, which related to s. 101 of the 1972 Act. In his judgment, Colman J had considered that this section was limited to decision-making as opposed to what was called the 'ministerial' part of the local authority's functions. Neill LJ did not consider s. 101 in any detail. However, Gibson LJ said it could not be limited in this way: as in s. 111, 'functions' had its ordinary and natural meaning of the powers and duties of a local authority.

The question then became whether s. 111 could be used as a means of escaping the strait- **6.31** jacket imposed by s. 101. Gibson LJ held that it could not:

> Section 111 (1) commences with words that make clear that the provisions of the section are not to conflict with other statutory provisions. It sets out what previously had been implicit and merely authorises the local authority to do what is calculated to assist the discharge by the local authority of its functions. Where the relevant function is that in section 19 [of the 1976 Act] to provide recreational facilities, section 111 cannot, in my judgement, be utilised by a local authority to procure another person to discharge the local authority's function in contravention of section 101.

Although Gibson LJ limits the application of his final sentence to s. 19, there is no reason in principle why it should be different for any other statutory function. He added that even if this was wrong, it would not be open to a local authority to use the power in s. 111 in a manner 'inconsistent with' the statutory controls on borrowing and expenditure. Again, the same principle could apply to any kind of statutory restriction.

**6.32**  It had been argued by counsel for the bank that if a local authority was able to devise a scheme that enabled it to avoid statutory restrictions that prevented its aims being achieved in a more straightforward way, this was not unlawful. The authority used in support of this was the case of *Attorney-General v Finsbury Borough Council* [1939] Ch 892. In this case the authority built an air raid shelter in spite of restrictions, by devising a scheme that enabled it to overcome these. The council was obliged to submit plans for air raid shelters to the Lord Privy Seal for approval. It was also obliged to obtain loan sanction from the Ministry of Health before borrowing. The council's application for loan sanction was refused since the Lord Privy Seal had rejected its plans on technical grounds. However, the local authority went ahead with its plans for constructing an air raid shelter on a clearance area. It entered into an arrangement with a company. It leased the land to the company, which then built the air raid shelter. The company then leased the land, together with the shelter, back to the local authority in exchange for payments, which, for the most part, represented the amortised costs of the capital expenditure. It was held that this was not a form of borrowing but a contract to pay for work by annual instalments over a period of years, which the authority was allowed to do. The scheme was therefore held to be *intra vires*. Gibson LJ expressed doubts as to whether the case would be decided the same way today since it was 'patently a device to evade a statutory restriction'. He concluded this part of his judgment by saying:

> For my part, I cannot see that it can be within the scope of section 111 for a local authority, wishing one of its functions to be performed but unable, without contravening statutory controls on borrowing and expenditure, to borrow or expend the funds necessary for the performance of that function and to guarantee the debts of that company, regardless of the statutory borrowing and expenditure limits.

Put in this way, it is not only the context of the statutory power in support of which s. 111 is invoked that needs to be examined, but also the purpose for which it is being used. If it is to evade a statutory restriction or control then it will be considered unlawful.

**6.33**  Neill LJ also said that he would have dismissed the appeal because the arrangements had been made for an improper purpose, namely the evasion of the statutory controls on borrowing and expenditure. Hobhouse LJ dismissed the appeal on a different ground, namely that by setting up the company and allowing it to develop the swimming pool complex the local authority had delegated the discharge of one of its functions to the company.

**6.34**  The Court of Appeal in this case appears to put a more restrictive interpretation on the LGA 1972 s. 111 than the House of Lords did in the *Hazell* case. The principle that it is necessary to examine the context of the alleged statutory function has been taken to mean that there needs to be a full enquiry as to the circumstances in which the section is being invoked. This enquiry will include examination of the motives for whatever action is being justified under s. 111. If the motive includes an attempt to escape the effect of statutory controls or to have one of the local authority's functions discharged other than in accordance with s. 101, then the use of s. 111 will be unlawful.

## Crédit Suisse v Waltham Forest London Borough Council

This was another Court of Appeal decision, heard at the same time as *Allerdale*, sharing many **6.35** of the same features and many of the same arguments. As in *Allerdale*, the council had provided a guarantee so that a company could raise capital. The object was again to enable the loan to be paid by the company, but when this failed to happen the local authority argued that it lacked the power to enter into the arrangements. In 1988, the London Borough of Waltham Forest, in common with other local authorities, was in a difficult position in trying to fulfil its obligations under the homelessness legislation. This imposed on local authorities a duty to ensure that accommodation was available for the homeless. At the same time, with the financial controls that were imposed by the Government, affording the cost of accommodation for the homeless became problematic. Bed and breakfast accommodation was available but both expensive and unsatisfactory.

The local authority entered into a scheme to provide additional housing. The scheme was to **6.36** raise money to finance the purchase of properties. These would be leased to the council for a period of three years less one day. (If they had been leased for a longer period the cost of the leases would have counted against the council's prescribed expenditure allocation under the rules then in force.) At the end of this period the properties were to be sold and the proceeds of the sale used to pay off the loan. A company was obtained and its name was changed to the North East London Property Company Limited (NELP). It had four directors, including two appointed by the council. The company then entered into a loan agreement with Crédit Suisse ('the bank'). This made up to £11m available to NELP to enable it to buy properties. At the same time, the council entered into an agreement with the bank to guarantee the payment of the sums payable by NELP under the loan agreement. The council also entered into agreements with NELP to grant the company the right to require the council to take a lease of property that it purchased and to indemnify the company against all losses arising out of the scheme. The success of the scheme was of course dependent on rising property values. This did not happen; in fact, values declined sharply during the period of the agreement. NELP was unable to repay the loan and eventually went into administrative receivership. The bank and the company both took action against the council to enforce the guarantee and indemnity respectively.

As in the *Allerdale* case, the council argued that the arrangements it had entered into were **6.37** *ultra vires* and therefore unenforceable. The case was heard at first instance after the High Court judgment in *Allerdale*. It came before Gatehouse J as an application for summary judgment under RSC Orders 14 or 14A. The local authority's argument was essentially that which had found favour with the House of Lords in the *Hazell* case: that where there is a detailed statutory code governing the way in which a local authority carried out a function, there is no room for the implication of powers outside that code. Here there was such a detailed code in the form of the provisions relating to homelessness in the Housing Act 1985 and the powers of a local authority to assist housing associations and with privately let housing generally contained in the Housing Associations Act 1985 and the Local Government Act 1988. It is noteworthy that these provisions gave express powers to give guarantees and indemnities in certain circumstances.

Gatehouse J found in favour of the bank. The difficulty with his judgment is that he did not **6.38** address the council's argument but simply said that he was 'not persuaded' by it, remarking that the facts were quite different from those considered by the House of Lords in the *Hazell* case. This is true but hardly a reason why the legal principles at stake should be different. The judge's conclusion is set out in the following passage:

> Here, the giving of the guarantee to the bank was a *sine qua non* of the scheme designed to fulfil the council's duty under section 65 [of the Housing Act 1985], and in my judgement, was 'calculated to facilitate, or was conducive to, or incidental to' the discharge of that function.

He therefore held that the giving of the guarantee and indemnity were permissible under the LGA 1972 s. 111. The local authority appealed.

**6.39**  The Court of Appeal allowed the appeal and, as in the *Allerdale* case, there were slightly different reasons in each judgment. There was also a greater level of regret about the conclusion that the Court felt compelled to reach. There are references to the 'laudable objects' of the scheme. The bank's argument was that the relevant functions were those under the homelessness provisions of the Housing Act 1985, and that the establishment of NELP and the provision of the guarantee and indemnity were calculated to facilitate, or be conducive or incidental to the discharge of these functions. Neill LJ repeated what he had said in *Allerdale* about the need both to identify the relevant statutory function and to look at the context in which it was made. Then he adopted the argument advanced on behalf of the local authority, 'that where Parliament has made detailed provisions as to how certain statutory functions are to be carried out there is no scope for implying the existence of additional powers which lie wholly outside the statutory code'. He therefore allowed the appeal.

**6.40**  Gibson LJ had three reasons for allowing the appeal: first, the scheme involved an impermissible delegation (see below); secondly, the guarantee and indemnity were too remote from the functions to fall within the scope of s. 111; thirdly, there is no scope for allowing such transactions where there is a detailed statutory code governing the way in which a local authority carried out its housing functions.

**6.41**  Hobhouse LJ based his judgment on acceptance of the argument that there was an improper delegation. He also added that the giving of the guarantee and indemnity was too remote to fall within the scope of s. 111:

> The primary exercise of any power that existed under section 111 was setting up, and taking a shareholding in the company. This was, on the plaintiffs' case, an exercise of the incidental power. The further transactions upon which the plaintiffs have to rely in this action are remote from the exercise of any function by the council and not incidental to it. The grant of the guarantee and the indemnity were to facilitate the borrowing by the company at advantageous rates. That is how it is put in the minute of the resources strategy committee from which I have quoted. The giving of the indemnity to the company had a similar character. Both documents were essentially aspects of an exercise in property speculation.

This follows from the House of Lords' rejection in the *Richmond* case of s. 111 being used indirectly. If the courts in future adopt the same approach as Hobhouse LJ, it will ensure that s. 111 is given a strict interpretation. He analysed it by looking first at the statutory function under the Housing Acts and then asking what was incidental to, or conducive to calculated to facilitate this? The answer to this was the establishment of the company. This meant that further transactions to help the company carry out its objects were automatically *ultra vires* as they did not directly facilitate the council's functions but only borrowing by the company.

The approach currently adopted by the courts in relation to s. 111 is illustrated by the    **6.42**
decision of the House of Lords in *Akumah v Hackney London Borough Council* [2005] 1 WLR
985. It was held that the regulation and control of parking was inherent in the management,
regulation and control of houses on a housing estate, pursuant to s. 21(1) of the Housing Act
1985. Even if it were not, Lord Carswell, considering s. 111, said he would have 'no hesitation
in holding that the regulation and control of the parking of vehicles in a housing estate
facilitates and/or is conducive to or incidental to the Council's discharge of its function of
the management of the houses in the estate'. This may be an indication of a move away from
the strict approach to the interpretation of s. 111.

## Conclusions to be drawn from the cases

Before moving on to consider the effects of an *ultra vires* contract, it is worth considering    **6.43**
what conclusions can be drawn from the *Richmond, Allerdale* and *Waltham Forest* cases to
assist those advising or dealing with local authorities.

In some ways this line of decisions simply reinforces the House of Lords' decision in the
*Hazell* case. A detailed statutory code governing the way in which a power or duty is to be
exercised will lead to the conclusion that it is inconsistent to use s. 111 to imply an additional power. Similarly, the way in which functions are to be funded is set out in
the statutory provisions regulating government finance. There is no power to imply an
additional power to raise finance outside these provisions.

When considering whether a proposed course of action is lawful it will be necessary to ask a    **6.44**
series of questions. What is the primary statutory power? If this does not give power to do
what is proposed, can the proposed action fall within the scope of s. 111? This question will
need to include consideration of whether all the action proposed is sufficiently proximate, or
whether it is too remote, applying the test of Lord Lowry in the *Richmond* case and Hobhouse
LJ in the *Waltham Forest* case. Next, consider whether there is any proposed delegation of
functions and, if so, whether this is lawful. This will involve considering not only whether
the local authority decision-making bodies have the power to take the decisions, but also
whether the arrangements involve delegation of functions to outside organisations: if they
do, it will be unlawful. And it needs to be borne in mind that the word 'functions' in s. 101 of
the 1972 Act has the same meaning as in s. 111; it is not confined to 'ministerial' powers or
mere decision-making. Next, can the decision be impugned on any other basis, such as
failure to consult, procedural irregularity, or other illegality? Finally, and perhaps most
importantly there needs to be an objective assessment of the risks. Are the proposed
arrangements sensible? Are there risks attached to them? If so, how great are the risks and
what are the consequences to the authority if everything that can go wrong does go wrong?

---

## B   THE CONSEQUENCES OF *ULTRA VIRES* ACTS

If a local authority has entered into a contract that has been found to be *ultra vires*, what does    **6.45**
this mean in financial terms? Can there be any claim to make good the loss that has been
incurred by the local authority or any other party? The answer depends on the nature of the
transaction.

### Restitution and unjust enrichment

**6.46**    If there has been a contract of a purely financial nature, such as interest rate swaps, then it will be possible for both parties to claim the payments back: *Westdeutsche Landesbank Girozentrale v Islington London Borough Council* [1994] 1 WLR 938. This arose from the consequences of the *Hazell* case. Although the London Borough of Hammersmith and Fulham was by far the largest player among local authorities in the swaps market, many local authorities had entered into these transactions. Following the House of Lords' decision, large numbers of writs were issued by the parties to swap contracts, claiming back the payments made under them. These claims were for the most part made on the ground of 'total failure of consideration' and were mostly defended on the basis of 'change of position' or (what amounted to the same defence) estoppel. The argument was essentially that because the party that had benefited from the contract had changed its position in reliance on the payment, normally by spending it, the party claiming it back was estopped from doing so.

**6.47**    When the matter came before Hobhouse J, as he then was, at first instance, he ordered that the London Borough of Islington should return the payment that the bank had made, less the payments it had made. (The bank had made only one payment since this was a 'front-loaded' swap in which a large initial payment by the bank was balanced by a series of interest level-related payments by the authority throughout the life of the swap contract.) The judge founded this decision on the basis that there simply was no consideration (i.e., absence of consideration) rather than failure of consideration. When as a result of this, one party was unjustly enriched, there was an obligation on that party to repay the extent of the unjust enrichment. This analysis was upheld by the Court of Appeal. The basis on which restitution was ordered was not appealed to the House of Lords, only the award of interest. It was also held at first instance that it made no difference whether the transaction was completed in the sense that the swap contract had run its life or was still in existence when it was decided that swap contracts were *ultra vires*. (This aspect of the judgment was not appealed.)

**6.48**    The fact that a party has suffered no loss does not prevent it claiming restitution on the basis of unjust enrichment: *Kleinwort Benson v Birmingham City Council* (unreported, 9 May 1996). In this case the bank had 'hedged' the interest rate swap transaction that it had entered into with the council. In other words, it had entered into a matching transaction in which the payment profile was reversed. The effect of this was that every time the bank made a payment to the council, it received an equivalent payment from the counterparty in the other transaction. It was argued that because of the payments received under this matching transaction, the bank should not be entitled to restitution. This argument was rejected by the Court of Appeal. It held that the right to restitution arose when it was unjust that the payee should retain the payments. It did not require actual loss on the part of the payer.

### Interest

**6.49**    There was also the question of interest. Was it payable and, if so, should it be simple or compound? This depended on the nature of the claim. Was there only a personal claim for restitution on the basis of unjust enrichment, or was there also some kind of equitable claim on the basis of a resulting trust? The question is crucial since there is no power to award compound interest in personal claims: Supreme Court Act 1981, s. 35A. However, both the High Court and the Court of Appeal considered that there was also an equitable claim, with the result that the funds were held on a resulting trust for the bank. This gave the courts power to award compound interest in equity. This conclusion was reached mainly on the basis of a rather problematic House of Lords' decision, *Sinclair v Brougham* [1914] AC 398, in which it was held that investors in a banking operation that was subsequently held to be *ultra vires* had an equitable claim for the return of the amounts they had deposited.

Islington appealed to the House of Lords on the question of interest only. By a majority, the   **6.50** House reversed the Court of Appeal decision on this point, and held that there was only power to award simple interest. Their Lordships held unanimously that there was no equitable remedy for the bank in this case. By a majority, they decided that *Sinclair v Brougham* was wrongly decided and should no longer be followed. Two of the Law Lords, Lord Woolf and Lord Goff, would have been prepared to dismiss the appeal on the basis that the equitable power to award compound interest could also be exercised in respect of personal claims. This would have been, as was freely admitted, a piece of judicial legislation. The majority of the Law Lords, who took a more conservative view of the role of a supreme court, considered that it would be inappropriate to change the law in this way, especially as Parliament had twice within living memory legislated on the power to award interest and had not taken the opportunity of amending the law. Interest rate swaps are in some ways a special case. Most of the transactions that an authority enters into will not be financial; they will involve the supply of works, goods, or services. In these cases the notion of restitution becomes much more problematic. It is simply not possible to undo a contract for services: the services will already have been provided. However, in those circumstances it is established that the person who provided the services will normally be entitled to payment on a quantum meruit basis.

## Partially *ultra vires* transactions

What if one part of a transaction was *ultra vires* and the other was not? In these circum-   **6.51** stances, can the lawful part of the transaction be severed so that it is enforceable? This argument was raised in the *Allerdale* case. In that case it was a purely academic point because the court had by this time found that the whole scheme was *ultra vires*. The Court of Appeal held that the right approach when considering an application to sever a contract in this way was to ask whether, if the lawful part was isolated, a fundamentally different contract would result. Neill LJ referred to the speech of Lord Oliver in *R v Inland Revenue Commissioners-ex parte Woolwich Equitable Building Society* [1990] 1 WLR 1400 at p. 1413:

> One has to ask . . . the question whether the deletion of that which is in excess of the power so alters the substance of what is left that the provision in question is in reality a substantially different provision from that which it was before deletion.

Using this test the court unsurprisingly found that it would not have been possible to sever in the *Allerdale* case. The provision of the time-share units was an integral part of the scheme. It is thought that rarely will there be schemes or arrangements in the local authority context in which severance is a possibility.

## C THE WELL-BEING POWER

### Background

6.52 There was for many years a debate about whether local authorities should benefit from a relaxation in the *ultra vires* rule or even whether the rule should be reversed so that authorities should be empowered to undertake any activities which were not specifically forbidden. The Government's initial approach to this was put forward in the White Paper Modern Local Government—In Touch with the People. It proposed to impose a duty on local authorities to promote the economic, environmental, and social well-being of their areas. In the end, when the Local Government Act 2000 was enacted, it was decided to give local authorities a power rather than a duty. However, it is clearly a power which local authorities are expected to exercise. Thus, although the use of the well-being power itself is discretionary there is a duty on all local authorities to produce a community strategy explaining how they intend to exercise the power. It is difficult in the circumstances to imagine a local authority not exercising the power at all.

### The well-being power

6.53 Under s. 2 of the LGA 2000 a local authority has power to do anything which they consider is likely to achieve one or more of the following objects:

- the promotion or improvement of the economic well-being of their area,
- the promotion or improvement of the environmental well-being of their area,
- the promotion or improvement of the social well-being of their area.

The use of the expression 'one or more' makes it clear that each of the three components of the power can be used either alone or in combination. It is very much a matter for individual local authorities to decide what is likely to achieve the well-being of their area. It is interesting that in the Parliamentary debates on the legislation there were attempts by members of opposition parties to limit the effects of the subjective wording of this section. However, the fact that it is worded subjectively does not provide any immunity from judicial review.

### The uses of the power

6.54 The power can be exercised in relation to or for the benefit of:

- the whole or any part of the local authority's area, and
- all or any persons resident or present in the area.

The first of these classifications means that, for instance, an authority could use the well-being power to promote a scheme for neighbourhood renewal even if it would not have any wider impact. The second allows it to be used for initiatives which would benefit only those staying in the area temporarily such as students, tourists, or business visitors.

6.55 Under s. 2(4) there is a list of activities for which the power can be used. This is clearly not exhaustive. It is a list of examples but its breadth shows how wide-ranging the power is. The list allows an authority to use the power to:

- incur expenditure;
- give financial assistance to any person;
- enter into arrangements or agreements with any person;
- co-operate with, or facilitate or co-ordinate the activities of any person;
- exercise on behalf of any person any functions of that person;
- provide staff, goods, services, or accommodation to any person.

The words 'incur expenditure' are intended to make it clear (as if there was any doubt) that this is a funding power, not just a piece of guidance as to how a local authority should go about its activities.

The ability to give 'financial assistance' shows that the power also allows payments to be **6.56** made to others. Such payments do not need to be grants, although the power could be made to make grants, such grants being subject to such conditions as the authority believes to be necessary or appropriate. The power could be used to make loans or to give guarantees. Such financial assistance can be given to any person. The word 'person' has its ordinary statutory meaning. It therefore includes public bodies, incorporated bodies whether established for gain or not, and unincorporated bodies.

It is difficult to see that the ability to 'enter into arrangements with any person' really adds **6.57** anything. There are no restrictions on local authorities entering into arrangements or agreements in exercising any of their powers. However, these words are a reminder that authorities need to consider themselves as civic leaders to a much greater extent than previously. Guidance on local authority strategic partnerships published by the Government emphasises the need for local authorities to co-ordinate strategic partnerships to deliver local initiatives. These need to involve the private and public sectors as well as community and voluntary groups. The lead role which authorities should be taking in this respect is further emphasised by the reference to co-operating with or co-ordinating the activities of any person.

A particularly intriguing provision is the power to 'exercise on behalf of any person any **6.58** functions of that person'. On the face of it, this is an extraordinarily wide power which enables local authorities to exercise a range of responsibilities which could otherwise be outside their powers. The guidance advises that this will 'enable local authorities to take on functions currently undertaken by other service providers'. The example given is s. 8 of the Health Act 1999 which enables local authorities and health authorities to carry out functions on behalf of one another by agreement. However, the word 'person' is not confined to service providers. It could include bodies carrying out administrative functions and commercial organisations. Provided that an appropriate agreement with the other body can be reached, the provision provides scope for authorities to take on a wide range of new functions. The guidance states in relation to this power that it 'does not transfer any statutory responsibility or accountability for the carrying out of that function'. This must be very doubtful. There would have to be some written contractual arrangement for the authority to carry out another person's functions. It is difficult to see how this could exclude accountability on the part of the body which was actually carrying out the work.

## Limitations on the power

**6.59**  There are two specific limitations on the power, spelt out in s. 3 of the Act. It cannot be used if there is a 'prohibition, restriction or limitation' on a local authority undertaking a particular activity. The other limitation is that the power cannot be used for raising money. The cases on the interpretation of the well-being power have confirmed its wide-ranging nature. Only one has concerned the legality of any action taken by an authority under the power. Instead, they have mainly concerned attempts by individuals to persuade the courts that an authority's power was wide enough to permit them to provide the services which that individual was requesting and that other statutory provisions did not prevent the use of the power. Thus in *R (Theophilus) v Lewisham London Borough Council* [2002] EWHC 1371 Admin the court held that s. 2 could be used to provide support to a student to enable him to pursue a degree course abroad although this was outside the existing regulations governing student support. In *Lambeth London Borough Council v Grant* [2004] EWCA Civ 1711 the Court of Appeal held that s. 2 could be used by the local authority to pay for the cost of transporting Ms Grant (who was an illegal overstayer) back to Jamaica.

**6.60**  The first important case on the interpretation of the well-being power was *R v Enfield London Borough Council, ex parte J* [2002] LGR 390. This concerned a judicial review of the decisions of the local authority refusing financial assistance to the claimant and her two year old daughter. J had entered the UK in 1995 and had overstayed the period permitted on her visa. She gave birth to a daughter in 2000. She had, during her ante-natal care, been diagnosed as HIV positive. She applied for indefinite leave to remain in the UK, an application which had not been determined at the time of the court hearing. She was asked to leave the flat where she had been living and sought financial assistance from the local authority in obtaining accommodation. The local authority made an assessment of her needs under the National Health Service and Community Care Act 1990 and the Children Act 1989 which concluded that she did not have needs. She claimed entitlement to accommodation under s. 21(1)(a) of the National Assistance Act 1948 which imposes a duty on local authorities to provide accommodation for persons who 'by reason of age, illness, disability or any other circumstances are in need of care and attention which is not otherwise available to them'. The local authority were provided with evidence from her GP which explained that she was HIV positive, that lack of food and shelter could have a seriously adverse effect on her health both because her living conditions would make it less easy for her to take medication regularly and because of the increased stress which would result. The local authority confirmed their original assessment. J applied for judicial review of these decisions.

**6.61**  Under s. 115 of the Immigration and Asylum Act 1999 those who overstay their authorised period of residence are excluded from claiming state benefits. Section 116 of that Act added a s. 21(1A) to the National Assistance Act 1948:

> A person to whom section 115 of the Immigration and Asylum Act 1999 (exclusion from benefits) applies may not be provided with residential accommodation under subsection 1(a) if his need for care and attention has arisen solely—
>
> (a)  because he is destitute; or
> (b)  because of the physical effects, or anticipated physical effects, of his being destitute.

The questions for the court were therefore whether s. 2 of the 2000 Act was a wide enough power to enable the authority to give the claimant the assistance she sought and, if so, whether s. 21(1A) constituted a 'prohibition, restriction or limitation' which prevented the exercise of the power.

The court held that the power in s. 2 LGA 2000 was sufficiently wide-ranging to allow the **6.62** authority to provide the assistance sought by the claimant. There was considerable debate about whether the court was excluded from exercising this power as a result of the provisions of s. 3. In addition to the restriction in s. 21(1A) referred to above there are limitations in sections 159 to 161 of the Housing Act 1996 and s. 118 of the Immigration and Asylum Act 1999. The effect of these parts of the Housing Act is to provide that an authority shall allocate housing accommodation only to those who are qualified to be allocated it. The provisions in the IAA 1999 prevent local authorities from allocating accommodation to those subject to immigration control. On the face of it, there would seem to be clear evidence that Parliament intended to exclude those in the category of the claimant from being provided with accommodation.

However, Elias J held that there was no 'prohibition, restriction or limitation' which pre- **6.63** vented the use of s. 2 in this case. He said of s. 2, approving the submissions of Philip Sales on behalf of the Secretary of State:

> It is drafted in very broad terms which provide a source of power enabling authorities to do many things which they could not hitherto have done. In my view, a 'prohibition, restriction or limitation' is one which will almost always be found in an express legislative provision. I do not discount the possibility that such might arise by necessary implication, but I would have thought that would be very rare.

He went on to refer to the Guidance given by the Government on s. 3 which advises that any **6.64** restriction, prohibition or limitation must be expressly spelt out in the legislation. He doubted whether it must always do so as a matter of construction of s. 3. He then added:

> Of course, where Parliament has conferred a positive power to do X, it will by implication have denied the right power to be exercised to do Y, but that is merely saying that Parliament has defined a clear boundary for marking out the scope of the power. In my view it would be inapt to describe the area where no power has been conferred as constituting a 'prohibition, restriction or limitation' on the power which is contained in an enactment.

He also quoted, without saying whether he approved of it or not, a submission from Philip **6.65** Sales to the effect that even when a statute imposed an express restriction or limitation 'it will be necessary in each case to scrutinise the legislation carefully to see whether, properly analysed, it is intended to provide a bar to its exercise at all, or whether it is merely intended to prevent the power being exercised under the particular legislation in which the restriction is to be found'.

It can be concluded from the above that there are three potential factual situations: **6.66**

(a)  the statute says that the authority can do X but says nothing about Y;
(b)  the statute says that the authority can do X but cannot do Y;
(c)  the statute says the authority can do X and qualifies the power to do Y in a way that falls short of an unambiguous prohibition.

In the case of (a) it is clear that s. 2 can be used to fill the gap. In the case of (b) this is a prohibition under s. 3 and s. 2 cannot be used to do Y. In the case of (c) the terms of the Act will need to be considered with care to see if it does prevent the exercise of the power.

**6.67**  This was the essence of the argument before the Court of Appeal in *R (Khan) v Oxfordshire County Council* [2002] EWCA Civ 309. Mrs Khan was a Pakistani national who had been granted leave to enter the UK to live with her husband. She left her husband because of his violence. She applied to the Council for assistance. The Council assessed her needs but concluded that they had no power to provide her with accommodation because s. 21(1A) of the National Assistance Act (quoted above) prevented them from using either s. 21 of the NAA or s. 2 of the LGA 2000 for this purpose. The argument advanced on behalf of Mrs Khan in the Court of Appeal was that s. 21(1A) referred to accommodation being provided under s. 21(a) but did not actually prohibit accommodation being provided under any other enactment. However, the Court of Appeal held that s. 21(1A) had to be given its natural meaning and it could not be circumvented by s. 2 of the LGA 2000. Dyson LJ added that if the prohibition in s. 21(1A) was trumped by s. 2, the prohibition in s. 3 would be severely emasculated and of no practical effect in relation to pre-existing legislative schemes since they could not refer to the LGA.

## Community strategy

**6.68**  Although the promotion of well-being was not made a duty of local authorities, there is a duty under s. 4 for each authority to prepare a strategy (known as the community strategy) for promoting and improving the economic, social, and environmental well-being of their area and contributing to the achievement of sustainable development within the United Kingdom. The local authority must consult and seek the participation of such persons as they consider appropriate when preparing or modifying their community strategy. They must also have regard to any guidance issued by the Secretary of State. Guidance was issued in December 2000: Preparing Community Strategies: Guidance to Local Authorities.

---

## KEY DOCUMENTS

Using the new power to promote well-being LGA Powerpack 2000

Power to promote or improve economic, social or environmental well-being ODPM
    Guidance 2001

Promoting well-being: making use of councils' new freedom, Inlogov

Doing the future, LGIU

Powering up: making the most of the power of well-being LGA 2003

Preparing Community Strategies: Guidance to Local Authorities DETR December 2000

# 7

# TRADING AND CHARGING POWERS

## A INTRODUCTION

There are two areas of activity to be considered in this chapter: the power of local authorities **7.01** to trade with each other, which is long-established, and the power, introduced for the first time by the LGA 2003, of local authorities to trade with the private sector. The latter is largely a new departure for local government. Until a specific power was created, any trading activity with the private sector was considered to be *ultra vires*.

## B TRADING POWERS

### The Local Authorities (Goods and Services) Act 1970

This Act gave local authorities power to trade with each other and also trade with other **7.02** public bodies. It provides that (s. 1(1)):

a local authority and any public body within the meaning of this section may enter into an agreement for all or any of the following purposes, that is to say:

(a) the supply by the authority to the body of any goods or materials;
(b) the provision by the authority for the body of any administrative professional or technical services;

(c)   the use by the body of any vehicle, plant or apparatus belonging to the authority and, without prejudice to paragraph (b) above, the placing at the disposal of the body of the services of any person employed in connection with the vehicle or other property in question;

(d)   the carrying out by the authority of works of maintenance in connection with land or buildings for the maintenance of which the body is responsible;

and a local authority may purchase and store any goods or materials which in their opinion they may require for the purposes of paragraph (a) of this subsection.

**7.03**   Under s. 1 (3) any agreement made pursuant to the above subsection may contain such terms as to payment or otherwise as the parties consider appropriate. As there is no specific provision confining the payment provisions to covering the authority's costs, there is no reason why authorities should not make a reasonable profit from these arrangements that can be used to subsidise its other activities. Section 1 (2) provides that:

Nothing in paragraphs (a) to (c) of the preceding subsection authorises a local authority:

(a)   to construct any buildings or works; or

(b)   to be supplied with any property or provided with any service except for the purpose of functions conferred on the authority otherwise than by this Act.

These are curious classifications. Even giving the words 'administrative, professional or technical' their widest meanings, it is difficult to see how they can be interpreted as including carrying out works of construction. The fact that the draftsman felt it necessary to make this plain though, is a good indication that s. 1 (1) should be given a wide interpretation.

**7.04**   The section allows local authorities to provide various goods, materials, services, etc., to 'public bodies'. The Secretary of State is able to designate by order that persons who carry out functions of a public nature shall be public bodies for the purposes of the Act. A very large number of orders has been made under this section. These include all registered social landlords. It has been reasonably easy for local independent bodies, such as companies set up to deliver a local authority project where a separate legal entity is needed in order to achieve a certain level of independence, to be designated as public bodies under the provisions of the 1970 Act.

**7.05**   There was for some time a degree of controversy about the extent of a local authority's powers under the 1970 Act. The Audit Commission advised that the powers of a local authority to undertake 'principal trading' were limited to the use of 'spare capacity' and that consequently, local authorities that took on staff specifically to provide goods or services for other authorities were acting beyond their powers. Different advice was given by what was then the Department of the Environment.

**7.06**   The legality of a local authority taking on extra staff to provide goods and materials for other authorities was decided in the case of *R v Yorkshire Purchasing Organisation, ex parte British Educational Suppliers* [1997] 95 LGR 727. The Yorkshire Purchasing Organisation (YPO) had been set up by a group of local education authorities to enable them to take advantage of the additional discounts, etc., they could achieve by bulk purchasing. By the time of the challenge, YPO had grown to be a substantial business employing a sizeable number of staff and with a large turnover. It did not simply purchase goods for which it was informed there was a demand. It bulk purchased goods and then stored them in warehouses to supply to authorities that needed them. It was held that there was nothing unlawful about these arrangements. Everything that the YPO undertook was permitted under s. 1 of the 1970 Act.

## Powers to trade other than the LA (Goods and Services) Act 1970

If, before the Local Government Act 2003, a local authority wished to trade outside the ambit of the 1970 Act, then its powers to do so were extremely limited. They were restricted to a number of specific provisions. The Civic Restaurants Act 1947 allows local authorities to set up public restaurants. This power appears to have been little used. Nearly all catering facilities provided by local authorities have been connected with the provision of leisure facilities. Section 19 of the Local Government (Miscellaneous Provisions) Act 1976 gives local authorities wide powers to provide leisure facilities and charge for them. This includes the power to set up catering facilities in connection with leisure and recreation facilities. Under s. 38 of the same Act local authorities are also empowered to sell spare capacity on any computer system. The authority is under a duty to obtain a price for the use of such facilities that would be regarded as commercially reasonable. **7.07**

## The trading power in the Local Government Act 2003

A new power to enable local authorities to trade in any activities related to their functions was introduced by the Local Government Act 2003 s. 95. This enables the Secretary of State to make an order authorising certain authorities to trade in any function related activity. The power was brought into effect by the Local Government (Best Value Authorities) (Power to Trade) (England) Order 2004. The order applies only to best value authorities that have been classified as 'excellent', 'good' or 'fair' under their comprehensive performance assessment (see chapter 17). These authorities are authorised to do for a commercial purpose anything which they are authorised to do for the purpose of carrying out any of their ordinary functions. **7.08**

This means that the authorities do not simply have power to trade in activities which they are expressly authorised to do by statute. Thus, local authorities' activities which they have to undertake in order to carry out their functions effectively, such as building cleaning, are included, as well as professional services, such as architecture, building surveying and financial and legal services. The power to trade is therefore very wide indeed. The indication so far is that there is at present no widespread enthusiasm among authorities to start using these powers. A survey by the LGA (reported in Local Government Chronicle 2/12/04) indicated that only 2 per cent of local authorities had started using them and that 80 per cent had no plans to do so. **7.09**

## The interaction between the 1970 Act and 2003 Act powers

There is no reason in principle why a company established by a local authority for the purposes of trading with the private sector should not trade with the public sector as well. The Guidance seems to indicate that it is anticipated that such public to public trading activities will continue to be undertaken mainly under the powers in the 1970 Act: **7.10**

> Existing *public to public* trading activities under the *Local Authorities (Goods and Services) Act 1970* ('the 1970 Act') will remain. These will operate in parallel with the s. 95 trading power.

Applications from bodies seeking public body designation under s. 1(5) of the 1970 Act will not receive Ministerial approval where it appears that the body seeking the designation is largely a local authority sponsored vehicle designed perhaps to avoid the statutory framework in sections 95 and 96 of the Act, or to facilitate quasi private trading opportunities for local authorities categorised as 'weak' or 'poor' under the CPA. The powers contained in the Trading Order are primarily concerned with *public to private* trading. (paragraph 19)

**7.11** There are some practical difficulties about this. The power to trade under the 2003 Act is much wider than that under the 1970 Act. Thus there are activities that could be carried out for other authorities under the power to trade, which should be outside the powers given by the 1970 Act, such as carrying out works of construction and maintenance.

**7.12** The types of activity in which a local authority is likely to want to trade in will probably be of interest both to the private and the public sectors. For instance, an authority developing computer applications to assist in its functions could seek to market these to local authorities, other public bodies, and private sector organisations. It is hard to see why the public sector side of the business should be undertaken by the authority itself, while the private sector elements of what would essentially be the same operation should be carried out separately through a company. However, local authorities will have an incentive to preserve this divide. Undertaking trading directly by the authority will be more cost effective than undertaking it through a company. The authority will not have to pay corporation tax, will be able to re-claim VAT and will not be subject to the requirements of the Companies Acts.

**7.13** The powers in the 1970 Act are of course available to all authorities, whereas those in the 2003 Act are available only to those with a CPA of 'fair' or above. The Government is alive to the potential for the 1970 Act being used as a way of allowing authorities assessed as being 'weak' or 'poor' to carry out a degree of trading. However, being designated as a public body under the 1970 Act does not give a body any additional powers to trade. All it does is enable a local authority to provide it with goods and services under the 1970 Act. There is nothing to stop a local authority, whatever its designation, exploiting the opportunities for trading under the 1970 Act to the fullest extent possible. Nor is there anything to prevent it deriving a profit from these activities. Such a local authority could, if it wished, set up a company to trade on its behalf, provided the trading activities did not exceed the boundaries set out by the 1970 Act. The setting up of such a company would not require ministerial consent.

**7.14** Nor is it clear what is meant by 'quasi private trading' in the guidance. The dividing line is perfectly clear. If a body is a 'public body' within the meaning of the 1970 Act, then a local authority can use the powers under that Act to trade with it. If it falls outside this definition then a local authority can only trade with it by exercising the powers in the 2003 Act. It is possible to imagine a scenario whereby a local authority suggests to a private organisation that it could set up as a 'public body' to receive the benefit of services from a local authority. However, such a body is not the type of vehicle which is likely to be designated as a 'public body' under the 1970 Act.

## Re-categorisation of trading authorities

**7.15** Since the power to trade is exercisable only by authorities categorised as 'fair' or above, it would be illogical for an authority that was re-categorised as 'weak' or 'poor' to continue trading. On the other hand, an authority in this situation could not reasonably be expected to wind up its operations overnight. The Trading Order deals with this by allowing a two year period within which an authority must either regain a CPA of 'fair' or above, or else cease trading.

The consequences of this are of course, that arrangements must be made for the various **7.16** relationships entered into by the company to be terminated. The Order provides for this to happen automatically. Any 'agreement or arrangement entered into for the purpose of facilitating the exercise of (the trading power) shall cease to have effect at the end of the period of two years beginning with the date on which this Order ceases to apply to the authority'. The Guidance explains that this means that from the second anniversary of the date when the order ceased to apply (i.e., the date of re-categorisation), the agreement will be 'incapable of performance'. However, it will not be void. This presumably means that it will no longer be lawful for any party to such an agreement to supply goods and services or make payments to another party pursuant to the terms of such an agreement. The fact that the Order simply refers to an 'agreement or arrangement' means that if there is more than one other party to the agreement, such an agreement will be unenforceable, even between parties other than the local authority company. However, any rights and obligations accrued up until the date of the second anniversary will still be capable of enforcement.

The Guidance gives advice about which types of agreement will be affected by this rule: **7.17**

> This provision will apply to any agreement which the authority may have entered into with the trading company (e.g. for the supply of works, goods or services) and also any other arrangement entered into by the authority with the trading company (which will include the acquisition of shares, giving of grants and secondment of employees etc). Any other agreements or arrangements entered into by the trading company outside of the agreements or arrangements with the authority will remain unaffected.

The difficulty with this advice is that the Order does not simply confine its effects to agreements and arrangements with the authority. It refers to all agreements that were entered into 'for the purposes of facilitating the exercise of the trading power'. Any arrangements entered into for this purpose will no longer be enforceable whether they were made with the authority or not. A company set up purely to exercise the trading power will cease to be able to function.

There are a number of possible ways of dealing with this. The Guidance suggests that break **7.18** clauses should be inserted into the relevant contracts so that, if a local authority loses its power to trade, it can extricate itself from these arrangements without being sued for breach of contract. The Guidance also advises that, in the event of arrangements being terminated under these provisions, there may be a loss to the trading company, so compensation may be payable. It advises that the level of compensation (or a formula for determining it) should be included in the original contract, since it could be that an authority's bargaining position will be weak if it has to negotiate this when it exercises the break clause. This surely depends on the circumstances. If the company is simply a local authority vehicle, then it has no bargaining power. Whether or not there is a break clause, it faces all its contractual arrangements coming to an abrupt end. It will also depend on what type of contractual arrangements exist. The exercise of a break clause in a contract for services would not normally give rise to a right to compensation. If there is in existence a contract for works to be undertaken, then it would be unreasonable to expect this to be ended without the contractor undertaking the works being compensated.

**7.19** Financial institutions and investors in trading companies will also require reassurance about what would happen in the event that an authority loses its trading powers. There will therefore be a need for exit arrangements to be built in to all financial agreements. This will include agreements relating to shares and to loan arrangements. There are a number of possible options for exit arrangements. These include:

(a)　The authority selling its share in the company.
(b)　The company being wound up.
(c)　The company being sold as a going concern.

**7.20** The first of these options only works if the company has third-party shareholders. It is only likely to be an option where the business can carry on under its own steam. If it is primarily dependent on seconded local authority staff to run it or on facilities and/or services which are being provided by the authority and which it would be difficult to obtain elsewhere, then this is not likely to be a viable option. The Guidance sensibly advises that the arrangements need to be decided on in advance and set out in the Shareholders' Agreement and Articles of Association. It also suggests that the local authority could benefit from a put option, i.e., an arrangement whereby it has a right to require the other shareholders to purchase the shares in accordance with a pre-agreed formula. As an alternative to the put option, the Guidance proposes a class of redeemable shares that could be redeemed by the local authority and paid for out of profits in the event that the authority lost its trading powers. The price paid on redemption would need to be calculated in accordance with a pre-set mechanism.

**7.21** The second option may be the only practicable alternative if the trading company is either wholly owned by the authority or is effectively a creature of the authority. The guidance advises that if an authority wishes to reserve this option, it will need to ensure that there are break clauses in agreements and arrangements between the trading company and third parties. Whilst the guidance advises that the exercise of these will give rise to the payment of compensation, this will depend on the circumstances.

**7.22** If it is likely to result in better value for money, a local authority that has to part company with a trading company should consider selling it as a going concern. There will need to be a competitive process to ensure that the best price is obtained.

## The power to trade and the well-being power

**7.23** One of the main anticipated uses of the well-being power is to assist with economic development. This includes power to give financial assistance. (The well-being power is of course available to all authorities, irrespective of their CPA.) This means that a local authority could use the well-being power to invest in a company. It could not only buy shares, but also participate in the running of the company. There is nothing in principle preventing an authority from owning a major interest in a company as a result of financial assistance provided under this power. If the authority considers that such an arrangement is likely to achieve 'the promotion or improvement of the economic well-being of the area' then there is power to enter into it under the LGA 2000. If the company is successful and is in a position to pay dividends, there is nothing to stop the authority benefiting from this.

However, there is a distinction between having an interest in a company pursuant to the **7.24** well-being power and trading through a company. If the primary motivation is to promote or improve the economic well-being of the area, then this is an exercise of the well-being power. If the aim is simply to make a profit, then this is an exercise of the trading power and can only be undertaken after complying with the conditions in the 2004 Order.

To confuse matters still further, the well-being power is an ordinary function of a local **7.25** authority, which can be the subject of local authority trading activity. This is in spite of the prohibition on using the well-being power as a means of raising money. This can come about as a result of a local authority deciding to carry out an activity pursuant to its well-being power. An example might be arranging seminars on management for people setting up new businesses. An authority might easily consider this likely to achieve an improvement in the economic well-being of its area. It could lead to new businesses being established, being well-managed, being more likely to succeed and create new wealth.

A local authority carrying out an activity pursuant to its well-being powers could then trade **7.26** in that activity in accordance with powers given to it under the Trading Order. This is because the power to trade in function-related activities is itself a primary power, which is conferred on certain local authorities by the Trading Order. So a local authority trading in an activity which it undertakes pursuant to its well-being power will not be relying on the well-being power. It will instead be relying on the separate power to trade. Thus, the prohibition on raising money will have no application. So to return to the example of management training seminars, a local authority that had decided to provide such training in exercise of its well-being powers could then set up a company to carry out the same activity (inevitably to a different audience) in order to make a profit.

## C   CHARGING POWERS

Before the enactment of s. 93 of the 2003 Act, local authorities had power to charge for **7.27** services only when there was a specific statutory provision authorising it, or such a power arose by necessary implication. This restrictive approach was the result of the House of Lords' decision in *R v Richmond upon Thames Borough Council, ex parte McCarthy and Stone* [1992] 2 AC 48.

The new charging power applies to discretionary services, i.e. services which an authority **7.28** has a power but not a duty to provide. Section 93 of the Local Government Act 2003 provides that a best value authority may charge a person for providing a service to him if:

(a)   the authority is authorised, but not required, by an enactment to provide the service to him; and

(b)   he has agreed to its provision.

Thus the person receiving the service must be aware of the charge before the service is provided and must agree to it being imposed.

Under s. 93(2) there is no power to charge if the authority: **7.29**

(a)   has power apart from this section to charge for the provision of the service; or

(b) is expressly prohibited from charging for the provision of the service.

If there is another statutory power to charge for the service, the authority must rely on that. If a statute provides that a service should be provided free of charge, the power in s. 93 cannot be used as a means of imposing a charge.

**7.30** There is a duty on the authority levying the charge 'to secure that, taking one financial year with another, the income from charges. . . . does not exceed the costs of provision': s. 93(3). This applies separately in relation to each kind of service. So if a local authority makes a surplus in one financial year, there is an obligation on it to make an adjustment so that the surplus is used for subsidising the service in the next financial year.

**7.31** Subject to the other provisions in the section a local authority may:

(a) charge only some persons for providing a service;
(b) charge different persons different amounts for the provision of a service.

Thus a local authority could charge nothing or a reduced charge for, say, local residents and community groups.

### Guidance on charging

**7.32** The ODPM has published guidance on the use of this power: General Power for Best Value Authorities to Charge for Discretionary Services—Guidance on the Power in the Local Government Act 2003.

**7.33** This gives advice on the types of service for which a charge can be made. Discretionary services include discrete areas of activity as well as extensions to existing services. In certain circumstances it seems that a local authority providing a statutory service which it is obliged to provide free of charge could make a charge for an enhanced service. Discretionary services include services provided under the well-being power in s. 2 Local Government Act 2000. Among the examples given of the type of discretionary service provided by authorities are advice on planning applications, loans of works of art to businesses and residents, and assistance to vulnerable young people and people leaving hospital.

**7.34** It also provides advice on charging arrangements. It indicates that it is legitimate for authorities to take into account any initial capital investment/set-up costs when assessing charges. It also advises about the administrative arrangements which need to be made in connection with charging which it states as being as follows:

(a) the terms and conditions under which the service is provided;
(b) details of the charges, any discounts, and how the charges will increase;
(c) billing arrangements.

### Differences between trading and charging

**7.35** As is pointed out in the Guidance on the Power to Trade, there are four main differences in the two powers:

(a) charging relates to discretionary services only, whereas the power to trade is for all services,

(b) all best value authorities can use the charging power but the trading power can be used only by those designated as excellent, good, or fair under the CPA,

(c) charging is limited to the cost of providing the service, whereas trading can make a profit,

(d) the power to trade is exercisable only through a company.

---

## KEY DOCUMENTS

Local Government (Best Value Authorities) (Power to Trade) (England) Order 2004 (SI No. 2004/1705)

General Power for Local Authorities to Trade in Function Related Activities Through a Company—Guidance on the Power in the Local Government Act 2003 (ODPM July 2004)

General Power for Best Value Authorities to Charge for Discretionary Services—Guidance on the Power in the Local Government Act 2003 (ODPM November 2003)

# 8

# BY-LAWS AND LOCAL LEGISLATION

## A INTRODUCTION

By-laws and local legislation are both means by which local authorities may enlarge their **8.01** powers. Both are mainly used for the purpose of regulating activities within an authority's area. There are important differences, both in the procedure for making them, and in how they can be applied.

By-laws can be made by an authority itself, subject to confirmation by the relevant Secretary **8.02** of State. Local legislation, however, needs to be approved in accordance with the full legislative process in both Houses of Parliament. By-laws will apply only in the area of the authority which made them. Local legislation can be promoted by one authority on behalf of other councils and will apply in the area of any authority which is able to benefit from the provisions and which adopts them.

## B　BY-LAWS

### Power to make by-laws

8.03　By-laws are, in some people's mind, almost synonymous with local authorities. Park-keepers, dog wardens, highways inspectors, and market inspectors may all be responsible for the investigation and prosecution of offences against by-laws. For the purposes of this book by-laws can be considered as being laws operating within an individual authority's area. Very frequently, a by-law is more limited in its scope than this, operating only in particular areas, such as parks or housing estates. (Although this book is exclusively concerned with the position of local authorities, by-laws can be made by other bodies as well.)

8.04　In spite of its age the leading case on by-laws is *Kruse v Johnson* [1898] 2 QB 91, in which by-laws were described by Lord Russell CJ in the following terms:

> A by-law, of the class we are here considering, I take to be an ordinance affecting the public, or some portion of the public, imposed by some authority clothed with statutory powers ordering something to be done or not to be done and accompanied by some sanction or penalty for its non-observance. It necessarily involves restriction of liberty of action by persons who come under its operation as to acts which, but for the by-law, they would be free to do or not do as they please. Further, it involves this consequence—that, if validly made, it has the force of law within the sphere of its legitimate operation.

8.05　There are numerous powers allowing local authorities to make by-laws for various purposes. In addition, there is a general power contained in s. 235 of the LGA 1972 to make by-laws for the good rule and government of the whole or any part of the local authority's area and for the prevention and suppression of nuisances therein. The words 'good rule and government' are extremely wide and in theory give the local authority power to legislate over a consider-able range of issues. However, there are two important restrictions. First, the by-laws must be confirmed by the Secretary of State. By-laws are currently the responsibility of the Office of the Deputy Prime Minister (ODPM). In practice they will be approved only if they are to deal with a problem which the Government recognises as appropriate for the use of by-laws. They will normally have to follow a model form to ensure consistency. Secondly, by-laws cannot be used as a way of extending an authority's range of responsibility. So if a by-law sought to extend a local authority's power into fields which were not its statutory responsibility, it would be *ultra vires*.

8.06　Another important limitation is contained in s. 253(3) of the LGA 1972:

> By-laws shall not be made under this section for any purpose as respects any area if provision for that purpose as respects that area is made by or is or may be made under, any other enactment.

This does not simply mean that s. 235 can be used only when there is no other suitable by-law making power; if there is any other statutory provision which is, or could be, used to deal with the mischief which the by-law would be aimed at, then there is no power to make the by-law. Thus, if a statutory provision made a particular course of conduct unlawful, but did not create a criminal offence, then it would not be open to a local authority to make a by-law making that course of conduct a criminal offence. If there was a statutory provision allowing regulations to be made that could be used to suppress a nuisance, a local authority could not make a by-law to deal with the same nuisance even if no regulations had in fact been made. The words 'as respects that area' in s. 253(3) mean that if, for instance, a local Act or by-law made something unlawful in Manchester but not anywhere else, then it would be open to local authorities elsewhere to make by-laws covering the same matter.

## Requirements of by-laws

The requirements which must be met for a by-law to be valid are summarised in the judgment of Lord Diplock in *Mixnam's Properties Ltd v Chertsey UDC* [1964] 1 QB 214:   **8.07**

1. It must be reasonable.
2. It must be certain in its terms.
3. It must not be repugnant to or conflict with any other law, whether statute or common law.
4. It must be within the powers given by the statute under which it is made.

## Unreasonableness

The leading case of *Kruse v Johnson* [1898] 2 QB 91 was concerned with the validity of a by-   **8.08**
law which made it an offence to play music or sing within fifty yards of a dwelling-house after being asked to desist. A person who was convicted of breaching this by-law argued on appeal to the Divisional Court that the by-law should be struck down as being unreasonable. The Court upheld the validity of the by-law with Lord Russell CJ remarking that by-laws made by local authorities which were bodies of a representative character which were entrusted with delegated authority by Parliament should generally be supported, although if by-laws were unreasonable the courts should not be slow to strike them down. He then went on to explain what he meant by unreasonable:

> If, for instance, they were found to be partial and unequal in their operation as between classes; if they were manifestly unjust; if they disclosed bad faith; if they involved such oppressive or gratuitous interference with the rights of those subject to them as could find no justification in the minds of reasonable men, the court might well say, 'Parliament never intended to give authority to make such rules; they are unreasonable and *ultra vires*.' But it is in this sense, and in this sense only, as I conceive, that the question of unreasonableness can properly be regarded. A by-law is not unreasonable merely because particular judges may think that it goes further than is prudent or necessary or convenient or because it is not accompanied by a qualification or an exception which some judges may think ought to be there.

The above passage still represents an accurate summary of the law. It appears therefore that a   **8.09**
test of unreasonableness even more stringent than the *Wednesbury* test will need to be satisfied before a court will strike a by-law down as unreasonable. If a by-law requires people to do something which they have no legal right to do, then it will be struck down as unreasonable: *Arlidge v Islington Corporation* [1909] 2 KB 127.

## Uncertainty

The courts have displayed a degree of inconsistency about the circumstances in which a by-   **8.10**
law will be held to be uncertain. In *United Bill Posting Co Ltd v Somerset County Council* (1926) 42 TLR 537, the council had made a by-law prohibiting advertisements which were visible

from highways, railways, and waterways and which 'disfigure the natural beauty of the landscape'. This might be thought to be a highly vague and subjective question, but the court declined to strike the by-law down on the ground of uncertainty. However, in *Scott v Pilliner* [1904] 2 KB 855, a by-law to prevent 'selling or distributing any paper or written or printed matter devoted wholly or mainly to giving information as to the probable result of races, steeplechases, or other competitions' was held to be bad on the ground, among other things, of uncertainty, though it is not clear why it should have been thought that it was in any way difficult to interpret its terms.

**8.11**   Local authorities have ceased to regard it as their duty to stop people from knowing the racing results. However, local authorities have tried to use their by-law making powers to suppress other types of perceived nuisance, as illustrated by the attempts of Adur District Council to regulate gliding. A practitioner of the sport of hang-gliding was prosecuted for flying over a pleasure ground. A by-law forbade persons from flying any glider, manned or unmanned, in any pleasure ground. It was conceded that the terms of this by-law were broken by flying over the ground. However, it was accepted by the Divisional Court that the by-law was void for uncertainty. A by-law of this nature needed to make it clear to anyone hang-gliding whether, at a given time, they were committing a criminal offence or not. A lower level beneath which gliders must not fly therefore needed to be specified: *Staden v Tarjanyi* (1980) 78 LGR 614.

**8.12**   This decision does not sit easily with the more recent decision of the Court of Appeal to the effect that by-laws should not be struck down for uncertainty unless they are meaningless: *Percy and Others v Hall* [1996] 4 All ER 523. This case concerned the HMS Forest Moor and Menwith Hill Station By-laws 1986. The plaintiffs, protesting against a military installation, were arrested on numerous occasions for breaches of these by-laws. Then, in *Bugg v DPP* [1993] QB 473, the by-laws were held to be void for uncertainty. The plaintiffs sued the constables who arrested them for wrongful arrest and false imprisonment, and the Attorney-General for breach of statutory duty in making invalid by-laws. The judge at first instance held that he was bound by the *Bugg* case to hold that the by-laws were invalid, but considered that the constables were entitled to a defence of lawful justification. The Court of Appeal held that the by-laws were valid. Simon Brown LJ approved a passage in the speech of Lord Denning in the case of *Fawcett Properties v Buckinghamshire County Council* [1961] AC 636 at p. 676, as a guide to the interpretation of by-laws. In that case the House of Lords were considering whether the words 'agricultural population' in a planning condition were so uncertain as to be unenforceable. The local authority had taken this phrase from the statute. Lord Denning, having remarked that the assertion of unenforceability was a 'bold submission' held that a statute could be void if it was meaningless but not because it was uncertain:

> . . . But when a statute has some meaning, even though it is obscure, or several meanings, even though there is little to choose between them, the courts have to say what meaning the statute has to bear, rather than reject it as a nullity. As Farwell J put it when speaking of a statute: 'Unless the words were so absolutely senseless that I could do nothing at all with them, I should be bound to find some meaning, and not to declare them void for uncertainty': see *Manchester Ship Canal Co v Manchester Racecourse Co* [1900] 2 Ch 352 at 360–361.

**8.13**   The plaintiffs' argument, which had succeeded in the *Bugg* case, was that the by-laws were invalid as they failed to provide adequate information about the protected area. Gibson LJ remarked that as this was a common feature of by-laws, the decision would be of wide application. The argument for the plaintiffs was that the words 'lands belonging to the Secretary of State' made it impossible for anyone walking in the area to know what land was being referred to. It was held that this was not the right test. Provided that the description identified the protected area by whatever means, the test was satisfied. The test of interpretation set out in *Fawcett Properties v Buckinghamshire County Council* [1961] AC 636 was the right one. It was wrong that the test of certainty should vary according to whether what was being considered was an enactment, a by-law, or another form of delegated legislation.

## Conflict with existing law

A by-law will also be struck down if it conflicts with or is inconsistent with or repugnant to existing statute or common law. Clearly, a by-law cannot be used as a means of changing the law. A by-law which directly contradicts the existing law will obviously be bad. However, if a statute regulates an activity so that it is lawful in certain circumstances, a by-law which seeks to outlaw it altogether will be void on this ground: *Powell v May* [1946] KB 330. In this case a by-law forbidding betting in a public place was held to be bad since existing statute law allowed this provided that certain conditions were complied with. **8.14**

There can be by-laws which create strict liability offences. However, this will only be possible if the statute from which the by-law making power derives allows this. Otherwise, a by-law creating a strict liability offence is liable to be struck down as unlawful. The fact that the same general subject matter is regulated by statute does not prevent a local authority from making a by-law prohibiting something which is not prohibited by statute. For instance, a by-law prohibiting the keeping of noisy animals 'which shall be or cause a serious nuisance to residents in the neighbourhood' was not repugnant to a provision in the Public Health Act 1936 regulating animals 'kept in such place or manner as to be prejudicial to health or a nuisance' since that provision did not refer at all to noise made by animals: *Morrisey v Galer* [1955] 1 WLR 110. **8.15**

## Outside statutory powers

A by-law cannot go beyond the statutory power under which it is made. Thus if the statute allows a local authority to regulate an activity, that power cannot be used to forbid it: *City of Toronto Municipal Corporation v Virgo* [1896] AC 88. Similarly, if the statute contains a list of matters which can be regulated then this list cannot be added to by the local authority. A statutory provision allowing by-laws to be made to compel the removal of 'dust, ashes, rubbish, filth, manure, dung and soil' could not be extended to cover snow: *R v Wood* (1855) 119 ER 400 5 E & B 49. **8.16**

## Lawful justification

If individuals are arrested and prosecuted under by-laws which are subsequently held to be invalid, those who have carried out the arrests and prosecution will have a defence of lawful justification provided that they have not exceeded their powers: *Percy v Hall* [1996] 4 All ER 523. **8.17**

## Procedure

**8.18**  The procedure for making by-laws is set out in s. 235 of the LGA 1972. First, the by-law has to be made under seal. In practice, the first step is usually discussion and correspondence with the confirming authority, normally the ODPM, about the necessity for and the acceptability of the proposed by-law. Only when this is sorted out will the authority proceed to have the by-law made. The decision on whether to make the by-law will normally be taken by full council, but there is no legal reason why it cannot be delegated. If the by-laws follow a standard model then the fast track procedure can be used. If they do not, then there needs to be an application for provisional approval before the by-laws are made. There will then be a subsequent application for confirmation. The procedure is explained in Home Office Circular 25/1996.

**8.19**  After the by-law has been made under seal, the local authority must announce its intention to submit it for confirmation. This is done by publishing a notice to this effect in one or more local newspapers. This must give at least one month's notice of the intention to seek confirmation and must state that the proposed by-law is open to inspection at the council's premises and that anyone can purchase copies. If the confirming authority confirms the by-law, it will also fix a time when it is to come into effect. The council have to make copies of the by-law available at their offices for public inspection and for sale.

## Penalties and enforcement

**8.20**  The penalty for breach of a by-law will be contained in the enabling statute. This will be a fine. In the case of a continuing offence, there may also be a daily penalty. There are no statutory provisions which allow imprisonment as a penalty for breach of a by-law. However, where it is necessary to deal with the relevant mischief, it is possible for by-laws to give other powers to local authorities, such as powers of confiscation.

**8.21**  Unless the statute places specific restriction on who is allowed to prosecute, anybody can initiate proceedings for breach of a by-law: *R v Stewart* [1896] 1 QB 300. Even if the statute does provide that only the authority can initiate proceedings, it is still open to the police to do so: Local Government (Miscellaneous Provisions) Act 1982, s. 12(1).

**8.22**  It is open to anyone prosecuted for breach of a by-law to argue the invalidity of the by-law by way of defence: *R v Reading Crown Court, ex parte Hutchinson* [1988] QB 384. However, there is a distinction between challenges to substantive validity, where the instrument founding the prosecution was bad on its face, and challenges to procedural validity: *Bugg v DPP* [1993] QB 473.

**8.23**  In *Boddington v British Transport Police* [1998] 2 All ER 203 the House of Lords held that a defendant in criminal proceedings could challenge the legality of a by-law or an administrative decision made under it, unless there was a clear Parliamentary intention to the contrary. From 1 January Network South Central applied the smoking prohibition contained in by-law 20 of the BRB by-laws to all trains within its area. The defendant was convicted of smoking on one of these trains. On appeal by way of case stated, it was argued that he should be permitted to argue the invalidity of the decision to extend the smoking ban to all trains. The Divisional Court indicated that this was a matter which needed to be raised by way of judicial review. However, Mr Boddington's appeal to the House of Lords was allowed on this point of law. There was no need to show that the by-law was 'bad on its face' before such a defence could be considered. In the event though the House of Lords considered that the railway company did nothing unlawful and that the by-law was valid.

## Severance

If a by-law is unlawful, it may in certain circumstances be possible to sever the unlawful **8.24** part from the permissible part and maintain a conviction on the basis of what remains: *DPP v Hutchinson; DPP v Smith* [1990] 2 AC 783. These cases arose out of the demonstrations at Greenham Common. By-laws were made prohibiting persons from entering certain parts of the Common. These were made under the Military Lands Act 1892 s. 17(2). This provision, however, made it clear that the rights of common over the land were not to be prejudicially affected. The by-law on its face prohibited those having rights of common along with the rest of the population. Smith and Hutchinson did not assert any rights of common and were convicted. Their convictions were upheld by the Divisional Court on the basis that if those making the by-laws had appreciated the fact that they should not interfere with rights of common, then they would have framed them correctly. The House of Lords, allowing the appeals, held that this was the wrong approach. The court should refrain from speculating about what the authority would have done if it had properly applied its mind to the nature of its powers. It should instead apply the double test set out in the speech of Lord Bridge (at p. 804). The two aspects of this test are 'textual severability' and 'substantial severability':

A legislative instrument is textually severable if a clause, a sentence, a phrase or a single word may be disregarded, as exceeding the law-maker's power, and what remains of the text is still grammatical and coherent. A legislative instrument is substantially severable if the substance of what remains after severance is essentially unchanged in its legislative purpose, operation, and effect. Only if both tests are satisfied can severance take place.

## Injunctions and damages

It is possible to grant an injunction to restrain breach of a by-law. The case of *Burnley Borough* **8.25** *Council v England* (1978) 77 LGR 227 concerns the rights of dogs and their owners. The council made a by-law banning dogs apart from guide dogs from certain pleasure grounds. A number of objectors to this by-law arranged a mass protest of dog walkers with their dogs. On the first occasion this took place the council did not prosecute anybody. When it heard that another protest was being organised, the council applied for an injunction. This was granted. The court held that a prima facie case had been made out as to the validity of the by-law and that serious damage to the public interest was likely if an injunction was not granted. The court also took into account the difficult position which the police and park wardens would be in when faced with mass disobedience of this kind. It is likely that the injunction would not have been granted in this case to restrain individual as opposed to collective acts of disobedience. However, this does not mean that an injunction would never be granted to restrain an individual breach. If repeated prosecutions proved ineffective in deterring an individual, then it is likely that a court would be sympathetic to an application for an injunction.

**8.26**    Only when it is intended that the by-law should provide a civil remedy does it allow someone who suffers as a result of a breach to take an action for damages.

### Waiver

**8.27**    A local authority has no power to waive its own by-laws. In *Yabbicom v King* [1899] 1 QB 444, when the urban district council approved a plan which was contrary to its own by-laws, it was held that the purported approval was unlawful and it was open to the successor authority, the City of Bristol, to take enforcement proceedings in respect of the house which was built pursuant to it.

### Repeal

**8.28**    A local authority can repeal its own by-laws, but it requires the consent of the confirming authority: Intepretation Act 1978, s. 4. If an Act containing by-law making powers is repealed, any by-laws made under it are automatically repealed as well. The only exception to this is if the statute contains some saving provision to preserve the validity of the by-laws. If the by-law making power is re-enacted, then any by-laws made under the replaced provision retain their validity: Interpretation Act 1978, s. 17(2)(b).

## C   LOCAL LEGISLATION

### Power to promote private legislation

**8.29**    Another way in which local authorities may acquire powers is by promoting a local Act of Parliament. Clearly, the vast majority of powers which local authorities have derive from public legislation. Local legislation can be used to give additional powers for which a convincing case can be made. Private bills have to be deposited by 27 November each year, following advertisement in the press and the London Gazette. The bills will then be checked to ensure that all formalities have been complied with, although there is discretion to waive standing orders.

**8.30**    Parliament (normally two officials, one from the House of Lords and one from the House of Commons) then agrees in which House the bill should proceed. Local legislation being promoted by local authorities will usually start in the House of Lords. At this stage it will become apparent whether petitions are being presented against the bill. If there is a petition against one or more of the clauses in the bill, the opposed clauses will be referred to a Select Committee. In the House of Lords this consists of five Lords; in the Commons, it consists of three MPs. Both the promoters and the petitioners will then normally be represented by counsel. Witnesses will usually be called by each side to lend support to their arguments and will be cross-examined by the opposing counsel, and may also be questioned by the committee members who will then make a decision. If the whole of a bill is opposed in principle, an unusual occurrence, this is dealt with first. Then, if the Committee decides that a bill should proceed, it continues to hear the opposed clauses. Additional clauses may be added and clauses may be amended to take account of petitioners' objections. In addition, undertakings may be given as a way of settling the objections in a petition. Such undertakings will have the force of court orders and can be enforced in court.

Clauses that are unopposed do not automatically become law. They are normally examined **8.31** by the Committee on unopposed bills. If a clause is covered by existing legislation, it will be disallowed, as will a clause with which the Committee disagrees on policy grounds. Generally, provisions that are opposed by the Government are unlikely to succeed. They will often be the subject of discussion with the relevant Government department. Clauses might be opposed by the Government for reasons other than being contrary to policy. For instance, the Government might feel that a particular problem should more appropriately be remedied by national, rather than local legislation. If an important question of principle is involved, it is possible for an unopposed clause to be referred to a Select Committee.

All local authorities, apart from parish and community councils, have power to promote **8.32** private legislation: LGA 1972, s. 239. The decision must be made at a full council meeting and requires the support of a majority of the members of the council, i.e., not just those present. There is also a requirement to advertise the meeting in the local press at least 30 clear days before it takes place. The local authority must still, of course, comply with the ordinary statutory provisions about notice. After the bill has been deposited in Parliament, there must be another meeting of the full council to confirm the decision to promote the bill. This meeting must take place 'as soon as may be' (presumably less stringent than 'as soon as possible') after the period of 14 days has expired following the bill's deposit in Parliament. This must again be advertised in the local press at least 30 days before it takes place, and again, a majority of the members of the council must vote to continue with the promotion of the bill. If they do not, then the bill must be withdrawn.

When the Greater London Council and the Metropolitan County Councils were abolished, **8.33** power was given to any London Borough to promote a bill including provisions requested by another London Borough. (The Common Council of the Corporation of London also counts as a London Borough for this purpose.) Similarly, a bill promoted by a metropolitan district council may include provisions requested by another metropolitan district council within the same county. Councils who wish to have the benefit of these provisions must again have the two council meetings, one before the deposit of the bill and the other as soon as may be after the expiration of 14 days following its deposit. Again, these must have been the subject of at least 30 days' clear notice in the local press. There is power for any participating council to contribute to the costs of promotion. In practice in London the City of Westminster promotes private bills on behalf of itself and other London authorities that wish to participate. This normally includes all London Boroughs with the exception of the Corporation of London, which promotes its own legislation if it considers that it is required.

## Construction

It is a convention that private Acts of Parliament are construed more strictly than public **8.34** Acts. The reason for the principle was stated by Lord Esher MR in *Altrincham Union Assessment Committee v Cheshire Lines Committee* (1885) 15 QBD 597 at p. 603:

> In the case of a public Act you construe it keeping in view the fact that it must be taken to have been passed for the public advantage, and you apply certain fixed canons to its construction. In

the case of a private Act, which is obtained by persons for their own benefit, you construe more strictly provisions which they allege to be in their favour, because the persons who obtain a private Act ought to take care, that it is so worded that that which they desire to obtain for themselves is plainly stated in it. But, when the construction is perfectly clear, there is no difference between the modes of construing a private Act and a public Act, and, however difficult the construction of a private Act may be, when once the court has arrived at the true construction, after having subjected it to the strictest criticism, the consequences are precisely the same as in the case of a public Act. The moment you have arrived at the meaning of the legislature, the effect is the same in the one case as in the other.

## Validity

**8.35**    There can be no challenge to the validity of an Act of Parliament once it has been passed. In *Pickin v British Railways Board* [1974] AC 765, an optimistic application was made to declare a private Act invalid on the grounds of misrepresentation and breaches of standing orders. Inevitably, it was held by the House of Lords that the courts had no power to examine these issues or to impugn the validity of an Act of Parliament.

## Special Parliamentary Procedure

**8.36**    There is also a little used means of acquiring additional powers, the Special Parliamentary Procedure Order. The procedure that needs to be followed will be set out in the Act giving power to use this procedure. The Minister will then make the Order. There are requirements to advertise in the London Gazette and, if the provision concerns a particular area, a local newspaper circulating in that area. The notice must allow for objections to be lodged and explain the procedure for making such objections. If there are objections, these must be considered by the Minister, who must hold a public inquiry, unless satisfied that this is unnecessary because of special circumstances.

**8.37**    Once the Order is laid before Parliament, petitions may be lodged, whether objecting to the whole of the Order or seeking amendments to it. These are reported to both Houses of Parliament and either may order that the Order be annulled. If it is not, then it may be referred to a joint committee. Unless there is a resolution to the contrary, an Order that has petitions against the principle of it will always have to be considered by the joint committee. The committee then has to report, and may either report on the Order unamended or amend it. The order will then come into force. This will be on the day the report is made to Parliament or, if it has been amended, on the day fixed by the relevant Minister.

---

## KEY DOCUMENTS

Home Office Circular 25/1996 Arrangements for confirmation of local authority by-laws

# 9

# ELECTIONS

## A  REGISTRATION OF ELECTORS

### Registration officer

The responsibility for maintaining a register of those entitled to vote in local elections falls   **9.01**
to the registration officer. In England it is the responsibility of every district council and
London borough to employ such an officer for any constituency or part of a constituency
coterminous with or situated in the district or borough. In Wales the same responsibility is
that of the council of every county or county borough. The registration officer is obliged,
under s. 9 of the Representation of the People Act 1983 to maintain:

(a)  a register of parliamentary electors for each constituency or part of a constituency in the
     area for which he acts; and
(b)  a register of local government electors for the local government areas or parts of local
     government areas included in the area for which he acts.

The two registers ought to be combined so far as is practicable with those who are only   **9.02**
entitled to vote in one type of election being marked appropriately. The registers must
contain the following information:

(a)  the names of the persons appearing to the registration officer to be entitled to be registered in it;

(b)  the qualifying addresses of the persons registered in it; and

(c)  in relation to each such person, that person's electoral number.

The electoral numbers are allocated by the registration officer and this should be done in such a way as to ensure that, as far as reasonably practicable, the numbers run consecutively in each separate part of the register.

**9.03**  A person is entitled to be registered in the register of local government electors for any electoral area if on the relevant date (essentially the date on which the declaration is made) he—

(a)  is resident in that area;

(b)  is not subject to any legal incapacity to vote (age apart);

(c)  is a qualifying Commonwealth citizen, a citizen of the Republic of Ireland, or a relevant citizen of the Union; and

(d)  he is of voting age (18 years of age. A person who is not 18 is entitled to be registered if he will be 18 within 12 months and is not to be treated as entitled to vote in an election until his 18th birthday.).

Those who are subject to legal incapacity are mental patients detained in hospital, prisoners serving prison sentences having been convicted of a crime, and those disqualified from voting. A 'qualifying commonwealth citizen' means a citizen of a commonwealth country who either does not require leave to remain in the UK under the immigration legislation or who has such leave. A 'relevant citizen of the Union' means a citizen of a member state of the EU other than the Republic of Ireland.

**9.04**  The features of residence for the purposes of electoral registration as decided by the Court of Appeal in *Fox v Stirk* [1970] 2 QB 463 are as follows (The case was decided under the previous legislation but the guidance provided by this case is still applicable.):

(a)  a person may have more than one residence;

(b)  temporary presence at an address does not make a person resident at that address;

(c)  temporary absence from an address does not mean that a person has ceased to be resident at that address.

**9.05**  Further guidance on residence is set out in s. 5 of the Representation of the People Act 1983. This applies when considering the question of whether a person is resident at a particular address on the relevant date for the purposes of s. 4. It provides that 'regard shall be had, in particular, to the purpose and other circumstances, as well as to the fact, of his presence at, or absence from, the address on that date'. It goes on to provide that if a person is 'staying at any place otherwise than on a permanent basis, he may in all the circumstances be taken to be at that time—

(a)  resident there if he has no home elsewhere, or

(b)  not resident there if he does have a home elsewhere'.

This is of little practical help and does not add anything to the existing law.

**9.06**  Section 5(3) provides some more specific guidance on the issue of when residence can be regarded as interrupted by living elsewhere. Residence in a dwelling is not to be taken as interrupted by reason of a person's absence to perform any duty 'arising from or incidental to any office, service or employment held or undertaken by him if—

(a) he intends to resume actual residence within six months of giving up such residence, and will not be prevented from doing so by the performance of that duty; or

(b) the dwelling serves as a permanent place of residence (whether for himself or for himself and other persons) and he would be in actual residence there but for his absence in the performance of that duty'.

Temporary periods of unemployment are to be disregarded. Section 5(3) also applies to **9.07** absences caused by attendance on courses provided by an educational institution. Mental patients, prisoners on remand, and homeless persons can make a declaration of local connection either giving an address where correspondence can be sent or stating that he can collect correspondence from the registration officer's office. He also has to provide an address (the 'required address') where he would be residing, has resided, or where he spends a substantial amount of his time. The effect of such a declaration is that the person who made the declaration is treated as resident for registration purposes at the required address.

## B FREQUENCY OF ELECTIONS

The Secretary of State is empowered to make an order providing that the scheme for election **9.08** of councillors to a principal council should be one of three options. These options are set out in s. 85 of the LGA 2000.

The first option is for a scheme under which— **9.09**

(a) the term of office of councillors is four years,
(b) the elections are held in a given year and every fourth year after it,
(c) all the councillors are elected in each year in which the elections are held, and
(d) the councillors retire together.

The second option is for a scheme under which—

(a) the term of office of councillors is four years,
(b) the elections are held in a given year and every second year after it,
(c) one half (or as nearly as may be) of the councillors are elected in each year in which the elections are held, and
(d) one half (or as nearly as may be) of the councillors retire in each year in which the elections are held.

The third option is for a scheme under which—

(a) the term of office of councillors is four years,
(b) the elections are held in a given year and every year after it other than every third year after it,
(c) one third (or as nearly as may be) of the councillors are elected in each year in which the elections are held, and

(d)   one third (or as nearly as may be) of the councillors retire in each year in which the elections are held.

The aim of these options was to promote greater accountability by having more frequent local elections. The intention was that there would normally be elections of one-third of the authority's membership for unitary authorities, and two year alternating elections in those parts of the country where there was a two-tier system.

## C   PROCEDURE FOR ELECTIONS

### Nomination procedure

**9.10**   The procedure for elections is set out in the Local Elections (Principal Areas) Rules 1986 (SI No. 1986/2214). The process begins with the publication of the notice of the election by the returning officer. This must follow the prescribed form set out in the rules. This informs those who wish to stand in the election where their nomination papers are to be lodged and the date by which this must be done. Candidates who wish to stand in the election must complete the nomination papers. Again there is a prescribed form in the rules. They need to have a proposer and a seconder and the assent of eight other electors for that electoral area. These people all need to sign the forms. (For parish and community council elections there only needs to be a proposer and a seconder.) The candidate either needs to be standing for a registered political party (i.e. a party included on the list of political parties maintained by the Electoral Commission) or does not purport to represent a political party (either by describing himself as an independent or by not including a description). If a description is included it must not exceed six words. (In the case of parish and community elections individuals can also stand for elections as representatives of 'minor parties' i.e. parties which only intend to contest parish and community elections.) The description needs to be authorised by a certificate issued by or on behalf of the party's registered nominating officer.

**9.11**   The importance of complying strictly with these formalities is illustrated by the case of *R (on the application of Beer) v Balabanoff* (2002) *The Times* 25 April. The certificate authorised the use of the description 'Liberal Democrat'. The nomination papers used the term 'Liberal Democrat Focus Team'. The returning officer rejected them and on a subsequent challenge, it was held that he was entitled to do so. The result was that all the Liberal Democrat candidates were unable to take part in the Council elections for the London Borough of Harrow that year.

### Election agent

**9.12**   A person must be named, by or on behalf of each candidate for an election, as that candidate's election agent. Except in the case of elections to the London Assembly, where the same agent must act for all candidates, the candidate may appoint himself as the election agent. In the case of elections for the Mayor of London and the London Assembly there can also be sub-agents. The candidate is responsible for the acts of his election agent whether or not they were authorised by him: *Coventry Case, Berry v Eaton and Hill* (1869) 20 LT 405. The declaration must be made and signed by the election agent or accompanied by a written declaration of acceptance signed by him. The appropriate officer (the returning officer in the case of elections for the Mayor of London or the London Assembly, in all other cases the proper officer of the authority) must give public notice of the appointment of the election agent. The election agent must have an office to which all claims, notices, legal process, and other documents may be sent. The address of the office must be declared to the appropriate officer at the time that the appointment of the agent is declared and must be stated in the public notice of the name of the agent. The office must be:

> . . . within the local government area or in the constituency or one of the constituencies in which the area is comprised or in a Welsh county or county borough, or London Borough or district, which adjoins it, and that of a sub-agent shall be in the area within which he is appointed to act.

If no election agent is appointed, the candidate will be deemed to have appointed himself as his election agent.

---

## D   ELECTION EXPENSES

All election expenses incurred by or on behalf of a candidate must be paid by or through that **9.13** candidate's election agent. The candidate may himself pay 'personal expenses' which are defined as including 'reasonable travelling expenses of the candidate, and the reasonable expenses of his living at hotels or elsewhere for the purposes of and in relation to the election'. In the case of most local elections this is likely to refer only to travel expenses.

Election expenses are defined by s. 90A of the RPA 1983 as 'expenses incurred in respect **9.14** of—

(a)   the acquisition or use of any property, or
(b)   the provision by any person of any goods, services or facilities

which is or are used for the purposes of the candidate's election after the date when he becomes a candidate at the election'.

Where the property, goods, services, or facilities concerned are not used exclusively for the purposes of the candidate's election, an apportionment has to take place. If property, goods, services, or facilities are provided to a candidate free of charge or at a discount of more than 20 per cent of the market value or applicable commercial rate, then the value provided to the candidate is treated as an election expense.

Election expenses are limited to the maximum amount for each candidate. The maximum **9.15** currently for local government elections other than for the Mayor of London or the London Assembly is £242 together with an additional 4.7p for each entry in the register of electors. If election expenses are incurred in excess of the maximum amount, 'any candidate or election agent who—

(a)   incurred, or authorised the incurring of, the election expenses, and
(b)   knew or ought reasonably to have known that the expenses would be incurred in excess of the maximum amount,
shall be guilty of an illegal practice'.

Incurring expenses to promote or procure the election of a candidate are not permitted **9.16**

unless they have been incurred by the candidate, the election agent or individuals authorised in writing by the election agent if they are incurred on account—

(a)  of holding public meetings or organising any public display; or
(b)  of issuing advertisements, circulars or publications; or
(c)  of otherwise presenting to the electors the candidate or his views or the extent or nature
     of his backing or disparaging another candidate; or
(d)  in the case of an election of the London members of the London Assembly at an ordi-
     nary election, of otherwise presenting to the electors the candidate's registered political
     party (if any) or the views of that party or the extent or nature of that party's backing or
     disparaging any other registered political party.

This does not restrict the publication in a newspaper or a periodical or in broadcasts of items
about the election. There is also a permitted sum which can be lawfully incurred for these
purposes being for local government elections £50 together with an additional 5p for every
entry in the register of local government electors for the electoral area in question.

9.17  There is a requirement to make a return as to election expenses. It must be made by the
      candidate's election agent within 35 days of the date on which the result of the election is
      announced. It must contain—

(a)  a statement of all election expenses incurred by or on behalf of the candidate; and
(b)  a statement of all payments made by the election agent together with all bills or receipts
     relating to the payments.

It must be accompanied by a declaration made by the election agent in the appropriate form.
Failure on the part of a candidate or election agent to make the return or otherwise comply
with these requirements is an illegal practice.

---

## E   VOTING

### Methods of voting

9.18  The manner in which electors may vote is now set out in Schedule 4 to the Representation of
      the People Act 2000. Under paragraph 2 a person may vote in one of the following ways.

(a)  He may vote in person at the polling station allotted to him unless he is entitled to an
     absent vote (i.e. a vote by post or by proxy).
(b)  He may vote by post if he is entitled to vote by post.
(c)  He may vote by proxy if he is entitled to vote by proxy unless before a ballot paper has
     been issued to him for a proxy, he applies at the polling station allotted to him for a
     ballot paper to vote in person, in which case he may vote in person there.
(d)  If he is not entitled to an absent vote but cannot reasonably be expected to attend at his
     allotted polling station, because of his employment as a constable or by the returning
     officer for a purpose connected with the election he may vote in person at any polling
     station in the electoral area.

9.19  Under paragraph 3 all that is required for entitlement to vote by post is registration in the applicable register of electors and that the application meets the prescribed requirements (under the Registration of the People (England and Wales) Regulations 2001 (SI No. 2001/341). The requirements are purely formal; any elector is entitled to a postal vote. The requirements for being allowed to vote by proxy are if the elector:

(a) is or will be registered as a service voter;
(b) cannot reasonably be expected to go to his allotted polling station or vote unaided there by reason of blindness or other physical incapacity;
(c) cannot reasonably be expected to go to his allotted polling station because of the general nature of his or his spouse's occupation, service, or employment or his or his spouse's attendance at a course at an educational institution;
(d) cannot go from his qualifying address to his allotted polling station without making a journey by air or sea.

A person may have an absent vote at a particular election or generally. The registration officer must keep two lists of absent voters, one consisting of those entitled to postal votes, the other listing those entitled to vote by proxy.

## Pilot voting schemes

Under s. 10 of the RPA 2000 local authorities can apply to the Secretary of State to use pilot voting schemes for any local election. A scheme can make provision differing in any respect from that made under or by virtue of the RPA as regards one or more of the following: **9.20**

(a) when, where, and how voting at the elections is to take place;
(b) how the votes cast at the elections are to be counted;
(c) the sending by candidates of election communications free of charge for postage.

Following any such pilot scheme, the Electoral Commission must prepare a report on it, assessing its success in terms of facilitating voting or the counting of votes, encouraging voting or enabling voters to make informed decisions. If the Electoral Commission so recommends, the Secretary of State can extend the scheme to local government elections generally or any particular description of such elections.

---

## F  ELECTION PETITIONS

### Grounds for petition

An election can be questioned by way of an election petition on the following grounds: **9.21**

(a) that the person whose election is questioned was at the time of the election disqualified;
(b) that the person whose election is questioned was not duly elected;
(c) that the election was avoided by corrupt or illegal practices;
(d) that corrupt or illegal practices or illegal payments, employments, or livings have so extensively prevailed that they may be reasonably supposed to have affected the result;
(e) that the candidate or his election agent has personally engaged a canvasser or agent who is disqualified from voting because he was convicted of corruption or convicted or reported for a corrupt or illegal practice in relation to an election.

The petition may be presented by four or more persons who voted or had the right to vote at the election or by a candidate. The person whose election is questioned and the returning officer may be made respondents. The petition has to be in the prescribed form and presented in the prescribed manner to the High Court. Petitions must normally be brought within 21 days of the date of the election. If it is on the ground of corrupt or illegal practices it can be presented within 28 days of the date of the alleged act.

## Hearing of petition

**9.22** An election court is presided over by a commissioner. There is a list of no more than five such commissioners appointed annually. The petition is tried in open court. Witnesses may be called and cross-examined. At the conclusion of the trial of the petition, the court must determine whether the person whose election is complained of, or any and what other person was duly elected, or whether the election was void. The determination is final as to the matters at issue on the petition. The report must also state whether any corrupt or illegal practice has or has not been proved to have been committed by or with the knowledge and consent of any candidate at the election, and the nature of the corrupt or illegal practice. If a candidate is reported guilty personally or by his agents, his election is void. There are also numerous offences which may potentially be committed in connection with elections.

**9.23** A recent example of an election being declared void was the petition in relation to two local elections in Birmingham wards: *In the matter of a local government election for the Bordesley Green Ward of the Birmingham City Council held on 10th June 2004: In the matter of a local government election for the Aston Ward of the Birmingham City Council held on 10th June 2004* LTL 14/4/2005. The election court was presided over by Richard Mawrey QC. It was clear that there was a large increase in the number of postal votes applied for in comparison with previous years. Individual voters were refused ballot papers because they had been placed on the absent voters' list without their knowledge. There was found to be evidence of large numbers of ballot papers being stolen either by the theft of postal voting packages or by theft from the electors themselves. They were then admitted to the count as votes for the Labour Party candidates. In the Aston ward it was considered that there were at least 1,000 forged ballot papers. Electoral fraud had determined the result in favour of the Labour Party in these two wards. Corrupt and illegal practices were so prevalent that the results were declared void and the respondents guilty of corrupt and illegal practices.

---

## KEY DOCUMENTS

Local Elections (Principal Areas) Rules 1986
Representation of the People (England and Wales) Regulations 2001

# 10

# LOCAL AUTHORITY COMPANIES

## A INTRODUCTION

There are a number of reasons why local authority companies have assumed increased **10.01**
importance in recent years. The best value regime, the introduction of strategic partnerships, and private finance transactions as well as the encouragement which councils have
received to be innovative, have all meant that some local authorities have felt the need to at
least consider setting up a company at some stage. For some functions, setting up a company
has been a means of obtaining access to further benefits from the Government. For instance,
the setting up of arm's length management organisations (ALMOs) to take over the management of a local authority's housing stock have enabled local authorities to obtain greater
investment in their housing. ALMOs are typically companies limited by guarantee wholly
controlled by the local authority. With the advent of powers for local authorities to trade
with the private sector, authorities which wish to take advantage of these powers will have to
set up (or join forces with) a company in order to do so.

There have been for a number of years specific statutory powers for local authorities to set up **10.02**
or participate in companies. Local authorities have also relied upon their power under LGA
1972, s. 111 to do anything that is conducive or incidental to or calculated to facilitate any of

their functions to set up companies. The Widdicombe Committee expressed concern about the trend and recommended legislation to make it clear that it was *ultra vires* for a local authority to set up a company in the absence of an express statutory power. This recommendation was not accepted by the Government. However, it was accepted that greater statutory controls were needed. A number of local authority companies at this time were being used as vehicles for ingenious schemes to avoid the effect of controls on borrowing and expenditure.

**10.03** The controls induced by the Local Government and Housing Act (LGHA) 1989 divided local authority companies into three types: controlled, influenced, and minority interest. The Act also gave power for the Secretary of State to make regulations to ensure that controlled and influenced companies were subject to the same kind of legal controls and restrictions as local authorities themselves. The exact nature of the controls was to be spelt out in the regulations and these were a long time coming. Six years after the legislation, the Local Authorities (Companies) Order 1995 finally appeared. The effect of all these provisions is complex. Controlled companies were already divided into two types: those that were at 'arm's length' and those that were just plain controlled. The 1995 Order then introduced another category: the 'regulated' company. The precise effect of all these provisions will need to be taken into account if a local authority company is being considered.

**10.04** The provisions set out in Part V of the LGHA 1989 listed the different categories of local authority company. All types of company are caught by these provisions. Under s. 67 of the Act a company is defined as:

> . . . a body corporate of one of the following descriptions—
>
> (a)   a company limited by shares;
> (b)   a company limited by guarantee and not having a share capital;
> (c)   a company limited by guarantee and having a share capital;
> (d)   an unlimited company; and
> (e)   a society registered or deemed to be registered under the Industrial and Provident Societies Act 1965 or under the Industrial and Provident Societies Act (Northern Ireland) 1969.

The last is important, since it brings in many voluntary organisations that may be registered as industrial and provident societies, including many housing associations.

## B   CONTROLLED COMPANIES

**10.05** Section 68 of the LGHA 1989 defines controlled companies and arm's length companies. A company is controlled by a local authority if:

(a)   it is a subsidiary of the local authority by virtue of s. 736 of the Companies Act 1985; or
(b)   the local authority has power to control a majority of the votes at a general meeting (i.e., the local authority has effective control of more than half the shareholding);
(c)   the authority has power to appoint or remove a majority of the board of directors of the company; or
(d)   the company is under the control of another company which, by virtue of these provisions, is under the control of the local authority.

Section 68 (3) ensures that control of voting rights is given a wide meaning. It provides that **10.06** power to control a majority of powers at a general meeting means:

> . . . a power which is exercisable—

(a) in the case of a company limited by shares, through the holding of equity share capital in any one or more of the following ways, namely, by the local authority, by nominees of the local authority and by persons whose shareholding is under the control of the local authority; or

(b) in the case of any company, through the holding of votes at a general meeting of the company in any one or more of the following ways, namely, by the local authority, by a group of members of the company the composition of which is controlled by the local authority and by persons who have contractually bound themselves to vote in accordance with the instructions of the local authority; or

(c) partly in one of those ways and partly in the other.

This is the same set of elaborate anti-avoidance mechanisms that can be seen elsewhere in the 1989 Act, particularly in the provisions governing capital controls.

A person's shareholding is under the control of the local authority if the right to the share- **10.07** holding arose because of some action that the authority took or refrained from taking and the authority (acting alone or jointly with others) can require the person to transfer that shareholding: LGHA 1989, s. 68(5).

For a controlled company to be an 'arm's length' company, there first needs to be a resolution to that effect by the local authority. Companies can be arm's length for one financial year at a time, and the resolution must be made before the beginning of the financial year to which it relates. During the whole of the financial year, the following conditions must be satisfied (LGHA 1989, s. 68(6)):

(a) that each of the directors of the company was appointed for a fixed term of at least two years;

(b) that, subject to s. 68(7) below, no director of the company has been removed by resolution under s. 303 of the Companies Act 1985;

(c) that not more than one-fifth of the directors of the company have been members or officers of the authority;

(d) that the company has not occupied (as tenant or otherwise) any land in which the authority has an interest, otherwise than for the best consideration reasonably obtainable;

(e) that the company has entered into an agreement with the authority that the company will use its best endeavours to produce a specified return on the assets;

(f) that, except for the purpose of enabling the company to acquire fixed assets or to provide it with working capital, the authority has not lent money to the company or guaranteed any sum borrowed by it or subscribed for any securities in the company;

(g) that the authority has not made any grant to the company except in pursuance of an agreement or undertaking entered into before the financial year (within the meaning of the Companies Act 1985) of the company in which the grant was made; and

(h) that the authority has not made any grant to the company the amount of which is in any way related to the financial results of the company in that period.

Section 68(7) provides that the Secretary of State is given powers to direct that removal of a director may be disregarded for the purposes of (b) above. However, such a direction must not be given if the director was removed with a view to influencing the management of the company for other than commercial reasons.

---

## C  INFLUENCED COMPANIES

**10.08**  Local authority influenced companies are defined by the LGHA 1989, s. 69. A company is local authority influenced if:

(a)  it is not a banking or insurance company or a member of a banking or insurance group; and

(b)  there is a business relationship, as defined in s. 69(3) between the company and the authority; and

(c)  one of the conditions below is satisfied.

The conditions referred to in (c) are as follows (s. 69(1)):

(a)  at least 20 per cent of the total voting rights of all the members having the right to vote at a general meeting of the company are held by persons who are associated with the authority as mentioned in s. 69(5); or

(b)  at least 20 per cent of the directors of the company are persons who are so associated (for an industrial and provident society the word 'directors' means the members of the committee of management); or

(c)  at least 20 per cent of the total voting rights at a meeting of the directors of the company are held by persons who are so associated.

**10.09**  This leaves two questions to be answered by the remaining provisions in s. 69: What is meant by 'business relationship'? What is meant by 'associated with'?

The 'business relationship' test is defined by LGHA 1989, s. 69(3), and there is such a relationship if at any time one of the following requirements is fulfilled:

(a)  within a period of 12 months, which includes that time the aggregate of the payments to the company by the authority or by another company that is under the control of the authority represents more than one-half of the company's turnover, as shown in its profit and loss accounts for the most recent financial year for which the company's auditors have made a report on the accounts or, if there is no such account, as estimated by the authority for the period of 12 months preceding the date of the estimate or for such part of that period as follows the formation of the company;

(b)  more than one-half of the company's turnover referred to in (a) above is derived from the exploitation of assets of any description in which the local authority or a company under the control of the authority has an interest (disregarding an interest in land which is in reversion of a lease granted for more than seven years);

(c)  the aggregate of—

(i)  grants made either by the authority and being expenditure for capital purposes or by a company under the control of the authority, and

(ii)  the nominal value of shares or stock in the company which is owned by the authority or by a company under the control of the authority, exceeds one-half of the net assets of the company;

(d) the aggregate of—

    (i)   grants falling within (c) (i) above,

    (ii)  loans or other advances made or guaranteed by the authority or by a company under the control of the authority, and

    (iii) the nominal value referred to in (c)(ii) above, exceeds one-half of the fixed and current assets of the company;

(e) the company at that time occupies land by virtue of an interest which it obtained from the local authority or a company under the control of the local authority and which it so obtained at less than the best consideration reasonably obtainable; and

(f) the company intends at that time to enter into (or complete) a transaction and, when that is done, there will be a business relationship between the company and the authority by virtue of any of (a) to (e) above.

('Net assets' is to be construed in accordance with s. 152(2) of the Companies Act 1985. It means the aggregate of the company's assets less the aggregate of its liabilities. 'Fixed and current assets' is to be construed in accordance with Schedule 4, paragraph 7 of that Act. They comprise intangible assets, such as intellectual property, tangible assets, such as land and buildings, investments, as well as debts and stock.)

This is a complicated set of conditions but can be simplified into a series of questions:    **10.10**

- Does more than half the company's turnover consist of payments from the local authority or exploitation of a local authority asset?
- Do more than half the company's assets consist of grants or loans made by the authority and/or shares owned by the authority?
- Does the company occupy land which it obtained from the authority at less than the best consideration reasonably obtainable?
- Is the company intending to enter into a transaction as a result of which the answers to any of the above questions will be yes?

The definition of 'associated with the local authority' is just as complicated, and s. 69(5) **10.11** shows a similar attention to detail in trying to ensure that every route for avoidance is closed off. This subsection provides that a person is:

. . . at any time associated with the local authority if—

    (a)  he is at that time a member of the authority;

    (b)  he is at that time an officer of the authority;

    (c)  he is at that time both an employee and either a director, manager, secretary or other similar officer of a company that is under the control of the authority; or

    (d)  at any time within the preceding four years he has been associated with the authority by virtue of paragraph (a) above.

Section 69(6) brings in other categories of persons who are treated as associated with the **10.12** local authority 'if and to the extent that the Secretary of State by Order so provides'. In summary the categories are as follows:

(a)   employment by a person providing advice in connection with the company;

(b) having been a member of the authority or an officer of the company within the last four years;

c) being the spouse or business partner of an employee of the authority;

d) holding an office in a political association that formed part of the description on the ballot paper of any member of the local authority.

---

## D   REGULATED COMPANIES

**10.13**   Section 70 of the LGHA 1989 gives the Secretary of State powers to set out what controlled and influenced companies may and may not do. These powers were exercised when the Local Authorities (Companies) Order 1995 was introduced. As if the situation were not complicated enough already, this Order brought in yet another category, the 'regulated company', which includes all local authority controlled companies and some (but not all) influenced companies.

**10.14**   The Order defines a regulated company as a company that for the time being is either:

(a) a controlled company; or

(b) an influenced company which—

    (i) is an unlimited company or an industrial and provident society, or

    (ii) satisfies either or both of the following conditions:

        (1) that if it were a company registered under the Companies Act 1985 it would be treated as having the right to exercise, or as having actually exercised a dominant influence over the company in question. (Exercising a 'dominant influence' means having 'the right to give directions with respect to the operating and financial policies of that undertaking which its directors are obliged to comply with, whether or not they are for the benefit of that undertaking' (s. 10A, Companies Act 1985);

        (2) that if it were a company registered under the 1985 Act it would be required to prepare group accounts in respect of the company in question. (Under s. 227 of the Act, group accounts must be prepared by a parent company for all companies within that group.)

**10.15**   Various restrictions applicable to regulated companies are set out in paragraphs 4 to 8 of the 1995 Order. A regulated company must state on all relevant documents that it is controlled or influenced by a local authority as the case may be, and name the authority or authorities. 'Relevant documents' means documents of a kind mentioned in s. 349(1)(a) to (d) of the Companies Act 1985, as follows:

(a) business letters;

(b) notices and other official publications;

(c) bills of exchange, promissory notes, endorsements, cheques and orders for money or goods purporting to be signed by or on behalf of the company;

(d) bills of parcels, invoices, receipts, and letters of credit.

**10.16**   A regulated company is not permitted to:

(a) pay more than the maximum amount by way of remuneration or expenses to a director who is also a member of a local authority. (The maximum amount for remuneration is the maximum that would be payable as attendance allowance for a councillor, and the maximum for expenses is the maximum subsistence allowance that would be payable to a councillor.)

(b) publish any material that the local authority would be prohibited from publishing by s. 2 of the Local Government Act 1986 (which prohibits the publication of 'political' material by local authorities).

Regulated companies must also provide 'such information and explanation about the affairs of the company' as the local authority's auditor may require for the purposes of auditing the local authority's accounts and such information as the Audit Commission may require for the purposes of carrying out its statutory duties.

There are also duties on regulated companies to provide information to members of their local **10.17** authority and to the authority itself. To any member a regulated company must provide 'such information about the affairs of the company as the member reasonably requires for the proper discharge of his duties' (Art. 7(1)). But this duty does not 'require a company to provide information in breach of any enactment, or of an obligation owed to any person' (Art. 7(2)). To the authority the company must provide 'such information about the affairs of the company as that authority may require for the purposes of any order for the time being in force under s. 39 (revenue accounts and capital finance) of the 1989 Act' (Art. 8(1)). Such an order allows the company's revenue and capital expenditure and receipts to be treated as those of its authority. This information must be provided within such reasonable time as may be specified by the authority and in such form as the authority may reasonably require (Art. 8(2)).

The 1995 Order also contains two provisions that relate purely to controlled companies. **10.18** First, all controlled companies have to obtain the Audit Commission's consent to the appointment of an auditor. Secondly, controlled companies that are not arm's length companies have to arrange for the minutes of general meetings to be available for public inspection for a period of at least four years from the date of the meeting. However, this does not require a company to disclose anything where this would be a breach of any enactment or a breach of an obligation owed to any person.

Certain types of company are excluded from the 1995 Order. These are set out in the Schedule **10.19** to the Order and are as follows:

1. Public transport companies within the meaning of s. 72 of the Transport Act 1985.
2. Public airport companies within the meaning of Part II of the Airports Act 1986.
3. Companies under the control or subject to the influence of a Passenger Transport Executive.
4. Companies that by virtue of s. 73 of the 1989 Act are to be treated as under the control or subject to the influence of two or more authorities (see below) where each of those authorities is a Passenger Transport Executive.
5. Companies which—
   (a) have companies of the type referred to in paragraphs 1 to 4 above as their holding companies, and
   (b) would, if those holding companies were local authorities be under the control of the authorities.

## E MINORITY INTEREST COMPANIES

**10.20** Apart from the exceptions set out below, local authorities require the consent of the Secretary of State to have minority interests in companies. Section 71(2) of the 1989 Act provides that:

> Except with the approval of the Secretary of State, in relation to a company to which this subsection applies, a local authority may not—
>
> (a)  subscribe for, or acquire, whether in their own name or in the name of a nominee, any shares or share warrants in the company;
> (b)  become or remain a member of the company if it is limited by guarantee;
> (c)  exercise any power, however arising, to nominate any person to become a member of the company;
> (d)  exercise any power to appoint directors of the company;
> (e)  permit any officer of the authority, in the course of his employment, to make any such nomination or appointment as is referred to in paragraph (c) or paragraph (d) above; or
> (f)  permit an officer of the authority, in the course of his employment, to become or remain a member or director of the company.

If the Secretary of State gives approval this can be either general or may relate to any specific matter or company.

**10.21** The exceptions are companies which, if the action referred to above were taken, would be controlled companies (and which are therefore subject to other rules) and companies specified for the purpose by the Secretary of State. The Secretary of State has specified for this purpose companies in which a person associated with the authority (see above) is a director or has a right to vote at a general meeting: Local Authorities (Companies) Order 1995, article 11. This excludes regulated companies (which are subject to the controls referred to above) and companies specified in the Schedule (i.e., those excluded from the effect of the Order and listed above). For all minority interest companies, authorities must ensure that those who are disqualified from being members of a local authority do not become directors, members or authorised representatives (within the meaning of s. 375 of the Companies Act 1985: somebody authorised by the directors or governing body of a company that owns shares in another company to represent it at meetings of that other company) of authorised companies.

**10.22** Members or officers of a local authority who have become members or directors of an authorised company by any of the means set out below must make a declaration to the authority, in such form as it may require, of any remuneration or reimbursement of expenses that is received from the company. The means are as follows:

(a)  a nomination made by the authority; or
(b)  election at a meeting of the company at which voting rights were exercisable (whether or not exercised) by the authority or by a person bound to vote in accordance with the instructions of the authority; or
(c)  an appointment made by the directors of another company, the majority of whom became directors of that company at which voting rights were exercisable as mentioned in (b) above.

In addition, if a member or officer has been appointed in the manner set out above, or has been authorised to act as the authority's representative under s. 375 of the Companies Act 1985, the authority must make arrangements for members of the authority to question that member or officer about the activities of the company. This may be done during the course of proceedings of the authority (i.e., a council meeting) or of a committee or sub-committee of it. This provision does not require the member or officer to disclose any confidential information.

## F  LOCAL AUTHORITY INFLUENCED TRUSTS

The Secretary of State has power by statutory instrument to make the LGHA 1989, s. 69 (which **10.23** concerns local authority influenced companies) applicable to non-charitable trusts, and may adapt its provisions. If this power is exercised, the rest of Part V of the 1989 Act applies to such trusts in the same way as it applies to companies (LGHA 1989, s. 72). Different provision may be made for trusts as opposed to companies. This power has not yet been exercised.

## G  LOCAL AUTHORITIES ACTING JOINTLY

Where a company would not be treated as under the control of any one authority, but would **10.24** be if two or more authorities acting together were treated as a single authority, then the company is treated as being under the control of each of those authorities. For local authority influenced companies, the position is slightly more complex. They are treated as being under the influence of more than one authority only if the conditions set out in subsection (3) are fulfilled. These are as follows:

(a)  that at least one of the conditions in LGHA 1989, s. 69(3)(a)–(e) (10.09 above) (i.e., the 'business relationship' test) would be fulfilled—
    (i)  if any reference therein to the company being under the control of a local authority were a reference to its being under the control of any one of the authorities in the group or of any two or more of them taken together; and
    (ii)  if any other reference therein to the local authority were a reference to any two or more of the authorities in the group taken together; and
(b)  that at least one of the conditions in LGHA 1989, s.69(1)(a)–(c) (10.09 above) (i.e., the 'one-fifth influence' test) would be fulfilled if the reference to a local authority were read as a reference to the group of local authorities referred to in (i) or (ii) above; and
(c)  if it is paragraph (a) that is being satisfied (at least one-fifth of the voting rights) at least one person associated with each authority within the group has the right to vote at a general meeting of the company; and
(d)  if it is paragraph (b) or (c) that is satisfied (at least one-fifth of the directors or one-fifth of voting rights on the board of directors) at least one person associated with each authority within the group is a director.

Where two or more local authorities have set up a joint committee, anything done or any power exercisable by that committee, sub-committee, or officer of the authority acting under delegated powers, is treated as done or exercisable by each of the participating authorities: LGHA 1989, s. 73 (5).

## H   DELEGATED POWERS

**10.25**　For the purposes of the provisions of the 1989 Act about companies, anything done or any power exercisable by any committee, sub-committee, or officer of the authority acting under delegated powers, is treated as being done or exercisable by the authority.

## I   DIRECTORS' LIABILITY

**10.26**　When the members or officers of a local authority serve as directors of a company, they owe an independent duty to the company in their capacity as directors. They cannot therefore simply agree to carry out the instructions of the authority that appointed them. If a company continues to trade when it can no longer meet its debts, there can be personal liability for the directors. It is possible to obtain insurance against such liability. The need for officers and members to think carefully before agreeing to become company directors is dramatically illustrated by the case of *Burgoine v Waltham Forest London Borough Council and Another* [1996] *The Times*, 7 November.

**10.27**　The council decided to provide a water park through the medium of a company. Two senior officers were appointed as directors. The company later went into liquidation. It became apparent also that because of the case of *Crédit Suisse v Waltham Forest London Borough Council* [1996] 4 A11 ER 176, both the setting up of the company and the appointment of the officers were *ultra vires*. The liquidator took the view that there had been wrongful trading on the part of the company and therefore sought a contribution to its debts. The officers had benefit of an indemnity that was incorporated into their contracts of employment. The council agreed to indemnify the employees against claims relating to defaults 'committed . . . in or about the pursuit of their duties on behalf of the council while acting within the scope of their authority'. The officers sought to rely on the indemnities. However, the council, relying on the advice of its auditor, resisted this, arguing that the losses incurred as company directors could not be claimed under these indemnities. The court agreed with the auditor. Since the council had no power to appoint them as company directors, they could not have been pursuing 'their duties on behalf of the council' or 'acting within the scope of their authority'.

**10.28**　Officers and councillors who are asked to serve as company directors will need to bear in mind the duty they owe the company. They will also need to give careful consideration to the wording of any indemnity that they are offered and will need to consider appropriate insurance if necessary.

**10.29**　Under the Local Authorities (Indemnities for Members and Officers) Order 2004 (SI No.

2004/3082) local authorities now have power to provide indemnities in relation to any action of, or failure to act by, the member or officer in question, which—

(a) is authorised by the authority; or

(b) forms part of, or arises from, any powers conferred, or duties placed, upon that member or officer, as a consequence of any function by that member or officer (whether or not when exercising that function he does so in his capacity as a member or officer of the authority)—

    (i) at the request of, or with the approval of the authority, or

    (ii) for the purposes of the authority.

The power to grant an indemnity can extend to acts or omissions beyond the power of the authority if it was believed that it was within the powers of the authority and the belief was reasonable. The indemnity can also extend to acts or omissions which are subsequently found to be beyond the powers of a member or officer if he reasonably believed that the act or omission was within his powers. There is a restriction for the consequences of crime, fraud, deliberate wrongdoing, or recklessness but an officer or member can be indemnified for the costs of their defence in criminal proceedings. Local authorities can take out policies of insurance instead of providing an indemnity. **10.30**

---

## J COMMUNITY INTEREST COMPANIES

The Companies (Audit, Investigations and Community Enterprise) Act 2005 allows for a new type of company to be established. These are called community interest companies. It may be that, for certain types of local authority enterprise, they could be a suitable vehicle. They will not be allowed to distribute profits or assets. They will have to adopt a suitable constitution and satisfy a community interest test i.e. whether a reasonable person could consider the community interest company's activities to benefit the community. They will be able to issue shares which pay a dividend to investors. They will have a lighter regulatory regime than charities and will have no special tax status. **10.31**

---

## KEY DOCUMENTS

Local Authority (Companies) Order 1995 (SI No. 1995/849)
Local Authorities (Indemnities for Members and Officers) Order 2004 (SI No. 2004/3082)
Community Interest Company Regulations

# 11

# LOCAL AUTHORITIES AS LANDOWNERS

## A  INTRODUCTION

Local authorities are landowners on a very large scale. Land used for a wide variety of **11.01** functions, such as housing and education, is owned by local councils. In addition, they own parks and other open spaces and various facilities for leisure and recreation. They are also likely to own other land within their area, which may not be held for a specific purpose and that can be used for commercial purposes to subsidise a local authority's other activities.

Local authorities cannot simply behave as any other landowner by doing as they please with **11.02** the land, subject only to planning controls and other legal requirements. They can purchase land only if they need it for one of their functions; they must have regard to their functions in acting as landowners. Their powers to sell land are also controlled by legislation. Unlike ordinary citizens, however, local authorities do have the power to deprive other people of their land against their will by exercising their powers of compulsory purchase. In addition, there are some constraints on changing the use of land. Land which is used for one purpose may not always automatically be switched to another purpose.

## B  ACQUISITION OF LAND

Under s. 120 of the Local Government Act 1972, a local authority may buy land by agree- **11.03** ment, whether inside or outside their area for:

(a)  any of their functions; or

(b)  the benefit, improvement, or development of their area.

In order to use this power to buy land, it does not matter that the authority has no immediate use for the land. Under s. 120 (2) they may also buy land for future, rather than immediate use. This power can be exercised by principal councils. Parish councils can also acquire land by agreement for the same purposes as principal councils. However, they cannot buy land for future use.

**11.04** There are also various powers for local authorities to buy land for specific purposes. The most important of these is the power in s. 227 of the Town and Country Planning Act 1990 which allows local authorities to acquire by agreement any land which they require for any purpose for which a local authority may be authorised to acquire land compulsorily under s. 226.

---

## C  COMPULSORY ACQUISITION

**11.05** Under s. 121 LGA 1972 a principal council can use its power of compulsory purchase to acquire land for any purpose for which it could acquire land voluntarily under LGA 1972 or any other enactment. Obviously, these powers will normally only be used when negotiations to buy land voluntarily have been unsuccessful. However, for certain types of large-scale re-development, e.g., a new town centre, a major commercial development, demolishing and re-building a housing estate, it will often be impracticable to buy out all the necessary interests without resorting to compulsory purchase powers. In addition, starting the CPO procedure will often be necessary for tactical reasons. Without activity towards a CPO going on in the background, a landowner may delay selling and become obstructive in the hope that the authority will be pressurised into paying a higher price than would normally be justified, rather than risk delay to a major re-development programme.

**11.06** There are certain limits to the use of the power under s. 121. The consent of the appropriate minister is always required for the exercise of CPO powers. There are also certain exclusions. This power cannot be used:

(a) for the purposes in s. 121 (1) (b), i.e., the benefit, improvement, or development of the area,

(b) for the purposes of any other function under the Local Authorities (Land) Act 1963,

(c) for any purposes where the statute authorising the acquisition expressly states that the acquisition may be by agreement only.

Parish councils cannot exercise compulsory purchase powers. Under s. 125 LGA 1972, parish councils can represent the case for a CPO to the district council for their area, which can then exercise CPO powers on their behalf.

**11.07** There are many other statutory powers of compulsory purchase. Generally, s. 121 should be regarded as a fall-back. The applicable minister will normally expect the appropriate CPO power to be used; for instance s. 17 of the Housing Act 1985 should be used for a housing re-development. Most important of all is the power under s. 226 of the Town and Country Planning Act 1990, which allows authorities to purchase land for the development, re-development, or improvement of their area, or for any purpose that it is necessary for them to achieve in the interests of proper planning of their area. The use of this power was considered by the court in *Chesterfield Properties PLC v Secretary of State for the Environment*

(1998) JPL 568. It was held that there was no need for the Secretary of State, when exercising his power to confirm the order, to consider the likelihood of the development being carried out. He could confirm the order provided he was satisfied that there was a genuine intention on the part of the authority to undertake the development. A summary of the steps that need to be taken to pursue a CPO through to its conclusion are set out at Appendix 2.

Any authority wishing to exercise CPO powers needs to bear in mind that it is a lengthy **11.08** process. As a minimum, the necessary steps will take a year; it is common for CPOs to take several years. The procedure for exercise of the smaller and less complex CPOs is likely to be speeded up by the introduction of the changes made by the Planning and Compulsory Purchase Act 2004. This includes the ability to use the written representations procedure for a contested CPO instead of having to have a full-blown public inquiry in every case.

Generally an authority embarking on a CPO will be expected to have tried to negotiate **11.09** where possible. However, it is often preferable to undertake negotiations in parallel with the CPO procedure. This may enable the authority to engage more easily with the potential purchasers and also convince them that the authority will exercise CPO powers if negotiations are unsuccessful. The Compulsory Purchase Order Circular (02/03) also recommends the use of alternative dispute resolution as a means of resolving disputes with landowners and objectors. The authority should also provide full information about its involvement and plans. The Circular advises authorities to make sure that the order is made correctly to begin with. It encourages authorities to seek initial advice from the Department over technical issues.

A local authority exercising CPO powers will also have to pay compensation. The elements **11.10** of compensation payable on a compulsory purchase are as follows:

* the open market value of the property;
* compensation for severance/injurious affection;
* compensation for disturbance and other losses not directly based on the value of the land.

Alternatively, if the property is of a type for which there is no general demand or market and the owner intends to reinstate it elsewhere, the payment could be based on the cost of reinstatement. A list of the relevant principles is set out in Appendix 3.

---

## D APPROPRIATION OF LAND

Generally, a local authority that owns land for one purpose is entitled to change the use **11.11** of that land, but it needs to go through a specific procedure authorising this known as appropriation. Under s. 122 (1) LGA 1972 a principal council may appropriate land for any purpose for which it is authorised to acquire land voluntarily, if the land is no longer required for the purpose for which it is held immediately before the appropriation. A similar power to appropriate land is available to parish and community councils: s. 126 LGA 1972.

Appropriation does not in itself affect any rights that a third party may have in the **11.12** land. Section 122(1) provides that 'the appropriation of land by a council by virtue of this subsection shall be subject to the rights of other persons, over or in respect of the land concerned'. Thus, the appropriation of land to an alternative use will not affect the enforceability of a restrictive covenant against the land. In *Dowty Boulton Paul Ltd v Wolverhampton Corporation (No 2)* [1976] 1 Ch 13 the Court of Appeal decided that the question of whether land was no longer needed for a particular purpose was a matter for that authority provided that it acted in good faith.

**11.13**  The Council in that case had leased land to the plaintiffs in 1935 for a period of 99 years or as long as the adjoining land was used as an aerodrome. The plaintiffs were also allowed to use the aerodrome for their business purposes. The Council resolved to discontinue the use as an aerodrome and use the land for other purposes including housing instead. The plaintiffs' challenge failed. Russell LJ alluded to the possibility that a challenge could be founded on the basis that such a decision was one that no reasonable authority could have made, as well as an allegation of bad faith. He also expressed the view that the words 'not required' in s. 163(1) of the LGA 1933 (the equivalent provision to s. 122) meant 'no longer required in the public interest of the locality'.

**11.14**  Special rules apply to the appropriation of land that forms part of a common, field, or allotment. The power under s. 122 (1) can be used only if the land does not exceed 250 sq. yards. The proposal needs to be advertised for two consecutive weeks in a local newspaper. The local authority also needs to consider any objections made. The local authority will need to be able to show that there was a genuine consideration of such objections, such as a report to the relevant decision-maker, summarising the objections and setting out the basis on which the decision is to be made.

---

## E   MANAGEMENT OF LAND IN LOCAL AUTHORITY OWNERSHIP

**11.15**  Local authorities still need to be guided by the relevant statutory provisions when carrying out management functions in relation to their land. If the land was acquired pursuant to a specific statutory power then the authority must be guided by that power. Land which has been otherwise devolved on a local authority needs to be managed in accordance with s. 120 of the LGA 1972. Relevant guidance is to be found in the judgments in *R v Somerset County Council, ex parte Fewings* [1995] 1 WLR 1037. The facts of the case are set out in chapter 13. What is relevant for the purpose of this chapter is that the court said that the governing statutory position for the management of the land was s. 120 of the LGA 1972 which provided that councils could hold land for the 'benefit, improvement or development of their area'. It was this that councillors needed to keep at the forefront of their minds when considering whether to ban stag hunting on land within their ownership in the Quantock Hills. They needed to focus on the questions of whether such a move would be to the benefit of or result in the improvement of their area. Since the relevant statutory provision was not even drawn to their attention, the decision was quashed.

## F  DISPOSAL OF LAND

Local authorities these days are more likely to be disposing of land than acquiring it. The **11.16**
best value regime and the difficulties that local authorities face in raising new capital mean
that they are likely to provide new building and facilities through partnerships with outside
bodies. These types of transactions will often include arrangements for the transfer of land.
The general rule is that local authorities cannot dispose of land for less than the best consideration reasonably obtainable unless the disposal is for a lease of less than seven years or
the consent of the Secretary of State is obtained. Under s. 128 of the LGA 1972 the Secretary
of State has power to issue general, as well as specific consents.

The number of cases in which the specific consent of the Secretary of State is likely to be **11.17**
required has been considerably reduced since the issue of the General Disposal Consent
2003. (Circular 06/03.) This removes the requirement on local authorities to seek the specific
consent of the Secretary of State where the undervalue (i.e., the difference between the
unrestricted use value of the land to be disposed of and the consideration actually accepted)
is less than £2 million.

Local authorities can dispose of land in accordance with the terms of this consent if they
consider that this will help it to secure the promotion or improvement of the economic,
social, or environmental well-being of its area. Local authorities will also need, where
appropriate, to have regard to their community strategy (see chapter 6). These criteria obviously derive from the well-being power in s. 2 of the LGA 2000. The consent, however, also
applies to parish councils, which do not benefit from the well-being power.

The criteria are widely drawn but this does not mean that every disposal at an undervalue of **11.18**
less than £2 million will be lawful. The authority will need to give careful consideration to
the circumstances of each proposed transaction and make an assessment of the benefits that
are likely to result from it. There will need to be a clear audit trail showing the factors which
the authority has considered in coming to its decision. It will also need to take the advice of a
qualified valuer about the amount of the undervalue.

The above consent only applies to land that can be disposed of under s. 123 LGA 1972. **11.19**
Different statutory provisions may apply depending on the purpose for which the land is
held. Land held for the provision of housing is subject to s. 32 of the HA 1985, which requires
the Secretary of State's consent to be obtained in connection with any disposal. Again, there
is power to make general consents, and a number of such consents have been made, listed
in the General Consents for the Disposal of Houses and Land dated 12 August 1999.

If a local authority wishes to dispose of land forming part of an open space, it must follow the **11.20**
procedure set out in s. 123 (2A) LGA 1972. This requires it to advertise the proposed disposal
for two successive weeks in a local newspaper, and consider any representations made in
response to these advertisements before deciding whether to proceed with the disposal. As
with the power to appropriate land forming part of an open space, (s. 122 (2A)) the authority
will need to show that it has considered the relevant objections.

In considering whether it is receiving the best consideration reasonably obtainable a local **11.21**
authority must generally adopt a commercial approach. Unless the disposal falls within the

general consent, the fact that a disposal helps to achieve other desirable objectives will be considered irrelevant. In *R (on the application of Lemon Land) v Hackney London Borough Council* (2001) 3 LGLR 871 it was held that a local authority was acting unlawfully in accepting a lower bid for the land because it meant that more jobs would be created locally.

**11.22**   The approach that local authorities are expected to adopt is illustrated by *R v Lancashire County Council, ex parte Telegraph Service Stations* (1988) *The Times* 25 June. Two opposing bidders were competing for a piece of land. The council decided to accept a lower price despite a later higher offer from the bidder whose interest had precipitated the decision to sell. It was held that, although the council was entitled to take ethical considerations into account, the desire to avoid 'gazumping' was insufficient to justify the council failing to carry out its statutory duty.

**11.23**   In certain circumstances the court will be prepared to intervene before the sale takes place by granting an order prohibiting the local authority from proceeding with it. In this case, land was being sold by auction but, before the auction took place, the council accepted an offer for the land from its tenants. The council then received a higher offer for the land, which was rejected. The court granted an order preventing the council from completing the sale while the court considered a judicial review of the decision not to accept the higher offer.

**11.24**   It will only be in exceptional circumstances that the court will interfere with a decision as to whether to proceed with a sale. In *Leeds City Council v Cobleigh* (1997) COD 69, the council was considering whether to sell land to the adjoining owner. The relevant planning permission had been granted but, following consultation with ward councillors, the authority decided not to go ahead with the sale. An application for judicial review by the adjoining owner was unsuccessful. It was held that the authority had not acted irrationally in granting the planning permission and then refusing to sell, and that it was entitled to take into account local opinion.

---

## KEY DOCUMENTS

Disposal of Land for Less than Best Consideration ODPM Circular 06/03
Compulsory Purchase Orders ODPM Circular 02/03
The Compulsory Purchase Procedure Manual (TSO)

# 12

# LOCAL GOVERNMENT OMBUDSMAN

## A  INTRODUCTION

A person who is aggrieved by the actions of a local authority may consider making a **12.01**
complaint to the Commissioner for Local Administration, popularly known as the Local
Government Ombudsman. The ombudsman concept—essentially an independent investigation and complaints service—was first applied to central government, the idea having
been borrowed from Sweden. It was introduced to local government by the LGA 1974. At
first complaints could be referred only by councillors. This restriction was removed in 1988.
The Commissioners' role was widened and their powers enlarged by LGHA 1989 to ensure a
greater level of compliance with recommendations.

Under s. 23 of the LGA 1974, two commissions were established, one for England and **12.02**
one for Wales. Each consists of one or more Commissioners, and also the Parliamentary
Commissioner, who is a member of both. In Wales, there is one Local Government
Commissioner; in England, there are three with responsibility divided between them on a
regional basis. It is also now possible for Advisory Commissioners to be appointed. The
bodies subject to investigation include all county councils, district councils and London
Borough Councils, the Corporation of London, the Isles of Scilly Council, and joint boards
where all the constituent authorities are local authorities.

### Making a complaint

**12.03**   Complaints must be made in writing to the Local Commissioner or to a member of a local authority. If made to a member, they must be referred by that member or another member of the same authority with the consent of the complainant or someone acting on their behalf with a request to investigate. The complaint needs to specify the action alleged to constitute maladministration. The exact nature of the maladministration does not need to be spelt out provided that there are details of the action that gave rise to the complaint: *R v Local Commissioner, ex parte Bradford Metropolitan City Council* [1979] QB 287. This case had its background in complaints about the way the local authority had dealt with a child care problem. A mother of two young children had left them in the care of a neighbour. They were later taken into care and placed with separate foster parents. Care orders were made following this. The children's mother applied to revoke the orders and appealed against the refusal to revoke. The appeal was unsuccessful. She then made a complaint to the Local Government Ombudsman, who decided to investigate. The complaints were formulated as follows:

(a)   The authority failed in its duty under the Children and Young Persons Act 1933.

(b)   A senior social worker said she would strongly oppose the mother having the children back as the girl suffered from fits, but later said that she did not so suffer.

(c)   The children were separated against the mother's wishes and assigned to different foster parents.

(d)   The senior social worker said that she would have the children adopted without the mother's consent and that they were placed with prospective adopters without consulting the mother.

**12.04**   The local authority applied for an order of prohibition to stop the investigation. At first instance, May J held that the Ombudsman was entitled to investigate complaints (a), (b) and (d), but should not investigate complaint (c) as there was no action alleged to constitute maladministration as required by s. 26(2)(a) of the 1974 Act. The authority appealed and the mother cross-appealed. In the Court of Appeal, Lord Denning MR considered the two opposing points of view: first May J's view that a 'complaint must allege not only that the complainant suffered injustice but also that it was due to maladministration which he must specify expressly or by necessary inference'; secondly, the view of the Parliamentary Commissioner (quoted from a lecture delivered to the Public Teachers of Law) that '. . . a complainant is usually specific about the injustice he has sustained but less so about the maladministration which causes the injustice. So the complaint, as I get it, usually starts with the injustice of which the complainant is naturally most aware and says little about the maladministration.' (The legislation under which the Parliamentary Commissioner operates does not have the equivalent of LGA 1974, s. 26 (2) (a).)

**12.05**   Lord Denning MR preferred the approach of the Parliamentary Commissioner. He felt able to depart from the literal words of the statute on the basis that this would 'promote the general legislative purpose' underlying the provision:

> It cannot have been intended by Parliament that a complainant (who of necessity cannot know what took part in the council offices) should have to specify any particular piece of maladministration. Suffice it that he specifies the action of the local authority in connection with which he complains there was maladministration.

Lord Denning's conclusion was therefore that the Ombudsman should be permitted to investigate all four complaints.

Complaints must be made within 12 months of the day on which the complainant first had notice of the matters alleged in the complaint, but this period can be extended if the Commissioner considers it reasonable to do so. **12.06**

Once a complaint is made and satisfies the above requirements, then the Commissioner 'may' investigate it. So there is a discretion. It will not normally be possible to take proceedings to compel the Commissioner to investigate a complaint: *Re Fletcher's Application* [1970] 2 All ER 527, decided by the Court of Appeal when considering the position of the Parliamentary Commissioner but the principles are the same. If the discretion was exercised improperly, though, there is no reason in principle why proceedings for judicial review could not be taken. **12.07**

There is another requirement before the investigation actually begins. The Commissioner must be satisfied that the complaint has been brought to the notice of the authority concerned and that it has had a reasonable opportunity to investigate and reply to it: LGA 1974, s. 26 (5). The Commissioners are generally keen on local settlements as opposed to formal investigations wherever possible and will therefore be especially reluctant to investigate a matter unless the authority has already been given a full opportunity of resolving it itself. In addition, once a preliminary examination of the issues has taken place, the Commissioner may suggest how a local settlement may be achieved, including proposals for the award of compensation. **12.08**

# B INVESTIGATIONS

## The nature of maladministration

An investigation can be commenced if it is claimed that a member of the public suffered injustice as a result of 'maladministration'. There is no definition of this word in the legislation, but when the provisions of the Bill that established the Parliamentary Commissioner were being considered, the Minister responsible, Mr. Richard Crossman, said that 'maladministration' encompassed 'bias, neglect, inattention, delay, incompetence, ineptitude, perversity, turpitude, arbitrariness and so on'. The majority of complaints would fall into the category of 'neglect, inattention [or] delay', often with a helping of incompetence and ineptitude. Only a small number of cases concern 'perversity, turpitude, arbitrariness and so on'. **12.09**

## Exclusions from investigation

There are various exclusions. The Commissioner should not investigate any of the following: **12.10**

(a) any action in respect of which the person aggrieved has or had a right of appeal, reference or review to or before a tribunal constituted by or under any enactment;

(b) any action in respect of which the person aggrieved has or had a right of appeal to a Minister of the Crown; or

(c) any action in respect of which the person aggrieved has or had a remedy by way of proceedings in any court of law.

However, there is a proviso. Matters falling within the above exclusions can still be investigated if the Commissioner is satisfied that 'in the particular circumstances it is not reasonable to expect the person aggrieved to resort or have resorted to it [i.e. the remedy]' (LGA 1974, s. 26 (6)).

**12.11** There is also a restriction designed to ensure that the Commissioner does not investigate areas of general policy. No investigation should be made that in the Commissioner's opinion affects most of the inhabitants of the area of the authority concerned. The other exclusions for local authorities are as follows (LGA 1974, Schedule 5):

(a) commencing or conducting court proceedings whether civil or criminal;
(b) commercial transactions, but excluding—
  (i) the acquisition or disposal of land
  (ii) transactions to discharge a statutory function, other than purchases of goods or services to enable the authority to discharge the function;
(c) personnel matters including appointments, dismissals, pay, discipline, or superannuation;
(d) matters concerning education, including both secular and religious teaching and conduct, curriculum, internal organisation, management, and discipline.

## Conduct of investigations

**12.12** The Commissioner has a wide discretion as to how investigations should be conducted. Normally an investigating officer will be appointed who will read the relevant files, interview the complainant, decide what other witnesses need to be seen and arrange times for interviewing them. These witnesses will usually be a series of local authority officers, interviewed in an office made available by the local authority. It is a requirement of the investigative procedure that the Commissioner allows the authority concerned, and any person alleged to have taken or authorised the action complained of, to comment on the allegations: LGA 1974, s. 28(1).

**12.13** Investigations must be held in private. Other than this Commissioners can adopt what procedure is considered appropriate in the circumstances. They can obtain information from such persons and in such manner as they see fit and may decide whether to allow those interviewed to be represented by solicitor, counsel, or otherwise: LGA 1974, s. 28(2). In practice, the main information will be gleaned from the local authority files and from interviewing officers. It is very unusual for anybody to be represented by a lawyer. There is provision to allow for expenses and compensation for loss of time: LGA 1974, s. 28(3).

**12.14** Local authorities are normally willing to cooperate with investigations. However, Commissioners do have substantial powers to ensure that they receive the information they need. They have the same powers as the High Court to require the attendance and examination of witnesses and in respect of the production of documents. This means that they can issue orders to compel witnesses to attend and to produce documents. To fail to comply with such orders or to fail to answer questions will be a contempt of court. Obligations to maintain secrecy or other requirements of confidentiality do not prevent the disclosure of information under these provisions, but nobody can be compelled to produce information or documents that they could not be required to disclose in civil proceedings before the High Court. This means that documents or information in respect of which privilege could be claimed need not be disclosed.

Obstructing Commissioners or their officers in the performance of their functions, or being guilty of any act or omission in relation to an investigation, is a contempt of court and may be dealt with as such by the High Court. Presumably, 'obstruction' has the same meaning as in criminal statutes of making it more difficult for the Commissioners' functions to be performed. **12.15**

## C REPORTS AND FINDINGS OF MALADMINISTRATION

When the Commissioner has conducted an investigation, or decided not to conduct an investigation, a copy of the report on the result of the investigation (or a statement of the reasons for not conducting an investigation) must be sent to: **12.16**

(a) the person who referred the complaint, if not the complainant;

(b) the complainant; and

(c) the authority concerned and any other authority or person who is alleged in the complaint to have taken or authorised the action complained of.

The last provision means that, although the finding of maladministration, if any, will be made against the local authority itself, copies of the report must also be sent to the individual officers alleged to have been responsible for or to have contributed to the action that is the subject of the complaint. Before sending out the report with its conclusions, the Commissioner will normally send out a draft to the interested parties, with the conclusions omitted, so that an opportunity is provided to comment on the factual findings before the report is finalised.

The report will not name the complainant or the officers concerned. They will be identified in the report only by pseudonyms. However, the name of a person or identifying particulars may be given if 'after taking into account the public interest as well as the interests of the complainant and of persons other than the complainant' the Commissioner considers it necessary. This will be rare. It is difficult to imagine circumstances in which this will be 'necessary'. However, those who have sought elected office are treated differently. If there is a finding of maladministration that involves a member of the authority concerned, and the maladministration also constituted a breach of the National Code of Local Government Conduct, then unless the Commissioner is satisfied that it would be unjust to do so, the report must name the member and specify the particulars of the breach: LGA 1974, s. 30(3A). **12.17**

### Publicity for reports

Once the report is ready, the local authority must, within two weeks, advertise this fact in newspapers (which will normally be the local newspapers) and give notice that for a period of three weeks, copies of the report will be available for inspection at the council offices at all **12.18** reasonable hours and copies may be made on payment of a reasonable charge. There is power for the Commissioner to direct that the report should be subject to these provisions 'taking into account the public interest as well as the interest of the complainant and of persons other than the complainant'. Public interest in these reports is usually very limited, though they may be the subject of brief reports in local newspapers and the local government press.

**12.19** Local authorities will also normally have an internal procedure for ensuring that the contents of reports are taken into account, that procedures are improved to ensure that the same mistakes are not repeated, and that any recommendations are given careful consideration.

## Findings of maladministration

**12.20** If there is a finding of maladministration by the Commissioner, this will in most cases be accepted by the authority. (Even if officers consider that in fact the conclusions are not justified, they will often be accepted anyway for the sake of good will, public relations, or simple apathy.) However, if the authority wishes to challenge the Commissioner's findings, this can be undertaken only by way of judicial review. If there is no basis for the Commissioner's findings, it will be appropriate for a declaration to be granted: *R v Local Commissioner- ex parte Eastleigh Borough Council* [1988] QB 855. In this case the Ombudsman had criticised the way in which the council carried out its building control functions and concluded that its failures had led to expenditure on works that would not otherwise have been incurred. The High Court and Court of Appeal held that this could not be sustained. In the circumstances, it was appropriate to grant a declaration that the Ombudsman's conclusion was unauthorised by law and of no effect.

**12.21** In *R v Local Commissioner, ex parte Croydon London Borough Council* [1989] 1 All ER 1033, one of the complaints was that the Ombudsman should not have investigated because there was a remedy in law available to the complainants, i.e., proceedings by way of judicial review. The court held that the Ombudsman should have appreciated this in the course of investigation, but that there was discretion to continue with the investigation in spite of the existence of this alternative remedy, and this discretion would have been exercised in favour of continuing with the investigation. Relief would therefore not be granted on this ground alone. However, the finding of maladministration was based on an assertion that the Education Appeal Committee simply followed the policy of the council. This was not sustained by the facts, so there were no grounds for the finding of maladministration. Again, a declaration was granted.

**12.22** The scope for judicial review is much wider now than it was when the Local Government Ombudsman first appeared on the scene in 1974. There are many types of behaviour which could now form the basis of an application for judicial review where previously an investigation by the Ombudsman would have been the only means of redress. This makes the proviso referred to in paragraph 12.10 above more important and the Ombudsman's task in deciding whether to apply it more difficult.

**12.23** In *R v Local Commissioner for Administration in North and North East England, ex parte Liverpool City Council* [2001] 1 All ER 462, the Council granted planning permission for a new stand for Liverpool Football Club. A long and detailed letter of complaint was sent by local residents to the Local Government Ombudsman who decided to investigate. She found maladministration in two respects:

1.  Six councillors were Liverpool Football Club season ticket holders and one regularly attended matches. They had voted on the scheme without declaring an interest, contrary to the National Code of Conduct. The only three members of the main opposition party who voted in favour of the scheme were season ticket holders. The Ombudsman concluded that 'a reasonable member of the public would have felt that it might have been a substantial influence on the way in which councillors voted'.
2.  The patterns of voting showed that the decision was heavily, perhaps decisively, influenced by a sense of party political loyalty. She considered that the system of agreed voting in a planning matter constituted maladministration. It rendered the subsequent debate in committee meaningless.

The High Court and the Court of Appeal rejected the Council's application for judicial    **12.24** review. The Court of Appeal held that:

1.  There was no need for the Commissioner to apply the legal test of bias when considering whether there was a breach of the code and whether this constituted maladministration.
2.  This was a clear case for the application of the proviso. Serious allegations had been made. These could best be investigated by the Commissioner with her resources and powers to order the production of documents. The ratepayers would have been unlikely to be able to do so in an application for judicial review 'having regard to the weaknesses of the coercive fact finding potential of judicial review'. The claimants were also a group in modest housing who were unlikely to have the means to pursue the remedy.
3.  This planning application should have been outside party politics. It was hard to see how what the Ombudsman described as 'heavy and perhaps decisive pressure' at the pre-meeting caucuses would be a 'material consideration' in exercising powers under s. 70 of the Town and Country Planning Act 1990.

This shows that the courts are likely to support a liberal approach by the Commissioners to the application of the proviso. If the matter requires greater investigation than the court in judicial review proceedings would be able to undertake, or if the complainants are of limited means, then the courts are unlikely to interfere with any decision of the Commissioner to apply the proviso.

## Compliance

In the LGHA 1989, further provisions were added to the 1974 Act to ensure a greater level of    **12.25** compliance with reports. Although in most cases authorities have always responded positively to reports, there was little effective action that the Commissioner could take before 1989 if they did not. The authority had to consider the report and notify the Commissioner of its response. If the Commissioner did not hear from the authority or was not satisfied with its response, the only remedy was to issue a further report. If the first report could be ignored, so could the second.

Under the new provisions in sections 31 and 31A of the LGA 1974, if the Commissioner    **12.26** reports that there has been injustice, there is a duty to ensure that the report is laid before the authority concerned. The authority then has a duty to consider it and within a period of three months or such longer period as the Commissioner may agree in writing, must notify the Commissioner what action it has taken or proposes to take.

**12.27**  If the Commissioner:

(a)  does not receive the above notification; or
(b)  is not satisfied with the action the authority has taken or proposes to take; or
(c)  does not hear from the local authority within a further period of three months from the date of the notification that it has taken the proposed action;

then a further report may be issued setting out these facts and making recommendations. The same procedure then has to be followed.

**12.28**  If, in relation to the further report, the Commissioner:

(a)  does not receive notification from the authority within the requisite three-month period (subject to any extension agreed in writing), or is satisfied before the end of this period that the authority does not propose to take any action; or
(b)  is not satisfied with the action the authority has taken or is proposing to take; or
(c)  does not hear from the authority within a further period of three months beginning at the end of the three-month period mentioned in (a) above that it has taken the proposed action;

the local authority may be required to make a public statement consisting of:

(i)  details of the action recommended in the further report that the authority has not taken;
(ii)  such supporting material as the Commissioner may require; and
(iii)  if the authority requires, a statement of its reasons for taking no action or for not taking the action recommended by the Commissioner.

**12.29**  The statement must be published in any two editions of a local newspaper within a fortnight. The newspaper must be agreed with the Commissioner, but in default of agreement it can be nominated by the Commissioner. There is unlikely in practice to be disagreement. Publication must be arranged for the earliest practicable date. If the authority fails to arrange for the publication of the statement, or the form of the statement cannot be agreed with the Commissioner within one month, then the Commissioner must arrange for publication and the cost of this must be reimbursed by the authority. The form of the statement must be taken to mean its wording. The last word as to what the statement says therefore belongs to the Commissioner.

**12.30**  The functions as regards consideration of reports are subject to the usual powers of delegation considered in chapter 4. However, if the local authority decides to take no action in respect of an adverse report, or action other than that recommended in the report, this is a matter that must be considered by the authority itself. If the criticism is of a joint committee or an education appeal committee, it must be considered by the committee concerned. If the authority or body is considering a report by any person or body with an interest in the report (for instance, an officer or department criticised in the Commissioner's report) then it is also necessary for them to consider a report by someone with no interest in the Commissioner's report. There is nothing to prevent this report being by another officer of the local authority provided that the officer concerned has no interest and no previous involvement. Members who are named and criticised in Commissioners' reports are not permitted to vote on any question relating to the report or any further report: LGA 1974, s. 31A(5). If, after consideration of a report, the local authority considers that a payment should be made to somebody or some benefit provided, there is specific statutory power to make payment or give the benefit: LGA 1974, s. 31(3).

## Reports on functions

Each of the Local Commissioners has a duty to prepare a report on the discharge of their **12.31** functions each year and submit it to the Commission: LGA 1974, s. 23(11). Every three years each Commission must conduct a full review of the operation of the statutory provisions and may make recommendations to the authorities that can be the subject of investigation and their representatives and to Government departments: LGA 1974, s. 23(12). The Commissions may also, after consultation with authorities and representatives, give general advice and guidance about good administrative practice: LGA 1974, s. 23(12A).

The Ombudsman service has been successful in providing a means of redress either where **12.32** court proceedings have been inappropriate, or where there is no legal remedy. More than the awards of compensation, which are usually small, it is the recognition that something has gone wrong and the taking of some action to rectify it that provides complainants with satisfaction. The Commissioners have always expressed a high degree of anxiety about non-compliance, although the level of deliberate failure to comply has always been low. It has become lower still since the introduction of the provisions in the 1989 Act, though it has not disappeared. When these provisions were introduced, the Government said that they would be monitored to see how effective they were. If there continued to be non-compliance, legislation would be introduced to make the recommendations legally enforceable. This now seems unlikely. Another issue is whether the increased availability of complaints procedures within authorities had led to the Local Government Ombudsman becoming less important than before. There has been a massive development in the last few years of internal complaints procedures within local authorities. Many of these are at least as effective as the service provided by the Commission and may be quicker and more accessible.

---

## KEY DOCUMENTS

Good practice guides are available on the Local Government Ombudsman website:
  <http://www.lgo.org.uk/guidance.htm>

# 13

# CHALLENGES BY WAY OF JUDICIAL REVIEW AND DEFENCE TO ACTIONS

## A  INTRODUCTION

**13.01**  Previous chapters have explained how local authorities acquire powers and how they may be exercised. This chapter considers how these decisions may be challenged. Inevitably, a large part of this chapter will deal with the topic of judicial review. It is outside the scope of this work to cover in detail this fascinating and still-expanding jurisdiction. The main purpose in outlining the law here is to show the kind of circumstances in which local authority decisions may be subject to judicial review. If at all possible, local authorities do not want their decisions challenged at all. This may of course be unavoidable. In general, though, even an unsuccessful challenge is likely to mean delay and possibly undesirable publicity. This chapter therefore concentrates on the areas of potential challenge and how these may be recognised. It also considers the circumstances in which local authorities' decisions may be challenged by way of defence to particular types of legal action. A judicial review checklist is set out at Appendix 4.

## B  ABILITY TO APPLY FOR JUDICIAL REVIEW

### Who can take proceedings for judicial review?

**13.02**  The law of England and Wales does not yet allow open access to the courts for the purposes of correcting unlawful decisions by public authorities. In order to take proceedings for judicial review, an applicant must show 'sufficient interest' in the subject matter of the decision. What constitutes sufficient interest will depend on the circumstances. Recently, the courts have adopted an increasingly broad approach to this question. Clearly, anyone whose own interests are affected by a decision will be permitted to take proceedings. Sometimes, these interests can be very wide. A parent can take proceedings about policy affecting a local authority's schools. A council tax payer or tenant can take proceedings about decisions which affect tax or rent levels.

**13.03**  Sometimes the court will be prepared to allow an individual acting as 'self-appointed guardian of the public interest' to challenge a decision. This is most likely to happen when there is no other more suitable candidate. Courts will be reluctant to allow unlawful decisions to go unchallenged on the basis of lack of standing of the applicant. It is probably not necessary for the person seeking to challenge a decision to have any stake in the outcome provided the challenge is not undertaken for an ill motive. In *R v Somerset County Council, ex parte Richard Dixon* (1998) 75 P & CR 175, Sedley J allowed a judicial review of a grant of planning permission commenced by a local citizen to proceed. The point was that public law was not about rights, although it might involve the invasion of private rights. It was about wrongs, such as the misuse of public power. In these circumstances someone with no particular stake in the outcome might wish and be well placed to draw the court's attention to an apparent misuse of power. If an arguable case for illegality could be made out on an application for leave, the court's only concern was to establish whether the challenge was being launched for an ill motive. In this case the applicant was neither a busybody nor a mere troublemaker and was entitled to challenge what he considered to be an illegality in a planning consent which would have an impact on the natural environment.

## Challenges to the authority's own decision

Whilst an authority cannot challenge its own decision, if it has made a decision which it **13.04** considers is unlawful, then the leader of the council can challenge the decision. This approach was accepted by the Divisional Court in *R v Port Talbot Borough Council, ex parte Jones* [1988] 2 All ER 207 and by the Court of Appeal in *R v Bassetlaw District Council, ex parte Oxby* LTL 11/12/97

## Pressure groups and unincorporated associations

The courts have been increasingly willing to allow pressure groups, such as Greenpeace to **13.05** challenge decisions the subject matter of which falls within their area of concern. It appears that even unincorporated associations are able to take judicial review, although there are conflicting decisions on this point. In *R v Darlington Borough Council and the Darlington Transport Co Ltd, ex parte The Association of Darlington Taxi Owners and the Darlington Owner Drivers Association* [1994] *The Times* 21 January the court struck out proceedings for judicial review initiated by two unincorporated associations on the ground that they did not have the necessary legal personality to commence proceedings. However, in *R v Traffic Commissioners for North Western Area, ex parte Brake* LTL 10/11/95 Turner J refused to set aside leave granted to an unincorporated association, doubting the authority of the *Darlington* case and preferring instead an earlier decision in which it had been decided that lack of incorporation was not a bar to a body commencing proceedings for judicial review: *R v Liverpool Corporation, ex parte Liverpool Taxi Fleet Operators' Association* [1972] 2 QB 299.

---

## C  JUDICIAL REVIEW PROCEDURE

### Letter before claim and response

The Pre-action Protocol for Judicial Review sets out the steps that parties should generally **13.06** follow before commencing an action for judicial review. It is not appropriate in urgent cases and in cases where the decision maker does not have the power to change the decision. However, it warns that 'Where the use of the protocol is appropriate, the court will normally expect all parties to have complied with it and will take into account compliance or non-compliance when giving directions for case management of proceedings or when making orders for costs.'

The claimant should send a letter of claim to the proposed defendant before commencing **13.07** any action for judicial review. The purpose of the letter is to identify the disputed issues and to see if litigation can be avoided. The standard format set out in Annex A to the protocol should normally be used. This requires the following details to be included:

1.   the name and address of the proposed defendant;
2.   details of the claimant;
3.   reference details;
4.   details of the matter being challenged;
5.   the issue (date and details of the decision, act or omission, a summary of the facts and why it is argued it is wrong);

6. details of the action the defendant is expected to take;
7. details of legal advisers;
8. details of interested parties;
9. details of any information sought;
10. details of any documents that are considered relevant and necessary;
11. the address for reply and service of court documents;
12. proposed reply date (14 days will usually be considered reasonable).

If a decision of a local authority is being challenged, the letter should be sent to the address on the relevant decision letter/notification, with a copy to the legal department. If it is a decision of a department or body for whom the Treasury Solicitor acts and the Treasury Solicitor has already been involved, a copy should also be sent to the Treasury Solicitor. A copy should be sent to interested parties.

**13.08**    The defendant should reply to the letter before claim, normally within 14 days and using the standard format at Annex B of the protocol. Defendants are warned that: Failure to do so will be taken into account by the court and sanctions may be imposed unless there are good reasons. The defendant can ask for more time, explaining the reasons why the time limit cannot be met and, where required, additional information may be requested. The response should cover the following:

1. the claimant's details;
2. the name and address of the defendant;
3. reference details;
4. the details of the matter being challenged;
5. response to the proposed claim (This includes whether the issue is conceded, either wholly or partly, the response to any request for disclosure of information and the reasons for any refusal. If it is an interim response and there is a realistic prospect of a settlement, details should be included.);
6. details of other interested parties;
7. address for further correspondence and service of court documents.

### Claim form and grounds

**13.09**    The procedure for judicial review is set out in practice direction 54: The process begins with submission of a claim form filed in the Administrative Court and served on the defendant. Under para 5.6 the claim form has to include or be accompanied by:

1. a detailed statement of the claimant's grounds for bringing the claim;
2. a statement of the facts relied on;
3. any application to extend the time for filing the claim form;
4. any application for directions.

The following documents are also required (para 5.7):

1. any written evidence in support of the claim or application to extend time;
2. a copy of any order that the claimant seeks to have quashed;
3. where the claim for judicial review relates to a decision of a court or tribunal, an approved copy of the reasons for reaching that decision;

4.  copies of any documents on which the claimant proposes to rely;
5.  copies of any relevant statutory material; and
6.  a list of essential documents for advance reading by the court (with page references to the passages relied on).

The claim form should also identify any interested party i.e. any person other than the claimant and defendant who is directly affected by the claim.

## Acknowledgement of service

A party who has been served with a claim form must file an acknowledgement of service **13.10** if he wishes to participate in the proceedings. This must be filed within 21 days of the date of service of the claim form and must state:

*   whether it is intended to oppose the application;
*   any person or body who is believed to be an interested party;
*   summary grounds for contesting the claim.

The defendant should also disclose relevant documents.

## Time limit

An application for judicial review must be made promptly and in any event within three **13.11** months of the date on which the grounds to make the claim first arose, normally the date of the decision being challenged. This does not mean that there is a three month time limit. Permission will be refused if the application is not made promptly, even if it is made within three months. There is power, sparingly exercised, to extend time beyond three months. Reasons for exercising this power might include the fact that the claimant was trying to pursue other remedies and the importance of the matters raised. The court will bear in mind the strength of the claim and the consequences of allowing the claim to proceed.

## Permission

Judicial review requires the permission of the Administrative Court before proceeding to a **13.12** substantive hearing. The issue of whether to grant permission will be decided by a judge reading the papers. He may refuse permission, grant it in whole or in part, or order a permission hearing. The judge considering whether to grant permission must consider whether the case is suitable for investigation at a full hearing. Permission will be refused if the judge considers the case to be unarguable. It may also be refused for delay, prematurity (e.g. if the decision being challenged is not final and might change), or the existence of an alternative remedy such as a statutory right of appeal.

If permission is refused, the claimant may renew it which means that it will be considered **13.13** at a permission hearing. The claimant will have been sent the judge's reasons for refusal. It is normal for the defendant to appear and be represented at the permission hearing though there is no obligation on him to do so, unless the Administrative Court so orders. It will frequently be an advantage for the authority whose decision is being challenged to appear at this stage to explain the context and reasons for the decision and it will often be relevant to point out the adverse consequences if permission is given. If permission is refused the application can be renewed before the Court of Appeal.

13.14    If permission is granted, the claimant has to pay the applicable fee within seven days and the defendant has to file his grounds of resistance and any evidence on which he relies with 35 days of the date of the order granting permission. The parties must submit skeleton arguments before the date of the substantive hearing (or warned date). These must be submitted 21 working days before in the case of the claimant, 14 working days before for the defendant and interested parties. Skeleton arguments must contain:

1. a time estimate for the complete hearing, including delivery of judgment;
2. a list of issues;
3. a list of the legal points to be taken (together with any relevant authorities with page references to the passages relied on);
4. a chronology of events (with page references to the bundle of documents);
5. a list of essential documents for the advance reading of the court (with page references to the passages relied on) (if different from that filed with the claim form) and a time estimate for that reading; and
6. a list of persons referred to.

At the same time the claimant must file a bundle of all relevant documents required for the hearing. This must include documents required by the defendant and any other party who wishes to make representations at the hearing. The hearing will be restricted to consideration of the documents and hearing the arguments of counsel. Oral evidence at a judicial review is rare. There is power to hear such evidence but it is to be used only in unusual circumstances.

---

## D    GROUNDS FOR JUDICIAL REVIEW

### General principles

13.15    The classic formulation of the grounds for judicial review is contained in the speech of Lord Diplock in *Council of the Civil Service Unions v Minister for the Civil Service* [1985] AC 374 at pp. 410–11:

(a) Illegality. This means that the decision-maker must understand correctly the law that regulates the decision-making power and give effect to it.
(b) Irrationality. Lord Diplock categorised this as meaning '*Wednesbury* unreasonableness' meaning 'A decision which is so outrageous in its defiance of logic or accepted moral standards that no sensible person who had applied his mind to the question to be decided could have arrived at it.'
(c) Procedural impropriety. This includes failing to observe the rules of natural justice, failing to act with procedural fairness and failing to observe rules expressly set out in the relevant legislation.

This is an admirably succinct summary. It has been referred to in numerous judgments since. However, it does contain an element of oversimplification. A reading of the cases shows a more complex and less easily classifiable jurisprudence. It should also be said that, as regards the second ground, many of the decisions that have been quashed on the grounds of irrationality demonstrated no lack of logic on the part of the decision-maker, and the concept of 'accepted moral standards' is notoriously slippery: judges, politicians and members of the public may all have their own ideas of what constitutes accepted moral standards. Lord Diplock did not rule out the addition of further grounds on a case by case basis, saying that he had in mind particularly the concept of 'proportionality', which was recognised as a ground of challenge in other European administrative law jurisdictions.

All of these will have a certain level of importance to local government. For the purposes of this chapter the grounds are summarised under the following headings: **13.16**

(a)  Fettering discretion
(b)  Failing to take into account relevant considerations
(c)  Taking into account irrelevant considerations
(d)  Irrationality
(e)  Improper purpose
(f)  Illegality
(g)  Procedural irregularity
(h)  Legitimate expectation
(i)  Lack of consultation
(j)  Lack of proportionality
(k)  The right to a fair hearing
(l)  Predetermination
(m) Bias.

## Fettering discretion

**Unlawfully delegating the exercise of discretion.** A body that is given a discretion is **13.17** normally expected to exercise it itself. It follows that it would be unlawful for individual officers, committees, or sub-committees to take decisions except in accordance with their delegated powers. In the same way, a decision cannot be delegated to an individual councillor or group of officers. A local authority cannot give its discretionary powers to third parties to exercise on its behalf. It can, however, exercise discretionary powers subject to the approval of third parties, provided that the final decision rests with the authority.

**Fettering exercise of discretion by policy.** Local authorities will often have policies about **13.18** how a discretion is to be exercised. In some areas, such as the allocation of grants for further education, it becomes almost impracticable to carry out these functions without some policy, rules, or guidance. (There is, for practical purposes, no difference between the three.)

What the authority must not do is adopt a policy to which it will always adhere regardless of **13.19** the circumstances of each individual case. The authority must 'never say never'. It must always leave open the possibility of departing from normal policy or reconsidering it in the light of changes or particular circumstances. This rule derives from *R v Port of London Authority, ex parte Kynoch* [1919] 1 KB 176, and was stated by Bankes LJ (at p. 184) in the following terms:

> There are on the one hand cases where a tribunal in the honest exercise of its discretion has adopted a policy, and, without refusing to hear an application, intimates to him what its policy

is, and that after hearing him it will in accordance with its policy decide against him, unless there is something exceptional in his case. I think counsel for the applicants would admit that, if the policy has been adopted for such reasons which the tribunal may legitimately entertain, no objection could be taken to such a course. On the other hand there are cases where a tribunal has passed a rule, or come to a determination, not to hear any application of a particular character by whomsoever made. There is a wide distinction to be drawn between these two classes.

Thus in *R v London Borough of Southwark, ex parte Udu* [1995] *The Times*, 30 October, it was held legitimate for a local authority to have a policy that it did not fund students for courses at private colleges and did not fund postgraduate courses when the student concerned had already received a grant for a first degree. The local authority had provided that it would be prepared to be willing to depart from the policy if circumstances warranted it.

**13.20**  The principle was supported by the House of Lords in *British Oxygen Co Ltd v Minister of Technology* [1971] AC 610. It was held that it did not matter if the policy was in effect a rule, provided that it allowed for the possibility of exceptions. The Board, which made grants for capital expenditure and equipment, had a policy of refusing applications where the cost of individual items was less than £25. An application for a grant for 20 oxygen cylinders was therefore refused. The House of Lords declined to declare this policy unlawful. The following passage from Lord Reid's judgment has been much quoted and probably provides the most helpful guidance when considering what approach an authority should adopt to these issues:

> The general rule is that anyone who has to exercise a statutory discretion must not 'shut his ears to an application' (to adapt from Bankes LJ . . .). I do not think there is any great difference between a policy and a rule. There may be cases where an officer or authority ought to listen to a substantial argument reasonably presented urging a change of policy. What the authority must not do is to refuse to listen at all. But a Ministry or large authority may have had to deal already with a multitude of similar applications and then will almost certainly have evolved a policy so precise that it could well be called a rule. There can be no objection to that, provided the authority is always willing to listen to anyone with something new to say—of course I do not mean to say that there need be an oral hearing.

The 'willingness to listen' referred to by Lord Reid must be construed as including a willingness to depart from the policy if the circumstances warrant it. Simply setting up a mechanism so that the authority can be seen to be going through the motions will not do: *Sagnata Investments Ltd v Norwich Corporation* [1971] 2 QB 614.

**13.21**  **Fettering exercise of discretion by agreement or estoppel.**  A local authority cannot by agreement divest itself of a power to exercise its discretion. Any clause to this effect in a contract will be invalid. Thus, for instance, a local authority cannot by contract bind itself to grant or refuse planning permission, or an entertainment licence, or any kind of discretionary grant. In *Stringer v Minister of Housing and Local Government* [1970] 1 WLR 1281, the council entered into an arrangement with Manchester University to discourage development in the area of the Jodrell Bank telescope. It then refused an application for planning permission based on this agreement. The decision was quashed on the grounds that the agreement was an unlawful fetter on the council's discretion.

**13.22**  However, local authorities can enter into agreements that restrict the exercise of their discretionary powers. In *Birkdale District Electric Supply Co Ltd v Southport Corporation* [1926] AC 355, a statutory electricity company had given a contractual undertaking not to charge higher prices than the neighbouring authority, Southport Corporation. The company had a statutory power to make such charges as it saw fit up to a prescribed maximum. The House of Lords held that the contractual undertaking was not unlawful. The company was still able to carry out its statutory function.

It is not easy to distinguish the *Birkdale* case from the decision in *Ayr Harbour Trustees v Oswald* (1883) 8 App. Cas 623. On acquiring a piece of land by compulsory purchase, the Trustees gave an undertaking not to develop part of it. This was held to be unlawful. The case was distinguished on the basis that the development of land was the sole function of the Trustees, so they were divesting themselves of their main powers. It is also probable, though, that there was a shift in judicial thinking between these two cases that has largely persisted. Nonetheless, it is not safe to assume that contractual restrictions will never be declared void by the courts. It can be said, however, that the more peripheral the restriction is, the less likely it is to be unlawful.   **13.23**

In this context a discretion is to be taken as meaning a specific statutory decision-making **13.24** power. The rule cannot be construed in such a way that a local authority can walk away from agreements freely entered into on the basis that it has a statutory power that it could, if it chose, exercise in a way that was contrary to the provisions of the agreement. An example of this was the case of *Dowty Boulton Paul Ltd v Wolverhampton Corporation* [1971] 1 WLR 204. The council had sold some land to the plaintiffs. It had already granted them a licence to use some neighbouring land as an airfield. While the licence was in force, the authority decided to build a housing estate over the land being used as an airfield. It argued that it was entitled to use the land for the purpose of exercising its statutory powers under the housing legislation and that this overrode the provisions of the licence. This argument received short shrift, with Pennycuick V-C pointing out (p. 210):

> Obviously, where a power is exercised in such a manner as to create a right extending over a term of years, the existence of that right pro tanto excludes the exercise of other statutory powers in respect of the same subject matter, but there is no authority and I can see no principle upon which that sort of exercise could be held to be invalid as a fetter upon the future exercise of powers.

Similarly, assurances given by a local authority that it will exercise its discretion in a particu- **13.25** lar way do not give rise to an estoppel unless the assurance is in itself a valid decision of the authority. Thus in *Southend-on-Sea Corporation v Hodgson (Wickford) Ltd* [1962] 1 QB 416, a builder had used a site in a builder's yard in reliance on a letter from the local authority informing him that this was the established use of the site and that no planning permission would be necessary. The authority later served an enforcement notice on him to compel him to cease this use. It was argued on his behalf that the authority was now estopped from denying its earlier statements. This argument was rejected: a local authority could not be estopped from exercising a statutory discretion.

In *R v East Sussex County Council ex parte Reprotech (Pebsham) Ltd* [2002] JPL 821 the House **13.26** of Lords rejected the idea that estoppel (which they described as a 'private law concept') could be applied to planning law. In this case an officer had given an opinion that electricity could be generated on the respondent's site without further permission. It was held that this could not have given rise to an estoppel. However, Lord Hoffmann said that in any event the concept of estoppel had no application in the field of planning. He added:

> It is true that in the early cases such as the *Wells* case [*Wells v Minister of Housing and Local Government* [1967] 1 WLR 1000] and *Lever Finance v Westminster (City) London Borough Council* [1971] 1 QB 222 Lord Denning MR used the language of estoppel in relation to planning law. At that time the public law concepts of abuse of power and legitimate expectation were very undeveloped and no doubt the analogy of estoppel seemed useful. In the *Western Fish* case [*Western Fish Products Ltd v Penwith District Council* [1981] 2 All ER 204] the Court of Appeal tried its best to reconcile these invocations of estoppel with the general principle that a public authority cannot be estopped from exercising a statutory discretion or performing a public duty. But the results did not give universal satisfaction: see the comments of Dyson J in the *Powergen* case [*R v Leicester City Council ex parte Powergen UK Ltd*] [2000] JPL 629, p. 638. It seems to me that in this area public law has already absorbed whatever is useful from the moral values which underlie the private law concept of estoppel and the time has come for it to stand upon its own two feet.

**13.27**  There is some suggestion in the case of *Re Liverpool Taxi Owners' Association* [1972] 2 All ER 589 that simple public statements by senior members of the council can constitute undertakings and therefore give rise to a duty not to depart from them, or at least, not to do so except in exceptional circumstances. The proposition of law that Lord Denning was trying to formulate in this case seems rather imprecise, though. It arose out of the increasing number of unlicensed private vehicles being used in Liverpool. There was a system of licensing that applied only to those cabs that had licences. The council was promoting legislation to bring these vehicles under the same system of control. The number of licensed vehicles was limited to 300. At a public meeting of the council the chairman of the relevant committee said that this number would not be increased until the private legislation had been enacted and come into force. He repeated this afterwards to the treasurer of the taxicab owners' association. The town clerk also wrote a letter saying that the chairman of the committee 'gave an undertaking in council that no plates in addition to the existing 300 would be issued until the proposed legislation had been enacted and had come into force'. Subsequently, and only a few months later, the council, confirming recommendations made by the committee and sub-committee, decided to increase the number of licences, first by 50, then by another 50, and finally to remove the limit.

**13.28**  The taxicab owners' association applied for leave to seek orders of mandamus, certiorari and prohibition. Leave was refused by the Divisional Court, but an appeal was successful and the Court of Appeal made an order of prohibition. The judgments of Roskill LJ and Sir Gordon Wilmer indicated that there was unfair treatment of the applicants and that they had a right to be heard before any decision was made that changed the publicly expressed policy. Force was given to this by the fact that the taxicab owners had previously been invited to make representations on the first occasion this issue was considered and also by the fact that the town clerk had written to them to say that they would be consulted about any change in policy.

**13.29**  More intriguingly, Lord Denning MR's judgment implies that the 'undertaking' given by the committee chairman was binding on the authority. He said first that there was a duty to consult with the owners before taking a decision that was adverse to their interests. He went on to say that 'the corporation were not at liberty to disregard their undertaking. They were bound by it so long as it was not in conflict with their statutory duty.' Then, after citing the principle in *Birkdale District Electric Supply Co Ltd v Southport Corporation* (above), he went on to say (p. 594):

> . . . But that principle does not mean that a corporation can give an undertaking and break it as they please. So long as the performance of the undertaking is compatible with their public duty, they must honour it. And I should have thought that this undertaking was so compatible. At any rate they ought not to depart from it except after the most serious consideration and hearing what the other party has to say: and then only if they are satisfied that the overriding public interest requires it. The public interest may be better served by honouring their undertaking than by breaking it.

When summarising the ways in which the corporation acted wrongly, Lord Denning MR concluded: **13.30**

> In the first place, they took decisions without giving the owners' association an opportunity of being heard. In the second place, they broke their undertaking without any sufficient cause or excuse.

It appears that in one short passage, three separate tests are formulated: first, an undertaking is binding unless it conflicts with a statutory duty; secondly, it is binding unless the authority is satisfied that the overriding public interest requires it to be broken; thirdly, it is binding unless there is sufficient cause or excuse for breaking it.

It is quite difficult to say whether local authorities need to have regard to this part of the judgment. The difficulty in applying it in practice is illustrated by *R v Secretary of State for Transport, ex parte Richmond London Borough Council* [1994] 1 WLR 74. One of the arguments that the applicants put forward as a ground for attacking the Secretary of State's decision was that he had gone back on an assurance that was previously given. This argument was based on the passages from the *Liverpool* case quoted above. Counsel for the applicants submitted that any policy change had to be justified by reference to the 'overriding public interest'. Laws J rejected this, commenting that the court could not be the judge of the decision-maker's policy: this rested with the decision-maker. However, this only meant that: **13.31**

> . . . a reasonable public authority, having regard only to relevant considerations, will not alter its policy unless it concludes that the public will be better served by the change. But this is no more than to assert that a change in policy, like any discretionary decision by a public authority, must not transgress *Wednesbury* principles.

But if there is nothing in Lord Denning's judgment in the *Liverpool* case other than *Wednesbury* principles, all the emphasis he placed on the need for special circumstances in order to renege on an undertaking was completely irrelevant. **13.32**

The following conclusions can probably be drawn:

(a) Public assurances given by leading representatives of the council are not to be regarded as undertakings in any legal sense of the term.

(b) If it is desired to change the publicly expressed policy, it is a matter for the local authority to decide whether this is justified.

(c) Particular care should be taken by local authorities when changing publicly expressed policies. They should take into account the public interest and also any representations which those affected by the decision may wish to make.

### Failing to take into account relevant considerations

**13.33**   This ground and the following two grounds are often considered under the single heading of 'irrationality'. However, they raise slightly different issues and, in a local authority context, require separate examination. All three grounds derive from the judgment of Lord Greene MR in the famous case of *Associated Provincial Picture Houses Ltd v Wednesbury Corporation* [1947] 2 All ER 680. Hence the expression 'Wednesbury unreasonableness'. At that time the word 'unreasonableness' was generally used as the main ground for judicial review. It could, of course, mean different things to different people. It has, as a concept, now largely been abandoned, it being accepted that public bodies may do many things that would be regarded as unreasonable in common parlance, but that would not be unlawful.

Lord Greene MR summarised thus:

> The court is entitled to investigate the action of the local authority with a view to seeing whether or not they have taken into account matters which they ought not to have taken into account, or, conversely, have refused to take into account or neglected to take into account matters which they ought to take into account. Once that question is answered in favour of the local authority, it may still be possible to say that, although the local authority had kept within the four corners of the matters which they ought to consider, they have nonetheless come to a conclusion so unreasonable that no reasonable authority could ever have come to it. In such a case, again, I think the court can interfere.

**13.34**   At first sight, the concept of relevant and irrelevant considerations seems to be problematic. It implies that, for any given decision, there are a certain number of matters that must be taken into account, no more, no less. The court will judge what these are, with the benefit of hindsight. In practice, decision-making is not quite so rigorous a process. Identifying the factors that a local authority must take into account is usually not difficult. There are some matters that it clearly must not take into account, though court cases about these usually concern the weight to be given to certain factors rather than the propriety of examining them at all. Between these extremes, the local authority must, of necessity, be given a wide measure of discretion to make decisions taking into account the issues that it considers relevant.

**13.35**   One factor that will always be relevant if the decision has financial consequences is the effect on the council tax payers. Failure to consider this issue or to give it sufficient weight will render the decision invalid: *Roberts v Hopwood* [1925] AC 578, *Bromley London Borough Council v Greater London Council* [1983] 1 AC 768. The *Bromley* case arose out of the 'fares fair' policy of the newly elected administration of the Greater London Council. They had in their election manifesto pledged substantial reductions to bus fares. These were then implemented after the election. Part of the additional subsidy was raised by way of an additional precept to the London Boroughs. The legality of the precept was challenged by the London Borough of Bromley. One of the matters raised was the duty owed by a local authority to those who pay its taxes. Lord Diplock, commenting on this point, said that it was well-established that (p. 829):

> ... a local authority owes a fiduciary duty to the ratepayers from whom it obtains monies needed to carry out its statutory functions, and that this includes a duty not to expend those monies needlessly but to deploy the full financial resources available to it to the best advantage.

In many cases, a statutory provision will lay down specifically matters that must be taken **13.36** into account. For instance, under s. 604A of the Housing Act 1985, local housing authorities must consider guidance given by the Secretary of State in deciding whether to take action relating to unfit houses or using their slum clearance powers. Sometimes the legislation will provide that the views of a certain category of people must be solicited and, if given, taken into account. Where there is a duty to consult, either statutory or implied (as there very often will be), there will always be a duty to consider the outcome of that process of consultation. In addition to taking into account those matters specifically prescribed by legislation, it is always necessary to take into account the statute from which the power is derived. If it can be said that the statute from which the power derives has a policy, there is a duty to give effect to that policy: *Padfield v Minister of Agriculture, Fisheries and Food* [1968] AC 997. This important principle is considered in more detail below.

The local authority may, in certain circumstances, have more general duties imposed upon it **13.37** such as the duty under the Local Government Finance Act 1988 to ensure that its expenditure does not exceed the amounts that it receives in any financial year. The local authority's own plans and policies may also be a relevant consideration. In any decision about planning matters, a local authority will be under an obligation to consider its local plan. It will also be obliged to consider its own future plans for the area: *Westminster Bank Ltd v Minister of Housing and Local Government* [1971] AC 508.

## Taking into account irrelevant considerations

An irrelevant consideration is often not as easy to identify as a relevant consideration. The **13.38** case law on irrelevant considerations is inextricably mixed with the law on improper purpose, though it is preferable for them to be considered separately: a decision vitiated by an improper purpose is best considered unlawful because of irrationality. Whether the courts will actually quash a decision on the ground that an irrelevant consideration was taken into account will usually depend on how much weight it was given. An irrelevant consideration that was considered only to a limited extent will not necessarily be fatal, though it might be if it was a major factor in reaching the decision. Thus, if political considerations (a desire either to support or oppose the policies of the government of the day, for instance) are a major factor in reaching the decision, it is likely to be quashed. In *R v Inner London Education Authority, ex parte Westminster City Council* [1986] 1 WLR 28, it was held by the Court of Appeal that the wish to persuade others of an essentially political point of view was an irrelevant consideration; and that since it had exercised a 'material influence' on the local authority's decision-making, the decision to expend money to provide literature and information about the effect of Government policy on education was quashed.

The manifesto commitments of the majority group are likely to be considered an irrelevant **13.39** consideration if given too much weight: *Bromley London Borough Council v Greater London Council* [1983] 1 AC 768. The decision here was quashed by the House of Lords partly because the council had regarded itself as bound by its manifesto commitment to reduce fares. Indeed, Lord Denning MR in the Court of Appeal advanced the view that it should be given no weight at all, which surely leaves out of account the reality of modern local government. It is suggested that Lord Diplock in the House of Lords took a more realistic view:

> . . . if the democratic system as at present practised in local government is to survive, the fact that he [a council member] received a majority of the votes of those electors who took enough interest in the future policies of the GLC to cause them to cast their votes, is a factor to which considerable weight ought to be given by him when participating in the collective duty of the GLC to decide whether to implement those policies in the circumstances that exist at the time that the decision falls to be made.

**13.40**    The crucial point, though, is that there is a duty to look at all the relevant circumstances that pertain at the time the decision must be made. Quashing the decision on this ground, Lord Diplock said (at pp. 830–31) that:

> . . . in exercising the collective discretion of the GLC . . . the members of the majority party by whose votes effective resolutions were passed, acted on an erroneous view of the applicable law in that from first to last they regarded the GLC as irrevocably committed to carry out the reduction of that amount that had been pre-announced in the election manifesto issued by the political party whose candidates formed a majority of the members elected.

Taking into account, or giving undue weight to extraneous factors that are not derived from the statute giving the power may also lead to decisions being quashed: *R v Secretary of State for Education and Science, ex parte Inner London Education Authority* (1986) 84 LGR 454, *Landau v Secretary of State for the Environment* [1992] COD 6.

### Irrationality

**13.41**    There is a distinction between this and the next ground, 'illegality'. It was formerly believed that the fact that a decision was irrational led the court to infer that there had been an error of law and that it was this that led the decision to be quashed. Lord Diplock in *Council of the Civil Service Unions v Minister for the Civil Service* [1985] AC 374 indicated that this was unnecessary. Irrationality was itself a ground for judicial review, and if a decision could be categorised as irrational then it could be quashed as unlawful. In describing what he meant by 'irrationality' Lord Diplock used the words that have since been quoted in most of the subsequent cases on this question and which are set out above. Both before and after Lord Diplock's seminal speech on the grounds for judicial review, judges used extreme language to emphasise the difficulty of attacking decision on this ground: 'perversity', 'verging on absurdity' or even 'taking leave of one's senses'. These phrases have all been applied in cases where relief was being refused. Where relief is granted, courts have tended, rather than categorise a public official or body's behaviour as 'perverse' or some other choice expression, to classify a decision as irrational for one of a number of specific reasons.

**13.42**    Courts have also emphasised that they are not concerned to make a judgment between reasonable views. They will intervene only if the decision has strayed so far from the precepts of reasonableness that it becomes irrational. However, this still obliges courts to reach judgments about the quality of decisions, albeit only in extreme circumstances.

The classifications of irrational decisions are neither exhaustive nor mutually exclusive, but may broadly be considered as follows.

**13.43**    **Discrimination.**    If a decision discriminates between different people, or different classes or groups of people, it will be unlawful if there is no rational basis for the discrimination. The most conspicuous example, though not involving a local authority, is *R v Immigration Appeal Tribunal, ex parte Manshoora Begum* [1986] Imm AR 385, in which a rule requiring applicants for admission on the basis of dependent parent status to have a standard of living substantially below that of their native country was struck down as unlawful, since it discriminated against applicants from less affluent countries.

Similarly, in *R v Barnet London Borough Council, ex parte Johnson* (1990) 88 LGR 73, it was held to be unlawful to prohibit political parties from participating in events at a local authority's parks.

**Interference with property rights.** This is likely to be more of an issue than human rights **13.44** in practice in a local authority environment. It will normally be regarded as irrational to interfere with property rights without good reason, unless there is a specific statutory provision allowing this. Thus it is unlawful to forbid alterations to property without good reason: *Repton School Governors v Repton RDC* [1918] 2 KB 133. It will also be unlawful to deprive a property owner of compensation by imposing a condition attached to planning permission to require road construction rather than using the Highways Act procedure: *Hall and Co Ltd v Shoreham-by-Sea UDC* [1964] 1 All ER 1, *Bradford City Metropolitan Council v Secretary of State for the Environment* (1986) P & CR 55.

**Absence of evidence.** If a decision-maker has come to a conclusion that depends on **13.45** certain evidence, the decision will be quashed if there is in fact no material on which the decision could properly have been based. (It is of course important that the decision is actually dependent on the evidence; if it was immaterial, then the decision will be allowed to stand). The same principle applies if the material on which a decision was based was plainly insufficient to justify it. A good example of this is the inspector who based his decision in a planning appeal on the conclusion that a development would partially obstruct an objector's view. In fact, there would have been a complete obstruction, and the decision was quashed on this basis: *Jagendorf v Secretary of State* [1987] JPL 771.

**Creation of arbitrary powers.** A decision that creates for a local authority an arbitrary **13.46** power is likely to be quashed on the ground of irrationality. For instance, the power to impose what conditions the corporation liked by way of agreement when granting permission for commercial activities on a beach was held to be unlawful: *Parker v Bournemouth Corporation* (1902) 86 LT 449. Depriving third parties of freedom of contract is also irrational: *Mixnam's Properties Ltd v Chertsey UDC* [1964] 1QB 214.

## Improper purposes

This is really a separate ground, both from taking into account irrelevant considerations and **13.47** from illegality resulting from the failure to give effect to the legislation's purpose. In *Hanks v Minister of Housing and Local Government* [1963] 1 All ER 47, Megaw LJ said that it was preferable to regard improper purpose as a question of whether an irrelevant consideration had been taken into account. This view was supported by Glidewell J in the *ILEA* case referred to above, but the courts have continued to declare activities *ultra vires* on the ground that they were undertaken for an improper purpose. Indeed, Glidewell J himself referred to the purpose of the *ILEA* decision as his reason for quashing it. If a local authority makes a decision or carries out an activity that is ostensibly within its power, but that is made or carried out for an improper purpose, it will have acted unlawfully.

**13.48**    What, then, is an improper purpose? Here the courts show a certain level of distrust of politicians being motivated by political motives, especially if those motives are to do with political issues that do not directly relate to the authority's statutory functions. Thus, as with irrelevant considerations, political campaigning with a view to influencing public opinion about central government policy or the activities of individual businesses will always be unlawful. Examples include the 1986 *ILEA* case referred to above and *R v Lewisham London Borough Council, ex parte Shell UK Ltd* [1988] 1 All ER 938, in which a boycott of Shell products in order to put pressure on the company to end its business activities in South Africa was held to be unlawful on the ground that this was an improper purpose.

**13.49**    Revenge is an improper purpose: *R v Derbyshire County Council, ex parte Times Supplements Ltd* [1991] 3 Admin LR 241. Newspapers in The Times group had published attacks on the County Council and its then leader. This lead to the Council deciding to cease advertising its vacancies in *The Times*, *The Sunday Times*, or any of *The Times* supplements, such as the *Times Educational Supplement*. The decision was quashed by the Divisional Court. Similarly, in *R v Ealing London Borough Council, ex parte Times Newspapers Ltd* (1987) 85 LGR 316, considered below, opposition to the way in which the industrial dispute with the print unions was conducted was an improper purpose for deciding not to stock in public libraries *The Times* and other titles published by the same group.

**13.50**    The pursuit of electoral advantage is an improper purpose: *Porter v Magill* [2002] 2 AC 357. (See chapter 24.) Devices to defeat the object of legislation will be regarded as being for an improper purpose. For instance, in *Backhouse v Lambeth London Borough Council* (1972) 116 Sol Jo 802, we have one of the rare examples of a witty local government decision. The council was opposed to the Housing Finance Act 1972, which necessitated rent increases for council tenants. It imposed the entire rent increase for the local authority on a single unoccupied house, increasing the rent from £7 to £18,000 per week. The decision was quashed. Similarly, the Court of Appeal decision in *Crédit Suisse v Allerdale Borough Council* [1994] 4 All ER 129 arose out of a scheme devised in order to develop a swimming pool without the local authority having to borrow the money itself. At first instance, the matter came before Colman J, who, in addition to quashing the decision on the basis that there was no power to enter into these arrangements, held that the scheme was *ultra vires* because it was for an improper purpose, namely to avoid the application of the statutory controls on borrowing. This aspect of the decision was also upheld by the Court of Appeal.

## Illegality

**13.51**    A decision may be challenged on this ground if the decision-maker has failed to understand the law that governs the decision-making and apply it properly. This is the proposition derived from Lord Diplock's speech in the *CCSU* case. However, it is not usually treated as a separate ground for judicial review in the way that Lord Diplock appears to be suggesting it should. It may be taken, in the local authority context, to mean two things: First, that there must be statutory power to take the proposed course of action. If there is not, the decision will be *ultra vires*. Secondly, any power must be exercised in such a way as to give effect to the purpose of the legislation from which it dervies. This is an important principle for local authorities and has particular relevance for those who have had to advise on the contents of committee reports.

The principle derives from *Padfield v Minister of Agriculture, Fisheries and Food* [1968] AC 997.   **13.52**
The case concerned a milk marketing scheme that was then in force. The producers sold their
milk to the Milk Marketing Board. There were 11 milk-producing regions and the price paid
for milk in each of the regions varied depending on the cost of transport. At the time of the
application, the prices had not been varied for some years and the producers in the South
East Region had evidence that transport costs had changed. They considered that this
entitled them to a larger share of the payments. They tried making representations to the
Milk Marketing Board but this was unsuccessful. They then wrote to the Minister asking him
to set up a committee of investigation. He was empowered to do this under the governing
statute, the Agricultural Marketing Act 1958, s. 19. The committee would be charged with
the duty, 'if the Minister in any case so directs, of considering and reporting to the Minister
. . . on . . . any complaint made to the Minister as to the operation of any scheme which in
the opinion of the Minister could not be considered by a consumers' committee'. If the
report found something amiss, the Minister could amend the scheme, revoke it, or direct
the Board to rectify matters.

Following this request a correspondence ensued, the Minister making it clear that he was   **13.53**
not minded to refer the matter to a committee of investigation. The Court of Appeal judgments focused on the reasons given in the letters written by civil servants on the Minister's
behalf. These were listed by Lord Denning as being, first, that if the complaint was upheld,
the Minister would be expected to make a statutory order, secondly that the complaint
raised wide issues and, thirdly, that it was a matter for the Milk Marketing Board rather than
the Minister. Lord Denning described the first two points as 'bad reasons' and the third as a
mistake as the final decision about prices rested with the Minister. Lord Denning would
have upheld the Divisional Court decision to quash the Minister's refusal, but he was out-
voted. It was left to the House of Lords to quash the Minister's decision, on slightly different
grounds.

Lord Reid started from the assumption that a discretion given by Parliament must have been   **13.54**
intended to be used to promote the policy and objects of the Act. He went on:

> . . . the policy and objects of the Act must be determined by construing that the Act as a whole
> and construction is always a matter of law for the court. In a matter of this kind it is not possible
> to draw a hard and fast line, but if the Minister, by reason of his having misconstrued the Act for
> any other reason, so uses his discretion as to thwart or run counter to the policy and objects of
> the Act, then our law would be very defective if persons aggrieved were not entitled to the
> protection of the court.

Similar principles lay behind a number of other cases. For instance, in *R v Liverpool City
Council, ex parte Ferguson* [1985] *The Times*, 20 November, the council, which was running out
of revenue as a result of having failed to set a balanced budget, resolved to dismiss all its
teachers. This decision was quashed by the Divisional Court. One of the grounds for quashing it was that it was not made for proper educational purposes. Functions that were being
exercised under the Education Act 1944 needed to be exercised for educational reasons.

Another example is to be found in *R v Ealing London Borough Council, ex parte Times News-*   **13.55**
*papers Ltd* (1987) 86 LGR 316. This had its origins in the industrial dispute between Rupert
Murdoch's News International Group and the print unions. Three local authorities acceded
to requests by the unions to cease stocking News International titles in their libraries during

the dispute. These decisions were challenged and the Divisional Court held that the councils were abusing their powers under the Public Libraries Act 1964. Their powers as library authorities had to be exercised for the benefit of the libraries, and their desire to show solidarity with the dismissed print workers was irrelevant to these functions.

**13.56**    Although not expressed to be based on *Padfield* principles the interesting case of *R v Somerset County Council, ex parte Fewings* [1995] 1 WLR 1037 belongs to this line of authority. It concerned an area of land in the Quantock Hills, called Over Stowey Customs Common, which had belonged to the council since 1921 and was used for amenity purposes. It was also used by the Quantock Staghounds for hunting red deer and had been so used for some years. Discussion about the use of the land for hunting had been a subject of debate within the council for some time. The issue had been considered by the planning and transportation committee, which decided to defer consideration of a ban on deer hunting until after a deer survey had been carried out and a land management plan agreed. Further reports were prepared by the National Trust and by a body called the Quantock Hills Joint Liaison Group, which included representatives of the relevant local authorities and the Countryside Commission. The latter report was directed specifically to the issue of hunting and recommended by a majority that it should be allowed to continue. Both reports were before the Environment Committee when it considered the issue on 7 July 1993. This committee recommended to the council that hunting should be allowed to continue.

**13.57**    The issue was then debated by the full council on 4 August 1993. The councillors had in front of them a paper circulated with the agenda, which concluded:

> In the final analysis people go hunting primarily because they find it a sport they enjoy. The county council must come to a decision, as the National Trust report said 'largely on the grounds of ethics, animal welfare and social considerations . . .' which are matters for members to decide.

The council decided to ban hunting on this land. The debate focused mainly on arguments about cruelty to animals involved in deer hunting. There was some discussion about alternative means of managing the herd in the event of hunting being forbidden. The council's decision was challenged by the hunt in an application for judicial review. In the Divisional Court, Laws J held that the council's resolution was unlawful and quashed it. He concluded that the council's powers as a landowner derived from s. 120 (1) (b) of the LGA 1972, which provides that:

> (1) For the purposes of . . . (b) the benefit, improvement or development of their area, a principal council may acquire by agreement any land, whether situated inside or outside their area.

Laws J held that the council exceeded this power when it took into account arguments about animal welfare and that it had failed to take into account the effect on the management and conservation of the herd. So this was basically a decision on *Wednesbury* principles, taking into account an irrelevant consideration and failing to take into account a relevant consideration.

**13.58**    The council appealed. The Court of Appeal, by a majority, dismissed the appeal, but on narrower grounds. The leading judgment of Sir Thomas Bingham, MR focused on the fact that the councillors' attention was not drawn to the governing statutory provision as the main reason why the decision was defective. The question the councillors should have been addressing was not whether they approved of hunting but whether it was for the benefit of the area that hunting should continue on the land. He considered that the passage at the end of the paper that councillors were given did not 'express or exhaust the statutory test and could well be read as an invitation to councillors to give free rein to their personal views'. A letter was written to the hunt after the resolution was passed asserting that it was for every landowner to decide what activities he wished to allow on his land. This appeared to equate private and public landowners. The failure to refer to the statutory governing test was not a purely formal omission since councillors failed to appreciate that their personal views had to be related to the issue of the benefit of the area.

The lesson of this case for those writing or advising on reports that may be subject to chal- **13.59** lenge is clear. It is imperative that the governing statutory provision is set out in the report and councillors directed to the test that they have to apply in order to make a decision. Nonetheless, there does seem to be something artificial about this. Presumably this was an issue on which most councillors had views, and they were not likely to be swayed from them during the course of a debate. Neither would the fact that the statutory test was set out in a report have prevented them from airing these views in much the same terms at a council meeting. It would be an easy matter to produce a report setting out the test and a set of minutes recording that the statutory test had been applied. In these circumstances, the decision would presumably be unchallengeable, though it would not in fact have meant that the decision-making process was any different.

## Procedural irregularity

This may properly be regarded as a separate ground from failure to observe the rules of **13.60** natural justice. These are dealt with separately as they are of importance to local authorities only in specific situations. The ground of procedural irregularity is of more considerable general importance. In explaining why he classified this head as procedural irregularity rather than a failure to observe the rules of natural justice or failure to act with procedural fairness, Lord Diplock said ([1985] AC 374 at p. 411):

> This is because susceptibility to judicial review under this head covers also failure by an administrative tribunal to observe procedural rules that are expressly laid down by the legislative instrument by which its jurisdiction is conferred, even when such failure does not involve any denial of natural justice.

He might have added that, even where the legislative instrument does not expressly lay down any procedural rules, the courts may well be willing to imply them, and then quash decisions for non-observance of these.

Where there are procedural rules, they must be observed to the letter. However, a failure to **13.61** do so does not automatically render a decision invalid. The courts would be reluctant to strike down decisions in circumstances where this would have far-reaching consequences, for some purely technical defect that did not adversely affect the rights of anybody. In order to avoid this, the courts have divided statutory requirements into those that are mandatory and those that are directory. The word 'directory' is a misnomer. There is still a legal obligation to comply with such requirements; it is only that the consequence of a failure to comply will usually be less serious.

**13.62**   In general, breach of a mandatory requirement will render the resulting decision invalid and therefore liable to be quashed. However, it should always be remembered that the grant of relief is at the discretion of the court. In *London and Clydesdale Estates Ltd v Aberdeen District Council* [1980] 1 WLR 182, it was held that leaving a notice in a mail box 200 yards from the bungalow where the intended recipient lived, at the entrance to his drive, may have been a breach of the requirement to serve it at his 'usual place of abode' but would not justify granting relief. However, the breach of another mandatory requirement, by failing to place a notice in the register of planning applications at least 21 days before the resolution granting planning permission was passed, meant that there was no power to pass the resolution. It was therefore void.

**13.63**   It is often not easy to predict what requirements are likely to be treated by the courts as mandatory and which as directory. This is because this judgement will often depend on the particular circumstances in which the rules are being considered, whether the failure resulted in prejudice, and which choice would best serve the interests of justice. It would perhaps have been preferable to develop more coherent guidelines about how to decide which provisions are mandatory and which directory and consider factors such as prejudice only when deciding whether to grant relief. In the present state of law, it is conceivable that the same provision could be held to be mandatory in one case and directory in another, depending on the circumstances. Requirements that information about statutory rights be given, or that consultation takes place will always be treated as mandatory. Requirements that reasons be given, will normally be treated as mandatory. In some cases, courts may be prepared to treat rules as directory provided that the object of the procedure was achieved irrespective of whether the rules themselves were actually observed.

## Legitimate expectation

**13.64**   The phrase 'legitimate expectation' was described in *R v North and East Devon Health Authority, ex parte Coughlan* [2001] QB 213 as being an abuse of power which involves 'reneging without adequate justification, by an otherwise lawful decision, on a lawful promise or practice adopted towards a limited number of individuals' (p. 245). A failure to consult may be a breach of a legitimate expectation, but it is wider than this, and of such importance to local authorities that it is dealt with separately below.

**13.65**   The case of *R v Devon County Council, ex parte Baker* [1995] 1 All ER 73 concerned the closure of residential homes. The applicants' arguments were based on a failure to consult but the judgment of Simon Brown LJ contains an interesting analysis of the ways in which the phrase 'legitimate expectation' is used. He identified four categories:

1.   The phrase may be used to denote a substantive right: an entitlement which the claimant asserts cannot be denied him. The authorities show that the claimant's right will only be found established when there is a clear and unambiguous representation on which it was reasonable for him to rely. In this sense, it is like an estoppel.

2.  It may refer to the claimant's interest in some ultimate benefit which he hopes to attain (or retain). The expectation arises not because the claimant asserts a right to a benefit but because the law recognises his interest in it because of the requirements of procedural fairness. The interest cannot be withdrawn or denied without the opportunity for comment and without the authority providing rational grounds for any adverse decision. (The expectation of remission of prison sentences was one example quoted: *O'Reilly v Mackman* [1982] 3 All ER 1124.)

3.  It may refer to the fair procedure itself, in the sense that the claimant has a legitimate expectation that the public body will act fairly towards him. However, this is an unhelpful use of the term. There needs to be an interest in which there is a legitimate expectation and which is protected by the requirement to act fairly.

4.  It may require that a particular procedure, not otherwise required by law in the protection of an interest, must be followed consequent upon some specific promise or practice. If an authority has given an assurance, in this situation it is bound by it, whether it was an express promise or implied because of an established practice.

*Coughlan* also concerned the closure of a residential home. Ms Coughlan had been seriously **13.66** injured in a road accident. She was tetraplegic, doubly incontinent, and was partially paralysed in the respiratory tract. She and seven other seriously disabled people had moved in 1993 from a hospital which the health authority wished to close to Mardon House, a facility for the long-term disabled. At the time of the move the residents were given an assurance that this would be their home for life. The health authority undertook a public consultation exercise about the closure of Mardon House. This followed advice from the NHS that general nursing care should be provided by the local council rather than the health authority. The health authority considered that the residents of Mardon House fell into this category. Following the consultation exercise, it decided to close Mardon House. It decided to transfer responsibility for Ms Coughlan's care to the local authority, but no new residential placement had been identified at the time the decision to close was taken. On an application for judicial review of the closure decision, the judge at first instance quashed the decision on the ground, inter alia, that Ms Coughlan and the other residents had been given a clear promise that Mardon House would be their home for life and the health authority had not established any overriding interest which entitled them to go back on that promise.

On appeal by the health authority, the Court of Appeal considered the question of what the **13.67** court's role should be when considering the situation of a member of the public who as a result of a promise or other conduct has a legitimate expectation that was not fulfilled by a public body. The starting point is to ask what that person could legitimately expect. There are at least three possible outcomes:

(a) The court may decide that the public body is obliged to bear in mind its previous policy or other representations giving it the weight it thinks right but no more, before deciding whether to change course. In these circumstances, the court is limited to reviewing the decision on *Wednesbury* grounds.

(b) The court could decide that the promise or practice induces a legitimate expectation of, for example, being consulted before a particular decision. In these circumstances the court will require consultation to take place unless there is an overwhelming reason to resile from it. The court will itself judge the adequacy of the reason for the change of policy, taking into account the requirements of fairness. (Consultation is only one example of this.)

(c)  If the court considers that a lawful promise or practice has induced a legitimate expectation of a substantive benefit, not simply procedural, the court can decide whether to frustrate the expectation is so unfair that to take a new and different course will amount to an abuse of power. In this case, once the legitimacy of the expectation is established, the court's task is to weigh the requirements of fairness against any overriding interest relied on for the change in policy.

**13.68**  Once the court has decided into which category a case falls its role will be different in each case:

(a)  The test will be rationality and whether the public body has given sufficient weight to the implications of not fulfilling its promise.

(b)  The test will be whether the decision was procedurally fair.

(c)  The test will be whether there is a sufficiently overriding interest to depart from what has been agreed.

As Lord Woolf MR correctly pointed out, the difficult question will often be into which category the decision should be allotted. This is crucial since these are the types of local authority decisions which are frequently challenged and what the authority needs to do to avoid a challenge will depend on what category the decision fits into. The cases which belong in the first category are those where the claimant has no more than an expectation that whatever policy is in force at the time will be applied to him. Cases involving the early release of prisoners have been held to fall into this category, e.g. *In re Findlay* [1985] AC 318. What is the difference between a procedural and a substantive expectation? Woolf MR said that there is likely to be a substantive benefit where the expectation is confined to one person or a few people, giving the promise or representation the character of a contract. The importance of the promise to the claimant and the consequences to the authority will also need to be considered. In *Coughlan's* case the Court of Appeal had no hesitation in placing this in the third category. The reasons were that the consequences were immensely important to Ms Coughlan, that there was a promise given to a small number of people and that the consequences for the health authority were likely to be financial only. The decision to quash the health authority's decision was upheld.

**13.69**  This case gives important guidance to public bodies on the issue of legitimate expectation. Once an authority has identified that there is a category of potential claimants who may have some kind of legitimate expectation, the first challenge will be to identify to which of Lord Woolf's three categories the decision should be assigned. Where there is a general policy and potentially a large number of people who could be affected by it, this is likely to be a category (a) situation. Examples might be housing allocation policies or policies about discretionary grants. Where the decision is of more importance to the affected individuals, though involving comparatively large numbers and without a specific promise or commitment having been made, then it is likely to fall into category (b). If, as in *Coughlan*, it is of major importance to the affected individuals and there has either been a specific promise or a policy applied to a small number of people, then it is likely to be classified in category (c).

Once it has identified what category of legitimate expectation it is faced with, a local **13.70** authority contemplating a decision in these circumstances needs to consider what it should do to protect itself from challenge. There is first a need to establish exactly what was said to whom when and what policies were in force at the relevant time. It is necessary to consider what these communications would have meant to the applicants. In the *Coughlan* case, some of the correspondence from the health authority, without giving a specific commitment that Mardon House would be the residents' home for life, would certainly have been understood by them in this way. (It goes without saying that authorities need to consider carefully the consequences of giving commitments which appear reasonable at the time but could be more difficult to fulfil several years later.) Second, consultation will always be important. This issue is dealt with more fully below. Third, it is necessary to consider the type of potential applicant. The more vulnerable the affected group are, the more sympathetic the court is likely to be. It follows that the public authority will have to take more efforts if it is to satisfy the courts that the rights of those affected have been fully taken into account and that steps have been taken to ensure that the adverse effects are minimised. Fourth, and connected with this, there needs to be consideration given as to what can be done, in a concrete way, for the affected individuals. Crucial to the decision in the *Coughlan* case was the Court's view that the way the health authority had acted amounted to an abuse of power. The decision might well have been different if the health authority had identified a comparable facility for Ms Coughlan and a clear plan showing that it would take all reasonable steps to ensure that the move went as smoothly as possible. (There are of course practical issues here. Trying to identify alternative placements before a decision to close a facility has been taken could be both a waste of resources and unnecessarily disruptive. An authority's planning process will need to take account of this.) Fifth, the authority needs to have clear and well thought out reasons for its decision and to be in a position to show that it has carried out a balancing exercise. (The Court of Appeal in the *Coughlan* case was dismissive of the health authority's 'financial reasons' for closing the facility. Of course it is understandable that a court confronted with a vulnerable applicant needing a particularly high level of care will tend to sympathise with that applicant rather than arguments about the type of care not being cost effective. What the court does not see in areas where resources are finite, is the potential beneficial use to which these resources could be put if they were being used more efficiently.)

## Lack of consultation

Implied procedural requirements almost invariably concern the duty to consult. The **13.71** question of consultation is of major importance for local authorities. Although in practice local authorities do consult widely, and are responsive to public opinion, their decisions are often challenged on this ground. The issue therefore merits consideration in some detail. The first question is obviously that of who needs to be consulted. If the duty to consult is statutory, and reapplicable legislation sets out those who have to be consulted, the courts will be reluctant to extend this right to others. Similarly, if the statute leaves the consulting authority with an element of discretion about who should be consulted, the exercise of this discretion can be challenged only on the basis that the selection was irrational.

**13.72**  If the duty to consult is implied, those who will be directly affected by the decision must always be consulted. In the case of a decision with potentially far-reaching consequences, it will also be necessary for those indirectly affected to be consulted. Others may have acquired the right to be consulted on the basis of legitimate expectation, either because of their position, because they have previously been consulted about the same or similar matters, or because of assurances given by the authority.

**13.73**  The requirements as to consultation are neatly encapsulated in the following criteria, used by Hodgson J in *R v Brent London Borough Council, ex parte Gunning* (1986) 84 LGR 168:

(a)  Consultation must take place when the proposals are still at a formative stage.
(b)  Sufficient reasons must be given for any proposal to permit of intelligent consideration and response.
(c)  Adequate time must be given for consideration and response.
(d)  The outcome of the consultation must be conscientiously taken into account when the proposals are finalised.

Some comments about the above are needed. As to the first requirement, there obviously needs to be a proposal of some kind before consultation begins. Consultation cannot be a brainstorming exercise. On the other hand, if consultation does not begin until the local authority is almost irrevocably committed to a particular course of action, it is likely that the court will find the procedure defective on the ground that consultation took place at too late a stage.

**13.74**  The adequacy of the information provided will depend on the nature of the subject matter of the consultation. It must be intelligible. Generally, it should state the action proposed, the reasons for it, and the facts and assumptions on which it is based. Especially where there is a small number of consultees who may be significantly affected by the proposals, it may be necessary for the implications for those affected to be spelt out. There is no need for those being consulted to be shown the representations made by other consultees.

**13.75**  There can be no firm guidance on what constitutes adequate time for consideration and response. Where the consultation is a statutory requirement, the statute itself will often prescribe the required time. Where it does not, or where the consultation requirement is implied, it will depend on the nature and complexity of the proposals and the amount of information that needs to be considered. It may also depend on how urgently a decision needs to be taken. A few days will be insufficient for any but the simplest of proposals. Four weeks would seem to be a reasonable starting point in most cases, although a longer period may be needed in exceptional circumstances. An applicant who alleges that the time given was too short should normally request extra time when the consultation is taking place rather than waiting until after the decision is made and raising it as a ground for judicial review.

**13.76**  It is preferable for a consulting body to show that the representations made to it during the consultation process have been taken into account by it. In local authorities this may best be done by a report to the decision-maker explaining the outcome of the consultation process.

Proposals are of course frequently amended before being implemented, and it may be because of the consultation process. The question then arises of whether there is an obligation to consult on the amended proposals. This could of course go on forever, preventing decisions from being taken at all. The general rule is that if the amendments are so substantial that the result is a new proposal, then further consultation should take place: *Legg v Inner London Education Authority* [1972] 3 All ER 177.

## Proportionality

This means that the means of achieving an end should be proportionate to that end—a **13.77** grand way of saying that, in the old cliché, a sledgehammer should not be used for cracking nuts. It is unclear as yet whether proportionality is recognised as being a principle of domestic administrative law. The idea has received support but there has not been a pure domestic administrative law challenge which succeeded on this basis. The possibility was first raised by Lord Diplock in the *CCSU* case. The applicant sought to rely on this principle in *R v Secretary of State for the Home Department, ex parte Brind* [1991] 1 AC 696. The House of Lords rejected the claim on its merits. However, two members of the House expressed serious reservations about the principle on the basis that it drew the judiciary into examining the merits of the decision itself rather than the decision-making process. This is disingenuous. When courts examine the rationality of decisions they have already embarked on an examination of the merits of those decisions.

In *R (Alconbury) v Secretary of State for the Environment* [2001] 2 WLR 1389 Lord Slynn said **13.78** (p. 1407):

> I consider that even without reference to the Human Rights Act 1998 the time has come to recognise that this principle is part of English administrative law, not only when judges are dealing with Community acts but also when they are dealing with acts subject to domestic law. Trying to keep the *Wednesbury* principle and proportionality in separate compartments seems to me to be unnecessary and confusing.

In *R (Daly) v Secretary of State for the Home Department* [2001] 2 AC 532 Lord Cooke of **13.79** Thorndon said he considered it would be widely recognised that *Wednesbury* was a retrogressive decision in English administrative law in that it suggested only an extreme degree of unreasonableness can lead to a decision being declared invalid by the judiciary. These statements, though, do not simply mean that proportionality can now be regarded as a ground for judicial review. In *R (Association of British Civilian Internees: Far East Region) v Secretary of State for the Home Department* [2003] QB 1397 Lord Phillips MR said that he had difficulty in seeing what the justification there was for retaining the *Wednesbury* test. However, he pointed out that in *R v Secretary of State for the Home Department, ex parte Brind*, the House of Lords had rejected the idea of using proportionality as their test and applied *Wednesbury* principles instead. The issue of proportionality is one that needs to be borne in mind both by decision-making bodies and by those who wish to consider how their decisions may be attacked.

## The right to a fair hearing

The right to a fair hearing is well established, but there are two exceptions to this: first, **13.80** the statutory procedure must itself be insufficient to achieve justice, and secondly, the application of the rule must not frustrate the purpose of the legislation: *Wiseman v Borneman* [1971] AC 297. Thus, where the Act lays down an appeal procedure or an opportunity for making representations, it is unlikely that a court will imply an additional right to be heard: *R v Birmingham City Council, ex parte Ferrero Ltd* (1991) 155 JP 721 and *R v Secretary of State for the Environment, ex parte Hammersmith and Fulham London Borough Council* [1991] 1 AC 521.

**13.81**   There are essentially two elements to the rule: it requires both full notification of the case against and an opportunity to answer it. Notification of the case against the person affected by the decision requires that the reasons for the proposed course of action be given. In *R v Enfield London Borough Council, ex parte T.F. Unwin (Roydon) Ltd* [1989] *The Times*, 16 February, the local authority removed a contractor's name from its approved list without notifying the company of its intentions and the reasons for them. This was held to be unfair and the decision was quashed.

**13.82**   The case against includes all the material on which the decision-maker's assessment is based. Thus, if there is factual material that is going to be relevant to the outcome of the decision-making process, this needs to be disclosed and a reasonable opportunity of responding must be given. This rule does not extend to policy considerations. So if a local authority is going to be guided by policy considerations in reaching a decision, there is no need for it to explain these and provide an opportunity for argument against them. However, when the decision-making body is quasi-judicial, it does apply to arguments. If it is intended to decide an issue on the basis of an argument that had not been canvassed before it, there is a duty for the decision-making body to advise the party affected and give them an opportunity of addressing the argument.

**13.83**   The extent of disclosure of relevant material required will depend on the nature of the decision-making process. In judicial or quasi-judicial proceedings, this needs to be scrupulous. Thus in *R v Army Board of the Defence Council, ex parte Anderson* [1991] 3 All ER 375, it was held that a soldier complaining of racial discrimination was entitled (subject to any public interest immunity) to see all the material that the Board had seen. Where the decision is more of an administrative nature, then it will suffice that the nature, rather than the detail of the material, is disclosed.

**13.84**   The requirement that an opportunity must be given to correct the case against means that allegations must be made at a time when it is practicable for such rebuttal to be made. So if a hearing is taking place, it is a denial of natural justice for crucial allegations to be made only in a closing speech: *Tudor v Ellesmere Port & Neston Borough Council* [1987] *The Times*, 8 May. A postponement of the decision, or an adjournment of the hearing, may be necessary to give parties sufficient time to prepare their response. In these circumstances a refusal to adjourn or postpone will constitute a denial of natural justice.

### Pre-determination

**13.85**   Pre-determination is a separate issue from bias. Pre-determination is where a body effectively surrenders its independent judgement. Bias is where there is a perceived danger that the decision-maker favours one side of the argument. The distinction between the two is not absolutely clear-cut. The same type of evidence may be used to found an allegation of pre-determination that is used to found an allegation of bias. Bias does not need simply to relate to personal interests. The distinction is that to succeed in a claim that a decision should be quashed because it was pre-determined, the evidence needs to show that there was in fact such a surrender of independent judgement as to amount to pre-determination. Bias is concerned with the appearance of a decision. In order to succeed in a claim for bias it is not necessary to show that the decision-maker was in fact biased.

A decision can also be quashed on the ground of pre-determination without it being **13.86** unreasonable on *Wednesbury* principles. The reasons were explained in the judgment of Ouseley J in *Bovis Homes Ltd v New Forest District Council* [2002] EWHC 483 (Admin): (As this is primarily a case about bias, it is dealt with in more detail below.)

> There is obviously an overlap between this requirement [to avoid pre-determination] and the commonplace requirement to have rational regard to relevant considerations. But, in my judgment, the requirement to avoid pre-determination goes further. The further vice of pre-determination is that the very process of democratic decision-making, weighing and balancing relevant factors and taking account of any other viewpoints, which may justify a different balance, is evaded. Even if all the considerations have passed through the pre-determined mind, the weighing and balancing of them will not have been undertaken in the manner required. Additionally, where a view has been pre-determined, the reasons given may support that view without actually being the true reasons. The decision-making process will not then have proceeded from reasoning to decision, but in the reverse order. In those circumstances, the reasons given, would not be true reasons, but a sham.

The practical consequences of this are clear. If a decision is in fact pre-determined, the fact that it is made to 'look right' by showing that the decision-making body had in front of it a report setting out the relevant issues, will not cure its illegality. However, the following case is an example of how the process of decision-making can add to the likelihood of the decision being quashed.

*R v Teesside Development Corporation, ex parte William Morrison Supermarket plc and Redcar* **13.87** *and Cleveland Borough Council* (1998) JPL 23 concerned a decision of an urban development corporation. Development corporations are statutory bodies charged with the regeneration of a particular area. They are also given the functions of the local planning authority for that area. The potential for conflict is obvious: if the Corporation is of the view that a proposed development will assist in the regeneration of its area, then it has a duty to proceed with it. However, as a planning authority, they have a duty to approach decisions about planning permission in an open and unprejudiced way.

The Teesside UDC needed to consider the redevelopment of Middlesbrough Dock. ASDA had **13.88** come forward with an offer of £7m for the land and a proposed development which appeared to answer their requirements. The conduct of the UDC board following this approach appeared to show that they were determined for it to proceed rather than conduct an independent evaluation of the planning merits. Before any consultation had taken place, the board resolved to approve the application subject to the agreement of Middlesbrough Borough Council and a positive retail impact assessment. The report from planning consultants which was then commissioned by the UDC was, in its own words 'geared towards minimising the chances of call-in of the applications and maximising the chance of success should a public inquiry result'. The report to the board was also essentially one-sided, arguing the merits of the application rather than setting out the arguments for and against it in a dispassionate way. There were other problems. The board received factually incorrect information that ASDA intended to keep another of their nearby stores open for a period of at least three years. They were also told that they could ignore the representations of a committee set up by five local borough councils to consider and comment on strategic planning matters.

**13.89**   The decision was quashed. Sedley J described the UDC as having made a 'fundamental error of approach'. They had 'elevated the regeneration potential of the proposal to a level at which objective judgment of its planning merits was foreclosed'. This therefore amounted both to adoption of an inflexible policy in favour of a proposal and surrender of the UDC's judgment as a planning authority.

**13.90**   As an object lesson in how not to go about making a sensitive decision this would be difficult to beat. There are several important conclusions to be drawn. (These are not confined to the field of planning.)

(a)   The decision-making body should not ordinarily make an interim or provisional decision. There are some circumstances in which this is required by statute. However, a body must always leave itself in a position where it can take into account all relevant factors when making its decision. In this case the board had resolved to support the application unless there was either a negative retail impact assessment or opposition from Middlesbrough Borough Council. This amounted to a strong indication of a closed mind.

(b)   When seeking independent advice about the merits of a forthcoming decision both the brief and the advice itself need to be couched in neutral terms. This is not the same as objectivity. Advice can be objective but still amount to an argument in favour of one particular point of view. (Seeking advice before a decision is made is a very different matter from seeking advice once it has been made and needs to be justified in a public forum such as a public inquiry.)

(c)   Although officers' reports will frequently contain recommendations, these need to be made in the context of a balanced appraisal of the competing points of view. The arguments for and against each of the possible decisions need to be set out. In this case the report had essentially been an argument in favour of granting permission. One-sided reports are always a mistake.

(d)   There is an obligation to be particularly scrupulous when the decision-making body has an interest in the outcome of the decision. This is a well-established legal proposition in planning matters: *Steeples v Derbyshire County Council* [1985] 1 WLR 256 pp. 288–289.

(e)   The lower the degree of public scrutiny, the greater the obligation on the body to act with scrupulous fairness. In this case Sedley J commented that the UDC board met behind closed doors, did not need to publish its agenda materials and minutes, and consisted of individuals who did not need to stand for election. For local authorities, it seems that decisions taken by cabinet without the public being present or decisions taken by officers need to be approached in a particularly careful and objective manner.

(f)   There is a need to report the outcome of consultation fairly. Sometimes the decision-making body can and should be advised not to take particular responses into account. (For example, the effect on house prices of a new development.) In general though the outcome needs to be reported and the decision-maker needs to take it into account.

## Bias

It has long been established that public decision-making must be free from bias. However, **13.91** the appellate courts have had some difficulty in deciding exactly how the test should be formulated. The test of 'reasonable suspicion' (applied by the Court of Appeal in *Metropolitan Properties Co (FGC) Ltd v Lannon* [1968] 3 All ER 304) was replaced by the House of Lords in *R v Gough* by a test of whether there was a 'real danger' of bias. However, when the House of Lords came to consider the issue again in *Porter v Magill* [2002] 2 AC 357, they settled on a slightly different test (p. 494):

> The question is whether the fair-minded and informed observer, having considered the facts, would conclude that there was a real possibility that the tribunal was biased.

This is arguably a more stringent test than that formulated in *R v Gough* in that a 'real possibility' represents a lower threshold than a 'real danger'. However, this is modified by the introduction of the 'fair-minded and informed observer' who is assumed to have considered all the facts.

In *Porter v Magill* it was argued that the auditor was biased because of the way in which he **13.92** expressed and announced his provisional conclusions. The auditor was required under the terms of the statutory framework within which he was working to make provisional findings. However, he chose to make these at a press conference, and described the conduct of those he was investigating as 'disgraceful, improper and unlawful'. Taking into account all the facts, the House of Lords concluded that a fair minded and informed observer would not have concluded that there was a real possibility of bias. The auditor, although using somewhat florid language to describe the behaviour of the Westminster councillors and officers, was careful to describe his findings as provisional and gave a fair hearing to those whose behaviour he impugned, as witnessed by the fact that he changed his mind about some of those who he was originally minded to make findings against.

The rule against bias also applies to non-judicial administrative decisions. In *R v Secretary of* **13.93** *State for the Environment and Another, ex parte Kirkstall Development Campaign Ltd* [1996] *The Times*, 20 March, a community action group was seeking to challenge a planning decision by Leeds Development Corporation on the grounds that it was contaminated by the undeclared interests of its members. It was argued on behalf of the corporation that non-judicial bodies such as development corporations were governed by a different set of rules. Sedley J rejected this submission. He considered that there were sound reasons for not restricting the test in *Gough* in the way suggested. Public or individual interests might be more radically affected by administrative decisions than by the decisions of courts and tribunals. The principle applied generally to bodies exercising powers of this nature, whether elected or appointed. However, the applicants in this case failed on the facts.

Having an opinion about a matter before making a decision about it will not disqualify a **13.94** councillor from participating in the decision-making process. Obviously, members of a local authority are expected to have policies and opinions about matters affecting their area. However, if they make clear that they intend to adhere to that view irrespective of the arguments they hear or the material that is put before them, then the decision cannot stand. Similarly, if an authority binds itself by contract to follow a particular course of action where it is required to exercise a judgement, then any subsequent decision on this issue is likely to be quashed on the ground of bias: *Steeples v Derbyshire County Council* [1984] 3 All ER 468.

**13.95**    A situation that is not uncommon in local authorities is that a committee is required to hear appeals against or reviews of decisions of officers, other committees, or sub-committees. These will normally be of a judicial or quasi-judicial nature so that the rules of natural justice will be applied rigorously. In the case of an appeal or review of a committee or sub-committee decision, it is imperative that none of the members who made the first decision is sitting on the committee that is charged with reconsideration. In the case of a decision originally made by an officer, the committee should ensure that the officer concerned is not giving an impression of having the ability to influence the decision-making process in a 'behind the scenes' manner. For instance, the seating arrangements should be such that the officer cannot be considered as forming part of the tribunal. If the committee wishes to deliberate in private, this should be in the absence of the officer. The same strictures apply when a decision is being made on the recommendation of an officer.

**13.96**    An example of the type of conduct which will lead to a local authority decision being set aside on the grounds of bias is *Bovis Homes Ltd v New Forest District Council* [2002] EWCH 483 (Admin). The Council when adopting its local plan acted in some respects contrary to recommendations made by a planning inspector following the local plan inquiry. Bovis alleged that the chairman of the committee had been biased and that the committee had failed to approach the adoption process with an open mind. Ouseley J quashed the committee's decision. Its reasons for rejecting the inspector's recommendations were legally inadequate. There had been no proper attempt to identify and grapple with the issues raised by those recommendations. The chairman was also a member of a local interest group which had a particular view of the recommendations. It was held that her membership of this group would have led a fair-minded observer to conclude that there was a real danger of bias on her part and her presence at and participation in the relevant meeting vitiated the decision. Members of the committee also brought with them a draft resolution which had been prepared earlier. They adopted this without amendment or qualification. This gave the impression that they had attended the meeting with closed minds.

**13.97**    Another decision of Ouseley J's on a similar issue at about the same time fell on the other side of the line. *R v Camden London Borough Council, ex parte Laura Cummins* [2001] EWCH Admin 1116 concerned a challenge to the grant of planning permission for the redevelopment of a leisure centre at Swiss Cottage. One of the grounds for challenge was that the Council had unlawfully allowed its interests as landowner/manager of the leisure centre and applicant and promoter for the development to influence what should have been an independent consideration of the planning merits. It was argued therefore that the Council's decision was biased and predetermined and that material considerations had been ignored. The decision to grant planning permission had been made by the full Council. There were councillors attending the meeting who sat on the committee responsible for management of the land and they had not disqualified themselves.

**13.98**    There could not be any serious challenge on domestic law grounds founded on the fact that the Council had determined a planning application relating to its own land. The relevant regulations provided that, if a Council had an interest in land which was the subject of a planning application, it was for the authority to decide the application unless it was called in by the Secretary of State. There were various provisions in the regulations designed to ensure separation between the decision-making body and those within the Council who had contrary interests. Allowing the decision to be made by the full Council rather than a planning committee created a difficulty in applying this process of separation. There was no requirement in the regulations to exclude an interested councillor in these circumstances.

Ouseley J declined to quash the decision. He said that the question in determining bias was **13.99** whether there was a real danger that a councillor's decision would be influenced by personal interests or whether a fair-minded observer would perceive such a danger. A non-pecuniary interest could give rise to such a perception of bias. Here, however, councillors in the relevant committees did not have a personal interest that required them to be disqualified under the Local Government Code of Conduct. They had not closed their minds or made their decision in accordance with a pre-determined view. The membership of a committee which owned or managed the land was insufficient to disqualify a councillor. The recommendations of these committees were not, in any event, binding on the Council. An allegation of bias could not be sustained unless there was a danger that councillors were influenced by extraneous personal interests. Whilst there could have been a greater degree of separation of functions, there had been no pre-determination and the Council had not been prevented from fairly considering the relevant planning merits.

The tests for bias which Ouseley J applied in the above cases need to be treated with some **13.100** caution as these decisions were made without knowledge of the House of Lords' new formulation of the rule in *Porter v Magill*. He referred to a 'real danger' of bias whereas the test now favoured by the House of Lords refers to a 'real possibility'. He also indicated that the source of bias must necessarily be some external personal interest. This was not the conclusion of the House of Lords in *Porter v Magill*. It is plain from that decision that behaviour or statements indicating a predisposition to a particular point of view could lead to a decision being quashed on the grounds of bias.

The 'real possibility' test formulated in *Porter v Magill* was applied by Richards J in *R v Enfield* **13.101** *Borough Council, ex parte Costas Georgiou* [2004] EWCH 779 (Admin). This concerned a planning committee decision. Three members of the planning committee had also sat on the Council's Conservation Advisory Group ('CAG') and in that capacity had supported a number of the planning applications. They subsequently sat on the planning committee which approved these decisions. The judge concluded that there had been a real possibility of bias. He said the test was:

> ... whether, for the point of view of the fair-minded and informed observer, there was a real possibility that the planning committee or some of its members were biased in the sense of approaching the decision with a closed mind and without impartial consideration of all relevant planning issues.

He qualified this by cautioning against applying the test in too rigid a manner: **13.102**

> That is a question to be approached with appropriate caution, since it is important not to apply the test in a way that will render local authority decision-making impossible or unduly difficult. I do not consider, however, that the circumstances of local authority decision-making are such as to exclude the broader application of the test altogether.

It is likely that, if it was made clear that the planning committee members who were members of CAG were considering the matter afresh, with an open mind and taking into account all relevant factors, the decision would not have been quashed. This was a finely balanced decision.

**13.103**   Less finely balanced was the quashing of the planning permission in the case of *R v Harlow Borough Council, ex parte Chadani* [2004] EWHC 1883 (Admin). The Council had granted permission for a major redevelopment of Harlow Town Centre. The claimant owned commercial premises which were affected by the proposed development. Prior to the planning permission being granted the chairman of the planning committee (Councillor Garrett) had a number of telephone conversations with the claimant. During the course of these he had suggested that the claimant should be flexible over the amount of money he wanted for his land, referred to the possibility of it being compulsorily purchased, and suggested that the claimant could be given an alternative site. These telephone conversations were recorded by the claimant. The chairman of the planning committee had also discussed the proposed development with the Chief Executive and was involved in discussions with the developers. Richards J commented that Councillor Garrett 'appeared to be acting in effect as a broker in trying to resolve the problem created by the claimant or at least keep everyone in discussion with a view to resolving that problem'. He concluded that what Councillor Garrett had said in these telephone conversations would 'cause a fair-minded and informed observer to conclude that there was a real possibility that he had made up his mind in favour of the proposed development and that he would approach the decision on the planning application with a closed mind and without impartial consideration of all relevant planning issues'.

**13.104**   In *R v Pembrokeshire Coast National Park Authority* [2004] EWHC 2907 (Admin) an application was made to quash a planning permission granted by the National Park Authority (NPA) for a holiday village scheme (Bluestone). This was part of a wider development. The other part (Waterworld) lay outside the area of the NPA's jurisdiction and within that of Pembrokeshire County Council. By the time the application came to be considered by the NPA, the county council had already granted planning permission for Waterworld and approved a £1m loan in connection with Bluestone. Ten of the fifteen members of the NPA were Pembrokeshire councillors. This included two who had approved the loan. Jack J declined to quash the permission. Referring to the matters relied on by the claimants as grounds for applying for judicial review, he concluded:

> I do not consider that individually the ten matters relied on would suggest to the 'fair-minded and informed' observer that there was a real possibility of bias by reason of an approach with closed minds. The cumulative effect is more difficult to gauge. Grains that may be insignificant by themselves may be bound together to make a significant ball.

He considered that it came down to whether the county councillors had 'taken a proper approach' at the relevant meetings and concluded that they had.

**13.105**   It is not easy to draw from these cases simple guidance about the circumstances in which councillors should be advised to withdraw on the grounds of bias. Generally it is very unwise for councillors who will have a key decision-making role to be publicly associated with support for or opposition to a proposal before they have to make a formal decision on it. There is nothing to stop councillors who have supported a proposal in a different forum being on the body which makes a decision about it, but they need to approach the decision afresh. What will lead to a decision being quashed is difficult to predict. It is best to err on the side of caution, but this is not always easy advice to follow in a world where local decision-making is subject to extensive consultation and shared among various elected and non-elected bodies, many of which have overlapping membership.

## E    REMEDIES

The first point to make is that in judicial review proceedings, all remedies are discretionary. If **13.106** the court does not consider any useful purpose would be served by making an order, then it will decline to make one. The traditional public law remedies are certiorari (now referred to as a quashing order), prohibition (prohibiting order), and lastly mandamus (mandatory order) which compels somebody to do something. The court can also grant a declaration (now a very commonly sought remedy), an injunction, and, in certain limited circumstances, damages. These orders form the subject of a book in themselves; they are dealt with very briefly here.

An injunction can be granted against a public body in judicial review proceedings. It oper- **13.107** ates in the same way as mandamus and prohibition. An injunction could be granted either to forbid a local authority from doing something, or to compel it to do something. The great advantage is that it can be granted on an interim basis. With the Crown Office having become more congested over recent years, this provides an opportunity to ensure that remedies do not lose their purpose simply because of the passage of time.

Many issues fall to be decided between public bodies that need to establish the legal position **13.108** in order to act in accordance with it. Thus, as between an authority and its auditor, if the auditor considers that the local authority is acting unlawfully, a declaration will normally be the appropriate remedy to seek. However, the Divisional Court cannot be used as an advanced form of counsel's opinion. It will not provide answers to legal questions unless they form part of a current dispute. For instance, if a local authority is proposing to take a course of action that its auditor thinks may be unlawful, the parties cannot go ahead and clear up the question of legality before the authority decides whether to proceed by making an application to the court.

Damages cannot be awarded as a matter of course in judicial review proceedings. However, if **13.109** the applicant has also made a damages claim joined with the application for judicial review and the court is satisfied that if the claim had been made in an ordinary action damages would have been awarded, then damages may be awarded.

## F    CHALLENGES AS DEFENCES TO LOCAL AUTHORITY ACTIONS

The legality of a local authority decision can also be challenged by raising it as a defence to **13.110** an action taken by the authority in reliance on the decision. There is no need for the challenge to be made by way of judicial review. This was decided by the House of Lords in *Wandsworth Borough Council v Winder* [1984] 3 WLR 1254. In this case the local authority had imposed large rent increases on its council tenants for two consecutive years. Mr. Winder, who was the tenant of a council flat, continued paying rent at the old rate. When the authority took possession proceedings, he counterclaimed for a declaration that the rent increase was void and of no effect on the basis that the authority was in breach of its duty to impose 'reasonable' charges for the accommodation. In Mr. Winder's view the increased charges were unreasonable.

**13.111**   The local authority argued that the parts of the defence that impugned the legality of the rent increase and the counterclaim should be struck out. It claimed that the only procedure by which the increase could be challenged was by way of judicial review. The authority relied on two House of Lords' decisions, *O'Reilly v Mackman* [1983] 2 AC 237 and *Cocks v Thanet District Council* [1983] 2 AC 286. However, in both these cases, there was a need for the legality of rent increases to be established quickly. If Mr. Winder's defence succeeded it would create considerable administrative problems and financial difficulty. Lord Fraser of Tullybelton rejected these arguments:

> In any event, the arguments for protecting public authorities against unmeritorious or dilatory challenges to their decisions have to be set against the arguments for preserving the ordinary rights of private citizens to defend themselves against unfounded claims.

He continued:

> It would in my opinion be a very strange use of language to describe the respondent's behaviour in relation to this litigation as abuse or misuse by him of the process of the court. He did not select the procedure to be adopted. He is merely seeking to defend proceedings brought against him by the appellants. In so doing he is seeking only to exercise the ordinary right of any individual to defend an action against him on the ground that he is not liable for the whole sum claimed by the plaintiff. Moreover, he puts forward his defence as a matter of right, whereas in an application for judicial review, success would require an exercise of the court's discretion in his favour.

So, Mr. Winder was allowed to run his defence, which was, in the event, unsuccessful.

---

## KEY DOCUMENTS

Pre-action protocol for judicial review

# 14

# HUMAN RIGHTS

## A INTRODUCTION

The European Convention on Human Rights was incorporated into UK law by the Human **14.01**
Rights Act 1998. This has important implications for local authorities. It is unlawful for
them to act in a way which is incompatible with a 'Convention right'. Many of the Convention rights are relevant to local authority functions. The Act allows those aggrieved by
the failure of a public authority to act in accordance with a Convention right to take
proceedings directly against that authority in the UK courts. The UK has long been a signatory to the European Convention on Human Rights, but before the Human Rights Act,
a complainant who wished to complain about a breach of the Convention would have
to pursue his complaint first to the European Commission on Human Rights and then to

the European Court of Human Rights. Now a complainant can apply directly to a domestic court.

**14.02** The Convention rights are defined under s. 1(1) of the Human Rights Act as being:

(a)  Articles 2 to 12 and 14 of the Convention,

(b)  Articles 1 to 3 of the First Protocol,

(c)  Articles 1 and 2 of the Sixth Protocol,

as read with Articles 16 to 18 of the Convention.

The complete list of Convention rights is set out at Appendix 5. In this chapter it is intended to consider each right in turn and its relevance to local authorities.

---

## B   PUBLIC AUTHORITIES

**14.03** Under s. 6 of the Act it is 'unlawful for a public authority to act in a way which is incompatible with a Convention right'. However, an authority is not acting unlawfully if, because of primary legislation, it could not have acted differently or if it was giving effect to or enforcing primary legislation which was not compatible with Convention rights. The remedy of the aggrieved person in these circumstances is to seek a declaration of incompatibility. A local authority is clearly a public authority for the purposes of the Act. Thus it must ensure that it does not itself infringe any of the Convention rights. If another body carries out functions on behalf of a local authority, it may also be a public authority for the purposes of the Act. Under s. 6 of the Act the phrase 'public authority' includes 'any person certain of whose functions are of a public nature'.

**14.04** In *Donoghue v Poplar Housing and Regeneration Community Association Ltd* [2001] 4 All ER 604 the Court of Appeal decided that the defendant registered social landlord was a public authority. Poplar HARCA had taken over its housing stock from the London Borough of Tower Hamlets following a large scale voluntary transfer of the stock. It had on its board five members of Tower Hamlets Borough Council. It also acted under the guidance of the Council. The Court of Appeal emphasised that a body could exercise both public and private functions and would be a public authority for the first set of functions but not the second. Section 6(3) means that hybrid bodies, who have functions of a public or private nature are public authorities, but not in relation to acts which are of a private nature. The Court of Appeal quoted the conclusion from the High Court judgment: '. . . the role of Poplar is so closely assimilated to that of Tower Hamlets that it was performing public and not private functions. Poplar is therefore a functional public authority, at least to that extent. We emphasise that this does not mean that all Poplar's functions are public.'

**14.05** In *R v Leonard Cheshire Foundation, ex parte Heather* [2002] 2 All ER 936 the Court of Appeal held that the foundation was not exercising a public function when accommodating the elderly, even though the applicants were long-stay residents who had been placed in the home and whose places were funded by the local authority social services department on the grounds that there was no difference between the services provided to local authority funded residents to those provided to private residents, and that the Foundation was not exercising statutory functions. However, a first instance case has decided that the managers of a private hospital were acting as a 'public authority' when caring for a compulsorily detained patient under the Mental Health Act 1983, both because there was a statutory duty placed directly on them (regulation 12, Nursing Homes and Mental Nursing Homes Regulations 1984) and because the detention was compulsory: *R v Partnerships in Care Ltd, ex parte A and others* [2002] 1 WLR 2610.

---

## C  PROPORTIONALITY, DEFERENCE, AND THE MARGIN OF APPRECIATION

The concept of proportionality is extremely important in considering whether an authority's **14.06** conduct could fall foul of the Convention. It was an important concept in the administrative law of a number of European countries before being used by the European Court of Human Rights as a means of judging whether there has been an interference with a right granted by the Convention. The concept of proportionality is relevant in two main situations which will often need to be considered by public authorities:

(a)  A number of the Convention rights are 'qualified' in that interference with such rights can be justified on the grounds that it is 'necessary in a democratic society'.

(b)  A number of other Convention rights expressly allow for a public authority to restrict them if there are relevant and sufficient grounds for so doing.

The way in which the concept of proportionality has been expressed by the European Court **14.07** of Human Rights has varied. There has been a tendency to apply the test more rigorously when more fundamental freedoms are at stake. The test as derived from *Handyside v UK* (1976) 1 EHRR 737 and *Sunday Times v UK* (1979) 2 EHRR 245 is as follows:

(a)  The interference or restriction must be in response to a 'pressing social need'.

(b)  It must be proportionate to the legitimate aim pursued.

(c)  There must be 'relevant and sufficient' reasons to justify it.

The UK courts flirted with the idea of introducing proportionality as a separate free-standing **14.08** ground for judicial review before the enactment of the Human Rights Act: *R v Secretary of State for the Home Department, ex parte Brind* [1991] 1 AC 696. There are clearly similarities between the concept of proportionality and that of *Wednesbury* unreasonableness. A decision could fall foul of the concept of proportionality without being *Wednesbury* unreasonable. A decision that interfered with human rights for a reason which was important to a section of the population but did not answer a pressing social need would not be irrational in the *Wednesbury* sense, indeed it might be perfectly reasonable but it would not be justifiable as an interference with human rights. Similarly, a decision could be disproportionate without being irrational.

Lord Steyn in *R (Daly) v Secretary of State for the Home Department* [2001] 2 AC 532 referred in **14.09** his speech (p. 547) to three concrete differences between the traditional approach to judicial review and proportionality approach. First, the doctrine of proportionality may require the reviewing court to assess the balance the decision-maker has struck, not merely whether it is within the range of rational or reasonable decisions. Secondly, the proportionality test may go further than the traditional grounds of review inasmuch as it may require attention to be directed to the relative weight accorded to interests and considerations. Thirdly, even the heightened scrutiny test developed in *R v Ministry of Defence, ex parte Smith* [1996] QB 517 (the idea that courts scrutinise executive decisions with particular care when fundamental rights were at stake) is not necessarily appropriate to the protection of human rights. The European Court of Human Rights considering that case in *Smith and Grady v UK* (1999) 29 EHRR 493 found that the threshold had been placed too high. It excluded consideration of whether the limitation on the right was necessary in a democratic society in the sense of meeting a pressing social need and whether the interference was proportionate to the legitimate aim being pursued.

**14.10**   A local authority making a decision which it knows may be scrutinised for possible breach of a Convention right will therefore have to consider whether it could withstand a challenge bearing in mind the principles of proportionality set out above.

**14.11**   The doctrine of margin of appreciation owes its origins to the principles on which the Commission allowed states to derogate from Convention rights. Essentially the idea is that state governments have the knowledge of what is happening in their own countries and are, on the face of it, better equipped than a Strasbourg court to decide what measures are required to deal with the situation. However, it is a margin only. If States, whether legislatures or courts, extend beyond what the European Court of Human Rights regards as necessary, then it will not hesitate to intervene.

**14.12**   In the local government context the doctrine of margin of appreciation has sometimes been applied in a way that suggests that it is equivalent to Wednesbury unreasonableness. For instance, in his dissenting judgment in the Court of Appeal, in *R v Somerset County Council, ex parte Fewings*, Simon Brown LJ referred to there being a category of considerations which the decision-maker may have regard to if he considered it right to do so. 'There is, in short, a margin of appreciation, within which the decision-maker may decide just what considerations should play a part in his reasoning process.' Simply as a way of saying that there are some issues which one decision-maker (or member of a decision-making body) would consider to be relevant which another might consider to be irrelevant, this is unproblematic. (It may be that this was all that this statement was intended to express: the argument in *Fewings* appears very much to have been advanced as *Wednesbury* grounds rather than human rights grounds.) However, the notion of margin of appreciation is different from that of *Wednesbury* unreasonableness. There are no real grounds for believing that it applies to individual decisions of an individual public authority instead of a legislature or court. Nor is there any reason to believe that interference with human rights could be justified on the grounds that it was reasonable to do so. The decisions of the ECHR are consistent in saying the grounds for interference are narrower than this.

**14.13**   A slightly different concept from that of margin of appreciation (though sometimes confusingly expressed in similar terms) is the notion of deference. The ECHR has made it clear that a degree of deference should be accorded to policy decisions made through a democratic process. In other words it will be more reluctant to interfere with judgements made in this context. It is reasonable to assume that this will also apply to decisions made by locally elected bodies. There is also a principle that a degree of deference will be accorded to expert judgements. This is particularly relevant to local authorities where in fields such as planning and social services decisions are made either by experienced officers or by members with access to expert advice.

## D TORTURE, INHUMAN, OR DEGRADING TREATMENT

Article 3 provides that, 'No one shall be subjected to torture or to inhuman or degrading **14.14** treatment or punishment.' The case of *Z v UK* [2001] 2 FLR 612 was brought by the children whose claims for negligence had been considered by the House of Lords in *X v Bedfordshire County Council* [1995] 2 AC 633. The children claimed breaches of Articles 3, 6, and 13. The breach of Article 3 was not contested by the Government.

Under the Convention there is an obligation on the Contracting Parties to secure to **14.15** everyone within their jurisdiction the rights and freedoms in the Convention. This requires States to take measures to ensure that individuals are not subjected to inhuman or degrading treatment, including such treatment by individuals. These measures should provide effective protection for children and other vulnerable people against abuse which the appropriate authorities knew or ought to have known about. In this case the children's condition had come to the notice of the authority four and a half years before they were taken into emergency care at the insistence of their mother. In that period they had suffered appalling neglect and physical and psychological injury. The case makes it clear that social services authorities which fail to protect children from neglect or abuse will be in breach of Article 3.

## E FAIR TRIAL

Article 6 provides that; 'In the determination of his civil rights and obligations . . . everyone **14.16** is entitled to a fair and public hearing within a reasonable time by an independent and impartial tribunal established by law.' Various aspects of the planning system within the UK have been attacked on the grounds that it fails to comply with Article 6. These attacks began before the implementation of the Human Rights Act and culminated in the case of *R (Alconbury Ltd) v Secretary of State for the Environment* [2003] 2 AC 295. Since the system successfully withstood these attacks, in spite of moments of danger, the issue is not in itself of much practical importance. However, it is worth considering these cases since they are important in forming the approach which courts will adopt in deciding whether quasi-administrative systems, such as that operating in the field of town and country planning, satisfy the requirement for a fair hearing before an impartial and independent tribunal.

*Bryan v UK* (1995) 21 EHRR 342 concerned the position of inspectors hearing planning **14.17** appeals. The applicant had been required, under the terms of an enforcement notice, to demolish buildings which had been erected without planning permission. He argued before the European Commission for Human Rights and then, subsequently, the European Court of Human Rights that the inspector's decision did not satisfy Article 6. The Court concluded:

(a)  the applicant had a fair hearing before the inspector,

(b)  the inspector was not an independent and impartial tribunal because of the ability of the Secretary of State to make the decision himself if his policies were in issue,

(c)  the ability of the applicant to appeal to the High Court meant that Article 6(1) was satisfied even though that appeal was on points of law only and did not provide for a full rehearing.

**14.18**  The approach of the UK planning system appeared to the court to be both reasonable in itself and typical of such systems in other European countries. It was not considered unjust that there was no rehearing on the facts. If Mr Bryan had chosen to appeal to the High Court:

> . . . while the High Court would not have substituted its own findings of fact for those of the inspector, it would have had the power to satisfy itself that the inspector's findings of fact or the inferences based on them were neither perverse nor irrational.
>
> Such an approach by an appeal tribunal on questions of fact can reasonably be expected in specialised areas of the law such as the one at issue, particularly where the facts have already been established in the course of a quasi-judicial procedure governed by many of the safeguards required by Article 6(1). It is also frequently a feature in the systems of judicial control of administrative decisions found throughout the Council of Europe member states. Indeed, in the instant case, the subject matter of the contested decision by the inspector was a typical example of the exercise of discretionary judgment in the regulation of citizens' conduct in the sphere of town and country planning.

**14.19**  The above decision was followed in *Chapman v UK* [2001] *The Times* 30 January. In the case of *R (Alconbury) v Secretary of State for the Environment* [2001] 2 WLR 1389 the House of Lords considered the alleged incompatibility with Article 6 of the following powers of the Secretary of State in the planning system:

(a)  the power to 'recover' applications for planning permission to decide them himself under paragraph 3 of Schedule 6 to the Town and Country Planning Act 1990,

(b)  the power to 'call-in' applications under s. 77 of the Act, and

(c)  the power to approve an improvement scheme to a road junction under the Highways Act and subsequently approve the CPO which would enable that scheme to be carried out.

It was argued that the Secretary of State should not have a role as both maker of policy and as decision-maker in individual cases. The Divisional Court decided that the powers of the Secretary of State were incompatible with Article 6(1) but that the Secretary of State would not be acting unlawfully in exercising these powers since Article 6(2) applied, i.e. the Secretary of State was following legislation which could not be interpreted in any other way. The House of Lords reversed the Divisional Court's finding of incompatibility.

**14.20**  The House of Lords considered that the existence of the possibility of challenging the Secretary of State's decision by way of judicial review meant that there was a sufficient degree of judicial control to render these decision-making processes Article 6 compliant. It was accepted by the House of Lords that the disputes concerned the determination of 'civil rights' within the meaning of Article 6(1). They took the view that when the decision at issue was a matter of administrative policy there was no need for the reviewing body to have full power to redetermine the merits of the decision. The House of Lords were also concerned about democratic accountability. It was not the function of courts to review the policies of decisions taken by Ministers, and that to embark on such an exercise would be undemocratic.

The emphasis placed by the House of Lords on the conclusion that, because the decisions in **14.21** question were matters of policy rather than fact, there was no need for a full rehearing, led to further challenges. These were argued on the basis that, if there was a factual dispute, then there either needed to be a full hearing before an independent and impartial tribunal to determine this or a full rehearing by the court hearing the appeal. The House of Lords decision in *Alconbury* therefore inadvertently opened up a whole new front on which administrative decisions could be attacked on the grounds of breach of Article 6.

The speech of Lord Hoffmann provides the clearest illustration of this. He devoted quite a lot **14.22** of his speech to considering the opinion of Mr Nicolas Bratza in the *Bryan* case. This opinion, was to the effect that 'Article 6 did not require that a court should have the power to substitute its view for that of the administrative authorities on matters of planning policy or expediency'. He then looked at the requirement that a reviewing court should have 'full jurisdiction' in the context of whether the High Court hearing a planning appeal on a point of law could be described as having such jurisdiction.

> It appears to me that the requirement that a court or tribunal should have 'full jurisdiction' cannot be mechanically applied with the result that, in all circumstances and whatever the subject matter of the dispute, the court or tribunal must have full power to substitute its own findings of fact and its own inferences from those facts, for that of the administrative authority concerned. Whether the power of judicial review is sufficiently wide to satisfy the requirements of Article 6 must in my view depend on a number of considerations, including the subject matter of the dispute, the nature of the decision of the administrative authority which is in question, the procedure, if any which exists for review of the decision by a person or body acting independently of the authority concerned and scope of that power of review.

Lord Hoffmann relied on Mr Bratza's opinion for the notion that a tribunal could be more **14.23** or less independent, depending on the nature of the dispute it had to decide. On policy matters a planning inspector was not independent and it was undesirable that he should be. However, as a fact finder,he was an expert tribunal acting in a quasi-judicial manner. This approach was adopted by the European Court of Human Rights in the *Bryan* case which referred to the 'safeguards' which applied to the public inquiry procedure: 'the quasi-judicial character of the decision-making process; the duty incumbent on each inspector to exercise independent judgment; the requirement that inspectors must not be subject to any improper influence; the stated mission of the Inspectorate to uphold the principles of openness, fairness and impartiality'. He then concluded that the Divisional Court had mis-understood *Bryan*. They had believed that, whatever the nature of the decision, the 'safe-guards' referred to above were essential before a limited review such as an appeal on a point of law or a judicial review would satisfy Article 6. He then drew the following conclusion:

> If, therefore, the question is one of policy or expediency, the 'safeguards' are irrelevant. No one expects the inspector to be independent or impartial in applying the Secretary of State's policy and this was the reason why the court said that he was not for all purposes an independent and impartial tribunal. In this respect his position is no different from that of the Secretary of State himself. The reason why judicial review is sufficient in both cases to satisfy Article 6 has nothing to do with the 'safeguards' but depends on the *Zumtobel* principle of respect for the decision of an administrative authority on questions of expediency. It is only when one comes to findings

of fact, or the evaluation of facts, such as arise on the question of whether there has been a breach of planning control, that the safeguards are essential for the acceptance of a limited review of fact by the appellate tribunal.

**14.24** The compatibility of a local authority's decision-making process on planning matters was considered in *R (Adlard) v Secretary of State for the Environment* [2002] 1 WLR 2515. The case concerned the site at Craven Cottage, the ground of Fulham Football Club. A previous application for redevelopment had been granted by the Secretary of State following a public inquiry but the permission was eventually quashed because no environmental impact statement had been submitted, as was required. A further application for redevelopment was submitted in 2000. Objectors requested that the new application should be called-in to be determined by the Secretary of State. This would have enabled a public inquiry to take place. The Secretary of State declined, so the matter was determined by the planning committee of the local authority. There was no opportunity for the objectors to make oral representations about the proposed development.

**14.25** The procedure was challenged on the ground that failure to grant the objectors the right to make oral representations deprived them of the right to a fair hearing, contrary to Article 6. The objectors were unsuccessful before the High Court and appealed to the Court of Appeal. Simon Brown LJ relied heavily on the judgment of Laws LJ in the Court of Appeal judgment in *Begum* to the effect that there was a greater need for procedures akin to a conventional means of finding fact (cross-examination, access to documents, and a strictly independent decision-maker) if the statutory scheme systematically involves fact-finding. If, on the other hand, it involves judgement or the exercise of a discretion, the court is more likely to be satisfied with a decision-maker who acts more as an expert than as a judge. This approach was not recommended by the House of Lords when they came to hear the appeal in the *Begum* case. (See below.)

**14.26** Simon Brown LJ concluded that the planning process was 'towards that end of the spectrum where judgment and discretion, rather than fact-finding, play the predominant part'. He concluded:

> I can find no warrant, whether in domestic or in Strasbourg jurisprudence, for concluding that where, as in Runa Begum's case and as again here, the administrative decisions taken at first instance are generally likely to turn on questions of judgment and discretion rather than on findings of fact, the statutory scheme must provide for an oral hearing at that initial stage. On the contrary, I have reached the clearest conclusion that the statutory scheme as a whole is plainly compliant with Article 6 and that there is no need to resort to the Secretary of State's call-in power to make it so.

**14.27** The case of *Runa Begum v Tower Hamlets London Borough Council* [2003] 2 AC 430 concerned the application of Article 6 to a review of a decision about housing needs. The issue was whether the procedure whereby a senior housing officer of a local authority makes a decision about whether an offer of accommodation was suitable, subject to a right of appeal only to the county court on a point of law, satisfied the requirement for a person's civil rights to be determined before an independent and impartial tribunal.

**14.28** Runa Begum was separated from her husband and was no longer welcome at her mother's house. She sought assistance from the Council on the basis that she was threatened with homelessness. She and her child were given temporary accommodation and the authority satisfied itself that it had a duty to rehouse her. It made her an offer of accommodation which she rejected, claiming that the area in which the flat she was offered was situated was frequented by drug addicts and racists, that the block it was in was frequently visited by her estranged husband, and that she was attacked by two youths after visiting the flat. She requested a review of the decision under s. 202 Housing Act 1985. The procedure for the review is set out in the Allocation of Housing and Homelessness (Review Procedures) Regulations 1999. The review must be carried out by an officer who was senior to the officer who made the original decision and who had not been involved in that decision. In this case the review was conducted by the Council's rehousing manager who, after making various enquiries, concluded that Ms Begum's refusal of the offer of accommodation was unreasonable. This decision meant that the Council considered it had discharged its duties towards Ms Begum.

There is an appeal against a review of a decision to the county court on a point of law. **14.29** Ms Begum appealed but before her appeal was heard the Court of Appeal gave judgment in the case of *Adan v Newham London Borough Council* [2002] 1 WLR 2120. The appeal in the county court in the *Adan* case was heard just after the Human Rights Act 1998 had come into force. The judge allowed Mr Adan's appeal on the ground of irrationality and directed that the review should be conducted by a different reviewing officer who, in terms of independence and impartiality, complied with Article 6.

The Council appealed to the Court of Appeal who set aside the judge's order on the grounds **14.30** that he had no power to make what amounted to an order of mandamus. The Court then went on to consider the effect of Article 6 on these types of decision. It was conceded that the applicant's 'civil rights' were engaged and that the reviewing officer was not an independent and impartial tribunal. The issue was whether the composite procedure of an internal review by an officer subject to a right of appeal to the independent county court satisfied Article 6. The Court of Appeal's conclusion was that the composite procedure would not be sufficient if the housing officer conducting the review had to 'resolve a dispute of fact which [was] material to the decision'. The majority of the Court of Appeal thought that where the authority considered it likely that there would be material disputes of fact they should contract out their reviewing functions to a third party.

It is worth pausing at this point and considering some of the practical problems which might **14.31** have been presented if the Court of Appeal decision in *Adan* had been allowed to stand.

(a) It would not necessarily be easy to tell in advance which cases of review were likely to throw up material issues of fact. A local authority would have to adopt a cautious approach and contract out all those reviews where a dispute of fact could potentially be relevant.

(b) The purpose of allowing authorities to contract out reviews was to give them flexibility. They could contract out if they considered this was likely to be more efficient or economic. The purpose of allowing contracting-out was not to provide independence. If this had been the aim, then the legislation would have provided for an external review by somebody independent to be part of the scheme.

(c) The type of reconsideration by a different officer provided for in the regulations on homelessness decisions is a common process both in local authorities and other public bodies. To require every such decision which involved a material dispute of fact to be referred to somebody outside the organisation would be extremely burdensome.

**14.32**   Ms Begum's appeal was then heard in the county court and was successful. The judge hearing her appeal considered, with some reluctance, that he should follow the reasoning of the majority of the Court of Appeal in the *Adan* case. The Court of Appeal allowed the Council's appeal. Laws LJ said that one could not have different systems of adjudication according to the degree of factual dispute. One had to look at the scheme (i.e. Part VII of the Housing Act 1985: the whole legal regime relating to homelessness) as a whole. If it was systematically likely to throw up issues of primary fact it might be necessary to have either an independent review or a full right of appeal. If, on the other hand, it was systematically likely to require the exercise of a discretion or the application of policy, then an appeal limited to a judicial review would be sufficient.

**14.33**   Ms Begum appealed to the House of Lords. There were three issues to be considered:

(a)   Whether the decision of the reviewing officer was a determination of Ms Begum's 'civil rights' within the meaning of Article 6.

(b)   Did the reviewing officer constitute an 'independent and impartial tribunal' so as to satisfy Article 6?

(c)   If not, did the composite procedure of an administrative decision and the appeal to the county court satisfy Article 6?

**14.34**   Lord Hoffman reviewed the way in which the European Court of Human Rights had dealt with the extension of Article 6 into administrative decisions. It was presumably not originally anticipated that 'civil rights' would at one stage extend beyond remedies for civil wrongs such as loss caused by a tort or breach of contract into redress for administrative decisions made by public authorities. The ECHR has long been clear about the potential difficulties which would be caused by requiring every administrative decision to be approached in a quasi-judicial manner. It took the view that in these types of cases, the opportunity of an appeal was sufficient to satisfy the requirements of Article 6. The question was, what sort of an appeal? In UK law these types of decision could often only be challenged by way of judicial review. This type of arrangement was typical of the legal systems of many countries which were signatories to the Convention. In *Kaplan v UK* (1980) 4 EHRR 64, 90 paragraph 161, the Court commented:

> An interpretation of Article 6(1) under which it was held to provide a right to a full appeal on the merits of every administrative decision affecting private rights would therefore lead to a result which was inconsistent with the existing, and long-standing, legal position in most of the contracting states.

**14.35**   There were two ways in which such an arrangement could be argued to satisfy Article 6, one suggested by the European Commission for Human Rights, the other being the approach favoured by the European Court of Human Rights. The Commission's approach was to say that the administrative decision called into question is not of itself a determination of civil rights or obligations. However, a question as to whether the decision-maker had acted lawfully when taking the decision would involve a determination of civil rights or obligations so that access to an independent and impartial tribunal would be required.

The Court's approach has been to analyse the engagement of Article 6 with administrative **14.36** decisions in the following way:

(a) An administrative decision is a determination of civil rights and obligations and, on the face of it, requires access to an independent and impartial tribunal.

(b) If the decision-maker is not independent it is permissible to consider whether a 'composite procedure' of administrative decision together with a right of appeal to a court is sufficient.

(c) It will be regarded as sufficient if the appellate or reviewing court has 'full jurisdiction' over the administrative decision.

(d) The expression 'full jurisdiction' need not mean that the court has jurisdiction to re-examine the merits of the case but 'jurisdiction to deal with the case as the nature of the decision requires'.

In the House of Lords it was argued that the review of the suitability of the accommodation **14.37** for Ms Begum required a set of procedures and safeguards which would have rendered it virtually a judicial hearing. The argument was developed on foundations provided by the ECHR decision in *Bryan v UK* (1995) 21 EHRR 342 and a remark in the speech of Lord Hoffman in *Alconbury*. In support of his argument counsel for Ms Begum relied on the passage in the ECHR judgment in *Bryan* quoted above which listed the 'safeguards' inherent in the public inquiry procedure and the passage in Lord Hoffmann's speech in *Alconbury* quoted in paragraph 14.23 above, particularly the sentence at the end in which he referred to the safeguards as being essential for acceptance of a limited review of fact by the appellate tribunal in cases which involved findings of fact.

Lord Hoffmann clearly regretted the way in which he expressed the above conclusion, **14.38** describing it as an 'incautious remark'. He dealt with the argument by considering the context in which the decision in *Alconbury* was made. The issue simply did not arise in that case because it was only concerned with policy issues. He then distinguished *Bryan* from Ms Begum's circumstances as the findings of fact in an enforcement appeal were of a quasi-criminal nature, binding on the appellant in future criminal proceedings. It was important to consider the context in which findings of fact were made. Certain decisions such as breaches of the criminal law needed to be made by the 'judicial branch of government'. But when it came to administration of a social welfare scheme such as the allocation of housing, the court would look at the requirements of efficient administration. A more complex review procedure could eat into the funds that would otherwise be available for social welfare expenditure. Lord Hoffmann went on to disagree with the conclusion of Laws J that the test for whether it is necessary to have an independent fact-finder depends on the extent to which the scheme is likely to involve disputed issues of fact. He concluded on this point:

> In my opinion the question is whether, consistently with the rule of law and constitutional propriety, the relevant decision-making powers may be entrusted to administrators. If so, it does not matter that there are many or few occasions on which they need to make findings of fact.

There were two other issues which needed to be considered. The House of Lords unanimously **14.39** rejected the argument that the rehousing officer was herself an independent and impartial tribunal (which would have meant that it was unnecessary for there to be a right of appeal). Lord Hoffmann's response was that one of the purposes of Article 6 was to uphold the rule of law and the separation of powers. If an administrator was to be regarded as an independent and impartial tribunal then this would preclude the possibility of judicial review and place that administrator above the law. He referred to a line of cases in which the Swedish government had been found to be in breach of Article 6 because there was no means of judicially reviewing Government decisions.

**14.40**   The argument was perhaps too readily rejected. There is nothing in the Strasbourg case law to suggest that the expression 'independent and impartial tribunal' must always be a member of the judiciary. In *Buckley v UK* the only reason why the ECHR considered that a planning inspector was not an independent and impartial tribunal was because of the ability of the Secretary of State to take the decision-making powers away from the inspector and decide the matter himself. The local authority had no power to remove the decision from its rehousing officer. The Swedish cases came about because of the fact that the Swedish constitutional set-up did not allow an adequate procedure for judicial review of Government action. It cannot be concluded from them that the fact that someone can be described as an administrator automatically excludes them from being independent and impartial. In spite of the unequivocal nature of the House of Lords' conclusion on this point, it may be anticipated that there will be further arguments in the future on this issue.

**14.41**   The third issue, whether Ms Begum's civil rights were engaged, was not decided by the House of Lords at all, though the case proceeded on the assumption that they were. The reason for this was that the case law in the ECHR has not yet resulted in a clear line being drawn as to where the civil rights of the individual are separated from the state's 'core prerogatives'. Thus the issue of entitlement to sickness allowance has been held by the ECHR to involve determination of a 'civil right': *Feldbrugge v The Netherlands* 8 EHRR 425, but disputes over taxation have fallen on the other side of the line: *Ferrazzini v Italy* (2001) 34 EHRR 1068. The extension of the concept of 'civil rights' to the right to social housing would go beyond the existing case-law of the European Court and the House of Lords did not feel able to do so.

**14.42**   The Court of Appeal in the case of *R (McLellan) v Bracknell Forest Borough Council* [2002] QB 1129 were not so reticent. It concluded that Article 6 needed to be satisfied when a local authority served notice of determination of an introductory tenancy. Waller LJ said that Article 6 could be engaged where there was an administrative decision which affected the rights of individuals. He relied on a passage from the speech of Lord Clyde in *Alconbury:*

> It is thus clear that Article 6(1) is engaged where the decision which is to be given is of an administrative character, that is to say one given in an exercise of a discretionary power, as well as a dispute in a court of law regarding the private rights of the citizen, provided that it directly affects civil rights and obligations and is of a genuine and serious nature.

Waller LJ took the view that a decision about the property rights of a tenant were of a 'genuine and serious nature' and that there would probably have been a requirement for an independent review even if the legislation had not specifically allowed for it. He took the view that the requirements of Article 6 were satisfied because there was a right to a full review before a review panel. This, although internal to the local authority, followed quasi-judicial procedures, allowing the tenant to appear before it, be legally represented, call witnesses, and question the Council's officer. If the decision to terminate the tenancy was upheld by the review panel, then the county court judge had no discretion about whether to make an order for possession but could adjourn the hearing to allow the tenant to take proceedings for judicial review. He concluded that there was no reason to believe that the review procedure would not be operated fairly and that its existence, together with the possibility of a challenge by way of judicial review if there was any unfairness or infringement of Convention rights satisfied Article 6. This case is also relevant in considering the effect of Article 8 and is considered further below.

## F   PRIVATE AND FAMILY LIFE, THE HOME, AND CORRESPONDENCE

Article 8 provides as follows:                                                                14.43

1.   Everyone has a right to respect for his private and family life, his home and his correspondence.
2.   There shall be no interference by a public authority with the exercise of this right except such as is in accordance with the law and is necessary in a democratic society in the interests of national security, public safety or the economic well-being of the country, for the prevention of disorder or crime, for the protection of health or morals, or for the protection of the rights and freedoms of others.

This article impacts on a wide range of local authority functions. A local authority can interfere with individuals' homes using their powers in the fields of planning and compulsory purchase, and as providers of housing. They have power to intervene in families in their capacity of social services authorities, especially in the field of child protection.

The ECHR considered the compatibility with Article 8 of some aspects of English child care   14.44
law in *Scott v UK* [2000] 1 FLR 958. The removal of a child from his or her parents was clearly an interference with family life. However, in some circumstances it could be argued that it was necessary in a democratic society and that it protected the health of children and their rights. In the *Scott* case the applicant, who was an alcoholic, had her child removed from her care and subsequently freed for adoption. She complained about two aspects of the local authority's treatment of her. First, she alleged that they had failed to look at her case and consult her properly in September 1993 when the decision to seek a freeing order was made. Secondly, she claimed that from June 1993, when the full care order was made, the local authority was outside the court's jurisdiction.

The court took the view that the appropriate authorities 'enjoy a wide margin of appreci-   14.45
ation' in assessing the necessity of taking a child into care. However, stricter scrutiny is required for any further limitations, such as restrictions placed on parental rights and access or on the legal safeguards designed to secure the effective protection of the rights of parents and children to respect for their family life, where such further limitations might entail the danger that the family relations between the parents and their child are effectively curtailed.

The court rejected the notion that the decision-making process had been unfair or that it   14.46
had failed to involve the applicant sufficiently. There was a complaint that she had been excluded from the meeting at which the decision to abandon the plan for rehabilitation had been made. However, this was an internal meeting and the applicant had been invited to the relevant case conferences and review meetings. The decision to free her child for adoption

was subject to a narrower margin of appreciation because of its definitive nature. However, the domestic court could not be criticised for making the freeing order. It was not convinced that the applicant was able to rid herself of her alcohol problem and it was not in the child's interests to remain in temporary placements.

**14.47**   For local authorities the only real conclusion of the case is the need to ensure that parents are involved at every stage of the planning process, which has long been the practice of social workers dealing with child care cases. The operation of the procedures to protect children from abuse or neglect have been accepted as necessary in a democratic society to protect children's rights. Particularly cogent justification will be needed to justify orders that are likely to have the effect of ending contact between a child and his or her parents.

**14.48**   The case of *South Buckinghamshire District Council v Porter* [2003] 2 AC 558 concerned the approach to be taken by the courts when considering whether to grant injunctions to prevent breaches of planning control. The House of Lords considered appeals in three cases. In all of these the appellants were gypsies who had bought land but had been refused planning permission to station their caravans on that land. It was argued on behalf of the appellants that the power to grant an injunction under s. 187B of the Town and Country Planning Act 1990 gave the judge a discretion which should be exercised as an original jurisdiction not a review power. The court had to address the issues arising under Article 8 and reach its own decision on whether the removal of the gypsies was proportionate to the public interest in preservation of the environment. On behalf of the local authorities it was argued that a judge exercising his s. 187B jurisdiction was more or less bound to grant an injunction unless it could be shown that the local authority's decision was flawed on *Wednesbury* grounds. The court's jurisdiction was only supervisory. Only when it came to deciding whether to commit someone to prison for breach of an injunction did factors such as personal hardship come into play.

**14.49**   Both the Court of Appeal and the House of Lords trod a path between these two extreme positions. In exercising its jurisdiction under s. 187B an English court was prohibited from acting in a way which was incompatible with the Convention including Article 8. The court therefore had to consider when deciding whether to grant an injunction 'whether such relief is proportionate in the Convention sense, and grant relief only if it judges it to be so'. This would involve taking into account the individual circumstances of the applicants.

**14.50**   Until the House of Lords' decision in *Harrow London Borough Council v Qazi* [2003] 3 WLR 792 it was assumed that possession proceedings automatically involved a prima facie violation of Article 8 which would always need to be justified under Article 8(2). This meant that whenever there was a challenge, the particular statutory scheme under which possession was sought needed to be scrutinised by the court in order to examine whether it was Article 8 compliant. An example of the approach previously taken is the Court of Appeal decision in *R (McLellan) v Bracknell Forest Borough Council* [2002] QB 1129. Both the applicants were tenants who had been granted introductory tenancies, which provided for a one year probationary period before the tenant was given a secure tenancy. Since then the Court had no discretion about whether to grant a possession order if the authority applied for it, the use of introductory tenancies made it easier for the authority to identify tenants who were going to behave in an anti-social way, or fail to pay their rent. The authority could then easily regain possession of the accommodation they were occupying.

It was argued on behalf of Reigate Borough Council that Article 8(1) was simply not engaged. **14.51**
A tenant would know the basis on which he or she became a tenant. They knew that the
statutory provisions which governed the granting of introductory tenancies applied to
them. If the Council followed the rules, and complied with the statutory requirements, this
could not amount to a lack of respect for the tenant's home. Although there was some
support for this argument in the decisions of the Commission the problem that it faced at
this stage was that there were two earlier decisions in which distinguished judges had seen it
as axiomatic that Article 8 was engaged when eviction was being considered.

Sedley LJ said in *Lambeth London Borough Council v Howard* (2001) 33 HLR 636 (p. 644 **14.52**
para 30):

> Respect for a person's home is neither an absolute concept nor an unqualified right. I do find
> myself puzzled by the learned judge's remark that Article 8 'at first sight . . . has no application
> to the present circumstances'. It seems to me that any attempt to evict a person, whether
> directly or by process of law, from his or her home would on the face of it be a derogation from
> the respect, that is the integrity, to which the home is prima facie entitled.

Woolf CJ took the same approach in *Poplar HARCA v Donoghue* [2002] QB 48 (p. 70 para 67):

> To evict the defendant from her home would impact on her family life. The effect of Article 8(2)
> is therefore critical.

Waller LJ said that the wording of Article 8(2) made it clear that the argument put forward by **14.53**
counsel for Reigate BC was not the proper approach to the article. It was under Article 8(2)
that it had to be considered whether an eviction was in accordance with the law. Turning to
the question of whether the scheme for introductory tenancies complied with Article 8,
Waller LJ concluded that it did. He also approved the procedure recommended in *Manchester
City Council v Cochrane* [1999] 1 WLR 809 which was that if a judge hearing a possession case
relating to an introductory tenancy considered there were arguable grounds for judicial
review, he should adjourn to allow this to happen. On the question of the scheme as a whole
it was concluded that Parliament had decided that such a scheme was in the interests of
tenants generally and local authorities, that it contained important safeguards, and that
there was no reason think that individuals' rights would be infringed without remedy from
the courts. A similar approach was taken by the Court of Appeal in relation to assured
shorthold tenancies: *Poplar HARCA v Donoghue* [2002] QB 48 and non-secure tenancies:
*Sheffield City Council v Smart* [2002] LGR 467.

The argument that there was no infringement of Article 8 in cases where the landlord **14.54**
required a tenant to leave accommodation which was granted to the tenant as a qualified or
limited home was successful in *Harrow London Borough Council v Qazi* [2003] 3 WLR 792. The
council granted Mr Qazi and his wife a joint secure tenancy of council owned premises in
1992. They lived together there until 1998 when Mrs Qazi moved out with her daughter to
go and live with her mother. Mrs Qazi served a notice to quit on the local authority, bringing
the tenancy to an end. Mr Qazi applied to become tenant of the property himself. The
council took possession proceedings. The judge in the county court decided that the premises were no longer Mr Qazi's 'home' for the purposes of Article 8 so that article was not
'engaged'. This went further than the argument which was rejected in the *Bracknell* case,
which did not assert that the premises were not the applicant's home. Mr Qazi's appeal to
the Court of Appeal was successful, and the case was remitted to the county court to

determine whether interference with Mr Qazi's right to a home was permitted by Article 8(2). The council appealed to the House of Lords.

**14.55** There were two conflicting views of the ECHR on the issue of what constituted a home. In *S v UK* (1986) 47 DR 274 the applicant carried on occupying a house of which her partner had been a tenant but to which she had no legal right to succeed. The Commission said that since the local authority was entitled to possession, the house could no longer be regarded as the applicant's home for the purposes of Article 8. However a broader view was taken in *Buckley v UK* 23 EHRR 101:

> . . . the concept of 'home' within the meaning of Article 8 is not limited to those which are lawfully occupied or which have been lawfully established. 'Home' is an autonomous concept which does not depend on classification under domestic law. Whether or not a particular habitation constitutes a 'home' which attracts the protection of Article 8(1) will depend on the factual circumstances, namely the existence of sufficient and continuous links.

**14.56** The House of Lords were unanimous in preferring the *Buckley* approach, and decided that the flat where Mr Qazi lived was his home for the purposes of Article 8. They also concluded that Article 8 was 'engaged' in the sense that it was applicable. However, according to the majority this did not mean that there was any issue under Article 8(2) to be decided. Lord Hope considered two decisions of the Commission to consider what the ECHR would make of the issue as to whether the interference was permitted by Article 8(2). In one, *Ure v UK* (Application no 28027/95) 27 November 1996, the facts were quite similar to *Qazi* in that a joint tenant had left, then served notice to quit, leaving the person left in the premises with no tenancy. The applicant, who remained in the flat, claimed that his right to respect for his home had been breached. The Commission noted that domestic law allowed a leaving co-tenant to bring a tenancy to an end. It rejected allegations that, in the particular circumstances of the case, the authorities had behaved in an arbitrary fashion. In *Wood v UK* (1997) 24 EHRR CD 69 the applicant complained that her rights under Article 8 had been breached when her house was repossessed because she had failed to meet repayments on a loan for which the house was being used as security. Her application was held to be inadmissible.

**14.57** Lord Hope concluded that he would expect the European Court to attach much importance to the fact that it was clear from the outset of the joint tenancy that it could be terminated by a notice to quit from either of the joint tenants. He concluded that a claim for breach of Article 8 in Mr Qazi's situation was unarguable. Having begun by asking the question as to whether the interference was justified under Article 8(2) he appears to conclude that the question did not arise because the obtaining of possession in circumstances such as Mr Qazi did not involve a breach of Article 8(1) (p. 821):

> I do not say that the right to respect for the home is irrelevant. But I consider that such interference with it as flows from the application of the law which enables the public authority landlord to exercise its unqualified right to recover possessions, following service of a notice to quit which here terminated the tenancy, with a view to making the premises available for letting to others on its housing list does not violate the essence of the right to respect for the home under Article 8(1). That is a conclusion which can be applied now to all cases of this type generally.

**14.58** Lord Millett also concluded that the court hearing a possession action would have to decide whether the landlord was entitled to an order for possession as a matter of ordinary domestic law. Once it concluded this, there would be nothing further to investigate. Making or enforcing a possession order to which a landlord was entitled did not involve any want of appropriate respect for a person's home: p. 827:

> I would accordingly endorse the observations of Moses J in *R (Gangera) v Hounslow* [2003] EWHC 794 (Admin) that in proceedings between private parties the court does not act incompatibly with Article 8 by making or enforcing a possession order without considering questions or proportionality. I also agree with him that it makes no difference that the landlord is a public authority. In most cases the statutory scheme established by Parliament will provide the object-ive justification for the council's decision which need not be demonstrated on a case by case basis: see *Wandsworth London Borough Council v Michalak* [2003] 1 WLR 617, 631–632. In the exceptional case where the applicant believes that the local authority is acting unfairly or from improper or ulterior motives, he can apply to the High Court for judicial review. The availability of this remedy, coupled with the fact that an occupier cannot be evicted without a court order, so that the court can consider whether the claimant is entitled as of right to possession, is sufficient to supply the necessary and appropriate degree of respect for the applicant's home.

Lord Scott concluded that Article 8 could not be used as a means of giving the defendant additional property rights that he would not otherwise have.

What then can be deduced from the case law?                              **14.59**

1.  A person's home for the purposes of Article 8(2) need not be premises that the person is occupying lawfully. It depends on whether there are sufficient and continuous links with that unit of accommodation.
2.  If a person is occupying premises without any legal entitlement to do so, e.g. a squatter, a person remaining in possession without a tenancy, then lawfully seeking possession is not a breach of the obligation to respect that person's home. There is therefore no need to consider whether that interference falls within Article 8(2).
3.  It remains an open question whether in certain circumstances ending a qualified right to occupation could be argued to be a breach of Article 8(1). In these circumstances the statutory scheme under which possession was being sought would have to be justified as falling within Article 8(2). As a practical issue, most of the circumstances which will be relevant for local authorities (introductory tenancies, non-secure tenancies, assured shortholds) have been held to be Article 8(2) compliant. However, the possibility of such challenges was not ruled out by *Qazi*. The prospect of any further such challenge being successful is remote.
4.  A local authority is not immune from judicial review in taking and implementing decisions about possession proceedings. A decision to issue a notice to quit would be judicially reviewable. It would be open to an occupier if it was considered that there was an arguable case, to say that because of the fact that the authority had behaved unlaw-fully, there was a breach of Article 8 in the circumstances of that case.

Article 8 may need to be considered whenever local authorities pass on information about **14.60** people. Such disclosures may constitute an interference with a person's private and family life, home and correspondence. An example of this is the case of *R v Wakefield Metropolitan Council, ex parte Robertson* [2002] 2 WLR 889. The claimant requested that the electoral regis-tration officer should not disclose his name and address on the electoral register to com-mercial organisations. The registration officer refused his request. Mr Robertson challenged his decision on three grounds:

(a) breach of Article 14 of the Data Protection Directive (This aspect is considered in chapter 16.);

(b) contravention of Article 8;

(c) breach of Protocol 1 Article 3 in that there was an unlawful interference with his right to vote as this right was made conditional on his consent to the sale of his personal particulars to commercial organisations.

**14.61** The court held that on the face of it, Article 8 was engaged. There was a need to consider not just the information which was being disclosed but the use to which it would be put. The local authority had a legitimate objective in providing the information. However, selling the information on without giving the individuals on the register a chance to object was a disproportionate way of achieving this objective. This was particularly true in the context of technological advances which made it easy to spread the information widely and speedily. There was therefore a breach of the claimant's Article 8 rights.

**14.62** The court also held that, if and to the extent that the Representation of the People Regulations made the right to vote conditional on a person's acquiescence in the sale of his personal details to a commercial organisation, they contravened Protocol 1 Article 3. The restriction could only be justified by reference to the principles in *Clerfayt v Belgium* (1987) 10 EHRR 1. The problem again was that there was no right to object. This made the restriction unjustifiable and disproportionate.

**14.63** The courts have continued to be unsympathetic to attempts to use Article 8 as a means of establishing a right to housing. An example of this is *Lambeth London Borough Council v Grant* [2005] 1 WLR 1781. Ms Grant had come to the UK on a visitor's visa which expired. She then made unsuccessful applications for leave to remain. Her children joined her in the UK. She applied again for leave to remain on compassionate grounds. An assessment was carried out by the local authority under the Children Act 1989. This concluded that it would be in the best interests of the children if they returned to live in Jamaica. The Council offered to pay for her and the children's flights to Jamaica and to accommodate them for a long enough period for the travel arrangements to be made. This decision was quashed by the High Court on the grounds that the failure of the local authority to provide temporary accommodation was a breach of Article 8. The Court of Appeal said that Ms Grant and her children had no right to be accommodated and could not create such a right by applying for leave to remain. The Council could not act in a way that breached the family's Convention rights. However, these rights had been safeguarded by the authority's offer to pay for the flights to Jamaica and accommodate them in the meantime.

**14.64** The courts have also had to consider whether in certain circumstances a failure to comply with a statutory duty to provide assistance could amount to an infringement of Article 8. The European Court of Human Rights has always been reluctant to interpret the Convention as a requirement that a particular level of welfare support must be provided. This has applied both to financial provision and assistance with housing. Thus in *Andersson and Kullman v Sweden* (1986) 46 DR 251 a complaint that the government had failed to provide financial assistance to enable the applicant to stay at home with her children was rejected as inadmissible by the Commission. In *Marzari v Italy* (1999) 28 EHRR CD 175 a disabled man complained about the accommodation which had been provided for him by the local authority. The court rejected the complaint on the basis that it was not its function to review decisions about allocation of housing made by local authorities. However, it made it clear that there were circumstances in which Article 8 could impose positive obligations, as well as simply a duty not to interfere.

The extent of these obligations was considered by the Court of Appeal in *Anufrijeva v*      **14.65**
*Southwark London Borough Council* [2004] 2 WLR 603. The claimants were Lithuanian asylum seekers who sought damages from the local authority under s. 8 of the Human Rights Act for alleged breaches of Article 8, arguing that the Council had failed to discharge its duty under s. 21 of the National Assistance Act 1948 to provide them with accommodation which met the needs of one member of the family. The claim was unsuccessful in the High Court. The claimants' appeal was heard together with the appeals of two other asylum seekers who claimed damages for alleged maladministration in the Home Office in dealing with their asylum applications.

There was an earlier High Court decision in which Article 8 was held to impose a positive      **14.66**
duty on a local authority: *R (Bernard) v Enfield London Borough Council* [2003] LGR 423. This concerned a disabled woman who was accommodated with her husband and their six children in extremely cramped conditions, lacking in privacy, and unable to use the toilet. Sullivan J held that the Council was also in breach of Article 8 of the Convention on the basis that their failure to act on the assessments of the claimant's needs 'showed a lack of respect for the claimants' private and family life'.

The Court of Appeal in *Anufrijeva* concluded that Sullivan J was right to accept that Article 8      **14.67**
was capable of imposing on a state a positive obligation to provide support. They indicated that this obligation was only likely to exist in extreme circumstances, saying that it was 'hard to conceive of a situation where the predicament of an individual will be such that Article 8 requires him to be provided with welfare support, where his predicament is not sufficiently severe to engage Article 3'. In other words the failure to help must be at the kind of level where the circumstances in which the individual is condemned to live without such support amounts to torture or inhuman or degrading treatment. This is a high threshold, impliedly higher than that used by Sullivan J in the *Bernard* case in which he rejected the claim that there was a breach of Article 3 (albeit with some reluctance). The court added that 'Where the welfare of children was at stake Article 8 may require the provision of welfare support in a manner which enables family life to continue.' Thus in *R (J) v Enfield London Borough Council* [2002] EWHC 735 (Admin) where the claimant was homeless and faced separation from her child, it was common ground that, if this occurred, Article 8(1) would be infringed. The appeal in the *Anufrijeva* case was dismissed.

The case also considered the question of the circumstances in which administrative delay      **14.68**
could constitute a breach of Article 8. The approach of the ECHR and the Commission has been not to find that there was a breach of Article 8 unless there was substantial prejudice to the applicant. Cases involving the custody of children need to be dealt with expeditiously in order to comply with Article 8 because such delay may determine the outcome of the dispute as in *H v UK* (1987) 10 EHRR 95. The Court of Appeal said that the approach of the Strasbourg court showed 'sound sense'. The need to have regard to resources when considering the obligations imposed on a state by Article 8 was also emphasised. When considering whether the threshold of Article 8 had been reached it was necessary to consider both how culpable the failure to act was, and how severe the consequences were. The 'more glaring the

deficiency—the easier it will be to establish the necessary want of respect. Isolated acts of even significant carelessness are unlikely to suffice.'

---

## G  FREEDOM OF EXPRESSION

**14.69**  Article 10 provides that everyone has the right to freedom of expression.

Local authorities will not often have to grapple with issues arising under Article 10. There may be questions about the extent to which, in a given case, children can be protected from the effects of adverse publicity. The approach taken by the courts is that the freedom of the press and media is important and should not be lightly interfered with. Even if there is publicity involving children, the issue in deciding whether publication should be restrained will not be considered purely by reference to a child's welfare. There needs to be a balance between the freedom to receive and impart information and ideas and the desirability of protecting children from harm. This approach is illustrated by the decision of the Court of Appeal in *Re H* [1994] 1 FLR 519. The case concerned a transsexual who had care of his children. There had been considerable media interest and a judge granted an injunction from taking or permitting any act likely to expose the children to any form of publicity. The Court of Appeal considered this to be too wide. The order was varied to ensure that the father did not have dealings with the media from the property where he lived with the children or in the children's presence.

**14.70**  In a very different context the issue of freedom of expression was also a factor in the case of *Ahmed v UK* [2000] 29 EHRR 1 which concerned the political restrictions on certain categories of council officers. The Commission declared that the complaints of four council officers who were prohibited from taking part in political activities because of the terms of their employment were admissible. They all held politically restricted posts. One was a solicitor who wanted to stand as a candidate for membership of a local authority, but was unable to do so. Two were senior planning officers who had been obliged to resign from positions which they held in their local Labour parties. The last was the Head of Committee Services for a local authority who had been active in local politics and a frequent speaker at public meetings but who had been obliged to cease these activities when his job became politically restricted.

**14.71**  By a majority the European Court of Human Rights rejected the argument that these restrictions were contrary to Article 10. It held that they were prescribed by law, were in pursuit of a legitimate aim, and that they were necessary in a democratic society. The argument that they were not prescribed by law was based on the fact that the interpretation and implementation of the regulations was entrusted to individual local authority employers, a process which was likely to promote inconsistencies. This argument was rejected by the Court which said there was no evidence to this effect. As regards the legitimacy of the aim, the Government argued that the purpose of the restrictions was the protection of democracy, which had been recognised as legitimate by the court in *Vogt v Germany* (1996) 21 EHRR 205. The applicants argued that this purpose would only be invoked in circumstances where there was a threat to the stability of the constitutional or political order. The court said that this interpretation would overlook the interests served by democratic bodies such as local authorities and the need to secure their proper functioning.

The main arguments concerned freedom of expression. The court took the view that the **14.72** Widdicombe Committee, which had recommended political restrictions, had identified a pressing social need. There were specific instances of abuses by council officers. It emphasised that the organisation of local democracy can vary from state to state according to national traditions. In the UK the system was historically based on having a permanent corps of politically neutral senior officers who were above factional politics and answerable to the council as a whole. The court also considered that the regulations had been made in such a way as to impair the applicants' rights as little as possible. The restrictions had been focused and a substantial proportion of officers had the opportunity to apply for an exemption. The court did not consider the restrictions to be a disproportionate interference with the applicants' rights.

Where disciplinary sanctions are imposed on councillors because of what they say, Article 10 **14.73** needs to be considered: *Sanders v Kingston* 2005 *The Times* 26 June. The case concerned the leader of Peterborough Council who, during the course of an interview, was reported to have said that the people of Northern Ireland should apologise for killing soldiers and hang their heads in shame for involving the English in their quarrel. Following an investigation by an ethical standards officer, the matter was referred to a case tribunal who found that he had brought the Council into disrepute and disqualified him from being a councillor. On appeal to the High Court it was argued that the penalty was a breach of Mr Sanders' freedom of expression. It was held that Article 10 was engaged and the tribunal were wrong not to have considered it at all. Disqualification was a disproportionate sanction. The court substituted a period of suspension of one year from acting as leader of the council.

## H  DISCRIMINATION

Article 14 prohibits discrimination on any ground. In *Chapman v UK* (2001) 33 ECHR 18 the **14.74** applicants had claimed breaches of both Article 8 and Article 14, in the refusal by the local planning authority to allow her to build a bungalow on a green field site. The European Court of Human Rights held, by a majority, that there was no breach on the facts of this case. The interference with the rights of the applicant and her family had to be weighed against the damage to the environment. The decision was not disproportionate.

The need for care not to discriminate on the grounds of lifestyle is illustrated by the case of **14.75** *Clarke v Secretary of State for the Environment, Transport and the Regions* [2002] EWCA Civ 819. The applicant was a romany gypsy whose application to station his caravan on land which he owned had been refused. The inspector hearing the appeal had taken into account the fact that the applicant had received an offer of alternative modern accommodation which he said was unsuitable for his and his family's lifestyle. The inspector's decision was quashed on the ground that it could be a breach of Articles 8 and 14 to force someone to take accommodation which was unsuitable for their lifestyle. The inspector should have stated whether he had taken this into account. It also needs to be remembered that the categories of grounds for discrimination in Article 14 is not closed. It will include physical and mental incapacity: *R (Pretty) v DPP* [2002] 1 AC 800.

---

## I PROTECTION OF PROPERTY

**14.76** In *Stretch v UK* 4277/98 (2004) the European Court of Human Rights held that the operation of the *ultra vires* rule in a way that deprived a person of a property right was a breach of Article 1 Protocol 1. In this case Mr Stretch had taken a building lease from Dorchester Council for 22 years with an option to renew for a further 21 years. It was argued on behalf of the successor authority West Dorset District Council that there was at the time the original lease was granted no power to grant an option. This argument succeeded in the High Court and Court of Appeal. Leave to appeal to the House of Lords was refused. An application was made to the European Court of Human Rights who held that possessions included legitimate expectations that a person will enjoy a property right. The interference caused by the operation of the *ultra vires* doctrine, which deprived Mr Stretch of his property right altogether, was disproportionate. The case is an example of the wide meaning that the courts will give to property rights and the need of local authorities to be aware of this.

---

## J EDUCATION

**14.77** Article 2 of the First Protocol provides that:

> No person shall be denied the right to education. In the exercise of any functions which it assumes in relation to education and to teaching, the State shall respect the right of parents to ensure such education and teaching in conformity with their own religious and philosophical convictions.

**14.78** The nature of the right to education was explored in the *Belgian Linguistics case (No.2)* (1979–1980) 1 EHRR 252. The case concerned the policies of the Belgian government to require schools to teach in a particular language depending on the area in which they were situated. The court held that such a policy did not infringe the right to education. In the course of its judgment the court clarified the nature and scope of this right:

(a) Although the article was formulated in the negative, it did enshrine a 'right'.

(b) The negative formulation indicated that the Contracting Parties did not recognise such a right to education as would have required them to establish at their own expense, or to subsidise, education of any particular type or at any particular level.

(c) All member states of the Council of Europe had a general and official educational system, so there was no requirement on a state to establish such a system.

(d) The right to education necessarily implied the right to be educated in the national language or one of the national languages.

(e) The first sentence of Article 2 guaranteed the right of access to educational institutions existing at any given time. It was also necessary for the recipient of the education to have official recognition of the studies he had completed.

(f)   The Convention implied a just balance between the protection of the general interest of the community and the respect due to fundamental human rights, while attaching particular importance to the latter.

The meaning of the expression 'religious and philosophical convictions' was considered by **14.79** the European Court of Human Rights in *Campbell & Cosans v UK* (1982) 4 EHRR 293. That case concerned parental objections to the use of corporal punishment in schools. The Court held that the obligation to respect religious and philosophical convictions did not extend just to educational instruction. It included the organisation and financing of public education, the supervision of the educational system, and questions of discipline. The expression 'philosophical convictions' meant such convictions as were worthy of respect in a democratic society and not incompatible with human dignity. The obligation to respect parental convictions was a duty. It could not be overridden by saying that a balance needed to be struck with conflicting views.

The issue of the right to education was considered by the Court of Appeal in *R (Holub) v* **14.80** *Secretary of State for the Home Department* [2001] 1 WLR 1359. The case concerned a family who sought judicial review of a decision to refuse exceptional leave to remain in the UK on the grounds that this would disrupt their daughter Luiza's education, contrary to Article 2 of the First Protocol. The application was refused by the judge and the parents appealed. The Court of Appeal accepted as an accurate statement of the law the following passages from Lester and Pannick, Human Rights Law and Practice (1999) paragraphs 19.45 and 19.46:

> The general right to education comprises four separate rights (none of which is absolute): (i) a right of access to such educational establishments as exist; (ii) a right to an effective (but not the most effective possible) education; (iii) a right to official recognition of academic qualifications . . . As regards the right to an effective education, for the right to education to be meaningful the quality of the education must reach a minimum standard.

The court concluded that there would be no breach of Luiza's Article 2 rights to return her to **14.81** her native country Poland. The Convention did not give the right to education in a particular country, Poland had a well developed education system, and there was no reason to conclude that Luiza would be denied an effective education there.

Similarly there is no denial of an effective education in removing a disruptive pupil to **14.82** another room if he is in fact provided with an education. The educational needs of the other children also need to be taken into account: *P v National Association of Schoolmasters/Union of Women Teachers* [2001] IRLR 532.

The issue of parental convictions has also received attention from the UK courts. Due weight **14.83** needed to be given to religious convictions that a child should be educated in a single sex school. In this case, the form which allowed parents to list their preferences did not provide for parents to give reasons for their decision. In these circumstances there needed to be a means of ascertaining the parents' convictions and these should be taken into account. The decision to refuse the applicant's daughter admission to a single sex school was quashed: *R (K) v Newham London Borough Council* [2002] EWHC Admin 405.

In the case of *R (Williamson) v Secretary of State for Education and Employment* [2003] 1 All **14.84** ER 385 it was argued that (in contrast to the *Campbell & Cosans* case) belief in corporal punishment was a 'religious and philosophical conviction' and that refusing to allow private schools to practise it (which was the effect of s. 548(1) of the Education Act 1996) was a breach of Article 2 of Protocol 1. The parents asserted that the use of mild corporate punishment formed part of their fundamental Christian beliefs. Their claim was dismissed at first instance on the ground that their belief in corporal punishment was a belief in the efficacy of corporal punishment rather than an 'article of faith'. The Court of Appeal held that the belief that corporal punishment was an integral part of the education of children was both a belief under Article 9 and a religious conviction under Article 2 of Protocol 1. It did not have to constitute an 'article of faith' as there was no distinction between articles of faith and other religious convictions. However, since the punishment could be performed by the parents themselves, the prohibition did not constitute an interference with their religious beliefs or a failure to respect their rights.

## K　FREE ELECTIONS

14.85　Article 3 of the First Protocol provides that the Contracting Parties 'undertake to hold free elections at reasonable intervals by secret ballot, under conditions which will ensure the free expression of the people in the choice of legislature'. The legislature does not mean the national parliament. It depends on the constitutional arrangements of the state concerned: *Mathieu Molin and Clerfayt v Belgium* (1988) 10 EHRR 1. There are two aspects as to whether a body is or forms part of a legislature (*Clerfayt, Legros v Belgium* 42 DR 212):

(a)　whether the body has an independent (or inherent) power to issue decrees with the force of law;

(b)　a consideration of the nature of the laws made by that body.

In this case the court rejected the notion that the power to make by-laws constituted legislative power. A similar approach was adopted by the European Court of Human Rights whenever the Convention was invoked to protect local authorities from changes or interference by the government.

14.86　Thus a challenge to the abolition of the Greater London Council failed: *Edwards v UK* (1986) 8 EHRR 96. The Commission looked at the UK's constitutional arrangements and concluded that they did not provide for subordinate bodies such as the GLC to exercise legislative powers. The GLC had been created by statute and its powers, although considerable, themselves derived from statute. The GLC did not have any primary rule-making power. It was subject to the ultimate control of Parliament and Parliament could therefore vote for its abolition. For similar reasons arguments that metropolitan councils were immune from abolition because of Article 3 Protocol 1 were rejected by the Commission: *Booth-Clibborn v UK* (1985) 43 DR 236.

## L　COMPENSATION

14.87　The Court of Appeal in *Anufrijeva v Southwark London Borough Council* considered both the circumstances in which compensation should be awarded and the principles governing the amount of compensation. This issue had previously been considered by Stanley Burnton J in *R (KB) v South London and South West Region Mental Health Tribunal* [2003] 3 WLR 185, a claim by mental patients whose rights to liberty (Article 5) had been infringed by delay in processing their claims before mental health tribunals. The following principles will apply:

1. Where there is no pecuniary loss involved, a breach of a Convention right will not automatically lead to an award of compensation. It is necessary to consider whether the other remedies are sufficient vindication.
2. Courts dealing with claims for damages for maladministration need to adopt a broad brush approach. This is an issue which can generally be decided by looking at the correspondence and witness statements.
3. The complainant's own responsibility for what happened should be taken into account.
4. The court should bear in mind the principles laid down by the Human Rights Act. The remedy has to be 'just and appropriate' and 'necessary' to afford 'just satisfaction'. The approach is equitable.
5. The scale and manner of the violation can be taken into account. (In *Aksoy v Turkey* (1996) 23 EHRR 553 damages were awarded to the father of the applicant who had been tortured in detention and since died.)
6. The manner or way in which the violation took place may be sufficiently serious to justify an award of compensation. (In *Halford v UK* (1997) 24 EHRR 523 non-pecuniary damages were awarded for unlawful telephone surveillance partly because of the improper purpose for which the police intended to use the recorded material.)

When assessing compensation, courts should take into account the guidelines issued by the Judicial Studies Board, awards of the Criminal Injuries Compensation Board and awards for maladministration made by the Parliamentary Ombudsman and the Local Government Ombudsman.

# 15

# PROVISION OF INFORMATION AND PUBLICITY

## A INTRODUCTION

There are various powers for local authorities to publicise their activities. In addition, there **15.01** are some duties compelling them to make certain information available to the public. There are restrictions on what local authorities can do by way of information and publicity. The statutory restrictions were imposed as a result of high-profile 'political' campaigning by some authorities during the 1980s, and in particular that of the Inner London Education Authority against education cuts.

---

## B   POWER TO MAKE INFORMATION AVAILABLE

**15.02**   Under s. 142 of the LGA 1972, local authorities have wide powers to provide information about and publicity for their activities, as well as the activities of other local authorities, government departments and voluntary organisations. Section 142 (1) is in the following terms:

> A local authority may make, or assist in the making of arrangements whereby the public may on application readily obtain, either at premises specially maintained for the purpose or otherwise, information concerning the services available within the area of the authority provided either by the authority or by other authorities mentioned in subsection (1B) below or by government departments or by charities and other voluntary organisations, and other information relating to the functions of the authority.

The 'authorities mentioned in subsection (1B)' are all other local authorities, boards or committees that carry out functions that would otherwise fall to be undertaken by two or more authorities. The power is therefore not lost as a result of setting up joint arrangements for the discharge of functions, or even by delegation of functions to an outside body where this is permitted.

**15.03**   Section 142(2) provides local authorities with further powers to undertake the following:

(a)   arrange for the publication within their area of information relating to the functions of the authority; and

(b)   arrange for the delivery of lectures and addresses and the holding of discussions on such matters; and

(c)   arrange for the display of pictures, cinematograph films or models or the holding of exhibitions relating to such matters; and

(d)   prepare, or join in or contribute to the cost of the preparation of, pictures, films, models or exhibitions to be displayed or held as aforesaid.

**15.04**   Lastly, local authorities may assist voluntary organisations, meaning non-public but non-profit making bodies, to provide for individuals (s. 142(2A) LGA 1972):

(a)   information and advice concerning those individuals' rights and obligations; and

(b)   assistance, either by the making or receiving of communications or by providing representation to or before any person or body, in asserting those rights or fulfilling those obligations.

This power cannot be used for the purposes of political campaigning in the sense of trying to persuade the public of the correctness of the local authority's point of view: *R v Inner London Education Authority, ex parte Westminster City Council* [1986] 1 WLR 28 (see also chapter 13). However, Glidewell J did say in that case that explanations as to the effect of legislation could come within the definition of 'information' in this section. There is Scottish authority to the effect that slogans alone, even when accompanying a local authority's logo, could not constitute 'information' for these purposes: *Stated Case by the Commission for Local Authority Accounts in Scotland relating to the City of Edinburgh District Council* [1988] *The Times*, 18 April.

---

## C  DUTIES TO PROVIDE INFORMATION

**15.05** Local authorities are also under a duty to provide information about certain matters, under ss. 2–4 of the Local Government, Planning and Land Act 1980. There is also power to make codes. These are advisory, but regulations can be made to compel observance of them. The only regulations that have been made have since been revoked. The codes concern the preparation of an annual report and financial information and information to be provided with planning applications. Local authorities are generally good at preparing and providing annual reports, some of which are quite impressive publications. The Annual Report Code contains recommendations about what the report and financial statement should contain. It recommends that there should always be details of revenue and capital expenditure. There should be comments on changing patterns of expenditure. General statistics for major services should be included, showing the scale of service provision, client group and numbers if applicable, usage of the service and measures of cost. There should also be key service indicators that can be used to measure performance.

**15.06** In addition, all principal councils (essentially counties, districts, unitary authorities and London boroughs) must keep a register containing the following information (s. 100G LGA 1972):

(a)  the name and address of every member of the council and the wards they represent;
(b)  the members of each committee and sub-committee, including the names, addresses and functions of non-councillor members who are entitled to speak;
(c)  the powers delegated to officers, identified by the job title of the officer concerned.

The authority must also keep available for public inspection a summary of the rights to attend committee meetings and rights to documents conferred by Parts VA and XI of the LGA 1972.

---

## D  RESTRICTIONS ON LOCAL AUTHORITY PUBLICITY

**15.07** Restrictions were introduced by the LGA 1986. This legislation derived from a recommendation of the Widdicombe Committee that there should be a ban on local authorities producing publicity material of an expressly party political nature. There is no doubt also that the Government was unhappy about the campaigns against cuts in local government expenditure and other Government policies during the early part of the 1980s. Section 1(1) of the LGA 1986 provides that:

(1)  A local authority shall not publish any material which, in whole or in part, appears to be designed to affect public support for a political party.

**15.08**  Section 1(2) gives further guidance on when material should be regarded as falling foul of this restriction:

(2)  In determining whether material falls within the prohibition regard shall be had to the content and style of the material, the time and other circumstances of publication and the likely effect on those to whom it is directed and, in particular, to the following matters—

    (i)  whether the material refers to a political party or to persons identified with a political party or promotes or opposes a point of view on a question of political controversy which is identifiable as the view of one political party and not another;

    (ii)  where the material is part of a campaign, the effect which the campaign appears to be designed to achieve.

A local authority is not allowed to give money or financial assistance to another organisation or person to publish material that it could not lawfully publish itself.

**15.09**  The Secretary of State has power to make one or more codes of recommended practice as to local authority publicity and related matters. These codes are not mandatory, but local authorities must have regard to the contents of any code before making any decision about publicity. Before exercising these powers the Secretary of State must consult local authority associations and any local authority that it appears desirable to consult. This will presumably apply if the Secretary of State has it in mind to include something in a code that is directed at the activities of one particular local authority. Any code made under these provisions and any revisions of any such code must be laid for approval before both Houses of Parliament.

**15.10**  The current Code of Practice is set out in Department of the Environment Circular 20/88 Welsh Office Circular 16/88, as amended by DETR Circular 06/2001. Generally it advises that publicity should be as objective as possible. If commenting on proposals from the Government it should be 'objective, balanced, informative and accurate' rather than 'prejudiced, unreasoning and political'. Public funds should not be used, the Code warns, to 'mount publicity campaigns whose primary purpose is to persuade the public to hold a particular view on a question of policy'. It also warns that particular care should be taken when publicity is issued immediately before an election or by-election. Local authorities have to keep separate accounts of their expenditure on publicity.

**15.11**  There is no doubt that the LGA 1986 has had an important inhibitory effect. Publicity material distributed by local authorities now tends to concentrate on the business of the local authority and its area rather than on wider political issues, though this may represent a political change as well as the effect of the legislation. What will fall foul of s. 1 of the Act is very largely a matter of impression. It is sensible for all local authorities to invite a lawyer to scrutinise any material that may contain anything that could be regarded as politically controversial. Balance is also important. If a publication contains the names and photographs of and quotations from councillors of the majority group, it is often sensible to include similar details of representatives of the minority party or parties.

## E  FREEDOM OF INFORMATION

The Freedom of Information Act 2000 (FOIA 2000) came into force on 1 January 2005. It **15.12** provides to the public at large a general right to information held by public authorities. It applies to all local authorities. The Act first provides the general right of access to information, and the procedural requirements surrounding requests for information. Then Part II of the Act sets out the categories of information which are exempt from disclosure.

### Scope

Under Schedule I Part II, the Act applies to all local authorities in England and Wales includ- **15.13** ing parish councils, the GLA, the Corporation of London, and the Scilly Isles. It applies to bodies which are wholly owned by local authorities. Under s. 6(2)(b) a company is wholly owned by a local authority if it has no members except:

(i)   that public authority or companies wholly owned by that public authority, or

(ii)  persons acting on behalf of that public authority or of companies wholly owned by that public authority.

Therefore an arm's length management organisation set up to manage an authority's housing stock, of which the authority was the sole shareholder or guarantor, would fall within the requirements of the Act. A company in which an authority held only a part interest would not.

For this purpose 'company' means any corporate body: s. 6(3). There is power for the **15.14** Secretary of State to designate a person (which will normally mean an organisation) who:

(a)  appears to the Secretary of State to exercise functions of a public nature, or

(b)  is providing under a contract made with a public authority any service the provision of which is a function of that authority.

### The right to information

Under s. 1 of the Act, any person making a request for information to a public authority is **15.15** entitled:

(a)  to be informed in writing by the public authority whether it holds information of the description specified in the request, and

(b)  if that is the case, to have that information communicated to him.

The right belongs to 'any person'. It is not necessary to establish any kind of interest or standing. The motive of the person making the request is also irrelevant (except in the case of vexatious requests). An authority is not entitled to enquire into the motives of a person making a request. It may be in order to find out about a commercial competitor. It may be simply to make mischief. It makes no difference to the requirement to respond to the request.

There are, strictly speaking, two separate rights contained within s. 1: a right to know **15.16** whether the authority possesses the information and a right to have the information communicated. In practice, only the second right is important. There is power to require a fee to be paid. If the authority has sent the applicant a notice requiring him to pay a fee, then there is no requirement to provide the information unless the fee is paid within three months of the date of the notice. The fee is fixed by regulations.

**15.17**  The authority must comply with a request for information promptly and in any event not later than the twentieth working day following the date of receipt of the request: s. 10(1). If the authority has given a notice to the applicant requiring payment of a fee, the period from the date of that notice until the date of receipt of the fee is ignored in calculating the twenty working days. If an authority has required further information from the applicant in order to identify and locate the requested information and has informed the applicant of this requirement, then the obligation to comply with s. 1(1) does not take effect until the applicant has supplied this further information:

**15.18**  Section 11 sets out the means by which the information is to be communicated to the applicant by the authority. The applicant may request that the information be communicated by one of the following means, namely:

(a)  the provision of a copy of the information in permanent form or in another form acceptable to the applicant;

(b)  the provision of a reasonable opportunity to inspect a record containing the information;

(c)  the provision of a digest or summary of the information in a permanent form or in another form acceptable to the applicant.

The authority has a duty to give effect to the applicant's preference, so far as reasonably practicable. In deciding whether a particular means of communication is reasonably practicable, an authority may have regard to all the circumstances, including the cost. If an authority does decide that a particular means of communication is not reasonably practicable, then it must notify the applicant of the reasons for this. Subject to the above requirement, an authority may comply with a request for information by communicating it by any means which are reasonable in the circumstances.

**15.19**  There are exemptions if the information would be disproportionately expensive (which for these purposes means the same thing as time-consuming) to provide and for vexatious and repeated requests. Under s. 12 an authority is not obliged to comply with a request for information if it estimates that the cost of complying with the request would exceed the appropriate limit. The appropriate limit is prescribed by regulations. It is currently £450 for local authorities. (For central government it is £600.) This is intended to equate to about two and a half days of officer time. Even if the cost of providing the information would exceed the appropriate limit, the authority is still obliged to notify the applicant whether it has the information except in the very unlikely event that the cost of answering this question would in itself exceed the appropriate limit. Where the cost of providing the information exceeds the appropriate limit and disclosure is not otherwise required by law, the authority may charge a fee for its disclosure, subject to a maximum prescribed by the Secretary of State.

**15.20**  An authority is not obliged to comply with a vexatious request for information. If a person has previously made a request for information, the authority is not obliged to comply with a request for the same information from the same person unless a reasonable interval has elapsed between the two requests.

There is a general duty on authorities to help applicants and would-be applicants for infor- **15.21** mation. Under s. 16(1) it is the duty of a public authority 'to provide advice and assistance, so far as it would be reasonable to expect the authority to do so, to persons who propose to make, or have made, requests for information to it'. An authority which has complied with the code of practice made by the Secretary of State is to be taken to have complied with the above duty.

Authorities are also under a duty to adopt and maintain publication schemes. Under s. 19(1) **15.22** it is the duty of every public authority:

(a) to adopt and maintain a scheme which relates to the publication of information by the authority and is approved by the Information Commissioner;
(b) to publish information in accordance with its publication scheme; and
(c) from time to time review its publication scheme.

Section 19(2) sets out the requirements of a publication scheme. It must:

(a) specify classes of information which the public authority publishes or intends to publish;
(b) specify the manner in which information of each class is, or is intended to be, published; and
(c) specify whether the material is, or is intended to be, available to the public free of charge or on payment.

The Commissioner has power to approve model schemes.

## Exemptions

Part II of the Act sets out the grounds on which an authority can claim exemption from **15.23** disclosure. The fact that information falls within one of the exemptions does not mean that an authority cannot disclose it. Subject to any right of action to which the authority may expose itself by such disclosure, it is a matter for the authority to decide whether it gives out the information or not. A number of exceptions are absolute. In these cases, if the exemption applies, the authority is not obliged to disclose the information. The remaining exemptions require the application of a further test: whether, in all the circumstances of the case, the public interest in maintaining the exemption outweighs the public interest in disclosure.

Many of the exemptions set out in Part II have no application to local authorities, being **15.24** concerned with national security, Parliamentary privilege etc. The following is a list of the exemptions on which a local authority may wish to rely, and whether they are absolute exemptions. The exemptions are explained in more detail below:

• Information accessible to the applicant by other means (s. 21)—Absolute
• Information intended for future publication (s. 22)
• Information about investigations and proceedings by public authorities (s. 30)
• Information relating to law enforcement (s. 31)
• Court records (s. 32)—Absolute

- Information held by auditors relating to audit functions (s. 33)
- Information the disclosure of which would prejudice the effective conduct of public affairs (s. 36)
- Environmental information covered by regulations (s. 39)—see further below
- Personal information (s. 40)—Partly absolute—see further below
- Information provided in confidence (s. 41)—Absolute
- Information covered by legal professional privilege (s. 42)
- Trade secrets (s. 43)
- Information which the authority is prohibited from disclosing (s. 44)—Absolute.

**15.25**   Where an authority is refusing a request for information because of one of the exemptions it must give the applicant a notice which:

(a)   states that fact,
(b)   specifies the exemption in question, and
(c)   states (if it would not otherwise be apparent) why the exemption applies.

**15.26**   If the authority is relying on an exemption which is not absolute and is claiming that the public interest in maintaining the exemption outweighs the interest in disclosure then it can either:

(a)   state that no decision about the application of the exemption has been reached and give an estimate as to when the decision will be made, or
(b)   provide a notice stating that in all the circumstances of the case, the public interest in maintaining the exemption outweighs the public interest in disclosing the information.

An authority is not obliged to make a statement of the type referred to at (b) above if, or to the extent that, the statement would involve the disclosure of information which would itself be exempt information. (It is difficult to see how this is likely to be relevant for local authorities.)

**15.27**   If the authority is refusing the request because the cost is above the appropriate limit it must, within the twenty working day time limit, send the applicant a notice stating this fact. The authority must also, within the same time limit, send such a notice to the applicant if it is refusing the request because it is vexatious or because it has provided the same information before. There is an exception to this if:

(a)   the authority has given a notice to this effect to the applicant in relation to a previous request, and
(b)   it would be unreasonable in all the circumstances to expect the authority to serve another notice.

Any notice of refusal must:

(a)   contain particulars of the authority's complaints procedure in respect of disclosure of information or state that the authority does not have such a policy, and
(b)   give details of the right to apply to the Commissioner for a decision as to whether the request has been dealt with in accordance with the statutory requirements (see further below).

## Absolute exemptions

### Information accessible to the applicant by other means

If information is reasonably accessible by means other than applying for it under the FOIA **15.28**
2000 then the authority have an absolute right not to disclose it. Thus if information is
already in the public domain, if it has been published or is available on the internet, or is
required to be disclosed under other legislation, then the FOIA 2000 cannot be used as a
means of obtaining it. Information can be regarded as reasonably accessible even if available only on payment. An authority cannot simply refuse a request under the FOIA 2000
on the basis that information would be provided on request anyway unless the provision of
the information is in accordance with the authority's publication scheme and any charge for
the information is specified in, or determined in accordance with the scheme.

## Court records

Information is exempt if it is held by an authority only by virtue of it being contained in: **15.29**

(a) any document filed with, or otherwise placed in the custody of a court, for the purposes
of legal proceedings (thus information in the pleadings, lists of documents etc themselves will be exempt, but the information which they contain will often be available in
other documents);
(b) any document served upon, or by, a public authority for the purposes of legal proceedings (this will include pleadings etc even if they have not been filed at court, though
it probably does not include correspondence about litigation);
(c) any document created by a court or the administrative staff of a court, for the purposes
of legal proceedings.

All three of the above categories must relate to a 'particular cause or matter'. Documents
created for the purposes of legal proceedings generally do not fall within this exemption.

There is also an exemption for tribunals and inquiries. In this context, though, an inquiry **15.30**
means any inquiry or hearing held under any provision contained in or made under any
enactment. Thus inquiries set up by the Secretary of State such as the Cleveland Inquiry
chaired by Elizabeth Butler-Sloss would benefit from this exemption. Inquiries set up by
authorities themselves, such as the inquiry into events following the death of Victoria
Climbié would not. For these purposes information is exempt if it is held only by virtue of
being contained in:

(a) any document placed in the custody of a person conducting an inquiry or arbitration,
for the purposes of that inquiry or arbitration;
(b) any document created by a person conducting an inquiry or arbitration, for the
purposes of that inquiry or arbitration.

## Information provided in confidence

Section 41 provides that information is exempt if: **15.31**

(a) it was obtained by the public authority from any other person (including another public
authority); and

(b)   the disclosure of the information to the public (other than under the Freedom of Information Act) would constitute a breach of confidence actionable by that or any other person.

There is no definition in the Act of the word 'actionable'. It has a range of possible meanings. On the face of it, this could mean no more than that there is an arguable case for such an action. However, in the debates in the House of Lords on the Second Reading Lord Falconer said that it meant that such an action would be successful. This also accords with the advice given in the Code of Practice. This means that it will be necessary for an authority to consider, when they are confronted with a request for information which they believe may be confidential, to consider whether such disclosure could give rise to a successful claim for breach of confidence.

15.32   Confidentiality may arise as a result of a contractual agreement that such information should remain confidential. The fact that information is expressed in an agreement to be confidential does not of itself render that information confidential. It must still have the necessary quality of confidence. In any event, authorities cannot simply contract out of the obligations in the FOIA. Under the Code of Practice authorities are advised that they should enter into confidentiality obligations in contracts only when there is good reason to do so. Where a local authority is considering agreeing in a contract that information is confidential, it needs to satisfy itself that there is a good reason for this. It would be ill-advised to agree that whole contracts are in themselves confidential.

15.33   In addition confidentiality may arise by implication. The circumstances in which this arises are set out in the speech of Lord Goff in *Attorney-General v Guardian Newspapers (No 2) Ltd* [1990] 1 AC 109:

(a)   the information must not be generally accessible or in the public domain and is not trivial or useless,

(b)   the information must have been imparted in circumstances which import a relation of confidence.

The third element referred to by Lord Goff, an unauthorised use of the information to the detriment of the confidant, may no longer exist, and if it does exist, it may be satisfied by the disclosure of that information to persons to whom the confidant did not want it disclosed.

15.34   In addition to the above principles, there is a further consideration to which authorities need to have regard when considering whether to disclose information, which is that in certain circumstances the interest of the confidant in maintaining the confidentiality of his information and the public interest in maintaining obligations of confidentiality may both be outweighed by the public interest in disclosure. There are a number of principles to which authorities will have to have regard when considering this. For the purposes of considering a request under the FOIA, though it is important to bear in mind that an authority may have to consider not only whether the information is protected by confidentiality, but also whether an action to protect it is likely to be defeated by a claim that the public interest in its disclosure outweighs the confidentiality obligations.

## Personal information

Under s. 40 of the FOIA 2000 there are exemptions for personal data as defined in the **15.35**
Data Protection Act 1998. The first exemption provides that information is exempt if it
constitutes personal data of which the applicant is the data subject. In this context 'personal
data' means data which relate to a living individual who can be identified—

(a) from the data, or
(b) from the data and other information which is in the possession of, or is likely to come
into the possession of, the data controller (i.e. the person processing the information).

and 'data subject' means an individual who is the subject of personal data. The reason for
this exemption is that the applicant would be entitled to this information under the Data
Protection Act. There is no purpose served by having overlapping rights.

Information is also exempt if it is personal data of which the applicant is not the subject and **15.36**
one of the following conditions is satisfied:

(a) disclosure would contravene one of the data protection principles (for the purposes of
the FOIA 2000 the usual exemption for manual data does not apply—see chapter 16),
(b) disclosure would be likely to cause damage or distress,
(c) the information is exempt under Part II of the Data Protection Act from the provisions
in that Act giving rights of access to personal data.

## Information which the authority is prohibited from disclosing

This exemption (s. 44) applies if the disclosure of the information by the public authority **15.37**
holding it:

(a) is prohibited by or under any enactment,
(b) is incompatible with any Community obligation (i.e. it would be a breach of EU law), or
(c) would constitute or be punishable as a contempt of court.

Various statutory provisions which would prevent disclosure of information are being
considered for repeal.

## Exemptions which require the application of the 'balancing test'

In the case of the following exemptions the authority must judge whether the public interest **15.38**
in maintaining the exemption outweighs the public interest in disclosing the information
before deciding whether to disclose it.

## Information intended for future publication

Information is exempt under s. 22 if: **15.39**

(a) the information is held by the public authority with a view to its publication, by the
authority or any other person, at some future date (whether determined or not),
(b) the information was already held with a view to such publication at the time when the
request for information was made, and

(c)  it is reasonable in all the circumstances that the information should be withheld from disclosure until the publication date.

## Information held for investigations and proceedings

**15.40**  Information is exempt under s. 30(1) if it has at any time been held by the authority for the purposes of:

(a)  any investigation which the public authority has a duty to conduct with a view to it being ascertained whether a person should be charged with an offence or whether a person who has been charged with an offence is guilty of it,

(b)  any investigation conducted by the authority which may lead to the institution of criminal proceedings which the authority has power to conduct, or

(c)  any criminal proceedings which the authority has power to conduct.

The above exemptions seem to be dependent on there being an actual investigation in progress or at least being planned. There is then a separate series of exemptions which do not depend on there being an actual investigation or criminal proceedings in progress or under consideration.

**15.41**  Under s. 30(2)(a) information is exempt if it was obtained or recorded by the authority for the purposes of its functions relating to:

(i)    investigations falling within (a) or (b) above,

(ii)   criminal proceedings which the authority has power to conduct,

(iii)  investigations (other than those falling within (a) or (b) above) which are conducted by the authority for any of the purposes specified in s. 31(2)—see below),

(iv)  civil proceedings which are brought by or on behalf of the authority and arise out of such investigations.

There are numerous powers and duties for local authorities to undertake criminal proceedings and investigations, under legislation regulating food hygiene, consumer protection, town and country planning, highways enforcement, protection of private tenants from harassment etc.

**15.42**  There are two other features worth noting about this exemption. One is that it is not limited in time. It does not matter how long ago the investigation took place or whether any proceedings were ever instituted. The other is that the exemption applies whether or not its disclosure would prejudice or affect in any way the outcome of the investigation or proceedings. (The authority does of course need to apply the 'balancing test' as this is not an absolute exemption.)

## Law enforcement

**15.43**  Under s. 31 information which falls outside the information exempted by s. 30 is exempt if its disclosure would, or would be likely to, prejudice:

(a)   the prevention or detection of crime,

(b)   the apprehension or prosecution of offenders,

(c)   the administration of justice,

(d)  the assessment or collection of any tax or of any imposition of a similar nature,

(e)  the operation of immigration controls (this may occasionally have relevance to local authorities),

(f)  the maintenance of security and good order in prisons and other places where people are lawfully detained (this is rarely likely to be of relevance to the local authorities),

(g)  the exercise by a public authority of its functions for any of the purposes specified in subsection (2)—see below,

(h)  any civil proceedings brought by or on behalf of a public authority arising out of an investigation conducted for any of the purposes specified in subsection (2) below or by virtue of any other statutory powers.

The purposes specified in s. 31(2) (referred to in s. 30(2)(a)(iii) and s. 31(1)(g) and (h)) are as follows:

(a)  ascertaining whether any person has failed to comply with the law,

(b)  ascertaining whether any person is responsible for any conduct which is improper,

(c)  ascertaining whether circumstances which would justify regulatory action in pursuance of any enactment exist or may arise,

(d)  ascertaining a person's fitness or competence in relation to the management of bodies corporate or in relation to any profession or other activity which he is, or seeks to become authorised to carry on,

(e)  ascertaining the cause of an accident,

(f)  protecting charities against misconduct or mismanagement (whether by trustees or other persons) in their administration,

(g)  protecting the property of charities from loss or misapplication,

(h)  recovering the property of charities,

(i)  securing the health, safety and welfare of persons at work, and

(j)  protecting persons other than persons at work against risk to health or safety arising out of or in connection with the actions of persons at work.

## Audit functions

This exemption only applies to public authorities which have functions relating to the **15.44** auditing of the accounts of other public authorities or examining the economy, efficiency and effectiveness with which other public authorities use their resources. It would therefore apply to the Audit Commission or the National Audit Office or the various Government inspectorates. It would not apply to internal auditors and departments having these functions within authorities. Nor would it apply to a private firm undertaking audit functions as the firm would not be a public authority.

## Information the disclosure of which would be prejudicial to the effective conduct of public affairs

This is intended to be a narrow exemption, and is only rarely going to available to local **15.45** authorities. However, it is relevant, first because authorities may have information which relates to Government business and because there could be circumstances in which an authority's own information is exempt on this ground.

Information is exempt if, in the reasonable opinion of a qualified person, its disclosure:

(a)  would, or would be likely to, prejudice the maintenance of the convention of the collective responsibility of Ministers of the Crown, or the work of the Executive Committee the Northern Ireland Assembly, or the executive committee of the National Assembly for Wales,

(b)  would, or would be likely to, inhibit the free and frank provision of advice, or the free and frank exchange of views for the purposes of deliberation, or

(c)  would otherwise prejudice, or would be likely otherwise to prejudice, the effective conduct of public affairs.

**15.46**  In the case of the Greater London Authority the qualified person is the Mayor of London. In the case of a functional body under the Greater London Authority Act (i.e. Transport for London, the Metropolitan Police Authority, and the London Development Agency) it is the chairman of that body. In the case of any other public authority (this includes all other local authorities) it is:

(a)  a Minister of the Crown,

(b)  the public authority if authorised for this purpose by a Minister of the Crown, or

(c)  any officer or employee of the public authority who is authorised for this purpose by a Minister of the Crown.

The relevant Minister for these purposes is the Lord Chancellor. For local authorities the monitoring officer has been designated as the qualified person. The opinion must be 'reasonable'. The Information Commissioner has advised that a decision will be reasonable if it falls within the range of decisions open to a rational decision-maker. This is very much a *Wednesbury* test. Unless a decision is absurd, outrageous, made in bad faith, or without regard to relevant considerations, it is likely to be considered reasonable.

## Environmental information

**15.47**  Under s. 74 of the Act the Secretary of State has power to make regulations relating to the disclosure of environmental information. The Environmental Information Regulations 2004 (SI No. 2004/3391) came into effect on 1 January 2005 at the same time as the Act itself. They give effect to the 'Aarhus Convention', the Convention on Access to Information, Public Participation in Decision-making and Access to Justice in Environmental Matters signed at Aarhus on 25 June 1998. They make provision for substantial public access to environmental information. Under s. 39 of the Act information is exempt if the public authority holding it—

(a)  is obliged by the Environmental Information Regulations to make the information available to the public in accordance with these regulations, or

(b)  would be so obliged but for any exemption contained in the regulations.

This is consistent with one of the main policies of the Act which is that if a type of information is available under another regime, then that regime should govern the terms of its disclosure.

## Legal professional privilege

Information is exempt under s. 42 of the Act if a claim to legal professional privilege could be **15.48** maintained in respect of it. There are two types of legal professional privilege: privilege which relates to litigation and privilege in respect of legal advice. Once litigation has commenced or is in contemplation privilege attaches to communications which relate to that litigation whether between the solicitor and his client, the solicitor and other parties, or the client and other parties: *Wheeler v Le Marchant* (1881) 17 Ch D 675.

Legal privilege also attaches to advice from a solicitor. This must be related to the perform- **15.49** ance of the legal adviser's professional duty, though it does not need to relate specifically to legal issues. Legal advice privilege only applies to communications between a solicitor and his client. It should not be assumed that every officer within a local authority is a client for this purpose. In order to count as a client for this purpose the officer needs to have been employed as the agent of the authority in order to obtain legal advice. Other employees will not count as clients for this purpose and advice given to them will not be exempt. For the purposes of this exemption it makes no difference whether the authority is represented in litigation by or whether the applicable advice is given by an in-house or external legal adviser.

## Trade secrets

Under s. 43 information is exempt if it constitutes a trade secret. This term is not defined **15.50** in the Act. However, case law (*Thomas Marshall (Exports) Ltd v Guinle* [1979] Ch 227) has established the following principles:

(a) the owner of the information must believe that the release of the information will be injurious to him or advantageous to his rivals or others;
(b) the owner must believe that the information is secret;
(c) the owner's belief in (a) and (b) above must be reasonable;
(d) the information must be judged in the context of the trade or industry concerned and in the context of a particular trade or industry information may be regarded as a trade secret even if it does not fulfil the requirements of (a) to (c) above.

---

## KEY DOCUMENTS

Code of Practice—Freedom of Information
Code of Recommended Practice on Local Authority Publicity
Environmental Information Regulations (SI No. 2004/3391)
Aarhus Convention—The Convention on Access to Information, Public Participation in
 Decision-making and Access to Justice in Environmental Matters, 25 June 1998

# 16

# DATA PROTECTION

## A INTRODUCTION

Local authorities keep large amounts of data. Their functions as tax collectors, dispensers of **16.01** benefits and landlords, their responsibilities for the environment, the roads, and as protectors of children and the vulnerable, mean that they will need to keep large amounts of information about individuals. This means that local authorities will need to be particularly concerned about the legal implications of processing data. The Data Protection Act 1998 (DPA) transposes into UK law the EU Directive 95/46 on the protection of individuals with regard to the processing of personal data and the movement of such data. Under Article 1 of the Directive the Member States must protect the rights of individuals to privacy with respect to the processing of personal data.

The DPA sets out the principles which those who keep personal data must observe when **16.02** processing it. The emphasis in this legislation is on safeguarding the rights of the individual. One of the difficulties local authorities face is that they have pressures in other directions. They are required to disclose information under the Freedom of Information Act and the provisions in the Local Government Act dealing with access to information. They are encouraged to share information with other agencies in order to assist in combating crime and anti-social behaviour. Complying with legislation to protect the privacy of the individual in terms of ensuring that disclosure of personal information is carried out only in accordance with strict rules is, in this context, challenging.

## B   DEFINITIONS

**16.03**   In order to understand the regime under the DPA, it is necessary to consider some of the main terms used in the Act and their definitions.

**16.04**   'Data' is defined as information which:

(a)   is being processed by means of equipment operating automatically in response to instructions given for that purpose,

(b)   is recorded with the intention that it should be processed by means of such equipment,

(c)   is recorded as part of a relevant filing system or with the intention that it should form part of a relevant filing system,

(d)   or does not fall within paragraph (a), (b), or (c) but forms part of an accessible record as defined by s. 68 i.e. a health record, an educational record, or accessible public record. (All these phrases are given more detailed definitions in the Act.)

**16.05**   A 'relevant filing system' must be structured and/or indexed. In the case of *Durant v Financial Services Authority* [2003] EWCA Civ 1746 it was defined as a system:

1.   in which the files forming part of it are structured or referenced in such a way as clearly to indicate at the outset of the search whether specific information capable of amounting to personal data of an individual requesting it under section 7 is held within the system and, if so, in which file or files it is held; and

2.   which has, as part of its own structure or referencing mechanism, a sufficiently sophisticated and detailed means of readily indicating whether and where in an individual file or files specific criteria or information about the applicant can be readily located.

It is clear from the above definition that the Act is not only concerned with information stored on computer. Information kept in manual records will also be covered by the Act. However, the information does need to be stored as part of a system in order for it to be covered by the Act.

**16.06**   One of the most important definitions in the Act is that of 'personal data'. This means data which relate to a living individual who can be identified—

(a)   from those data, or

(b)   from those data and other information which is in the possession of, or is likely to come into the possession of, the data controller,

and includes any expression of opinion about the individual and any indication of the intentions of the data controller or any other person in respect of the individual. The fact that a person can be identified from the data does not itself make it personal. It is the second part of the definition i.e. the expression of opinion and indication of the intentions which makes it so. A person who is the subject of personal data is known in the Act as the 'data subject'.

**16.07**   The word 'processing' has for the purposes of the Act, a very wide definition. It is not simply confined to passing on information. It means 'obtaining, recording or holding the information or data or carrying out any operation or set of operations on the information or data, including—

(a)   organisation, adaptation, or alteration of the information or data,

(b)   retrieval, consultation, or use of the information or data,

(c)   disclosure of the information or data by transmission, dissemination, or otherwise making available, or

(d)   alignment, combination, blocking, erasure, or destruction of the information or data.

The 'data controller' is the person who (either alone or jointly or in common with other persons) determines the purposes for which and the manner in which any personal data are, or are to be, processed. The 'data processor' means any person who processes the personal data on behalf of the data controller. So the data processor is the person or body who makes the decision about what happens to personal information. The data controller is the person who actually executes the decision by passing on the data (or processing it in some other way).   **16.08**

There is a category of personal data which receives a higher degree of protection under the Act, which is called 'sensitive personal data' (see below para 16.12). This consists of information as to:   **16.09**

(a)   the racial or ethnic origin of the data subject,

(b)   his political opinions,

(c)   his religious beliefs or other beliefs of a similar nature,

(d)   whether he is a member of a trade union,

(e)   his physical or mental health or condition,

(f)   his sexual life,

(g)   the commission or alleged commission by him of any offence, or

(h)   any proceedings for any offence committed or alleged to have been committed by him, the disposal of such proceedings, or the sentence of any court in such proceedings.

## C   THE DATA PROTECTION PRINCIPLES

Schedule 1 to the Act sets out the Data Protection Principles. These are the eight principles which govern the processing of personal data. They are as follows:   **16.10**

1.   Personal data shall be processed fairly and lawfully and, in particular, shall not be processed unless—

　　(a)   at least one of the conditions in Schedule 2 is met, and

　　(b)   in the case of sensitive personal data, at least one of the conditions in Schedule 3 is also met.

2.   Personal data shall be obtained only for one or more specified and lawful purposes, and shall not be further processed in any manner incompatible with that purpose or those purposes.

3.   Personal data shall be adequate, relevant and not excessive in relation to the purpose or purposes for which they are processed.

4.   Personal data shall be accurate and, where necessary, kept up to date.

5.   Personal data processed for any purpose or purposes shall not be kept for longer than is necessary for that purpose or those purposes.

6.  Personal data shall be processed in accordance with the rights of data subjects under the Act.
7.  Appropriate technical and organisational measures shall be taken against unauthorised or unlawful processing of personal data and against accidental loss or destruction of, or damage to, personal data.
8.  Personal data shall not be transferred to a country or territory outside the European Economic Area unless that country or territory ensures an adequate level of protection for the rights and freedoms of data subjects in relation to the processing of personal data.

**16.11**  Schedule 2 of the Act sets out the conditions, one of which needs to be satisfied for personal data to be processed lawfully. They can be summarised as follows:

1.  The data subject has consented to the processing.
2.  The processing is needed to perform a contract to which the data subject is a party or to take steps which have been requested by the data subject with a view to entering into a contract.
3.  It is needed to comply with a legal obligation to which the data controller is subject (but this does not include a contractual obligation).
4.  It is needed to protect the vital interests of the data subject. (Interpreted by the Commissioner as meaning matters of life or death—a strikingly restrictive interpretation.)
5.  It is necessary for the administration of justice, for exercising any function conferred on a person by or under any enactment, a government function or another function of a public nature exercised in the public interest by any person. (This is the condition under which much disclosure of information between local authorities will be justified. However, there are certain requirements in relation to this, including advising the data subject of any purposes which would not be obvious to him.)
6.  It is necessary for the purposes of the legitimate interests of the data controller or those to whom the data are disclosed, except where it is unwarranted because of the rights, freedoms, or legitimate interests of the data subject.

**16.12**  Schedule 3 sets out the circumstances in which the processing of sensitive personal data is allowed. This list provides an additional set of more stringent safeguards which apply in addition to the list set out in Schedule 2 and which apply only to sensitive personal data as described above. These can be summarised as follows:

1.  The data subject has given his explicit consent to the processing of the personal data.
2.  The processing is needed to perform or exercise a legal right or obligation of the data controller in connection with employment.
3.  The processing is needed to protect the vital interests of the data subject or another person. This must be a situation where the data subject must be unable to give consent or the data controller cannot reasonably be expected to obtain consent or, in the case of another person's vital interests, consent has been unreasonably withheld.
4.  The processing is carried out in the course of its legitimate activities by a non-profit making body which exists for political, philosophical, religious, or trade-union purposes. There are additional safeguards required.
5.  The information in the personal data has been made public by the data subject.

6. The processing is needed in connection with legal proceedings or prospective legal proceedings, to obtain legal advice, or for the purpose of establishing, exercising, or defending legal rights.
7. It is necessary for the administration of justice, for the exercise of statutory functions or government functions. (This is narrower than condition 5 in Schedule 2 as it does not include other functions exercised in the public interest.)
8. It is necessary for medical purposes and is carried out by a health professional or a person who owes an equivalent duty of confidentiality.
9. It relates to racial or ethnic origin and is needed for equal opportunities monitoring.

The Secretary of State has power to make orders adding to the above list.

In Schedule 1 Part II there is a set of requirements as to the way in which the data protection **16.13** principles are to be interpreted. Under paragraph 1, in deciding whether personal data are processed fairly, regard must be had to the method by which they were obtained and in particular whether anybody was misled about the purposes for which the data was to be used. Data are to be treated fairly if they are information received from a person who is authorised under an enactment to supply it or is required to supply it under an enactment or a convention or instrument imposing an international obligation on the UK.

Paragraph 2 which also relates to the first principle provides that data is not to be treated as **16.14** being processed fairly unless the data controller has ensured as far as practicable that the data subject has certain information made available to him:

(a) the identity of the data controller,
(b) if he has nominated a representative, the identity of that representative,
(c) the purpose or purposes for which the data are intended to be processed, or
(d) any further information which is necessary, having regard to the specific circumstances in which the data are or are to be processed, to enable processing in respect of the data subject to be fair.

The policy is therefore that the data subject knows who is passing on the information and why.

As regards the second principle (requirement for specified and lawful purposes), the purposes **16.15** can be specified in a notice given by the data controller to the data subject, or in a notice given to the Commissioner under Part III of the DPA. The fourth principle (requirement for accuracy) is not to be treated as contravened if:

(a) having regard to the purpose or purposes for which the data were obtained and further processed, the data controller has taken reasonable steps to ensure the accuracy of the data, and
(b) if the data subject has notified the data controller of the data subject's view that the data are inaccurate, the data indicate this fact.

Thus, complete accuracy is rightly regarded as unattainable. If a data controller has done his best and includes any corrections of alleged errors with the data, he will not be in breach of the principle.

The sixth principle (requirement to process in accordance with rights of data subjects) is only **16.16** to be regarded as breached when there is a breach of one of the following sections of the DPA:

(a)  s. 7 (requirement to supply information to data subject),

(b)  s. 10 (prevention of processing likely to cause damage or distress),

(c)  s. 11 (prevention of processing for purpose of direct marketing),

(d)  s. 12 (rights in relation to automated decision making).

**16.17**  The seventh principle (need to take appropriate measures against unlawful or unauthorised processing of data) requires the following:

(a)  a level of security appropriate to the harm that would result from disclosure and the nature of the data to be protected;

(b)  reasonable steps to ensure the reliability of employees who have access to the data;

(c)  if the processing is to be carried out by a data processor, sufficient guarantees are needed about security measures and the controller must take reasonable steps to ensure compliance with those measures;

(d)  if it is to be carried out by a data processor it must be undertaken under a written contract under which the data processor has to act on the data controller's instructions and which requires the data processor to comply with the obligations of the seventh principle.

---

## D   THE RIGHTS OF DATA SUBJECTS

**16.18**  There is a right for data subjects to find out what information is held about them. There is a right first to be informed about whether any personal data about him is being held, and if there is, to be given by the data controller a description of—

(a)  the personal data of which that individual is the data subject,

(b)  the purposes for which they are being or are to be processed, and

(c)  the recipients or classes of recipients to whom they are or may be disclosed.

**16.19**  The request needs to be made in writing and the appropriate fee (usually £10) must be paid. This can raise the difficult issue of whether this request can be complied with if it would involve disclosing information about another individual. The data controller is not obliged to comply with the request unless—

(a)  the other individual has consented to the disclosure of the information to the person making the request, or

(b)  it is reasonable in all the circumstances to comply with the request without the consent of the other individual.

**16.20**  In deciding whether it is reasonable to disclose without the other person's consent, account must be taken of the following:

(a)  any duty of confidentiality owed to the other individual,

(b)  any steps taken by the data controller with a view to seeking the consent of the other individual,

(c)  whether the other individual is capable of giving consent, and

(d)  any express refusal of consent by the other individual.

Under s. 10 of the DPA there is a right to request a data controller to stop or not to begin **16.21** processing data on the ground that it would cause substantial damage or substantial distress to him or another and that damage or distress is or would be unwarranted. The data controller must respond within 21 days, either saying he has complied or intends to comply with the request or giving his reasons for not doing so. The applicant has a right to apply to the court to stop a data processor from processing data for failing to comply with such a request.

Under s. 11(1) of the DPA individuals can stop their personal data being used for the **16.22** purposes of direct marketing:

> An individual is entitled at any time by notice in writing to a data controller to require the data controller at the end of such period as is reasonable in the circumstances to cease, or not to begin, processing for the purposes of direct marketing personal data in respect of which he is the data subject.

It was held in *R (Robertson) v Wakefield Metropolitan District Council* [2002] 2 WLR 889 that this provision applied to the electoral register. An elector can therefore claim his right to object by sending a notice in writing to the local authority.

## Compensation

There is also a power to obtain compensation under the DPA if an individual has suffered **16.23** damage by reason of any contravention by a data controller of any of the requirements of the Act. An individual who suffers distress by reason of a contravention is entitled to compensation if he has also suffered damage and the contravention relates to the processing of personal data for the special purposes i.e. the purposes of journalism or artistic or literary purposes. It is a defence for the data controller to prove that he took such care as in all the circumstances was reasonably required to comply with the requirement concerned. Under s. 14 there is power for a data subject who considers that any data about him is inaccurate to apply to a court for an order that the data controller should rectify, block, erase or destroy those data and any data which contains an expression of opinion based on the inaccurate data.

## Offences

There are various offences under the DPA. These include a data controller failing to notify **16.24** the Commissioner either of the fact that processing is taking place or of changes that have been made to that processing. The Commissioner also has power to serve an enforcement notice on a data controller who the Commissioner is satisfied has contravened or is contravening any of the Data Protection Principles. The notice can require the data controller to take or refrain from taking the steps specified in the time required by the notice and/or to restrain from processing either any personal data or personal data of the type specified in the notice. The recipient can apply to the Data Protection Tribunal to cancel or vary the notice. Failing to comply with a notice is a criminal offence.

## KEY DOCUMENTS

Data Protection Directive 95/46/EC
Data Protection Act 1998 Legal Guidance (Information Commissioner)
Compliance advice issued by the Information Commissioner:

- Council Tax: Secondary Use of Personal Information
- Electoral Register: Use in light of the Robertson case
- Local Authorities: Disclosures to Elected Members
- Local Authorities: Advice to Elected Members
- Local Authorities: Data sharing

(The above can be found on the Information Commissioner's website: <http://www. informationcommissioner. gov.uk>)

Public Sector Data Sharing Guidance on the Law—Department of Constitutional Affairs
  November 2003
Public Sector Data Sharing—A Guide to Data Sharing Protocols—Department of Constitutional Affairs November 2003

(The above can be found on the Department of Constitutional Affairs website: <http://www. dca.gov.uk>)

The Department's toolkit on data sharing is also useful: <http://www.dca.gov.uk/foi/ sharing/toolkit/index.htm>

# 17

# BEST VALUE

## A INTRODUCTION

One of the commitments of the incoming Labour government in 1997 was to abolish com-   **17.01**
pulsory competitive tendering and replace it with a duty requiring local authorities to
achieve best value in delivering their services. Compulsory competitive tendering ('CCT')
had been introduced by the Local Government Act 1988. This followed earlier legislation,
the Local Government, Planning and Land Act 1980, which introduced compulsory competition for building works. The 1988 Act required authorities to seek competitive tenders
for a variety of major services, including refuse collection, street cleaning, and ground maintenance. The legislation set out in detail the tendering process which authorities were
obliged to follow. The process of CCT was later extended to a variety of 'white collar' services
in 1993.

Under the CCT regime authorities were obliged to set up separate direct labour organisations   **17.02**
with separate trading accounts. It became clear what the costs of providing these services
were as the rules required a rigid separation of these accounts from those of other local
authority services. However, this did not necessarily mean that authorities entered

wholeheartedly into the spirit of competition. As the 1988 White Paper Modern Local Government—In Touch with the People expressed it:

> CCT made the costs of services more transparent. But its detailed prescription of the form and timing of competition led to unimaginative tendering, and often frustrated rather than enhanced real competition.

---

## B  THE BEST VALUE DUTY

### The nature of the best value duty

**17.03**  The basic requirements of the proposed best value regime were spelt out in the 1997 consultation paper 'Implementing Best Value—A consultation paper on draft guidance' and the 1998 White Paper referred to above. The key features of the new framework were described as follows:

(1)  The authority would have to establish authority-wide objectives and performance measures. There would be some national performance indicators imposed on local authorities.

(2)  There would be an agreed programme of fundamental performance reviews set out in a local performance plan.

(3)  The authority would carry out the performance reviews of selected areas of expenditure.

(4)  It would also set and publish performance and efficiency targets in its local performance plan.

(5)  There would be a process of independent audit/inspection and certification.

(6)  In the last resort there would be power for the Secretary of State to intervene.

**17.04**  These proposals were enacted in the Local Government Act 1999. They apply to all local authorities as well as various other public bodies such as police, fire, and waste authorities. The general duty of best value is set out in s. 3 of the Act in the following terms:

> A best value authority must make arrangements to secure continuous improvement in the way in which its functions are exercised, having regard to a combination of economy, efficiency and effectiveness.

**17.05**  There are a number of important points which arise from this. First, the duty is not expressed in absolute terms. It is a duty to 'make arrangements to secure continuous improvement'. The Government decided against imposing a duty to ensure that in carrying out its functions it actually had to achieve these in the most cost-effective way. In this the best value duty differs from the duty of an authority to achieve the best consideration reasonably obtainable when they dispose of land. The Government were apparently concerned that if there was an absolute duty anyone who thought that there was a more efficient way of providing a service could challenge the authority.

Second, though not expressed in absolute terms, the duty is, if taken literally, an onerous one. There is no scope for services to reach a satisfactory level and then remain at that level. An authority must strive for improvement, even if it does not always manage to achieve it. Third, the requirement for authorities to have regard to what are called the

'3Es' is not new. The phrase was used in the Local Government Finance Act 1982, as one of the issues which auditors needed to investigate. Under the Audit Commission Act 1998, auditors are required to ensure that any body whose accounts they are auditing has 'made proper arrangements for securing economy, efficiency and effectiveness in its use of resources'.

A local authority does not need to disregard its existing policies to ensure compliance with **17.06** the best value regime. However, best value is a factor to which it has to have regard when discharging its functions. In *R v Camden London Borough Council, ex parte Bodimeade* LTL 18/4/ 2001 a decision to close a residential home was quashed partly because of the extent to which the concept of best value was given precedence over other relevant factors which the Council should have considered. The report recommending closure was criticised, as the way in which the notion of 'best value' was allowed to predominate over other established considerations was 'inapposite and unlawful'. The obligation to carry out a best value review did not render nugatory the established policy of having a 'needs led' approach.

## Consultation requirements

Under s. 3(2) there is a duty to consult those who pay for or use local services. In deciding **17.07** how to fulfil its best value duty, an authority must consult:

(a) representatives of persons liable to pay any tax, precept or levy to or in respect of the authority,
(b) representatives of persons liable to pay non-domestic rates in respect of any area within which the authority carries out functions,
(c) representatives of persons who use or are likely to use services provided by the authority, and
(d) representatives of persons appearing to the authority to have an interest in any area within which the authority carries out functions.

This is a wide duty but it is worth noting that it extends only to representatives of these groups, not the groups themselves. The authority has a degree of discretion in deciding what constitutes a representative. This is defined in s. 3(3) which states that ' "representatives" in relation to a group of persons means persons who appear to the authority to be representative of that group'.

The Secretary of State has power to specify both 'performance indicators' and 'performance **17.08** standards': s. 4(1). The indicators are the factors against which an authority's performance can be measured. The standards specify the levels of achievement which best value authorities may be required to reach. There is a specific requirement on best value authorities in exercising their functions to meet any performance standards specified by the Secretary of State. There is an obligation on the Secretary of State to consult representatives of the best value authorities concerned and such other persons as he sees fit. The aim in specifying performance indicators and standards must be to 'promote improvement of the way in which the functions of best value authorities are exercised, having regard to a combination of economy, efficiency and effectiveness'. (The '3Es' are a recurring mantra of the legislation.) The Secretary of State must also take into account any representations made by the Audit Commission.

## C BEST VALUE REVIEWS

**17.09** The power to require authorities to carry out best value reviews is contained in the Local Government (Best Value) Performance Plans and Reviews Order 1999 (SI No. 1999/3251). This has been amended twice, by SI No. 2002/305 and SI No. 2003/662. There was originally a requirement for authorities to review all their functions over a five year cycle. However, this was revoked, in the light of experience, by SI No. 2002/305. There is still a requirement on local authorities to review their functions. However, the change allows authorities to decide what the priorities in terms of reviewing services should be. This enables them to focus on what really matters; this decision may be led by an authority's comprehensive performance assessment (CPA) or other factors.

**17.10** Two sets of guidance have been published on the best value duty which provide advice on how reviews should be carried out. There was the guidance following the original legislation: Local Government Act 1999: Part I Best Value DETR Circular 10/99 and further guidance following the changes made in the 2002 Order, Local Government Act 1999: Part I Best Value and Performance Improvement. This includes advice on how to ensure that the 4Cs (see para 17.17 below) are addressed in undertaking reviews. In the 1999 guidance considerable emphasis is placed on the importance of consultation. There have never been any statutory requirements set out in relation to consultation (although there is power to give statutory guidance on this under s. 3(4)). The guidance recommends that practical advice on consultation in different circumstances is best provided within the local government community itself. It also refers to advice available from Improvement and Development Agency (I&DeA) and the joint DETR/Democracy Network publication *Guidance on Enhancing Public Participation* (October 1998).

**17.11** There is also considerable emphasis in the 1999 guidance about competition. Although the Government was committed to abolishing CCT which they considered to have too rigid and mechanistic an approach to competition, it was also made clear that competition was an important factor in establishing whether an authority was obtaining best value. The 1999 guidance contained exhortations that authorities should approach competition positively with an awareness of the opportunities for innovation and partnership which were available from working with the private and voluntary sectors. It emphasised that the Government was committed to variety in the way services were delivered and plurality among service providers.

**17.12** This includes advice about researching options in developing supply markets. The advice is that, once the process has highlighted the need for certain improvements, authorities should have discussions with potential suppliers (from the private and voluntary sectors as well as the public sector) and see what benefits could be delivered by bringing new providers into the market. This, as a matter of practical advice, may overestimate the capacity of authorities to create new markets. It is though, an invitation to look at new ways in which authorities can work with the private and voluntary sectors in order to deliver quality services, often by means other than simply seeking competitive tenders for a package of work.

**17.13** The 1999 guidance recommends that authorities should explore:

- the service developments that are anticipated in response to best practice, legislation, or user views,

- the current market for the provision of the service(s),
- new combinations of service which the marketplace suggests could deliver best value,
- the alternative ways to procure the service(s).

It also suggests that the following ways of engaging with the markets should be considered:    **17.14**

- holding discussions with selected private and voluntary sector providers,
- sending a questionnaire to suppliers to ask how they could add value,
- discussing existing experience with other authorities who have contracted the service from an external provider,
- holding a contractors' briefing day to explain the objectives of the authority and to elicit their views.

There are in addition a number of steps which it is suggested authorities might consider    **17.15**
taking in order to encourage new suppliers to enter the market or enable existing suppliers to
become more competitive:

- basing requirements on outcomes to allow for and encourage innovative methods of provision (This depends on the type of service. There are many local authority services which are of a fairly mechanistic nature where it makes little difference whether requirements are based on outputs or inputs—the method of service delivery is likely to be the same.);
- grouping activities to reflect prospective market competencies (Again the scope for this might have been thought to be limited. However, many local authorities have now grouped together numerous disparate services, usually customer-focused, in order to encourage interest and investment from large providers.);
- packaging work appropriate to the market (This has always been a factor in exposing local government work to competition. Some fields of activity are usually associated with fairly large providers, such as the waste industry; others such as ground maintenance are more often associated with small and medium-sized firms.);
- being clear about intentions (This seems obvious. If a local authority intends to develop long-term relationships with suppliers, then it needs to say so.);
- developing an understanding of the potential sources of supply (The guidance recommends that early discussions with prospective suppliers can help in shaping the optimum size, composition, and length of contracts, whilst ensuring the fairness, openness, and transparency required by EC procurement rules. This may not be as straightforward as the guidance suggests. An authority engaging in discussions with suppliers needs to make it clear that this is an information-gathering exercise and not part of any tendering process.);
- being clear in advance whether there will be an in-house bid for the work (This appears to be a relic from the days of CCT. It is likely that authorities will be clear by the time they start engaging on any tendering exercise whether they want the service to be provided in-house or not.).

The wording of the order follows s. 5(4) of the Act. In relation to the functions specified in    **17.16**
the order the authority is required to—

(a)  consider whether it should be exercising the function (Some functions are duties of local authorities; others are simply powers. The fact that an activity has always been

undertaken by an authority is not a good reason for thinking that it should continue to
be. The authority needs to look at the activities it is undertaking where it has no duty
to do so and consider whether continuing to carry out these activities is a good use of
its resources.);

(b) consider the level at which and the way in which it should be exercising the function
(This is another reminder of the need to ask some far-reaching questions when carrying
out these reviews. Are there services being provided which are not needed, or are not
needed at the level they are currently being provided? Could they be better provided in
a different way? Would there be improvements in service, greater cost-effectiveness or
efficiency if they were provided by someone other than the authority?);

(c) consider its objectives in relation to the exercise of the function (In some ways the most
fundamental question of all: what is the authority trying to achieve by carrying out this
activity?);

(d) assess its performance by reference to any performance indicator specified by it or set by
the Secretary of State (Clearly, this is going to be an important part of any review. The
purpose of having performance indicators is to use them as a means of judging the
authority's performance.);

(e) assess the competitiveness of its performance by reference to the exercise of the
same function, or similar functions, by other best value authorities and commercial and
other businesses (This is an important point. It invites, not a simple comparison
between the authority's performance and that of other authorities in carrying out the
service, but also a comparison with businesses who are engaged in similar types of
activity.);

(f) consult other best value authorities and commercial and other businesses about the
exercise of the function (A continuing theme of this legislation is the importance
of consultation. This type of consultation may involve obtaining advice as well as
feedback and ideas for future service provision.);

(g) assess its success in meeting any performance standard which applies in relation to the
function (Again, this will always be important. There is obviously a need to judge
whether standards are being achieved.);

(h) assess its progress towards meeting any relevant performance standard which has been
specified but which does not yet apply (The Secretary of State may indicate that he is
intending to set a particular standard. While this is still in the transitional stage, i.e. it
has been introduced but does not yet apply, the authority should assess its progress
towards achieving it.);

(i) assess its progress towards meeting any relevant performance target (Guidance may
require authorities to set targets. If it does, then assessment of progress towards meeting
these will be important.).

**17.17** The requirements in carrying out a review are summarised in the guidance as follows.
Authorities should:

- challenge why, how and by whom a service is being provided;
- secure comparison with the performance of others across a range of relevant indicators,
  taking into account the views of both service users and potential suppliers;
- consult local taxpayers, service users, partners and the wider business community in the
  setting of new performance targets;

- use fair and open competition wherever practicable as a means of securing efficient and cost-effective services.

These are known as the 4Cs: challenge, compare, consult, and compete.

The difficulties of authorities in challenging why and how a service is provided were com-  **17.18**
mented on in Circular 03/2003. The problems in having a fundamental rethink about whether and how services should be provided were also referred to in the Audit Commission report on the introduction of best value *Changing Gear* and a study into the impact of best value from the University of Cardiff *The Impact of Best Value in English Local Government* September 2002. However, the advice about how authorities should face up to the process of challenge does not offer much in the way of practical suggestions about how this should be undertaken. There is advice that such a process should typically involve the following:

- elected members, especially executive members and senior managers throughout the review process;
- staff, particularly front-line staff, who have knowledge of the current service;
- service users, and when appropriate the wider community;
- 'third parties' who can bring an external perspective.

The requirement to consult trade unions, employee representatives, and staff has been given statutory effect by an amendment to Article 6 of SI No. 1999/3251. The process by which the authority should undertake this is a matter for the authority to decide.

The revised guidance also includes advice on how authorities should assess the competitive-  **17.19**
ness of their functions. It suggests that simply market testing services at regular intervals is not in itself an appropriate means of ensuring service improvement. Some of the criticism of the process of market testing such as the imposition of costs and the potential distortion of the market for service provision appear to be arguments against the notion that there should be a process of genuine competition. There are always costs associated with tendering. The difficulty is that without a process of competition it is difficult to assess whether comparative information about providing a service is borne out within the reality of the market. As far as potential distortion of the market is concerned, this may be dependent on the nature of the competitive exercise. A genuine competition will, provided there is a reasonable market for the provision of the services, not involve any distortion. However, an invitation to submit theoretical prices in the absence of a real competition, cannot be regarded as a test of the market. Those submitting information will judge their response according to what they think the recipient wants to hear, rather than what is likely to be a competitive bid.

The guidance also makes it clear that authorities should not simply think in terms of either  **17.20**
maintaining an in-house service or outsourcing it. It recommends that other options including partnerships with other public, private, and voluntary sector bodies should be considered. The process of competition also involves looking at how procurement is managed throughout the authority. The *Byatt Report* recommended that authorities should have a clear policy for procurement and recommended that procurement expertise should be a central feature of the best value process. The Circular advises that authorities should consider their procurement practices to ensure that maximum value was being obtained from them.

The guidance suggests that third parties (whether from the private or voluntary sectors or from other authorities) may be able to question and challenge the authority's approach and that they can bring their own perspective to bear on the design and scrutiny of services.

**17.21**   The guidance gives some suggested options for future service delivery. These are the type of ideas which authorities should be considering:

- the cessation of the service, in whole or in part;
- the creation of a public-private partnership, for instance, through a strategic contract or a joint venture company;
- the transfer or externalisation of the service to another provider (with no in-house bid);
- the market-testing of all or part of the service (i.e. the in-house provider bids in open competition against the private or voluntary sector);
- the restructuring or re-positioning of the in-house service;
- the re-negotiation of existing arrangements with current providers where this is permissible;
- the joint commissioning of delivery of the service.

---

## D   PERFORMANCE PLANS

**17.22**   Best value authorities are also required to prepare a best value performance plan for each financial year. The object of this exercise is to explain to local people what the authority's objectives are and set out its assessment as to how well it is doing in achieving them. The requirements as to what such plans must contain are set out in s. 6 of the Act.

**17.23**   The requirements as to the contents of a plan as set out in s. 6(2), are as follows:

(a)   to summarise the authority's objectives in relation to the exercise of its functions;

(b)   to summarise any assessment made by the authority of the level at which and the way in which it exercises its functions;

(c)   to state any period within which the authority is required to review its functions;

(d)   to state the timetable the authority proposes to follow in conducting a review;

(e)   to state any performance indicators, standards, and targets specified or set in relation to the authority's functions;

(f)   to summarise the authority's assessment of its performance in the previous financial year with regard to performance indicators;

(g)   to compare that performance with the authority's performance in previous financial years or with the performance of other best value authorities;

(h)   to summarise the authority's assessment of its performance in the previous financial years or with the performance of other best value authorities;

(i)   to summarise its assessment of its progress towards meeting any performance standard which has been specified but which does not yet apply;

(j)   to summarise its assessment of its progress towards meeting any performance target;

(k)   to summarise any plan of action to be taken in the financial year to which the plan relates for the purposes of meeting a performance target;

(l)  to summarise the basis on which any performance target was set, and any plan of action was determined, in relation to a function reviewed in the previous financial year.

Each best value authority must publish its plan by 30 June in the year before the financial year to which the plan relates.

The purpose of the plan is to provide local people and anyone else who may be interested **17.24** with a clear picture of the aims of the authority and how effective it is in achieving these. There is obviously going to be a huge amount of information which could potentially be made available as part of such a plan. The guidance emphasises the importance of summarising the relevant service plans, inspectors' reports, and details of reviews without overloading the plan with information. However, there needs to be a clear audit trail showing where such supporting information can be accessed.

Following the introduction of the process of comprehensive performance assessment (see **17.25** below), the Government has issued new requirements on what a performance plan must include. Requirements that the authority should summarise its assessment of the level and way in which it exercises its functions have been removed. There is no longer a need to include information which is available from other sources. The current requirements as to the contents of performance plans are set out in Annex E of Circular 03/2003. The relevant requirements are as follows:

(a)  A brief summary of the authority's strategic objectives and priorities for improvement. (The advice goes on to state that this should be drawn from the authority's overall vision, community strategy, its corporate planning processes, and the opportunities and weaknesses identified in its CPA where applicable.)

(b)  CPA scores, as presented in the Audit Commission's scorecard, where applicable.

(c)  Progress in, and future plans for, delivering local and national priorities including:
  - progress over the past 3 years in implementing improvement measures including those identified in best value reviews and audit and inspection recommendations;
  - outcomes from, or impact of, improvement measures implemented over the past 3 years;
  - plans for improvement over the current and subsequent 2 years, including best value review and inspection programmes for the current year and, if available, future years. Those authorities that are categorised overall as poor and those that are categorised as weak with a score of 1 in corporate capacity and are engaged in recovery planning should reflect key elements of their recovery planning arrangements in their Performance Plan.

(d)  Details of past, current and planned performance against local and national performance indicators, including:
  - actual performance over the past year on:
    - all best value performance indicators,
    - indicators used to measure progress against Local PSA targets where applicable, and
    - local indicators set by the authority to measure performance in priority areas;
  - details of the performance targets for the past year as set out in the last year's Performance Plan for all BVPIs and other indicators referred to above;

- targets for the current year and the subsequent 2 years, for all BVPIs, and local indicators set by the authority to measure performance in priority areas. These must have regard to nationally set standards and floor targets applying to the relevant year.

(e) A brief summary of financial information. This should record budgeted and actual (or estimated) income and expenditure for the past financial year, and provide a brief explanation of any significant variation. It should also include planned income and expenditure for the current year.

(f) A brief statement on contracts. Authorities should state and certify that all individual contracts awarded during the past year which involve a transfer of staff comply, where applicable, with the requirements in the Code of Practice on Workforce Matters in Local Authority Service Contracts. (This is set out in Annex D to Circular 03/2003.)

---

## E  AUDIT AND INSPECTION

**17.26**  There is in addition a requirement for each authority to have their performance plans audited by their auditor. This audit takes the form of an inspection to establish whether the plan was prepared and published in accordance with s. 6 and any order or guidance issued under that section. (The latest guidance is Circular 02/2003.) An auditor carrying out a best value inspection has the same rights to documents and information as an auditor carrying out a statutory audit of an authority's accounts. Once the inspection has been carried out, the auditor must issue a report:

(a) certifying that he has audited the plan,

(b) stating whether he believes that it was prepared and published in accordance with section 6 and any order or guidance under that section,

(c) if appropriate, recommending how the plan should be amended to accord with section 6 and any order or guidance under that section,

(d) if appropriate, recommending procedures to be followed by the authority in relation to the plan,

(e) recommending whether the Audit Commission should carry out a best value inspection of the authority under section 10 (This is a more formal and far-reaching type of inspection than a best value audit. See paragraph 17.29 below.),

(f) recommending whether the Secretary of State should give a direction under section 15 (This is the Secretary of State's power to intervene in the running of an authority. See paragraph 17.32 below.).

**17.27**  The auditor's report must be ready by 30 June of the financial year to which it relates. A copy must be sent to the authority and the Audit Commission. (The Commission may be the authority's auditor but need not be.) If the report recommends formal action by the Secretary of State then a copy must also be sent to the Secretary of State. The auditor must have regard to any code of practice issued by the Audit Commission. There is a duty on the Commission to prepare, and keep under review such a code prescribing the way in which auditors are to carry out their functions when carrying out an inspection.

**17.28**  Once an authority has received a report from its auditor following an inspection it must publish it. If the auditor makes a recommendation falling within (c) to (f) above, the authority must prepare a statement of

(a)  any action which it proposes to take as a result of the report, and
(b)  its proposed timetable.

The statement must be prepared within 30 days of the date on which the authority received the report. If the report specifies a shorter period, then the statement must be prepared within that shorter period. If the report recommended that the Secretary of State should give a direction under s. 15, then a copy of the report must also be sent to the Secretary of State, within the required timescale.

## Audit Commission inspection

The Audit Commission has the power to carry out an inspection of any authority to check    **17.29**
that it is complying with its obligations in relation to best value. Such an inspection could be directed by the Secretary of State. It could begin as a result of a recommendation of an auditor or it could be initiated by the Audit Commission itself. If the Secretary of State is considering giving a direction, he must consult the Commission first. Any officer, servant or agent carrying out an inspection has a right of access at all reasonable times to any premises of the authority concerned and to any document which appears to him to be necessary for the purpose of the inspection. In addition an inspector:

(a)  may require a person holding or accountable for any such document to give him such information and explanation as he thinks necessary, and
(b)  may require that person to attend before him in person to give the information or explanation or to produce the document.

Failure to comply with a requirement of an inspector is a criminal offence, punishable by a fine not exceeding level 3 on the standard scale.

Once the Audit Commission has carried out an inspection of an authority under these    **17.30**
powers it must issue a report. Such a report—

(a)  must mention any matter in respect of which the Commission believes that the authority is failing to comply with its best value obligations, and
(b)  may, if it mentions a matter under paragraph (a) above, recommend that the Secretary of State gives a direction under section 15.

The Commission must send a copy of the report to the authority concerned. It may (i.e. it    **17.31**
does not have to) publish the report and any information in respect of it. If the report recommends that the Secretary of State gives a direction under s. 15, the Commission must as soon as reasonably practicable:

(a)  arrange for that recommendation to be published, and
(b)  send a copy of the report to the Secretary of State.

If the report states that the Commission believes that the authority is failing to comply with its best value duty this fact must be recorded in the next performance plan prepared by the authority. The performance plan must also record any action taken by the authority as a result of the report.

## F   POWER OF SECRETARY OF STATE TO INTERVENE

**17.32**   Under s. 15, the Secretary of State has power to intervene if he considers that an authority is failing to comply with its best value obligations. The power can be exercised by the Secretary of State on his own initiative. Although both the process of audit of an authority's plan by its auditor and a formal inspection by the Audit Commission could recommend an intervention by the Secretary of State, there is no need for either type of recommendation to have been made before such an intervention takes place. Under s. 15, the Secretary of State may direct:

(a)   that an authority should prepare or amend a performance plan (If a local authority fails in one of its most basic duties, to prepare a performance plan, then it can be told to do so. There is also power for the Secretary of State to amend the plan if he considers that it does not represent compliance with the statutory requirements.);

(b)   that an authority should follow specified procedures in relation to a performance plan (This does not necessarily amount to an amendment of a performance plan. It could refer to a plan which has not yet been prepared.);

(c)   that an authority should carry out a review of its exercise of specified functions (This could be because an authority is failing to observe the spirit of the legislation and failing to review functions where a review is necessary. This power may have become more important since the requirement to review all functions over a five year period has been repealed.);

(d)   that a local inquiry should be held into the exercise by a local authority of specified functions (This would be a formal inquiry to which the rules relating to public inquiries held under s. 250 of the Local Government Act 1972 would apply.);

(e)   that a specified function of an authority should be exercised by the Secretary of State or a person nominated by him for a period specified in the direction or for as long as the Secretary of State considers appropriate (This is the most draconian of the intervention powers available to the Secretary of State. Powers to run key services could be removed from an authority for an indefinite period.);

(f)   that an authority must comply with any instructions of the Secretary of State or his nominee in relation to the exercise of that function and provide such assistance as the Secretary of State or his nominee may require for the purpose of exercising the function (This is a slightly less draconian power which allows the Secretary of State to dictate how an authority exercises a function.).

**17.33**   Under sections 15(7) and (8) the Secretary of State has power to make regulations and amendments to legislation to deal with the situation which could arise if he was exercising the functions of a local authority in circumstances where he had a role to play in respect of that function in his capacity of Secretary of State. The example given in Parliament was that if the Secretary of State was exercising the functions of a local planning authority it would be difficult for him then to determine an appeal against his own decision. Before giving any direction under s. 15 the Secretary of State must give the authority concerned an opportunity to make representations about:

(a)   the report (if any) as a result of which the direction is proposed, and

(b)   the direction proposed.

If the proposed intervention arises as a result of a recommendation in a report made by **17.34** the authority's auditor under s. 7, the Secretary of State must consider the authority's formal response setting out what action it proposes to take (provided this is received by the Secretary of State within one month of the date of the report) before giving any direction under s. 15.

The Secretary of State can intervene without seeking representations or waiting for a formal **17.35** response if he considers that he has to make a direction urgently. If he does this he has to inform the authority concerned and representatives of authorities of the direction and the reasons for its urgency.

### Protocol on intervention

There is a Protocol on Central Government Engagement in Poorly Performing Local Author- **17.36** ities. This is set out as Annex B to Circular 03/2003. It derives from an agreement between the Government and the LGA called the Framework for Partnership which was signed in November 1997 by the Deputy Prime Minister on behalf of the Government and the Chairman of the LGA on behalf of local authorities. It was intended to provide for discussion between the Government and the LGA to discuss how intervention powers would be used. The aim of the Protocol is to set out the principles which will underpin the engagement of central Government with local authorities. The aim is to keep intervention to a minimum. The authority will be expected to prepare a recovery plan and adhere to it. However, if intervention is necessary, the Secretary of State may require a local authority within a specified period to:

- prepare or amend a recovery plan;
- make sure a function is carried out so as to achieve specified objectives or priorities;
- take consultancy advice;
- appoint interim management;
- enforce appropriate levels of delegation;
- secure the function from a specified provider or put the function out to tender;
- appoint a nominee to exercise certain specified functions of the authority;
- take any other action that will secure the necessary improvements.

## G   COMPREHENSIVE PERFORMANCE ASSESSMENT

The introduction of Comprehensive Performance Assessments (CPAs) has done much to **17.37** raise the profile of local government. Although local government generally attracts little public attention, many people will know into which category their local authority falls. Although the process of assessment and many of the conclusions have been much criticised, the categories are generally recognised as giving a fair overall picture of each authority's performance. There are substantial advantages, aside from good publicity in being in a high category and some dangers in being categorised as 'weak' or 'poor'. The wish to achieve an improved assessment has proved a powerful motivator in many authorities.

The proposal to introduce comprehensive performance assessment was first made in the **17.38**

December 2001 White Paper *Strong Local Leadership Quality Public Services*. The idea was to provide a simple and basic overview of the effectiveness of each authority, and this is how it has turned out. Services are assessed and judged according to a series of criteria. Local Councils are given marks out of five. Following the Government proposal, the Audit Commission produced a consultation paper in March 2002 setting out their proposals as to how the whole system would work. The outcome of the consultation was then considered by the Commission which published a formal response *CPA Consultation Summary—Responses to the Audit Commission's Consultation Draft Delivering CPA*. The process began with single tier authorities and county councils. There was continued consultation with authorities as the process was undertaken throughout 2002.

**17.39** The CPA process derives from the best value legislation. However, there was originally no legislative scheme which directly supported the CPA. There was some criticism of this at the time the process was introduced and some doubts were expressed about whether the power under which this process was purportedly being undertaken, s. 10 of the LGA 1999, could legitimately be used for this purpose. The issue was not tested in court and the CPA is now carried out in accordance with the duties imposed on the Audit Commission by s. 99 of the LGA 2003:

(1) The Audit Commission must from time to time produce a report on its findings in relation to the performance of English local authorities in exercising their functions.

(2) A report under sub-section (1) must (in particular) categorise each English local authority to which the report relates.

**17.40** The CPA is a continuously developing process and will change according to experience. However, the basic structure has been put in place. There are two elements of the CPA, the services assessment and the corporate assessment. These result in a final assessment. This was seen in some quarters as mechanistic and unimaginative. The justification for focusing on front-line services is that, inevitably, these are what the consumer of services will experience and therefore the basis on which the public will judge an authority. As far as corporate assessment is concerned, the Government's view, expressed in the 2001 White Paper, was that failures on the ground could often be traced back to political or management failures at the authority's centre. This is plainly right, as there is a clear correlation between authorities where it has proved impossible for members to show clear political leadership and failing services. In a febrile political atmosphere it has often proved difficult for both members and officers to focus on the task of improving services.

**17.41** When assessing services the Commission looks at both the quality of the services currently being provided and capacity for improvement. The Commission both collects its own data and relies on data received from other inspectorates, such as those responsible for social services, education, and benefit fraud. The data is then collated and measured against a matrix which produces a score. The process is summarised briefly below and set out in detail in the Audit Commission's publication *Comprehensive Performance Assessment Framework 2004*.

**17.42** The corporate assessment is undertaken in two parts, a self assessment by the authority and then a corporate assessment by the Commission. The key areas which a corporate assessment is intended to address are as follows:

- how the council has determined its ambitions and priorities;
- how the council uses its corporate capacity and systems to drive forward the organisation; and
- how the council measures the progress it is making

This approach was outlined by the Audit Commission in *Guidance for Single Tier and County Councils on the Corporate Assessment Process.*

The self assessment ought to be a rigorous process of appraisal of the authority's achieve-   **17.43** ments and its progress in terms of service delivery. A continuing theme of the Audit Commission has been the need for authorities to demonstrate self-awareness. A major concern about local authority performance has been complacency. There is perceived to be a tendency for authorities which are mediocre performers to believe there is no scope for service improvement and a widespread belief among poorly performing authorities that they are doing their best in difficult circumstances. It was to counter such beliefs that the process of self assessment was considered to be necessary. The self-assessment must be approved by the Chief Executive and the Leader of the Council concerned. The process of self-assessment is also being extended to the services element of the assessment.

The self assessment needs to consist of a scene-setting section and a corporate assessment.   **17.44** The scene setting should explain the major challenges facing the authority and other information about the area which are relevant in determining corporate priorities. The corporate assessment then needs to be undertaken by the authority focusing on the four questions identified as important by the Audit Commission. The Commission then undertakes its own corporate assessment.

The four questions which the Audit Commission see as key in carrying out the corporate   **17.45** assessment are as follows:

- What is the council trying to achieve?
- How has the council set about delivering its priorities?
- What has the council achieved/not achieved to date?
- In the light of what the council has learned to date, what does it plan to do next?

Scores are awarded against each of these and they are judged on the basis of the following nine themes:

- Ambition
- Focus
- Prioritisation
- Capacity
- Performance management
- Improvements achieved
- Investment
- Learning
- Future plan.

The first three of these relate to the first of the top level questions, the fourth and fifth, to the second question, the sixth and seventh to the third question, and the eighth and ninth to the fourth question. The key issues are what the council has achieved and what the council is doing to ensure that it achieves its objectives in the future. The emphasis is on action either in terms of securing improvements or in terms of positive steps towards securing future improvements.

**17.46**   Once both the services assessment and the corporate assessment have been carried out, they are combined to produce the final assessment. This is a single word conclusion placing the authority in one of the following five categories:

- Excellent
- Good
- Fair
- Weak
- Poor.

**17.47**   On the services element of the CPA some services are weighted so they are given more importance than others. For instance, education and social services are given weightings so that the assessments in these areas have twice the importance of the assessment for housing or the environment. There are three rules designed to ensure that local authorities failing in core services, especially in the key areas of education and social services, do not achieve high ratings overall. These are:

(a)   An authority must have at least three stars on education, social services combined star rating and financial standing to be categorised as excellent.

(b)   An authority must score at least two stars on education, social services star rating and financial standing to be categorised as fair or above.

(c)   An authority must score at least two stars on all other core services to be categorised as excellent.

### Audit Commission v Ealing London Borough Council

**17.48**   The way in which the Audit Commission used assessments carried out by other bodies was challenged by Ealing London Borough Council. The challenge was successful at first instance but the Audit Commission's appeal was allowed: *The Audit Commission for England and Wales v Ealing London Borough Council* [2005] EWCA Civ 556. The London Borough of Ealing was categorised as 'weak' in the round of comprehensive performance assessments which took place in 2004. This was because they had scored zero stars in the assessment which the Commission for Social Care and Inspection (CSCI) had carried out on their social services function. Thus, in accordance with the rule referred to at (b) above, the council could not be categorised as anything higher than weak. It would have been categorised as at least 'fair' and might have been categorised as 'good' if it was not for the application of this rule.

**17.49**   The council challenged their categorisation on the ground that the Audit Commission had, by the application of the rule stated above, subordinated their decision to the categorisation by CSCI. In doing so, it was argued, they had fettered themselves by allowing another body, CSCI to dictate the outcome of the process. If there were to be rules set for the CPA process then they had to be the Audit Commission's rules, not those of another body. The main argument advanced on behalf of Ealing was that the Commission had fettered their discretion. There are a series of cases in which decisions have been overturned because the decision-maker applied an inflexible rule which allowed of no exceptions and thereby prevented himself from exercising the discretion which had been imposed on him.

Walker J quoted the following passage from *Lavender v Minister of Housing and Local Government* [1970] 1 WLR 1231:  **17.50**

> . . . [the Minister] has said in language which admits of no doubt that his decision to refuse permission was solely in pursuance of a policy not to permit minerals . . . to be worked unless the Minister of Agriculture was not opposed to their working . . . It seems to me that by adopting and applying his stated policy he has in effect inhibited himself from exercising a proper discretion (which would of course be guided by policy considerations) in any case where the Minister of Agriculture has made and maintained an objection . . . Everything else might point to the desirability of granting permission, but by applying and acting on his stated policy, I think the Minister has fettered himself in such a way that in this case it was not he who made the decision for which Parliament has made him responsible. It was the decision of the Minister of Agriculture not to waive his objection which was decisive in this case, and while that might properly prove to be the decisive factor for the Minister when taking into account all material considerations, it seems to me quite wrong for a policy to be applied which in reality eliminates all the material considerations save only the consideration, when that is the case, that the Minister of Agriculture objects. This means, as I think, that the Minister has, by his stated policy, delegated to the Minister of Agriculture the effective decision . . . where the latter objects . . .

Walker J considered that this passage could be applied to the situation in which the Audit Commission found itself. By applying the automatic rule that their CSCI rating meant that they could not be categorised higher than 'weak', they had eliminated all the Audit Commission's own considerations about the factors which would have influenced Ealing's categorisation.

However, the Court of Appeal concluded that the way in which the Audit Commission  **17.51** approached their task did not offend the principle stated in the passage quoted from the *Lavender* case above. A crucial issue for the Court of Appeal was that the CSCI assessment was carried out in accordance with a set of publicly available rules, not as a result of judgments made about the quality of an authority's services. Keene LJ quoted from the witness statement of the Director of Performance and Improvement at the Audit Commission:

> . . . the social services star rating is not based on the subjective judgment of the Chief Inspector, but is arrived at by the application of a set of transparent and objective rules to those judgments. There is no discretion involved in translating those judgments into a star rating.

The Court of Appeal drew a distinction between the policy in the *Lavender* case which meant  **17.52** that the Minister's decision in any individual case was dictated by the decision of another Minister and the Audit Commission's practice of adopting another body's assessment:

> here the Audit Commission has in effect adopted as its own a series of weightings, produced by the CSCI, which result in a star rating in an entirely predictable way. In our view it is entitled to do that. It is not delegating its decision in any individual case to the CSCI, since the CSCI does not make any such individual decision once it has arrived at the 'scores'. It is simply that the Audit Commission has itself decided to adopt certain principles for achieving its categorisation.

It concluded that there was no injustice to authorities in this since they could challenge the scores arrived at by CSCI. Nor was there any reason in principle why the Commission should not have an inflexible rule. There was no reason for allowing authorities to make representations. Such representations would in any event be impossible for the Commission to judge since they would involve looking at the scores arrived at by a specialist directorate.

## KEY DOCUMENTS

Implementing Best Value—a Consultation paper on draft guidance 1997 ODPM Consultation Paper

Modern Local Government—In Touch with the People 1998 White Paper

Guidance on Enhancing Public Participation October 1998 DETR/Democracy Network

Local Government (Best Value) Performance Plans and Reviews Order 1999 (SI No. 1999/3251)

Local Government (Best Value) Performance Plans and Reviews Amendment and Specified Dates Order 2002 (SI No. 2002/305) and 2003 (SI No. 2003/662)

Guidance on Best Value DETR Circular 10/99

Guidance on Best Value ODPM Circular 03/03

Changing Gear (Audit Commission)

The Impact of Best Value on English Local Government (2002) Cardiff University

Strong Local Leadership Quality Public Services 2001 White Paper

Comprehensive Performance Assessment Consultation Summary (Audit Commission)

Comprehensive Performance Assessment Framework—Guidance to Single Tier and County councils (Audit Commission)

# 18

# CONTRACTS AND PROCUREMENT

## A  INTRODUCTION

There has, over the last few years, been an increased awareness of the importance of local **18.01** authority procurement, and the importance of ensuring that it is undertaken efficiently. Local authority procurement is estimated to have a value of about £40bn each year. It is a sizeable chunk of the economy and the potential for benefits through improvements to procurement practices has been recognised. At the same time local authority contracting has been affected by a number of factors, some of which are relevant to important sectors of the economy and others which affect the whole range of Government activity. Broadly they fall into the following categories:

1.  The abolition of compulsory competitive tendering and its replacement by the best value regime. This has removed the legal obligation to go through a tendering process

for a range of services but encouraged authorities to consider new ways of delivering these services.

2. A focus on improvements within local authority procurement generally. This was initiated by the Byatt report into local authority procurement. The Government has since responded and the ODPM/LGA have put forward their proposals for a national procurement strategy for local government.

3. A new approach to construction projects. These are a major part of local government procurement. The Egan report 'Rethinking Construction' found that the problems in the construction industry were partly a result of too many individual tendering exercises and the absence of long-term partnering arrangements. Local authorities involved in construction projects may well now adopt the type of approach favoured by Egan, using partnering forms of contracts instead of traditional standard forms.

4. The requirement for efficiency savings across the public sector. The Gershon review had identified the need for savings within local authorities, which is placing local authorities under pressure to ensure that best value is delivered through contracting.

5. Encouragement for local authorities to enter into private finance transactions and strategic partnerships. These issues are considered in the next chapter.

6. Changes to the EU procurement rules. The new combined consolidated directive contains a number of features designed to make the complex framework of the EU procurement rules more flexible and easier to operate.

7. Developments in connection with staff transfers. Consultation has recently taken place on changes to the Transfer of Undertakings (Protection of Employment) Regulations 1981. The Government has also made clear that where functions are transferred, the expectation will be that the rights of the employees are protected, which will include protection of pension rights and equivalent rights for those joining an outsourced workforce.

8. The proposals for e-government. This includes a target for all transactions to be able to be undertaken electronically.

Some of these issues do not relate to local government law and therefore fall outside the scope of this book. This is not the place for a detailed discussion of the implications of the Egan report, the Gershon, review, or proposed e-government initiatives. However, the Byatt report and the Government and local authority response to it have very important implications for local authority procurement and are worth considering in some detail.

## B   THE BYATT REPORT

**18.02**   The Local Government Procurement Taskforce (chaired by Sir Ian Byatt) was established to carry out a review of 'the state of procurement and commissioning skills and practice in local government in the light of the requirements of Part 1 (Best Value) of the Local Government Act 1999, and its objective of continuous improvement in the economy, efficiency and effectiveness of local services; and to make recommendations'. The review was jointly commissioned by the LGA and DETR in July 2000. The Byatt report 'Delivering Better Services for Citizens' was published in June 2001. It made a total of 39 recommendations falling into three headings:

- The procurement function within an authority
- Making markets work better
- Tender design, tender evaluation and contract management.

The complete list of recommendations is set out in Appendix 7 below.

The first three recommendations relate to the alignment of procurement and best value. **18.03** The issue of authorities' strategic objectives and priorities for improvement is addressed in its comprehensive performance assessment. This, and the recommendation about staff involvement are both reflected in the 2003 best value guidance. There is more detailed guidance in 'Working Together for Best Value: promoting employee and trade union involvement.'

The following three recommendations express the view that authorities should have a **18.04** corporate procurement function. The corporate strategy should be a succinct and strategic document rather than a full explanation of the Council's tendering procedures, though it should refer to the Council's main procurement policies. Most larger authorities now have a central procurement team, though small authorities may tap into the resources of larger authorities or make pooled arrangements. In practical terms, it is often of major importance for authorities to have a central procurement function. The tendencies for ad hoc arrangements to turn into long-term practices and the use of the same supplier for reasons of convenience are frequent vices in large organisations and can prove extremely costly.

The next three recommendations are to do with looking at an authority's current practices. **18.05** The use of framework arrangements can result in lower prices and reduced transaction costs. The recommendation about the involvement of elected members and their responsibility for scrutinising and monitoring the procurement process is seen as a priority by the Government and the LGA. There is a need to ensure that members are trained so that they can carry out this role effectively. Similarly training is required for those engaged in procurement (Recommendation 14). This, and the funding for such training are issues being considered by I&DeA and the local government employers. E-procurement is also a priority. The Government has funded pathfinder projects and said that further work will be supported.

The Government has indicated that local authorities should prepare a guide on how to do **18.06** business with their council and publish it, including placing it on their website with a register of contracts and a schedule of contracts to be awarded in the near future (Recommendation 21). The Audit Commission have developed a set of performance indicators for local government. The LGA and Government have supported the idea that buying consortia should review their business plans and that they should consider the possibility of collaboration on large projects. The question of standardisation (Recommendation 27) also received support from the LGA and the Government. Standardisation of documentation is capable of reducing cost. However, it needs to be targeted and there needs to be guidance on its use. The inappropriate use of standardised documents could prove to be a false economy.

The final set of recommendations related to legislation, all of which were on the agenda. **18.07** The EU procurement rules have been changed in ways which allow for more flexible forms of procurement. There has been legislation to allow local authorities to trade with the private sector, in s. 95 LGA 2003. The requirements set out in the Cabinet Office Statement of Practice on Staff Transfers in the Public Sector have been given legislative effect in the LGA 2003. There has been consultation on revisions to the TUPE Regulations (see Chapter 3).

## C  THE NATIONAL PROCUREMENT STRATEGY

**18.08**  Following the publication of the Byatt report and the Government/LGA response, the National Procurement Strategy for Local Government was published in October 2003. The main features of this are as follows:

- An emphasis on the importance of procurement and the intention to create regional centres of excellence to develop procurement expertise, disseminate good practice, and provide advice.
- A proposal for councils to measure progress by means of performance indicators covering the implementation of the National Procurement Strategy, operational buying, and major projects.
- Advice about how councils should provide leadership, strategic direction, and building capacity for procurement. Further details of what the strategy advises councils to do is set out below.
- New strategic objectives of partnering and collaboration. Partnering is described as the creation of sustainable partnerships between councils and suppliers in the public, private, social enterprise, and voluntary sectors for the delivery of services and the carrying out of major projects, including construction. Collaboration is the process of bringing councils and other public bodies together at local, regional, and national levels to combine their buying power and create shared services.
- Objectives in respect of e-Procurement. The strategic objectives are to reduce the time taken in procurement and reduce transaction costs. Councils are also encouraged to use e-Marketplaces.
- Objectives in terms of stimulating markets and achieving community benefits. Councils should engage actively with suppliers and use procurement to help deliver corporate objectives.

There are specific targets attached to each of the strategic objectives.

**18.09**  The steps which councils ought to take in order to provide leadership and direction are:

1. Demonstrate political leadership of procurement. There should be a member 'procurement champion'.
2. Demonstrate managerial leadership of procurement. There should be a chief officer champion of procurement to ensure procurement is seen as a strategic rather than a technical issue.
3. Implement a corporate procurement strategy. This will set out the contribution procurement can make to the authority's strategic objectives.
4. Establish a centre of excellence in procurement and project management. Single tier and county councils should set up a corporate procurement team. Smaller councils

should consider shared procurement services, partnering, or linking to regional centres of excellence.

5. Carry out a skills audit and implement a training and development programme. This should enable councils to assess their need for new posts, for advice from other councils or consultants, and their training needs.

6. Review and redesign procurement processes. This involves mapping the procurement process for major projects and goods and then redesigning the processes to reduce the time taken, the number of steps involved, and the cost.

7. Review and revise procurement procedures. There needs to be a means of examining these to ensure they incorporate legal obligations, adequate internal controls, and best practices.

8. Maintain transparency. This includes publishing a procurement plan, keeping a corporate contracts register, publishing a Selling to the Council guide on a website and complying with the publication and reporting requirements of the public procurement directives.

9. Audit compliance. This requires systems to ensure compliance with mandatory policies and procedures including legal obligations.

10. Ensure early involvement. There should be early involvement of procurement officers in strategic reviews and of other advisers in procurement projects.

11. Make best use of buying power. This will include setting up framework agreements and corporate contracts to obtain maximum discounts.

12. Implement an appropriate e-Procurement solution. This includes implementing an e-Procurement strategy and using e-Marketplaces.

13. Manage major procurements as projects and introduce gateway reviews. The core principles of project management should be applied.

14. Manage contracts and supplier relationships. This is to be seen as a crucial part of project management.

15. Measure performance of the procurement function. The effectiveness of the delivery of the corporate procurement strategy depends on this.

What then are the practical implications of this for local authorities, particularly local **18.10** authority lawyers? First, it is to be expected that local authority procurement functions will be centralised to a greater extent than before. This will require standardised procedures. It is also likely to mean that the authority operates through a standardised set of contracts. This may have both advantages and disadvantages. Standardisation can streamline the process, but many local authority lawyers will have experience of clients trying to use unsuitable standard documents for contractual arrangements for which they are inappropriate. It will mean that procurement is likely to be undertaken through a core team of experienced and expert officers rather than having a variety of local arrangements which have grown up piecemeal over the years. This is likely to be beneficial to authorities in obtaining good value for money. There should be early involvement of expert procurement officers in any procurement exercise and early involvement of lawyers in major procurement exercises and complex contractual arrangements. Because of the increasing importance of e-procurement, it is to be expected that there will be disputes and queries about contractual arrangements made electronically. Since there will also need to be a full awareness of both the procurement rules within an authority and the contractual framework within which they are operating, there is likely to be an increased demand for training in these areas.

---

## D   THE LOCAL GOVERNMENT (CONTRACTS) ACT 1997

**18.11**  One of the difficulties in encouraging local authorities to engage more with the private sector was the suspicion of the private sector, and in particular funders, that when public sector bodies made contractual arrangements which subsequently turned out to be unwise they could look to the government and the courts to protect them, if necessary at the expense of a private sector partner particularly if there was a way of contriving that the principal loser was a large bank rather than a poorly advised local authority. The decisions in *Hazell v Hammersmith and Fulham London Borough Council* and the *Crédit Suisse* cases meant that there was a lack of confidence in entering into major and complex contractual arrangements with local authorities. At the same time, one of the priorities of the incoming Government in 1997 was to encourage local authorities to enter into PFI transactions and strategic partnerships with the private sector. The Local Government (Contracts) Act was designed to provide a means of ensuring that, if a contract was found to be beyond an authority's powers, the private sector investor would be compensated rather than simply being expected to bear the loss.

**18.12**  The scheme of the Act is that local authorities can provide certificates to the effect that a transaction is within their powers. If they provide such a certificate then there is a presumption that the contract is lawful. If the contract is found to be unlawful, then there will be 'relevant discharge terms' which set out what will happen if, in spite of the presumption that the contract is lawful, the court nevertheless decides that the contract is outside the authority's powers. Such discharge terms will normally provide that the contractor should be compensated in much the same way as if the contract had been terminated because of a default by the Council. If there are no relevant discharge terms then the contractor is compensated in the way it would have been if there had been a repudiatory breach by the local authority.

**18.13**  Section 1 of the Act provides for the first time a general power for local authorities to enter into contracts. Of course, local authorities have been entering into contracts since their formation and there has never been a serious issue about the power of the councils to do this. Nonetheless it was considered important in the context of this piece of legislation to spell out the power. It did so in the following terms:

> Every statutory provision conferring or imposing a function on a local authority confers power on the local authority to enter into a contract with another person for the provision or making available of assets or services or both, (whether or not together with goods) for the purposes of, or in connection with, the discharge of the function by the local authority.

This does no more than give effect to what had always been understood to be the legal position. Under s. 1(2) if a person makes a loan or provides finance for the other party (i.e. the private sector party) to the contract then the local authority also has power to enter into a contract with the funder or any insurer of or trustee for the funder in connection with the original contract. The purpose of including the reference to insurers and trustees is to cover anybody who might be granted step-in rights.

Section 2 is really the essence of the legislation. It provides that, if a local authority certified **18.14** that it had power to enter into a contract, then that contract is treated as if the authority did have power to enter into it. This is a rather odd concept, that a statutory body can acquire a power simply by asserting that it has such a power:

> Where a local authority has entered into a contract, the contract shall, if it is a certified contract, have effect (and be deemed always to have had effect) as if the local authority had had power to enter into it (and had exercised that power properly in entering into it).

A certified contract is one to which the certification requirements set out in s. 3 of the Act apply. The above subsection is still subject to the power of the court to examine the legality of the contract in proceedings for judicial review. Nor does it affect the right of any party to challenge the authority in respect of the way in which they went about the procurement process.

Section 3 sets out the certification requirements. A local authority must have issued a **18.15** certificate (whether before or after a contract is entered into):

(a)  including details of the period for which the contract operates or is to operate,
(b)  describing the purpose of the contract,
(c)  containing a statement that the contract is or is to be a contract falling within section 4(3) or (4),
(d)  stating that the local authority had or has power to enter into the contract and specifying the statutory provision, or each of the statutory provisions, conferring the power,
(e)  stating that a copy of the certificate has been or is to be given to each person to whom a copy is required to be given by regulations,
(f)  dealing in a manner prescribed by regulations with any matters required by regulations to be dealt with in certificates under this section, and
(g)  confirming that the local authority has complied with or is to comply with any requirement imposed by regulations with respect to the issue of certificates under this section.

A draft pro forma of a certificate to be provided under the Act is set out at Appendix 6. The certificate must have been signed by the person who is required under the regulations to sign it. The authority must have obtained the consent of every other person with whom it has entered or is to enter the contract. Once it has issued a certificate a local authority must ensure that, throughout the contract period, a copy of the certificate is available for inspection by the public and that people can obtain copies of it for a reasonable fee.

Under s. 5, it is provided that s. 2(1) does not apply to any determination or order made in **18.16** relation to a certified contract on—

(a)  an application for judicial review, or
(b)  an audit review.

The expression 'audit review' is defined in s. 8. It covers all the statutory functions of auditors in relation to local authorities.

**18.17** If a court is of the opinion that the authority did not have power to enter into a certified contract (or exercised its power improperly in entering into it), but considers that the contract should have effect, the court can order that the contract should be treated as if the local authority always had power to enter into it and had exercised that power properly in entering into it.

**18.18** Under s. 6 even a determination in a judicial review or an audit review cannot affect the enforceability of any relevant discharge terms relating to the contract. The idea is that even if the contract itself is outside the powers of the authority, the discharge terms remain. The 'relevant discharge terms' means terms—

(a) which have been agreed by the local authority and any person with whom the local authority entered into the contract,

(b) which either form part of the contract or constitute or form part of another agreement entered into by them not later than the day on which the contract was entered into, and

(c) which provide for a consequence mentioned in subsection (3) to ensue in the event of the making of a determination or order in relation to the contract on an application for judicial review or an audit review.

The consequences mentioned in subsection (3) are as follows:

(a) the payment of compensatory damages (measured by reference to loss incurred or loss of profits or to any other circumstances) by one of the parties to the other,

(b) the adjustment between the parties of rights and liabilities relating to any assets or goods provided or made available under the contract, or

(c) both of these things.

**18.19** If a certified contract is found by a court not to have effect, and there are no relevant discharge terms then the other party or parties to the contract are entitled to be paid such sums by the local authority that they would have been entitled to be paid if the contract—

(a) had had effect until the time the determination or order was made (i.e. the determination or order that the contract does not have effect),

(b) had been terminated at that time by acceptance by him of a repudiatory breach by the local authority.

---

## E   THE EU PROCUREMENT RULES

**18.20** The requirements of EU law on public procurement are set out in directives. There are three directives which regulate contracting by public authorities, covering contracts for works, supplies, and services. All these were transposed into national law by means of regulations. There is now a consolidated procurement directive which consolidates these three directives and makes some amendments to them. This has not yet been transposed into UK law and some of its procedures cannot be used until the relevant regulations have been made. However, since it is anticipated that the relevant regulations will be made at about the time this book is published, the summary below deals with the law as set out in the consolidated procurement directive.

In general the requirements of the directives are to ensure that there is a fair opportunity for   **18.21**
contractors and suppliers across the EU to compete for public sector contracts. The essential
features of the directives are:

(a)  Contracts must be advertised in the Official Journal of the European Union (OJEU) to
allow contractors from all EU Member States to compete.
(b)  Potential contractors can only be rejected for certain specified reasons.
(c)  Contracts may only be awarded by following the procedures set out in the directives.

The existing directives and the regulations which implement them are as follows:

- Council Directive 93/37 (the Works Directive) implemented by the Public Works
Contracts Regulations 1991
- Council Directive 93/36 (the Supplies Directive) implemented by the Public Supply
Contracts Regulations 1995
- Council Directive 92/50 (the Services Directive) implemented by the Public Services
Contracts Regulations 1993.

## The Treaty of Rome

Article 30 of the Treaty of Rome applies to all local authority contracts, of whatever type   **18.22**
or value. This forbids Member States of the EU from imposing quantitative restrictions on
trade between themselves or equivalent measures. Such restrictions or measures will include
such matters as specifying standards which are exclusively national and which would
therefore make it difficult for contractors from other Member States to comply with them.
The general principles of EU law are satisfied by following the requirements of the procurement directive. However, it needs to be remembered that, although in practice the prospect
of a challenge may be low in the case of a local authority contract which falls outside the
requirements of the directive, the general laws of the EU apply to all public sector procurement, not just those contracts which fall within the scope of the directive. These essentially
require that those invited to tender must be chosen on the basis of objective criteria and the
rules set at the outset of the tendering process will continue to be followed by the contracting authority. The nature of the project must not be changed materially during the process
of the negotiation from that which was originally advertised. Equality of treatment between
Member States also requires that specifications etc recognised in one Member State should
be recognised in them all.

## Consolidated procurement directive

For the most part, the consolidated directive simply reflects changes in procurement practice   **18.23**
which have been taking place over the last few years. They make allowances for different
methods of procurement, especially those involving new technology. The main changes are
as follows (the changes discussed here are those which the consolidated procurement directive makes to the earlier directives covering works, supplies, and services. There are also
changes to the utilities directive which is outside the scope of this work):

- Allowance is made for framework agreements i.e. call-off contracts where suppliers/
providers commit to carrying out work on agreed terms for a fixed period.

- Provision is made for central purchasing bodies. If the procurement rules have been followed by such a body, then they are deemed to have been followed by its constituent bodies.
- Electronic auctions are permitted. This is a process whereby bids are submitted electronically against the authority's specification.
- Dynamic purchasing systems are allowed. These are a framework which allows suppliers to join by submitting a bid at any time during the framework's existence.
- A new procedure, called competitive dialogue, has been introduced. This is for use in complex projects where it may not be possible to identify the best solution in advance. It allows for innovative solutions to be put forward.
- There is clarification of the circumstances in which social and environmental issues can be taken into account.

**18.24** One of the features of the EU procurement rules is the set of rigid timescales for each step in the procurement process. These were of course formulated before electronic means of communication could be used. There are changes in the consolidated directive to take account of this. Notices can be submitted for publication on the Commission's procurement website: <http://www.simap.eu.int>. If this is done, tender periods in the open procedure and the period for requests to participate in the other procedures can be shortened by seven days. If documentation is available electronically the tender periods in the open and restricted periods can be shortened by five days. This is additional to the reduction for electronic transmission of notices.

**18.25** There have been changes to the articles covering the selection of tenderers and award criteria (Articles 44, 45 and 53). There is now a requirement to exclude those convicted of corruption, organised crime, or fraud. There is also a need to provide more information about the evaluation process. The weighting given to each criterion used to judge what is the most economically advantageous tender will need to be disclosed. These types of contract will often be awarded as a result of an evaluation using a complex scoring system. The system will need to be objective and justifiable in case there should be a challenge. There is also now a provision allowing relevant environmental and social requirements to be specified. This needs to be done with precision and in detail so tenderers will know where they stand.

### The thresholds

**18.26** The directives and the regulations which implement them apply only to contracts above the thresholds currently set out in Article 7 of the consolidated procurement directive. Of course at the outset of a contract, particularly if it is for supplies or services, it may be very difficult for an authority to know what it is going to spend. There are therefore rules to ensure that contracts which are likely to exceed the thresholds are subject to the full rigours of the procurement rules. Article 9 of the revised procurement directive provides that, in order to calculate the estimated value of public contracts, framework agreements, and dynamic purchasing systems:

> The calculation of the estimated value of a public contract shall be based on the total amount payable, net of VAT, as estimated by the contracting authority. This calculation shall take account of the estimated total amount, including any form of option and any renewals of the

contract. Where the contracting authority provides for prizes or payments to candidates or tenderers it shall take them into account when calculating the estimated value of the contract.

The rules previously required that, if there were options in supplies or services contracts, **18.27** then the contract was valued on the basis that the consideration is the highest amount which could be paid on the assumption that all options are exercised. The change of the wording to 'take into account' presumably means that the estimate can place a value on the option bearing in mind the likelihood of it being exercised rather than simply assume that it will be exercised. The same approach can presumably be applied to renewals and prizes. The estimate must be valid at the time the required notice is sent to the OJEU or, if no notice is required, at the moment at which the contracting authority commences the contract award-ing procedure. No works project or proposed purchase of a certain quantity of supplies or services can be subdivided for the purpose of avoiding the application of the rules. Where the contract is a public works contract, account has to be taken of the value of any supplies necessary for executing the works and placed at the contractor's disposal by the contracting authority. If a proposed work or purchase of services or proposal to purchase supplies of a particular type may result in contracts being awarded at the same time in the form of separate lots, account has to be taken of the total estimated value of such lots.

In the case of public supply contracts relating to the leasing, hire rental, or hire purchase of **18.28** products, the value for the purposes of calculating the estimated value is as follows:

(a)  if it is a fixed term contract and the term is less than or equal to 12 months, the total estimated value for the term of the contract or, if the term is greater than 12 months, the total value including the estimated residual value (i.e. the value for the period after the expiry of the 12 month period);

(b)  if there is no fixed term or there is a term which cannot be defined, the value to be used is the monthly value i.e. that which the authority expects to pay each month, multiplied by 48.

If there are public supply or service contracts which are regular in nature or which are **18.29** intended to be renewed within a given period, the contract value must be based on the following:

(a)  either the total actual value of the successive contracts of the same type awarded during the preceding 12 months or financial year adjusted, if possible, to take account of the changes in quantity or value which would occur in the course of the 12 months following the initial contract;

(b)  or the total estimated value of the successive contracts awarded during the 12 months following the first delivery, or during the financial year if that is longer than 12 months.

Which method is chosen is a matter for the authority, but it must not choose with a view to **18.30** avoiding the application of the rules. One of the difficulties is deciding what constitutes a 'type' of service or supply for this purpose. The test usually suggested is that if they are usually obtained from the same provider then they should be regarded as belonging to the same type. This test causes some problems. With some services and supplies there are few providers catering for a wide range of demand. The application of this test could therefore mean types of service or supply which would on a commonsense basis be regarded as disparate being counted together for this purpose.

### Contracting authority

**18.31**  Public works, supply, and services contracts all have to be made by a contracting authority. The definition of 'contracting authority' is the same in each of the directives and also in each set of regulations. It includes local authorities, fire authorities, and police authorities, as well as joint authorities and joint education boards. In addition, certain other quasi-public bodies are included. If a body is set up 'for the purpose of meeting needs in the general interest' and:

(a)  is financed wholly or mainly by another contracting authority; or

(b)  is subject to management supervision by such an authority; or

(c)  more than half its board of directors or members are appointed by such an authority, or, if it is a group of individuals, more than half of them are appointed by such an authority;

then it will also be a 'contracting authority' for the purpose of these rules. Thus registered social landlords fall within the definition of 'contracting authority' because of the extent to which they are publicly financed. Local authority companies, depending on the nature of their financing arrangements, may also fall within this definition.

### Contracts which are within the scope of the rules

**18.32**  In the consolidated procurement directive 'public contracts' are defined as 'contracts for pecuniary interest concluded in writing between one or more economic operators and one or more contracting authorities and having as their object the execution of works, the supply of products or the provision of services within the meaning of this directive'.

**18.33**  Public works contracts are defined as contracts for the carrying out of work or works (as listed in Schedule 1 to the 1991 Regulations, now Annex 1 of the consolidated procurement directive) or engagements of a person to procure a work corresponding to specified requirements by any means. Thus an authority cannot evade the effect of the rules by the use of an intermediary. There is a distinction between 'works' and 'work'. 'Works' are the activities set out in Schedule 1 to the Regulations; 'work' is the outcome of any works 'sufficient to fulfil an economic or technical function'. This is therefore essentially a distinction between the finished product and the activity required to produce it. Public supply contracts include the purchase, lease, rental, or hire purchase, with or without option to buy, of what are called 'products' in the directive and 'goods' in the Regulations. The definition is very wide: all supplies of 'products' are included, whatever their nature. Public services contracts are defined in the combined directive as 'public contracts other than public works or supply contracts having as their object the provision of services referred to in Annex II'. This is different from the definition in the 1993 Regulations which defines 'public services contracts' as contracts under which an authority 'engages a person to provide services' (subject to various exceptions).

### Overlaps between works, supplies, and services contracts

**18.34**  If there is a contract which might be covered by more than one set of rules, because it includes elements which fall within more than one set, how is it decided which set of rules should apply? As between works and supplies, the new directive provides that 'A public contract having as its object the supply of products and which also covers, as an incidental matter, siting and installation operations shall be considered to be a "public supply contract".' As between supplies and services, the contract is a public services contract if the value of the services exceeds that of the products covered by the contract. A comparison of the two values is all that is needed. The directive is silent on the question of how the question is to be addressed if there is a combination of works and services. In the case of *Gestion Hotelera Internacional SA v Communidad Autonoma de Canarias* [1994] ECR I-1329 it was held that the test was whether the works were incidental to the services provided.

## Tendering procedures

There are three procedures which may be adopted for the tendering process. These are the **18.35** open, restricted, and negotiated procedure. In the combined directive there is also a competitive dialogue procedure. Local authorities can choose which of the open or restricted procedure they wish to follow. The competitive dialogue procedure and negotiated procedures can be applied only in the circumstances set out in the applicable articles.

The competitive dialogue procedure is governed by Article 29. The authority must follow **18.36** these rules:

(a)  the contract must be a 'particularly complex contract';
(b)  the contracting authority must consider that the use of the open or restricted procedure will not allow the award of the contract;
(c)  the contract must be awarded on the sole basis of the award criterion for the most economically advantageous tender;
(d)  the authority must publish a contract notice setting out their needs and requirements, which they have to define in that notice and/or in a descriptive document.

Once the candidates have been shortlisted, in accordance with the applicable provisions of the directive, then the authority opens a dialogue with the selected candidates the aim of which is to identify and define the means best suited to satisfying the authority's needs. They may discuss all aspects of the contract with the chosen candidates during this period. There is an obligation on authorities to ensure equality of treatment among all tenderers. In particular they must not provide information in a discriminatory manner which may give some tenderers an advantage over others. Authorities must not reveal to the other participants in a competitive dialogue any solutions proposed or confidential information communicated by a participant in the dialogue without that candidate's agreement.

There is provision for the process to take place in a series of stages: 'Contracting authorities **18.37** may provide for the procedure to take place in successive stages in order to reduce the number of solutions to be discussed during the dialogue stage by applying the award criteria in the contract notice or the descriptive document. The contract notice or descriptive document shall indicate that recourse may be had to this option.' The dialogue continues until the authority can identify the solution or solutions which are capable of meeting its needs. The directive says 'if necessary by comparing them'. It is difficult to see how this choice can be made without some kind of comparison being made. Once the dialogue is concluded the authority must inform the parties and ask them to submit their final tenders on the basis of the solution(s) put forward during the dialogue. These tenders must contain all the elements necessary for the purpose of the project. (This presumably means that they must, for instance, include detailed drawings of any buildings to be constructed and detailed method statements setting out how services are to be provided.) The tenders can, at the request of the authority, be 'clarified, specified and fine-tuned'. However, this must not involve changes to the 'basic features of the tender', or variations which are likely to distort competition or have a discriminatory effect.

**18.38**   Following this, authorities must assess the tenders received on the basis of the award criteria set out in the contract notice or descriptive document and choose the most economically advantageous tender. There is then scope for post-tender clarifications: 'At the request of the contracting authority, the tenderer identified as having submitted the most economically advantageous tender may be asked to clarify aspects of the tender or confirm commitments contained in the tender provided this does not have the effect of modifying substantial aspects of the tender or of the call for tender and does not risk distorting competition or causing discrimination.' This does not provide scope for post-tender negotiations over substantive issues. Authorities may specify prices or payments to the participants in the dialogue. This is interesting. It is already frequent for authorities to say to tenderers how much they can afford. This provision allows an authority to specify how much they will pay and seek the best solution within this amount.

**18.39**   The above process does at least allow for some discussion with tenderers. The notion that every aspect of the contract could be included within the invitation to tender so that an offer could be accepted and a contract concluded without further discussion between the parties, was never practical when large and complex contracts were being considered. Some kind of post-tender discussions were inevitable. This was why the negotiated procedure was recommended by HM Treasury for PFI contracts, even though it never appeared to fit comfortably. However, the competitive dialogue does appear to be potentially wasteful in both time and resources. There may be a number of tenderers. If, in a complex project, discussions are taking place with all of these and all of them are required to incur substantial expenditure on providing solutions and preparing a very detailed final bid, then this will have an effect on project costs as contractors will try to recoup the costs of tendering. It will also involve a large commitment of resources on the part of the authority as discussions will need to take place with a number of tenderers simultaneously.

**18.40**   The negotiated procedure allows authorities to negotiate the terms of the contract with a chosen contractor. The negotiated procedure might be preceded by a contract notice. The circumstances in which authorities can use this procedure after publication of a contract notice are as follows:

(a)   in the event of irregular tenders or the submission of tenders which are unacceptable under national provisions compatible with Articles 4, 24, 25, 27, and Chapter VII, in response to an open or restricted procedure or a competitive dialogue insofar as the original terms of the contract (If authorities are negotiating with all those who submitted tenders which satisfy the criteria in Articles 45 to 52 then they need not publish a contract notice before starting the negotiations.);

(b)   in exceptional cases, when the nature of the works, supplies, or services or the risks attaching thereto do not permit prior overall pricing;

(c)  the nature of the services is such that contract specifications cannot be established with sufficient precision to permit the award of the contract by selection of the best tender according to the rules governing open or restricted procedures (The directive mentions services within category 6 of Annex II A, and intellectual services such as services involving the design of works.);

(d)  in respect of public works contracts, for works which are performed solely for purposes of research, testing, or development and not with the aim of ensuring profitability or recovering research and development costs.

When using the negotiated procedure following the publication of a prior notice, authorities **18.41** are to negotiate about the tenders to adapt them to the authority's requirements and seek out the best tender in accordance with Article 53 i.e. the lowest price or the most economically advantageous tender. There is an obligation to treat all tenderers equally and in particular not to provide information in a discriminatory manner which may give some tenderers an advantage over others. The procedure can take place in successive stages.

There are also circumstances in which authorities can award public contracts by a negotiated **18.42** procedure without publication of a contract notice in the following circumstances.

For public works, supply, and services contracts:

(a)  when no tenders or no suitable tenders or no applications have been submitted in response to an open procedure or a restricted procedure, provided that the initial conditions of contract are not substantially altered and on condition that a report is sent to the Commission if it so requests;

(b)  when, for technical or artistic reasons, or for reasons connected with the protection of exclusive rights, the contract may be awarded only to a particular economic operator;

(c)  insofar as is strictly necessary when, for reasons of extreme urgency brought about by events unforeseeable by the contracting authorities in question, the time-limit for the open restricted or negotiated procedures cannot be complied with. The circumstances invoked to justify the urgency must not in any way be attributable to the contracting authority.

For public supply contracts only:

(a)  when the products involved are manufactured purely for the purpose of research, experimentation, study or development; this provision does not extend to quantity production to establish commercial viability or to recover research and development costs;

(b)  for additional deliveries by the original supplier which are intended either as a partial replacement of normal supplies or installations or as the extension of existing supplies or installations where a change of supplier would oblige the contracting authority to acquire material having different technical characteristics which would result in incompatibility or disproportionate technical difficulties in operation and maintenance; the length of such contracts as well as that of recurrent contracts may not, as a general rule, exceed three years;

(c)  for supplies quoted and purchased on a commodity market;

(d)  for the purchase of supplies on particularly advantageous terms, from either a supplier which is definitively winding up its business activities, or the receivers or liquidators of bankruptcy, an arrangement with creditors, or a similar procedure.

For public service contracts only, when the contract concerned follows a design contest and must, under the applicable rules, be awarded to the successful candidate or to one of the successful candidates; in the latter case, all successful candidates must be invited to participate in the negotiations.

For public works contracts and public service contracts:

(a) for additional works or services not included in the project initially considered or in the original contract but which have, through unforeseen circumstances, become necessary for the performance of the works or services described therein, on condition that the award is made to the economic operator performing such works or services—when such additional works or services cannot be technically or economically separated from the original contract without major inconvenience to the contracting authorities, or— when such works or services, although separable from the performance of the original contract, are strictly necessary for its completion. But the aggregate value of contracts for additional works or services must not exceed 50 per cent of the amount of the original contract;

(b) for new works or services consisting in the repetition of similar works or services entrusted to the economic operator to whom the same contracting authorities awarded an original contract, provided that such works or services are in conformity with a basic project for which the original contract was awarded according to the open or restricted procedure.

### Advertising rules

**18.43** **Notices.** Contracting authorities are, if (but only if) they are going to take advantage of the option of shortening time limits for receipt of tenders as set out in Article 38(4), required to publish prior information notices setting out:

(a) for supplies, the estimated total value of the contracts or framework agreements by product area (see below) they intend to award over the following 12 months where the total estimated value is equal to or greater than EUR 750 000;

(b) for services, the estimated total value of the contracts or framework agreements in each of the categories listed in Annex II A (see below) where the total estimated value is equal to or greater than EUR 750 000;

(c) for works, the essential characteristics of the contracts or framework agreements which they intend to award the estimated value of which is equal to or greater than the applicable threshold for works contracts (see above).

A contract notice (i.e. a notice advertising the contract and inviting responses as opposed to a prior indicative notice) must be published where a contracting authority wishes to award a public contract by the open or restricted procedure or by the negotiated procedure under Article 30 (use of negotiated procedure with publication of a contract notice) or a competitive dialogue under Article 29. Contracting authorities which wish to set up a dynamic purchasing system must make their intention known by publishing a contract notice. If they simply wish to award a contract based on an existing dynamic purchasing system they must make their intention known by publishing a simplified contract notice. Although notices are mandatory for the purposes set out in this paragraph, an authority is entitled to place voluntary notices in the OJEU for public contracts which fall outside the requirements of the directive. Often this will be a sensible idea. Since there are many contractors who use the OJEU as a means of finding out information about potential tenders, this can be a good way of encouraging competition.

Notices are required to contain the information mentioned in Annex VII A of the directive. **18.44** They must also include any other information deemed useful by the contracting authority. Notices may be sent by electronic means. Any other means of forwarding them is acceptable but if authorities wish to take advantage of the accelerated procedure set out in Article 38(8) notices must be sent by electronic means or telefax. The format and procedures for transmission of notices are set out in Annex VIII of the directive, which also contains the required technical characteristics. If notices are transmitted by electronic means in the correct format they will be published no later than five days after they are sent. Otherwise they will be published within 12 days. Notices should not exceed 650 words.

An authority may not publish a notice at national level before the date on which the notice **18.45** is sent to the Commission. It is of course common for notices to be published both in the OJEU and in the domestic trade press. Authorities should therefore be careful about the date on which notices are sent to the trade press so that this rule is not infringed. A notice published at national level must not contain information other than that contained in the notice sent to the Commission. Authorities should keep proof that a notice was sent. They will receive from the Commission a confirmation of the publication of the information, which will include the date of publication. This will constitute proof of publication.

## Time limits

The time limits are set out in Article 38. These are minimum time limits. Authorities must **18.46** 'take account in particular of the complexity of the contract and the time required for drawing up tenders'. This is without prejudice to the minimum time limits set out in the Article. There are clearly some types of contract for which it would not be appropriate to use the minimum time limits. For instance in a complex PFI contract it will normally be inappropriate to allow less than three months for preparation of a tender.

**Open procedures.** The minimum time limit for receipt of tenders (obviously there is no **18.47** stage dealing with requests to participate/submission of expressions of interest) is 52 days from the date on which the contract notice was sent. If a prior information notice was published this period can be shortened, normally to 36 days but never to less than 22 days.

**Restricted procedures.** The minimum time limit for receipt of requests to participate is **18.48** 37 days from the date on which the contract notice is sent. If a prior information notice was published this period can be shortened, normally to 36 days (scarcely a generous reduction) but never to less than 22 days. The minimum time limit for the receipt of tenders is 40 days from the date on which the invitation to tender is sent.

If a notice has been drawn up and transmitted by electronic means, the above time limits can **18.49** all be shortened by seven days. If, from the date of publication of the notice, the contracting authority offers unrestricted and full direct access by electronic means to the contract documents and any supplementary documents, the time limits can be shortened by a further five days. This five day reduction can be added to the seven day reduction referred to in the above paragraph. These electronic procedures may be sensible for an authority to undertake, even if they do not intend to take advantage of the shorter time limits to which this entitles them.

18.50   In the case of restricted procedures and negotiated procedures where there has been prior publication of a contract notice, if urgency renders the time limits set out in Article 38 impracticable, authorities may fix:

(a)   a time limit for the receipt of requests to participate, not less than 15 days from the date on which the contract notice was sent (10 days if it was sent by electronic means);

(b)   in the case of restricted procedures, a time limit for receipt of tenders, not less than 10 days from the invitation to tender.

### Reports

18.51   An important innovation in the combined directive is the need for reports setting out their decisions on the various issues arising in the course of a tendering process. This means that these issues need to be considered carefully and that the authority is clear about its justification for each decision it makes. The Commission may request copies of these reports or the main features of such reports. Each report must, at a minimum, contain:

(a)   the name and address of the contracting authority, the subject matter and value of the contract, framework agreement, or dynamic purchasing system;

(b)   the names of the successful candidates or tenderers and the reasons for their selection;

(c)   the names of the candidates or tenderers rejected and the reasons for their rejection;

(d)   the reasons for the rejection of tenders found to be abnormally low;

(e)   the name of the successful tenderer and the reasons why his tender was selected and, if known, the share of the contract or framework agreement which the successful tenderer intends to subcontract to third parties;

(f)   for negotiated procedures, the circumstances which justify the use of these procedures;

(g)   as far as the competitive dialogue is concerned, the circumstances justifying the use of this procedure;

(h)   if necessary, the reasons why the contracting authority has decided not to award a contract or framework agreement or to establish a dynamic purchasing system.

### Shortlisting

18.52   Whichever procedure is chosen, the selection of the successful tenderer will be a two stage process. First various criteria are used to exclude particular tenderers, then the award criteria are applied to select the most economically advantageous bid. (Though it could be that the lowest price is used as the award criterion except with the competitive dialogue procedure.) Except in the case of the open procedure where there is no separation of the stages of request to participate and submitting a bid, this will be divided into two separate steps.

18.53   In the cases of restricted procedures, negotiated procedures with publication of a contract notice, and competitive dialogue procedure, it is open to the authority to restrict the numbers invited to tender, provided that the number is sufficient to ensure genuine competition. The minimum number is five in the case of the restricted procedure and three in the cases of the negotiated procedure with publication of a contract notice and the competitive dialogue procedure.

The reasons for which a bidder can be rejected may be summarised as follows:                **18.54**

(a)  conviction for participation in a criminal organisation, corruption, fraud, or money laundering;
(b)  bankruptcy, winding up or administration;
(c)  conviction for any offence concerning his professional conduct;
(d)  being guilty of grave professional misconduct;
(e)  failing to fulfil obligations relating to the payment of social security contributions;
(f)  failing to fulfil obligations relating to the payment of taxes;
(g)  serious misrepresentation in supplying information or failing to supply information for the purposes of this rule;
(h)  failure to be a member of an appropriate trade or professional organisation;
(i)  inadequate economic or financial standing;
(j)  inadequate technical and/or professional ability;
(k)  failure to comply with quality assurance standards;
(l)  failure to comply with environmental management standards.

Some of the above criteria are simply of a pass/fail nature. A tenderer who has been  **18.55** convicted of corruption cannot expect to have the precise nature of the offence taken into account in deciding whether he is invited to tender. Some of them, however, will need to be measured or scored. Generally, a set of shortlisting criteria will need to be drawn up in advance in all but the very simplest tendering exercise. It is imperative that this is adhered to in order to avoid the risk of challenge. This does not mean, however, that all tenderers who pass a pre-determined threshold necessarily need to be invited to tender. If this was the position, there would be no point in specifying the number of bidders who would be invited. It is sufficient that there are good grounds, based on the criteria listed above, for choosing the shortlisted tenderers.

Two of the criteria require some further explanation. Economic or financial standing can be  **18.56** established by one or more of the following references:

(a)  appropriate statements from banks or, where appropriate, evidence of relevant professional risk indemnity insurance;
(b)  the presentation of balance sheets, where publication of the balance sheet is required under the law of the country in which the economic operator is established;
(c)  a statement of the undertaking's overall turnover and, where appropriate, of turnover in the area covered by the contract for a maximum of the last three financial years available, depending on the date on which the undertaking was set up or the economic operator started trading, as far as the information on these turnovers is available.

Contracting authorities have to specify, in the contract notice or invitation to tender, which of these references they will accept and what other references must be provided. If the bidder is unable, for a valid reason, to provide the references required, he can prove his financial standing by other means which the authority considers appropriate.

**18.57** There is a list of the means by which evidence of the bidder's technical abilities may be furnished. What is appropriate will depend on the nature, quantity, or importance, and use of the works, supplies, or services.

    (a) A list of the works carried out over the last five years with certificates of satisfactory execution for the most important works. In the case of services or supplies, a list of the principal deliveries effected or the main services provided over the past three years, with evidence of the deliveries and services provided.

    (b) An indication of the technicians or technical bodies involved especially those responsible for quality control.

    (c) A description of the technical facilities and measures used by the supplier or service provider for ensuring quality and the undertaking's study and research facilities.

    (d) Where the products or services to be supplied are complex or required for a special purpose, a check carried out by or on behalf of the contracting authorities.

    (e) The educational and professional qualifications of the service provider or contractor and/or those of the undertaking's managerial staff and, in particular, those of the person or persons responsible for providing the services or managing the work.

    (f) In appropriate cases, for public works and services contracts an indication of the environmental management measures the bidder will be able to apply.

    (g) The average annual manpower of the service provider or contractor and the number of managerial staff for the last three years.

    (h) The tools, plant, or technical equipment available to the service provider or contractor.

    (i) An indication of the proportion of the contract which the services provider may subcontract.

    (j) Samples, descriptions, and/or photographs of the products to be supplied and certificates of conformity of products.

**18.58** For particular contracts tenderers may, for the purposes of both economic and financial standing and for technical and/or professional ability rely on the capacities and/or abilities of other entities, whatever the nature of the links which it has with them. It must be able to prove to the relevant authority that it has the resources of these bodies available to it. If there is a group of entities bidding then the bidder may rely on the resources available within that group. The directive uses the term 'economic operator'. This includes contractors, suppliers, and service providers. A bidder cannot be rejected on the grounds that it is not a legal entity. (However, some means will have to be found of enforcing the contract which must of its nature be with a legal entity. Normally the situation will not arise as bidders will almost always be incorporated. If they are not and are not willing to become incorporated or to form a partnership, then a contract would have to be made with one or more individuals.) A bidder in the form of a group cannot be required as a condition of bidding that it forms itself into a legal entity. However, it can be required to form a legal entity for the purposes of entering into a contract.

## Contract award criteria

**18.59** Contracting authorities when selecting the criteria for the award of public contracts must base their awards on one of the following:

(a) when the award is made to the tender most economically advantageous from the point of view of the contracting authority, various criteria linked to the subject matter of the public contract in question, for example, quality, price, technical merit, aesthetic and functional characteristics, environmental characteristics, running costs, cost-effectiveness, after-sales service and technical assistance, delivery date, and delivery period or period of completion, or

(b) the lowest price only.

If the authority decides to award the contract to the most economically advantageous tender, it has to specify the relative weighting which it gives to each of the criteria they have chosen to use. Before the process of evaluating bids commences an authority will have to have worked out how it will go about scoring each bid against its specified criteria. This will include deciding the relative importance of each of the criteria and allocating weightings accordingly. These weightings must now be disclosed by being specified in the contract notice or in the contract documents, or, in the case of a competitive dialogue, the descriptive document. The weightings can allow for a range with an appropriate maximum spread. If it is not possible for demonstrable reasons to allocate weightings the authority must specify the criteria in descending order of importance.

---

## F  NON-COMMERCIAL CONSIDERATIONS

Under s. 17 of the LGA 1988 local authorities are forbidden from taking into account **18.60** non-commercial considerations when deciding whether to place a contractor on a select list, when shortlisting or selecting tenderers in supply and works contracts, and when approving the appointment of sub-contractors. Failure to comply with these provisions gives rise to a potential claim for damages from an aggrieved contractor. The complete list is set out in s. 17(5):

(a) the terms and conditions of employment by contractors of their workers or the composition of, the arrangements for the promotion, transfer or training of, or the other opportunities afforded to, their workforces;

(b) whether the terms on which contractors contract with their sub-contractors constitute, in the case of contracts with individuals, contracts for the provision by them as self- employed persons of their services only;

(c) any involvement of the business activities or interests of contractors with irrelevant fields of Government policy;

(d) the conduct of contractors or workers in industrial disputes between them or any involvement of the business activities of contractors in industrial disputes between other persons;

(e) the country or territory of origin of supplies to, or the location in any country or territory of the business activities or interests of, contractors;

(f) any political, industrial, or sectarian affiliations or interests of contractors or their directors, partners, or employees;

(g) financial support or lack of financial support by contractors for any institution to or from which the authority gives or withholds support;

(h) use or non-use by contractors of technical or professional services provided by the authority under the Building Act 1984 or the Building (Scotland) Act 1959.

This is not of much relevance to most local authority procurement practice now. However, it was seen as at least a theoretical potential obstacle to the achievement of best value and it was also thought that it could conflict with the advice that authorities were being given about the TUPE Regulations. The Local Government Best Value (Exclusion of Non-Commercial Considerations) Order 2001 (SI No. 2001/909) provides that (a) and (d) in the above list cease to be non-commercial considerations in relation to the best value requirements under Part I of the LGA 1999 or where there is a transfer of staff to which TUPE may apply.

---

## KEY DOCUMENTS

Delivering Better Services for Citizens (the Byatt Report) June 2001
National Procurement Strategy for Local Government ODPM/LGA October 2003
Directive on co-ordination of procedures for the award of public works contracts, public supply contracts and public service contracts
Local Government Best Value (Exclusion of Non-Commercial Considerations) Order 2001 (SI No. 2001/909)

# 19

# PUBLIC/PRIVATE PARTNERSHIPS

## A INTRODUCTION

The phrase 'public/private partnership' has been used to cover a variety of types of transaction **19.01** which local authorities carry out with the private sector. These include private finance transactions (PFIs), externalisations of local authority services, and long-term partnership arrangements. This chapter will focus mainly on two types of transactions which are of particular importance to local authorities: PFIs and strategic partnerships. The ways in which these terms have been used has not always been consistent. At one point it was recommended in a review of PFI that PFIs should be renamed as public/private partnerships. However, that expression had by this time already been commonly used in a much wider sense. Since the private finance initiative began in 1992, it is hardly accurate to describe it as an initiative, but the name has stuck. The type of transactions which are referred to in this chapter as PFIs and strategic partnerships are described below, but it needs to be remembered that these terms are not precise and there are a wide range of deals which can be described as falling within these headings.

A PFI transaction is an arrangement whereby a private sector provider will build or otherwise **19.02** provide an asset for a public authority at its own expense and then recoup the capital cost of its provision by virtue of being awarded a long-term contract (normally 25 years) to manage the facility which it provided. The 'asset' need not be a building. It could be equipment and software, as in the case of an ICT PFI. It could be major repairs, as would be the case with a housing PFI. The finance would typically be borrowed and repaid over the period of the long-term contract. An important element of PFI is that the main risks in relation to the project are taken by the contractor. A major incentive for local authorities to use PFI is the fact that for approved schemes the Government will pay the authority PFI credits i.e. added revenue payments which are intended to cover the capital costs of the scheme. There may or may not be a transfer of staff to the private sector provider.

A strategic partnership is a transaction in which a private sector partner agrees to provide **19.03** certain services for the council over a reasonably long period, will normally take over the employment of the council's staff who were providing these services, and also provide capital investment, typically in information and communications technology. The benefits to the council of such an arrangement will be that the security of the long-term contract will enable the private sector partner to invest in a way which would be more difficult for the local authority. It will sometimes involve the staff providing the services being moved to different premises. This type of strategic partnership will often be used for what are often referred to as corporate and transactional services such as human resources, finance, revenues and benefits, and ICT support. It may also involve the provision of improved means of access to the council's services for members of the public. An example of this will be the provision of call centres. The long-term nature of the partnership should place an incentive on the provider to ensure that high quality services are being provided and on both parties to try to resolve amicably the problems which will inevitably occur. There needs to be a shared interest in making the contract work.

---

## B   PFI TRANSACTIONS

**19.04**   The private finance initiative was introduced by the Government in the early 1990s as a means of enabling public assets to be provided by the private sector. The early PFIs were important projects for the Government or for health authorities. They involved prisons, hospitals, and other major construction works. The potential extension of the principle to local authorities soon became apparent. In 1996 the Government made amendments to the capital finance regulations to enable local authorities to enter into PFI transactions without these counting as credit arrangements. (It also made available Government funding in the form of PFI credits so that for approved schemes the local authority would receive additional grant to enable it to pay for the capital element of the charge to the contractor who paid for the initial capital outlay.) The first local authority PFI was Colfox School for Dorset County Council. The PFI in local government began to take off in 1997. In particular the enactment of the Local Government (Contracts) Act 1997 allowed local authorities to 'certify' the legality of contracts and make arrangements for repayment of loans if transactions were found to be *ultra vires*. This allayed many of the fears of the private sector (especially funders) about becoming involved in the local authority market after the cases of *Hazell v Hammersmith and Fulham London Borough Council*, *Crédit Suisse v Allerdale Borough Council* and *Crédit Suisse v Waltham Forest London Borough Council*.

**19.05**   The typical PFI transaction is an arrangement whereby the private sector partner is required to design, build, finance, and operate a new facility. (This is why these schemes are sometimes referred to as DBFOs.) To take a school as an example, the local authority will make the land available and the contractor will build a school on it at its own expense, normally using borrowed money. There is no payment at this stage. The design of the school is the responsibility of the contractor, though it will obviously be approved by the local authority. Once it is built, the contractor will maintain the buildings and provide facilities management services at the school in return for a regular payment known as the unitary charge. The steps which need to be undertaken by a local authority undertaking a PFI transaction are set out below.

**Preparation of an outline business case.**   The idea of a PFI transaction may have come   **19.06**
about as a result of a best value review or an examination, either internal or external, of how
a service could be improved or made more cost-effective or how an identified need for capital
investment was to be met. The authority will at some stage have to undertake a full options
appraisal, setting out the alternatives to a PFI, always including a 'do nothing' option. This
will include a public sector comparator i.e. a comparison with what it would cost the authority to undertake the transaction using its own borrowing capacity and resources. The outline
business case (OBC) needs to address these issues. The OBC is the document which is
initially submitted to the Government by the authority for approval of PFI credits.

**Submission to Government and PRG Review.**   This stage takes place whenever an author-   **19.07**
ity is seeking PFI credits from the Government. A local authority can still undertake a PFI
without Government financial support, which may be because there are aspects of the
project or the local authority's requirements which would be inconsistent with the
requirements imposed by Partnerships UK (PUK) and the Treasury on a project in receipt of
Government funding, or it may be that the timescale does not fit. A local authority undertaking a PFI which is not being supported by PFI credits needs only to comply with the
generally applicable legal requirements. The outline business case is subitted to the applicable Government department. This will depend on the nature of the project. The DfES
approve education projects, the DOH social services projects, and the ODPM most other
types of scheme. The sponsoring department then submits the OBC to the Projects Review
Group (PRG). This is a cross-departmental group which has the function of deciding whether
the projects which it considers are suitable for funding from the Government. This process
will include scrutiny of the proposal by the Office of Government Commerce. If the project
passes the PRG stage the authority will proceed to seek bidders.

**Advertising and the OJEU notice.**   Normally the project will need to be advertised in the   **19.08**
OJEU to comply with the European procurement rules. Some types of project may not,
strictly speaking, need to be advertised in the OJEU. For instance a social services project
where most of the expenditure would be on the provision of care services would fall outside
the requirements of most of the rules. However, the placing of an OJEU advertisement is
likely to be good practice in any event. It may also be a good idea to advertise in trade
journals or other publications which are likely to be seen by potential bidders. The advertisement, and in particular the way in which the project is described in it, needs to be drafted
with care. It is quite common, in these types of project, for the authority to change its
requirements or for new ideas to emerge during the course of the bidding process. If these
represent a substantial departure from the description of the project contained in the original advertisement, then this could mean the local authority having to readvertise. The pre-
qualification questionnaire will contain questions designed to obtain information about the
financial standing, capacity, and ability of the potential bidder. Since the project is likely to
be governed by the EU procurement rules, the information sought at this stage must be
limited to the information which the authority is entitled to take into account for shortlisting tenderers in accordance with those rules. However, it is necessary to obtain some details
of the contractor's relevant experience.

**Choosing the preferred bidder.**   Since the Government's recommended approach is that   **19.09**
the negotiated procedure under the EU procurement rules should be used, the document to

be sent out to the shortlisted tenderers will normally be called an invitation to negotiate (ITN). When the consolidated procurement directive is transposed into UK law, there is an alternative procedure which may be suitable, the competitive dialogue procedure. There may, however, be a stage before this known as an invitation to submit outline proposals (ISOP). This may be required where the exact scope of the project is not clear and may need to be refined as a result of suggestions from the market. An invitation to submit an ISOP will not contain the same level of detail as an ITN. It will not require the same sort of detailed response. Instead, the authority will explain the outcomes it requires and invite proposals in general terms as to how these might be achieved. (It is in general hard to see why this type of research could not have been done as part of a soft market testing exercise rather than as part of a bid process.)

19.10    The ITN will be sent out to the shortlisted tenderers. There will ideally be three or four of these. The information required will include details of the tenderer's detailed proposals for providing the assets and the services. This will include detailed architectural drawings and method statements about the way in which the services will be provided. It will also be usual to include a draft project agreement and invite the tenderers to mark up on the copy any clauses they consider to be unacceptable, though amendments to the Treasury standard documentation will not normally be allowed. The ITN will also need to include a payment mechanism, setting out the arrangements for payment, indexation and deductions for failure to perform the services satisfactorily, or for failure to ensure that the facilities are available. The bidders will be invited to submit their financial models. These set out the basis of the financing of the project, the anticipated costs and income, and the underlying assumptions.

19.11    **Tender evaluation.**   Following receipt of the tenders, they will have to be evaluated. This will need to follow an objective, almost mathematically precise process. This is because of the requirements in the EU procurement rules that the factors which the authority will take into account when selecting the final bidder must be listed in the advertisement or the tender documentation in order of importance. This in effect means that the scoring mechanism will need to be explained in the ITN.

19.12    **Best and final offer.**   There may be yet another stage between the ITN and the appointment of the preferred bidder which is the invitation to submit a best and final offer (BAFO). The tenderers will have submitted a very large amount of detailed information with their bid. However, after this, there may still be further information required and many points which need to be clarified and negotiated. It may still be difficult to select the preferred bidder without another round of competition. This may also concentrate the minds of the bidders in putting forward their best possible price. The BAFO documents will normally be sent only to the final two bidders. This will not involve as much work and information as the preparation of a bid. It will concentrate on the areas where the bids were weakest and where further information/clarification is required to enable the authority to make their final decision.

19.13    **Final business case.**   The final business case will need to be submitted to the sponsoring department in order to obtain PFI credits. The final business case will contain essentially the same things as the OBC but there will now be detailed information setting out the details of the successful bid and the bid price. If there are derogations from the standardised documentation, they need to be reported as part of this process. Unless these amendments are acceptable to PUK (Partnerships UK, the body responsible for advising HM Treasury on these issues) they will have to be renegotiated until PUK are satisfied with them. Without PUK approval, the PFI credits will not be released.

**Commercial and financial close.** Theoretically once the preferred bidder has been chosen **19.14** the agreement and production of final contract documentation should be a relatively straightforward matter. However, there are frequently further complex discussions prior to the contract documentation being signed. This will include discussions over the detailed design, the service specifications and method statements for service delivery, the payment mechanism, and the terms of the project agreement and ancillary documents. At this stage, the external funders will usually undertake their own due diligence exercise and this may lead to new issues being raised. There are in theory two stages, commercial close when the terms of the transaction are agreed between the council and the contractor, and the contract is entered into, and financial close when the loan agreement and other supporting documentation is entered into and the final figure for the unitary charge can be calculated. In practice the two stages are undertaken at the same time.

There are a number of legal issues which need to be considered in all PFI transactions: **19.15**

1. The standardised documentation must be used. The latest set of documentation is the Standardisation of PFI Contracts Version 3 (SOPC3) published by HM Treasury in March 2004. The only acceptable derogations will be those that are project specific, are needed in the context of some features of that particular project, and therefore require amendment to the drafting. PUK will not accept changes to the essential commercial position represented by the documentation nor will it accept attempts to improve on or clarify the wording. There is also standardised local government documentation, published by 4Ps, but the use of this is not mandatory.

2. There are often delays connected with the grant of planning permission. Further work is likely to be required on the designs following preferred bidder appointment. There may be delays in granting planning permission. Funders will often not be willing for financial close to take place until three months after commercial close, so that the risk of the decision to grant planning permission being challenged by way of judicial review is minimised.

3. The contractor will usually be a company set up for the sole purpose of delivering the project, a special purpose vehicle. The finance is usually project specific, i.e. the security is the future income stream derived from the payments of the unitary charge. This means that the funders will themselves need to investigate the project. They will usually appoint a separate firm of lawyers to represent their interests, and certain aspects of the transaction may be unacceptable to the funders even if it is acceptable to the contractor.

4. The process to be followed for PFI transactions does not fit well with the EU procurement rules. The Treasury Taskforce Private Finance Technical Note No. 2 suggests that PFI transactions can be undertaken using the negotiated procedure. It refers to the Regulation 10(2)(c) of the Public Works Contracts Regulations, allowing the negotiated procedure to be used in the following situation:

> Exceptionally, when the nature of the work or works to be carried out under the contract is such, or the risks attaching thereto are such, as not to permit prior overall pricing.

They suggest that the equivalent provision in Regulation 10(2)(c) of the Public Services Contracts Regulations allows the negotiated procedure to be used in these types of contracts:

> Where the nature of the service to be provided, in particular in the case of intellectual services or services specified in category 6 Part A of Schedule 1 (of the Services Regulations), is such that specifications cannot be drawn up with sufficient precision to permit the award of the contract using the open or restricted procedure.

As indicated above, the competitive dialogue procedure may provide a suitable alternative when this is available.

## C   STRATEGIC PARTNERSHIPS

**19.16**   The development of strategic partnerships has a more complex history than that of PFI. That was the extension of a Government initiative to local authorities made attractive by virtue of Government subsidy. A variety of factors have led authorities to enter into strategic partnerships. The traditional approach to the provision of local authority services was that the authority hired the staff and got on with the job. There were some authorities in the 1970s which outsourced to private contractors services which had previously been provided in-house. In the 1980s and the early part of the 1990s under the Local Government, Planning and Land Act 1980 and the Local Government Act 1988 local authorities had to expose a large number of services to competition. Although this led to local authorities setting up separate units to deliver these services and separate trading accounts for them, it did not lead to large-scale private sector penetration of this market. Competitive pressures were undoubtedly brought to bear on local authorities but the majority of contracts were awarded to the in-house provider often with little competition.

**19.17**   The introduction of the best value regime was undoubtedly a factor in encouraging strategic partnerships. Local authorities began to question whether different methods of providing their services could be more cost effective. There was no longer the hostility felt towards private sector providers which there had been during the period when competition was compulsory. More protective labour laws and changing economic circumstances have probably played their part as well. At a time when the Transfer of Undertakings (Protection of Employment) Regulations were not applied to the public sector, a private contractor winning a contract would be likely to lead to compulsory redundancies. Now when a service is taken over by the private sector the expectation will be that the workforce is transferred and that their terms and conditions of employment will remain the same.

**19.18**   Another factor has been the experience of PFI transactions and other outsourcing initiatives. This has meant that there are now within the public sector the management and project skills to undertake this type of transaction and members and senior officers who have the vision and political will to carry them through. Finally there has been the change in thinking about how major construction projects should be managed. Long-term partnerships with a service provider are in some ways the logical extension of the thinking behind the Egan report which recommended a constructive partnership approach to major building projects.

The Government has seen the advantages of strategic partnerships and encouraged local **19.19**
authorities to enter into them. The potential benefits of private sector involvement in managing local authority assets were one of the recommendations in a Government examination of Public Private Partnerships in 2000: Public Private Partnerships: The Government
Approach. An early contribution in terms of Government support for strategic partnerships
was the publication of the paper Supporting Strategic Service Delivery Partnerships in Local
Government—A Research and Development Programme published by the DTLR in April
2001. This summarised the main features of strategic partnership transactions and committed the Government to providing practical advice and assistance to enable authorities to
enter into this type of deal. A Strategic Partnering Taskforce was set up to undertake a
research and development programme into the use and potential of strategic partnerships
within local authorities. The Taskforce delivered its final report in March 2004. This extolled
the benefits of strategic partnerships and made a number of recommendations as to how
local authorities should approach them. They see a number of key advantages to local
authorities in adopting a strategic partnering approach:

- They help to secure a step-change in efficiency and remove cultural and organisational
  barriers to improvement.
- They can add significantly to an authority's capacity to re-engineer service delivery.
- They can provide investment and address wider community objectives.
- They provide impetus to refocusing service delivery on the service user.
- They can bring economies of scale that authorities cannot address in any other way.
- They engender constructive, collaborative relationships with service-delivery partners
  that provide flexibility for the future and innovation in approach.

It will be noted that all the above bullet points apart from the first and last (which are also **19.20**
really potential rather than guaranteed benefits) talk about what strategic partnerships 'can'
do. This is why the planning stage is crucial. There is a need to be clear, and set out in the
contractual documentation what the authority's expectations are and what the private sector partner will be required to deliver. The Taskforce final report warns that a local authority
should have realistic expectations and give early consideration to:

- the likely cost of what is being planned and the available savings;
- the value for money and affordability of the strategic partnership.

## Procedure for letting a strategic partnership

There is no strict necessity for a local authority to follow the type of procedure which it **19.21**
needs to undertake for a PFI when it wants to apply for credits. A strategic partnership could
be started on a wing and a prayer. However, this would be most inadvisable and there is
advice about how to undertake the planning stage. The Taskforce publication From Vision to
Outline Business Case advises that authorities should follow a similar type of planning
process to that which would be used for PFI projects. Authorities should carry out a baseline
assessment, a strategic outline case (setting out how in essence how they intend to deliver
the project), an options appraisal (including a full evaluation of the potential alternatives),
an outline business case, and an implementation plan.

As with PFI contracts, it is likely that most strategic partnerships will need to be advertised in **19.22** the OJEU since they will be public service contracts and will almost certainly be above the relevant threshold. It is also likely to be advantageous to advertise in the trade press. Since it is possible that the decision to enter into a strategic partnership may have been preceded by soft market testing, many of those who might be interested in bidding for the project may already be aware that it is likely to be tendered. Again a questionnaire will be sent to those who respond to the advertisement. A shortlisting process will then take place. This might involve the use of an ISOP but this is very unlikely to be necessary. As with a PFI transaction, it is not sensible to crowd the field with potential tenderers as the completion of the invitation to negotiate will be a complex document and substantial time and resources will be needed to put together a credible bid. Again, it is likely that the assessment of bids will require an evaluation as to which is the most economically advantageous. There may be a further refinement of the process involving a best and final offer from the final two bidders but, as with PFI, this is likely to add to the length of the procurement process.

**19.23**  There are a number of ways in which strategic partnerships have a slightly different emphasis from PFIs.

1.  There is not quite the same emphasis on capital investment. One of the main purposes of most PFIs is the provision of a major capital asset. Much of the standard documentation for PFIs is concerned with ensuring that funders are compensated in the event that the contract is terminated. Although this is a potential issue in strategic partnerships, the contracts will be more service-focused and the protection of funders' interests will not be paramount. Many may not involve any external funding.

2.  The contract period will typically not be as long as PFI transactions, with fifteen years being typical rather than twenty-five. This is a long enough period to make significant investment from the private sector partner worthwhile, but permits slightly more flexibility for an authority in planning for the long term.

3.  As with PFI there is a transfer of risk. However the risk is not so much in terms of responsibility for an asset (which will be the main focus in many PFIs) but for the delivery of customer satisfaction and taking the lead in resolving problems in the provision of services.

4.  There is likely to be a greater emphasis on innovation and improvements in efficiency than with PFI transactions. With PFI some authorities will be embarking on the project because they see it as the most cost-effective means of providing a new asset. Many of the services provided as part of a typical PFI transaction, such as facilities management and maintenance do not readily lend themselves to startling innovations. The driving force behind a strategic partnership is more likely to be a need for improvement in service delivery and efficiency gains.

5.  The relationship is more likely to rely on a genuine partnership approach of the type proposed by the Egan report. Whereas a PFI contract will define a relationship based on clearly defined roles, a strategic partnership is more likely to place emphasis on a joint approach to problem solving and a co-operative spirit in delivering improvements. Most large strategic partnerships have a detailed governance structure to facilitate decision-making.

**19.24**  There are a number of issues in strategic partnerships which lawyers involved in these types of transaction will need to consider carefully.

1.  There is at present no standardised documentation. Although there are various templates in existence, and a procurement pack is currently being prepared by the 4Ps, there is not a standard which has reached the same state of development as the PFI documentation. Nor is there a market norm in the sense that this exists in the PFI market. Since the range of transactions which can be classified under the heading of strategic partnership is much wider than those which can be called PFIs, the development of a standard form is much more problematic. The use of standardised documentation can effectively be enforced by the Government since acceptance of the standard terms is a pre-condition of access to Government funding in the form of PFI credits. There is no such means of enforcement with strategic partnerships. It will be a matter for the parties to negotiate between themselves.

2.  The nature of the arrangement as a genuine partnership creates difficulties in the preparation and drafting of the contract documentation. Contracts are a means of expressing the terms of a commercial bargain between the parties. In the case of strategic partnerships, they also need to be a means of conveying and recording the expectations of the parties about how the partnership arrangements will work in practice. In some instances this will need rethinking the traditional role of the lawyer and drafting clauses which provide a framework for the operation of the partnership rather than setting out a detailed mechanism for every aspect of the contract. To work effectively, the arrangement will need to provide clear benefits to both sides.

3.  To an even greater extent than PFI, the services will be described in a way which is based on outcomes rather than inputs. The specification will be prepared by those with a knowledge of their service and a clear understanding of what they want to achieve. Nonetheless the way in which these requirements are expressed in terms of contractual requirements will sometimes be quite difficult.

4.  Since one of the major reasons for an authority to enter into a strategic partnership will be to enable the contractor to provide services in innovative ways, there will need to be a means of capturing this at the time the contract is entered into. However, inevitably, such innovations will only emerge during the course of the contract as the obstacles which occur in the provision of the services give rise to ideas for new means of overcoming these. In addition new technologies may emerge or be developed during the course of the contract. This will mean that the contract will need to be flexible enough to accommodate and even anticipate future change in a way that will enable the authority to control and benefit from the process. This means that the change control mechanism will need to be carefully drafted.

5.  Sometimes the existence of a strategic partnership will allow the contractor to develop ideas and solutions including systems and software which lend themselves to future commercial exploitation. Since the authority is providing the means for this intellectual property to be developed, there needs to be a means for ensuring that it shares the benefits with the contractor. It also needs to be considered who is best placed to develop and exploit these ideas and solutions.

6.  The property issues may be more complex than they are with other types of transaction. Whereas outsourcing a contract may mean allowing a contractor to have a lease or licence of office or depot space, or if the contractor has its own facilities, moving the operation so that land and buildings are released, there may be a wide variety of arrangements suitable for a strategic partnership. This could include the possibility that

staff will be relocated not immediately but at some stage in the future. Provision will need to be made for this at the outset.

7. Whereas only a small proportion of PFI transactions are likely to involve the transfer of staff, most strategic partnerships will involve such a transfer. Large-scale transfers are frequently difficult to manage and there is not a clear market agreement as to how the risk of pre-transfer claims which have not yet been made should be dealt with. There will be a need to ensure that the provisions of the Cabinet Office Guidance Staff Transfers in the Public Sector Statement of Practice and the guidance set out at Annex D to Circular 03/03 are followed. There are alternative ways of dealing with staffing issues. These have included secondment of the relevant employees and sub-letting the contract back to the council so that the staff remain council employees.

8. Some types of strategic partnerships may require an initial investment from the council. This will not usually be in the form of a grant or loan. The capital investment is more likely to be contributed by the contractor. It is more likely to be in the form of access to facilities or infrastructure. In these circumstances, particular care will need to be taken that the investment does not amount to the provision of state aid. (See chapter 20.) This will usually not be a problem because the preferred tenderer will have been chosen as a result of open competition. However, extra care will be needed when the transaction comes about as a result of an approach by an organisation to the authority or if the suggestion arises in the context of post-tender negotiations.

9. The flexibility needed to negotiate a contract where the parameters may not be entirely clear at the outset means that the letting of strategic partnerships will often not fit easily with the somewhat rigid requirements of the EU procurement rules. If new suggestions arise following the initial advertisement they need to be scrutinised to ensure that the proposed change is permissible. It is a feature of these types of transactions that new services are often added incrementally. The potential scope of the contract needs to be reflected in the initial OJEU notice.

---

## KEY DOCUMENTS

Standardisation of PFI Contracts Version 3 HM Treasury March 2004

Standardisation of Local Authority Contracts—Contracting to Achieve Best Value OGC 2002

Treasury Taskforce Private Finance Technical Note No. 2

Public Private Partnerships—The Government Approach 2000

Supporting Strategic Service Delivery Partnerships in Local Government—A Research and Development Programme April 2001

From Vision to Outline Business Case—Report of Strategic Partnering Taskforce March 2004

Procurement packs offering guidance on various types of PFI transaction are available from 4Ps: <http://www.4Ps.gov.uk>

# 20

# COMPETITION AND STATE AID

## A COMPETITION LAW

There are circumstances in which local authorities will be affected by competition law, and **20.01** it is quite likely that the need for advice on this issue will increase in the future, particularly if a local authority becomes heavily involved in trading. At present, competition law has impacted on local authorities only when they have been accused of abusing their dominant position within a market, having an effective monopoly in relation to certain types of economic activity within an area.

The Competition Act 1998 replaced a complex web of legislation about restrictive trade practices with a new statutory regime closely modelled on Article 81 of the Treaty of Rome. There were a number of advantages to this approach. In particular, it harmonises EU and UK law and allows UK courts interpreting the Act to benefit from the case law of the ECJ in interpreting the terms of the Treaty.

The following are prohibited under s. 2(1) of the 1998 Act: **20.02**

Subject to s. 3, agreements between undertakings, decisions by associations of undertakings or concerted practices that—

(a)  may affect trade within the United Kingdom, and

(b)  have as their object or effect the prevention, restriction, or distortion of competition within the United Kingdom.

With the substitutions of the words 'within the United Kingdom' for 'between Member States', in (a) and 'United Kingdom' for 'Common Market' at the end, the wording of the section is taken directly from Article 81. The section also contains an illustrative list of activities that would breach s. 2(1), again taken directly from Article 81.

**20.03**  Subsection (1) applies, in particular, to agreements, decisions, or practices that—

    (a)   directly or indirectly fix purchase or selling prices or any other trading conditions;

    (b)   limit or control production, markets, technical development, or involvement;

    (c)   share markets or sources of supply;

    (d)   apply dissimilar conditions to equivalent transactions with other trading parties, thereby placing them at a competitive disadvantage;

    (e)   make the conclusion of contracts subject to acceptance by the other parties of supplementary obligations, which, by their nature or according to commercial usage, have no connection with the subject of such contracts.

It needs to be stressed that the above list is illustrative, not exhaustive. An agreement may fall foul of s. 2(1) without being mentioned in the above list. Local authorities need to be aware of these provisions when carrying out tendering and when engaged in commercial activities themselves. There is no doubt that potentially the word 'undertaking' can apply to local authorities. The word 'undertaking' is not defined in the 1998 Act, or in the Treaty of Rome. However, it has been interpreted by the ECJ as meaning every entity engaged in an economic activity regardless of the legal status of the entity and the way in which it is financed. It does not matter that the activity is not profit making: *Distribution of Package Tours During the 1990 World Cup* [1994] 5 CMLR 253, but the competition rules have no application to the exercise of powers of a public authority: *Wouters v Algemene Raad van de Nederlandse Orde van Avocaten* [2002] 4 CMLR 913.

**20.04**  So far the aspect of competition law that has had the largest impact on local authorities has been the prohibition on abuse of a dominant position, which is contained in s. 18 of the Act and that again, essentially follows the wording of the Treaty. Section 16(1) provides that

> Subject to section 19, any conduct on the part of one or more undertakings, which amounts to the absence of a dominant position in a market, is prohibited if it may affect trade within the United Kingdom.

**20.05**  There is an illustrative list of conduct (very similar to the list under s. 2) that may constitute such abuse set out in subsection (2):

    (a)   directly or indirectly imposing unfair purchase or selling prices or other unfair trading conditions;

    (b)   limiting production, markets, or technical development to the prejudice of consumers;

    (c)   applying dissimilar conditions to equivalent transactions with other trading parties, thereby placing them at a competitive disadvantage;

    (d)   making the conclusion of contracts subject to acceptance by the other parties of supplementary obligations which, by their nature or according to commercial usage, have no connection with the subject of the contracts.

**20.06**  Local authorities acting as purchasers of residential care services have been found to be acting as undertakings for the purpose of s. 18 above by the CCAT (the Competition Appeals

Tribunal, which considers appeals against decisions by the Director General of Fair Trading (DGFT) under the Competition Act). The complaint was brought by a company called BetterCare, which asked for a ruling from the DGFT that a Health and Social Services Trust (Northern Ireland local health authority) abused its dominant position in that, having an effective monopoly on the purchase of residential care services in its area, used this power in order to drive down prices to unnecessarily low levels. The DGFT rejected the complaint but it was upheld by the CCAT, which held that the contracts between the Trust and its suppliers were commercial contracts and in entering into them the Trust was acting as an undertaking engaged in economic activity.

This conclusion would obviously have serious implications for local authorities, extending **20.07** far beyond the residential care market. Authorities are often in a position of having a monopoly of this type within their area and complying with the conflicting duties of ensuring best value and at the same time not using the position to impose unfairly low prices would seem to involve a very difficult balancing act. However, the decision in *BetterCare* has been undermined by the decision of the Court of First Instance on a very similar point: *Federación Nacional de Empresas de Instrumentación Científica, Médica, Técnica y Dental (FENIN) v Commission of the European Communities* [2003] 5 CMLR 1. In this case a group representing suppliers of medical goods and equipment to the Spanish health service complained to the European Commission about the length of time taken to pay members' invoices. They claimed this was a breach of Article 82 in that the health service, when purchasing goods, was acting as an undertaking within the meaning of Article 82, in managing the public health service. The Commission rejected the complaint. Its role as provider of health services could not be separated from its role as a purchaser of goods and equipment for this purpose. The Commission's approach was endorsed by the CFI. The court concluded:

(a) The concept of an undertaking covered any entity engaged in an economic activity, regardless of its legal status and the way in which it was financed.

(b) The characteristic feature of an economic entity was offering goods and services in a given market, not simply the business of purchasing. The activity of purchasing could not be separated from the question of the use to which the goods were subsequently put.

(c) An organisation that purchased goods, not to offer goods and services as part of an economic activity but to use them for a different activity, e.g., one of a purely social nature, did not act as an undertaking simply because it purchased these goods. The health service was therefore not acting as an undertaking for the purposes of EU competition law.

# B  STATE AID

State aid which distorts or has the potential to distort competition is unlawful under Euro- **20.08** pean law. If a government or public authority provides financial aid to a business this has the potential to give that business an advantage as against other businesses across the European Union. It could therefore distort competition and affect trade. For this reason state aid, except in certain circumstances, is contrary to the European Community Treaty.

**20.09**    This is an issue of particular concern to local authorities within the UK as they now have extensive powers to make grants and provide assistance to businesses and non-profit making bodies in order to assist in regeneration or bring benefits to their areas. Any schemes which involve providing any kind of advantage or subsidy need to be carefully scrutinised in order to ensure they do not infringe the rules against state aid. The consequences of making unlawful state aid can be drastic. The European Commission has power to recover unlawful aid, which could have a seriously adverse effect on the recipient as well as be embarrassing to the authority which granted the aid.

**20.10**    Article 87 (1) of the EC Treaty provides as follows:

> Save as otherwise provided in this treaty, any aid granted by a Member State or through State resources in any form whatsoever, which distorts or threatens to distort competitors by favouring certain undertakings or the production of certain goods shall, insofar as it affects trade between Member States, be incompatible with the Common Market.

State aid therefore has five characteristics:

1. It is granted by the State or through State resources.
2. It favours certain undertakings or the production of certain goods.
3. It distorts or threatens to distort competition.
4. It affects trade between Member States.
5. It confers an advantage on the recipient.

**20.11**    Anything, other than general measures of economic policy, which confers a benefit on the recipient, is capable of constituting an aid. As was pointed out by the ECJ it is wider than a subsidy. An aid . . .

> . . . places emphasis on its purpose and seems especially devised for a particular objective which cannot be achieved without outside help. The concept of an aid is nevertheless wider than that of a subsidy because it enforces not only positive benefits such as subsidies themselves, but also interventions which, in various forms, mitigate the changes which are normally included in the budget of an undertaking and which without them being subsidies in the strict sense of the word, are similar in character and have the same effect.
> *De Gezamenlijke Steenkolenmijnen in Limburg v High Authority* [1961] ECR 1.

However, when in the case of *R (BT3G Ltd) v Secretary of State for Trade and Industry* [2001] LS Gaz R 35, the Court of Appeal had to consider whether the fact that Vodafone and Orange were able to delay their payments for mobile phone licences because of their need to become separate companies, the Court of Appeal expressed doubts as to whether the fortuitous effect of the operation of contractual conditions could constitute state aid within the meaning of Article 87.

### Provision of aid through the state

**20.12**    The first of these criteria does not just include government grants. It includes payments made by local authorities and private bodies if the aid originates from state resources. Thus, for instance, a local authority could not avoid the application of the state aid rules by channelling funds through a company. However, it must involve some actual or potential financial liability on the part of the state. (This could include an opportunity cost e.g. providing one body with access to some infrastructure which the authority could not then subsequently exploit by providing access to another body.) Anything that was undertaken for a regulatory purpose would not constitute state aid even if it had the effect of favouring certain enterprises at the expense of others.

## Undertakings and selectivity

As regards the second criterion, the aid does not necessarily need to be made to a business in the conventional sense of the term. An organisation does not need to be a company in order to be an undertaking for these purposes. A partnership or a self-employed individual could be undertakings. So could a company which was wholly or partly owned by a local authority. Nor does an undertaking have to be a self-contained legal entity. An organisation could be partly an undertaking for these purposes and partly not an undertaking.  **20.13**

The issue is whether there is a market in the type of goods or services which the beneficiary of the aid is supplying. Thus aid to a charity or non-profit making body can be state aid if there are other bodies in competition with them on a commercial basis. If it is intended to provide money to an organisation which is charitable but where there may be an argument that they are in competition with the private sector, then it is necessary to ensure that the aid is not used to subsidise any economic activity which the charity may be carrying out. This does not necessarily need to be achieved by setting up a separate legal entity (though this is often the solution for charities because of the tax position). It would need to be shown that the aid towards purely charitable activities was accounted for separately from that where there was an economic activity. However, certain organisations are not undertakings. These include schools (other than private schools), universities, and hospitals which will treat anyone. Thus aid which might be unlawful if given direct to a recipient could be lawful if supplied through a university. Giving a research grant to a company could be unlawful state aid though giving it to a university would not be even if individual companies derived benefits from this.  **20.14**

Any aid or benefit which is available only on some kind of selective basis is likely to be found to give a selective advantage. If it is available only to businesses within a particular region, or a particular sector or to businesses of a particular size or businesses which produce certain specified goods or services then it is likely to be unlawful. This restriction could easily prevent a local authority from taking up an offer with a business which would involve that business being given some kind of competitive advantage. One solution to this is to ensure that a process of competition has been undertaken. Once a tendering process has been gone through it would be very difficult to argue that the aid was being provided on a selective basis.  **20.15**

The principle against which the Commission judges whether state aid is giving a selective advantage is called the market investor principle: *Belgium v EC Commission* [1986] ECR 2263. If a public authority is conferring an advantage on a private enterprise by giving a grant, loan or guarantee, or buying shares in it, then this will not be unlawful if the authority could demonstrate that a market investor in the same situation would do the same thing when confronted with a similar set of circumstances. Obviously this will not always simply be a question of looking at whether something was a good investment. There may be no market against which to judge whether a market investor would have behaved differently. In  **20.16** these situations, which could for instance include disposal of publicly owned land, the Commission will look at whether what the authority were doing could be justified on a commercial basis. Thus disposal of land at an undervalue would be regarded as a strong indication that state aid was being provided. This is obviously putting authorities very much in the position of trading entities with their eye on the potential profit rather than having regard to the wider benefits to their area. Investment in infrastructure which is available to enterprises on an equal footing will not constitute state aid.

### Distortion of competition

**20.17** The third criterion will very often be fulfilled if the others are. The Commission may regard even small amounts of aid as having the potential to distort competition. The fact that a business is small and local may not be sufficient grounds for it to be regarded as outside the state aid rules. Even small local businesses potentially face competition from other companies from elsewhere in the EU particularly in the case of goods and services which can be traded or commissioned on the internet. In the opinion of Advocate-General Capotorti in the case of *Philip Morris v Commission of the European Communities* [1980] ECR 2671 he expressed doubt about the argument that Article 92(1) needed to be read as if it referred to a 'material' distortion (or threat of distortion) of competition (p. 2699).

### Affecting trade between Member States

**20.18** The fourth criterion is also easily fulfilled. The fact that the aid benefits a type of business where there are not generally competitors from across the EU tendering for the work will not prevent it being unlawful. The European Court of Justice has interpreted this criterion strictly. Selective aid, even of a very small amount, is regarded as affecting trade. However, single businesses with only an immediate local market could be regarded as outside this criterion.

In *France v Commission of the European Communities* [1980] ECR 4075 Advocate-General Lenz recommended a restrictive approach. Having referred to the extensive exceptions to the rule against the provision of state aid he concluded:

> . . . it cannot be assumed that there should be further unwritten exceptions to the prohibition of aid. Therefore the argument that minor hindrances to competition and intra-Community trade should be allowed within the framework of Article 922 of the EEC Treaty cannot be upheld.

**20.19** The Court concluded that there was no need to show that an undertaking itself exported in order for there to be an effect on trade between Member States and a distortion of competition:

> . . . aid to an undertaking may be such as to affect trade between the Member States and distort competition where that undertaking competes with products coming from other Member States, even if it does not itself export its products. Such a situation may exist even where there is no overcapacity in the sector at issue. Where a Member State grants aid to an undertaking, domestic production may for that reason be maintained or increased with the result that, in circumstances such as those found to exist by the Commission, undertakings established in other Member States have less chance of exporting their products to the market in that Member

State. Such aid is therefore likely to affect trade between Member States and distort competition. (pp. 4087–8, para 19)

However, there is a de minimis threshold. This is that an undertaking receiving less than **20.20** EUR 100,000 over a three year period is regarded as not having a significant effect on competition. There are three exceptions to this:

(a)  transport, though further consideration is being given to extending the threshold to this area;

(b)  agriculture, because of the subsidies already provided under the common agricultural policy, though there is a de minimis threshold of EUR 3,000 over three years;

(c)  where there is a breach of the rules of the world trade organisation, for instance by seeking to boost the domestic products of an individual state.

If de minimis aid is given by a public authority it must be given pursuant to a grant and the grant offer must specify that it is being provided pursuant to the de minimis allowance. It is possible for a single organisation to have more than one de minimis threshold if the separate parts of that organisation are operating in different markets.

## Provision of an advantage

Aid need not simply be in the form of money. Anything which confers an advantage can be **20.21** state aid. This could include, for instance the provision of guarantees, or access to infrastructure. However, providing for the cost of something which could not be provided by the market because it would be uneconomic to do so, will not constitute state aid. A typical example of this is the provision of transport services to remote locations.

## Guarantees

The question of the extent to which a guarantee can constitute state aid may be important to **20.22** local authorities, particularly as they are empowered to provide guarantees in order to support their power to promote the well-being of their area. Clearly, a guarantee that does not affect trade between Member States will not constitute state aid. However, this will be comparatively rare—see below. The Commission has published a notice on this issue (Commission Notice on the application of Articles 87 and 88 of the EC Treaty to State Aid in the form of guarantees OJ [2000] C 71/7).

Paragraph 4.2 sets out the circumstances in which an individual guarantee does not **20.23** constitute state aid. (All the criteria below must be fulfilled.)

(a)  the borrower is not in financial difficulty;

(b)  the borrower would in principle be able to obtain a loan on market conditions from the financial markets without any intervention by the state;

(c)  the guarantee is linked to a specific financial transaction, is for a fixed maximum amount, does not cover more than 80 per cent of the outstanding loan or other financial obligations (except for bonds and similar instruments), and is not open-ended;

(d)  the market price for the guarantee is paid (which reflects, amongst other [things] the amount and duration of the guarantee, the security given by the borrower, the borrower's financial position, the sector of activity and the prospects, the rates of default, and other economic conditions).

**20.24**   Paragraph 4.3 sets out the conditions that must be fulfilled in order for a State Guarantee Scheme (i.e., a scheme set up to grant individual guarantees) not to constitute state aid.

(a)   the scheme does not allow guarantees to be granted to borrowers who are in financial difficulty;

(b)   the borrowers would in principle be able to obtain a loan on market conditions from the financial markets without any intervention from the state;

(c)   the guarantees are linked to a specific financial transaction, are for a fixed maximum amount, do not cover more than 80 per cent of each outstanding loan or other financial obligations (except for bonds and similar instruments) and are not open-ended;

(d)   the terms of a scheme are based on a realistic assessment of the risk so that premiums paid by the beneficiary enterprises make it, in all probability, self-financing;

(e)   the scheme provides for the terms on which future guarantees are granted and the overall financing of the scheme to be reviewed at least once a year;

(f)   the premiums cover both the nominal risks associated with granting the guarantee and the administrative costs of the scheme, including where the state provides the initial capital for the start-up of the scheme a normal return on that capital.

## Exceptions

**20.25**   Certain types of aid are seen as compatible with the rule against state aid. Article 87(2) provides that the following are not to be regarded as state aid:

(a)   social aid granted to individual consumers granted without discrimination in relation to the origin of the products concerned;

(b)   aid to make good damage by natural disasters or exceptional occurrences.

Floods, marine pollution arising from tankers being wrecked, and the cost of insurance following the 9/11 attacks on the world trade centre have all been defined as natural disasters or exceptional occurrences, but epidemics affecting British agriculture such as BSE and foot and mouth have not been.

**20.26**   Under Article 87(3) certain types of state aid may be regarded as permissible:

(a)   aid to facilitate development of certain economic activities or of certain economic areas, where such aid does not adversely affect trading conditions and competition to an extent contrary to the common interest;

(b)   aid to promote economic development of areas where there is an abnormally low standard of living or serious unemployment;

(c)   aid to promote an important project of common European interest or to remedy a serious disturbance in the economy of a Member State;

(d)   aid to promote culture and heritage conservation;

(e)   other categories which may be proposed by the European Commission and specified by the Council of Ministers.

The operative word set out above is 'may'. The list set out above does not provide a series of exemptions. It is a list of the types of aid which could be authorised by the Commission if they are given prior notification and a good enough reason. The Commission has produced a series of block exemptions (similar to the general consents for the disposal of land by local authorities). If aid falls within one of these exemptions, there is no need for prior notification. However, the Commission must still be informed once the grant has been given.

## Small and medium sized enterprises

There is an exception to the state aid rules in the case of small and medium-sized enterprises (SMEs) currently contained in Regulation 70/2001 (in force until 31 December 2006). This block exemption does not apply: **20.27**

(a) to activities linked to the production, processing, or marketing of products listed in Annex I to the Treaty (essentially food products);
(b) to aid to export related activities;
(c) to aid contingent on the use of domestic over imported goods.

SMEs are enterprises which: **20.28**

(a) have fewer than 250 employees;
(b) have either an annual turnover not exceeding EUR 40m or an annual balance sheet total not exceeding EUR 27m;
(c) are independent in that not more than 25 per cent of the capital or voting rights is owned by an enterprise or jointly by several enterprises which fall outside the definition of a SME.

Aid outside any scheme is allowed if it fulfils the requirements of the Regulation and specifically refers to the Regulation. Aid schemes are allowed if the scheme expressly refers to the Regulation and any aid that could be awarded under it expressly refers to the Regulation. Aid for investment (subject to intensity limits) and for consultancy services (provided the aid does not exceed 50 per cent of the costs of such services) are allowed. **20.29**

There is a requirement (Article 7) that, before work on the aided project is started: **20.30**

• either an application for aid has been submitted to the Member State by the beneficiary, or
• the Member State has adopted legal provisions establishing a legal right to aid according to objective criteria and without further exercise of discretion by the Member State.

## Land

The provision of land at an undervalue by a public authority is likely to constitute state aid. There is a requirement to go through a competitive bidding procedure before disposing of land, or failing this an independent expert valuation needs to obtained. The authority should try to dispose of the land at the market value. After a reasonable effort has been made to do this, a discount of up to 5 per cent of the value is permissible. **20.31**

## Obligation to notify and investigation procedure

Under Article 93(3) of the Treaty: **20.32**

The Commission shall be informed, in sufficient time to enable it to submit its comments, of any plans to grant or alter aid. If it considers that any such plan is not compatible with the Common Market having regard to Article 87, it shall without delay initiate the procedure provided for in paragraph 2. The Member State shall not put its proposed measures into effect until this procedure has resulted in a final decision.

**20.33**  The obligation to notify applies to both aids which Member States consider to be outside Article 87(1) and also those considered to be fully compatible under Article 87(2). The obligation also extends to all changes other than those of a purely formal or administrative nature which cannot affect the evaluation as far as compatibility with the Common Market is concerned: Regulation 794/04. There is a standard form for notifications set out in Regulation 794/2004. From 1 January 2006 this is to be submitted electronically. The procedure for scrutiny is set out in Regulation 659/1999. The Commission has to examine the notification. If after a preliminary examination the Commission finds:

(a)  that the measure does not constitute aid, it must make a decision to this effect;

(b)  that there are no doubts as to the compatibility of the measure with the Common Market, it must make a decision to this effect, recording which exception under the Treaty applies;

(c)  that there are doubts as to the compatibility of the measure with the Common Market, it initiates the formal investigation procedure.

If the Commission have not reached any of these decisions within a period of two months of notification (which includes receipt of any additional information requested) then the aid is deemed to be authorised.

**20.34**  The formal investigation procedure involves summarising the relevant issues of fact and law and setting out a preliminary assessment. The Member State and other interested parties are invited to make comments, normally within one month. The Member State can also comment on the comments made by interested parties, again normally within one month. The Commission then reaches one of the following decisions:

(a)  that the measure does not constitute aid;

(b)  that the doubts as to compatibility have been resolved (a positive decision);

(c)  a positive decision which can be considered compatible if conditions to which it is subject are complied with (a conditional decision). This can also be subject to monitoring obligations;

(d)  that the aid is not compatible with the Common Market (a negative decision).

---

## KEY DOCUMENTS

Treaty of Rome

Commission Notice on the application of Articles 87 and 88 of the EC Treaty to State aid in the form of guarantees OJ [2000] C 71/7

Commission communication on State aid elements in sales of land and buildings by public authorities OJ [1997] C 209/3

Council Regulation (EC) 659/1999—detailed rules for the application of Article 93

Council Regulation (EC) 794/2004—application procedure OJ [2004] L 140.1
Commission Regulation (EC) 70/2001 on the application of Articles 87 and 88 of the EC
Treaty to small and medium-sized enterprises
Commission Regulation (EC) 68/2001—training aid
Commission Regulation (EC) 69/2001—de minimis aid

# 21

# LOCAL AUTHORITIES AND THE LAW OF TORT

## A  INTRODUCTION

There have been a number of important developments in the law of tort as it affects local **21.01** authorities in recent years. The most significant of these have been in the field of negligence. There is little sympathy in the courts now for arguments that particular classes of activity ought to be protected from the consequences of imposing a duty of care on the ground that they are too sensitive or that this might result in an excessively cautious approach on the part of a local authority. Nor does the existence of a duty of care to an employer any longer count as an argument against owing a duty of care to others who might rely on an officer's advice. The way in which the law of tort is likely to impact on local authorities is now highly unpredictable.

## B  VICARIOUS LIABILITY

A local authority is liable in tort for the acts of its servants in the same way as any other **21.02** employer. The law on vicarious liability has recently been reconsidered by the House of Lords in *Lister v Hesley Hall Limited* [2001] 2 WLR 1311. The issue has always presented a difficulty. In order to find that the employer is liable for a wrong committed by its employee, then there must be some link between the employment and the wrongful act, otherwise employers would be assuming liability for the personal lives of their employees. In the case of negligence, the policy considerations are reasonably clear-cut. To what extent should an employer be liable because an employee uses his place of work as a base for his criminal activities? The issue is of particular concern to local authorities because of the degree of responsibility which they have for care of the vulnerable.

**21.03**    In order for the employer to be held liable for the acts of its employee the employee must have been acting in the course of his employment. The test traditionally used by courts to decide whether a wrongful act is deemed to be in the course of a person's employment is called the Salmond test: '. . . if it is either (1) a wrongful act authorised by the master, or (2) a wrongful and unauthorised mode of doing some act authorised by the master'. In the case of *Trotman v North Yorkshire CC* [1999] LGR 584 (overruled by the House of Lords in *Lister*—see below) the Court of Appeal struggled with the application of the Salmond test to the situation of a deputy headmaster who had sexually assaulted a handicapped teenager on a foreign holiday. Butler-Sloss LJ remarked: 'availing himself of that opportunity [to carry out sexual assaults on the boy] seems to me to be far removed from an authorised mode of carrying out a teacher's duties on behalf of his employer. Rather it is a negation of the duty of the Council to look after the children for whom it was responsible.' This approach would effectively rule out vicarious liability for criminal offences committed against the vulnerable by those responsible for their care.

**21.04**    The House of Lords in *Lister v Hesley Hall Limited* took a different approach. The claimants in this case had been resident in a boarding house attached to a school which was owned and managed by the defendants. The boarding house was under the day to day control of a warden, who systematically sexually abused the boys there. Subsequently he was charged with these offences and sentenced to seven years' imprisonment. The question was whether the defendants were liable for the acts of their employee, the warden. In the county court the judge found the defendants liable, holding that although the acts of abuse were not themselves committed in the course of his employment, the defendants were liable for the warden's failure to report the harm that would flow from the acts of abuse and that did flow from them once they had taken place. In other words, the school was liable, not for the sexual abuse, but for the warden's failure to notify his employers that it was taking place. The Court of Appeal allowed the defendant's appeal.

**21.05**    The claimants' appeal to the House of Lords was unanimously allowed. Before the hearing in the House of Lords the law reports of two important decisions of the Canadian Supreme Court on vicarious liability had become available: *Bazley v Curry* (1999) 174 DLR (4) 45 and *Jacobi v Griffiths* (1999) 174 DLR (4) 71. These established a test as to whether it was 'fair' to hold an employer liable for the tortuous conduct of its employees. The House of Lords adopted a slightly different approach, emphasising the need to consider whether the wrongful act was so closely connected with the employment that it would be 'fair and just to hold the employers vicariously liable' (Lord Steyn p. 1323). Lord Hobhouse indicated that the crucial issue to consider was 'to ask what was the duty of the servant towards the plaintiff which was broken by the servant and what was the contractual duty of the servant towards his employer' (p. 1335).

## C   MISFEASANCE IN A PUBLIC OFFICE

The tort of misfeasance in a public office is a means of ensuring that those who have suffered   **21.06**
as a result of abuses of power have a means of redress. It appears that the first successful
action for misfeasance in a public office was *Ashby v White* (1703) 1 Smith's LC (13th edn.)
253, in which it was held that an elector who was wrongly denied the right to vote by a
returning officer could establish a cause of action. In the early twentieth century the Court of
Appeal denied the existence of the tort: *Davis v Bromley Corporation* [1908] 1 KB 170. However, during the course of the twentieth century it enjoyed a revival to the extent that in
*Dunlop v Woollahra Municipal Council* [1982] AC 158 it was described by the Privy Council as
'well-established'. The decided cases indicate that it has generally been used as a tort of last
resort, used only when it is clearly going to be difficult to establish liability for breach of
statutory duty or negligence.

The elements of the tort are now set out in the House of Lords' speeches in *Three Rivers District*   **21.07**
*Council v Bank of England (No. 3)* [2003] 2 AC 1, a case which arose from the collapse of
the Bank of Credit and Commerce International SA ('BCCI'). The origins of the Bank
of England's alleged liability lay in the Banking Act 1979 which introduced a system of
licensing banks in the United Kingdom. BCCI, which had been established before the
Banking Act came into force, was granted a licence by the Bank of England in 1980. It
carried on business until 1991 when it collapsed, causing losses to thousands of depositors.
It transpired that senior officials had been engaged in fraud on a spectacular scale and that
this was what had led to its collapse. It was alleged that senior officials within the Bank of
England were guilty of misfeasance in a public office in that they continued to grant licences
to BCCI even when they should have been aware of its obvious failings. The action was taken
by some 6,000 investors who had incurred losses as a result of the collapse. The House of
Lords was not making a final judgment in the case. Its purpose was to set out the elements of
the tort of misfeasance in a public office so that this could be applied when dealing with the
remainder of the litigation.

Lord Steyn described the rationale of the tort as being 'that in a legal system based on the   **21.08**
rule of law executive or administrative power may be exercised only for the public good and
not for ulterior or improper purposes: *Jones v Swansea City Council* [1990] 1 WLR 54'. He then
set out the ingredients of the tort:

(1) The defendant must be a public officer. This refers to the 'office in a wide sense'. A local
    authority can itself be liable for misfeasance quite apart from having vicarious liability
    for the acts of its employees.
(2) The claim must relate to the exercise of power by the public officer. The ordinary
    principles of vicarious liability apply to the tort: *Racz v Home Office* [1994] 2 AC 45.
(3) The public officer must be acting in bad faith in the sense that he must either display
    malice or be acting without an honest belief that his act is lawful. Thus there are two
    different types of liability:
    - Targeted malice. This is when a public officer specifically intends to injure a person
      or persons. This is bad faith in the sense that power is exercised for an improper or
      ulterior motive.

- Where a public officer acts knowing that he has no power to do the act complained of and that the act will probably injure the plaintiff.

The Court of Appeal in *Bourgoin SA v Minister of Agriculture, Fisheries and Food* [1986] QB 716 warned against drawing too rigid a distinction between the two limbs of the tort and emphasised 'the need to establish a deliberate and dishonest abuse of power in every case'.

There was an argument about whether this limb of the tort could be satisfied by recklessness on the part of the public officer. Lord Steyn held that it could in the sense that it would be satisfied by showing that 'the public officer acted with a state of mind of reckless indifference to the illegality of his act': *Rawlinson v Rice* [1997] 2 NZLR 651. (See further below.)

(4) The claimant must have a sufficient interest to found a legal standing to sue. It had been argued that the plaintiff needed to establish 'an antecedent legal right or interest' and an element of 'proximity'. This argument was rejected. Lord Steyn concluded that this was not needed as a controlling mechanism. Both the state of mind on the part of the defendant which needed to be proved and the requirements in relation to causation were sufficient to keep the tort within reasonable bounds.

(5) It must be shown that the act of misfeasance caused the above loss. This was a question of fact.

(6) The defendant must have foreseen the losses to the claimant as a probable consequence of its act. This was the formulation which Clarke J arrived at when considering these issues at first instance. The Court of Appeal were divided on the issue, with the majority favouring a test which required it to be shown that the defendants knew that their actions would cause loss to the plaintiff. Auld J, dissenting, considered that all losses which were reasonably foreseeable should be recoverable. The reasoning of the House of Lords was that, bearing in mind the special nature of the tort, reasonable foreseeability would be insufficient. However, the test proposed by the majority of the Court of Appeal was unduly restrictive; it would 'emasculate the tort'.

**21.09**   The tort can be founded on conduct by a public officer which would, at first sight, appear to be more akin to defamation rather than misfeasance. An illustration of this is *Cornelius v Hackney London Borough Council* [2002] EWCA Civ 1973. Mr Cornelius had been employed as an accountant by the local authority. He discovered a number of frauds and corrupt irregularities which he passed to the Council's Director of Finance. The Council dismissed him, alleging that his conduct had been 'irresponsible and unprofessional'. He was later exonerated by the Employment Appeal Tribunal. The action for misfeasance in a public office concerned letters, reports, and press statements made by the Chief Executive, members, and senior officers of the Council which, it was alleged, made further criticism of Mr Cornelius' professional competence and integrity. It was claimed that this had damaged his professional reputation and harmed his employment prospects. He argued that the statements by the officers amounted to an abuse of their position as officers and that the Council was vicariously liable. It was argued on behalf of the Council that there was no exercise of a power by a public officer. This argument relied on the House of Lords' decision in *Calveley v Chief Constable of the Merseyside Police* [1989] AC 1228. In that case, it was alleged that misfeasance arose from a misleading report which was made by an officer to the deputy Chief Constable. Lord Bridge in the House of Lords held that this could not constitute 'an act done ... in the exercise or purported exercise of a power or authority vested in him as investigating officer'.

The Council argued that since writing a report could not come within the concept of the **21.10** exercise of power or authority, then still less would the writing of letters, so the claim for misfeasance should be struck out. However, the Court was also referred to the decision in *Peter Elliott v Chief Constable of Wiltshire Constabulary* [1998] *The Times* 5 December. The allegation was that a police officer had supplied details of the plaintiff's convictions to the press. The Vice-Chancellor said that the officer had obtained the information because he was a police officer and, when giving the information to the news editor he was acting in his capacity of and because of his office of police officer. This was illustrated by the fact that he identified himself as a police officer and spoke on behalf of the police in making statements such as 'We do not want him down here.' In that case, the Vice-Chancellor refused to strike out the claim.

In the *Cornelius* case Lord Justice Waller suggested that in the above reasoning 'a distinction **21.11** is being drawn between a public officer exercising a power and a public officer abusing his position as a public officer'. He went on to remark that, although Mr Cornelius' statement of claim was not alleging an exercise of a power, it was alleging that the Chief Executive and others were abusing their position as public officers. This raised three questions:

(1) Was the position of the Chief Executive and members such a public office that liability for its abuse could give rise to a claim by someone in Mr Cornelius' position?
(2) Could the Council be vicariously liable for the Chief Executive or servants or agents of the Council abusing their position?
(3) Could the facts if proved establish that the Chief Executive or other members of the Council did abuse their public office?

Waller LJ answered the first two questions in the affirmative. He entertained doubts about the third. However, as it was a question of fact, and the facts had not been fully established because this was a preliminary hearing, it would not be right to strike out the claim. The above reasoning is very difficult to follow. The exercise of power by a public officer was held in the *Three Rivers* case to be one of the essential elements of the tort. The allegation that the public officer abused his position as a public officer does not amount to the same thing. However, in the light of the *Cornelius* case, public statements by officers and members need to be scrutinised not only for possible defamatory content but also to consider whether they could form the basis of a claim for misfeasance.

## D   BREACH OF STATUTORY DUTY

There is a separate tort which gives a right of action against a public authority for breach of, **21.12** or failure to carry out, its statutory duty. However, the circumstances in which it is possible to take action for breach of statutory duty are very limited. They are summarised in the speech of Lord Browne-Wilkinson in the case of *X v Bedfordshire County Council* [1995] 2 AC 633. The case mainly concerned allegations of negligence (which are discussed below) but also involved allegations of breach of statutory duty against a series of public authorities arising from the ways in which they carried out their education and social services functions. In an ordinary case, the breach of statutory duty does not give rise to any private law cause of action. It must be shown that, as a matter of construction of the statute:

(a)  the statutory duty was imposed for the protection of a limited class of the public; and

(b)  Parliament intended to confer on members of that class a private right of action for breach of that duty.

If the statute provides another means of enforcing this right, this will normally indicate that the statute was intended to be enforced by these means. However, this is not decisive.

**21.13**   The House of Lords in these cases decided that there could be no cause of action for breach of statutory duty in the fields of child abuse or special educational needs. As regards the Children Act 1989, it was introduced primarily for the protection of a limited class, namely children at risk and it originally contained only limited machinery for enforcing the statutory duties imposed. However these were the only pointers that an action for breach of statutory duty might exist. The decision whether to take care proceedings and the various duties of the local authority were all dependent on a subjective exercise of judgement. This was inconsistent with a right to take action for breach of statutory duty. As regards the issue of special education, the Education Act 1981 required the close involvement of parents at every stage and provided for extensive rights of appeal. Parliament could not have intended there to be a right to sue for damages as well.

## E   NEGLIGENCE

**21.14**   The leading case on negligence as it affects local authorities is *X v Bedfordshire County Council* [1995] 2 AC 633. Five appeals to the House of Lords were heard together. In two of them ('the abuse cases') it was alleged that the Council (and in one of the cases, the health authority and a psychiatrist employed by it) was negligent in the way in which it responded to allegations of child abuse. The other three cases ('the education cases') concerned allegations of negligence in the way in which authorities had provided education to children with learning difficulties. The actions had all been struck out as disclosing no reasonable course of action. The Court of Appeal had upheld the decision to strike out the abuse claims but allowed the appeal in the negligence claims in the education cases.

**21.15**   The Bedfordshire case was an action brought by the Official Solicitor on behalf of five children. For a period of about five years, it was alleged, the social services department of the authority received reports of abuse, neglect, and ill-treatment of the children. Although there had been case conferences, the children's names were not placed on the at-risk register. It was not until 1993, six years after the concerns about the children were first raised, that the local authority instigated care proceedings. The claims alleged that the defendants had been in breach of their statutory duty and had been negligent.

**21.16**   The Newham case concerned an investigation into alleged sexual abuse. A child of four, M, was interviewed, at the behest of the social services department, by a psychiatrist, in the presence of a social worker. They identified the abuser as the mother's cohabitee. The child had simply given the first name of her alleged abuser and it was wrongly assumed that this referred to the mother's cohabitee of that name. The social services department concluded that M was unsafe at home and that her mother would be unable to protect her from further abuse. M was removed from her mother's care and placed with foster parents.

In the first of the education cases (the Dorset case), the plaintiff, E, had dyslexia. He attended **21.17** the local primary school and, following a request by his parents for assessment, the local authority produced a statement of special educational needs. This named his primary school as suitable for him. The parents disagreed and moved him to a fee-paying boarding school for children with dyslexia. Following two statements of special educational needs (the first revised statement being quashed in judicial review proceedings), E was placed at a maintained school chosen by his parents. E took proceedings against the County Council based on allegations of breach of statutory duty and negligence.

The Hampshire case concerned a child who had learning difficulties at the school he **21.18** attended from 1978 until 1985. These problems were raised by the parents with the head teacher on many occasions, but it was not until 1984 that there was a referral to an education advisory service. This referral resulted in a conclusion that the child had a serious handicap. There were still problems at the private school to which the child had transferred. Following a request by the parents, the defendant authority drew up a statement of special education needs in 1989, which concluded that the child had 'a severe specific learning difficulty'. The child took proceedings against the county council alleging negligence on the part of the head teacher and the advisory service.

In the Bromley case it was alleged that the authority had failed to make proper arrangements **21.19** for a child's schooling by failing at times to ensure that he had a school place and by placing him at special schools when he did not have a serious disability and failing to assess his educational needs. He alleged breach of statutory duty and negligence on the part of the authority.

In the leading speech Lord Browne-Wilkinson first gave an extensive summary of the law **21.20** and then applied it to the facts of each case. His summary of the law relating to breach of statutory duty has been explained above. He first considered the issue of whether action could be taken against a public authority based on the careless performance of a statutory duty in the absence of any other common law right of action. He concluded that it could not. There was a dictum in *Geddis v Proprietors of Bann Reservoir* (1878) 3 App. Cas. 430 to the effect that 'an action does lie for doing that which the legislature has authorised if it be done negligently'. Lord Browne-Wilkinson concluded that that this had been taken out of context and that *Geddis'* case needed to be treated as a decision that the fact that they were acting in pursuance of a statutory duty could not provide a public authority with a defence if they were exercising that statutory duty carelessly.

He then went on to analyse the circumstances in which a claim could be made against an **21.21** authority on the basis of a common law duty of care. These may fall into three types:

(a) a claim that a statutory duty gives rise to a common law duty of care on the part of the authority to do or refrain from doing a particular act;
(b) a claim that in the course of carrying out a statutory duty the authority has brought about a relationship that gives rise to a duty of care at common law;

(c)   an employee of the authority, while carrying out a statutory function was under a duty of care for which the authority is vicariously liable.

There was a need to draw a distinction between

(a)   allegations that the local authority owed a duty of care in the manner in which it exercises a statutory discretion, and

(b)   allegations that a duty of care arises from the manner in which the statutory duty has been implemented in practice.

A decision to close a school was an example of a) and the actual running of the school, an example of b).

21.22   Local authorities are normally given discretion as to how they carry out their duties. If what an authority has done falls within the ambit of that discretion, then it cannot be actionable at common law. This was the law as established by the leading case of *Home Office v Dorset Yacht* [1970] AC 1004. (In that case, three officers were in charge of a group of boys from Borstal who were staying on an island. Seven of the boys escaped because of the inadequate supervision by the officers and caused damage to a yacht. The House of Lords held that the Home Office could be liable.) However, Lord Browne-Wilkinson disagreed with the approach of Lord Diplock in that case, which was that an action had to be *ultra vires* in a public law sense before it was actionable.

21.23   Lord Browne-Wilkinson went on to say that in deciding whether an action by an authority was outside the ambit of its discretion, the court needed to assess the relevant factors taken into account by the authority in exercising the discretion. (It may be remarked at this stage that although Lord Browne-Wilkinson criticised Lord Diplock's attempt to introduce public law concepts into private law claims, this notion of assessing the factors that were taken into account seems to derive from a public/administrative law approach. It is also a reasonable way of analysing a decision taken by a meeting or a senior officer in the light of reports and advice from others. However, it becomes a very difficult exercise when applying this kind of analysis to the way in which individual officers—teachers, social workers etc. go about their jobs on a day to day basis).

21.24   Lord Browne-Wilkinson went on to say:

> Since what are under consideration are discretionary powers conferred on public bodies for public purposes the relevant factors will often include policy matters, for example social policy, the allocation of finite financial resources between the different calls made upon them or (as in *Dorset Yacht*) the balance between pursuing desirable social aims as against the risk to the public inherent in so doing. It is established that the courts cannot enter upon the assessment of such 'policy' matters. The difficulty is to identify in any particular case whether or not the decision in question is a 'policy' decision.

21.25   He concluded that if any of the factors relevant to the exercise of the discretion include matters of policy, the courts cannot adjudicate on these. Therefore the court could not decide that such an exercise was outside the ambit of the statutory discretion. Again, it is worth pointing out the sheer difficulty of applying an intellectual test of this nature to the circumstances that give rise to negligence claims. The *Dorset Yacht* case is a good example. The allegations against the Borstal officers concerned had nothing to do with the relative weight given to 'desirable social aims' against the risks to the public. It was simply that they failed to do their job by going to bed instead of keeping a watch on the young offenders in their charge with the consequence that they escaped and caused damage to other people's property.

Lord Browne-Wilkinson summarised the position as being that a complaint was 'justiciable' **21.26** if it alleged carelessness, not in the taking of a discretionary decision to do some act, but in the practical manner in which that act has been performed. If a complaint was justiciable, then the question of whether there was a common law duty of care had to be decided in accordance with the usual principle laid down in *Caparo Industries PLC v Dickman* [1990] 2 AC 605.

(a) Was the damage to the plaintiff reasonably foreseeable?
(b) Was the relationship between the plaintiff and the defendant sufficiently proximate?
(c) Is it just and reasonable to impose a duty of care?

The question of whether there was a common law duty of care also had to be influenced by the statutory framework within which the acts complained of were done. A common law duty of care could not be imposed on a local authority if the observance of such a common law duty of care would be inconsistent with, or have a tendency to discourage, the performance by the local authority of its statutory duties.

Lord Browne-Wilkinson also considered the issue of vicarious liability. In some of the cases **21.27** the claims were based on the authority's vicarious liability for the actions of its employees. The distinction was important. The authority might not be under a direct duty even if the employee was. The extent of the direct duty owed by an authority might differ from that owed by a professional to a patient. A local authority under a direct duty of care would still be liable for the negligent acts and omissions of its employees. It could only act through its employees.

He then summarised how he would deal with each of the cases. **21.28**

(1) Does the statutory provision give rise to a private law claim in damages? (Breach of statutory duty—see above).
(2) Is a common law duty of care owed?
   (a) Is the negligence in the exercise of a statutory discretion involving policy consider-ations? If the answer to this question is yes, the claim fails.
   (b) Were the acts complained of within the ambit of the discretion? If the answer to this question is yes, the claim also fails. If the answer is no, the third question must be considered.
   (c) Is it appropriate to impose a common law duty of care on the local authority? (This last question is decided in accordance with the *Caparo* principles, see above).

Where vicarious liability was alleged, it would be considered as follows:

(a) Is the duty of care alleged to be owed by the employee of the authority consistent with the proper performance of his duties to the authority? If the answer to this question is no, the claim fails. If the answer is yes . . .
(b) Is it appropriate to impose on the servant the duty of care alleged? (Again, this last question is to be decided in accordance with the principles laid down in the *Caparo* case.)

**21.29**  Applying the first set of principles to the Bedfordshire case, he concluded that it would be wrong to strike out the claim on the basis that it involved unjusticiable policy questions. For the most part the decisions in child care cases involved practical questions rather than policy issues, although if there were, for instance, questions about the level of resources allocated, there might be a reason why the claim should fail. He said the claim might well fail on the grounds that it was within the ambit of a discretion of the local authority. However, he concluded that it would be wrong to strike out the claim for this reason since it might be possible for the plaintiff to show at trial that the decisions of the local authority were so unreasonable that no reasonable authority would have reached them. (This is another example of Lord Browne-Wilkinson sliding back into a public law way of thinking. Although this formulation was referred to in the *Dorset Yacht* case, it derives of course from *Wednesbury*, where it was referred to as irrationality—the third ground of *Wednesbury* unreasonableness. It is an inherently unsuitable test to use when focusing, not on an individual decision, but on a failure to act. To characterise the allegations in the Bedfordshire case as a series of decisions, in the way Lord Browne-Wilkinson does, is inappropriate. The stated criticism of the authority was that its officers failed to apply their minds in such a way as to enable them to respond effectively to the history of reports and abuse that they were receiving.)

**21.30**  He then turned to consider whether, in accordance with the *Caparo* principles, the authority owed a duty of care. The tests of foreseeability and proximity were satisfied. So the question was: is it just, fair and reasonable to impose a common law duty of care on the local authority in relation to the performance of its statutory duties to protect children? He concluded that it was not. He agreed with Sir Thomas Bingham MR who had stated in his judgment in the Court of Appeal in the Bedfordshire case that in general the law should provide remedies for wrongs and that there would need to be powerful counter-considerations for this principle to be overridden. However, he concluded that there were such considerations in this case.

(1)  A common law duty of care would cut across the statutory system set up for the protection of children at risk. This was multi-disciplinary, involving other agencies such as the police and health professionals.

(2)  There were other remedies available. There was a statutory complaints procedure as well as the possibility of a complaint to the local ombudsman.

(3)  In deciding whether to develop novel categories of negligence, the court should proceed incrementally and by analogy with decided cases. The nearest analogies were cases where it had been sought to establish liability on the part of the police or statutory regulators of financial dealings. The courts had not imposed a common law duty of care in these fields and should exercise great care in imposing a duty of care on those 'charged by Parliament with the task of protecting society from the wrongdoings of others'.

**21.31**  He also decided against imposing a duty of care on the individual social workers in the child abuse cases, for the following reasons:

(1)  The system for child protection is multi-disciplinary. It would be unfair to impose a duty of care on only one of the participant bodies. To impose such a duty on them all would cause insuperable problems in terms of disentangling who had responsibility for what, in terms of contributing to the alleged negligence.

(2) Social services authorities have a delicate task in dealing with children at risk. They are criticised both for reacting too readily and for failing to act.

(3) If a liability in damages was imposed it may be that local authorities would adopt a more cautious and defensive approach to the way in which they carry out their duties.

(4) The social workers and psychiatrists were retained by the local authority to advise the authority, not the plaintiffs. The correct analogy is with a doctor retained by an insurance company to examine an applicant for life insurance. The doctor does not as a result of this examination come under a duty of care to the person he examines. The situation of a building surveyor who is instructed by a building society is different, since he is aware that the purchaser will buy a property relying on the survey report.

Then Lord Browne-Wilkinson applied the same principles to the education cases. From this he concluded:     **21.32**

(1) Although the carrying out of the duties under the Education Act 1981 involved the exercise of a statutory discretion, this was unlikely to involve policy considerations.

(2) Even if decisions about what to include in a statement of educational needs were made carelessly, in order to succeed it would be necessary to show that they were so careless that no reasonable authority would have reached them. This was very unlikely, but it could not be said that it was impossible without knowing all the facts. The claim could not be struck out on this ground. (Here the two concepts of carelessness and irrationality appear to be muddled. A course of action could be appallingly careless without being remotely unreasonable, in the public law sense. Similarly it is not possible to quash a decision in a public law claim on the grounds that it was taken so carelessly that it is *Wednesbury* unreasonable.)

(3) It was foreseeable that if the powers relating to special education were exercised carelessly, children with special educational needs would suffer damage. (Proximity is not specifically mentioned. It appears to have been assumed.)

(4) Nonetheless it would not be right to superimpose a duty of care in respect of special education functions for the following reasons:
   • The parents are closely involved in the decision-making and have various rights of appeal. There could therefore be a duplication of remedies.
   • There was a risk that many hopeless and vexatious cases would be brought.
   • There was no category of case by analogy with which it would be right to impose a direct duty of care.

(5) In the case of an educational psychology service offered to the public, the authority was in the same position as any private individual or organisation offering a service. It comes under a duty of care. (This conclusion was based on a mistaken view of the facts. Local authority educational psychology services are established to advise the authority. They are not services offered to the public at large.)

(6) Schools have responsibility for the education needs of their pupils as well as their physical well-being. In these circumstances a head teacher has a duty of care in relation to such educational needs.

Lord Browne-Wilkinson's speech in the Bedfordshire case remains the most lucid and comprehensive explanation of the relevant legal principles. A summary of the questions     **21.33** to be posed in order to establish whether a duty of care exists against a public authority in any given case is set out in Appendix 8. The general conclusion from this case might be thought to be that extreme caution would be exercised before extending the concept of a duty of care into areas of public sector activity where the nature of the authority's functions are complex and delicate. However two factors have meant that, following this case, authorities have faced increasing difficulty in persuading courts to strike out claims not based on established legal principles. One of the reasons for this is the increased reluctance of courts to strike out claims without fully establishing the facts. The second is the impact of human rights law.

21.34   From the point of view of local authorities a considerable burden is imposed on them if a case is taken to trial, even if it fails. Documents need to be assembled, witnesses traced, and professional fees incurred. If claims succeed the amounts payable need to met from public funds or from insurance. Establishing the boundaries of public sector liability is therefore an issue with intensely practical implications.

21.35   The difficulty of predicting whether a duty of care will be found in a particular area of activity is illustrated by important cases since *X v Bedfordshire County Council*. It might have been predicted that the reasons listed by Lord Browne-Wilkinson for refusing to impose a duty of care in relation to decisions whether to take children into care would equally apply to actions alleging negligence in the way authorities looked after children who were in their care. It might also have been predicted that, if Lord Browne-Wilkinson had correctly understood the nature of an educational psychology service, then claims alleging negligence by educational psychologists would be dismissed on the grounds that they were providing a service to the authority rather than to the users of the service, and this is what would happen in cases where the facts were fully established. However, the House of Lords has since the *Bedfordshire* case both refused to strike out cases alleging negligence in relation to decisions about children in care and restored a judgment awarding damages for negligence in the way in which an educational psychologist did her job.

21.36   *Barrett v Enfield London Borough Council* [2001] 2 AC 550 concerned a man who had previously been in the care of the defendant local authority. He was, along with his sister, placed with foster parents. He had several changes of social worker. He was placed in a children's home before going to live with his former social worker who acted as his foster parent. He had in all nine placements before leaving care at the age of 17. He saw his mother only twice, when he was aged 14 and 15. He claimed that the way in which the local authority had placed him in various children's homes and foster placements, separated him from his sister, failed ever to consider the possibility of adoption or rehabilitation with his mother, led him to suffer damage and injury. This included a psychiatric illness causing him to harm himself, his involvement in criminal activities, the failure of his marriage, his inability to find work, and an alcohol problem.

21.37   His claim was struck out as disclosing no cause of action. The Court of Appeal upheld this decision. His appeal to the House of Lords was unanimously allowed. Three members of the House gave substantive speeches. Lord Browne-Wilkinson felt unable to strike out the claim. He said that what had happened in the education cases heard with *X v Bedfordshire County Council* was a graphic illustration of the dangers of striking out cases when the facts had not been properly established. In that case, influenced by his erroneous remarks about the nature of an educational psychology service, the claim had succeeded. It had been followed by other successful claims. This showed (apparently) that it was important that these cases were decided on real facts deduced from evidence rather than hypothetical facts assumed for the purpose of a strike out claim.

The second reason for Lord Browne-Wilkinson's refusal to strike the claim out was the **21.38** decision of the European Court of Human Rights in *Osman v UK* (1999) 29 EHRR 245. The Osmans took a claim against the police alleging negligence in connection with a criminal investigation. This claim was struck out by the Court of Appeal: *Osman v Ferguson* [1993] 4 All ER 344. They had applied a previous House of Lords' decision that it was not just and reasonable to impose on the police a duty of care in connection with the pursuit and prevention of crime: *Hill v Chief Constable of West Yorkshire* [1989] AC 53. The ECHR held that this constituted a breach of Article 6(1) of the Convention: 'In the determination of his civil rights and obligations ... everyone is entitled to a fair and public hearing ...'. The ECHR decision implied that by applying a precedent the courts in the UK had effectively given the police an immunity. The implication of this decision was that a general rule that a duty of care would not be imposed in a particular class of case could not be applied. Each case would have to be considered on its own merits. This part of the *Osman* decision was reversed in *Z v UK* (see below). However, it caused considerable consternation to Lord Browne-Wilkinson. He thought that if the court struck out the *Barrett* case there would be an appeal to the ECHR and a finding that this was a breach of Article 6. He therefore considered that it was 'difficult to say that it is a clear and obvious case calling for striking out'.

Lord Slynn and Lord Hutton did not consider the *Osman* case. However, they thought that **21.39** this case was distinguishable from *X v Bedfordshire County Council*. They concluded that:

(a)  The multi-disciplinary nature of decisions about children at risk was not applicable. Once children were in care they were the responsibility of the local authority.
(b)  The other remedies (complaints, Local Government Ombudsman) were not sufficient.
(c)  There were other analogous cases. These included cases which established that schools owed duties to their pupils, those running prisons to their detainees, and hospitals to their patients.

A further set of education cases came before the House of Lords in *Phelps v Hillingdon London Borough Council* [2001] 2 AC 619. The main conclusion of these cases was that, contrary to the indication given in Lord Browne-Wilkinson's speech in *X v Bedfordshire County Council*, professionals who are employed by a local authority to advise them may still be liable in negligence to third parties if those parties were going to rely on that advice.

The *Phelps* case concerned a child who was referred to her education authority's school **21.40** psychological service. The educational psychologist did not consider that she had specific learning difficulties. Later she was privately diagnosed as being dyslexic. The child took legal proceedings based on the alleged negligence of the educational psychologist, claiming that her failure to diagnose dyslexia meant that she missed out on appropriate treatment or educational provision which would have mitigated her condition. The judge at first instance held that the educational psychologist owed a duty of care to the plaintiff and made findings that she was negligent and that the plaintiff's condition was worse as a result than it would otherwise have been. He awarded damages. The authority's appeal was allowed by the Court of Appeal who held that:

1.   The educational psychologist did not owe a duty of care to the plaintiff since she was employed by the authority to advise them. This was not a service available to the public at large.
2.   On the facts there was no negligence.
3.   Even if there had been negligence, the evidence did not establish that it worsened the plaintiff's condition.

21.41   The Court of Appeal decision was reversed by the House of Lords. They held that:

1.   A person exercising a skill or profession might owe a duty of care in its performance to those who might foreseeably be injured if due care and skill were not exercised.
2.   Such a duty of care did not depend on the existence of a contractual relationship between the person causing and the person suffering the damage.
3.   An educational psychologist owed such a duty of care. The fact that she owed duties to the education authority did not exclude the existence of a duty to the child.
4.   If an educational psychologist was asked to advise about a child's future educational provision and it was clear that parents and teachers were going to rely on that advice, then a prima facie duty of care arose.
5.   The authority were vicariously liable for such a breach even though the breach occurred in the performance of a statutory duty.
6.   The relationship between the plaintiff and the educational psychologist created sufficient nexus for the duty of care to arise.
7.   The judge had been entitled to find the educational psychologist in breach of that duty and the authority vicariously liable for such breach.

The implications of the above decision for local authorities are considerable, extending far beyond the field of educational psychology. It means that, if a local authority employee is advising his employer and others are going to rely on his advice, there is a likelihood that there will be a duty of care to those who rely on the officer's advice.

21.42   The issue of human rights can also now have an effect on the circumstances in which a duty of care will arise. In *Z v UK* [2001] 2 FLR 612 four of the five children whose claims were struck out by the House of Lords in *X v Bedfordshire County Council* successfully argued before the European Court of Human Rights that there had been a breach of Articles 3 (inhuman and degrading treatment) and 13 (right to an effective remedy) because they had not been able to obtain redress in the courts. However, they found that there had not been a breach of Article 6 (right to a fair hearing) either by using the striking out procedure or by determining as a preliminary issue whether it was just and reasonable to impose a duty of care. This part of the decision reversed the decision of the same court in *Osman v UK*.

21.43   Potential claims for negligence against professionals in the field of child abuse have been considered twice by the House of Lords since the *Barrett* case. In *W v Essex County Council* [2001] 2 AC 592 the claimants were foster parents. They had received assurances from the Council that no sexual abuser would be placed with them. They also received specific assurances from a social worker that the 15 year old by who was placed with them was not a sexual abuser. He abused their own children, who were aged between 8 and 12. The foster parents and the children sued the local authority in negligence. The foster parents claimed that they had suffered psychiatric illness as a result of the abuse of their children. The judge struck out all the claims apart from the children's claim in negligence. This decision was upheld by the Court of Appeal but unanimously reversed by the House of Lords who held that:

1. On the alleged facts it was arguable that there was a duty of care owed to the parents and a breach of that duty by the defendants.
2. Whether or not the claim was justiciable depended on an investigation of the full facts so it was not an appropriate case for striking out.
3. It could not be said that the type of psychiatric injury alleged was outside the type which the law recognises.
4. The categorisation of those claiming to be primary or secondary victims of negligence was still developing.
5. It was not conclusively shown that the parents in this case fell outside the category of primary victims.
6. There had to be some temporal and spatial limitations on those claiming to be secondary victims but the concept of 'immediate aftermath' of an incident had to be assessed on the particular facts of the situation; it was not necessary for the parents to have discovered the abuser immediately after the abuse had taken place.
7. The parents' claim was not so clearly bad that they should be prevented from pursuing it to trial.

The case of *D v East Berkshire Community Health NHS Trust* [2005] 2 WLR 993 concerned **21.44** wrong diagnoses of child abuse. One child suffered from severe allergies. The paediatricians believed that this was a case of Munchausen's syndrome by proxy, i.e. that the mother had invented the child's symptoms. In another case the child suffered from Schamberg's disease which manifested itself in purple patches on the skin. The child's symptoms were considered to be bruising resulting from abuse. In the third case the child had osteogenesis imperfecta (brittle bone disease). The resulting fractures were diagnosed as being non-accidental injuries. The parents claimed negligence against the relevant health authorities (and in one case, the local authority). In each case the judge had determined as a preliminary issue that no duty of care was owed by any of the defendants on the ground that it was not fair, just, and reasonable to impose such a duty. The Court of Appeal upheld this decision as did, by a majority, the House of Lords. Lord Bingham's dissenting speech contains the most interesting analysis of the current state of the law. Summarising the position which had been reached after the *Barrett* case referred to above, he concluded:

1. It was accepted that a claim may lie against a local authority arising from childcare decisions in certain circumstances.
2. It was generally undesirable to strike out claims arising in uncertain and developing areas of the law without a full exploration of the facts.
3. The notion of an exclusionary rule conferring immunity on particular classes of defendant was rejected.
4. The policy factors which had weighed with the House in *X v Bedfordshire County Council* did not have the same weight once a child had been taken into care.

**21.45**   He also went through the policy issues given for rejection of the claims in *X v Bedfordshire County Council* and applied them to the circumstances of the present case:

1.   The difficulties of ascertaining and allocating responsibility. This did not preclude a claim by the child in the *Phelps* case so it was difficult to see why it should preclude a claim by a parent.

2.   The delicacy of the task faced by professionals in this field. This is not generally recognised as a reason for not requiring the exercise of reasonable skill and care.

3.   The possibility of authorities adopting a more cautious and defensive approach. On the contrary, it was more likely to induce a sense of professional responsibility.

4.   The risk of conflict between social worker and parents. The parents and child's interests were generally regarded as consonant.

5.   The availability of other remedies. The law had been found wanting here: *Z v UK*.

6.   The principle that the categories of negligence should be developed incrementally and by analogy with existing cases. To accept a claim by parents as arguable in these circumstances involved no massive extension of a prima facie duty of care.

**21.46**   However, the majority upheld the striking out. The difficulty the parents faced was the question, why should they be in a different position from any other suspected perpetrator? It was not argued that health professionals in these types of circumstances owed a duty of care to everyone who might be suspected. The parents' argument was that they were in a special position. Reliance was placed on Article 8 of the Convention on Human Rights and its reference to respect for family life. The issue of conflict of interest was in Lord Nicholls' view, the most important consideration:

> . . . when considering whether something does not feel 'quite right' a doctor must be able to act single-mindedly in the interests of the child. He ought not to have at the back of his mind an awareness that if his doubts about intentional injury or sexual abuse prove unfounded he may be exposed to claims by a distressed parent.

**21.47**   He then adds his opinion that health professionals are made of 'sterner stuff' than to let such considerations influence their judgement. However, he considers that the seriousness of child abuse as a social problem means that the duty owed to a child should not be 'clouded by imposing a conflicting duty in favour of parents or others suspected of having abused the child'. He goes on to say that parents should not be kept in the dark or their interests ignored. However, it will be in the child's interests for suspected abuse to be investigated thoroughly. It will not be in the parents' interests for this to happen. He considered that the appropriate level of protection for the parents was the same as that afforded to persons suspected of crimes generally, i.e. that the investigations should be carried out in good faith.

**21.48**   The changes in this area of law in recent years mean that it cannot be predicted with certainty that there will not be further extensions of the duty of care. There is even the possibility of the concept of the duty of care being abandoned altogether and replaced by a different basis for a finding of negligence. Lord Nicholls referred to this possibility in the above case. He referred to the difficulties of identifying the parameters of the tort, particularly in fields involving the discharge of statutory functions by public authorities. Sometimes, particularly when considering claims under the Human Rights Act it is appropriate for a court to look back over everything that has happened. The court then decides whether the end result is acceptable by making 'a value judgment based on more flexible notions than the common law standard of reasonableness and does so freed from the legal rigidity of a duty of care'. This radical idea was rejected in this case on the ground that it would lead to a period of uncertainty. Abandoning the duty of care was, in Lord Nicholls' view, unlikely to clarify the law without some, as yet unidentified control mechanism which recognises that sometimes acts and omissions will not lead to liability even though loss might be foreseeable.

## F   DECEIT

Local authorities can be liable in deceit. The tort of deceit has the following elements:    **21.49**

(a) a false material representation of fact by the defendant;
(b) the defendant knew that the representation was false or did not believe in its truth or was reckless as to its truth or falsity;
(c) the representation was made with the intention that it should be acted on by the claimant, or persons including the claimant, in a manner that resulted in damage to him;
(d) the misrepresentation had induced the claimant to act to his detriment.

The case of *Slough Estates plc v Welwyn Hatfield District Council* [1996] 2 PLR 50, simply   **21.50** applied the existing law to the actions of a local authority. Nonetheless, it is worth considering the circumstances of the case since they illustrate both the dangers to local authorities of making misrepresentations—however well-intentioned—in the course of commercial negotiations and the potential for large-scale losses if an authority is found to have practised deceit.

Slough Estates (Slough) was, in 1982, granted planning permission to develop a large   **21.51** shopping complex in the town centre (the Howard Centre). Slough later became aware of a proposed development by another company, the Carroll Group, three miles away, called Park Plaza. Slough was concerned about the sustainability of its own proposed development, bearing in mind that another was going to take place such a short distance away. The Council was keen on both schemes going ahead. It had a strong financial interest in the Park Plaza scheme going ahead as it held a long leasehold interest in the site and was to be paid £11m by the developers. Its lease to the Carroll Group incorporated a tenancy mix agreement (TMA) designed to ensure that the tenants in the Park Plaza scheme were, for a period of five years, connected with the leisure industry. In fact, the Council secretly relaxed the requirements of the TMA while continuing to assert to Slough and to the public generally that it intended to enforce its terms. Slough went ahead with the development of the Howard Centre, relying on these representations. When Slough made a loss out of the development of the Howard Centre, it sought to recover these losses from the Council.

The judge held that the assertions by the Council that it intended to enforce the TMA   **21.52** constituted a continuing misrepresentation, which it knew to be false. Slough had been induced by these false representations to continue developing the Howard Centre at a loss. The Council was therefore liable in deceit. Judgment was given to Slough in the sum of £48.5m. This figure was calculated by adding up the total costs incurred by Slough in developing the Howard Centre and deducting its current value. The Council argued that this was inappropriate, since it failed to take into account the fall in property values that had taken place and did not measure the loss that would not have been incurred if the representations were true. Nonetheless, this was the measure of damages the judge decided to apply, on the basis that in the case of a transaction induced by fraud, the whole risk falls on the fraudulent defendant, and the court does not speculate on what might have happened if the fraudulent representations had not been made.

# 22

# LOCAL GOVERNMENT FINANCE—REVENUE

## A INTRODUCTION

Until 1988, local taxation took the form of rates (a form of which had existed since 1601), a **22.01** charge on property, both commercial and residential, which had to be paid by the occupiers of the property and also imposed liability on owners. The tax was based on the rateable value of the property, an assessment of the amount of rental income that would be achieved by letting it. The LGA 1988 introduced a new system for England and Wales. It had been introduced in Scotland the previous year. Commercial rates were to be assessed centrally instead of locally. More radically, domestic rates were abolished and replaced by a sum fixed by each authority and payable by each adult, called in the legislation the 'community charge' but popularly known as the 'poll tax'. This in its turn was replaced by a new system based on the 'council tax', which represents a reversion to a property-based tax but with a personal tax element. (The system for national non-domestic rates, (NNDR) introduced by the Local Government Finance Act 1988, remained unchanged.)

Although there are currently no plans to abolish council tax, the Government is looking at **22.02** options for reform. In July 2004 the Balance of Funding Report was published. This was a report from a steering group set up by the Government and chaired by the then local government minister, Nick Raynsford. It included representatives from the main political groups on the LGA, local government officers, and independent experts. The main options considered by the review were the return of responsibility for business rates to local authorities and the introduction of a local income tax. The return of business rates to local control was supported by the LGA who pointed out that the share of local government funding paid by business had reduced since NNDR was introduced (because there is an inflation cap on NNDR). They also argued that localisation would encourage more effective partnerships with businesses and increase accountability. The idea was opposed by representatives of business who argued that the current political system protected businesses against unaffordable increases.

22.03   The Review group received representations from CIPFA setting out the administrative difficulties in setting up any kind of local income tax which allowed local authorities the power to vary tax rates themselves. They concluded that these needed further examination. They recommended that any consideration of local income tax should be as a supplement and not as a replacement for council tax. They also considered a variety of other possible taxes such as local vehicle taxes, local sales taxes, and taxes on property transfers. They concluded that none of these could achieve a significant shift in the balance of funding. The group concluded that council tax should not be abolished. There are arguments in retaining a property tax, particularly as council tax yields high collection rates. However, they did consider that some reforms were needed. It advised that there were strong arguments for shifting the balance of funding so that more revenue was raised locally if the means of doing so were both feasible and desirable.

22.04   In July 2004 the Government announced that it had set up an independent inquiry into local government funding. This is being undertaken by Sir Michael Lyons. The main purposes of the Lyons inquiry as far as funding is concerned are to:

(a)   make recommendations for the reform of council tax taking into account the revaluation of domestic property;

(b)   assess the case for giving local authorities more flexibility to raise additional revenue;

(c)   analyse the options for shifting the balance of funding, which will include looking at the possibility of a local income tax, reforms to business rates, and other possible local taxes and charges.

The inquiry has now been widened to consider the functions of local government generally.

---

## B   COUNCIL TAX

22.05   The method of valuing property for the purposes of council tax is much cruder than under the rating system. Properties are valued in eight broad bands, from A to H, with A being the lowest and H the highest. It is calculated on the assumption that two people are living in each property. If only one person is living there, the amount is discounted by 25 per cent. council tax is payable on residential property. The term used in the legislation is 'chargeable dwelling'. It includes any property which would have been subject to rates under the old system but is not subject to NNDR or otherwise exempt. They may be exempted by the legislation itself or by an order made by the Secretary of State. Under the Act, premises may be excluded by order. The exclusions are complex but include many types of unoccupied dwellings, student accommodation, and separate dwellings in a single property occupied by a dependent relative.

22.06   Each property in respect of which council tax is payable is on a list. It was the responsibility of listing officers under the 1992 Act to prepare a valuation of each property. This places it in one of the eight valuation bands. The original list was compiled in time for the introduction of the tax in 1993. The valuation on the list is supposed to be based on the assumption that it is sold on the open market by a willing vendor. The list is not regularly updated. Pending a further comprehensive valuation, for which there is at present no date fixed, the list can be altered only in four circumstances:

(a) the value has increased and there has been a sale of the freehold or a grant of a lease of seven years or more;

(b) there has been a decrease in value due to demolition of part of the property, works of adaptation to meet the needs of the disabled, or a physical change in the locality of the property;

(c) a property which was previously composite i.e. only partly used as a dwelling, ceases to be composite;

(d) the proportions of domestic/non-domestic use within a composite property have changed.

## Liability for council tax

The following are liable to pay council tax in respect of a chargeable dwelling: A person is **22.07** liable on a given day if on that day—

(a) he is a resident of the dwelling and has a freehold interest in the whole or any part of it;

(b) he is such a resident and has a leasehold interest in the whole or any part of the dwelling which is not inferior to another such interest held by another such resident;

(c) he is both such a resident and a statutory, secure, or introductory tenant of the whole or any part of the dwelling;

(d) he is such a resident and has a contractual licence to occupy the whole or any part of the dwelling;

(e) he is such a resident;

(f) he is the owner of the building.

If more than one person is liable, then they are jointly and severally liable. The 'owner' in **22.08** relation to any dwelling means the person as regards whom the following conditions are fulfilled—

(a) he has a material interest in the whole or any part of the dwelling; and

(b) at least part of the dwelling or, as the case may be, of the part concerned is not subject to a material interest inferior to his interest.

A 'resident' means a person over 18 who has the dwelling as his sole or main residence.

## Calculation of council tax

In order to set its council tax each year, a local authority needs to go through a number **22.09** of steps:

(a) Calculate its budget requirement. This means that it must work out what it needs to spend in the next financial year. It then needs to consider the amount of money it will receive from other sources, i.e., revenue support grant, national non-domestic rates, other grants, and other sources of income. The budget requirement will be the shortfall, in other words the amount it needs to raise by way of council tax in order to meet its expenditure for the following year.

(b) Calculate its council tax base. This is found by multiplying 'the total of the relevant amounts for that year for each of the valuation bands which is shown or likely to be shown for any day in that year in the authority's valuation list as applicable to one or more dwellings situated in its area' by the authority's estimate of its collection rate for that year. The formula (A × B) is derived from the Local Authorities (Calculation of Council Tax Base) Regulations 1992 (SI 1992 No. 612).

(c) Notify the council tax base to major precepting authorities, i.e., county councils, police authorities, and fire and civil defence authorities.

(d) Calculate the basic amount of tax. This is done by deducting from its budget requirement the income it will receive from revenue support grant, national non-domestic rates, and special grants, and then dividing the resulting figure by the council tax base. The formula used in the legislation is:

$$\frac{R-P}{T}$$

(e) Calculate the amount of any 'special items' (that relate to part only of an authority's area) and aggregate these.

(f) Recalculate the basic amount of tax to take account of the special items referred to above. This is done in one of two ways:

(i) For the area to which no special items apply, the aggregate of special items ((e) above) is divided by the council tax base ((b) above) and the resulting figure is deducted from the basic amount of tax ((d) above). The formula is:

$$B-\frac{A}{T}$$

(ii) For the area(s) to which special items apply, there is added to this amount a figure to take account of the special items. This figure is calculated by dividing the amount of the special item by the amount of the council tax base for the area to which it relates. The formula for this is:

$$\frac{S}{TP}$$

(g) Calculate the amount of tax applicable for each valuation band. This is done by dividing the number applicable to that valuation band (which is contained in s. 5(1), Local Government Finance Act 1988: A:6, B:7, C:8, D:9, E:11, F:13, G:15, H:18) by the number applicable to band D. This is then multiplied by the figure calculated for the basic amount of tax (see (d) above; (f) above where there are special items). The formula is described in the legislation as:

$$A\times\frac{N}{D}$$

(h) Calculate the amount of tax payable for each dwelling. By this time the authority will have received details from major precepting authorities of the amounts they require. These will be expressed in terms of amounts for each valuation band, the precepting authority having undertaken much the same process as the billing authority. The two figures are added together to give the amount of tax payable for each category of dwelling.

The above process has to be completed by 11 March in the financial year preceding that for which council tax is being set. However, it is not to be treated as invalid if it is set after this date (though losses that occur as a result of setting the tax late may constitute unlawful expenditure).

The amount for each category of dwelling cannot be set before the earlier of:

- 1 March in the financial year preceding that for which the council tax is being set;
- the receipt of the last precept from a precepting authority.

If the amount is set earlier than this, or the authority has not carried out the calculations outlined above, then the tax set is invalid. This means there will be no legal obligation to pay it and no legal power to collect it.

There will of course be some difficulty for a local authority if it sets a council tax without having received the necessary details from a major precepting authority. There would be a need for a substituted council tax to be set. A substituted council tax can also be set, provided that it is a reduction and not an increase, if the local authority goes through a process of recalculation of the figures referred to above, provided that the same figures are used for the amount that it estimates it will receive from grants and national non-domestic rates and for the council tax base. Therefore, if the figure used for the council tax base was wrong, or the authority receives less than it expected from the Government in grants, it will not be able to recoup the shortfall by raising the council tax.

## Council tax capping

The rules relating to council tax capping were changed by the Local Government Act 1999 **22.10** which inserted Chapter IVA into the Local Government Finance Act 1992. Under s. 52B, if in the Secretary of State's opinion the amount calculated by an authority as its budget requirement for a financial year is excessive, he may exercise his power to designate or nominate the authority. Essentially, 'designate' means that a cap will be applied in that financial year and 'nominate' means a warning that a cap is likely to be applied in respect of the following financial year. The question of whether an amount is excessive must be determined in accordance with a set of principles determined by the Secretary of State. He may also place local authorities in categories for this purpose and, if he does so, must apply the same set of principles to each category. If the Secretary of State designates an authority for the year under consideration, he must notify them in writing of—

(a) the designation;
(b) the set of principles determined for the authority under s. 52B above;
(c) the category in which the authority falls (if he determines categories under s. 52B above);
(d) the amount which he proposes should be the maximum for the amount calculated by the authority as its budget requirement for the year;
(e) the target amount for the year, that is, the maximum amount which he proposes the authority could calculate as its budget requirement for the year without the amount calculated being excessive;

(f) the financial year as regards which he expects the amount calculated by the authority as its budget requirement for that year to be equal to or less than the target amount for that year (assuming one to be determined for that year).

**22.11** An authority has 21 days to respond, either challenging the designation and giving reasons, or accepting the maximum proposed by the Secretary of State. If the amount is challenged the Secretary of State may, after taking into account the information provided by the authority and any other information he thinks is relevant, make an order specifying the maximum amount for that authority's budget requirement. An order may also be made if the authority does not respond. If the authority accepts the amount, the Secretary of State simply needs to send a notice confirming that authority's maximum budgetary requirement. Following nomination, the Secretary of State is able to follow the process of designation, which takes effect in the following financial year. The procedure is essentially the same.

## C   GRANTS

**22.12** Although council tax is the only part of its income over which a local authority has significant control (apart from fees and charges, which usually account for very little, commercial rents, which usually account for not much more and domestic rents, which are dealt with separately), it does not form a large part of most local authorities' budgets. It now accounts for only 11 per cent of local government expenditure. The largest share is accounted for by revenue support grant, the amount given by central government to local authorities to allow them to provide a reasonable level of services insofar as the sums that can be raised by council tax and rates fall short of their requirements.

**22.13** The procedure for calculating revenue support grant is set out in sections 77 to 83 of the LGFA 1988. For each financial year the Secretary of State must make a determination of the amount of grant which will be available for the year and the amount which will be payable to authorities. This is set out in the local government finance report which must be laid before the House of Commons. This must also set out the basis on which the grant is to be distributed among the receiving authorities. Once the report has been approved, the Secretary of State needs to calculate the amount each authority should receive. Following this calculation the Secretary of State is under a duty to pay these amounts to the authorities. There is power to make an amending report at any time before the end of the financial year following the financial year concerned. Essentially the same procedure is followed in Wales by the National Assembly for Wales: sections 84D–84P. There is also power to pay additional grant if the Secretary of State is of the view that there have been fresh circumstances affecting local authority finances since the original approval. It is extremely difficult for local authorities to challenge assessments made under these provisions. Under the previous system for rate support grant the House of Lords held that for the courts to interfere with the Secretary of State's decision on the grounds of *Wednesbury* unreasonableness would require highly exceptional circumstances: *R v Secretary of State for the Environment, ex parte Nottinghamshire County Council* [1986] AC 240.

## D NATIONAL NON-DOMESTIC RATES

Since the Local Government Finance Act 1988, rating has survived only for non-domestic **22.14**
premises. Its level is controlled centrally. Local businesses no longer need concern themselves about the spending plans of their local authorities: what they pay will not be affected.
However, their representatives still have to be consulted about their local authority's
expenditure proposals each financial year.

The collection and enforcement of the non-domestic rate is still the responsibility of local
authorities. In addition, the basis for liability for rating remains the same as it was before
the 1988 Act: it is still based on occupation. The meaning of the word 'occupation' has
developed through a series of cases. The best summary is that given by Tucker LJ in *John
Laing and Son Ltd v Assessment Committee for Kingswood Assessment Area* [1949] 1 KB 344 at
p. 350:

> First, there must be actual occupation; secondly, that it must be exclusive for the particular
> purposes of the possessor; thirdly, that the possession must be of some value or benefit to the
> possessor; and fourthly, the possession must not be for too transient a period.

Since unoccupied buildings would otherwise fall through the net, the statute provides that **22.15**
the owner is liable for rates on unoccupied property: s. 45 LGFA 1988. The phrase 'non-
domestic' is unhelpfully defined in the Act as meaning 'a hereditament which consists
entirely of property which is not domestic, or is a composite hereditament': s. 64(8). (Obviously a composite hereditament means that it is partly domestic and partly non-domestic.)
Domestic property includes not only living accommodation but yards, gardens, and out-
houses used in connection with such accommodation, private garages, and private storage
premises.

Rates are assessed on the rateable value of the property: the rent which the owner could **22.16**
reasonably be expected to receive if the property was let on the basis that the tenant paid all
necessary outgoings. However, where this principle is difficult to apply, the Secretary of
State is given power to make regulations so that other assumptions can be used. This power
can only be exercised to prescribe cases and prescribe alternative methods of assessment:
LGFA 1992 Schedule 6, paragraph 3. The actual rates which each occupier has to pay are
determined by a multiplier set by the Secretary of State. This is then applied nationally. Each
year it may be increased by the retail price index, though it is open to the Secretary of State to
specify a lower figure. Although collection is in the hands of local authorities, the receipts are
subject to a central pooling system. The basis on which they are to be distributed to local
authorities is set out in a report which has to be approved by the House of Commons.

Liability is determined on the basis of rating lists. There are both local lists and a national **22.17**
list, both compiled by valuation officers appointed for this purpose by the Inland Revenue.
The local lists contain details of all non-domestic premises within the authority's area, the
rateable value, whether it is wholly non-domestic or whether it is composite, and whether it
or any part of it is exempt. The national list contains the same details for special cases such as
railways and the electricity, water and telecommunications industries. There is a duty to
maintain the list and regulations assume the existence of an implied power to alter the list.
This may be done on the valuation officer's own initiative, or as a result of representations

made by the local authority or any other 'person aggrieved'. There is a duty to notify the ratepayer and the local authority within six weeks of the amendment. If someone considers that the rateable value recorded in the list is wrong, or that any detail is wrongly included or excluded, there is a right of appeal to a valuation tribunal. This must be made within six months of the person becoming the occupier of the premises concerned or, if the grievance derives from a change, within six months of the change.

**22.18**   There are certain categories of property which are exempt from national non-domestic rates, most of which are derived from exemptions under the old system. Land which is held wholly or mainly for charitable purposes, or land which is unoccupied but which will next be used for such purposes is exempt from 80 per cent of rates, provided that the ratepayer is either a charity or trustees for a charity (sections 43 and 45 LGFA 1988). The charity does not have to be registered; whether it is a charity is a question of fact. However, if it is registered, this will be regarded as conclusive evidence that it is a charity. The 80 per cent relief is mandatory. The local authority also has a discretion to give relief of up to 100 per cent.

**22.19**   Discretionary relief may also be given to various voluntary organisations and other bodies. Broadly speaking these are non-profit making organisations which are clubs or concerned with recreational objects or social welfare, or are for religious or scientific purposes, or for the promotion of the arts. Crown property, places of public worship, including ancillary administrative and organisational activities, agricultural property and premises used for the training or welfare of disabled people are exempt. There are further exemptions for certain categories of unoccupied property and there are other miscellaneous exemptions such as those applying to diplomats. The council also has power to remit rates on the ground that if it did not do so, the ratepayer would suffer hardship: s. 49 LGFA 1988.

**22.20**   Rates are normally paid by equal monthly instalments. If a payment is missed, a reminder notice is served. If the ratepayer fails to pay the instalment within seven days of this, the whole amount becomes due. Rates due from ratepayers on the local list can be enforced by means of an action for civil debt or by distress. For ratepayers on the central list, only actions for civil debt can be used. If after distress is used, the value of the goods seized is insufficient, a warrant for committal to prison can be made. The period of imprisonment must not exceed three months (though the debtor will be released if the amount is paid earlier) and the warrant cannot be made unless the magistrates are satisfied that the failure to pay was the result of wilful refusal or culpable neglect. If the levy of distress is excessive, this will give rise to a right to claim damages. Such a levy may also be prevented by the grant of an injunction: *Steel Linings Ltd and Harvey v Bibby & Co* [1993] RA 27. However, this power will be exercised only in exceptional circumstances. In this case, goods which were vital to the company's business and had a value of £46,340 were seized for a rate debt of £7,358.

## KEY DOCUMENTS

Balance of Funding Report
Council Tax (Exempt Dwellings) Order 1992 (SI No. 1992/558)
Local Authorities (Calculation of Council Tax Base) Regulations 1992 (SI No. 1992/612)

# 23

# LOCAL GOVERNMENT FINANCE—CAPITAL

## A INTRODUCTION

The Local Government Act 2003 replaced the complex capital finance regime of the Local **23.01** Government and Housing Act 1989 with a simpler and more flexible system. This is described below but its main features can be summarised as:

(a) a general power for local authorities to borrow subject to limits which they determine for themselves and any national limits imposed by the government;
(b) a simplified system of credit arrangements (i.e. transactions entered into by local authorities which have same economic effect as borrowing);
(c) a simplified definition of capital receipts;
(d) a power to invest.

The new regime gives local authorities a greater degree of freedom in relation to capital **23.02** finance than they have previously enjoyed. It also relies more heavily on the conventions and principles of good accounting practice than the controls which it replaces. There is an emphasis in both the legislation and in the CIPFA Code of Practice (which advises authorities on its implementation) on prudence and affordability. The guiding principle behind the legislation is that it is primarily for local authorities to manage their own capital finance but they must do so sensibly.

## B   BORROWING

**23.03**   The LGA 2003 allows a local authority to borrow money:

(a)   for any purpose relevant to its functions under any enactment, or

(b)   for the purposes of the prudent management of its financial affairs.

The provision in (b) thus allows authorities the flexibility to change their loan arrangements if they consider they need to do so to manage their finances better. This need not be connected with the purpose for which the money was borrowed.

**23.04**   Section 2 sets out the controls on borrowing. Local authorities cannot borrow money if doing so would result in a breach of either:

(a)   the limit which the local authority determines for itself under s. 3 (see below), or

(b)   any limit which is imposed on it by the Secretary of State (this power is contained in s. 4 and is described below).

Local authorities may borrow only in sterling, unless they have Treasury consent to borrow in another currency. The above borrowing controls apply to all local authority borrowing, including borrowing under earlier statutory provisions.

**23.05**   Section 3 sets out the authority's duty to determine its borrowing limit in refreshingly clear language:

> A local authority shall determine and keep under review how much money it can afford to borrow.

Under Regulation 2 of the Local Authorities (Capital Finance and Accounting) (England) Regulations 2003, authorities must have regard to the CIPFA Code:

> In complying with their duties under section 3(1) and (2) (duty to determine affordable borrowing limits) a local authority and the Mayor of London shall have regard to the code of practice entitled the 'Prudential Code for Capital Finance in Local Authorities' published by CIPFA, as amended or reissued from time to time.

**23.06**   The determination of the authority's borrowing limit may be made only by the authority i.e. this must be done at a full Council meeting. It cannot be delegated.

The Secretary may set two types of limit on local authority borrowing: national limits applicable to all local authorities generally, and specific limits for individual local authorities. Section 4(1) provides that:

> The Secretary of State may for national economic reasons by regulations set limits in relation to the borrowing of money by local authorities.

Under s. 4(2):

> The Secretary of State may by direction set limits in relation to the borrowing of money by a particular local authority for the purpose of ensuring that the authority does not borrow more than it can afford.

**23.07**   The first of the above powers relates to the Government's need to control the level of national borrowing. Local authority debt forms part of the public sector borrowing requirement, and control of this forms part of national economic policy. The second is a power of intervention to stop individual local authorities behaving, in the eyes of the Secretary of State, irresponsibly. It can be seen as the capital finance equivalent of council tax capping. The Secretary of State may set different limits for different types of borrowing.

If a national limit has been set under s. 4(1) a local authority which has 'headroom' under **23.08** such a limit (i.e. spare borrowing capacity) may transfer it to another local authority. If headroom is transferred, then, for the purposes of the rest of the capital finance provisions, the transferor authority's borrowing limit is treated as reduced by the transferred amount and the transferee authority's limit correspondingly increased. Under s. 5 there is an exception for temporary borrowing, which provides that the limits determined under sections 3 and 4 are treated as increased by the amount of any payment which:

(a) is due to the authority in the period to which the limit relates, but
(b) has not yet been received by it.

The exception does not apply to any payment if the delayed receipt was taken into account in arriving at the limit.

If a local authority borrows outside its powers, the lenders will still be able to enforce the **23.09** loan agreement. Under s. 6:

> A person lending money to a local authority shall not be bound to enquire whether the authority has power to borrow the money and shall not be prejudiced by the absence of any such power.

## C CREDIT ARRANGEMENTS

Credit arrangements are transactions which enable local authorities to obtain a benefit on **23.10** terms that the consideration for that benefit is payable at a later date. Without being loans, they have the same economic effect as loans. If there were no restrictions over this type of transaction, it would be easy for an authority to circumvent the controls on borrowing by, for instance, obtaining an asset on delayed payment terms. Under s. 7 'a local authority shall be taken to have entered into a credit arrangement where:

(a) it enters into a transaction which gives rise to a liability on its part, and
(b) the liability is a qualifying liability'.

This raises two questions. What is meant by a liability? Which types of liability are qualifying liabilities?

Under s. 7(2) a transaction is treated as giving rise to a liability on the part of the authority if: **23.11**

(a) it falls in accordance with proper practices to be treated for the purposes of the authority's accounts as giving rise to such a liability, or
(b) it falls in accordance with regulations made by the Secretary of State to be treated as falling within paragraph (a).

The only type of transaction which is specified as a capital receipt in the 2003 Regulations is a variation of an earlier arrangement. If a local authority varies a transaction entered into before 1 April 2004 in such a way that, although the original transaction was not a credit arrangement, the agreement as varied would be (under either the old or the new rules), then the variation counts as a credit arrangement.

**23.12**  Under s. 7(3) a qualifying liability is any liability *other than:*

(a)  a liability to repay money (i.e. borrowing does not of itself create a qualifying liability since this is governed by other provisions in the legislation);

(b)  a liability in respect of which the date for performance is less than 12 months after the date on which the transaction giving rise to the liability is entered into (i.e. it does not count as a qualifying liability if the period during which the obligation on the authority is outstanding is less than 12 months);

(c)  a liability of a description specified for the purposes of this provision by regulations made by the Secretary of State.

**23.13**  The following have been specified as *not* being credit arrangements:

(a)  liabilities that do not arise from a transaction which results in the local authority being required, in accordance with proper practices, to recognise a fixed asset in any balance sheet (i.e. transactions which do not result in a capital asset for a local authority are not credit arrangements);

(b)  liabilities for retirement benefits appropriated to a pension reserve in accordance with proper practices.

**23.14**  The main concern about credit arrangements is that they could allow an authority to exceed its borrowing limit. Provided that it does not do this, then an authority is free to enter into credit arrangements. Section 8 sets out the provisions for control of credit arrangements. Under s. 8(1) a local authority may not enter into, or vary, a credit arrangement if doing so would result in a breach of:

(a)  the borrowing limit which the local authority determines for itself (under s. 3), or

(b)  any limit for the time being imposed on it by the Secretary of State (under s. 4), either national or specific to that authority.

**23.15**  Under s. 8(2) the costs of the credit arrangement or the variation is equated, for the purposes of this section as an amount of money borrowed. Entering into or varying a credit arrangement is treated as borrowing an equivalent amount to the cost of the arrangement or variation. Regulation 6 of the 2003 Regulations provides that the cost of a credit arrangement or variation of such an arrangement 'shall be the amount of the liability in respect of that arrangement or variation which is shown, in accordance with proper practices, in the authority's accounts'.

## D   CAPITAL RECEIPTS

**23.16**  The rules whereby a proportion of capital receipts had to be paid towards debt redemption have been abolished. Instead there is power for the Secretary of State to make regulations providing that such receipts must be used for certain types of capital expenditure, debt redemption or, in the case of receipts from the disposal of housing land, paid to the Government. The definition of capital receipt in contained in s. 9(1):

> Subject to subsection (3), references in this Chapter to a capital receipt, in relation to a local authority, are to a sum received by the authority in respect of the disposal by it of an interest in a capital asset.

Under s. 9(2):

> An asset is a capital asset for the purposes of subsection (1) if, at the time of the disposal, expenditure on the acquisition of the asset would be capital expenditure.

Capital expenditure is defined in s. 16(1): **23.17**

> Subject to subsection (2), references in this Chapter to capital expenditure, in relation to a local authority, are to expenditure of the authority which falls to be capitalised in accordance with proper practices.

Thus if an item of expenditure is properly treated, in accounting practice, as an item of capital expenditure, it is treated as such for the purposes of the legislative regime. Normally expenditure on assets such as buildings, vehicles and equipment, is treated as capital expenditure. Expenditure on salaries, running costs and consumables is revenue expenditure.

Under s. 16(2) the Secretary of State can make regulations: **23.18**

(a) to define certain types of local authority expenditure as being or not being capital expenditure, and
(b) to make a direction defining expenditure of a particular authority as being or not being capital expenditure.

Section 9(3) is another regulation-making power, allowing the Secretary of State:

(a) to exclude sums received from the disposal of a capital asset from being treated as capital receipts, and
(b) to provide that sums received by a local authority from sources other than the disposal of a capital asset should be treated as a capital receipt.

The following are specified (regulations 7–9) *as being capital receipts*: **23.19**

(a) repayment of a loan, grant or other financial assistance if it had been advanced for the purposes of capital expenditure;
(b) disposal of a mortgage portfolio relating to housing land;
(c) payments made to redeem a local authority's share of shared ownership property under Schedule 6A Housing Act 1985.

The following are specified (regulations 9 and 10) as *not to be treated as capital receipts*:

(a) capital receipts under £10,000;
(b) amounts received under an operating lease or a finance lease if, in accordance with proper practices, such amounts should be credited to a revenue account.

If sums are payable to the authority before they are actually received, they are treated for the purposes of the capital finance regime as being received at the time they were payable.

**23.20**    Section 10 covers non-money receipts. This prevents authorities from circumventing the rules by engaging in 'barter' type arrangements. It allows the Secretary of State to make regulations applying section 9 to cases where:

(a)  a local authority makes a disposal of the kind mentioned in subsection (1) of that section (i.e. disposal of a capital asset) and the consideration for the disposal does not consist wholly in money payable to the authority, or

(b)  a local authority receives otherwise than in the form of money anything which, if received in that form, would be a capital receipt under that section.

**23.21**    Section 11 allows the Secretary of State to make regulations providing for the use of capital receipts by a local authority. Under s. 11(2), such regulations may:

(a)  make provision requiring an amount equal to the whole or any part of a capital receipt to be used only to meet—
(i)   capital expenditure, or
(ii)  debts or other liabilities;

(b)  make provision requiring an amount equal to the whole or any part of a capital receipt to be paid to the Secretary of State.

**23.22**    The power to require amounts to be paid to the Secretary of State applies only to receipts derived from the disposal of an interest in housing land, i.e. land in respect of which income and expenditure fall within the authority's housing revenue account. Under the 2003 Regulations the Secretary of State must be paid a proportion of capital receipts in respect of housing land:

75 per cent of the amount received for the disposal of a dwelling
50 per cent of amounts received in respect of other housing land.

Under regulation this amount is to be treated as reduced by:

(a)  the administrative costs of and incidental to the disposal;

(b)  expenditure incurred on improving the land during the previous three years;

(c)  an amount (determined by the authority) up to the amount of the authority's capital allowance.

The capital allowance means amounts spent on facilitating the disposal of land, providing affordable housing or on regeneration projects.

---

## E   INVESTMENTS

**23.23**    Under s. 12 a local authority may invest:

(a)  for any purpose relevant to its functions under any enactment, or

(b)  for the purposes of the prudent management of its financial affairs.

# F THE PRUDENTIAL CODE

CIPFA have published the Code to which authorities in England and Wales must have regard **23.24** when carrying out their functions under Part I of the LGA 2003. The Code recommends the setting and monitoring of a series of 'prudential indicators'. These consist of a series of requirements for local authorities. They provide that each local authority should make estimates as to its capital expenditure needs, set limits for its borrowing and other indicators designed to ensure that it follows good treasury management practice and is not exposed to unnecessary risk.

The objective of the Code is to provide a framework for local authority capital finance to **23.25** ensure that, for individual local authorities:

(a) capital expenditure plans are affordable;
(b) external borrowing and other long-term liabilities are within prudent and sustainable levels;
(c) treasury management decisions are taken in accordance with professional good practice.

There are a number of matters to which the local authority must have regard when setting its **23.26** prudential indicators:

(a) affordability, e.g. implications for levels of council tax and Council housing rents;
(b) prudence and sustainability, e.g. implications for external borrowing;
(c) value for money, e.g. carrying out options appraisals where appropriate;
(d) stewardship of assets, e.g. asset management planning;
(e) service objectives, e.g. strategic planning for the authority;
(f) practicality, e.g. achievability of the forward plan.

The key prudential indicators (i.e. the issues in respect of which the authority should set **23.27** targets and then monitor its performance against those targets) may be summarised as follows.

Over a three year period:

- the estimated ratio of financing costs (i.e. all the costs of borrowing) to net revenue stream (i.e. all revenue to be received by the authority);
- the estimated impact of capital investment decisions on the council tax.

Local authorities which are housing authorities and have a housing revenue account need to do separate calculations for the housing revenue account (HRA) and non-HRA elements and consider the impact on rents as well as the council tax.

The authority also needs to look at the following over a three year period: **23.28**

- estimates of capital expenditure;
- estimates of capital financing requirement (i.e. the underlying need to borrow for capital purposes);
- the authorised limit for external debt (i.e. the authorised limit for borrowing plus other long-term liabilities);
- the operational boundary for external debt (i.e. the maximum level of external debt based on a prudent, but not worst-case scenario).

**23.29**   The local authority needs to ensure that over the medium term net borrowing is only for a capital purpose. A key indicator is that net external borrowing should not exceed the total capital funding requirement of the preceding year plus any additional estimated capital financing requirements of the current and following two years.

**23.30**   In addition there are the following prudential indicators designed to ensure good treasury management:

- compliance with the CIPFA Code of Practice for Treasury Management in the Public Services;
- upper limits on fixed interest rate and variable interest rate exposures;
- upper and lower limits for the maturity structure of borrowings;
- upper limit for principal sums invested for periods longer than 364 days.

---

## KEY DOCUMENTS

Local Authorities (Capital Finance and Accounting) (England) Regulations 2003 (SI No. 2003/3146)
Prudential Code for Capital Finance in Local Authorities CIPFA
Code of Practice for Treasury Management in the Public Services CIPFA

# 24

# LOCAL GOVERNMENT FINANCE—AUDIT

## A INTRODUCTION

Local authorities have been subject to a statutory duty to have their accounts audited since **24.01** the nineteenth century. Their auditors are now chosen by a statutory body, the Audit Commission. A local authority auditor may be a member of the Audit Commission's own staff or of an independent firm of accountants. He or she must have an appropriate accountancy qualification.

## B CODE OF AUDIT PRACTICE

There is an obligation on the Audit Commission to produce a Code of Audit Practice: s. 4 **24.02** Audit Commission Act 1998. This has to 'embody what appears to the Commission to be the best professional practice with respect to the standards, procedures and techniques to be adopted by auditors'. It must be produced at least every five years and is subject to approval by both Houses of Parliament. The Commission may revise the code between approvals. Before preparing the code or altering it, the Commission has to consult such local authority associations as appear to be concerned and such accountancy bodies as it considers appropriate. The Commission must publish the code from time to time and must send copies of it and any alterations to the Secretary of State who has responsibility for laying them before Parliament. Auditors have a duty to comply with the code when carrying out audits of accounts.

**24.03**     The current version of the code is the Code of Audit Practice 2005 for local government bodies. Under paragraph 15 it states that: 'Auditors are required to audit the financial statements and to give their opinion, including—

- whether they present fairly the financial position of the audited body and its expenditure and income for the year in question
- whether they have been prepared properly in accordance with relevant legislation and applicable accounting standards.'

Under paragraph 16 auditors 'should provide reasonable assurance that the financial statements:

- are free from material mis-statement, whether caused by fraud or other irregularity or error
- comply with statutory and other applicable requirements
- comply with all relevant requirements for accounting presentation and disclosure.'

---

## C   THE DUTIES OF AUDITORS

**24.04**     The best summary of the general nature of the local government auditor's office is contained in a well-known passage from the judgment of Lord Denning MR in *Asher v Secretary of State for the Environment* [1974] 2 WLR 466 at p. 472:

> The district auditor holds a position of much responsibility. In some respects he is like a company auditor. He is a watch-dog to see that the accounts are properly kept and that no one is making off with the funds. He is not bound to be of a suspicious turn of mind: see *In re Kingston Cotton Mill Co. No.2* [1896] 2 Ch 279; but if anything suspicious does turn up, it is his duty to take care to follow it up: see *In re Thomas Gerrard & Son Ltd* [1968] Ch 455. In other respects, however, the duties of a district auditor go far beyond those of a company auditor. He must see whether, on the financial side, the councillors and their officers have discharged their duties according to law. He must listen to any elector who makes objection to the accounts. He must make his own investigation also. If he finds that the councillors or the officers, or any of them, have expended money improperly, or unreasonably, or allowed it to be so expended, it is his duty to surcharge them: see *Roberts v Hopwood* [1925] AC 578 and *Pooley v District Auditor No. 8 District* (1964) 63 LGR 60 and in The Court of Appeal (1965) 63 LGR 236.

**24.05**     Apart from the reference to surcharge which has since been abolished the above remains a fair summary of an auditor's duties. More specifically the statutory duties of auditors are contained in s. 5 of the Audit Commission Act 1998.

They have to satisfy themselves:

(a)   that the accounts are prepared in accordance with the Accounts and Audit Regulations and that any other statutory requirements have been complied with;

(b) that proper practices have been observed in the compilation of the accounts;
(c) that the authority has made proper arrangements for securing economy, efficiency, and effectiveness in its use of resources;
(d) that the authority has made arrangements for collecting, recording, and publishing performance information.

---

## D  RIGHTS TO DOCUMENTS AND INFORMATION

Auditors' rights to documents and information are extensive, and clearly they need to be. **24.06**
The have a right of access at all reasonable times to all documents 'relating to' the authority which appear to them to be necessary for the purpose of carrying out their functions under the 1998 Act: s. 6(1). Under s. 6(2) an auditor may—

(a) require a person holding or accountable for any such document to give him such information and explanation as he thinks fit,
(b) if he thinks it necessary, require the person to attend before him in person to give the information or explanation or to produce the document.

There is also a separate power to require officers or members to give such information or explanation as the auditor considers necessary, and to require them to attend before an auditor for this purpose.

Documents which 'relate to' the authority need not be held by the authority. Documents in **24.07**
the possession of, for instance, contractors carrying out work for the authority, can be demanded by auditors under ACA 1998 s. 6: *R v Hurle-Hobbs, ex parte Simmons* [1945] KB 165 which concerned a similar, earlier provision. In this case the applicant was the senior partner of a firm of accountants. His firm acted as auditors to a company, Hortensia Garages, which made a claim against the London County Council. This claim was subject to an audit, and as a result the local authority's auditor needed to see the company's accounts. A notice was sent to the applicant requiring him to produce these documents. (This notice was served under the previous legislation, contained in the LGA 1933, but the provisions were essentially the same.) On the first occasion the accountant appeared but failed to produce the required documents, saying he did not have the documents which the auditor wanted and would need his client's consent to release any documents which he did possess. (The statutory duty to produce documents does of course override the ordinary duties of client confidentiality.) When he failed to respond to subsequent notices, he was served with a subpoena ad testificandum. He applied to the High Court to have this set aside. The application was successful, for reasons considered below, but it was accepted that the auditor was entitled to the documents he sought. It was said that the auditor had functions of a 'judicial nature':

> The auditor being in that position, and being charged with a duty under the Act of holding an audit and taking action in certain events, requires evidence to be available to him so that he may perform his duty. It is very desirable, therefore, that he would be armed with sufficient powers to bring that evidence before him. It would indeed, be absurd to suppose that he could perform his duty if he were unable to obtain the materials he required.

**24.08** It is an offence to fail without reasonable excuse to comply with any requirement of an auditor under these provisions. There can be a continuing daily penalty for failure to comply. It has been held that there is no other power to compel people to appear and produce documents: *R v Hurle-Hobbs, ex parte Simmons* [1945] KB 165. The facts of this case were considered above. In response to a second notice the accountant failed to appear. As a result, he was fined. He failed to respond to a third notice and was served by a subpoena ad testificandum. This was set aside by the court (Viscount Caldecote CJ at p. 171):

> I have come to the conclusion that the right view is that Parliament intended to exclude the powers exercisable by the King's Bench Division, and that a person who is in the position of a district auditor who is charged with certain duties must rely on the weapons which Parliament has given him and not on some other weapons which in other circumstances might be available.

**24.09** This decision seems to be inconsistent with local authorities' powers to obtain injunctions to restrain breaches of criminal offences when criminal proceedings have proved ineffective. It may be that today, if an auditor faced with similar was a recalcitrant, and had tried and failed to obtain important documents by criminal proceedings, a court would be more sympathetic to such an application. Failure to comply can be defended only on the ground of 'reasonable excuse'. In *R v Reid* [1973] 3 All ER 1020, it was held, in a very different set of factual circumstances, by the House of Lords that a mistake of law could not be a reasonable excuse. There is also a statutory duty on the part of the local authority which is having its accounts audited to provide the auditor with 'every facility and all information which he may reasonably require for the purposes of his functions' under the ACA 1998 s. 6(5).

---

## E PUBLIC INSPECTION AND RIGHT OF CHALLENGE

**24.10** Under s. 14(1) of the ACA 1998 a local government elector for the area of a body subject to audit, may

(a) inspect and make copies of any statement of accounts prepared by the body under s. 27 (which allows for regulations to be made as to the keeping of accounts);

(b) inspect and make copies of any report, other than an immediate report, made to the body by an auditor; and

(c) require copies of any such statement of report to be delivered to him on payment of a reasonable sum for each copy.

A document which a person is entitled to inspect under this section may be inspected by him at all reasonable times and without payment. A person who has custody of a document and obstructs a right of access being exercised under this section is guilty of an offence.

**24.11** In addition, under s. 15, ACA 1998, at each audit all 'persons interested' are allowed to inspect the accounts which are to be audited and all 'books, deeds, contracts, bills, vouchers and receipts relating to them' and to make copies of the accounts and the other documents. It is necessary to establish some legal or financial interest: *Marginson v Tildsley* (1903) JP 226. A person is entitled to arrange for the inspection to be carried out by an accountant acting on his behalf: *R v Bedwellty UDC, ex parte Price* [1934] 1 KB 333. In this case the council had objected to the accountant being allowed access to the books on the basis that he was not a ratepayer of the area and also because he acted for utilities with which the council was negotiating. It was held that the expression 'person interested' also extended to skilled agents otherwise the purpose of the provision would be defeated. The word 'contracts' includes supplementary documents which also form part of the contract such as schedules of rates but not background documents such as time sheets: *Hillingdon London Borough Council v Paullsen* [1977] JPL 518.

Under s. 15(2) there is power to question the auditor: 'At the request of a local government **24.12** elector for any area to which the accounts relate, the auditor shall give the elector, or any representative of his, an opportunity to question the auditor about the accounts.' There is an exclusion for personal information i.e. information which relates to payments to officers and employees. There is a right to make objections at the audit under s. 16(1):

> At each audit of accounts under this Act . . . a local government elector for an area to which the accounts relate, or any representative of his, may attend before the auditor and (in accordance with subsection (2)) make objections—
>
> (a) as to any matter in respect of which the auditor could take action under s. 17; or
> (b) as to any other matter in respect of which the auditor could make a report under s. 8.

Under s. 16(2) no objection may be made unless the auditor has received written notice of the proposed objection and the grounds on which it is made.

The above provision does not mean that there has to be a hearing. As Woolf LJ said in *Lloyd v* **24.13** *McMahon* [1987] AC 625 at p. 662:

> The fact that the elector is required to attend to make an objection does not mean that today the auditor is required to inquire into the objections in public or to hear oral representations or evidence relating to the objection.

---

# F AUDITOR'S REPORTS

Once the audit of the accounts has been concluded, the auditor has a duty to enter on the **24.14** statement of accounts:

(a) a certificate that the audit has been completed in accordance with the requirements of the Act; and
(b) an opinion on the relevant statement of accounts.

The auditor also has to decide whether, in the public interest, a report needs to be made **24.15** and whether this needs to be made immediately rather than at the conclusion of the audit (s. 8 ACA 1998). Once a report has been made the authority has a duty to consider it: s. 11 ACA 1998. This duty also applies to any other written recommendation of an auditor who states in it that it should receive such consideration. The authority must follow these steps:

(a) the report must be considered at a meeting of the full council;
(b) at the meeting the authority is under a duty to decide whether the report requires the

authority to take action, or whether the recommendation is accepted, and what action, if any, is to be taken in response to the report;

(c)   the auditor must be notified of the decisions taken at the meeting;

(d)   the meeting has to be held within four months of the report, or such longer period as the auditor may agree;

(e)   the meeting has to be advertised in a local newspaper at least seven days before it takes place and details must be given of its purpose and the subject matter of the report or recommendation;

(f)   a summary of the decisions must be published in a local newspaper.

In addition, if the report under s. 8 is an immediate report, members of the public are entitled to:

(a)   inspect the report at all reasonable times without payment and copy it or parts of it; and

(b)   have a copy given to them on payment of a reasonable sum.

**24.16**   There is also an obligation on the part of the authority to publish in one or more local newspapers a notice which:

(a)   identifies the subject matter of the report; and

(b)   states that any member of the public—

    (i)   may inspect the report, and

    (ii)   may make copies of it, or any part of it.

The notice must give details of the times within which and the place(s) at which the report may be inspected. Every member of the authority must be sent a copy of the report. An auditor who has made an immediate report may also notify any person he thinks fit of the fact that he has made such a report, and may supply a copy of the report, or of any part of it, to any person he thinks fit.

**24.17**   The question of whether reports can be challenged by way of judicial review has not been decided. In *R v Arthur Young (a firm), ex parte Thamesdown Borough Council* [1989] *The Independent* 16 February the auditor argued that there could be no application for judicial review as no decision had been made which could be subject to any prerogative order. The issue was left open to be decided at the substantive hearing which in the event never took place.

## G   UNLAWFUL EXPENDITURE

**24.18**   Under s. 17 of the Act:

> Where it appears to the auditor carrying out the audit of any accounts under this Part of this Act . . . that an item of account is contrary to law he may apply to the court for a declaration that the item is contrary to law.

If the court grants the application then, in addition to making the declaration, it may order rectification of the accounts. The earlier power to require those responsible to repay any unlawful expenditure was abolished in 2000.

**24.19**   If an auditor decides not to apply for a declaration, there is a right of appeal for anyone who made an objection under s. 16(1)(a). Once an objector has been notified in writing of an auditor's decision not to apply for a declaration, then the auditor can be required to give reasons for the decision. On the hearing of such an appeal, the court has the same powers that it would have on hearing an auditor's application for a declaration. What, then, are the kinds of matter that can be regarded as contrary to law? First, it is clear that if the way in which an item is dealt with in the accounts is illegal then it may be contrary to law even if no unlawful expenditure was incurred: *Randall v District Auditor for Tendring District Council* (1980) 79 LGR 207. In this case the Tendring District Council had entered into a contract to build a playground for the Lawford Parish Council. The District Council undertook the building work itself using its own workforce. Following a dispute about the quality of the works there was an objection against this expenditure. The auditor rejected the complaint, but an appeal to the High Court was allowed. The District Council could have built the playground itself and this would have been perfectly lawful. However, it was not lawful for them to contract with the Parish Council to undertake these works. In these circumstances the amounts were held to be contrary to law even though the legal formalities surrounding the way in which the works were carried out made no difference to the amount of the expenditure.

Secondly, it has been assumed that the test for deciding whether a decision is contrary to law **24.20** is the same as that for considering whether it would be quashed on an application for judicial review. Thus concepts such as '*Wednesbury* unreasonableness' (see chapter 13), which were developed in response to the requirements of administrative law, are used to decide whether public funds have been unlawfully spent. This approach may have been inevitable since these concepts lay ready to hand, some of them encapsulated in handy catch-phrases, but there is no logical reason why the test should be the same. The principles of administrative law were brought about to prevent people being adversely affected by arbitrary decision-making by public authorities. The purpose of allowing an auditor to apply for a declaration that expenditure is contrary to law is for the protection of the inhabitants of the area, to stop money being spent on their behalf being used for unlawful purposes. It is arguable that this calls for a stricter test. A person who is unfairly treated by the local authority may have no remedy other than judicial review. It may be thought that, provided there is statutory power, it is very much a matter for elected members as to how the local authority's money is spent, especially as the local inhabitants have another weapon at their disposal, albeit a crude one, namely the ballot box.

One of the leading cases on the interpretation of the phrase 'contrary to law' is *Pickwell v* **24.21** *Camden London Borough Council* [1983] 1 All ER 602. The judgments in that case have been influential in determining how auditors exercise their powers and are worth examining in some detail. The facts of the case took place against a background of what has come to be known as the 'winter of discontent' in 1978/9, when there was a series of industrial disputes as wage negotiations broke down when employers followed the 5 per cent maximum pay norm laid down by the then Labour Government as a means of controlling inflation. Negotiations over local authority manual workers' pay became protracted and were taking place while a series of strikes in support of the national pay claim was going on. These strikes were proving highly disruptive. In Camden, the ruling Labour Group decided to negotiate a settlement outside the national negotiations. They offered a wage of £60 per week and a 35-hour working week. This was accepted and the employees returned to work. Shortly afterwards the national claim was settled on much less favourable terms as far as the employees were concerned. The following year, a nationally negotiated cost of living increase was added to the manual workers' pay packets rather than absorbed within the margin by which their remuneration exceeded that of other local authority manual employees.

**24.22**  The auditor applied to court for a declaration that the payments by which the locally agreed settlement exceeded the national pay award were contrary to law, and for an order surcharging the councillors who voted for them. The auditor's application relied heavily on the decision of the House of Lords in *Roberts v Hopwood* [1925] AC 578. The argument that the auditor appears to have pursued was that this case is authority for the proposition that manifestly excessive wage increases are in themselves unlawful. This argument was not helped by the fact that the auditor's calculations of the amounts that should be surcharged were themselves flawed. It is highly unlikely that any surcharge would have been imposed even if the court had found that unlawful payments had been made.

The trouble with relying on *Roberts v Hopwood* was that this decision was not based simply on the size of the pay award. Rather, the payments in that case were unlawful because they were not a genuine exercise of the power to pay wages at all. Gifts or gratuities were instead being made in a purported exercise of the power to pay wages. The only reason put forward in that case for paying £4 per week was to be a 'model employer'. It was not guided by any economic considerations at all. This was, as the judges in Camden had little hesitation in pointing out, very different from the agonising that had taken place in Camden before the manual workers' strike was settled.

**24.23**  There were two judgments in the Divisional Court. The first, that of Forbes J, was closely tied to what he referred to as the *Wednesbury* principles and that he summarised as follows:

(a)   an authority must not be affected by immaterial or ignore material considerations;

(b)   an authority must not act in such a way that it can be said of it that no reasonable authority, properly directing itself to what was material, could have concluded that it was entitled so to act; and

(c)   in reviewing the acts of an authority the court will not substitute its own view of how a discretion should be exercised for that of the authority entrusted by Parliament with the discretion.

**24.24**  Forbes J went on to consider the nature of the court's jurisdiction. Previously, under the Public Health Act 1875 and the LGA 1972, it had been for the auditor to decide whether an item was contrary to law and whether anybody should be surcharged. But in s. 161 of the LGA 1972 this was replaced by a discretionary power on the part of the auditor to make an application to the court. The onus was therefore on the auditor to prove that an item was contrary to law.

The general principle, according to Forbes J, was that the local authority had to have regard to the interests of its ratepayers, but it had to have regard to other interests as well. Only if it could be shown that it deliberately tipped the balance in favour of one interest over the others, whether this is regarded as taking into account an irrelevant consideration or acting in a way that no reasonable authority could act, would it be unlawful. The judge drew support for this principle from *Re Hurle-Hobbs* [1944] 2 All ER 261. In this case the authority had a contract for refuse collection. The contractor's costs increased as a result of the war. The local authority negotiated an increase in the payments to the contractor although it was not contractually obliged to do so. The court, when considering the lawfulness of these additional payments, declined to draw an inference that the council was concerned only with the interest of the contractor. It had, on the evidence, taken into account the right considerations, and was mainly motivated by a wish to maintain the high standard of service that it had been receiving. In that case Lord Greene MR had also warned against the dangers of being wise after the event and applying an artificially high degree of logic to the problem:

> In considering a practical business problem, therefore, the court must always bear in mind that the persons whose actions it is judging are persons who had to carry their conclusions into action; that their problem was not merely an academic one to be solved on paper, but a problem which had to be solved then and there by some practical action. Therefore, in working out what it was reasonable to do, the court must endeavour to avoid treating it as though the practical solution was a matter that could be arrived at by some purely logical process of weighing the obvious factors in the case. It must be remembered that most business problems present more than one possible solution. Events may prove that one was better than the other, but that does not mean that a person who has chosen what turns out to be the less desirable solution has thereby acted unreasonably. There may be six possible solutions, one of which turns out to be the right one, but that is perfectly consistent with any of the other five being a solution to which a reasonable business man could at the time quite easily have come.

Forbes J also made the point that the issue of reasonableness has to be judged on the basis of how matters looked at the time the decision was made. It cannot be judged by looking at how they turned out to have been. In the circumstances, Forbes J found himself unable to draw any inference that the council 'ignored relevant material, was guided by improper motives, or acted in such a way as no reasonable authority could properly act'.

The second judgment, that of Ormrod LJ, is in some ways more interesting. Within it can be **24.25** found the suggestion discussed above, that a stricter test than '*Wednesbury* unreasonableness' is needed to find that expenditure is contrary to law pursuant to these provisions. The judgment begins by referring to the 'invidious position' of the auditor as a 'quasi-prosecutor' who had to decide whether to launch proceedings and then conduct them. It is not clear why this is supposed to be invidious. In deciding whether to launch, and then conducting legal proceedings, the auditor is in the same position as any other plaintiff. Ormrod LJ goes on to consider the test that should be used when deciding whether an action is contrary to law. He adopts the arguments of counsel representing the borough and the individual councillors, that in order for this to be satisfied it must be shown that the local authority has exceeded or abused its statutory powers or a discretion which is entrusted to it by statute: it must have acted *ultra vires*. He goes on to say that a breach of the '*Wednesbury* principles' is not to be regarded as illegality in itself but only as evidence of illegality. The basis on which he would decide whether a decision is contrary to law is set out in the following passage (p. 625):

> ... However, some action or decisions may be so far out of line with the 'norm' or so self-evidently erroneous, that the court may be justified in drawing the inference that the local authority has purported to use the discretion, given it for one purpose, in reality to achieve an ulterior or collateral objective which is ultra vires. This argument directs attention to the quality or character of the decision itself, rather than to the methods by which it is reached.

Lord Ormrod LJ goes on to bemoan the tendency to treat expressions used by judges as if they were propositions of law in themselves, and remarks that this is especially true of the concluding passage in the judgment of Lord Greene MR in the *Wednesbury* case.

**24.26**    This approach is a contrast to both Forbes J's judgment and the way in which questions of illegality had been decided in earlier judicial review cases. Lord Greene MR's formula has been treated as a proposition of law both before and after the *Camden* decision. Indeed, it was in the judgment of Forbes J. Moreover, breach of the principles derived from it has been regarded as being in itself sufficient to render a decision unlawful. Ormrod LJ suggests that it is necessary to go on from there to decide whether the decision is so far outside the 'norm' that it should be regarded as unlawful. This is difficult to apply in practice. How far away a decision is from the 'norm' will be a highly subjective question. He also suggests that only if a decision is made for some collateral, unlawful purpose can it be considered *ultra vires*. This is probably too narrow. It is possible to imagine decisions made for proper purposes, in the sense that they could be justified by reference to a statutory power, but which were still unlawful in the sense that no reasonable authority could have reached them.

**24.27**    Ormrod LJ then considered the authorities, and in particular *Roberts v Hopwood*. He said that the headnote in the report of this case did not accurately reflect the ratio decidendi since it implied that it was the excessiveness of the wages that led to them being considered unlawful: in other words, a quantitative rather than a qualitative judgement. In reality the judgments of that case showed that the real reason why the decision was unlawful was that these payments were not wages at all but gifts or gratuities paid in purported exercise of the power to pay wages. The *Camden* decision was contrary to law only if it was made for some unlawful, extraneous purpose or was such that no reasonable authority could have made it. Lord Ormrod decided that the evidence did not justify either of these findings.

**24.28**    If there is no statutory authority that can be used for the payment, then it will be contrary to law: *Hazell v Hammersmith and Fulham London Borough Council* [1991] 1 All ER 545. Once a payment has been finally fixed by an authority then it is likely to be contrary to law if it is re-opened and an additional payment made. *Re Magrath* [1934] 2 KB 415 concerned the duties imposed on local authorities in respect of road fund licences from 1 January 1921. The Minister of Transport said that it would be prepared to give sympathetic consideration to representations that officers' salaries should be increased because of the additional duties that local authorities would have to undertake. Durham County Council took no action in 1921, but in 1925 increased its accountant's salary by £100 per annum. In 1931, it voted to give the accountant an additional payment of £700 on the basis that the council had received an additional £1,575 from the Minister for the road fund licence duties and only £600 had been paid to the officer. This additional payment was disallowed by the District Auditor and the members who authorised it were surcharged. The Court of Appeal, allowing an appeal from the High Court, held since there were no records that the 1925 salary increase was provisional, it was not open to the council to re-open the matter and make a further payment in respect of the earlier years. However, it accepted that it was not an appropriate case for surcharge.

**24.29**    *West Cheshire Water Board v Crowe* [1940] 1 KB 793 is another illustration of the same principle. The Water Board was allowed to borrow money for works and also to borrow to pay interest on borrowed moneys out of capital. It could also pay interest out of revenue. It then borrowed an amount rather in excess of the amount of interest paid so far in purported exercise of the power to borrow to cover interest payments, and credited this to a reserve fund. The Auditor disallowed this insofar as it represented interest already paid and the High Court upheld this decision. The power given was to borrow for the purposes of paying interest as it fell due. Once it had been paid that was an end to the matter and the Board could not use this power as a means of recouping the payments.

The fact that a payment has been incorrectly calculated does not mean that it will be **24.30** contrary to law. In *Livingstone v Westminster Corporation* [1904] 2 KB 109, the plaintiff was previously surveyor to the vestry of St. George. His office was abolished in May 1901, and he claimed compensation for loss of office in the manner the council asked him to do this and calculated this as being £518 per annum for a period of five years. This figure was agreed by the council. Part of this amount was disallowed and surcharged by the Auditor on the ground that an allowance for keeping a horse and carriage was not an emolument for which compensation should be given. (This case has contemporary relevance: similar arguments about cars forming part of severance packages are not unknown.) The council then decided to rescind the earlier resolution and substitute the amount of £432. The plaintiff appealed to the Treasury (which was then the proper procedure) and, failing to obtain redress, he commenced an action in the High Court. It was held that the amount of Mr. Livingstone's salary and emoluments was a mater of fact for the council. The court could not review this. Even if the amount was wrong, this did not mean that it was *ultra vires*. The resolution to rescind was therefore invalid and the surcharge was wrong.

Although the power to surcharge members and officers, thereby rendering them personally **24.31** liable for unlawful expenditure, was abolished by the LGA 2000, the cases on this topic remain important. First, the auditor has power to declare items of expenditure as being contrary to law. He can order rectifications of accounts. He can also seek injunctions to restrain unlawful expenditure. In addition, the monitoring officer (see chapter 3) is under an obligation to submit a report to the council if it has, or is about to, make a decision that is unlawful. The need for careful scrutiny of prospective local authority decisions is therefore as great as it ever was.

The leading case on unlawful expenditure is now the House of Lords' decision in *Porter v* **24.32** *Magill* [2002] 2 AC 357, the final appeal from the challenge to the decision of the auditor to Westminster City Council to declare amounts lost as a result of the council's designated sales policy as being unlawful and to surcharge those members and officers he judged responsible for it.

The facts: The City of Westminster had, since 1972, designated blocks of council property for **24.33** sale to approved applicants. Once a property in one of these blocks became vacant, it would be sold rather than re-let to someone on the housing waiting list. Following the 1986 local elections, in which the Conservative majority on the council was reduced to four, the leader (Dame Shirley Porter) and Deputy Leader (Mr. David Weeks), together with others, identified eight 'key wards' where success at the following council elections would be crucial to the aim of increasing the Conservative majority. This policy was called 'Building Stable Communities' (BSC). A policy was proposed whereby there would be a particularly high target for designated sales in these wards, the assumption being that by increasing the number of owner-occupiers, the implementation of the policy would also result in an increase in the number of Conservative voters.

**24.34**    The policy of increasing designated sales in the eight key wards was not supported by professional advice on the City Council's housing needs. A consultant's report prepared shortly before the policy was adopted recommended that the council needed to make available a supply of low and medium priced rented housing. A discussion paper was prepared following this report. This was intended to be presented to a body known as the chairmen's group, consisting of the chairmen of committees, but which officers also attended. It advised that the consultant's report did not justify the designated sales policy that had been proposed. It also recommended obtaining counsel's advice on the committee report. On the morning of the chairmen's group meeting, Dame Shirley Porter requested a revised note. There was a consultation with leading counsel that day. He advised that it would be unlawful for the Council to sell the proposed figure of 250 properties in the key wards alone. He advised that designation needed to take place across the whole of the city and for proper reasons. Following this, and a revised report from the Director of Housing, the chairmen's group agreed that they would increase the target for designated sales across the Council with a view to achieving the desired numbers of sales in marginal wards.

**24.35**    At the subsequent housing committee meeting, a report was presented by the chairman in which it was recommended that sufficient properties should be designated to produce 500 sales per annum. A list of properties was chosen for designation. 74 per cent of these were in the eight key wards. These proposals were agreed by the committee with the seven conservative members voting in favour and the five labour members voting against. Following this, monitoring reports were produced on the implementation of the policy. The report to the chairmen's group considered what progress was being made towards the sales targets in each of the key wards. The reports to the policy and resources committee (on which members of the opposition sat) did not mention the key wards.

**24.36**    In 1989 objections were made to the council by a number of local government electors and the auditor was appointed to investigate. Following a lengthy investigation the auditor made provisional findings against a number of members and officers. Following hearings he found that unlawful expenditure had been incurred and that Dame Shirley Porter, Mr. Weeks, Mr. Hartley (the chairman of the housing committee) and two officers, Mr. Phillips, the managing director and Mr. England, the director of housing, were guilty of wilful misconduct. Following an appeal to the Divisional Court, Mr. Hartley and the two officers were found not guilty of wilful misconduct. However, the findings and the surcharge against Dame Shirley Porter and Mr. Weeks were upheld. They appealed to the Court of Appeal, which by a majority, allowed the appeal. The auditor appealed to the House of Lords, which unanimously allowed his appeal.

**24.37**    The decision: The speech of Lord Bingham sets out the relevant legal principles and covers the issues of legal advice, consistency, and causation. He summarised the relevant legal principles as follows:

(1)  Powers conferred on a local authority may be exercised for the public purpose for which those powers were conferred and not otherwise. Lord Bingham quoted with approval the following passage from Lord Bridge's speech in *R v Tower Hamlets London Borough*

*Council, ex parte Chetnik Developments Ltd* [1988] AC 858 p. 872: 'Statutory power conferred for public purposes is conferred as it were upon trust, not absolutely—that is to say, it can validly be used only in the right and proper way which Parliament when conferring it is presumed to have intended.'

(2) Such powers are exercised by or on the delegation of councillors. It is misconduct in a councillor to exercise or to be party to the exercise of such powers otherwise than for the public purpose for which they were conferred. If powers are given on trust, a failure to use them for the purposes for which they were intended is a betrayal of that trust.

(3) If councillors misconduct themselves knowingly or recklessly it is regarded by the law as wilful misconduct.

(4) If the wilful misconduct of a councillor is found to have caused loss to a local authority, the councillor is liable to make good such loss to the council. Items (3) and (4) above are much less important now that the power to surcharge has been abolished.

(5) Powers conferred on a local authority may not lawfully be exercised to promote the electoral advantage of a political party. In support of this he quoted the following passage from the judgment of Farwell LJ in *R v Board of Education* [1910] 2 KB 165 p 181: 'If this means that the Board were hampered by political considerations, I can only say that such considerations are pre-eminently extraneous, and that no political consequence can justify the Board in allowing their judgment and discretion to be influenced thereby.'

The last of these was a principle with which the courts considering this case had difficulty. **24.38** Clearly, the reality of local politics, like national politics, is that politicians act with a view to political advantage. They pursue policies that they think will attract votes. To suggest otherwise would be quite unrealistic. However, to use power so as to manipulate the system in order to gain a political advantage was plainly an abuse of that power. Lord Bingham said that the overriding principle was not in doubt:

Elected politicians of course wish to act in a manner which will commend them and their party (when, as is now usual, they belong to one) to the electorate. Such an ambition is the life blood of democracy and a potent spur to responsible decision-taking and administration. Councillors do not act improperly and unlawfully if, exercising public powers for a public purpose for which such powers were conferred, they hope that such exercise will earn the gratitude and support of the electorate and thus strengthen their electoral position. The law would indeed part company with the realities of party politics if it was to hold otherwise. But a public power is not exercised lawfully if it is exercised not for a public purpose for which the power was conferred but in order to promote the electoral advantage of a political party.

There was an argument that political allegiance can properly play a part in local government. **24.39** There was a series of cases in which it was decided that councillors could lawfully support policies adopted by the parties to which they belonged but would not obviate their own responsibilities and their duty to exercise their own judgement. This was really a different issue. The objection to the policies pursued at the behest of Dame Shirley Porter and Mr. Weeks was not that councillors abdicated their responsibility in following the dictates of their party, but that they pursued a policy that had been designed purely to promote the interests of a political party.

It was argued on behalf of Dame Shirley Porter and Mr. Weeks that they acted in accordance **24.40** with their understanding of the legal advice that they had been given. Both the auditor and the Divisional Court rejected this argument. However, it found favour with the majority in the Court of Appeal. The House of Lords was clearly unimpressed with the argument. Lord Bingham identified what he referred to as two fatal weaknesses in the Court of Appeal's reasoning. The first was that Counsel (Jeremy Sullivan) had not been given access to all the information. He was asked whether the policy of designated sales in marginal wards to secure an electoral advantage for the conservative party was lawful and he advised that it was not. He should have been asked if, for the same purpose, the designated sales policy was extended across the City of Westminster in order to conceal the fact that sales were being targeted in the marginal wards, the policy would become lawful. This question was not put, as it would have been quite obvious what the answer would have been. The second fatal weakness, in Lord Bingham's view, was the history of 'pretence, obfuscation and pre-varication' that surrounded the policy from May 1987 onwards. This, he pointed out, was inconsistent with a belief that what they were doing was lawful. It was also argued that it was inconsistent of the Divisional Court to have cleared Mr. England, Mr. Phillips, and Mr. Hartley, but to have upheld the findings against Dame Shirley Porter and Mr. Weeks. This was the main reason why Kennedy LJ would have allowed the appeal. Lord Bingham dealt shortly with this point, remarking that, whilst there may have been an element of mercy in the Divisional Court's exoneration of Messrs Hartley, Phillips, and England, the case against the Leader and Deputy Leader ('the prime architect and midwife of this policy') was very strong.

24.41    Another argument advanced on behalf of Dame Shirley Porter and David Weeks was that the housing committee adopted the policy for lawful housing reasons. If there was an improper motive on the part of those who originally formulated the policy, then it no longer mattered as the causative link had been broken. This argument, which had impressed Schiemann J in the Court of Appeal, did not impress the House of Lords. Although neither Dame Shirley Porter nor David Weeks were members of the housing committee, two members of that committee, the chairman, Mr. Hartley and the vice chairman, Dr. Duff, were aware of the motivation behind this policy. This invalidated their votes. As for the backbench members, there was no informed exercise of judgement on their part, since the true purpose of the policy was never explained. There was therefore no break in causation.

24.42    There are important lessons to be drawn from this case, particularly for officers who are placed in the invidious position of being put under pressure by members to pursue policies that they consider may be unlawful. The House of Lords adopted a strict approach to the exercise of local authority powers. They reaffirmed that powers are given to members of local authorities on trust. If they are exercised for purposes other than the purposes for which they were given, then this is unlawful. Monitoring officers are under a duty to ensure that they are aware of and understand the purpose for which powers are exercised when decisions are being made. If they are for an unlawful purpose then they are under a duty to prevent this, if necessary by using the statutory mechanisms under s. 5 of the LGHA 1989.

24.43    The role of party politics in local government has been clarified. Councillors can and should promote policies that they consider will prove attractive to their electorate, with a view to being re-elected. However, to pursue policies to favour the interests of a political party is plainly unlawful.

The case also illustrates the importance of obtaining external, independent advice on sensitive issues. The advice being given to members by the City Solicitor was clear—the Council was not entitled to exercise its powers for an ulterior purpose. It is necessary to bear in mind that the purpose for which a power is exercised must be the genuine purpose. What happened in this case was that members subsequently went to great lengths to camouflage the real reason for their decisions. As was said by the City Solicitor's note: 'The advantages of sale were to be considered not from any ulterior motive but from the standpoint of what is right in view of the council's role as a housing authority.' The note advised seeking counsel's advice at an early stage. **24.44**

The problem was though that, once counsel's advice was obtained it was used, not to guide members into acting lawfully, but to claim that they believed they were acting in accordance with legal advice. What happened was that there was a meeting with Lady Porter in the morning, a consultation with counsel later that same day, and a revised note prepared for the chairmen's group that evening. It is not clear why everything needed to be so rushed. Although obviously Jeremy Sullivan advised that designated sales in marginal seats alone were unlawful, the response to this was to widen the number of wards in which the policy was to be applied. The unlawful motivation was disguised when it should have been abandoned. **24.45**

The lesson to be drawn is that it is essential when seeking external advice for the questions on which advice is to be sought to be set out in writing. The answers to these should be recorded in writing. If counsel's advice is sought, then, if it is not written, a note needs to be prepared of any advice given on the telephone or in conference, which needs to be approved by counsel. Specific legal clearance of reports on highly sensitive issues is also required. This is a necessary check on the legality of what the Council is doing. (It also ensures that the report is expressed in such a way that the authority is not unnecessarily exposed to the likelihood of challenge for legal policies.) If Jeremy Sullivan had seen the report presented to the housing committee, it would have been obvious how his advice was being used, and the committee would have received clear advice about the illegality of their proposed course of action. **24.46**

## H EXTRAORDINARY AUDITS AND OTHER POWERS

### Extraordinary audits

An extraordinary audit must be ordered by the Audit Commission. It will direct that it is carried out by auditors appointed by the Commission. Such an audit can be directed under s. 25 ACA 1998 if: **24.47**

(a) an application is made by a local government elector for the area; or

(b) it appears to be desirable to the Commission made under the ACA 1998 in consequence of a report by an auditor; or

(c) for any other reason.

There is also power for the Secretary of State to require the Commission to direct an extraordinary audit. If such an audit takes place, the auditor has the same powers as during an ordinary audit. However, there is no power for members of the public to inspect the accounts and supporting documents or to question the auditor. An extraordinary audit may be held on three clear days' notice in writing.

**24.48**  The Secretary of State has power to make regulations applying to bodies which have to have their accounts audited under the 1998 Act, providing for:

(a)   the keeping of accounts;

(b)   the form, preparation, and certification of accounts and of statements of accounts;

(c)   the deposit of the accounts of any body at the offices of the body or at any other place;

(d)   the publication of information relating to accounts and the publication of statements of accounts;

(e)   the exercise of the public's rights of inspection and objection and the steps to be taken by any body for informing local government electors for the area of that body of those rights.

**24.49**  A new power was added by the LGA 2000, the power to issue an advisory notice under s. 19A of the ACA 1998. (This replaces the rather more draconian power to issue prohibition notices.) Such a notice can be made if the auditor has reason to believe the body he is auditing or any officer of that body:

(a)   is about to make or has made a decision which involves or would involve the body incurring expenditure which is unlawful; or

(b)   is about to take or has taken a course of action which, if pursued to its conclusion, would be unlawful and likely to cause a loss or deficiency; or

(c)   is about to enter an item of account, the entry of which is unlawful.

**24.50**  An advisory notice has the following features:

(a)   it is addressed to the body concerned;

(b)   it specifies which of the above paragraphs is relevant and the decision, course of conduct, or item of account to which the notice relates;

(c)   it specifies that the notice will take effect on the day a copy of the notice is served on the person to whom it is addressed;

(d)   it requires the body or officer before—

(i)   making or implementing the decision,

(ii)   taking or continuing to take the course of action, or

(iii)   entering the item of account (as the case may be)

to give the auditor notice in writing (the auditor can specify the period of notice which must not exceed 21 days).

**24.51**  A copy of an advisory notice—

(a)   shall be served on the body to which, or to an officer of which, it is addressed,

(b)   in the case of a notice addressed to an officer, shall also be served on him, and

(c)   may be served on such other person or persons as the auditor considers appropriate.

Under s. 19A(6), within seven days of the date of the notice, the auditor must also serve a statement of his reasons for believing that the decision, course of action, or item of account would be unlawful.

While an advisory notice has effect it is not lawful for the body, or any officer of that body— **24.52**

(a)  where the notice relates to a decision, to make or implement the decision,

(b)  where the notice relates to a course of action, to take or continue to take the course of action, or

(c)  where the notice relates to an item of account, to enter the item of account,

unless and until the conditions set out in subsection (2) are satisfied. The conditions are—

(a)  that the body has considered, in the light of the advisory notice and the statement under s. 19A(6), the consequences of doing the thing mentioned in the paragraph of subsection (1) which is relevant,

(b)  that the body or officer has given the person who is for the time being the auditor of the accounts of the body the period of notice in writing required by the advisory notice under s. 19A(3)(d), and

(c)  that period has expired.

If a disposal of land which a body had contracted to sell becomes unlawful as a result of an advisory notice, the existence of the advisory notice does not prejudice any remedy in damages which may be available as a result of the body's failure to complete.

---

## KEY DOCUMENTS

Code of Audit Practice 2005 for local government bodies available on the Audit Commission website: <http://www.audit-commission.org.uk>

## Exempt information (Schedule 12A Local Government Act 1972)

1. Information relating to a particular employee, former employee or applicant to become an employee of, or a particular office-holder, former office-holder or applicant to become an office-holder under, the authority.
2. Information relating to a particular employee, former employee or applicant to become an employee of, or a particular officer, former officer or applicant to become an officer appointed by—
   a. a magistrates' court committee, within the meaning of section 19 of the Justices of the Peace Act 1979; or
   b. a probation committee within the meaning of the Probation Service Act 1993.
3. Information relating to any particular occupier or former occupier of, or applicant for, accommodation provided by or at the expense of the authority.
4. Information relating to any particular applicant for, or recipient, or former recipient of, any service provided by the authority.
5. Information relating to any particular applicant for, or recipient, or former recipient of, any financial assistance provided by the authority.
6. Information relating to the adoption, care, fostering or education of any particular child.
7. Information relating to the financial or business affairs of any particular person (other than the authority).
8. The amount of any expenditure proposed to be incurred by the authority under any particular contract for the acquisition of property or the supply of goods or services.
9. Any terms proposed or to be proposed by or to the authority in the course of negotiations for a contract for the acquisition or disposal of property or the supply of goods or services.
10. The identity of the authority (as well as any other person, by virtue of paragraph 7 above) as the person offering any particular tender for a contract for the supply of goods or services.
11. Information relating to any consultations or negotiations, in connection with any labour relations matter arising between the authority or a Minister of the Crown and employees of, or office-holders under, the authority.
12. Any instructions to counsel and any opinion of counsel (whether or not in connection with any proceedings) and any advice received, information obtained or action to be taken in connection with—
    a. any legal proceedings by or against the authority, or
    b. the determination of any matter affecting the authority (whether in either case, proceedings have been commenced or are in contemplation).
13. Information which, if disclosed to the public, would reveal that the authority proposes—
    a. to give under any enactment a notice under or by virtue of which requirements are imposed on a person; or
    b. to make an order or direction under any enactment.
14. Any action taken or to be taken in connection with the prevention, investigation or prosecution of crime.
15. The identity of a protected informant.

# APPENDIX 2

## Compulsory purchase order procedure (Acquisition of Land Act 1981)

1. Compulsory purchase order made in the prescribed form, describing by reference to a map the land to which it relates.
2. Notice published for two successive weeks in one or more local newspapers circulating in the locality in which the land comprised in the order is situated. The notice must be in the prescribed form and shall—
   (a) state that the order has been made and is about to be submitted for confirmation;
   (b) describe the land and state the purpose for which the land is required;
   (c) name a place within the locality where a copy of the order and of the map referred to in the order may be inspected; and
   (d) specify the time (not being less than twenty-one days from the first publication of the notice) within which, and the manner in which, objections to the order can be made
3. Notice in prescribed form served on every owner, lessee and occupier (except tenants for a month or any period less than a month) of any land comprised in the order—
   (a) stating the effect of the order;
   (b) stating that it is about to be submitted for confirmation;
   (c) specifying the time (not being less than twenty-one days from service of the notice) within which, and the manner in which, objections to the order can be made.
4. If no objections are made, or all objections are withdrawn, or the confirming authority is satisfied objections can be dealt with by the tribunal assessing compensation, the order can be confirmed.
5. If there are objections, these can be heard at a public inquiry or written representations can be made, following which the confirming authority can confirm the order with or without modifications.
6. Once the order has been confirmed the authority must publish a notice in two successive weeks in one or more local newspapers circulating in the locality in which the land comprised in the order is situated. The notice must be in the prescribed form and must:
   (a) describe the land;
   (b) state that the order has been confirmed;
   (c) name a place where a copy of the order as confirmed and of the map referred to in the order may be inspected at all reasonable hours.
7. Like notices and a copy of the order as confirmed must be served on every owner, lessee and occupier who was served in accordance with 3 above.
8. The local authority can then proceed to acquire the land either by serving a notice to treat or by making a general vesting declaration.
9. Compensation may be assessed by the Lands Tribunal if not agreed.

# APPENDIX 3

## Principles on which compensation for a compulsory purchase order is assessed (Land Compensation Act 1961)

1. No allowance shall be made on account of the acquisition being compulsory.
2. The value of the land shall, subject as hereinafter provided, be taken to be the amount which the land if sold on the open market by a willing seller might be expected to realise.
3. The special suitability or adaptability of the land for any purpose shall not be taken into account if that purpose is a purpose to which it could be applied only in pursuance of statutory powers, or for which there is no market apart from the requirements of any authority possessing compulsory purchase powers.
4. Where the value of the land is increased by reason of the use thereof or of any premises thereon in a manner which could be restrained by any court, or is contrary to law, or is detrimental to the health of the occupants of the premises or to the public health, the amount of that increase shall not be taken into account.
5. Where land is, and but for the compulsory acquisition would continue to be, devoted to a purpose of such a nature that there is no general demand or market for land for that purpose, the compensation may, if the Lands tribunal is satisfied that reinstatement in some other place is bona fide intended, be assessed on the basis of the reasonable cost of equivalent reinstatement.
6. The provisions of rule (2) shall not affect the assessment of compensation for disturbance or any other matter not directly based on the value of the land.

# APPENDIX

## Principles on which compensation for a compulsory acquisition is assessed (Land Compensation Act 1961)

# APPENDIX 4

## Checklist for judicial review

Claimant

- Defendant and address
- Details of any interested parties
- Previous correspondence including references
- Exact decision being challenged
- Identity of decision maker
- Grounds for review (facts, legal framework, who should be the witness)
- Action required (What action would prevent judicial review? What order should be sought?)
- Information needed, if any
- Documents needed, if any
- Whether interim relief is required
- Whether there is a need to apply for urgent consideration
- Whether there is a possible alternative remedy

Defendant

- Whether claimant has standing to bring claim
- Whether the action has been taken against the correct defendant
- Details of any interested parties
- Correspondence and reference details
- Whether the claim can or should be resisted
- Whether the action has been taken promptly or whether it is premature
- Details of the relevant factual background and relevant documents
- Whether there is a possible alternative remedy

# APPENDIX 5

## The European Convention on Human Rights

### PART1

### THE CONVENTION

. . .

### RIGHTS AND FREEDOMS

#### Article 2
#### Right to life

1. Everyone's right to life shall be protected by law. No one shall be deprived of his life intentionally save in the execution of a sentence of a court following his conviction for a crime for which this penalty is provided by law.
2. Deprivation of life shall not be regarded as inflicted in contravention of this Article when it results from the use of force which is no more than absolutely necessary:
   (a) in defence of any person from unlawful violence;
   (b) in order to effect a lawful arrest or to prevent the escape of a person lawfully detained;
   (c) in action lawfully taken for the purpose of quelling a riot or insurrection.

#### Article 3
#### Prohibition of torture

1. No one shall be held in slavery or servitude.
2. No one shall be required to perform forced or compulsory labour.
3. For the purpose of this Article the term 'forced or compulsory labour' shall not include:
   (a) any work required to be done in the ordinary course of detention imposed according to the provisions of Article 5 of this Convention or during conditional release from such detention;
   (b) any service of a military character or, in case of conscientious objectors in countries where they are recognised, service exacted instead of compulsory military service;
   (c) any service exacted in case of an emergency or calamity threatening the life or well-being of the community;
   (d) any work or service which forms part of normal civic obligations.

. . .

#### Article 5
#### Right to liberty and security

1. Everyone has the right to liberty and security of person. No one shall be deprived of his liberty save in the following cases and in accordance with a procedure prescribed by law:
   (a) the lawful detention of a person after conviction by a competent court;
   (b) the lawful arrest or detention of a person for non-compliance with the lawful order of a court or in order to secure fulfilment of any obligation prescribed by law;
   (c) the lawful arrest or detention of a person effected for the purpose of bringing him before the competent legal authority on reasonable suspicion of having committed an offence or when it is reasonably considered necessary to prevent his committing an offence or fleeing after having done so;

(d) the detention of a minor by lawful order for the purpose of educational supervision or his lawful detention for the purpose of bringing him before the competent legal authority;

(e) the lawful detention of persons for the prevention of the spreading of infectious diseases, of persons of unsound mind, alcoholics or drug addicts or vagrants;

(f) the lawful arrest or detention of a person to prevent his effecting an unauthorised entry into the country or of a person against whom action is being taken with a view to deportation or extradition.

2. Everyone who is arrested shall be informed promptly, in a language which he understands, of the reasons for his arrest and of any charge against him.

3. Everyone arrested or detained in accordance with the provisions of paragraph 1(c) of this Article shall be brought promptly before a judge or other officer authorised by law to exercise judicial power and shall be entitled to trial within a reasonable time or to release pending trial. Release may be conditioned by guarantees to appear for trial.

4. Everyone who is deprived of his liberty by arrest or detention shall be entitled to take proceedings by which the lawfulness of his detention shall be decided speedily by a court and his release ordered if the detention is not lawful.

5. Everyone who has been the victim of arrest or detention in contravention of the provisions of this Article shall have an enforceable right to compensation.

## Article 6
### Right to a fair trial

1. In the determination of his civil rights and obligations or of any criminal charge against him, everyone is entitled to a fair and public hearing within a reasonable time by an independent and impartial tribunal established by law. Judgement shall be pronounced publicly but the press and public may be excluded from all or part of a trial in the interest of morals, public order or national security in a democratic society, where the interests of juveniles or the protection of the private life of the parties so require, or to the extent strictly necessary in the opinion of the court in special circumstances where publicity would prejudice the interests of justice.

2. Everyone charged with a criminal offence shall be presumed innocent until proved guilty according to the law.

3. Everyone charged with a criminal offence has the following minimum rights:
   (a) to be informed promptly in a language which he understands and in detail, of the nature and cause of the accusation against him;
   (b) to have adequate time and facilities for the preparation of his defence;
   (c) to defend himself in person or through legal assistance of his own choosing or, if he has not sufficient means to pay for legal assistance, to be given it free when the interests of justice so require;
   (d) to examine or have examined witnesses against him and to obtain the attendance and examination of witnesses on his behalf under the same conditions as witnesses against him;
   (e) to have the free assistance of an interpreter if he cannot understand or speak the language used in court.

## Article 7
### No punishment without law

1. No one shall be held guilty of any criminal offence on account of any act or omission which did not constitute a criminal offence under national or international law at the time when it was committed. Nor shall a heavier penalty be imposed than the one that was applicable at the time the criminal offence was committed.

2. This Article shall not prejudice the trial and punishment of any person for any act or omission

which, at the time when it was committed, was criminal according to the general principles of law recognised by civilised nations.

## Article 8
### Right to respect for private and family life

1. Everyone has the right to respect for his private and family life, his home and his correspondence.
2. There shall be no interference by a public authority with the exercise of this right except such as in accordance with the law and is necessary in a democratic society in the interests of national security, public safety or the economic well-being of the country, for the prevention of disorder or crime, for the protection of health or morals, or for the protection of the rights and freedoms of others.

## Article 9
### Freedom of thought, conscience and religion

1. Everyone has the right to freedom of thought, conscience and religion; this right includes freedom to change his religion or belief and freedom, either alone or in community with others and in public or private, to manifest his religion or belief, in worship, teaching, practice and observance.
2. Freedom to manifest one's religion or beliefs shall be subject only to such limitations as are prescribed by law and are necessary in a democratic society in the interests of public safety, for the protection of public order, health or morals, or for the protection of the rights and freedoms of others.

## Article 10
### Freedom of expression

1. Everyone has the right to freedom of expression. This right shall include freedom to hold opinions and impart information and ideas without interference by public authority and regardless of frontiers. This Article shall not prevent States from requiring the licensing of broadcasting, television or cinema enterprises.
2. The exercise of these freedoms, since it carries with it duties and responsibilities, may be subject to such formalities, conditions, restrictions or penalties as are prescribed by law and are necessary in a democratic society, in the interests of national security, territorial integrity or public safety, for the prevention of disorder or crime, for the protection of health or morals, for the protection of the reputation or rights of others, for preventing the disclosure of information received in confidence, or for maintaining the authority and impartiality of the judiciary.

## Article 11
### Freedom of assembly and association

1. Everyone has the right to freedom of peaceful assembly and to freedom of association with others, including the right to form and to join trade unions for the protection of his interests.
2. No restrictions shall be placed on the exercise of these rights other than such as are prescribed by law and are necessary in a democratic society in the interest of national security or public safety, for the prevention of disorder or crime, for the protection of health or morals or for the protection of the rights and freedoms of others. This Article shall not prevent the imposition of lawful restrictions on the exercise of these rights by members of the armed forces, of the police or of the administration of the State.

## Article 12
### Right to marry

Men and women of marriageable age have the right to marry and to found a family, according to the national laws governing the exercise of this right.

. . .

## Article 14
### Prohibition of discrimination

The enjoyment of the rights and freedoms set forth in the Convention shall be secured without discrimination on any ground such as sex, race, colour, language, religion, political or other opinion, national or social origin, association with a national minority, property, birth or other status.

. . .

## Article 16
### Restrictions on political activity of aliens

Nothing in Articles 10, 11 and 14 shall be regarded as preventing the High Contracting Parties from imposing restrictions on the political activities of aliens.

## Article 17
### Prohibition of abuse of rights

Nothing in this Convention may be interpreted as implying for any State, group or person any right to engage in any activity or perform any act aimed at the destruction of any of the rights and freedoms set forth herein or at their limitation to a greater extent than is provided for in the Convention.

## Article 18
### Limitation on use of restrictions on rights

The restrictions permitted under this Convention to the said rights and freedoms shall not be applied for any purpose other than those for which they have been prescribed.

# PART II

# THE FIRST PROTOCOL

## Article 1
### Protection of property

Every natural or legal person is entitled to the peaceful enjoyment of his possessions. No one shall be deprived of his possessions except in the public interest and subject to the conditions provided for by the law and by the general principles of international law.

The preceding provisions shall not, however, in any way impair the right of a State to enforce such laws as it deems necessary to control the use of property in accordance with the general interest or to secure the payment of taxes and other contributions or penalties.

## Article 2
### Right to education

No person shall be denied the right to education. In the exercise of any functions which it assumes in relation to education and teaching, the State shall respect the right of parents to ensure such education and teaching in conformity with their own religious and philosophical convictions.

## Article 3
### Right to free elections

The High Contracting Parties undertake to hold free elections at reasonable intervals by secret ballot, under conditions which will ensure the free expression of the opinion of the people in the choice of legislature.

# APPENDIX 6

## Specimen certificate issued under section 3 of The Local Government (Contracts) Act 1997 (the 'Act')

This certificate is given by [          ] ('the Council') under Section 3 of the Local Government (Contracts) Act 1997 in respect of a [        ] Agreement dated [         ] ('the Contract') between the Council (1) and [        ] (2) ('the Company')

1  **Period of Contract**

The Contract operates (subject as provided therein) until [         ]

2  **Purpose of the Contract—S3(2)(B) of the Act**

The purpose of the Contract is to [        ]

3  **Contract Type—S3(2)(C) of the Act**

The Contract falls within Section 4(3) of the Act.

4  **Powers to enter into the Contract—S3(2)(D) of the Act**

The Council has power to enter into the Contract pursuant to Sections [         ] of [        ] and Section 1(1) of the Act.

5  **Copies of Certificate—S3(2)(E) of the Act**

A copy of this certificate is to be given to each person to whom a copy is required to be given by the Local Authorities (Contracts) Regulations 1997 (the 'Regulations') as follows:
5.1  pursuant to Regulation 3 of the Regulations, to the Company; and
5.2  pursuant to Regulation 4 of the Regulations, to the monitoring officer and auditor of the Council.

6  **Matters to be dealt with in the Certificate—S3(2)(F) of the Act and Regulation 6 of the Local Authorities (Contracts) Regulations 1997**

The main relevant functions, the discharge of which the Contract is calculated to facilitate, or is conducive to or incidental to, are those conferred by [        ]

7    **Compliance with Regulations—S3(2)(G) of the Act**

The Council has complied or will comply with all requirements imposed by regulations with respect to the issue of certificate under Section 3(2) of the Act.

8    **Consent of Other Parties to the Contract—S3(4) of the Act**

By clause [        ] of the Contract, the [            ] has consented to the issue of this certificate.

Signed this              day of                        [     ].

. . . . . . . . . . . . . . . . . . . . . . . . . . . . . . . . . . . . . . . . . . . . . . . . . . . . . . . . . . . . . . . . . . . . .

Being duly authorised by the Council and a non-statutory chief officer within the meaning given to that expression in Section 2(7) of the Local Government and Housing Act 1989.

## Byatt recommendations

1. Procurement expertise should be integrated into best value reviews and represented in every local authority on the body which oversees best value.
2. Best value reviews should incorporate a wide-ranging approach to a local authority's key strategic objectives and be aligned to outcomes rather than the existing patterns of service provision.
3. Local authorities should adopt policies which ensure the effective involvement of staff in service reviews and in the procurement process.
4. Local authorities should set out their procurement strategy in a document which includes principles and information on current and planned activities. This should be regularly reviewed and updated.
5. Local authorities should develop a corporate procurement function to collect information, oversee devolved buying, co-ordinate training and act as an internal source of expertise.
6. Smaller local authorities without the expertise to set up a corporate procurement function should work with others to share resources. The Local Government Association (LGA) should work with the private sector to build up centres of excellence available to such authorities.
7. Local authorities should review their procurement structures and processes as part of the best value review programme.
8. Local authorities should, at an early stage, map their procurement activities using techniques such as high/low risk and low/high value matrices. They should identify the areas where procurement resources can have most impact and the appropriate skills and techniques for each type of procurement.
9. Using the analysis set out in Recommendation 8, local authorities should seek to aggregate demand and reduce costs by setting up central contracts for commonly used items and by requiring consolidated invoices.
10. Elected members should take a strategic role in securing quality outcomes. This should include scrutinising the procurement processes and monitoring the outcomes of procurements. There should be clear political responsibility for procurement with appropriate training.
11. Local authorities should review their standing orders to ensure they promote efficient and effective procurement whilst maintaining safeguards of probity and good governance. Standing orders should be used positively to encourage good practice. Changes to standing orders should be accompanied by an effective education programme.
12. The Audit Commission should guide and train auditors and inspectors to support a strategic approach to procurement. This should emphasise a risk-based approach and aim to equip auditors and inspectors to deliver effective scrutiny in a mixed economy of service provision. The Audit Commission should continue to review its experiences of significant and large procurement exercises and disseminate the lessons learned from them.
13. To help local authorities, the Audit Commission should clarify the roles of inspectors and auditors in relation to procurement and seek to co-ordinate their activities locally.
14. Local authorities should identify all those engaged in procurement within the organisation and identify the skills needed in each post across the authority. It should set out a strategy to meet those needs, including the recruitment of suitable staff, training, and ways of retaining trained staff.
15. The Improvement and Development Agency (IDeA) and the Local Government Employers

Association) EO should lead on developing a suite of training programmes. This should particularly be developed in partnership with the Chartered Institute of Purchasing and Supply (CIPS) and the Society of Purchasing Officers in Local Government (SOPS). This should build on the work done by the Office of Government Commerce (OGC).

16. Pump-priming funding should be provided to support the development of training programmes to subsidise costs of local government staff who use the courses. This could be provided through the IDeA or EO as part of the annual settlement or through the funding referred to in Recommendation 18.

17. Local authorities should increase their use of simple forms of e-procurement such as purchasing cards and BACS payments. They should adopt a modular approach to the implementation of e-procurement solutions.

18. Government should consolidate its funding for improvements in local government's capacity into a single fund, designed to provide both revenue and capital support on a pump-priming basis for key priorities. Such a fund could usefully absorb the resources currently made available in support of PFI projects so as to allow a wider range of partnership options related to outcomes to be pursued.

19. Government funding for e-solutions (such as Local Government Online) should be used to support the development of a variety of different e-procurement models in local government. Projects should be designed to encourage joint working between local authorities.

20. Local authorities should identify the information they need about the markets for local authority goods, works and services. The LGA, together with the IDeA and the 4Ps, should lead in devising better systems of information.

21. Each local authority should produce a prospectus for suppliers. This could usefully be adapted from the procurement strategy document described in Recommendation 4. It should include the significant items which the council expects to buy in the future, with an indication as to how it will procure them.

22. A joint national forum, convened by the DTLR, the LGA and the CBI, should broker a dialogue between local authorities and suppliers. Matters affecting the wider local authority market should be raised and resolved in this forum. This should be underpinned by an open dialogue, conducted through a variety of media such as workshops, web enabled discussion groups, training and development opportunities and case studies.

23. Buying consortia should publish annual accounts and performance information which is sufficient to allow local authorities to make informed decisions.

24. Buying consortia should review their services and their structures in the light of the need to retain and win new business in a competitive environment. They should pay particular attention to the needs of smaller councils.

25. A project plan should be drawn up at the beginning of each procurement exercise, setting out all the strands of work, how they will be undertaken and the time for their completion.

26. The LGA and ODPM should explore how a Gateway project review process can be developed to support local authorities who are involved in major, complex or high risk projects. It should include a strategy for providing high quality project review teams with an understanding and experience of the commercial sector. It should take advantage of the work done by OGC.

27. Local authorities should, in conjunction with suppliers, rationalise their procurement processes, e.g., by using common documents and pre-qualification processes or by using websites to exchange information.

28. Each local authority should develop a corporate strategy for managing risk which recognises the trade-off between risk and reward. That strategy should be applied to individual procurement decisions.

29. The Audit Commission should continue to develop good practice on risk assessment for auditors and inspectors which supports a balanced view of the risks and benefits of various procurement techniques.

30. Local authorities, with the support of IDeA and other organisations, should develop evaluation criteria which incorporate quality and whole life costs. The criteria chosen should not detract from the need for clear and prioritised objectives. They should be agreed in advance and should be published, transparent and auditable.

31. The project plan for all major procurements should include a requirement for client managers to be recruited or receive training and development prior to contract award. It should specify the skills needed by their client manager. Wherever possible, client managers should be party to the negotiation of the contract. The skills needed by the client managers should be discussed with potential service providers.

32. Suppliers should provide managers who are experienced or trained to understand the local authority environment.

33. Suppliers should be prepared to adopt an open book approach to the contract in complex contracting environments where change is likely. The DTLR-led R&D programme Supporting Strategic Service Delivery Partnerships in Local Government should look at the definition of open book and its use.

34. Suppliers should help local authorities by publishing data to support performance measurement (though where they have legitimate commercial concerns about confidentiality, these should be respected and assured). This issue should be considered by the joint national forum.

35. Government should give a clear lead on how intelligent procurement might be achieved within the European public procurement rules.

36. Changes are required to the European public procurement rules to simplify them and make them more flexible. Changes should support the setting up of framework arrangements and greater use of discussion and negotiation.

37. Central government should use the opportunity presented by the recent review of legislation on partnership working to relax restrictions which prevent effective joint delivery of goods, works and services.

38. Local authorities and contractors should understand and make best use of statutory and non-statutory arrangements to protect the legitimate interests of staff during transfers, including TUPE regulations, the Cabinet Office Statement of Practice on Staff Transfers in the Public Sector and the provisions to allow admission to the local government pension scheme.

39. Central government and the LGA should set up arrangements to monitor the effects of TUPE and local government pension scheme regulations which particularly look at what happens on subsequent re-tender of contracts.

## Duty of care summary

Was the alleged negligence in the exercise of a statutory discretion involving policy considerations?

| Yes | No |
|---|---|
| Claim fails | Continue |

Were the acts complained of within the exercise of the discretion?

| Yes | No |
|---|---|
| Claim fails | Continue |

Was the damage to the claimant reasonably foreseeable?

| Yes | No |
|---|---|
| Continue | Claim fails |

Was the relationship between the claimant and the defendant sufficiently proximate to establish a duty of care?

| Yes | No |
|---|---|
| Continue | Claim fails |

Is it just and reasonable to impose a duty of care on the defendant?

| Yes | No |
|---|---|
| Continue | Claim fails |

Duty of care exists and claim must be judged on the facts.

# INDEX

# Tata vs Mistry

# Tata vs Mistry

The Battle for India's Greatest
Business Empire

Deepali Gupta

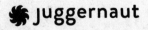

JUGGERNAUT BOOKS
KS House, 118 Shahpur Jat, New Delhi 110049, India

First published by Juggernaut Books 2019

10 9 8 7 6 5 4 3 2 1

P-ISBN: 9789353450397
E-ISBN: 9789353450403

Sketches by Deepika Rajjak

Typeset in Adobe Caslon Pro by R. Ajith Kumar, Noida

Printed at Nutech Print Services - India

*To my mother,*
*my harshest critic, staunchest supporter, and best friend*

# Contents

# Author's Note

This book is based on information obtained from various sources, including thousands of pages of public and court filings, over a hundred press reports, many hours of interviews, and several interactions and email exchanges with the parties involved and those who had a ringside view of events. I reached out to around fifty people for my research. They include current and former employees of the Tata Group, the Shapoorji Pallonji Group, board members, present and former, of Tata Group companies, and friends and family members of the protagonists. Parts of the book rely on court filings that have been sourced from the parties involved.

Many of the people who engaged with me did so anonymously because of the ongoing and high-profile nature of the case, the involvement of influential people, and to avoid taking a public stance on the question: whose side are you on? They were, or are, directly involved with the events narrated in the book. The quotes in the book are taken verbatim from documents or interviews. Where events unfold in dialogue form they have been reconstituted from minutes of meetings, or other such documents.

I started my journey of writing this book by reaching out to the offices of Cyrus Mistry and Ratan Tata, seeking comment and clarifications on their perspectives. Neither of them offered comment for the purpose of this book.

This book is not intended to support one or the other party. Nothing in this book is intended to disparage the persons involved or hurt their sentiments. I am a dispassionate observer and have portrayed the events neutrally as they unfolded.

Any loss, damage or disruption caused by this account is unintended.

# Cast of Characters

## Ratan Naval Tata

Ratan Naval Tata was chairman of the Tata Group from 1991 to 2012 and then for a brief period in 2016. He has been chairman of the the Tata Trusts, the largest shareholder of Tata Sons, since 2000. Popularly called RNT, he is known to hold himself and others to high standards. He is greatly admired by Tata Group employees and the business community for his friendly and gentle manner and strong values, and enjoys celebrity status.

The unmarried RNT has a small social circle. Even though he approaches eighty years of age, few can match his focus and determination.

## Cyrus Pallonji Mistry

Cyrus Mistry is the second son of the construction and real estate tycoon Pallonji Shapoorji Mistry. The Mistry family owns 18 per cent of Tata Sons, making them the second largest shareholders of the company. He joined the family business at twenty-three and led the Shapoorji Pallonji Group from strength to strength. Despite his privileged upbringing Mistry has remained grounded. Relatives described him as an 'old head on young shoulders'. He became a director of Tata Sons in 2006 and was chairman from December 2012 to October 2016. He is sharp and keeps his cards close to his chest. Married with two sons, Mistry lives in a closely knit joint family.

## Nirmalya Kumar

Nirmalya Kumar was part of Cyrus Mistry's core team at Tata Sons as group strategist, his only non-academic position in his career. Before that he was professor of marketing and director of the Aditya Birla India Centre at the London Business School. He has also taught at Columbia University and Harvard Business School, and has written eight books. Nirmalya writes a detailed blog on what's on his mind. He is now a Lee Kong Chian professor of marketing at the Singapore Management University and distinguished fellow at the INSEAD Emerging Markets Institute.

## Madhu Kannan

Madhu Kannan was also part of Cyrus Mistry's core team at Tata Sons. He was head of business development and public affairs, and became de facto in-charge of plan implementation. Before that, in 2008, Kannan had stepped down as MD of the New York Stock Exchange and took on the task of revamping the Bombay Stock Exchange in the aftermath of the global financial meltdown. He is now chief business officer for India and emerging markets at Uber India.

### Noshir A. Soonawala

Noshir A. Soonawala was till March 2019 a trustee of Tata Trusts. He has spent four decades in finance roles at the Tata Group. His last assignment was as finance director of Tata Sons. Financially astute, Soonawala is one of the few people who can talk to Ratan Tata as a peer. Soonawala's advice on managing funds, acquisitions and accounting is considered gospel in the Tata Group.

### R. Venkatramanan

R. Venkatramanan is a former executive assistant to Ratan Tata. Venkatramanan first came in contact with Ratan Tata while working at Videsh Sanchar Nigam Limited, a company that Tata acquired from the Indian government and rechristened Tata Communications. With nearly twenty years of working for profit and non-profit organizations, a law degree as well as an MBA, he

straddles both finance and strategy roles. He has served
as the managing trustee of the Sir Dorabji Tata Trust, one
of the key trusts that holds shares in Tata Sons, and also
as a trustee of several other Tata Trusts. Venkatramanan
was a board member of the Tata Group's low-cost airline
AirAsia India.

## C. Sivasankaran

Sivasankaran, a Chennai-born
businessman, is a telecom industry
veteran. He was promoter of Aircel,
which he sold to Malaysia's Maxis
in 2005, and was also an early
investor in Airtel and Idea. In
2006, Sivasankaran bought a 7 per cent stake in Tata
Teleservices. Sivasankaran would try to exit this
investment during Cyrus Mistry's tenure as Tata Sons
chairman under controversial circumstances. Flamboyant
and outspoken, Siva is everything the Tatas are not. He
is synonymous with big bungalows and a lavish lifestyle.
It is said that he was once close to Ratan Tata but that
is not the case any more.

## Nusli Wadia

Nusli Wadia, grandson of Muhammad
Ali Jinnah and son of Neville Wadia,
became chairman of Bombay Dyeing
and Britannia Industries at a young
age. He was a close associate of the

Tata Group and served on the boards of Tata Steel, Tata Chemicals and Tata Motors. Wadia was the godson of J.R.D. Tata. There was a time when he was considered the most probable candidate for Tata Sons chairmanship. Wadia and Ratan Tata were friends since RNT became the chairman of Tata Sons.

# 1

## The Suitable Boy

The monsoon inundated the streets of Mumbai in August 2010. It was the heaviest August rain the city had seen in over a decade. On the first Wednesday of the month, in a narrow lane, in a quaint corner of South Mumbai, the street market was oblivious of the electric atmosphere behind the stone walls of Bombay House. At this iconic Tata headquarters, most of the traffic was in the wires, as emails swished from one person to another, phones vibrated and occasionally people scurried over to each other preparing for what was going to happen. It was a momentous day and the tension was palpable: for the first time in its history the Tata Sons board was formally announcing the creation of a selection committee to find its next chairman.

Tata Sons, the main entity that works out of this heritage building, is the holding company – a company that owns and controls other firms – for nearly a hundred operating companies in the Tata Group, like Tata Motors, maker of the Indica car and owner of Jaguar Land Rover (JLR); Tata Steel, maker of steel products for cars and construction; Tata Chemicals, maker of Tata Salt; Tata Consultancy Services (TCS), India's biggest information technology outsourcing company; and Tata Global Beverage, maker of Tata Tea and Himalaya water and 50 per cent shareholder in Starbucks cafes in India. The chairman of Tata Sons is responsible for this sprawling empire, which has been headed by members of the Tata family for over 140 years. The retirement policy of Tata Sons was set up by sitting chairman Ratan Naval Tata (popularly known as RNT) after he joined in 1991. According to the policy, the directors of Tata Sons, including the chairman, had to retire at the age of seventy-five. It was going to be applied to the top job for the very first time as Ratan Tata would turn seventy-five in 2012, and before that a successor had to be found and trained under him.

On this Wednesday, Bombay House was abuzz because the upcoming announcement about the selection committee meant that Ratan Tata was really retiring. The search for a successor had been informally on for some time. Many people believed a suitor would never be found and the search was cosmetic. But Ratan Tata meant what he said about leaving.

The announcement would reveal the five selectors who had just met for the first time officially to undertake the arduous task of choosing the successor.

Surprisingly, Ratan Tata was not one of them. The names, which were revealed later that day, were:

- Noshir A. Soonawala – Ratan Tata's lieutenant and finance ace who had retired in 2010 from the post of non-executive vice chairman of Tata Sons. He was a trustee of the Tata Trusts
- Shirin K. Bharucha – lawyer with the Tata Group and a trustee of Tata Trusts
- Cyrus P. Mistry – Tata Sons shareholder and board member since 2006
- R.K. Krishna Kumar – director at Tata Sons, retiring in 2013, former head of Group companies like Tata Global Beverages and Indian Hotels (IHCL)
- Sushanta Kumar Bhattacharyya – a Tata outsider, UK politician (with title of Lord), founder of Warwick Manufacturing Group in the UK and friend of Ratan Tata

The rumour mill was still pegging Noel Tata as the likely successor. If an heir was to be nominated from the family, Noel Tata was the only eligible candidate in a family with few children. He also had the support of Pallonji Mistry, the head of the Shapoorji Pallonji (SP) Group, which had 18 per cent shares in Tata Sons who was the second largest stakeholder after the charitable Tata Trusts headed by Ratan Tata. Seven major trusts founded by Tata family members own around 65 per cent in Tata Sons.

To Noel Tata, Pallonji Mistry was father-in-law and Cyrus Mistry brother-in-law.

A few days earlier, Noel Tata had been promoted to MD of Tata International. It echoed Ratan Tata's elevation as chairman of Tata Industries in 1981, which turned out to be a precursor to his ascension as chairman of Tata Sons.

However, Ratan Tata had other plans. He had told a London newspaper that Noel Tata was not adequately exposed to diverse businesses to lead the Tata Group. Noel is Ratan Tata's half-brother from his father's second wife. The two reportedly had strained relations. Ratan Tata had made it clear that the next chairman need not be a Tata or even a Parsi. Parsis are a close-knit affluent community of an estimated 60,000 people of Zoroastrian decent.

Many in the community did not appreciate this declaration. Russi Mody, a former top executive at and once a contender for the chairmanship of Tata Sons, openly expressed his desire for a Parsi head for Tata even if it was not a family member.

The search committee cast its net far and wide. The August 2010 press statement issued by Tata Sons stated: 'The panel will look at suitable candidates from within the Group and professionals from India and overseas to find a replacement for Ratan Tata, who retires at the end of 2012.' Over the next months, fourteen potential candidates were evaluated and some of them interviewed more than once. The committee met eighteen times, sometimes at overseas locations.

Praise for Ratan Tata and the Group resounded in all corners of the corporate world. Here was a model showcasing that India's family-owned businesses were coming of age. It embodied the essence of professional succession planning. Institutes and academicians watched with admiration, acknowledging that 'letting go' is always a hard thing.

Newspapers bounded regularly with headlines naming potential successors. The contenders that reports named outside the Group were very qualified. Indra Nooyi was at the peak of her career as CEO of PepsiCo and knew consumer-facing businesses well, an aspect that the Tata Group was trying to crack. Her presence would introduce gender diversity in the Group's top management.

Arun Sarin was the former Vodafone global chief and had brought Vodafone to India with a whopping $11 billion investment after tough negotiations. Then, he dealt firmly with the Indian taxman who imposed a further $2 billion charge on the investment. Tata Teleservices would benefit from his telecom experience, and the Group with his ability to strike mega deals against all odds.

Anshu Jain had a meteoric rise to become the co-CEO of Deutsche Bank, the first non-European to do so. With the Indian financial sector poised to take off and Tata's plans to get into banking, his expertise would be an asset.

John Thaine, the former American chairman and chief executive of Merrill Lynch, and Carols Ghosn, chief of Renault–Nissan, were also considered, as Tata Motors entered a transformative phase for its consumer vehicles.

Keki Dadiseth, former chairman of Unilever in India and global executive director of the company, was a contender with whom Ratan Tata had interacted intermittently over a decade.

'Ratan is very hands-on with things he enjoys in a way that's not feasible for someone to come into the company at this point and do,' a Reuters news report quoted Bala Balachandran, a professor at the Kellogg School of Management, Illinois, USA, and a friend of Ratan

Tata. A Tata Sons press statement said, 'The Group would require someone with experience and exposure to direct its growth amidst the challenges of the global economy.'

Professor Balachandran said, 'The bigger challenge for any successor, and even more so for someone from outside the family, will be living up to the legacy and the constant comparisons that are bound to happen.'

Tata confidants said the committee believed appointing an insider would be a better choice. Internally, names that did the rounds included the finance director of Tata Sons Ishaat Hussain, brand custodian and human resources head R. Gopalakrishnan, former head of Tata Steel B. Muthuraman, chief of Tata Motors Ravi Kant, and former head of TCS, S. Ramadorai. Yet Ratan Tata preferred someone young. The retiring age for executives of the Tata Group was sixty-five and these aforementioned executives were set to retire in the next five years. Continuity had always proved to be an asset in the past. Jehangir Ratanji Dadabhoy Tata (J.R.D. Tata or JRD, as he was popularly known) was chairman for over half a century and launched the Group into many new businesses. His chairmanship was followed by Ratan Tata's two-decade-long stint, during which he centralized the Group, transforming the brand and foraying into large global acquisitions.

The committee looked for a candidate who would hold office for at least a decade to make any material difference to the Group. The younger insiders in the Group who reports said were being considered included N. Chandrasekaran, CEO of TCS, and Bhaskar Bhat, MD of Titan. Not many close to the unfolding events ascribed much significance to their candidature. Then, it dawned upon the committee that, while they were looking far and wide, the 'suitable boy' was sitting right before them!

The committee asked Cyrus Mistry to become a candidate. At first he refused. A little later when the search still came up short, Mistry was sounded again. He consulted his father, Pallonji Mistry, and others in the family and 'reluctantly' entered the race. The forty-four-year-old dropped out of the selection committee and served himself up for assessment. In October 2010, he was fielding questions from the selection committee like any candidate would.

In Mumbai parlance, Mistry was a true 'townie'. He went to the prestigious Cathedral and John Connon School in South Mumbai. He was known to be less flamboyant than his brother but close to his 'group of boys', recall friends and family. He went on to his bachelor's in civil engineering at Imperial College, London, and a master's in management at the London Business School. At twenty-three, Mistry joined the family construction business. Three years later, in 1994, he became the MD of Shapoorji Pallonji's flagship construction company. Mistry extended his company's product portfolio from construction to design and delivery of residential projects as well as projects in specialized sectors such as oil and railways. He also expanded his business internationally. In Cyrus Mistry's words, 'Shapoorji Pallonji is a company I have built bit by bit. Most of the people there have been part of a team, many of whom have worked with me for over twenty years. I would like to think I built a company that has world-class capability.'

In October 2010, Mistry requested the selection committee to excuse him from a meeting due to health reasons and instead answered on email the committee's questions on his vision and understanding of the Group.

Mistry had a larger vision for the Group. He wrote that the chairman of such a big group should have at least six years to effect change. He added it was time the articles of association or founding principles of Tata operating companies were modified to give Tata Sons rights to nominate a third of the board of directors of each operating company as long as Tata Sons held over 26 per cent in the operating company. Till such time, each company should have at least two directors from Tata Sons to ensure control of Tata Sons over its operational arms.

He also envisioned that over the span of the next five years the Group must incubate at least four major businesses, which would potentially be spun off into new companies. 'I believe the Tata Trusts can play a very important role here (managing the expanse and diversity of the Group), but it has to be well synchronized with the Group requirements,' wrote Mistry.

The meshing of young enterprise with wisdom of the old guard seemed to be an important theme running through all that he proposed. As a board member of Tata Sons, many had observed Ratan Tata turning to him for counsel.

Mistry seemed to tick all the right boxes. He was an entrepreneur. He was familiar with the Group, being a board member of Tata Sons. He had skin in the game with a financial stake of 18 per cent in Tata Sons that his family held. He was related to the Tata family, albeit indirectly – Cyrus's sister was married to Noel Tata. And as quoted in a *New York Times* report: 'He had a good relationship with Ratan Tata which was always seen as an important qualification for the job.'

Shirin K. Bharucha, who was representing the Tata Trusts on the selection committee, said in a television interview that Mistry was most qualified to 'grow into the role'. Mistry was the man who would further the philanthropic mission through the Tata Trusts.

Still, his appointment came as a big surprise to many.

The naysayers made all kinds of gloomy predictions. Some said that the Shapoorji business mindset would never fit into the Tata culture – which focused on diversity, people and philanthropy. Some predicted that he would pale before the grandeur of Ratan Tata. Many dismissed his single-company experience saying his vision would be myopic for the vastly diversified Group. His personal interests, some said, would come before the Group's well-being, and that the move favoured the Mistrys, who had long been rumoured to want control over the Tata Group. Perhaps these were just the lashings of aspiring contenders for the golden ticket whose hopes had been dashed. Yet, intentionally or unwittingly, these rantings sowed the seeds of doubt, as the events that unfolded subsequently suggest.

The division among Mistry's supporters and detractors was reminiscent of the time when Ratan Tata had himself taken over more than two decades ago. He often recalled

the day in March 1991 when J.R.D. Tata returned from
the hospital after undergoing a heart-related procedure,
and offered Ratan the bigger chair in the fourth-floor
boardroom. Ratan Tata became chairman later that year.
When JRD asked Ratan Tata if he should vacate his
office, he urged JRD to retain it.[1] He said, 'I did have
some concerns that Jeh would be in office every day, that
he would interfere and that he would forget that he was
not any longer the chairman, that he would be irritable
and render somewhat impotent the moves that I was
hoping to make.'

Yet, Ratan Tata's challenge did not come from
JRD. Instead, it came from Russi Mody, the long-time
lieutenant of J.R.D. Tata and chairman and MD of
TISCO, now Tata Steel. Mody had claimed chairmanship
and had even spoken to the press of his candidature.
Thereafter, when he did not get the post, he spoke in
public about the 'mismanagement' in the company at the
hands of Ratan Tata.

Ajit Kerkar, the chairman and managing director of
India Hotels Company Limited (IHCL) was another
heavyweight who opposed Ratan Tata's idea of a
centralized Group. Ratan had envisaged the Tata brand
as bigger than any of its operating companies and decided
that a brand charge be paid by all Group companies
to Tata Sons for using the brand name. The operating
companies at that time were often run by the individual
chiefs as their own fiefdoms. Neither the company names,
nor the brands they operated made it obvious they were
part of the Tata Group. Kerkar was one such chieftain.
He declared that IHCL that operated the Taj chain of

hotels did not use the Tata brand name and refused to pay the charge. He questioned Ratan Tata's move as being detrimental to shareholders. Tata negotiated these challenges to his authority with firmness. In a boardroom battle, Kerkar was forced out of his company, completing the purge of the old guard.

Under Ratan Tata, the Tata Group became a global brand. All companies under it benefited from the values of 'trust' and 'fairness' associated with the mother ship. Taking on challenges that no one thought possible had become his signature. In his two decades at the helm, Tata Steel made the large acquisition of Corus, the ailing European steel conglomerate, and Tata Motors acquired Jaguar, the world-renowned luxury car brand. Ratan Tata had conceived of manufacturing a car that every scooter-riding Indian would be able to afford – the Nano, for just Rs 1 lakh, a mere $2,000. Under Ratan Tata's leadership, Group revenues grew over 46 times to $83 billion, profits grew 51 times and market value 33 times.

Tata saw a similar future for Mistry and decided to make Mistry's rite of passage easier than his own had been. Therefore, Ratan Tata's glowing testimonial and endorsement of Mistry's candidature bore special significance. In the November 2011 announcement naming Mistry as his successor Tata said, 'He has been on the board of Tata Sons since August 2006 and I have been impressed with the quality and calibre of his participation, his astute observations and his humility. He is intelligent and qualified to take on the responsibility being offered and I will be committed to working with him over the next year to give him the exposure, the

Tata Sons chairman Ratan Tata with his successor-in-waiting Cyrus Mistry at an event in Mumbai in April 2012. They found occasions to smile together in the months leading up to Ratan Tata's retirement.

involvement and the operating experience to equip him to undertake the full responsibility of the Group on my retirement [in 2012].'

So began a one-year-long handover process with Ratan Tata as the master and Mistry as his apprentice. At several forums Ratan Tata endorsed Mistry to the staff and stakeholders of the Tata Group as Mistry accompanied him to get a handle on the Group's varied businesses.

Ratan Tata wrote in a letter to Group employees: 'The Tata Group will undoubtedly play an important role in the continued development of our country, providing leadership in various industrial segments in which they operate and living by the value systems and ethical standards on which our Group was founded. The future growth of the Group will be led in the coming years by Cyrus Mistry.'

His advice to Mistry was, 'Be your own man. Be yourself and just be driven by the fact that every act you do and every move you make has to stand the test of public scrutiny.'

A year went by all too quickly and soon it was 11 a.m. on 18 December 2012 – the day of Ratan Tata's last board meeting as chairman of the Group. Paying tribute to Ratan Tata, Cyrus Mistry said: 'The past year has been a great learning experience under the direct guidance of Mr Ratan Tata. The Tata Group is founded on strict values. We will face ups and downs, whatever may lie in our path. We are ready to face all the challenges that will come our way.'

Ratan Tata also offered his last words of advice as the chairman: 'How you deal with an aberration is a test of what you stand for rather than sweeping it under the carpet.' He expressed his availability for any advice that Mistry or other Group leaders would seek, but said he 'would like to make a clean break'.

The meeting ended and Mistry's watch began.

# 2

# The Board Meeting

**3 years, 10 months and 7 days later . . .**

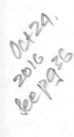It was another Monday. Bombay House was quiet. Mistry, just back from a routine overseas trip, sat in his room mulling over tough decisions that had to be made, preferably that day itself. Could he urge the Tata Sons board to go along with him? A forensic report had culminated in the discovery of a fraud in Tata's joint venture AirAsia. Mistry had placed that on the agenda of the meeting. A five-year plan for the Group, which had been going back and forth for several months, was also on the agenda. It included proposals for paring down loss-making investments, several of which were made during Ratan Tata's tenure as chairman. Mistry knew the pain points dragging down the Tata Group's performance on his fingertips. But resolution is never easy, especially if it involves shutting down businesses or selling assets. He called the pain points the

14

Group's 'hotspots'. Some of them certainly were touchy subjects.

Mistry had heard that some of the board members had met separately earlier that day. Perhaps they were discussing his proposals to sell businesses. What else could it be? The meeting was to start in a few minutes. It was best he went more prepared than usual.

As he sat there, unexpected visitors came to his room – Ratan Tata and Nitin Nohria. Nohria is the first Indian-born dean of Ratan Tata's alma mater – Harvard Business School. A few years ago the Tata Trusts had donated $50 million to fund an academic and residential building for the school to be named Tata Hall. It was the largest donation the university had ever received from an international donor. This had strengthened relations between the two men. After Ratan Tata's retirement, Nohria was nominated to the Tata Sons board by Tata Trusts, which Tata still headed. Nohria had been a board member of Tata Sons since September 2013.

Without any preamble Nohria brought up the rift between Tata Trusts (led by Ratan Tata) and Tata Sons (led by Cyrus Mistry). The Trusts disagreed with many of Mistry's plans and actions. Nohria said, 'Cyrus, as you know, the relationship between you and Ratan Tata has not been working.'[1] Ratan Tata was there, but quiet for the most part. Nohria offered Mistry two choices – resign or be voted out by the board. Mistry refused to quit. With that, the two visitors left his room, and Mistry made his way to the board meeting.

There was not much time to think. Mistry messaged his wife, Rohiqa, that he may soon be sacked. There was probably no time to consult a lawyer. Surely, there were some board members who would side with Mistry?

Mistry walked a few paces from his office to the boardroom to get the meeting started. This was the last stage in the game of chess.

Present in the room were:

Ratan Tata – chairman emeritus (an honorary member with none of the usual rights associated with board members)

Ishaat Hussain – finance director since 1998; career-long Tata professional

Vijay Singh – nominee of the Trusts since June 2013; former IAS officer with over forty-seven years of experience

Nitin Nohria – nominee of the Trusts since September 2013; dean of Harvard Business School and regular adviser to Piramal Enterprises companies

Ronendra (Ronen) Sen – independent director (a non-executive director on a company's board usually tasked to represent the interests of minority shareholders and uphold corporate governance) since April 2015; diplomat, India's Ambassador to the US between 2004 and 2009

Farida Khambata – independent director since April 2015; strategist at Cartica (an investment firm that acquires companies and controls their management in emerging markets), and former member of the International Finance Corp Management, a World Bank affiliate

Venu Srinivasan – independent director since 26 August 2016; chairman of TVS Motors

Ajay Piramal – independent director since 26 August 2016; chairman, Piramal Enterprises, credited with creating and divesting a pharmaceutical empire now focused on real estate and financial services

Amit Chandra – Trust-nominated director since 27 August 2016; MD, Bain Capital, part of the Asia leadership team and India head, also brother-in-law of Nitin Nohria

Mistry walked past some members to settle into the chairman's seat, which was marginally bigger than the others. The Tata Sons board had nine members: three trust-nominated members, four independent members and two executive members[2]: Mistry and Hussain.

What transpired after that can be best described as 'Gone in 60 minutes' because the meeting lasted just that long.

Mistry sat in the chairman's seat and initiated the meeting at 2 p.m. He was officially informed that Ratan Tata would be joining them.

Nohria: Tata Trusts has asked us to bring before the board a motion [not mentioned in the agenda].

Amit Chandra: We, the trust-nominated directors, held a meeting earlier this morning and have agreed to request Mr Mistry to step down as chairman. Mr Mistry, would you like to reconsider and resign before we initiate formal proceedings to change the board?

Mistry: I'd request Mr Tata to please say a few words.

Tata: At this stage, I am just an observer.

Chandra: Mr Mistry, do you have any views on the motion [to remove you as board chairman]?

Mistry: The motion, sir, is illegal. The Board, including all its members, must be informed at least 15 days in advance before such a motion can be put before it.

This set the tone for Mistry's refrain for the rest of the meeting. On everything else that ensued as well, Mistry noted his objection to no avail.

Chandra: We actually have obtained a legal opinion which suggests that in the current situation the notice is not necessary.

Mistry: Gentlemen, would you be so kind as to share this legal opinion. I am not aware of it and I do not agree with it.

Chandra: Mr Mistry is an interested party, I would like to bring this before other board members. For the purpose of this meeting, I propose Mr Singh act as chairman hereon. Let's put this to vote.

Ishaat Hussain: I would like to abstain from voting on this.

Farida Khambata: I would also like to abstain, please.

It was later said that Hussain and Khambata were caught unawares and were reluctant to make a hasty choice either way. While Khambata was brought to the Tata Group by Cyrus Mistry, Hussain had spent his whole career with the group.

The remaining six directors supported the motion and Mistry was now just a 'man' without the 'chair'. Khambata abstained from all resolutions proposed and passed during the rest of the meeting. Hussain voted in favour of all nine resolutions the board passed during the rest of the meeting.

The minutes of the board meeting show that first Vijay Singh became chairman for the rest of the meeting. He then proposed other resolutions that were not mentioned on the agenda. The first was to strip Mistry of all executive powers and annul all power he had been granted on behalf of Tata Sons. Then, the retirement age for directors that was set at seventy-five years was removed.

This was necessary because without that, Ratan Tata could not be nominated to the board.

Ratan Tata was nominated to the board as additional director and then made interim chairman. A selection committee was formed to appoint a new chairman. Finally, sixty-year-old Farokh N. Subedar, company secretary and chief operating officer, was given management control as the new chief executive of Tata Sons till a new leader could be identified.

Tata: We must recognize the work Cyrus has done over the last four years. It is important for the Group to move forward as seamlessly as possible. Cyrus, would you like to continue as a director on the board?

Mistry: Yes.

Chandra: Should we adjourn the meeting to consider this?

Mistry: Are we planning to make a public statement on what has happened here?

Hussain: Does Mr Mistry continue as the chairman of the Group companies? If not, this is a material change and the listed companies must report it to the stock exchanges.

[While Tata Sons is unlisted, its companies like Tata Steel, Tata Motors, Tata Consultancy Services and others are listed on public stock exchanges. The Tata Sons chairman typically is also nominated as the chairman of the top few of these companies as a measure of control. Cyrus Mistry was on the boards of seven such companies.]

Mistry: I will think this over and let you know.

Tata: Keeping directorship on the board is really up to you.

Khambata: Can we already announce this? There seems to be a question on the legality of these resolutions.

Chandra: I am not carrying the opinions, but they are from eminent lawyers and ex-Supreme Court judges.

Mistry: Could I please get copies of the written opinions? How can the rest of the board act without ever seeing these opinions? I would like to see these opinions today itself, please.

Chandra: Sure, we will check with the lawyers.

Tata: These are material developments to our company. What has happened here must be reported today itself. We should call a press conference.

All other items that Mistry had planned to discuss just over an hour ago were deferred to the next board meeting. His five-year plan was shelved without any further debate. Mistry was pushing for 'tough love' of some projects that the board members nominated by the Trusts – and Ratan Tata – still believed in.

Mistry walked back to his cabin. He checked with Subedar whether he should return for a handover the next day. Negative.[3] He was to wrap up his affairs and walk away without looking back.

Bombay House buzzed once again, readying for an explosive press announcement.

Three members of Mistry's group executive council – a five-member panel that deliberated all strategic moves of the Group companies – were sacked summarily that night in a very American fashion. 'It was literally like there was no need to come, your personal effects will be couriered to you,' quipped a former Tata employee. These were Nirmalya Kumar, Madhu Kannan and N.S. Rajan.

Insiders and senior executives at other Tata companies were rattled that everyone was on the watch list. Many of them searched through their emails. Were there any that could be perceived as backing the wrong horse, they wondered.

As things unravelled, it became clear that trouble had, in fact, been brewing for some time, but Mistry had shielded all his immediate executives from the struggle. So, this sudden announcement came as a shock to most of them. Only a few people, mostly lawyers, were aware of the differences between Ratan Tata and Cyrus Mistry. Even they never saw this move coming. Were these not friendly master–apprentice disagreements that could be resolved?

Evidently not.

Ratan Tata was no stranger to boardroom conflict. The sacking of Mistry was reminiscent of Russi Mody's dismissal at the start of Ratan Tata's career. Mody had run the Tata Group's highly profitable steel business like his own personal fiefdom. No one dared question him

Hemant Pithwa/The India Today Group/Getty Images

From left to right: Ratan Tata, J.R.D. Tata and Russi Mody at a meeting in New Delhi in January 1992 shortly after Ratan Tata became chairman of Tata Sons.

because he raked in unprecedented profits for the Group. Without the Tata Sons board approval, he nominated Aditya Kashyap as deputy MD of TISCO (now Tata Steel) and superseded another executive, J.J. Irani. It had possibly been part of his rebellion against Ratan Tata becoming chairman.

Soon after making the designation changes among TISCO's top brass, Mody left with Kashyap for London, as if it were business as usual. In the meantime, nothing was usual at Bombay House; Ratan Tata who had already earned his stripes in managing worker unrest, had taken the opportunity of Mody's absence to introduce and enforce a retirement age of sixty-five years for executives and seventy-five years for non-directors of all Group companies. Bitter about the retirement age as he was nearing sixty-five, Mody went public in his criticism of the Tata Group. For going against the Tata way he was asked to leave a month before he was due to retire.

The question that was on the minds of many corporate leaders was whether Ratan Tata imposed the retirement age in 1991 to ease out senior leaders at the time, and was he now looking to roll it back? When Mistry came in Ratan Tata was in favour of reducing the retirement age even for directors from seventy-five to seventy. There was no reason to do that except to remove any shadow of the past for Mistry.

By the end of that Monday, Cyrus Mistry had been removed as chairman of Tata Sons though he was still a member of the board. The official communication was succinct:

Tata Sons today announced that its board has replaced Mr Cyrus P. Mistry as chairman of Tata Sons.

The board named Mr Ratan N. Tata as interim chairman of Tata Sons. The board has constituted a selection committee to choose a new chairman ... The committee has been mandated to complete the selection process in four months.

The committee comprised Venu Srinivasan, Amit Chandra, Ronen Sen, Lord Kumar Bhattacharyya and Ratan Tata.

Milk processing cooperative Amul, known for its commentary on current events of national significance through its cartoon advertisements, featured Cyrus Mistry's hiring and firing.

When Cyrus Mistry took over as chairman, Amul had carried an advertisement showing Ratan Tata handing over a giant key with the Tata logo to him, with Jamsetji Tata watching on in the background.

The advertisement on the occasion of Cyrus Mistry's mysterious firing showed Ratan Tata sitting on a grand chair while Cyrus Mistry is shown standing, about to exit the stage.

Things had come full circle in under four years. Ratan Tata was chairman of Tata Sons once again.

# 3

# Mistry History

Mistry left Bombay House through an alternate exit. The press was already beginning to gather at the main entrance of the building. Along with Mistry was his childhood friend and well-known lawyer Apurva Diwanji, who whisked him away to a quiet conference room in another office to reflect on things. How had this come to pass? How was Mistry going to react?

His own family enterprise was steeped in history, one that was intertwined with that of the Tata Group. 'Over the last five decades our (family's) support for the Tata Trusts and the Tata Group has been one of guardianship. We ensured that we always did the right thing for the right reasons, regardless of consequences,' said Mistry.

Cyrus, as the younger of two brothers, did not bear the signature name that the eldest member of every generation bore. The eldest male family member in each generation had toggled between names Shapoorji Pallonji and Pallonji Shapoorji.

## The Mistry Family

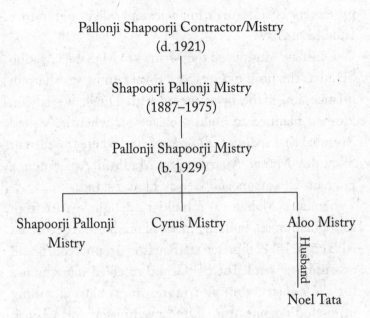

Pallonji Shapoorji Contractor/Mistry
(d. 1921)

Shapoorji Pallonji Mistry
(1887–1975)

Pallonji Shapoorji Mistry
(b. 1929)

Shapoorji Pallonji        Cyrus Mistry        Aloo Mistry
Mistry

Husband

Noel Tata

The family-run construction business first came to life in the late 1800s under Cyrus's great-grandfather, Pallonji Shapoorji Contractor. He partnered with a British citizen to form Littlewood Pallonji & Co. and built a cover for Mumbai's first water reservoir under the landmark Hanging Garden on the Peddar Road. The money from this venture, Rs 3,40,000, became the seed capital for the Group.

In 1900, Pallonji built the pavement around Mumbai's Chowpatty beach. By this time, Shapoorji Mistry, son of Pallonji Contractor and grandfather of Cyrus Mistry, barely a teenager, had joined the family business. While the SP Group was prospering and gaining a reputation for its execution ability, its most significant turn in fortune came when the Mistrys got recommendations from prominent businessman, financier and solicitor Framroze Edulji Dinshaw.

Dinshaw introduced the Mistrys to Maharaja Madho Scindia. The head of Gwalior's royal family was sharp in finance and made investments with Dinshaw's advice. He had planned to build a palace for when he visited Mumbai that spanned 20 acres of land where the current Samudra Mahal Apartments, Madhuli Apartments, Poonam Chambers and Ceejay House stand.

Samudra Mahal was a builder's delight. Apart from the opulent main building made of marble and decorated with crystal, it comprised staff quarters, tennis courts and a swimming pool. The SP Group received much praise for the construction and more orders started rolling in, including one from Dinshaw himself for a lavish bungalow in Pune. The bungalow later became a training centre for the Tata Group.

Now socializing with India's elite, the Mistrys took on construction of military barracks, hospitals and eventually ammunition factories. This gave the SP Group experience in a wide range of construction projects. Its wealth also soared.

In 1924, the Tata Group was looking to build its headquarters, Bombay House, on two plots of land that Jamsetji Tata had bought from the municipal corporation. Dinshaw, a close associate of the Tata Group, introduced them to George Wittet, the ideal architect for the building, and suggested Cyrus Mistry's grandfather, Shapoorji, as the contractor.

In 1936, Dinshaw died. Cyrus's grandfather bought

Dinshaw's financing company FE Dinshaw & Co (FED Ltd), for its small shareholding in various companies, most notably ACC Ltd.

By the late 1930s, the SP Group had become Tata's preferred contractor, building factories, townships and housing projects. Notable examples include that of Tata Chemicals in Mithapur, which was not just a factory but also a whole township. The SP Group was also fast altering Mumbai's skyline with structures such as the Bombay Central railway station, Mafatlal House, SBI Corporate Centre, Ambassador Hotel and The Oberoi at Nariman Point. The Group later went on to build Breach Candy Hospital, the Reserve Bank of India (RBI) headquarter, and the New India Assurance building, noted for the statuesque figures that adorn the façade.

The construction business under Cyrus Mistry's grandfather was growing at breakneck speed. So much so that his son, Pallonji, joined him at eighteen and learnt much of the business working on construction sites. He had the vision to add ancillary businesses such as an electrical supplier for construction. Pallonji also added a car dealership to the SP Group portfolio. Over the years as the Indian working landscape in both construction and real estate got tougher, Pallonji took his company to Muscat, Oman, for construction, while the Group shut its real estate operations.

Along the way both Cyrus Mistry's grandfather and father tried their hand at other ventures, but the ones that really flourished were construction and its affiliates. When Cyrus's father returned from Muscat he toyed with a short-lived aviation venture. He brought home seven helicopters in anticipation that they would be useful for spraying pesticides for the growing agricultural sector. However, landowners had small parcels of land that could not house a helicopter. There were no takers. The helicopters locked the SP Group's capital and created a cash crunch. This setback occurred around the time of a general election, and fortunately a politician requested Pallonji for six helicopters. Pallonji offered all seven, raking in both goodwill and financial returns on his investment.

*which politician?*

By 1975, the family had comfortably settled in a pent house apartment in a posh South Mumbai building – Windmere. Though Cyrus grew up in the lap of luxury, he watched his father put in hard work unassumingly. During the Mumbai monsoon, Pallonji would ride a truck to work, rather than miss a day.

Pallonji also had the foresight to plan for his two sons. In 1978, FED Ltd, Dinshaw's financing company that Cyrus's grandfather had bought, was rechristened Cyrus Investments. He divided his businesses and investments in two equal halves and Cyrus Mistry was made owner of Cyrus Investments, in which 50 per cent of the SP Group was vested, while Sterling Investments, which held the remaining 50 per cent, was given to Shapoorji Mistry.

The 18.4 per cent stake that the SP Group had come to hold in Tata Sons was also divided between Cyrus Investments and Sterling Investments. How Shapoorji Pallonji came to own this stake is a mixed bag of unusual events.

The popular misconception is that Dinshaw held 12.5 per cent in Tata Sons in his finance company FED Ltd. When Dinshaw died in 1936, J.R.D. Tata, still only a director in Tata Sons, did not have enough money to buy FED Ltd or its Tata Sons shares. The Mistrys bagged these shares when they bought FED Ltd. The truth: FED Ltd never held any shares of Tata Sons.

Tata Sons was formed by three family members – founder Jamsetji's sons, Sir Dorab J. Tata and Sir Ratan J. Tata, and their uncle, Ratanji Dadabhoy (RD) Tata. It became the investment vehicle for already existing Tata enterprises. The company Tata Sons was registered in 1917. Both Dorab J. Tata and Ratan J. Tata donated most of their equity to form charitable trusts. R.D. Tata's share was left to his eldest son J.R.D. Tata. A principled egalitarian, J.R.D. Tata shared this equity with his siblings Rodabeh, Dorab and Sylla. At this time, the Trusts held around 82 per cent in Tata Sons, while the rest was held by J.R.D. Tata and his siblings.

In 1965, Rodabeh decided to sell her shares. It is unclear why J.R.D. Tata did not buy them. In any case as Cyrus Mistry later recounted, J.R.D. Tata called on his grandfather Shapoorji to buy the shares so that they would not fall in the wrong hands. This was how, in January 1965, the Mistrys came to own 6 per cent of Tata Sons.

Pallonji then bought about 4.8 per cent more from the Sir Ratan Tata Trust in 1969, taking the SP Group stake in Tata Sons to 10.8 per cent. The last purchase occurred in May 1974 when Mistry's grandfather Shapoorji bought 6.7 per cent from J.R.D. Tata's younger brother Dorab.

Rumour has it that Dorab felt eclipsed by his elder brother and sold his stake in a fit of rage.

J.R.D. Tata was upset about this sale. It left more of the Tata Group in Shapoorji's hands (17.5 per cent) than with the Tata family and companies put together. At the time, the Tata Trusts, that held around 77 per cent of Tata Sons, were governed by public trustees – government – appointed administrators who oversaw the activities of the charities – under the Bombay Public Trust Act, 1950, and the Tata family had limited control on how they would vote. J.R.D. Tata asked that the founding principles of the company, or articles of association, be changed so that anyone acquiring new shares in the company would first need board approval. The earlier rule allowed existing shareholders in Tata Sons to acquire more from others without disclosure or permission. This way Shapoorji would not make a hostile takeover move against the family. The SP Group patriarch agreed.

Cyrus Mistry's father, Pallonji Mistry, in a letter forwarded to Ratan Tata in 2003, wrote, 'Mr J.R.D. Tata was upset about this transaction as it increased [the] Mistry family's stake in Tata Sons, but subsequently the matter was resolved … The Mistry family was approached by the Proposing Seller and at no point of time did they approach any of the Tata family members for sale of their shares.[1]

In a board meeting on 27 June 1974, the articles were amended to remove the line: 'A share may at any time be transferred to any member of the company'. Hereafter, Tata Sons shares could be transferred from a shareholder to only a legal heir. Any other exchange or purchase of

Tata Sons shares required approval from the board of directors, who held the right to reject it.

Pallonji Mistry is said to have had a big hand in smoothening matters between the SP Group and the Tata Group, for which he came to be known as the 'Phantom of Bombay House'. He was seldom seen, but his impact was always felt. As a general rule, Pallonji, despite having more stake than any Tata, rarely imposed his opinion on Tata's chairmen.

Pallonji's relations with RNT were also harmonious. They grew up together. A friend recalls that perhaps Ratan Tata's first driving experience was in Pallonji Mistry's car. It is safe to assume that RNT's appointment as chairman was not without Pallonji's support.

Pallonji's last boost in Tata Sons shares came in 1995, when the SP Group subscribed to a rights issue by Tata Sons, taking the stake from 17.5 per cent to 18.4 per cent.

Tata Sons had turned out to be one of the most successful investments for the SP Group. The rough cost of the first three acquisitions was Rs 35 lakh, and another Rs 69 crore in 1995, adding up to about $12 million. During Ratan Tata's tenure as chairman from 1991 to 2012, the SP Group received dividends of Rs 872 crore ($135 million) from Tata Sons.

~

Even while the equity holding discord was unfolding with J.R.D. Tata, Cyrus Mistry and his elder brother, Shapoorji, were growing up aware that some day they too would enter the family construction business of the SP

Group. They got along well and complemented each other.

As per an unspoken tradition, both boys were offered a car when they turned twenty-one. Shapoorji opted for a red Ferrari. Cyrus selected a discreet black Ford Sierra Cosworth. At twenty-three, Cyrus Mistry joined the family business after getting his engineering degree. He started to work on construction sites and worked with various departments before occupying a management office.

Cyrus, just like his father and brother, demonstrated keen business acumen. Under Cyrus and Shapoorji, the group grew to an eye-popping Rs 18,000 crore (approximately $3 billion) in 2011 or 600 times from just Rs 30 crore when they took over twenty years ago.

Shapoorji looked after the finance side of the group and eventually reopened its real estate business that had been shut since 1960. Cyrus, with his hawkish temperament and scientific inclination, took over the construction operations.

When he assumed charge as joint MD of the SP Group, Cyrus found its overseas operations languishing. He rebuilt the business and expanded the group to as many as forty-five countries. In 2000, after a mutual agreement between father and sons, the group bought the ailing infrastructure company Afcons, the turnaround of which can be credited to Cyrus Mistry, who was the SP Group's board representative in a non-executive role. The company went on to build some of the Delhi Metro's major stations.

In 2001, Cyrus completed construction of a 105 megawatt power plant in Samalpatti, after overcoming a major crisis that hit them in the initial stages. A few months into the project, their foreign partner walked out of the project. Cyrus managed to save face by convincing Ogden Energy to partner with and complete the project.

According to friends, Cyrus remained grounded despite his success at the SP Group which has built complex bridges, office buildings, low-income housing projects, and even an oil refining ship.

In a letter to Ratan Tata, Cyrus Mistry recalled occasions when the SP Group had also supported the Tata Group in its corporate and social responsibility initiatives. They built Tata Hospital in Kolkata below cost. In the aftermath of the 2004 tsunami, the SP Group helped Tata build rehabilitation housing. Some years later, in 2009, political discord forced Tata Motors to relocate their plant from West Bengal to Gujarat to build Nano cars. The SP Group delivered a factory faster than expected. In the same year, because Tata Motors was under financial stress, the SP Group agreed to take delayed payments over a span of eighteen months.[2]

The Tata Group accounted for 10–14 per cent of the SP Group's revenue and the relationship was symbiotic. Cyrus Mistry's father had been a board member of Tata Sons until his retirement in 2004 after which Cyrus Mistry had been inducted in 2006. Both Cyrus and Shapoorji had also been board members in some operational Tata companies.

In 2012, when Cyrus Mistry became chairman of Tata Sons, he had to leave the SP Group, which was a bittersweet pill – one that Mistry took nonetheless.

Cyrus Mistry's induction into the Tata Group had

been smooth. Once, after being nominated as chairman-to-be, on his way to a dinner reception in London, Mistry realized he had left his tie behind. Seated next to the always impeccably turned out Ratan Tata in the car, he could think of just one recourse – borrow the chauffeur's tie. That was the tie he sported through the evening.

Ratan Tata had himself had a tie situation some years ago at a shareholders' meeting. A keen shareholder had then commented that his tie was the same as the one in the annual report photo. 'Have you run short of ties?' the shareholder had quipped as Tata blushed.

The absurdity of the tie affairs had brought smiles to both Cyrus Mistry's and Ratan Tata's faces more than once. But on Monday, 24 October 2016, there were no smiles. Ratan Tata sat in the eye of the storm as everyone sought an explanation from him and Cyrus Mistry, who was smarting from what had just happened. What had gone so terribly wrong was still unclear and would only be revealed bit by bit much later.

Pallonji Mistry was unwell at this time and not in a position to intervene and fix matters between his friend and son. Something had snapped between Ratan Tata and Cyrus Mistry that only Pallonji could have de-escalated, according to a friend.

# 4

# The Morning After

There was little sleep for Cyrus Mistry on the night of 24 October. To the few colleagues he chose to talk to, he remained soft-spoken. Two of the three 'outsiders', or lateral hires into the Tata Group, on Mistry's general executive council – Madhu Kannan and Nirmalya Kumar – who had been sacked from the Tata Group on 24 October itself would become Cyrus Mistry's main support in the months to come. Right now though, the sudden events had just shocked them. As mentioned earlier, they were aware of some back and forth between Cyrus and the Tata Trusts over Cyrus's proposed changes to investments made during Ratan Tata's tenure as chairman, but had been well shielded from the magnitude of the problem. Like any good leader, Cyrus felt responsible for their fate too.

That night he started drafting a letter to the board of Tata Sons. The words would have to be carefully chosen. The facts were on his fingertips and the thoughts methodically catalogued in his mind. He had rehearsed them over and over for that fated board meeting. In a scathing five-page letter he predicted nearly $18 billion of potential write-offs in Tata companies as a result of poor investment decisions taken in the past.

By the afternoon of 25 October, this letter had found its way into the press.

So began the 'airing of dirty laundry', a phrase used liberally during the rest of the tussle that both sides had hidden so well all along.

In this letter, Cyrus criticized the board and the manner in which he was dismissed: 'I was shocked beyond words by the happenings at the board meeting of 24 October 2016. Apart from the invalidity and illegality of the business that was conducted, I have to say that the board of directors has not covered itself with glory. To "replace" your chairman without so much as a word of explanation and without affording him an opportunity of defending himself in a summary manner must be unique in the annals of corporate history . . . I am writing this letter to the board to emphasise the total lack of corporate governance and to point out the failure on the part of the directors to discharge the fiduciary duty, to the stakeholders of Tata Sons and of the Group companies. All this does not augur well for the future of the Group.'

Next Mistry took aim at Ratan Tata and listed out the problems that could be traced to Tata's term as chairman. These included an ailing steel business in the UK, bad buys of hotels under the Taj umbrella, losses on the Nano car project, entry into aviation which Mistry said was forced upon him, and a telecom business run into the ground before his appointment.

Mistry's letter was full of emotion and evoked much sympathy as he explained his journey with the Group. 'I took courage to overcome my initial reluctance and agreed to consider the position,' explained Mistry, as if to remind the board that he only took up the chairmanship of Tata Sons after the selection committee persevered in asking him. 'I am not sure if the original board members and Trustees truly appreciated the extent of the problems I inherited. I cannot blame them, for I myself, as a non-executive director [Mistry was appointed as a director of Tata Sons in 2006], did not have a clear grasp of the gravity of the issues involved.' Mistry said in the letter that not only were these problems created under Ratan Tata's leadership but also the board members received inadequate information to make informed decisions during that time.

'I cannot believe I was removed on grounds of non-performance,' Mistry protested in his letter. Just a few months ago, his work had been appreciated and the board had given him a raise along with the rest of the senior management. He continued, again targeting Ratan Tata: 'Prior to my appointment, I was assured that I would be given a free hand. The previous chairman was to step back and be available for advice and guidance as and when needed . . . I had to take many tough decisions with sensitive care to the Group's reputation as well as

contain panic amidst internal and external stakeholders
... I had to ease out hangers-on who are prone to flaunt
their proximity to power ... I hope you do realize the
predicament that I found myself in. Being pushed into
the position of a "lame duck" chairman, my desire was
to create an institutional framework for effective future
governance of the Group.'

These were all reasonable statements to make for a former
chairman. The Tata Group's silence on the matter swung
public sympathy towards the Mistry camp. Most people
were trying to come to grips with this new world in which
the Tata Group seemed like any other corporate.

For over a century, the Tata Group had come to be
identified as an employer safer and more upstanding than
the government. This hire-and-fire avatar was baffling.
Through a global economic meltdown, through local
scams, through disputed regulatory changes, being a
Tata employee had meant there would always be bread
on the table. Tata employees were considered secure from
upheavals in the economic environment or even from an
unkind boss.

In fact, in the 1970s and 1980s, the next best thing to
a government job was a job with the Tata Group. Even
today, many staffers across all levels, from clerks and peons
to directors, have clocked several decades at the company.
Loyalty was always rewarded, and the focal point of that
loyalty had been Ratan Tata, a lean, towering man with
a soft nature who noticed people no matter where they
stood in the pecking order. Employees at every level

had direct access to him. His former driver once needed money to fund his son's education in Australia. Ratan Tata was quick to help and also gave an additional amount for the driver to build a home locally.

Mistry, on the other hand, was a man of few words and mostly kept to himself. Within Bombay House he was perceived as less approachable than his predecessor. Even before the boardroom had decided it, the staff at Bombay House was ready to welcome their old chairman back. The leaked letter made it clear that Mistry was going to put up a fight. But the open warfare had expectedly incensed the Parsi community. A friend of Mistry's said, 'He should have taken his shares and negotiated a deal to get out of the Group. This letter is only eroding the value of his own investment!'

Gearing up for a legal challenge, the Tata Group filed a caveat in all the relevant company law tribunals, a special division of the judiciary to deal with matters that come under the Companies Act which largely governs business operations and disputes. The caveat alerted the courts that Mistry may file a suit against Tata Sons and before passing any order, even temporary, Tata Sons should be given a hearing. This way Mistry could not ask for a freeze on any decisions at Tata companies exparte, that is, without giving the Group a chance to explain.

'We haven't done or said anything yet. They [Tata Sons] are afraid that is why they are doing such things,' taunted a lawyer from the Mistry camp in response to the caveat.

It was time for Mistry to create his team and start lawyering up. Madhu Kannan took up the task of finding the right public relations representatives while Apurva Diwanji worked on roping in a legal team.

Mistry found himself with a smaller and less renowned legal team than Tata Sons. Leading the charge was his childhood friend Apurva Diwanji backed by his law firm Desai and Diwanji. He is known for his work in matters related to private equity, mergers and acquisitions, and capital markets. In his twenty-one years at this law firm, Diwanji also developed skills in stock exchange – related regulations.

Cyrus Mistry's father-in-law, Iqbal Chagla, helped strategize Mistry's course of action but never appeared in court. The son of the Bombay High Court's first Indian Chief Justice, M.C. Chagla, he is reputed for his legal mind and remarkable skill in litigation.

Despite Chagla's deep connections in the legal world and the affluence of the SP Group, it took Mistry a few attempts before he could finalize his legal and public relations representatives.

Mistry's team found that several of the PR agencies and lawyers they called had either been retained by or were in talks with Tata Sons for an engagement. Six PR agencies were working to malign Mistry, Nirmalya Kumar exclaimed.

Madhu Kannan phoned a few PR leaders, including the biggest one, Adfactors PR. He urged the PR firms to make their decisions only after listening to Mistry's side of the story. Some did, others did not. Most declined to work with Mistry. A week later, Adfactors PR received an offer from Tata Sons, which they accepted. Mistry finally signed Perfect Relations as his PR agency.

It wasn't easy for the lawyers either. Many were wary of going against the Tata Group. 'We get so much work from Tata Sons, can't make them an enemy,' said a senior partner from a South Mumbai law firm. Some refused to take sides. Darius Khambata, senior advocate in the Bombay High Court and former state advocate general, resigned from the post of trustee at the Tata Trusts and declined to work with Mistry, in order to maintain a neutral stance between Tata and Mistry. There was also the conspicuous absence of Zia Mody among the legal teams that were being shored up.

Mistry's team of lawyers finally comprised Janak Dwarkadas, Aryama Sundaram, Shyam Divan, Somasekhar Sundaresan – who had recently quit as partner at the J. Sagar Associates (JSA) law firm and started out on his own – and Sharan Jagtiani.

The Tatas, on the other hand, had been preparing for this for a month. Although very few on the team knew what they had been hired for. Nirmalya Kumar's comment that six PR agencies were doing the Tatas' bidding may have been an overstatement, but there were certainly four working on the problem within a week of the board meeting to remove Cyrus Mistry.

Avian Media had been recruited by the Tata Trusts ahead of the meeting, and later moved to work out of Bombay House. Edelman India was the official agency for Tata Sons and had reported to Mistry while he was chairman, so it was not looped in before Mistry was fired. Edelman took to handling press queries and communication in and out of the Tata headquarters. Adfactors PR was appointed for strategy and investor communications, with key emphasis on monitoring content and identifying journalists (and their potential sources) who were publishing stories damaging to the Tata Group. More discreetly, PR agency Ketchum Sampark advised the Tata Trusts on their publicity given that Mistry was expected to drag the charitable institutions into the thick of the controversy.

The Tatas' battery of legal eagles included Harish Salve, arguably the country's most expensive lawyer; Congress spokesman Abhishek Singhvi; Raian Karanjawala, managing partner of a law firm named after him; former finance minister P. Chidambaram; former Solicitor General of India Mohan Parasaran; former telecom minister Kapil Sibal; senior advocate at the Delhi High Court Rajiv Nayar; and top litigation law firms Karanjawala & Co and Shardul Amarchand Mangaldas. There was a clearly defined role for each of them.

News reporters thronged outside Bombay House with just one motto, 'Trespassers shall be interviewed'. Many of the lawyers were hounded with phone calls from newsrooms. The slightest hint of new information was splashed across television screens in big bold letters that said 'Exclusive'. The general public were no different from journalists. They yearned for information. In meetings, executives regularly refreshed their newsfeeds and every twist in the story was discussed threadbare in office pantries, by water coolers, in corridors and even in meeting rooms.

Tata's communications teams were asked to focus

internally on Tata employees. Ratan Tata's first priority was to return to business as usual at the Tata companies.

In a series of swift moves, N. Chandrasekaran, chief executive of TCS, the Tata Group's metaphorical cash cow, and Ralf Speth, CEO of Jaguar Land Rover (JLR), were nominated to the board of Tata Sons, clearly signalling that the two were in the running for the expedited search for a chairman. Next, Ratan Tata engaged with the senior leaders of the Group. 'I look forward to working with you as we have worked together in the past. An institution must exceed the people who lead it. I am proud of all of you, and let us continue to build the Group together,' Ratan Tata told them at a meeting held on 25 October 2016. 'The companies must focus on their market position vis-à-vis competition, and not compare themselves to their own past. The drive must be on leadership rather than to follow,' he said. Having somewhat calmed the nerves of an edgy Group that was wondering if the next announcement would be about the sacking of company executives, Ratan Tata retreated for the moment. He also reassured them he was assuming the role of interim chairman for the sake of stability and continuity.

Despite Mistry's letter, communication professionals at the Tata Group were initially asked to remain silent. A senior executive recalls being directed not to respond to 'fake news' and videos on YouTube that had popped up at an alarming rate discussing the losses of the Tata Group.

But when talk of the $18 billion write-off that Cyrus Mistry had predicted in his letter began to pick up, it was time for Tata's lawyers to speak up.

Mohan Parasaran said, 'The Tata board was well within its rights to remove Cyrus . . . It needed to be in a majority to remove him, which it was.' It is rumoured that in the run-up to the 24 October 2016 board meeting, Ratan Tata travelled to Chennai to meet Parasaran regarding the degenerating relations with Cyrus Mistry. It was Parasaran who had given the legal opinion that allowed for the change in the agenda of the board meeting to include Mistry's removal. Parasaran's opinion was now aired on national television and printed across newspapers. The other legal opinions Amit Chandra, one of the directors of Tata Sons, had mentioned in the board meeting included one from P. Chidambaram, and another from Justice (retd.) R.V. Raveendran, a former judge of the Supreme Court.

Addressing Mistry's comments on the need to sell assets or write off investments made by the Tata Group during Ratan Tata's time as chairman, Salve said emphatically on national television that there are two ways to address ailing assets – to 'ditch' them or nurse them back to health. A write-off would suddenly boost operating profit but, Salve said, Mistry's emphasis on profitability by writing off loss-making businesses did not fit with the overall ethos of the Group and was not in tandem with the opinion of the Trusts'. Remember, that the Trusts were headed by Ratan Tata and governed largely by Parsi loyalists of the Tata Group. Salve continued: the drive towards profit was overpowering the aim to build the institution. The Trusts believed that this profit focus would unwind the scale of the Tata Group. Salve added that some moves would affect the political goodwill Tata enjoyed. 'When Corus was purchased it was a commitment to the British government,' said Salve. 'This [removal of Mistry] is not for property or money. Tata is an institution,' he said. Salve seemed to gently goad Mistry into moving on without picking a fight despite his humiliation: 'The Tatas are institutions that are reputationally and financially very important to India. When it comes to governance of institutions, sometimes things don't go right. Changes have to be made. There is hurt; there is disappointment; sometimes even a sense of humiliation. But I am sure all the people concerned here know that they are not fighting for a piece of land or property. They will all rise to the occasion because the course of the Tata name is far bigger than the individuals.'

In fact the Tata Group was so reputed, Salve continued, that despite what Mistry said, 'if they [the Tata Group] were to go to the financial markets to raise money to tide over difficult times, the market will respond to them warmly.'

Then the ace lawyer took on Mistry's comment about being a 'lame duck' and said he knew what 'he was getting into' when he became chairman: 'I don't think Mr Mistry was made of such mild stuff that he would have allowed someone to push him around . . . It's not like he was a person who could be pushed and shoved around . . . When Mistry went in he knew the control the Trusts have exercised. He knew the architecture of the Group that he was getting into.'

Next came Abhishek Singhvi's brutal but honest comment: 'Tough luck and you go. This is a sad context.

No one is celebrating or doing a victory dance, [but] what's the point of the blame game? Last I heard there is nothing that prevents the change of the chairman.' Cyrus Mistry was not removed from directorship. He was merely excused from heading the company. 'Loss of confidence is a subjective thing. It happens across the world.' No one, courts or alternate boards, could sit in judgement over concrete events that led to the rupture in confidence, was Singhvi's refrain.

Singhvi's words struck hard in the Mistry camp. Getting fired is never easy, getting fired so publicly only made it harder. Yet, so far, Mistry had not moved the courts against Tata Sons. It was unclear if the boardroom battle would spill over into the courtroom. Mistry was still showing restraint. Other than the leaking of the letter, Mistry or his affiliates had not come into the open to give interviews or said anything rash.

Ratan Tata believed the leaked letter would be the extent of Mistry's counter to his dismissal. The teams at Tata Sons, other than the lawyers, were still instructed to remain quiet.

~

Mistry's letter and Salve's talk of building an institution over profit resonated in the stock market. At the close of trading on 26 October, the day after Mistry's scathing letter, the market capitalization of Tata's top listed companies fell by over Rs 23,500 crore ($3.6 billion). The steep fall in share prices led to a reaction from the stock exchanges. The Bombay Stock Exchange and the National Stock Exchange asked the Tata Group to explain the losses Mistry was talking about.

Spurred by the regulators' queries, Tata Sons came up with an official answer to Mistry's passionate letter.

Among other things, it was revealed that the board had rejected Mistry's plans on dealing with the problematic investments he was concerned about earlier than October.

The Group statement said:

It will be beneath the dignity of Tata Sons to engage in a public spat with regard to the several unfounded allegations appearing in his [Cyrus Mistry's] leaked confidential statement. These allegations are not based on facts or [on] the true state of affairs. It is convenient to put selective information in the public domain to defend one's point of view. There is a multitude of records to show that the allegations made by Mr Cyrus Mistry are unwarranted and these records will be duly disclosed before appropriate forums, if and when necessary, sufficiently justifying the decision made by responsible boards of directors . . .

The Tata way is to not run away from problems, or constantly complain about them, but [to] firmly deal with them and build a better tomorrow.

In his demeanour Mistry was always a polite person and had never shown an extrovert side. The Tata Group thus inferred that he would not descend into a more public battle. So it was decided that Tata would not engage in a field battle.

There was a time that people used to call Cyrus Mistry the son Ratan Tata never had. But now the relationship had completely frayed.

When Abhishek Singhvi spoke on Tata's behalf, he said, 'The reasons for Mistry's dismissal will include economic, moral, propriety and several other factors; sanskar and sanskriti had been breached.' Sanskar meaning values and sanskriti meaning culture that had been created over the 150-year history of the Group.

# 5

# More than Money

The beginnings of the Tata Group date back to the late 1800s. Brothers Nusserwanji and Dadabhoy Tata made a fortune in China trade. Their sons, Jamsetji Nusserwanji Tata and Ratanji Dadabhoy Tata, who were first cousins, preferred to strike out on their own rather than carry on their fathers' trade. They bought an oil mill in 1868 and converted it into a textile mill, marking the beginnings of the Tata Group. When the textile business started to do well, Jamsetji looked beyond it to other sectors.

In 1899, Jamsetji elected to build a hotel – the Taj Mahal Hotel – over the more cost-effective proposition of building himself a bungalow. There is a popular story that his motivation to start the Taj came from being denied entry into a hotel only for Europeans. The veracity of this story is unconfirmed, but whatever his reasons, Jamsetji built the Taj Mahal Hotel on the seafront in Colaba, Mumbai, adjacent to the Gateway of India.

The opulent building was designed so that guests

# Tata Family Tree*

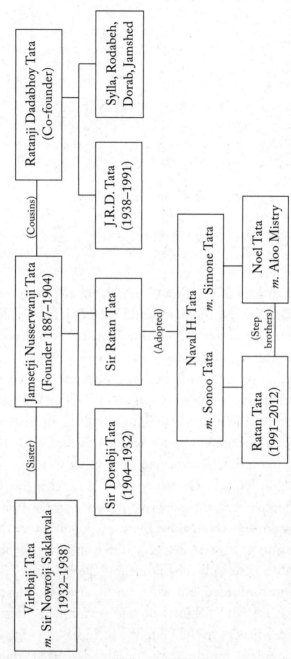

*The years shown here refer to duration as head of the Tata empire

staying in the top row of rooms that looked out on to the expanse of sea would feel like they were on a cruise. The hotel opened in 1903 and all guests were welcomed without discrimination. The textile business and now the hotel were doing well, but Jamsetji did not rest. Europe's industrialization was nearly a century old and Jamsetji saw the impending need for steel and power in India. He laid the foundation for these businesses but, in his lifetime, he was not able to grow either of them to a meaningful size. His dying wish was if the future leaders of his businesses could not grow what he had started, they should at least keep the status quo.[1]

Leading the charge after Jamsetji was Dorab Jamsetji Tata, Jamsetji's eldest son, supported by his younger brother Ratanji Jamsetji Tata and Jamsetji's cousin and partner Ratanji Dadabhoy Tata. The three came together in the early 1910s to form Tata Sons which was registered in 1917. Dorab became its chairman and took the mantle to complete what his father had started. In 1907, he formed Tata Iron and Steel, a company now called Tata Steel. The demand for steel gradually picked up, until there was a major boom during the First World War from 1914 to 1918. As the steel business flourished, Dorab focused on the power sector. Tata Sons acted as an agent to raise foreign funds for the fast-growing business.

Relying on new scientific advancement was in the DNA of the Tata Group. In 1915, when the prominent technology for power generation was using heat from burning coal, Tata Power started its first hydroelectric power generator in a dam in Khopoli to provide power to Mumbai. In 2018 the company provided 10,496 megawatts of power in the country through various methods of generation, including thermal power. Government-owned NTPC that distributes power across India generates around 55,000 megawatts.

The growing need for business funding was an opportunity for the Group to enter financial services with the Tata Industrial Bank in 1917. Alongside the bank, Tata added an insurance arm – New India Assurance, in 1919. In 1918, Dorab started yet another venture Tata Oil Mills Company (TOMCO), to make detergents, soaps and edible oils.

Expansion in these Tata enterprises was exponential till the post-war recession in 1919. Tata Steel was in the midst of a fivefold capacity expansion when steel and shipping prices became volatile and funds ran dry. In 1924, Tata Steel had a near-death experience. Dorab pledged all his property, even his wife's jewellery, to raise loans. When even that was not enough, the Group went to financier F.E. Dinshaw, who invested Rs 1 crore in the business. In return Dinshaw was promised 25 per cent of what Tata Sons made from Tata Power and 12.5 per cent of what it made from Tata Steel but he got no shares in Tata Sons. Revival of the business took time and effort.

Even as Dorab Tata continued to hold the reins of the growing Tata empire, a young Tata, Jehangir Ratan Dadabhoy Tata, Ratanji Dadabhoy Tata's son, was continuing the tradition of pioneering technology and innovation in business. Fascinated by the progress in air travel, J.R.D. Tata secured India's first pilot licence, and asked a reluctant Dorab to fund a venture in the sector – Tata Airlines. In 1932, JRD flew the country's first commercial flight carrying mail from Karachi to Mumbai.

Professionally, brothers Dorab and Ratan were taking the Tata Group to new heights but neither had an heir. In mid-1932 when Dorab passed away – Ratan had already died much earlier, in 1918 – the Group went into consolidation mode led by Nowroji Saklatwala, brother-in-law of Jamsetji Tata. In 1938, JRD took control of the Tata Group after Saklatwala's sudden passing and Tata's foray into new ventures resumed. JRD remained at the helm till 1991 and retired voluntarily at over 80 years of age – which is when Ratan Naval Tata took over.

In 1939 under JRD, the Group entered the salt and chemical businesses after taking over Okhlamandal Salt Works to form Tata Chemicals. It pioneered vacuum drying of salt and launched the brand Tata Salt. The company set up an industrial town in Mithapur to produce farm chemicals. The town now has its own power and cement units among other projects.

In 1945, as steam engines and railways proliferated, the Tata Group started the Tata Locomotive and Engineering company, TELCO, which morphed into Tata Motors – the Group's largest enterprise by turnover today. As the demand for steam engines dropped, JRD spotted another opportunity in motor vehicles. The Group set up a partnership with Daimler-Benz in 1954, creating commercial and consumer vehicles inspired by Mercedes designs over the next few decades.

JRD also launched the Group into the digital age with TCS in 1968. The company created computer software solutions for enterprises and emerged as a leading IT outsourcing company. Today, TCS is India's largest company in the IT outsourcing segment and the Tata Group's biggest wealth creator. It is also one of the companies in which Tata Sons still holds a significant majority share. The peculiarity of the Tata Group is that Tata Sons doesn't wholly own all of the Tata Group companies. The exigencies of fund raising for group companies meant that in some of them Tata Sons stake can be as low as 25 per cent. For example, in Tata Steel in the 1990s the Aditya Birla Group was the largest shareholder. The Tata Group's equity in the company reached a low of 2 per cent, before the Group clawed its way back to 27 per cent around the time when it bought out the Birla Group out in 2006.

~

The Tata family was as philanthropic as it was far-sighted in business. In 1904, when Jamsetji died, apart from power and steel, he left behind the dream of a science university, which led to the creation of the Indian Institute of Science in Bengaluru in 1911.

Jamsetji's stake in the Tata Group was passed to his two sons, Dorab and Ratan. The two willed their entire equity in Tata Sons towards philanthropic endeavours. That is how the Tata Trusts came into being. The first, the Sir Ratan Tata Trust, started in 1919.

The Trusts' objectives are multifarious. Among other things, they aim to promote academic and research excellence by sending Indian scholars overseas and setting up world-class academic facilities locally to educate the girl child. The Trusts funded the National Metallurgical

Laboratory and the National Centre for Performing Arts (NCPA). They also released funds to the Delhi School of Economics and Bombay University. Sir Ratan Tata Institute, or RTI, was formed for vocational skilling of women.

Dorab Tata later contributed his stake in Tata Sons to form a trust for international-scale research in blood disorders. Thereafter, seven Tata Trusts, each with a different objective, held around 82 per cent shares in Tata Sons and depended on dividends to pursue their activities. The Trusts, equity reduced in 1969 when Pallonji Mistry bought around 5 per cent from one of the Trusts. After that the seven Tata Trusts cumulatively held 77 per cent. The Trusts thus became a shareholder in Tata Sons, and Tata Sons is the promoter and a significant shareholder – though not necessarily the majority shareholder or even the largest shareholder – in Tata's operating companies. The Tata Trusts are charitable and as per the current law cannot buy equity in any company including the operating Tata companies. They can only hold on to their existing shares in Tata Sons but not add to them.

The founding principles or articles of association of Tata Sons empowered the Trusts to exercise majority rights. Post Indian Independence in 1947 came changes in the law and all public charitable trusts were taken over by government-appointed public trustees. The government-appointed trustees never appear to have interfered with business at Tata Sons. In the year 2000, however, the Tata Trusts were given an exemption to form their own governing board. This was how Ratan Tata came to head the Tata Trusts, the control of which he did not give up even after he ceased to be chairman of Tata Sons.

Despite the dependence of The Tata Trusts on the financial performance of the Tata Group, the Trusts never pressured Tata Sons to make quick profits or give dividends.

Tata Steel took on a large expansion and gave no dividends for over a decade. Tata Power struggled to convince distributors to accept hydroelectric power, at the time it was formed in 1915. It had to shell out money that could have gone towards dividends to buy and scrap steam engine power companies were using to nudge them towards hydroelectricity. Tata Oil Mills was duped by its consulting engineer, which resulted in significant losses in the 1930s.

After the Group realized the fraud, it took the company twenty-three years to generate its first dividend for shareholders. Tata Trusts showed forbearance through the years of strife. Tata companies also came to each other's help – when one company was struggling for cash, other cash-rich Tata companies would infuse funds. This led to each company holding shares in other Group companies, creating a web of crossholdings.

J.R.D. Tata said that the Tata Group had a 'remarkably consistent propensity, perhaps unavoidable in any pioneering and risky venture, for getting into difficulties in the early years of new projects, ultimately retrieving them by enormous and prolonged effort backed by a dour determination not to admit failure'.[2]

Like every business, the success came with its share of failures. Ventures in engineering, construction, electrochemicals, aeroplane building and sugar had to be shut down because they became unviable.

When India became independent from British rule in 1947, it adopted a socialist regime that frowned on private enterprise. The government nationalized the financial services sector, taking over New India Assurance and the Tata Industrial Bank, now Central Bank of India. The popularity and quality of Tata's aviation venture also made it an ideal target for the government to call it its own. The Tata Group had only recently renamed it Air India and now the government had taken it over. During later years, Tata Oil Mills and Lakmé were sold to Unilever because the Group did not consider these ventures worth retaining.

~

Ratan Naval Tata joined the Group in 1962, when he returned to India from the US to tend to his ailing grandmother. His father Naval Tata was the adopted son of Sir Ratan Tata, although it was his grandmother who largely brought him up. In 1955 he left India to study at Cornell University and later went to Harvard Business School. He was applying for a job at technology company IBM in India when J.R.D. Tata brought him into the fold of the family firm. He worked his way up in the Group with various assignments at Tata Motors, Tata Steel, TCS, Nelco and a few others. His roles ranged from working on the manufacturing shop floors to strategic representation overseas. In the early 1980s, Ratan Naval Tata was assigned charge of Tata Industries – a company that raises funds and incubates new businesses for the Group. Here he proposed his first plan to reinstate the significance of Tata Sons for Group companies. Since Tata Sons did not hold majority, and after cancellation of the management agent regime in the 1970s, operating companies' were only loosely tethered to the centre. Tata Sons was in no position to press on any decision-making in operating companies. Ratan Tata proposed a plan to reshuffle the Group's shareholding, including increasing Tata Sons hold on the group companies in a strategic plan in 1983. This would be a career-long pursuit of his.

A decade later, JRD nominated Ratan Tata as his successor when India was opening up its economy. In 1991, when Ratan Tata became chairman, the Tata Group was termed a 'loose confederation of companies' bound by J.R.D. Tata, who led it with charisma and with the personal regard individual leaders had for him.[3] Ratan Tata's plan to consolidate shareholding became even more important to prevent hostile takeovers in the sprawling Tata empire.

Soon after that, Ratan Tata asked all Tata Group companies to start paying royalty to Tata Sons for using the name 'Tata'. In 1995, Tata Sons launched a rights issue – in which shareholders of a company buy more shares to raise funds and increase the capital of a company. It diluted the Tata Trusts' stake to 65 per cent. As mentioned earlier, Pallonji Mistry ploughed in Rs 69 crore, taking the SP Group's shares to 18.4 per cent. Ratan Tata got Group companies to subscribe to the remaining rights issue, freeing cash to accumulate more shares in vulnerable Tata companies.

During his tenure, Ratan Tata launched Tata Motors' Indica car, the country's first completely indigenously manufactured passenger vehicle. Tata Motors also acquired well-known luxury carmaker JLR. Tata Tea acquired UK-based Tetley. Tata Chemicals acquired fertilizer chemical maker UK Brunner Mond and US-based soda ash maker US General Chemical Industrial Products in landmark deals in their segments. Tata Steel acquired the UK's Corus. Through it all, the consolidation of all Group company shares under Tata Sons and a methodical central control regime served Ratan Tata well.

In 2012, after Ratan Tata stepped down as Tata Sons chairman, he turned his complete attention to the Tata Trusts, which he continued to head. He was hoping to replicate the success of institutionalization at the charitable organizations.

Cyrus Mistry became the sixth chairman of the Group, the first one without a direct relation to the Tata family. He was the first chairman with no sway on the Tata Trusts – which made him answerable to the Trusts unlike his predecessors.

In his final board meeting as chairman of Tata Sons on 18 December 2012, Ratan Tata had made a prophetic statement: 'In the future, the chairmen of the Trusts and Tata Sons are not likely to be the same individual. It would be desirable to enter into an agreement between the major Trusts and Tata Sons to clarify the involvement of the Trusts . . .'

As soon as Mistry took centre stage at the Tata Group, he found he had more than one white elephant to deal with. He believed all his time and effort were needed to address five legacy hotspots – major ailing assets that could rake up right-offs worth $18 billion according to him. In the past he had also never seen the Tata Trusts so deeply engaged with the running of Tata Sons, but Ratan Tata was changing that. The Trusts were now exercising control like a majority shareholder.

Mistry viewed this control as a hindrance. He felt the Trusts' involvement with decision-making rendered the company's board useless. The Trusts should not and could not have so much say and veto power over Group decisions that it made the executives redundant, he argued.

Mistry was still chairman of seven major Tata Group companies. Even if he had lost the big seat in the Tata Sons boardroom he would try to hold on to the chair in the boards of these companies. Would the fifty-odd directors of the Group companies support him and agree with his assessment of the Trusts' interference? Would they support his bid and retain him as chairman even if he was no longer head of Tata Sons? He would soon find out.

# 6

# The Chase

After Tata Sons responded to the stock exchange on 27 October, things went quiet for a few days. The Tata Group hoped this might be the end of the public bitterness. The new powers at Tata Sons, led by Ratan Tata, hoped Mistry would resign from the boards of the Tata Group companies he was on, because he had only been on those boards as a nominee of Tata Sons. The Group, could then go on with business as usual. Was the fight over?

Tata's legal team were keen to find out what was happening in the Mistry camp who remained suspiciously tight-lipped. They wondered what Mistry was up to, since he had not moved a court of law against his sacking. The Tata Group soon realized Mistry would likely fight the battle through proxies. This was just the lull before the storm.

A slew of suits filed by small investors in Tata companies and public interest litigations were expected.

Sure enough, a few weeks later a class action suit was filed by six small investors in the Bombay High Court against Tata Sons, its directors and the trustees of the Tata Trusts, claiming over Rs 40,000 crore in damages and objecting to Mistry's removal from the boards of the Tata operating companies. This was noted as one of India's first class action suits, filed by law firm Makarand Gandhi and Co on behalf of six individuals, claiming their investment value had fallen because of Mistry's removal.

The share price of the Tata companies which the individuals held had fallen sharply in the days after 24 October 2016. Another suit was filed by well-known investor Janak Mathuradas and three others to stop Tata Sons from removing directors in operating companies.

The Tata lawyers probably expected share prices to bounce back once the dust had settled, and hoped the suits would lose steam over time. Little did they know that the real fight was going to unfold elsewhere.

The Tata Group spent this time reassuring its CEOs that the developments would not affect their businesses. Huddled in a room in Bombay House, Ratan Tata addressed twenty-five CEOs of the Group. A few others joined via video call. According to a statement issued at the end of the meeting, RNT had told them, 'The leadership of the companies [should] focus on their respective businesses, without being concerned about change in leadership.' He added that there may be future changes to the decisions that had been taken under Mistry but that the teams would be notified and taken into confidence before any change was effected.

Meanwhile, Madhu Kannan set up office in the SP

Group headquarters in Colaba, where Mistry strategized with his team, keeping journalists and investors in the loop.

In his blog, Nirmalya Kumar described this period as the time when Kannan and he worked tirelessly to help Mistry. Perhaps it was Mistry's misfortune that his detractors perceived these two core members of his team as part of the problem during Mistry's time as Tata chief. Even Mistry's friends were sceptical about the two. Kannan and Kumar, lateral entrants into the Tata ecosystem, were not welcomed wholeheartedly in the hierarchical structure of the Tata Group. Kumar allegedly regularly told everyone it was his task to create a vision and not to execute it. According to a senior executive at one of the Tata operating companies, some of his ideas were unrealistic. Nirmalya Kumar's visiting card, which he freely handed out, had no information on how to reach him directly. Was this meant to say he was unapproachable? This was not in keeping with the Tata ethos and did not enhanced his standing in the Group. It was in sharp contrast with the legendary kindness and open door policy of the Group's chairmen. Sudha Murthy, chairperson of the Infosys Foundation, recalls her initial years of working with the Tata Group, when J.R.D. Tata himself once kept her company as she waited to be picked up after nightfall. Even Cyrus Mistry's personal chauffeur apparently had the right to interrupt his meetings to remind him, 'Baba late ho raha hai' (Baba, it's getting late).

It wasn't just Kumar. Kannan was also associated with having an un-Tata-like approach, said an executive who quit Tata Sons after he claimed he was treated poorly during Cyrus Mistry's term as chairman.

But he clarified that this was not Mistry's way.

N.S. Rajan, Mistry's third lateral hire into his executive council, was also sacked by Tata Sons on the day of the board meeting. The labour unions in companies such as Tata Steel and Tata Motors were ruffled by Rajan's policies, such as performance-based remuneration. While many insiders admit this change was required, it came too suddenly and encountered a lot of resistance.

Mistry didn't have a long-standing relationship with Kumar, Kannan or Rajan. He had hired them for their expertise in their respective fields. Kumar was a professor at the London Business School. Kannan was CEO of the Bombay Stock Exchange. Rajan was Partner and Global Leader for People and Organization at Ernst & Young, one of the big four accounting firms. Mistry had always known that in the future the Tata Group would require an even mix of insiders and outsiders. The recruitment of these professionals was merely the execution of a vision he had shared while being interviewed for chairmanship. Over time, of course, he had come to depend on their counsel.

~

As executive chairman, Mistry was not a promoter, just an employee. His shareholding in Tata Sons had no bearing on or relevance to his appointment. His sudden dismissal had driven home the point. As an executive chairman, he was contracted like any other employee of

Tata Sons, answerable to the board and ultimately the shareholders. Most people weren't even aware Mistry was on a five-year contract. They assumed the prestigious seat was his for the keeping. The rift between Ratan Tata and Cyrus Mistry had run so deep that Mistry was not even allowed to serve his contract out – which would have ended in six months.

A court proceeding by Mistry at this time would have wasted this emotional advantage. No concrete reason had been offered for Mistry's unceremonious firing. Ratan Tata had in fact said at an employee forum that the reason would go with him to his grave. But in the business community, people were saying, 'You don't treat a person like this, and you certainly don't treat the chairman of the Tata Group like this.' Mistry by virtue of his filial roots had a deep connect with the business promoter community. There was some speculation that the SP Group would sell its stake in protest. Remember that in order to do so they would have to get Tata Sons to approve the buyer. Would Ratan Tata or the Tata Trusts be able to find a buyer? Who even had that kind of cash? The *Times of India* would later report that the Mistry family planned on keeping its stake in Tata Sons.

This was the time for reconnaissance. Mistry's team was testing the waters. He was still chairman of seven major Tata companies: Tata Motors, Tata Steel, TCS, IHCL, Tata Global Beverages, Tata Chemicals, and Tata Power. Each one would have to individually move against Mistry to remove him. By staying on as their chairman – which would mean he still enjoyed the trust of their boards – Mistry would not only score a moral victory and redeem his personal image, he would also remain in control of the Tata Group.

As Mistry and his team saw it, the allegations being levelled, most notably by the Tata Trusts, of failing performance and governance at Tata Sons did not translate into governance collapse in the operating companies. Mistry had worked with these teams and boards for nearly four years. In fact, Mistry's performance had been regularly commended at the board meetings of these companies. With Tata Sons owning as little as 25 per cent in some of these companies, and in some cases with Mistry being the only Tata Sons representative on the company boards, would it be able to edge Mistry out?

While maintaining a calm front, both parties were hard at work behind the scenes. Ratan Tata and Cyrus Mistry both met Prime Minister Narendra Modi. Ratan Tata later also met Finance Minister Arun Jaitley. Speculation after that hour-long meeting was that Tata had sought support for Mistry's exit from government banks and insurance companies that had investments in the Group. Tata reportedly also met senior officials at the Life Insurance Corporation, a significant stakeholder in Tata Steel, Tata Power and Tata Global Beverages. The government in its wisdom steered clear of the dispute. Mistry met a few other politicians. He received endorsement from Supriya Sule, member of parliament from Maharashtra and daughter of prominent politician Sharad Pawar.[1]

At this stage all actions remained civil. But the fighting was costing the Tata Group dearly. A ratings agency, Brickwork Ratings, downgraded the debt of Tata Steel

because of 'heightened management risk', indicative of
the uncertainty the imminent battle posed.

~

4 November 2016 was the day of a board meeting of
IHCL, the parent company of Taj Hotels. The meeting,
the first after Cyrus's sacking, had been planned before
the coup to discuss the quarterly financial results. The
directors reached Bombay House ahead of time. Press
reporters thronged outside, blocking the entrance. There
was even a physical scuffle between a lensman and a
security guard.

Cyrus Mistry and his brother Shapoor Mistry outside Bombay House
before the Indian Hotels Company Ltd's board meeting on 4 November
2016.

In the boardroom, the air was thick with suspense. Mistry had earlier called IHCL out as a lemon that he had inherited – one of the reasons being a languishing investment in a land parcel, Sea Rock in Bandra, Mumbai. Its development was stranded due to lack of funds. Moreover, this investment resided in a complex structure of companies, such that it was off the books of IHCL. Mistry now proposed that Tata Sons lend IHCL Rs 1,550 crore and bring the property within the fold of IHCL by collapsing the special purpose vehicle, or holding entity, that held Sea Rock. Then, Mistry proposed to write off the loan and initiate development of the property. The Tata Trusts had initially declined to vote on this resolution citing a technical rule. The board meeting went on for long. When they finally came out, the independent directors made an announcement to the stock exchange that said, 'Taking into account board assessments and performance evaluations carried out over the years, the independent directors unanimously expressed their full confidence in the chairman, Cyrus Mistry, and praised the steps taken by him in providing strategic direction and leadership to the company.'

The sympathy wave for Mistry was now tidal. He had won this round. He not only remained chairman of a significant operational Tata company but also scored a moral victory. Tata Sons may have sacked him but he was going to hold on to his position on the boards of the operating Group companies that were in a way more significant, being the real profit centres Tata Sons is designed to control. Mistry could control them as chairman irrespective of his removal from Tata Sons.

The victory was even more significant because the board comprised long-standing Tata associates, Keki Dadiseth and Deepak Parekh, the architect and head of HDFC Bank, both former contenders for the top job at Tata Sons. Other directors on the board were Nadir Godrej, MD Godrej Industries; Ireena Vittal, formerly a senior at consulting firm McKinsey and board member at several leading companies; Gautam Banerjee, senior managing director at private equity firm Blackstone; and Vibha Paul Rishi, former group strategy director at Future Group and former member of the Tata Administrative Services.

That was a long evening for the Tata camp. It was also the night they decided to end the silence. The gloves were coming off.

# 7

# The Silence Ends

The Tata Group began to execute their outreach programme. PR agency Adfactors started with managing shareholder communication and investor relations. Senior executives at Tata Sons contacted directors of the seven Group companies Cyrus Mistry was still chairman of, explaining to them how the fate of Tata companies depended on the Tata brand. Tata Sons held management control and received brand royalties from all Tata's operating companies which benefited from the affiliation. Being part of the group makes capital, both debt and equity, more accessible to the companies. If the image of Tata Sons took a beating, other companies of the Group would also suffer.

But more critically, sources told media that if the Tata Group were to withdraw support for IHCL and if Tata Sons revoked its guarantees there would be sizeable impact on the hotelier. Bankers speculated it could mean a 0.5–1 percentage point increase in interest costs for the company.

But things were about to get uglier. A steady flow of accusations and counter-accusations would follow in the days to come. All eyes were on the upcoming board meetings of other group companies. Mistry seemed determined on staying. It was simplistic, however, to think that he could continue on the companies' boards, as before – even if on some of the boards Tata Sons had no representatives other than Mistry.

Tata Sons took no chances. Five days after the Indian Hotels shocker, TCS, India's largest technology outsourcing company, with 74 per cent Tata Sons ownership, and Cyrus Mistry still as chairman, invoked a rule embedded in its founding principles. The rule stated that as long as Tata Sons held over 26 per cent stake in the company, it could nominate or remove the chairman of the board. Early on the morning of 9 November, Cyrus Mistry was removed as chairman of the TCS board and Ishaat Hussain was made interim chairman. Mistry called this an unlawful cloak-and-dagger approach. Tata Sons had notched an emphatic victory and with it made the statement that it was not to be trifled with. Mistry remained a board member but no longer headed the TCS board.

~

The Tata Group now had the task of ensuring Mistry's removal from the board of the six remaining major

Tata companies, including IHCL, of which he was still chairman. The obvious move for the Tata camp was to find directors on the boards who could take up their cause. Board members were actively sensitized to the need to remove Mistry from the chairmanship, said people directly involved.

On 10 November came the board meeting of Tata Chemicals, of which Tata Sons directly owned 19.4 per cent and with cross holdings in other Tata Companies held 30.8 per cent. Nusli Wadia, chairman of Bombay Dyeing and Britannia Industries, was a senior independent director on this one. All eyes were on him and there was a great deal of speculation on whose side he would take. He placed himself clearly in Mistry's corner. The Tata Chemicals board made an even more emphatic statement in favour of Mistry than the IHCL board. At the end of the board meeting, the independent directors issued another statement to the stock exchanges:

> [The independent directors] recalled and reaffirmed their earlier assessment and evaluation carried out in the year 2015 and 2016 of the chairman, the board, and its functioning.
>
> The independent directors unanimously affirmed their confidence in the board, its chairman and the management in the conduct of the company's business.
>
> The independent directors also reaffirmed that all the decisions taken with regard to the operations and business of the company had been taken by the Board unanimously and executed by the chairman and management as per the directions of the board.

The independent directors also wish to reassure all the stakeholders, management of the company and its subsidiaries, wherever located, of their full confidence and support.

During the board meeting Bhaskar Bhat, managing director of Titan and member of the Tata Chemicals board, had allegedly initiated talk of removing Mistry as chairman. But the independent directors of the board apparently united under Nusli Wadia in defence of Mistry. Bhat ultimately resigned from the board.

He said in his resignation letter, 'The contents as well as the spirit of the statement [of the independent directors] completely dilutes the views I expressed at the board meeting today, especially regarding the threat the company faces on account of loss of confidence of Tata Sons in the chairman of Tata Chemicals Limited. Several important issues of discomfort I expressed seem to have been totally ignored.'

Then in a show of support for Tata Sons, there was a signature campaign run by the staff of Tata Chemicals seeking Mistry's removal. This could partly be attributed to Ratan Tata's charisma and partly to the unions seeking relief from certain performance-based human resource policies Mistry and his team were pushing for. Shortly after this signature campaign, the union of workers at Tata Steel issued a statement in support of Ratan Tata. The Tata Motors union also followed suit.

At the Tata end, these board rebellions needed to be dealt with firmly. The shareholders had to be assured that the Tata Group was still the best falconer for the

operating companies. The following statement was put
out in which Tata Sons accused Mistry of betraying their
trust and scheming against them:

> The recent development in the IHCL now seems to
> reveal the true colours of Mr Mistry and his ulterior
> objective. Having been replaced as the chairman of
> Tata Sons, where the majority of the board and the
> major shareholders had expressed lack of confidence,
> Mr Mistry is trying to gain control of IHCL with the
> support of the independent directors of the Board. He
> has cleverly ensured over these years that he would
> be the only Tata Sons representative on the board of
> IHCL in order to frustrate Tata Sons' ability to exercise
> influence and control on IHCL. In hindsight, the trust
> reposed by Tata Sons in Mr Mistry by appointing him
> as the chairman four years ago has been betrayed by
> his desire to seek to control main operating companies
> of the Tata Group to the exclusion of Tata Sons and
> other Tata representatives. Indeed, this strategy of
> being the only Tata Sons representative on the boards
> of the operating Tata companies seems to have been
> a clever strategy planned and systematically achieved
> over the last four years. It is unfortunate that Tata Sons,
> acting in good faith, did not anticipate such devious
> moves by Mr Mistry and thereby did not inform the
> other directors of the operating companies about its
> dissatisfaction with Mr Mistry at the level of Tata Sons.
> However, we will now do whatever is required to deal
> with this situation.

To ensure the message was not distorted in press coverage, the Group published it in a full-page advertisement in all major dailies on 11 November 2016.

~

If Tata Sons was unable to edge Mistry out of the boards, the battle would have to be taken to the court of public opinion. A story was brought to the media's attention that showed Cyrus Mistry in poor light. A sexual harassment accusation against the IHCL chief executive, Rakesh Sarna, that had allegedly been brushed under the carpet by Mistry, was reported. The woman had not formally complained at IHCL, but was moved to an office in a nearby building – where she sat practically alone – into a role that reported to Tata Sons. In her resignation letter, which was shared with the press, she called this move a demotion. The news reports showed poor governance on Mistry's part, more so as he had hand-picked Sarna for the job.

Mistry refuted this strongly and on record, in a press statement:

> Mr Mistry was very upset as this [harassment] was absolutely against his belief of a safe work environment. Mr Mistry set aside time to meet with her [the complainant] and assured her that the Tata Group stands fully committed to support her.
>
> As an immediate action, with her concurrence, Mr Mistry initiated an interim measure of providing

an appropriate short-term alternate and safe work environment until the matter could be investigated and appropriately addressed. The Group HR head was directed to create an appropriate interim position. An interim senior role, directly reporting to a group executive council member in the corporate communications team was identified ... At her request to put the issue behind her, an enquiry was not set up at that point in time.

However, since this was a serious allegation and potentially a violation of the Tata code of conduct, Mr Mistry decided to institute a committee to investigate into the matter.

The investigation eventually cleared Sarna of wrongdoing in March 2017.

~

On 11 November 2016, the day after the Tata Chemicals board meeting, was the Tata Steel board meeting. Nusli Wadia was an independent director here too.

At the meeting that lasted six hours, another independent director, O.P. Bhatt, former chairman of the SBI, proposed Mistry's removal. Bhatt explained that the discord between Mistry and Tata Sons was costing Tata Steel dearly and therefore Mistry had to go. He cited the downgrade of the company's debt rating as an example.

'There were no fireworks, all the people in the room were of a certain age after which a high voltage conversation isn't even possible,' joked someone who was in that room. But each side tried to beat down the other. The independent directors faced a dilemma, as Nusli Wadia reminded them that voting against Mistry now would imply a U-turn on the stands they had taken in earlier board meetings. More importantly it was argued that there was no real risk related to a conflict with Tata Sons because Tata Steel had its own standing without the parent company.

The meeting ended without any resolution, and with the directors confused about where the consensus lay on the issue.

The matter would only be put to vote a few days later, in a circular resolution that directors sign on without a meeting. Mistry would go on to challenge this form of decision-making which was usually adopted only for routine and less significant matters. Independent directors, O.P. Bhatt and Mallika Srinivasan, chief executive of the agricultural automotive company Tractors and Farm Equipment Limited (TAFE), voted in favour of removing Mistry. Ishaat Hussain too stood for Mistry's removal. Wadia and Subodh Bhargava were alone in their opposition to change chairman. Since Mistry was an interested party, he could not vote on the matter. With that, O.P. Bhatt became chairman of the Tata Steel board and Mistry was again reduced to being just another board member.

~

The boards that met next were Tata Motors and Tata Global Beverages. Tata Sons owned 24 per cent of the latter and group companies owned 12 per cent more.

The board meeting of Tata Motors, in which Tata Sons held 29 per cent and Group companies another 6 per cent, lasted five hours, with the independent directors, including Nusli Wadia, reaffirming in a statement that all past decisions of the company had the directors' unanimous blessing. Although Mistry retained his chairmanship, it was a much weaker statement than the one IHCL had made.

The Tata Global Beverages board meeting on 15 November reversed the trend altogether. The meeting progressed in a similar but long-drawn version of the first one, as its minutes showed.

Present in the room were:
- Cyrus Mistry – chairman
- Harish Bhat – director, chief of Titan and Tata stalwart
- Mallika Srinivasan – independent director, chief of TAFE and wife of Tata Sons board member Venu Srinivasan
- S. Santhanakrishnan – independent director, partner in a chartered accounting firm
- V. Leeladhar – independent director, former RBI deputy governor
- Ranjana Kumar – independent director, former vigilance commissioner, government of India
- Ajoy Mishra – managing director and chief executive of Tata Global Beverages
- L. Krishnakumar – executive director of Tata Global Beverages

- Analjit Singh – independent director, founder and chairman of Max India
- Darius Pandole – independent director, private equity professional

Harish Bhat: I would like to introduce an item on the agenda that Mr Mistry should recuse himself and allow for appointment of another chairman. Secretarial standards allow us to introduce this item at this time.

Cyrus Mistry: How can you introduce this item when it was not part of the agenda?

Darius Pandole: It is not part of the board agenda. You would need to circulate such an item beforehand.

Analjit Singh to Harish Bhat: In what capacity can you introduce this item?

Harish Bhat: As a director, the law allows me to bring a new item to the board.

Mistry: Introducing a new item is not permissible by law. As chairman, I do not permit it.

Pandole: What is your reason for introducing this item?

Bhat: In view of aligning with the stakeholders' interests, we need to consider the proposal.

Analjit Singh: The board has no right to remove a sitting Chairman. That can be done only by the shareholders in the annual or extraordinary general meetings.

Santhanakrishnan: Chairmanship is decided by the board, the general body is not needed for this.

The company secretary [who sits in every board meeting and is tasked with documenting and ensuring smooth proceedings of meetings] confirms this and reads out a rule that the board is to appoint its chairman every year unless otherwise stated.

Analjit Singh: Does Mistry get appointed annually as per this rule?

Company secretary: His appointment as chairman remains till otherwise decided by the board.

Srinivasan: This is a legitimate motion, why are we not allowing it?

Mistry repeats that it is not legal and hence he does not allow it. Bhat calls for a vote on this.

Srinivasan: A discussion is at least a fair request.

Mistry, Pandole, Singh agree that introducing the new agenda item is illegal.

Santhanakrishnan: It is not illegal.

Singh: I have spoken to a top lawyer in Delhi. The board and its directors cannot introduce an item. The board also cannot change the chairman.

Bhat: We also have a legal opinion to the contrary.

Pandole: You cannot introduce an item and disrupt the meeting.

Singh: Let us deal with the other items. If at all, this would qualify under the 'Any Other Business' title on the agenda – an agenda which is lower in the order of proceedings. Besides, only a chairman can allow an item to be introduced under this head.

Bhat: This is a valid item and should be taken up.

Board votes to introduce an additional item to discuss the need to remove Mistry. Mistry, Pandole, Singh disagree. Mistry was recused from voting on grounds of conflict of interest as he was directly involved. Santhanakrishnan becomes interim chairman to conduct the vote. The vote passes . . . Santhanakrishnan becomes chairman for the rest of the meeting.

Bhat praises Mistry, but says this must be done keeping in mind the Tata brand, its suppliers, talent, global reputation, capital security, lending rates, credit rating and other synergies that Tata Global benefits from as a result of being part of the Group. Mistry no longer bring these resources to the table and would do well to resolve differences with Tata Sons.

Bhat: It is indeed personally challenging for me to stand here today and move this resolution, and I do so with a heavy heart. In such a difficult moment, I take recourse, with some adaptation, to what Shakespeare famously said in his play *Julius Caesar*. I move this resolution, ladies and gentleman, 'not because I love Cyrus Mistry any less, but because I love our company much more'.

Singh: Great spiritual discourse on governance, but it is unfortunate you are not factoring the uncharacteristic way this board is functioning. You need the chairman's consent, majority of directors and one independent director to move such a motion.

Mistry: Tata Sons process was not right and is being challenged.

Santhanakrishnan: Tata Sons decision is final, it has not been set aside.

Mistry's objections are noted. Srinivasan starts to say something, Analjit cuts in and reiterates objection, Santhanakrishnan says his objection has been noted and lets others speak.

Ranjana Kumar: There have been three to four years of great work done by Mr Mistry, but this fight with Tata Sons is worrying and he cannot be allowed to continue.

Singh: I agree with you that this tension is untenable but this is not the characteristic Tata way of doing things. It would be better to adjourn this meeting and get another legal opinion.

Krishnakumar: We have a legal opinion saying that it is fine.

The board votes to remove Mistry and replaces him with Bhat as chairman. Bhat proposes a resolution to ask Mistry to resign as director. Mistry cannot vote on this, Pandole and Singh oppose. Resolution passes.

Other items are deferred. Bhat calls the meeting to an end. Mistry opposes Bhat's right to end the meeting. Meeting ends at 5.25 p.m.

~

By the end of November Mistry was still chairman of IHCL, Tata Chemicals, Tata Motors and Tata Power. He had been removed as chairman of Tata Sons, Tata Global Beverages, Tata Steel and TCS, even though he continued to be a board member of these companies.

Seeing the mixed results of the board meetings, the Tata Group had changed its approach. At the board meeting of Tata Power, in fact, the company avoided all talk of removing Mistry from chairmanship. Instead, Tata Sons would initiate action to remove him from the board altogether. How? Tata could propose to remove Mistry as a director in shareholder forums. The Tata Group called special shareholder meetings or extraordinary general meetings of the companies to axe Mistry from the boards.

The Group most likely had preferred to first tap board members instead of moving shareholders outright as this action would seem vindictive, and paint Mistry as even more of a victim. But things were getting out of hand and drastic action had to be taken.

The role of the directors was irrelevant now. Several of them believed there was little good in standing against Tata Sons that would have its way in the end anyway. The directors were caught in the crossfire. Most were friends with both Mistry and Ratan Tata and had never imagined a situation like this. 'It wasn't for any love for Mistry that I stood up for him, it was because of a principle that as a director I had regularly thought one way,' recalls one of the directors. 'It was odd to be in that situation.'

Some directors refrained from attending meetings. Notably, Ireena Vittal missed the Tata Global Beverages meeting after facing the controversy in Indian Hotels. After refraining from voting on Mistry's removal from Tata Sons, Farida Khambata did not attend the next meeting.

No one liked to be in this position. Mercifully for them, the focus was already shifting to the shareholders.

# 8

# The Shareholders

Allegations between Tata Sons and Cyrus Mistry flew thick and fast. The news stories came mostly from unnamed 'sources': the PR machineries on both sides. Even when a story came directly from an official, it was still usually 'off the record'. Then, as the fight got uglier, the statements started coming straight from the two groups. Social media was also tapped to mobilize shareholder and public opinion. Twitter handles and hashtags such as @factsontata and #cyrusmistry popped up along with websites like Cyrus Mistry's official cyrusforgovernance. com and Tata's official version factsontata.com.

There was no evident logic for the exchanges, the accusations and counter-accusations. It was all tit for tat. To refute the attacks by 'The Office of Cyrus Mistry' the Tata Group called on senior executives, rather than directly involving Ratan Tata.

Mistry was accused of enriching his firm through contracts. He retorted that the Tata Group's companies had in fact not awarded any new contracts to Mistry's family firm during his tenure. In turn, he accused Ratan Tata of supporting old associates at the cost of the Group's interests. Dragged into the battle was the septuagenarian Arun Nanda, founder of the ad agency Rediffusion Y&R. Nanda, someone Mistry believed Ratan Tata trusted, had the Tata Group public relations contract and had subcontracted it to Edelman India, the agency on record for the Tata Group since 2011. Mistry accused Nanda's firm for getting a sweetheart deal and of doing work for the Tata Trusts at the expense of Tata Sons. Nanda explained that the original contract included work to be done for the Tata Trusts as well. According to a source, the contract, which was originally for five years, was extended by Cyrus Mistry himself for a sixth – but only after negotiating it down by Rs 6 crore–Rs 7 crore from nearly Rs 50 crore annually. Mistry in his accusations said Nanda's contract was for Rs 60 crore.

Thereafter Mistry's camp proceeded to accuse Ratan Tata of capricious decision-making at the Tata Group and called into question his governance of the Tata Trusts. In particular they described the acquisition of Corus by Tata Steel as overpriced and a result of Ratan Tata's ego. Tata Sons responded with a statement by Tata Steel CEO B. Muthuraman, that the acquisition was in fact well considered.

Mistry also alleged that Ratan Tata wanted to sell TCS to IBM in the 1990s, to which F.C. Kohli, the TCS chief during that time and widely considered the father of Indian IT, responded, 'I would like to reiterate that at no point at that time was there ever an intention of the

Tata Group to sell TCS to IBM.' In deference to Kohli's stature, Mistry revoked his statement confirming that he did not imply that a sale of TCS was ever considered.

Mistry accused Vijay Singh, one of the Tata Sons directors, of being a part of the Rs 3,600 crore scam involving procurement of special helicopters from AugustaWestland during his tenure as defence secretary. Singh denied the allegations stating that his tenure at the concerned ministry came after the period under investigation for the scam.

The Tata Trusts were also not spared. News reports suggested that some unspecified activities at the Trusts were 'unlawful'. Ratan Tata's control of the Trusts was called into question. 'The Trusts belong to the people and must be administered by the government,' said Mistry, who also filed this with the tax department, questioning how a charitable trust could award a high salary to its executive, R. Venkatramanan. This later yielded a response from the taxman that threatened to revoke the tax-free status of the Trusts if remuneration remained so high.

On its part, Tata Sons highlighted the soaring staff costs during Mistry's chairmanship, from Rs 84 crore in 2012–13 to Rs 180 crore in 2015 and other expenses from Rs 220 crore in 2012–13 to Rs 290 crore in 2015, even as dividends were declining. This was indicative of the higher amount Mistry and his team were being paid in comparison to the old guard.

Mistry defended his team, denying having taken commissions from other companies. This was an insinuation that the earlier remuneration structure hid what Tata Sons senior executives really earned. As for other expenses, Mistry said Rs 30 crore of the 2015 expenses was on Ratan Tata's office, largely comprising payments for chartered flights. A Tata supporter protested this charge, 'Using the company plane is . . . [part of] Ratan Tata's retirement terms that Mistry signed off on!'

~

These barbs were fired to win the battle of public perception and, in particular, influencing the shareholders of Tata companies.

The Tata Group had called special shareholder meetings or extraordinary general meetings for TCS and IHCL to axe Mistry from the company boards altogether, not just to remove him from the chairmanship. It was now only a matter of time that similar notices would be issued for Tata Motors, Tata Steel, Tata Global Beverages, Tata Chemicals and Tata Power. Tata Sons had called for shareholder meetings of its marquee companies between 12 and 26 December, the last one being of Tata Power.

Everyone knew Mistry's future on the boards of Tata companies would now be decided not by board members but by extraordinary general meetings of shareholders.

For decades, Ratan Tata had won hearts at major Group annual general meetings at the historical Birla Matoshri Hall near Bombay Hospital. Even after Mistry took over, Ratan Tata attended some of the meetings as chairman emeritus, always captivating the audience with his aura and charm. His celebrity status far surpassed that of Mistry, who remained out of the public eye during his tenure at the Tata Group. Could Mistry get the same support from shareholders as he had from several board members across companies?

Reaching out directly to the retail shareholder would have been difficult for Mistry to do. His first step, therefore, would be to address the proxy advisory firms – companies that advise shareholders on how to vote on agenda items at shareholder meetings. A good place to begin was Institutional Investors Advisory Services (IiAS), whose founder Anil Singhvi had openly supported Cyrus Mistry. But when the reports advising on voting strategy finally came in, the IiAS supported the removal of Mistry. While the IiAS report agreed that Mistry's dismissal was odd, it supported it because discord between the largest shareholder and management would be counterproductive for operating companies, indicating that Tata was more likely to win in the end.

Madhu Kannan and Mistry reportedly spent several hours on calls with two other proxy advisory firms – Institutional Shareholder Services (ISS) and InGovern, both of which eventually wrote notes supporting Mistry. The ISS in its proxy advisory for TCS (the only one that became public) wrote: 'At its core the dispute appears to reflect an internal power struggle within the unlisted holding company [Tata Sons], marked by cross-accusations of interference and poor decision-making, as well as independent director support for Mistry at some of the other listed Tata companies ... Neither Tata Sons as the proponent nor the board of TCS has provided ... compelling evidence that the proposal to remove him will be beneficial for TCS, or that his continued presence on the Board is expected to have a material negative effect on board governance or future performance. Additionally, support for Mistry from several independent directors at different companies seems to indicate Mistry was operating on the basis of a healthy distance from undue pressure. On this basis, support for the proposal is not considered warranted.'

InGovern recommended voting to retain Mistry on six companies that had called for extraordinary general meetings by the time the note was published. It did, however, point out that since the promoter holding in TCS was around 74 per cent, the resolution would pass irrespective of the vote.

The impact of these reports was unclear given that the opinion was divided amongst the advisory firms. So Mistry engaged the mutual fund managers, who held large blocks of shares in the Tata companies. Most of the significant shareholders sympathized with Mistry, but no one committed to supporting him. They agreed that the steps Mistry had taken at Tata Sons and at the Group companies had been beneficial for the shareholders, but funds do not operate by alienating the largest shareholder.

~

Pinned in a corner, Mistry decided it was time to directly reach out to the shareholders.

He once again in a letter to the shareholders told his story that led to the ignominy of being fired and answered some of the questions people had often asked him. He said, 'The Tata Group is no one's personal fiefdom: it does not belong to any individual, not to the trustees of

Tata Trusts, not to the Tata Sons directors, and not to the directors of the operating companies. It belongs to all the stakeholders, including every one of you.'[1]

Mistry claimed that during his tenure as chairman of Tata Sons he had been working selflessly without engaging with the media to increase his personal fame and profile. He would say: 'I did not join the Tata Group to craft a personal image for myself. I did not give any interviews to the press, but instead used my time to communicate widely to the internal community that mattered to me the most – the 6,60,000 employees of the Tata Group, who toil to build and maintain the good name of the Tata brand.'

Tata Sons sharply retorted in a public statement: 'Indeed, the Tata Group is no one's "personal fiefdom". After he became the chairman of Tata Sons, it is Mr Mistry who converted the Group into his "personal fiefdom", with his unilateral actions destroying precious institutional memory of the House of Tata.' In the statement, Tata Sons called Mistry's letter to the shareholders, a 'rehashed version from his earlier statements, press reports and leakages which we have forcefully rebutted'.

But Ratan Tata accused him of working in the shadows. Indeed, perhaps one of Mistry's biggest tactical errors was not having communicated enough when he was chairman. In fact, it was only as late as September 2016, well over three years after taking office, that any journalist was given access to Mistry's group executive council.

But the most telling things about Tata Group's statement was that it referred to a story critical of Cyrus Mistry that had appeared in the *Economist* just a month before his sacking. The fact that the Tata Group now referred to that story perhaps gives us a window into the reason – or at least the publicly stated reason: they wanted Mistry removed as Tata Sons chairman in the first place, and now from the boards of Tata Group companies.

The *Economist* piece was one of the first news stories that would chronicle Mistry's journey at the Tata Group. And it wasn't complimentary to him. In fact Mistry had realized the story might slam his stint at the Group when he received the final set of questions from the magazine. The Tata team under Mistry had reached out to modify the findings of the magazine, but to no avail.

In fact, in its statement Tata Sons referred to Mistry trying to control and suppress any negative messaging by saying, 'This attitude does not befit an old and venerable house like Tatas known for their fair play and transparency.'

The story titled 'Mistry's Elephant', carried in the 24 September 2016 issue, stung. 'Mr Mistry's peers might well look at the uninspiring financial performance of much of his Group since he took over in December 2012 and conclude they could do better,' it said. It went on to elaborate that a strategy to 'refocus' and cut flab of the Tata Group would have been a logical start for Mistry. But the Group, in spite of lower returns than cost of capital in seven of top nine companies, was not taking the hard calls.

'Far from slimming down, Tata is eyeing still further expansion: defence, infrastructure and financial services are the latest targets. There is a growing sense that it lacks the "refocus" gene altogether. Nearly four years into Mr Mistry's tenure, the listless performance that could once have been blamed on things like slowing Chinese demand seems to be entrenched. One former adviser to several Tata CEOs says that "the risk is that Tata uses its long-term emphasis and ethical way of doing business as an excuse to tolerate underperformance" . . . That the revered Mr Tata still chairs the Trusts that bear his name may make it trickier for Mr Mistry to be his own man . . . For the moment, however, he appears dangerously content just to sit atop what has grown into an impressive but lumbering pachyderm.'

When the piece was written, the rift between the Tata Trusts and Tata Sons – this is at the beating heart of the battle – was already beginning to show.

The magazine described the Trusts as 'murky and secretive' and validated that Mistry had been under an illusion if he had thought that he had a free hand.

In a forceful rebuttal in September 2016 itself Mistry's team pointed out that the Tata Group portfolio had outperformed indices in the stock market, and the cash flow was higher by 30 per cent over three years to exceed capital expenditure. The published rebuttal carried in the *Financial Express* on 27 September,[2] wrote off the *Economist* article as one that 'draws preconceived conclusions based on an inappropriate interpretation of selected data'.

From Mistry's perspective, Tata Sons calling out this article and validating the *Economist*'s had backfired on it. In its issue of 19 November 2016, the magazine wrote yet another article titled 'Ratantrum'. If the title was not telling, the article elaborated that the Tata Group's image for its good governance had taken a hit: 'That reputation has now been shredded owing to a brutal fight for control between Ratan Tata, the Group's 78-year-old patriarch, and Cyrus Mistry, his successor. The battle is bad for Tata, rotten for its outside investors who have tens of billions of dollars at risk and damaging to India. Mr Tata needs to get a grip before his legacy and the company are destroyed.'

In response to the Tata statement raking up the *Economist* article Mistry repeated that refocusing and cutting 'flab' – things the *Economist* accused him of not doing proactively – was precisely what he had been trying to do. He reiterated that he had identified and tried to address the Group's vulnerabilities as early as 2013. It was 'apparent that much of the Tata Group's capital was locked down in five "hotspots" [these were investments made by Tata companies during Ratan Tata's term as chairman] which were dragging down performance. These put the entire Tata Group at risk and needed tackling on a war footing'.

He then proceeded to point a finger at directors nominated to Tata Sons by the Trusts, stating that they were hindering him in resolving the hotspots and not necessarily placing the company's interests over those of the Trusts or Ratan Tata. The Trusts often breached protocol by interfering excessively, he said. For example, N.A. Soonawala, a trustee of the Tata Trusts but not a board member of Tata Sons, wanted to conduct discussions with the managements of Tata Group companies on the nitty-gritty of business. Mistry egged shareholders to move towards giving the power over the Trusts back to the government, rather than leave control with Ratan Tata. Mistry also urged shareholders to pay attention to the premeditation of his removal as three new directors had been appointed to the Tata Sons board weeks before the no confidence motion that saw his exit. Ajay Piramal and Venu Srinivasan were appointed as independent directors on 26 August 2016 on Ratan Tata's request, he pointed out. The beefing up of the board was clearly to shore up votes against him, Mistry said. The new directors did not have a right to judge him as they were not fully informed, he emphasized. He requested shareholders to ignore the outcome of the Tata Sons board meeting when they came to vote on his removal from Tata companies.

Ratan Tata also issued a personal letter that was delivered in hard copy to shareholders, which, in an apparent response to Mistry's talk of hotspots and write-offs, stated, 'We exit businesses only when we believe it is unviable.' The letter further said that operational teams had enjoyed freedom within the Group for years, indicating that Mistry was the first to complain. The name of Tata Sons is associated with operating companies to lend them credibility and strategic support, he explained. It is because of this that the Tata Group companies enjoy the trust of vendors and partners. A new leadership would stem the uncertainty, Ratan Tata assured, asking shareholders to vote Mistry off the Tata companies' boards. To buttress shareholder confidence, in December 2016, Tata Sons bought Tata Motors shares worth Rs 2,500 crore at a 10 per cent premium to the market price to shore up its stakeholding. The move formed 1.3 per cent of the total company equity.

~

But what was the constructive agenda for the Tata Group that Mistry presented to shareholders?

The Mission (why we exist):
To improve the quality of life of the communities we serve globally through long-term stakeholder value creation based on Leadership with Trust.

The vision (a dream with a deadline):
Twenty-five per cent of the world's population will experience the Tata commitment to improving the quality of life of customers and communities. As a result, Tata will be amongst the 25 most admired corporate and employer brands globally, with a market capitalization comparable to the 25 most valuable companies in the world.

As such Mistry was not able to effectively communicate his precise roadmap for achieving the Tata Group's long-term goals. His vision statement to shareholders was full of generalities and platitudes and left much wanting.

All it said, on concrete measures, was that there was the need to address the Group's 'five hotspots' which Mistry had earlier said would add up to a mammoth $18 billion write-off.

A senior Group executive said this seemed like the work of Nirmalya Kumar who proposed lofty end goals without quantifying the steps to achieve them. There lingered the dream to hit net worth of $500 billion by 2021, but the little steps towards that remained unarticulated.

~

In the battle between Ratan Tata and Cyrus Mistry, the shareholders of the Tata Group companies sided with Tata. When the TCS shareholder meeting, the first in the series of seven planned extraordinary general meetings, came up on 13 December, the voting that followed favoured Ratan Tata by 93 per cent. Of course, some 74 per cent of the votes were on account of Tata Sons shareholding, but big shareholders (such as LIC) abstained, giving Ratan Tata the leg-up. This was the beginning of the end for Mistry's bid to stay on the boards.

As the subsequent shareholder meetings came up, Mistry wrote letters to each company's investors separately, to no avail.

Eventually, before he could be embarrassed and voted off the boards at other shareholder meetings, Mistry conceded defeat the day before the shareholder meeting of IHCL, saying, 'The objective of effective reform and best interest of employees, public shareholders, and other stakeholders of the Tata Group (the very people I sought to protect as chairman) would be better served by my moving away from the forum of extraordinary general meetings.' And then Mistry resigned from all the boards of all Tata companies.

The courts were his only recourse now.

# 9

# Armed and Ready

It wasn't just Cyrus Mistry who was removed from the Tata Group company boards. The shareholders of Tata Steel, Tata Chemicals and Tata Motors voted Nusli Wadia out too. The notice to remove Wadia came on the day he had convened a meeting with some independent directors.

It all started when Wadia spoke in favour of Mistry at the Tata Chemicals board meeting. Wadia could have been Ratan Tata's staunchest supporter, but as events unfolded, Wadia and Tata ended up on opposite sides. After the board meeting, in which Mistry was retained as chairman, according to senior executives and board members of Tata Steel, meetings were held by Wadia to discuss how to support Cyrus Mistry further. Wadia had been on the boards of Tata Steel for over three decades and Tata Motors for about two decades. Though Mistry was sacked as chairman of Tata Steel, he retained the position at Tata Motors.

The Tata Group's retaliation against Wadia was more

acute perhaps because Ratan Tata felt betrayed by a friend and ally, or perhaps because Wadia had the power to sway other decision-makers. Either way, the move to sack Wadia himself from the boards was put in motion and it was decided that this matter, too, would be taken to the shareholders at the extraordinary general meetings.

~

Nusli Wadia loves a good fight. He fought for his business when he was twenty-six. He has litigated for possession of this home. He litigated and won when he was accused of being a Pakistani spy, on account of being the grandson of Muhammad Ali Jinnah. It took some boardroom and shareholder mobilization for him to buy biscuit maker Britannia. When Ratan Tata became the chairman of Tata Sons, Wadia fought to establish Tata against the satraps of the Group. He continues to fight to secure land left in FE Dinshaw's estate as the trustee of Dinshaw's trust. He was now fighting once more in Tata's boardrooms. Perhaps not as much for Cyrus Mistry as for his lifelong habit of taking a stand. 'He isn't fighting for Mistry . . . there is no special love for Mistry,' points out a lawyer. 'He's fighting for a principle.'

Wadia started his business career with a battle. He returned after completing his education in England, to join Bombay Dyeing, his father's business, in the late 1960s. In 1970, his father told him, he was selling the firm to settle overseas.

His father, Neville Wadia, backed by Pallonji Mistry, wanted to sell Bombay Dyeing & Manufacturing Co

Ltd, to R.P. Goenka, and planned to retire overseas. Young Nusli, who intended to expand the Wadia empire, was determined not to allow this to happen. He swung into action, and relied on advice from his godfather, J.R.D. Tata. He mopped up shares from his mother and sisters, and stirred up the employees of the Group into action. The employees forked out capital to buy shares, and blocked the deal with Goenka in support of Wadia. With that Wadia became the leader of Bombay Dyeing from the get-go – he didn't work his way to the top like other Parsi business scions. With JRD's help Wadia was able to assert his control over Bombay Dyeing and other Group companies.

When JRD was due to retire in 1991, Wadia, then forty-seven years of age, was even considered a potential successor to him. But, it was rumoured, that some years earlier, when it came to inducting Wadia on the Tata Sons board, Pallonji Mistry refused to allow it. So instead JRD appointed Wadia to the Tata Steel board in 1979 and the Tata Chemicals board later.

When JRD chose Ratan Tata to succeed him, Wadia supported his mentor's decision. Ratan Tata had worked on the shop floor and had risen over the previous decade assuming various roles at most major Tata companies including TCS. Boardroom wizardry was not quite his forte back then. He was generally retiring, little known and considered weak in front of stalwarts such as Russi Mody, Darbari Seth and Ajit Kelkar. Word on the street was that these strong operational heads of Tata group companies would soon marginalize Ratan Tata.

Wadia played a big role in proving the world wrong

about Ratan Tata. A magazine even called Nusli Wadia the corporate samurai of Ratan Tata. In fact, when Darbari Seth exited Tata Chemicals, it was seen as a personal victory for Wadia who helped edge him out. After the boardroom coup to overthrow Russi Mody, Wadia was rewarded with the post of vice president on the TISCO (now Tata Steel) board. Of course, at the time Wadia denied any prior knowledge of the impending reward. Tata and Wadia were often seen together, both professionally and socially. Friends of both the men say that Wadia may have expected a seat in the Tata Sons board at some point but this was never given to him. Ratan Tata instead nominated Wadia to the Tata Motors board in 1998.

Indeed Wadia was a close professional ally of Ratan Tata's. In 1997, *Indian Express* published illegally tapped phone conversations of Wadia. In those conversations, Wadia was heard lobbying for Tata Tea in Assam. The conclusion drawn by many from the tapped conversations was that Wadia shepherded Ratan despite Wadia's businesses being significantly smaller than the sprawling Tata Group. The tapped conversation led to some distance between Ratan Tata and Nusli Wadia. A *Times of India* report observed it was the first time in years that the two industrialists were not seen together at any major social event. Several people close to them say, though, that the drift was only for show.

In 1999, when Atal Bihari Vajpayee became prime minister, Wadia started spending more time in New Delhi. He had forged relations with Vajpayee and L.K. Advani over the years. People close to both Tata and

Wadia believe this was when the two really started to drift apart.

As mentioned earlier, Wadia has no special love for Mistry. Not many people know that Wadia was, in fact, skeptical of Cyrus Mistry's appointment as chairman of Tata Sons. Towards the end of 2011, when Mistry was about to be appointed, Ratan Tata wrote to Wadia informing him that Mistry had been chosen as the most suitable contender. Wadia wrote back saying that Tata was aware of his opinion on Mistry, but if Tata still chose Mistry, Wadia would support the decision.

Ratan Tata was still at the helm of Tata Sons. In 2012 he decided to re-enter the aviation business, after having lost Air India to the government after Independence. Wadia had already invested in GoAir by that time. But the airline was haemorrhaging cash, as was most of the sector. In 2012, foreign investment regulations in aviation were eased and the Tata Group opened discussions to invest in a new airline in partnership with AirAsia and Singapore Airlines. Rumour had it that Wadia had earlier invited Tata to become a co-investor in GoAir. When this did not happen and the Tata Group decided to start its own venture, Wadia blamed Ratan Tata for luring away Singapore Airlines, a potential investor for GoAir. Tata apparently told Singapore Airlines that they had the option of either partnering with him in a greenfield operation or going with Wadia. Singapore Airlines chose Tata.

The real discord between Tata and Wadia happened after Mistry's appointment. While the two men were too polite to air their anguish in public, the investment caused friction, say friends.

These events coincided broadly with Ratan Tata turning seventy-five and retiring from the board of Tata Sons and also from the board of Wadia's Bombay Dyeing. In an interview with *Business Standard*, Wadia said that Ratan Tata was welcome to stay on the board longer if he so wished. However, Rata Tata chose to retire from the Bombay Dyeing board also, as he handed over the reins of Tata Sons to Cyrus Mistry.

This is the background of the Ratan Tata–Nusli Wadia relationship as the tussle over the Tata Group companies' chairmanship raged on. Wadia became Mistry's ally. It was not clear till the Tata Chemicals board meeting, which side Wadia would take. As it turned out, he not only took Mistry's side, but after Tata Sons moved the shareholders to dismiss Wadia from the boards of Tata Steel, Tata Motors and Tata Chemicals, he also went on the offensive against Ratan Tata.

The Tata Group had accused Wadia of galvanizing the independent directors against Tata Sons and in favour of Cyrus Mistry. Wadia took umbrage to that. He asked Tata Sons to revoke the notice to remove him from the directorship of Tata companies, or face the courts! A few weeks and a couple of reminders later, two suits followed, in which Wadia accused Ratan Tata of defamation. The first suit claimed Rs 3,000 crore in damages, and the second was a suit alleging criminal defamation.

What had irked Wadia was Tata's attempt to 'gag' the independent directors – typically tasked with voicing unbiased opinions and upholding small shareholder interests. Wadia expressed his anguish in his letter to the shareholders of Tata Steel on the proposal to remove him as a board member: 'I was invited to join your company as a Director almost four decades ago by the late J.R.D. Tata, my mentor and godfather . . . The most important value that he taught me was that when one enters a boardroom, you leave your shares at the door, irrespective of whom you represent . . . It is both sad and unfortunate that Tata Sons and its interim chairman Ratan Tata are not only not practising this great tradition but effectively destroying it.'

Wadia, in his letter to Tata Steel shareholders, refuted the allegations against him, point by point:

Accusation: Acting in concert with Mistry.

Response: False and baseless.

Accusation: Acting against the Tata Group.

Response: I do not serve the Tata Group. I am independent. My fiduciary duty is to your company and not to an unidentified Tata Group.

Accusation: Acting as an interested party to harm the Tata Group.

Response: Baseless and defamatory and not worthy of a response.

Accusation: Galvanizing the independent directors.

Response: My independent director colleagues are independent-minded enough not to be galvanized by anybody, least of all by one of their peers.

Accusation: Putting Tata Steel Ltd and its future in grave jeopardy.

Response: This is false and untrue and is based on conjecture. No worker, employee, or manager or director of Tata Steel has ever complained of my conduct.

Accusation: No bona fides (no good faith towards the company).

Response: I have already sent notices for defamation to Tata Sons for harbouring a personal vendetta against me for not toeing their line. I believe that it is Tata Sons and its interim chairman who have vindictively issued this notice with malicious intent to remove me from the board of Tata Steel. I believe that it is their actions, which lack bona fides and in fact are malafide.

Proxy advisory firm, IiAS, which had advised shareholders to vote in favour of Mistry's removal from the Tata company boards, said that the proposal to remove Wadia was proof that the issue that arose between Tata and Mistry was personal rather than about replacing a non-performing management. In his letters, Wadia pointed out that it was only his removal that was sought, not that of other independent directors, not even those from Indian Hotels, who had endorsed Mistry before Wadia had done so. 'If they (independent directors) can be removed at the whim and fancy of a promoter, then their role is reduced to being "yes-men",' Wadia argued. He challenged the boards to open an enquiry to validate the allegations levelled against him by Tata Sons. The boards did not take the matter up. Wadia then said that the value of his contribution to the boards had been appreciated in the form of his reappointment over the years, which shareholders, including Tata Sons, had supported. Now, as events unfolded over just seventeen days, his work of a lifetime was being discredited.

Critically, Wadia also validated what Mistry had been saying about the bad investments that Tata companies had made during Ratan Tata's tenure, including the buying of Corus in the UK. Tata had been hailed then as the saviour of jobs in the UK's steel sector. British prime minister, Theresa May, on her maiden visit to India, commented that Tata had become the UK's largest manufacturing employer. Nusli Wadia provided a reality check: 'It is not the role of your company to save jobs in the UK nor to support its pension funds. The role of your board is to apply your funds to the most profitable growth opportunities which are quite obviously better served by investing in India where the returns are better and the company contributes to the industrial growth and development of India.'

Wadia also supported Mistry's claim on the intrusions of the Tata Trusts. According to him the Trusts had asked for company information before and after the Securities and Exchange Board of India (SEBI) had notified insider trading norms that came into effect in January 2015. Wadia's words screamed out of the pages of his letter to shareholders. He said he had also been instrumental in preventing Tata Steel, during Ratan Tata's tenure, from becoming a promoter of Tata Teleservices that had been burdened with debt, and was now staring at billions of dollars of write-offs.

Apart from Ratan Tata, Wadia's defamation suit named Tata Sons directors Ajay Piramal, Amit Chandra, Ishaat Hussain, Nitin Nohria, Ronen Sen, Vijay Singh, Venu Srinivasan, Ralf Speth, N. Chandrasekaran and F.N. Subedar as defendants.

A suit by minority shareholder and well-known investor Janak Mathuradas in the Bombay High Court also sought to block Wadia's removal by Tata Sons from the three operating companies. Initially, the Bombay High Court allowed the voting at the shareholder meetings to continue in which Wadia was voted off the boards. It later said that Wadia's place on the boards should be kept vacant in case he was reinstated after the court was done hearing the case.

In public, the move to eject Wadia had done more damage to Tata's case, even as the shock value of Mistry's dismissal was beginning to fade. Both the Tata Group and Mistry now readied themselves for their day in court at the National Company Law Tribunal (NCLT), a special division of the judiciary that deals with corporate matters.

# 10

# Mistry Goes to Court

Mistry tendered his resignation from the boards of Tata's operating companies on 19 December. Tata Sons responded quickly with a public statement the same day.

It said that Mistry had resigned because he knew that 'the overwhelming majority of the shareholders were not in support of his actions' and rejected his accusations as 'baseless, unsubstantiated and malicious'.

Ratan Tata said at a company shareholders meeting, 'These days are very lonely because the newspapers are full of attacks, most of them unsubstantiated but nevertheless very painful . . . It could have gone either way but your support has been overwhelming and remarkable. It has done more for my sense of goodwill today and this week than anything else that has happened.'

In these meetings Ratan Tata was gleefully welcomed by upbeat shareholders. In one, he even got a standing ovation.

The day after his resignation, Cyrus Mistry and his brother Shapoorji Mistry's firms filed a petition in the NCLT – against Tata Sons for mismanagement, leading to the detriment of the minority shareholders.

The petition was filed by Vinay Karve, the authorized representative for the two Mistry investment companies – Cyrus Investments and Sterling Investment Corporation – that each held 9.2 per cent of Tata Sons shares.

The lawsuit named Mistry as one of the twenty-three respondents. It was accompanied by a 900-page affidavit from Mistry supporting the petition, detailing emails, minutes of meetings, messages, documents and an emotional narrative of how in spite of being in charge, he really had not been in control.[1]

Mistry's affidavit and the other documents, evidences and submissions presented by both sides to the court paint a detailed picture of what exactly went wrong between Mistry and Ratan Tata in the months before his sacking. It is to this that we now turn in the rest of this book.

Broadly speaking, the issues we will encounter fall into three buckets: inter-personal friction between Cyrus Mistry and Ratan Tata; what the role of the Trusts should be in the running of Tata Sons and Tata Group companies; and, lastly, how the 'hotspots' should be dealt with and how the Tata Group should be turned around.

～

It took Mistry's lawyers eight weeks to prepare the document. They spent nights sifting through mails and records. The final dossier was less than a third of what they had gleaned through. In the affidavit, Cyrus asserted the crux of the matter: 'I sought to address the intuitive and unscientific mismanagement, imprudent decision-making and oppressive conduct [in Tata Sons] that I learnt of in my capacity as executive chairman. I had also found that some decisions were unfortunately tainted by utter lack of probity . . . My efforts at remedying the situation met with resistance, initially in polite terms and over time, in rising degree of resentment; eventually leading to events of 24 October 2016, when because of the inability to bear the remedial action that I had been taking, I was illegally removed . . . Operations of Tata Sons are being conducted purely to subserve the whims and fancies of Ratan Tata and Noshir Soonawala. The allegations [are] far from being an individualized personal attack.'

Mistry said that he had sent 555 emails to Ratan Tata over his tenure of just three years, which is indicative of the constant scrutiny he was under.

'It is unfortunate that Mr Mistry has not been able to graciously accept the decision of the very same board that appointed him,' said Tata in his reply. 'It was with a heavy heart that I came to terms with this realization that we had faltered in our judgement and choice of Mr Mistry and that the board had completely lost confidence in Mr Mistry's ability to steer and lead the company.'

The court filings revealed how deep-rooted the discord between Ratan Tata and Mistry was and how far back it went. As early as in September 2013, Ratan

Tata wrote a letter reminding Mistry that he had not yet separated himself from his shareholding in the SP Group and Tata Sons, a precondition that Mistry had been apprised of – and had agreed to – when he had accepted the chairmanship of Tata Sons. In this hand-written letter, Tata conveyed that Mistry's reluctance to distance himself from his shareholding in the SP Group and Tata Sons was surprising and not in keeping with the Tata Group's values.

Ratan Tata had proposed a structure, such as a blind trust, where the beneficiary – Cyrus Mistry – would have no insight into how the investments were being managed, or how its voting rights being used. If Cyrus put his Tata Sons shares in a blind trust he would have no control over voting. Mistry, rejecting blind trust as an instrument, suggested that he could safeguard against conflict of interest by adding appropriate clauses to the tender processes and contract documents involving the SP Group.

Tata disagreed. 'Over the past year I have made every effort to be supportive of all your actions and decisions, providing my views only if sought . . . I have ensured I do not become "a ghost in the corridor".' (Pallonji Mistry had come to be known as the Phantom of Bombay House.) But if push came to shove, he was willing to open a public debate on Mistry's conflict of interest. Mistry replied two days later apologizing for the delay in sorting this matter out. But he disagreed that there was any agreement to put his Tata Sons shares into a trust, saying, 'All our discussions on blind trust were to put all assets related to the Shapoorji Pallonji Group in a blind trust. Not to put any of my personal assets or the Tata Sons shares in a blind trust as that has no bearing on conflict of interest.'

No matter the structure, it was his family that must remain a beneficiary of his holding in the SP Group! 'If there is a rethinking on this, I would consider this a fundamental breach of trust,' Mistry wrote.

Ratan Tata said, 'I am unaware of what breach of trust there has been or what rethinking there has been by me.' He pointed out that for years the SP Group had been a preferred contractor and received large orders from Tata companies. Now, with Mistry at the helm, this arrangement could not be justified if it appeared to be lining the chairman's pockets.

Mistry took umbrage to this and said the SP Group was never given preferential treatment. All its bids had been competitive and work exemplary.

Tata made a pointed comment about a large Tata Steel contract given at an inflated cost in a single tender to the SP Group.

'I feel uncomfortable and mistrusted,' Mistry said.

Mistry then compiled a docket of related-party transaction policies followed by global leaders including General Motors, Prudential and Apple and shared it with Ratan Tata.

Ratan Tata commented that related-party transactions and conflict of interest were two different things. He compiled conflict of interest rules for the same companies and some others. Tata said Mistry was implementing what he preferred over what he had earlier committed to the selection committee. Tata recommended that Mistry remove himself from his family assets or discontinue business between the two groups Mistry was straddling.

'A full public discussion on the past, present and future compliance to the Tata code of conduct in letter and spirit would only be detrimental to the interests of the entire Group,' Mistry practically threatened. He chose the latter course. He sent a letter to all the operating companies of the Tata Group asking them not to give any further engineering and construction orders to the SP Group companies.

Ratan Tata thanked him for his resolution. But the sparring continued. In July 2014, Ratan Tata flagged a transaction between Tata Motors and SP Sterling Motors that exceeded Rs 100 crore. While Tata said he assumed this was a transaction that was initiated before Mistry's joining, he recommended that a list of all ongoing contracts with the SP Group be compiled with the timeline of their completion. Mistry obliged. The outcome did throw up several contracts running into a few hundred crore of rupees, all above board.

~

In August 2014, Mistry received another email from Ratan Tata on a different subject that gives us a peek into their relationship. Tata Motors had agreed to sell a property on the twenty-sixth floor of the World Trade Centre – a building on Cuffe Parade, a posh location in South Mumbai – to Tata Trusts. As per the agreement, payment for the purchase would span five years, but Tata Motors was now seeking it upfront. An upset RNT threatened to find another office for the Tata Trusts and asked for a refund of Rs 1.9 crore that the Trusts had

already spent on the woodwork and furnishings of the
World Trade Centre office, unless Tata Motors decided to
honour its original agreement. Mistry made Tata Motors
give the property to Tata Trusts on the original terms.

By 2015, the Trusts, headed by Ratan Tata, had held
up certain Tata Sons decisions, seeking more clarity
on them. Bharat Vasani, the general legal counsel of
the Tata Group, wrote to Mistry on 1 February 2015,
'We had to withdraw two resolutions from Tata Sons
EGM. To avoid confusion ask RNT and NAS [Noshir
A. Soonawala] to put down in writing what kind of
prior consultation they have in mind.' Vasani said that
Soonawala's communication could be construed as that
of a 'shadow director,'.

The Trust-nominated directors had also caused a delay
in putting into motion fundraising and debt recast plans
for Tata Motors and IHCL Mistry periodically received
emails from Vasani highlighting the involvement of the
Trusts in company matters. In one such email, Vasani
informed Mistry that a managing partner of a prominent
law firm had told him that there was a general impression
in the market that the Trusts control Tata Sons and Cyrus
does not have a free hand, but no one knows the exact
mechanism through which the Trusts exercise control.
In another email, Vasani quoted a well-known senior
advocate of the Bombay High Court asking him how he
operates in an environment where both the Trusts and
Mistry are giving contradictory instructions. In yet another
instance Vasani told Mistry that his view and possibly the
actions he was to carry out under Mistry's guidance were
irrelevant because the Trusts had taken charge.

Eventually, to address this issue, perhaps the biggest pain point of his tenure as chairman, Mistry compiled a set of governance guidelines on the working relationship between the Trusts and the executives of Tata Sons. In an email to Tata Sons director Nitin Nohria in May 2016, Mistry listed out the criteria he had used to formulate the guidelines:

- Trusts should have visibility of decisions taken by Tata Sons.
- Legacy ailing businesses would need Ratan Tata and Noshir Soonawala's inputs.
- For all else, the Trusts should refrain on commenting lest they make the Tata Sons board redundant.
- Directors nominated by the Trusts on Tata Sons board should not become 'telegraphic relays' of the Trusts.
- Separate the plan for Tata Sons from that of the operating companies [this meant that plans of operating companies would not be presented to Tata Sons board members, and in turn create distance between operating companies and the Trusts].
- The guidelines translated to lesser involvement of both Tata Sons and the Trusts in the operating companies.

As per the guidelines:
- Tata Sons would receive quarterly performance reports from operating companies and in turn collate results for the entire Group annually, with a rough forecast.
- Tata Sons would need to be informed of acquisitions by operating companies ahead of a shareholder resolution only if the ticket size exceeds Rs 1,000 crore or a quarter of the acquiring company's net worth (in sharp contrast

with the current norm to bring everything higher than Rs 100 crore to vote at Tata Sons board).

- If the transaction exceeds Rs 5,000 crore or 50 per cent of the company's net worth the trustees of the Tata Trusts would be included in discussions.
- Trust-nominated directors would discuss deviation from proposed plans with trustees only if the variation is over Rs 3,000 crore.
- Ratan Tata and Noshir Soonawala would be consulted on resolution of hotspots and possibly aviation.
- As per the guidelines, operating companies need not consult Tata Sons when appointing management or board members, because the Tata Sons representatives on each company board would have adequately applied themselves.

These guidelines increase the opacity of decision-making like mid-sized acquisitions and fundraising activities for even the Tata Sons board apart from the Trusts. It would allow fewer checks on and more flexibility for the individual companies. It would possibly shorten decision-making cycles. In the immediate term this would make Mistry the only common link between the operating company and the Tata Trusts since he was the only one from Tata Sons on the boards of several major Group companies.

Even as these guidelines were being worked on in the first half of 2016, news of the strain in relations between the Trusts and Mistry seemed to have leaked to the press. In April 2016, Mistry alerted Ratan Tata that the *Financial Times* was readying a piece on Tata Steel, which could negatively portray Tata Steel's history. Indicative of how brittle the relationship was, Ratan Tata wrote to Mistry that he was trying to show Tata in poor light and himself as someone who was fixing wrongs. 'With my hand on my heart, I can say that I have repeatedly taken actions and done my very best to protect your reputation and outstanding legacy,' Mistry wrote back to him. He quoted several instances when he had praised Tata. In fact, Mistry said when the *Indian Express* had posed questions about Ratan Tata's name surfacing in the Panama Papers scandal, he had instructed Bharat Vasani and Mukund Rajan, the communications head of the Group, to get Tata's name cleared.

Media reports did their bit in fuelling speculation about the Tata–Mistry rift. London-based Kumar Bhattacharyya, described as 'long-time Tata adviser', received probing questions from the *Financial Times* on whether there was a rift between Tata and Mistry. To the paper, Bhattacharyya had said that Mistry did nothing without consulting Ratan, and worked very hard.[2] 'They are in very close contact and meet often.'

Ratan Tata told Cyrus Mistry in an email on 5 April 2016, 'Today's actions become tomorrow's history. And the past cannot be blamed forever. What goes around comes around.'

~

By 2016 the relationship between Mistry and the Tata Trusts was completely frayed as a result of a number of smaller disagreements and the general oversight that the

Trusts was exerting on the operations of Tata Sons and
Tata Group companies. But the tensions between Mistry
and Tata were taken up a notch or two with Mistry's
controversial strategic vision for the Tata Group which
he presented to the Tata Sons board multiple times
including in June 2016, which they rejected. Ultimately,
the directors said this plan lacked vision, detail and clear
future goals. (Mistry's strategic vision in a presentation
he attached in his court affidavit can be seen in the
Appendix.)

In the plan Mistry detailed what to do with the five
'hotspots'.

In **Tata Teleservices**, Mistry proposed to buy minimal
spectrum (or airwaves on which mobile telecom signals
are transmitted) and bide time to find a buyer for the
business (Tata Docomo). The alternative would be to
write it all off and shut the business.

In **Tata Steel**, Mistry proposed to sell the Europe
business (Corus) even if the Tata Group didn't make a
return on its investment. The buyer would conceivably
take on the debt and pension liabilities that were weighing
Tata Steel Europe down. Mistry's logic was that the
Group had already invested Rs 1.1 lakh crore, yet a
turnaround had been elusive.

As for **Tata Power**, Mistry proposed two possibilities.
One was to shut the Mundra power plant (in Kutch
district, Gujarat) in which the Group had around Rs
15,000 crore invested and yet the plant had incurred a
Rs 6,200 crore loss. The other was that the Tata Group
could hunt for partners willing to shell out at least Rs
5,200 crore and invest this in increasing the capacity and

distribution of the unit. This he believed would turn the losses of the Mundra plant around.

In **IHCL**, Mistry saw no alternatives but to write off first Rs 1,256 crore on high-profile projects like Sea Rock in Mumbai and The Pierre in New York.

**Tata Motors** had a number of unrelated businesses. Mistry suggested selling those off. For example, Tata Technologies is a subsidiary of Tata Motors but does a mix of design (such as Tata Elxsi) and technology outsourcing (similar to TCS).

Mistry's identification of 'hotspots' and his plan for dealing with them could tarnish Ratan Tata's legacy. Several of the projects that Mistry wanted to sell off were in fact launched or acquired under Ratan Tata's leadership with great fanfare. But that wasn't the only reason for the Trusts' disappointment with Mistry's plan.

His proposal on increasing Tata Sons stake in Group companies was admittedly shy. To the Trusts this fell short of the recommendations he had made at the time of being interviewed for the post. But the move required cash and Tata Sons would do better to conserve it, in anticipation of exigencies such as payouts towards the telecom venture and its Japanese partner NTT Docomo, Mistry's strategy presentation said.

TCS shares could be sold to raise cash, but Mistry proposed to buy Tata Group company shares only when the prices were beaten down. That wait would be long.

As for the implementation of greater control on Tata operating companies, another of Mistry's promises, the plan belied reality. Many of the operating companies were drifting apart from the Group and Tata Sons, through a systematic reduction of control and influence by Tata

Sons over them,' said Ratan Tata. This was a cause for concern for the Trusts.

The overlap between directors of the operating companies and executives of Tata Sons was at an all-time low. Tata Sons historically exercised control over the operating companies through its shareholding and by nominating senior Tata Sons executives as board members even though the founding principles of the companies do not provide for directors to be nominated by Tata Sons.

Ratan Tata pointed out that although Mistry had proposed several divestment plans no significant divestments happened in the Tata Sons portfolio.

But Mistry justified this saying, 'I have also been sensitive to not take decisions as soon as I took over as this might be misrepresented as clean-up.'

~

Clearly the tension between Tata and Mistry had been brewing for long. Perhaps Mistry had seen his firing coming. As mentioned earlier, he was not pleased at the idea of inducting two new independent directors – Ajay Piramal and Venu Srinivasan – on the Tata Sons board in August 2016, but the Trusts had the right to nominate directors, and propriety demanded that he could not refuse the request of their nomination as it came from Ratan Tata himself. Instead of antagonizing the new directors at the outset, Mistry decided to bring them on board without much protest.

Now that Mistry was out, he questioned the independence and competence of the directors who voted him out. Out of the seven directors who had supported his dismissal, two had been appointed at the personal request of Ratan Tata and three as nominees of the Tata Trusts. Mistry challenged the independence of Nohria and Chandra, both Trust-nominated directors, as well as that of Piramal, flagging that the first two were related (they were brothers-in-law) and sat on the same boards as Piramal in several companies, including those of the Piramal Group. The vote of the newly appointed directors should be discounted because they did not know the Tata Group, said Mistry.

Yet, the minutes of a board meeting held on 15 September 2016 told another story. Amit Chandra and Ajay Piramal, two new directors, were adequately informed to advise on company matters. They made several suggestions regarding the plans of the Group and warned against entering some businesses that they thought would not fit within the group.

In their responses filed in court, Chandra and Piramal said that the business plan Mistry presented was not viable in execution; the financial projections were reliant on cash flows from existing ventures without any discussion on the generation of cash flows from new businesses.

The board members shot the plan down as one with little foresight. 'I found the five-year business plan presented by Cyrus Mistry to be lacking in substance, comprehension and strategy,' Amit Chandra said in his affidavit in response to Mistry's petition. He explained that the plan's success hinged mainly on TCS and did not factor in external economic influences. 'The current business plan was more of a cash flow statement.'

These directors vigorously countered Mistry's questioning of their independence. All of them had prominent professional statuses and long years of experience. Piramal even got personal as he made his point that sharing another board was not tantamount to collusion. He also sat on the board of an NGO called Pratham with Rohiqa Mistry, Cyrus Mistry's wife.

The suit brought on by Mistry was testament that the understanding – needed between the Trusts and Tata Sons – he had spoken of at the start of his stint had broken down. The suit went on to highlight in minute detail the alleged transgressions of Ratan Tata and the Tata Trusts.

# 11

# The Wish List

Mistry did not want to become chairman of Tata Sons again, and he did not want to sell his shares. It was a mystery what he really wanted. Everyone expected his lawsuit to shed light on what Mistry's objective was.

In the suit Tata Sons and Ratan Tata were accused of 'oppression and mismanagement' under the Indian Companies Act, 2013. The relevant sections affecting the case were 241 to 244.

Comparable precedent cases included an investor asking to appoint a board member at PTC India; financial investors moving against Religare promoters, Shivinder and Malvinder Singh; and small shareholders moving against the pharmaceutical holding company, Alembic. None of them had any significant outcomes.

Section 241 allows any stakeholder who believes that the conduct of the company undermines their rights to challenge the company's decisions in court and ask for a say in management. To be eligible to file under this provision, Section 244 says that the applicants must have 10 per cent equity or they must comprise 10 per cent of the total number of shareholders or 100 small individual investors, whichever is less.

The provision then lists out a series of actions that the court can take. For instance, the court can order a change in the company management. It can alter the articles of association or even set aside decisions that have been taken in the past. It can roll back transactions of the previous three months. It can remove and appoint directors and officials. Directors and officials could also be mandated to report company activity directly to the court.

The cases pending in court filed under the same section as Mistry's suit were different from his. In the other cases, inappropriate use of funds had taken place, unlike at Tata Sons. Still, Mistry's application requested the judge to:

- Keep a chairman from being appointed by the search committee that had been formed, appoint 'an administrator' who could manage the company's day-to-day business and dissolve the board of directors to form a new board, or appoint a retired judge as chairman of Tata Sons, and new independent directors to form a majority on the board till such time as business returned to normal after the suit.
- Prevent Ratan Tata and Noshir Soonawala from influencing decisions and stop Tata from attending board meetings.
- Prevent any dilution of the SP Group's stake in Tata Sons. (This could be done by issuing additional shares or forcing the SP Group to sell.)
- Reverse the decision of Ratan Tata and Trust-

nominated board directors of removing Mistry from the board of Tata Sons.

- Prevent further changes in the articles of association of Tata Sons without court approval.
- Investigate the role of the Trustees of the Tata Trusts in Tata companies and prohibit them from interfering.
- Initiate an independent forensic audit of the dealings of the Tata Group with two individuals -- these were dealings in which Mistry was alleging some impropriety. The two individuals were: C. Sivasankaran, who was a vendor partner and shareholder in Tata Teleservices, and Mehli Mistry, a long-time Tata Power vendor and friend of Ratan Tata's. Any findings were to be reported to the Serious Fraud Investigation Office of the Ministry of Corporate Affairs.
- Investigate Ratan Tata and Noshir Soonawala for insider trading using confidential, price-sensitive information they sought from time to time from Tata Sons, and possibly report this to the Serious Fraud Investigation Office.
- Similar to the Mehli Mistry and C. Sivasankaran investigations, Cyrus Mistry also wanted the appointment of a forensic auditor to reinvestigate the transactions executed by the Tata Group's AirAsia India with entities in India and Singapore to ascertain whether any funds had been diverted to any secret bank account of Mr Venkatramanan, managing trustee of the Tata Trusts at the time, and to recover monies that had resulted from this.
  - Strike down articles of association, or founding company principles that empower the Tata Trusts

to nominate directors and receive reports and plans
of the company.
- Prevent Tata Sons from initiating any new line of
business till the case is decided.
- Prevent sharing of unpublished information
between the Group's operating companies and Tata
Sons.
- Grant some of this as interim relief while the case
is being heard.

Mistry's requests did not reveal what he would finally
achieve from this battle. It was unclear who Mistry was
battling; there was no real punitive action he wanted
against Ratan Tata. Since he had expressly stated in his
court petition and representation to shareholders that he
did not want to be chairman, why did he want the post
to be vacant until his challenge was pending? Was he
hoping to be reinstated anyway?

If his concern was governance, were stability and
permanence not valuable for the Tata Group? Yet,
Mistry wanted the leader's chair to remain empty.
Mistry's supporters questioned the capabilities of the
current committee to appoint a new chairman. They also
questioned the decisions any such appointee would take.

With these slightly confusing prayers to the court,
arguments began before the NCLT, Mumbai bench.
It was a room where the two judges sat on one side
on a high table, separated by the court's officers from
a seating area of about thirty people including sundry
lawyers, applicants and journalists. The lawyers on this
matter alone were sufficient to fill the benches and seats.

Officials from both sides, journalists and law interns lined the narrow aisles, waiting to see how things would unfold.

Mistry explained to the court that Ratan Tata's interference loomed over all decisions he had wanted to make through his tenure. Going beyond the instances of personal animosity, issues of conflict of interest, and disagreement over the five-year plan discussed in the previous chapter, Mistry now gave specific examples of Ratan Tata meddling with business decisions that compromised the Group's opportunities in future. In each instance of interference, Mistry had to demonstrate that it affected the financials of Tata Sons, so as to prove that his interest as a minority shareholder was compromised for it to be considered by the judges as a valid argument in this case.

In 2013 he said that the Tata Trusts scuttled the application for a banking licence for the Group that was aimed at furthering its financial sector operations. Later in the same year he was made to enter joint ventures with AirAsia India and Vistara did.

In 2014, Mistry said that a fight with Japanese equity partner NTT Docomo in Tata Teleservices broke out over an exit for the Japanese company. The Tata Group had to pay a hefty amount. Mistry said Ratan Tata shielded his friend Sivasankaran, who also held equity in Tata Teleservices, from paying his share in the Docomo exit, causing a loss to Tata Sons. Also in 2014, a past decision to enter a joint venture with Piaggio in the charter plane segment created a dent in the finances of Tata Sons.

In 2015, the Trusts pulled support for a rights issue in Tata Motors, throttling growth capital for the company that had been incurring losses in India. Ratan Tata also influenced Tata Sons to buy shares in domestic airline venture AirAsia India from a local partner at a rich valuation when the airline was running in losses. Not only that, Tata arranged for one of his aides and Tata Trusts' managing trustee R. Venkatramanan to buy shares in this airline, accused Mistry trying to prove that there was personal wealth being amassed in Ratan Tata's moves.

In 2016, the Trusts held up a decision to sell the fertilizer business of Tata Chemicals that was making losses. Ratan Tata and his friend Lord Kumar Bhattacharyya wrecked negotiations to pare down loss making Tata Steel Europe.

Throughout his tenure till October 2016, Mistry said the Trusts, Ratan Tata and Noshir Soonawala asked for information that would affect share prices of the listed Tata companies – in violation of insider trading regulations.

These instances would become the focal episodes of Mistry's case to show how exactly Ratan Tata and the Tata Trusts allegedly interfered in his functioning. These instances are why, Cyrus Mistry asserted, he had to draw up the administrative framework (described in the previous chapter) that would govern the relationship between Tata Sons, the group companies and the Trusts.

~

If the allegations of financial impropriety and personal profiting that have been recounted so far were not enough, Mistry's next allegation shows how bad matters had become.

Despite repeated assertions that Mistry's appeal in court had no personal motive, he raked up a controversy from over two decades ago regarding Ratan Tata allegedly profiting at the cost of Tata Sons. He also dragged his own relative Mehli Mistry into the fray.

'The Mistrys are a close-knit and tight lipped family,' said someone close to them. So, an open battle between two Mistrys was disconcerting. Mehli Mistry was related to Cyrus Mistry from both his mother's and father's side. Mehli's and Cyrus's grandfathers were brothers. Both had separate businesses, established a few years apart from each other – one was a construction contractor (Shapoorji Pallonji Mistry), and the other a painting contractor named M. Pallonji. In fact, the two tossed work over to each other when needed.

Mehli's and Cyrus Mistry's mothers are sisters. Despite the recent discord between their sons, the two still talk to each other regularly, say friends. 'Can you imagine the spot it put their mothers in!' exclaims a common friend.

Mehli and Cyrus never ostensibly had any resentment between them, say friends. Even today, Cyrus Mistry and Mehli Mistry are co-invested in a joint venture. Despite the vast difference in the size of their businesses, there had never been any rivalry between Cyrus Mistry's SP Group and Mehli Mistry's M Pallonji Group. Mehli is older than Shapoorji and Cyrus. He is also quieter and more reserved than most others in the Mistry family. This he possibly has in common with Ratan Tata.

Mehli Mistry is a close friend of Ratan Tata and, in

1993 when they were neighbours, he helped Tata buy a property in Alibaug, signing as witness for the transaction, claimed Cyrus Mistry.

Then, there was the matter of a flat owned by Tata Sons in which Ratan Tata lived. It was in a prominent building – Bakhtawar – in South Mumbai, one of the poshest areas of the city. The flat was bought by Mehli Mistry's company in 2000. At that time, an amount of Rs 3 crore was paid to Ratan Tata to vacate and give up leasing rights over the property.

The amount was due to Tata Sons, not to Ratan Tata, said Mistry. He presented a document that said should Ratan Tata vacate the flat, its ownership and rights would be returned to the arm of Tata Sons that had allotted the flat to Ratan Tata in the first place. So, how could Ratan Tata have collected Rs 3 crore, asked Cyrus Mistry.

For Cyrus Mistry this was proof enough that money was being taken away from the shareholders of Tata Sons for the personal benefit of Ratan Tata, and his petition cited it even though it meant dragging a family member into the dispute. In fact one of his pleas to the court was that Ratan Tata should return this amount with interest to Tata Sons.

Cyrus Mistry also accused Ratan Tata of playing favourites with Mehli Mistry by giving Mehli contracts from Tata Power. 'It is surprising that in this day and age, assistance extended to friends is questioned,' said Mehli Mistry, referring to the help he extended to Ratan Tata in the property-related matters.

Ratan Tata said, 'An attempt has been made by Mr Cyrus Mistry to sensationalize an ordinary personal transaction which has no bearing at all on Tata Sons or contracts with M Pallonji and Tata Power.'

To most of Cyrus Mistry's fraternity, Cyrus Mistry's accusations were inappropriate.

Mehli Mistry pointed out that his company's relationship with the Tata Group pre-dated Ratan's tenure at the helm: 'Since around 1940 the M Pallonji Group of companies has performed contractual obligations and works for the Tata Group particularly with Tata Power. A cordial relationship has extended through the reigns of successive chairmen [of Tata Power], including Mr Naval Tata, Dr Homi Sethna, Mr Ratan Tata and Mr Cyrus Mistry on behalf of Tata Power. This cordial relationship also existed when Mr J.R.D. Tata was the chairman of Tata Sons.'

According to Mistry, terminating and retendering, in 2013, contracts given to M Pallonji saved Tata Power nearly Rs 200 crore ($30 million). Until then, the contracts were just getting renewed. Mehli's shipping company till then was getting more than two and a half times the quote of the lowest bidder in 2013.

He continued that Mehli had received contracts for barging (storing and moving of coal on floating vessels), dredging (removing silt and sediment from the bottom of a waterbody, such as a dam or river) and even shipping. This was, he pointed out, even though Mehli and his companies had no previous experience in the domain.

Mehli Mistry protested, 'There was no quid pro quo ... in the purchase of the Bakhtawar flat and Alibaug land by Mr Ratan Tata. Mr Tata is a friend, as a consequence of which I assisted him in the purchase of land at

Alibaug . . . The M Pallonji Group of companies has been carrying out contractual works for Tata Power since 1956, before I was even born. All contracts have been given to M Pallonji after following due processes . . . all procedures were adhered to and approvals were taken.'

In fact Mehli Mistry's company had helped Tata Power out of a crisis as a barging, dredging and shipping partner, Mehli said, adding that in 1993 Tata Power's earlier vendor overnight 'demanded additional sums from Tata Power Co Ltd to transport the coal and further threatened to abandon unloading and transport operations in the event their demands were not met. Unwilling to accede to their ransom-like demands, the then acting MD requested the M Pallonji Group for assistance in this time of crisis. The coal was transported by the M Pallonji Group and their team at a rate lower than the existing contract rate . . . averting a crisis.'

Mistry did not agree, and alleged that M Pallonji had amassed wealth and grew nearly 280 times in two decades at the cost of Tata Power and its shareholders. He used figures from the M Pallonji Group's reserves to make his point. He went on to add that when it came to cancelling Mehli's contract in 2013 to award it to someone else, Mehli tried to arm-twist the Tata Group.

In an email sent to S. Padmanabhan, a veteran of the Tata Group, and operations head of Tata Power for long, Mehli wrote that existing contracts locked Tata Power into availing facilities from the M Pallonji Group alone. He blamed lapses in delivery on a lack of communication between his team and the Tata team. Mehli's communication to the Tata Power team displayed managerial authority rather than vendor reverence. 'We cannot have the management taking decisions without our involvement and concurrence and then expect us to perform our part of the contract . . . Tata Power Co Ltd should leave all barging logistical issues to the contractors who have been awarded the job. We know what to do and what is best for the company.'

Mehli also said that competitive bidding in which Mistry had announced savings in, was an illusion. The bidding company had not factored certain costs which would pile up to higher than his bid.

Cyrus Mistry on his part continued, 'All these undue benefits would not have been possible without the patronage of Ratan Tata who was the chairman of Tata Sons and TPC (Tata Power Corporation) during the relevant period.'

Neither Mehli nor Ratan Tata once denied that they were friends. A leading Indian financial daily reported that when the SP Group celebrated its 150th anniversary in 2015 with a grand function at the NPCA at the tip of land in Nariman Point, Mumbai, Mehli Mistry and Ratan Tata sat in a quiet restaurant enjoying dinner alone and away from the celebrations. Ratan Tata said, '[Cyrus Mistry's firms] have smeared accusations that undue favours got extended at my behest to people with whom I shared a close relationship. In particular, they have contended that Mr Mehli Mistry received "undue benefits" at the cost of Tata Group companies solely on account of his close association with me . . . To say that my association with Mr Mehli Mistry was the sole reason for Tata Power to enter into contracts with Mr Mehli's companies is not only an unfortunate charge against me but paints in poor light Tata Power and its executive management including its board of directors over the years. It is further ironical that Mr Cyrus Mistry was a director on the board of directors of Tata Power from the year 1996 to 2006 and a director again from 2011 and chairman thereafter from 2012, and so the transactions were within his knowledge for years. Mr Cyrus Mistry continues to make such remarks without bringing on record any shred of evidence in his support.'

Tata Sons, the instrument that was being abused as per Mistry's lawsuit, remained unfazed by these accusations. It pelted the court with data and documents to prove Cyrus wrong. Tata Sons said that the relations between Ratan Tata and Mehli Mistry, or Mehli's rise over twenty years had no bearing on it. Events at Tata Power showed that all processes in which Mehli received contracts were open to everyone. Tata Power said that the 1993 dredging project was allotted after a tender process, which comprised three bidders including M Pallonji. The contract was renewed in July 2002 when Cyrus Mistry was on the board of Tata Power.

Finally, Tata Sons said that these allegations of mismanagement were not aimed at it, but targeted Tata Power. The petition in court had been filed against Tata Sons not Tata Power and it was not Tata Sons lookout to manage bidding and assigning of contracts to operating arms.

Adding fuel to the fire in the Mehli Mistry–Cyrus Mistry stand-off was a news report in the *Economic Times* on 21 November 2016 that said Mehli had warned Cyrus

Mistry, in an angry visit to Bombay House just a few months earlier, of 'repercussions if Mistry didn't "mend his ways"'.

Mehli Mistry of course denies this. 'I have not spoken with Mr Cyrus Mistry since I congratulated him on his appointment as chairman of Tata Sons sometime in 2012,' he said. But angry he certainly was with Cyrus Mistry for drawing him into this war with Ratan Tata. 'This is a deliberate attempt to malign me and Ratan,' Mehli said, adding that the allegation that he was behind the ouster was untrue. 'I was in Dubai when it happened. I came to know about it from the media only. I am not part of any Tata Group company or management. Ratan Tata is my friend and mentor, and I don't see any other reason for dragging my name into this controversy,' he told newspaper *Hindu BusinessLine*.

'His father was Phantom of Bombay House, he will go down as a self-professed lame duck,' Mehli Mistry observed wryly to the press, after being pulled into the public controversy. Mehli Mistry was not named as a defendant in Cyrus Mistry's suit because he had no relevant position in Tata Sons. The issue did not get too much attention. There were, however, others that would become central to the debate Mistry was stirring up regarding governance at the Tata Group. Mistry argued that the Tata Trusts were at the heart of it all.

# 12

# Toil and Trouble

The divided opinions on whether Tata was right in removing Mistry as chairman brought the spotlight on what Mistry had achieved during the time he held the post, which was nearly four years. The official line of the Tata Group was that Mistry had been removed for poor performance. But stock market investors and fund managers, who looked at the headline numbers, dividends and growth trajectory of the Group, were satisfied with Mistry's results.

Mistry never shied away from hard work and long hours. A quarter of his working hours, estimated at nearly 700 a year, were spent attending board meetings. The remainder of his time was spent in executive meetings, client meetings, and travelling to remote locations of operating companies. This hardly left much time for quiet reflection.

Mistry took charge in December 2012, disbanded old structures and assembled his team – called the Group

Executive Council (GEC) – by April 2013. It was similar in nature to a team Ratan Tata had set up when he became chairman. As mentioned before, the team comprised three members hired from outside the Tata Group and two from within. While Madhu Kannan (business development and public affairs), Nirmalya Kumar (group strategist) and N.S. Rajan (human resources) were lateral hires, from the insiders, Mistry designated Mukund Rajan, former executive assistant to Ratan Tata, as brand custodian, which included heading Group communications. A year later, in 2014, Mistry added Group veteran Harish Bhat to the elite council, removing Bhat as the chief executive of Tata Global Beverages.

Mistry would later say, 'We filled the vacuum in the leadership team with a judicious amalgam of maturing leaders from within the Group as well as lateral inductees who brought in fresh perspectives and new knowledge.'

The hierarchical nature of the Group meant that as chairman Mistry was revered by Tata employees, but the same acceptance didn't extend to Kannan and Kumar.

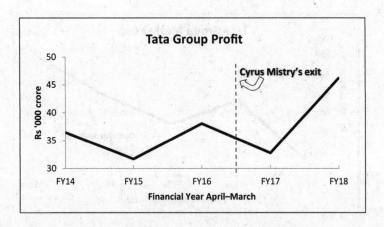

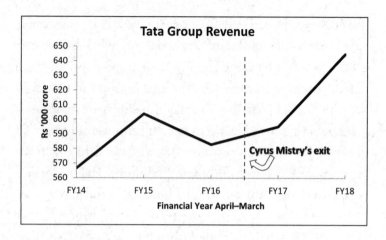

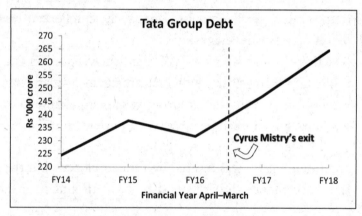

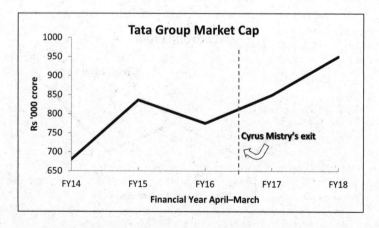

As a result, it was difficult for them to effect change. Mistry also created the role of the chief technology officer for the Group, saying, 'Mr Ratan Tata was deeply involved in promoting a technology-oriented culture in the Group. We are building on that strong foundation. The Group chief technology officer's role is to evangelize innovation within different Group companies.'

The one role Mistry was unable to fill was of group chief financial officer (CFO). The search for one was on. Meanwhile, Ishaat Hussain, who had held various finance positions within the Group over several decades and been second in command of former Group CFO Noshir Soonawala, took on the mantle of finance director at Tata Sons.

Mistry successfully engaged with the smaller companies in the Tata fold at an annual event he developed. It was held at the grand hall in the NCPA. This was a gathering of nearly 800 executives, not only Group CEOs, but also heads of finance, human resources and others. Small but profitable companies, such as Tata Elxsi, found a voice on this platform. Mistry's message was loud and clear. To find a spot under the sun, you need not be the biggest or oldest company in the Group, but be just a prime mover in your field.

This was a little threatening for the larger Group entities such as Tata Steel. Suddenly, relatively smaller companies found themselves advising their larger counterparts. Leaders in the more established Tata companies baulked at that.

Mistry also identified clusters of companies in four sectors – financial services, defence and aerospace, retail, and infrastructure. These were to be the future growth engines for the Group. The clusters were designed to increase synchronization between various Tata companies operating in common sectors and reduce internal competition. For example, in defence, there were seven entities that Mistry had hoped would consult each other when bidding for contracts. Or in retail, if multiple chains – Trent, Starbucks, Tanishq – wanted space in a similar location, such as a mall, they could jointly negotiate a lease deal. To improve coordination Mistry created posts of cluster heads.

Unfortunately, this became a fertile ground for office politics, and executives started lobbying and protecting their turf, defeating the purpose, at least to some extent, of the cluster groups. There was some infighting for the chief's position in a cluster. Between a CEO of a smaller company with more experience and a CEO of a bigger company with less experience, who would be chosen as the cluster head? Mistry's intention was to increase collaboration between chiefs of different companies in the same sector. Unfortunately this increased the internal competition.

Then there was the Group Strategy and Policy Forum. 'Here, we deliberated policy framework with CEOs of the Tata Group companies before rolling [the policy] out, to ensure alignment and practicality of implementation,' Mistry said, explaining his contribution to the Group in the run-up to shareholder meetings.

~

Mistry was at the helm for three and a half financial years. Fraught as these years were with 'interference' by Ratan Tata, as Mistry called it, showing results was his responsibility.

But Mistry also leaned on Ratan Tata. During his term Mistry drew extensively on Ratan Tata's inputs to grow certain businesses. For nearly two years, Mistry was acting as executive chairman, rather than non-executive, at Tata Motors as the company was yet to appoint a chief executive. He routinely sent teams to discuss conceptualization and design of new models of cars with Ratan Tata. He recalled a time when Jaguar was losing £245 million ($315 million) every quarter yet Ratan Tata insisted on keeping the product development programme. At the end of his chairmanship Jaguar's quarterly profit was around £300 million (approximately $400 million) per quarter. 'Today, we are reaping the fruits of Mr Tata's brave decision,' Mistry wrote in a letter to Soonawala in January 2016.

After retiring as chairman of Tata Sons, Ratan Tata started exploring and investing in the start-up space in his personal capacity. The Tata Group under Mistry also benefited from Ratan's new focus. In 2014 Ratan Tata invested in the online retailing platform Snapdeal, which at the time was a competitor to market leader Flipkart. After making the investment, Tata introduced Kunal Bahl, founder of Snapdeal, to Cyrus Mistry, recalls a person involved. The discussions between Bahl and Mistry's team resulted in the formation of Tata CliQ, one of the digital investments Mistry prided himself on, recalled a senior executive.

In an interview with tata.com in September 2016, Mistry said, 'I must here appreciate Mr Ratan Tata's leadership and vision to take the Tata Group global in the early 2000s, which has left us with a very strong platform. I think the onus is now on us to build on that, and to make sure that we not only have a global footprint, but that we create global mindsets . . . I continue to interact with Mr Tata, who is also the chairman of the Tata Trusts, our largest shareholder. I need to ensure there is good alignment on strategy between Tata Sons and the Tata Trusts.'

Mistry would later backtrack, saying he had only said that to appease egos.

~

While addressing shareholders in December 2016, Mistry asserted and documented his achievements at individual companies. 'We seeded next-generation businesses in the digital and healthcare space . . . our investment in growth over the last three years was in excess of $25 billion across the Tata Group.' He said he was unravelling the complicated shareholding structure between the Tata Group companies, by buying or moving the stake from operating companies to Tata Sons. For example, some shares in Titan were held by a Tata Steel subsidiary Kalimati and Tata Global Beverages. Under Mistry, Tata Sons bought these shares, freeing capital for the steel and tea maker. This he said was in the interest of shareholders, because an investor in steel may not be interested in buying shares in a watch maker, but if Tata

Steel held Titan shares, any shareholder buying Tata Steel shares would be at least partially exposed to the watchmaking segment.

To also provide steady financial progress, Mistry said he was focusing on services rather than businesses that are seasonal in nature. Cars or houses, for example, are bought at specific times in the year, around Diwali, for instance. During other months business tends to be much slower. But services like computer software for companies or call centres earn steady revenue year-round.

Mistry, till the end, maintained he had a hand and handle on each of the companies:

At Tata Steel, Mistry was questioning whether the time was ripe to move on from steel to other materials, such as graphene. Trouble was looming large in the UK arm of Tata Steel and Mistry was gearing up to address that. In a letter to Soonawala in January 2016, Mistry had emphasized the need to remain on positive terms with the UK government. A group official said, that he had planned reskilling, psychological therapy and other social programmes to contain any backlash in the UK, if the Group needed to shut operations there.

At TCS, Mistry said his biggest contribution was travelling around the world engaging customers. This he said more than doubled the customers buying services $100 million each and nearly doubled those generating $50 million–$100 million revenue for India's largest software outsourcing company.

As for the rest, N. Chandrasekaran, the CEO of TCS, and his team largely ran the company without much involvement from Mistry. When the centre tried to

influence any non-cosmetic aspects, it was kept at bay by
the TCS management. In fact, when Mistry had tried to
convince the cash-rich company to invest in the Group's
corporate jet, he had been turned down by TCS. Mistry's
decision not to meddle with a system that worked went
to his credit.

At IHCL, the company that owns the Taj group of
hotels, more than 80 per cent of its value, which includes
the money shareholders have invested, loans the company
has taken and assets it owns, had been written off during
Mistry's tenure. In fact around six months after he took
over, in July 2013 the shares hit a low of around Rs 38
a piece, nearly half of its highs from a couple of years
earlier. Yet, just before he left in 2016, the stock hit a
high of Rs 124 each. Mistry leveraged this in his appeal
to shareholders and the court.

At Indian Hotels, Mistry also undertook setting
leadership and strategy right. This involved changing
and training the leadership team of the company and
bringing in a new CEO with strong domain experience
and a thirty-five-year track record with a global hotel
chain. This last decision backfired, though not for any
fault of Mistry's. He brought in Rakesh Sarna to replace
the incumbent chief executive who had been at the helm
for nearly a decade and who was responsible, according
to Mistry, for many of the bad investments he had
been dealing with. But, as mentioned earlier, Sarna got
embroiled in a sexual harassment case and the employee
accused the Group, led by Mistry, of protecting Sarna at
her expense. Mistry had actually ordered an investigation

into the matter by a formal committee even though the employee had preferred not to complain officially.

Veiled accusations were also made that Mistry had been responsible for a stand-off with the New Delhi Municipal Corporation over the lease of the company's landmark Taj Mansingh Hotel. The corporation decided to auction the leasehold rights of the property to the highest bidder rather than renew the lease of Taj. The proposed lease amount made it unviable for the hotel to operate, the Group said. The auction was finally held in 2018 and was won by the Tata Group.

At Tata Motors, Mistry counted a revitalized product pipeline as yet another achievement. Of course he had often relied on Ratan Tata to design and plan the new cars. 'For the month of November [2016], our company became the third in sales, overtaking Mahindra & Mahindra. While there is a long way to go, we are on the path to significant improvements,' said Mistry.

Taking a leaf from Ratan Tata's playbook nearly a decade ago, Mistry also undertook a trip to the US, Europe and China to meet car dealers. Back home in India, he spent a day with fleet operators and drivers, eating at a dhaba with them. In the preceding years perhaps it was the lack of new cars that had been dragging Tata Motors' performance down in India. Thanks to the new line-up in 2018 when JLR, which had propped up Tata Motors' financials during Mistry's tenure, performed poorly it was Tata Motors India that offset the fall in profits.

At Tata Chemicals, Mistry was trying to sell their fertilizer business to get some cash and deal diplomatically

with the £120 million ($160 million) pension liability
of the company. The sale of its fertilizer business to Yara
Fertilizers was announced in August 2016, but completion
would still have to await approvals. The company was
expected to get around Rs 2,600 crore ($400 million)
from the sale.

At Tata Power, Mistry's achievement was restricted to
a reduction in losses. Mistry said he was unable to do more
because some decisions were held up in court. Tata Power
had sought the court's intervention to reprice the thermal
power it was supplying because coal prices had risen
sharply. Tata Power's contracts with power distributors
did not allow them to pass the costs forward which is why
they had to approach the courts. A judgement in Tata
Power's favour was finally pronounced by the Supreme
Court in December 2018.

When the opportunity for acquiring Welspun Energy's
renewable power arm, a solar power company based in
Delhi, came up, Mistry clinched it. While Mistry was
slammed for the way the deal was done, no one disputed
that the focus on renewable energy was the need of the
hour.

~

According to Mistry, the debate on his non-performance
– the ostensible reason for his sacking – was first
raked up in a letter written by Noshir Soonawala to
him in December 2015. The letter stated, 'One of the
presentations which you made to Mr RNT [Ratan
Naval Tata] and me a few weeks ago contained a useful

snapshot of each of the major listed companies.' Five years make a complete business cycle, therefore the numbers Mistry shared should show the best possible and worst-case performances of businesses at the Tata Group, said Soonawala's letter. In his analysis, Soonawala excluded the results of TCS, which he considered an outperformer in the Group. Large unlisted entities, such as Tata Teleservices, which had a significant negative impact too were kept separate in this study. According to Soonawala, at nine major listed Tata companies, the return on capital had fallen nearly 6 percentage points to 14 per cent.

The telecom business, Tata Teleservices (which operates under the name Tata Docomo), cost the Group dearly. A deal with Vodafone may have saved the venture, if one could have been stitched up. Mistry was in negotiations with the UK-based telecom major to sell Tata Teleservices. However, Vodafone eventually told Mistry that the deal was too complicated, and partnered with the Aditya Birla Group's Idea Cellular in March 2017 instead.

Barring Tata Motors, which owed its success to JLR, the market value of eight out of nine listed Tata Group entities remained flat. While net revenue had risen, profits had fallen. High capital expenditure had compromised net free cash flow. This was a key reason for the increasing indebtedness of the Group.

In 2015, the dividend payout by Tata Sons had fallen to Rs 780 crore from Rs 1,000 crore in Ratan Tata's last financial year. In fact half of the dividend of the year to March 2016 was from a one-time payout by TCS.

Soonawala's solution was to cut the Group's flab and focus on core areas as the Group had once done by selling Lakmé and Tata Oil Mills.

Mistry also wanted to cut the group's flab but they differed on their identification of what exactly was the flab. Mistry considered the 'hotspots' he had identified as the assets that ought to be sold. This included many of Ratan Tata's legacy projects in major Tata companies such as Tata Steel's Corus investment. Mistry conceded on the numbers but could not disagree more on the comment on his performance.

Mistry explained that the Group had lacked a succession plan. The reason for the fall in profits in spite of a rise in net revenues was that there had been a recent churn of top talent. The Group had hired a large number of executives from outside of Tata. This was Mistry's explanation for the increase in the wage bill.

The overall Group debt had risen not only as a result of capital expenditure, but also as a result of losses that could be traced to decisions taken before Mistry's time. In his reply, for the first time, Mistry also told Soonawala that the Group should realistically write off Rs 1,18,000 crore. The next five years would be a time for restructuring, recapitalizing and transformation for the Group, only then could a strategy for further growth be devised in 2020.

As for 'biting the bullet', Mistry's proposals to sell the 'hotspots' had been shot down by the board. Mistry explained that while the board had toyed with the idea of declaring bankruptcy in some cases, Mistry had preferred to avoid that. The impact this would have had on the Tata brand in the banking community would affect the Group in the long run.

The disharmony was caused by Mistry's focus on paring down or shutting ailing arms of major companies, such as Tata Steel and Tata Motors, in contrast with what the Trusts believed was needed. Apart from this action, Mistry's recommendation had been to sell TCS shares to raise funds, and he recalled an earlier occasion when he had proposed to Ratan Tata that Tata Sons itself should consider raising capital by issuing fresh shares accounting for 10 per cent of the total equity capital. This move would mean that the overall share of the Trusts would come down, and that of the SP Group, provided it subscribed to a potential share issue, would increase.

~

The *Economist* in its issue dated 24 September had said, 'Many people had . . . expected Mr Mistry to usher in change.' It is perhaps on this expectation that Mistry floundered. There was no big-bang change that was visible even if behind-the-scenes work was frenetic. The Trusts seemed to concur with this assessment. Mistry's achievements paled before the visionary planning Tata had expected of him. The target that had been set for Mistry was to take the Group to a value of $500 billion by 2021 – at the ten-year mark of Mistry's tenure.

Two years after Mistry was sacked, his successor as chairman, N. Chandrasekaran, or Chandra as he is popularly called, gave an interview to the magazine, the *Week*, saying he was creating management bandwidth before taking on any new projects. In his first year, Chandra closed a deal between the German steel company Thyssenkrupp and Tata Steel Europe whereby they would combine their European steel activities into a joint venture. The negotiations were initially started by Cyrus Mistry. Chandra also 'gave away' Tata Teleservices to Airtel in return for Airtel shouldering the company's liability to pay for spectrum. Nirmalya Kumar said that Chandra had in fact reaped the rewards of the seeds Mistry had sown. It is an open question whether Mistry's performance would have seemed better if he had written off the $18 billion and made it seem like Ratan Tata's fault. Mistry reasoned that he had not exposed the cumulative losses out of reverence to Ratan Tata. To Ratan Tata, however, Mistry was doing the opposite as he went about telling the board and possibly the press about the legacy 'hotspots'.

# 13

# A Trust Issue

Mistry narrated to the court what he meant when he said in his petition that he had been overshadowed by Ratan Tata. Retirement was necessary for a reason, believed Mistry. Ratan Tata and Noshir Soonawala, two years elder to Tata retired as vice chairman of Tata Sons in 2010, had hung up their boots but were not letting go, he said. They wanted to vet almost everything, approached Tata Group executives, vendors and bankers directly, going over Mistry's head, and even got involved with the nitty-gritty of Mistry's decisions.

In the initial period of his chairmanship, the Trusts asked Mistry questions politely and his responses were forthcoming. Over time, however, Mistry found that the trouble with sharing this information, particularly with Ratan Tata and Soonawala, was that Mistry got 'unsolicited' advice from them. 'RNT and Soonawala dug their heels in and created an environment of ambiguity [over who was in charge], refus[ed] to let go, and [created] a tyrannical breakdown of the rule of law and its replacement with the rule of men,' Mistry said.

After a certain age, a person becomes 'incapable of serving the institution', Mistry pressed the court, attributing the irritability of Tata and Soonawala to their age. Mistry pointedly said that advanced age compromises faculties and judgement. 'This is not a subjective issue.'

Mistry had never been answerable to anyone in his life, let alone two men he believed were past their prime. At the SP Group, Mistry's decisions had been accepted as supreme. He had a proven track record ever since his joining at the tender age of 23. Moreover, in his years as board member of Tata Sons since 2006 he never recalled operating company decisions being discussed in such detail. He only remembered one issue being as hotly debated: on whether or not to continue product development at the newly acquired loss-making JLR. There Ratan Tata had prevailed against the general grain. In contrast, Mistry was stuck relaying information back and forth to the Trusts.

He had not found any past record of information sharing with the Trusts. There was no pre-existing format for how this could be done. So why was it being asked of him?

'Shadow directors', 'super boards', and 'puppeteers' is what Mistry called Ratan Tata and Soonawala. Mistry too would find a way to stand his ground. Mistry's team wrote long, detailed reports about every Tata company and presented these documents to the board members, Ratan Tata and Soonawala 10–15 days before Tata

Sons board meetings. They contained minuscule details but buried in those pages was also information on the major decisions taken by the Group. It was difficult to read every word that was in those reports in ten – fifteen days. On one occasion, a person close to him recalls Noshir Soonawala commenting that these granular items should not be put up to the Trusts. Reports to the Trusts should only contain critical developments. A two-pager on major fundraising or acquisitions would be adequate, he said.

On one occasion information on an acquisition slipped the attention of the Trusts as it was embedded in a detailed document. The acquisition in question was Tata Power's purchase of Welspun's renewable energy arm. The deal was worth a whopping Rs 9,000 crore. By the time it was presented to the Tata Sons board in June 2016, the transaction had been more or less completed. Mistry said that it had found mention in a note circulated among the directors on 31 May, and no one had sought any further clarifications or raised concerns. Trust-nominated directors in the board meeting of June decided that they would put on record that they had not been looped into the decision and called it a 'breach' against the founding principles of the company or articles of association. Evidently, this made Cyrus Mistry uneasy. Negotiations began between the directors as to how to record the disagreement in the minutes. Eventually, talks broke down and two Trust-nominated directors – Nitin Nohria and Vijay Singh – stepped out to speak on the phone with Ratan Tata, holding up the meeting for over an hour. After conferring with him, the directors returned, a truce was brokered, and mutually agreeable wording for the minutes was arrived at.

Mistry cited this as an example of how Trust-nominated directors were taking instructions from Ratan Tata rather than making their own decisions. Ratan Tata was 'omnipresent' at Tata Sons, accused Mistry.

Ratan Tata did not agree. He said that while an acquisition of this size indeed could not be decided upon without the Trusts being taken into confidence, his telephonic conversation with Nohria and Singh was only to de-escalate the situation. Tata said all he did in that one hour on the phone call was to help arrive at appropriate phrasing of the minutes of the meeting that would be agreeable to both sides. Eventually, instead of recording that Mistry had broken the rules, the minutes only mentioned that the decision was 'at variance' with the articles of association.

In court, Mistry countered that he had, as per the rules, put up the decision of Tata Power to the board for voting. It was nowhere specified that prior clearance of the Tata Trusts was required for this. The directors in turn objected that there would be little reason to bring to vote a fait accompli as the purchase had almost gone through.

Mistry went on to narrate how Soonawala then hijacked the structuring of the deal. Soonawala asked to meet directly with the team at JM Financial that was working on how to arrange funds for the purchase of Welspun and what subsidiaries to route the money through. He asked them for alternative structures to the one that had been earlier approved by Mistry.

In what capacity was he doing this, Mistry questioned. He was only a trustee of the Tata Trusts, and not a Tata Sons board member, so why did he ask for this information from Tata Sons? Moreover, Mistry said that whenever Soonawala would write to him, he would always for form's sake say there was no need for a response because Soonawala knew he was wrong in asking for information in the first place, said Mistry.

Mistry went on to elaborate other instances in which the Trusts tried to sway decision-making in the Tata Group. The first was an aborted application for a banking licence. The RBI had invited applications for banking licences in 2013 and most large corporate groups were applying. To Mistry's mind, a banking licence could hold the key to future growth for the Tata Group's financial services business. In February 2013, just a few months into his tenure, he sent the application that he and his team had readied to Ratan Tata for his comments.

He was first censured for giving Ratan Tata only a week to comment on it, when he knew Tata would be travelling. 'There would be little I can add at this late stage, if any, regarding the decision that has been taken,' Ratan Tata wrote to Mistry. He further added that he would pass on the document to R. Venkatramanan, a trustee of the Tata Trusts, to see whether the application had any impact on the charitable organizations. Two days later, Ratan Tata sent a follow-up mail that said: 'It seems less than fair that barring two rather cursory discussions . . . there has been no detailed discussion with the Trusts – and that it is considered okay to merely send a copy of the application on Monday afternoon (with the knowledge that I would be away from Tuesday for the week), and state that the application had to be submitted by this Friday. All this is unfair and unwarranted.'

Clearly, Ratan Tata was furious at not having been given the chance to properly vet the application. The Group nonetheless submitted the application after about a week of mail exchanges. Ratan Tata was concerned about the extent of structural change that would be required of the Tata Group in order for it to comply with RBI eligibility regulations to run a commercial bank. The application was made with 'the clear understanding that the Trusts would have the opportunity to have a full presentation on the pros and cons of the proposed bank as also the alternative options, on the basis of which the Trusts could debate and decide on their position in the matter', Ratan Tata wrote to Mistry as part of the mail exchanges.

When it came to pass, Noshir Soonawala rejected the required restructuring of the Group as it affected the international operations of some of the companies. In November 2013, the Tata Group withdrew its banking application because it preferred not to conform to the stringent capital structuring norms for the licence. Soonawala even approved the final letter that went to the RBI to withdraw the application.

But that wouldn't be an isolated instance when Mistry tripped up on the requirements of the Trusts. Mistry also encountered resistance in early 2015. Ratan Tata and Soonawala stymied a rights issue to raise funds at Tata Motors. Mistry said Ratan Tata wrote to him expressing shock at a newspaper advertisement about a Rs 7,500 crore rights issue to raise funds in Tata Motors. Tata's letter called attention to the lack of discussion with the Tata Trusts as well as with the Tata Sons board regarding the fundraising. Mistry was annoyed. The approvals had been in place for over two years. He had already told Tata about the need to infuse funds. In fact a team had visited Soonawala in December 2014 and returned with the impression that he preferred a rights issue. Soonawala denied having supported the rights issue, 'This is, to say the least, not at all fair to me. I just don't work this way.' He acknowledged the meeting but said it had been tentative, and that there was no final laid-out timeline on the plan.

Five days after Ratan Tata's mail, Mistry replied, 'I am deeply concerned if you feel in any way I have taken the board of Tata Sons, the Trusts or you personally for granted or have not upheld the highest levels of transparency.' The fundraising approvals that Mistry cited were from 2013 and were general in nature about the need to raise funds for Tata Motors, Tata Steel and a couple of other companies. The Trusts said that as the majority shareholder, they needed specifics and an opportunity to debate such moves ahead of public announcements. Mistry wrote to Ratan Tata that the entire board of Tata Sons, including the nominee directors of the Trusts, and Soonawala, were aware of the plan. He assumed then that Ratan Tata would know of it too. Eventually the rights issue was offered although its size was curtailed. A volley of emails ensued that Mistry described as placating. At the end of this, it was clear that a structure of communication with the Trusts needed to be set up.

Ratan Tata said, 'What is needed is to agree on a form of acceptable communication or dialogue with the board of Tata Sons or principal shareholders of the operating company before such an issue is cleared by the underlying operating company. If not, we will unfortunately keep facing embarrassing confrontational positions in the public arena.'

Mistry found it embarrassing to withdraw, delay or modify proposals once they had been made public. It was sure to dilute his standing before his subordinates. 'If you or any of the stakeholders connected with the Trusts believe that we are directionally wrong, feedback should be given and corrections should be taken before it goes for formal approval to the board of the operating company,' he said. With this, Mistry said an informal channel of information flow would be set up between Tata Sons and the Tata Trusts, and Mistry would know for sure that his largest shareholder was on board before making proposals.

But it was not long before even this arrangement failed. Mistry started to lay down rules of what needed to be shared with the Tata Trusts. This would culminate in the rules described in chapter 10. For this, he referred to the insider trading norms, under the SEBI guidelines, according to which information that can affect the share price of a company must not be shared with anyone who does not need to know. Flouting these rules could lead to a punishment from the regulator. These regulations mean that information cannot even be shared with members of proprietor families in general, and therefore the Trusts were surely subject to the rules as well. How then could

Tata Sons share information about transactions and structures of deals with Ratan Tata and Noshir Soonawala who were not on the Tata Sons board?

Mistry shot off the shoulder of questions being raised by shareholders of operating companies about Tata Sons and the Trusts getting information on the companies before other shareholders. After Mistry had been fired, the *Times of India* reported that some foreign investors of Tata Motors had questioned the sharing of information with Tata Sons ahead of other shareholders of Tata Motors.

Mistry also presented legal opinions to the Trusts, showing that Tata Sons would be flouting rules if it shared information with the Tata Trusts. In fact, Mistry had even wondered if certain information of operating companies could be shared with Tata Sons itself. For this, too, he invoked legal opinions.

Caught in the crossfire was Darius Khambata, former advocate general of Maharashtra state, a trustee of the Tata Trusts and a junior of Iqbal Chagla, Cyrus Mistry's father-in-law. Mistry said that, according to Khambata, sharing information with the Trusts was against the rules. But Ratan Tata held otherwise.

After the board meeting in which Mistry was fired, Khambata quit the Trusts, leading everyone to believe he had agreed with Mistry. Khambata most likely only wanted to distance himself from the strife he had seen build up.

Then, in July 2016, Mistry sought the opinion of Somasekhar Sundaresan, who had left the law firm JSA to start his own practice. He would later also become a lead lawyer in Mistry's team, after the latter's dismissal. Incidentally, during his time as a journalist in the 1990s, Sundaresan is said to have developed a close relationship with Soonawala. Sundaresan is also considered to be an expert in SEBI matters. His opinion was that it was fine for operating companies to share information with Tata Sons because, before planning fundraising exercises and strategic decisions, the role of Tata Sons was significant. More importantly, the group companies had come to depend on Tata Sons for talent, personnel and support in times of need. Therefore, as long as Tata Sons did not trade in these shares while it had such information, it was essential for companies such as Tata Motors, Tata Steel and others to remain transparent and even share future plans with Tata Sons.

However, with the Tata Trusts the equation was not quite the same. Any information passed about these listed entities through Tata Sons or directly to the Tata Trusts was against the rules, Sundaresan said. This made an impact on the trustees. On two separate occasions in emails to Bharat Vasani, group legal counsel, Soonawala and Venkatramanan had asked that information should not be shared with them because it had insider trading implications.

Despite Sundaresan's opinion that there was a bar to passing information to trustees of the Tata Trusts, he said sharing of information with 'select trustees' – Ratan Tata and Noshir Soonawala – would still be acceptable given their track record with the Tata Group. 'Their long-standing experience and expertise in the running of the Tata Group companies can mean that Tata Sons and Tata Group companies can stand to gain from such experience.' The only condition Sundaresan had imposed was that each time information was shared with them, its reason needed to be justified.

It was based on Sundaresan's advice that Mistry had formulated a governance framework for the relationship between the Trusts and Tata Sons, as detailed in chapter 10 'Mistry Goes to Court'.

But in his lawsuit, Mistry said, 'Corporate governance guidelines that I had sought to get the board of directors of Tata Sons to adopt so that the communication between the listed Tata Group companies, Tata Sons and the trustees, in particular Ratan Tata and Noshir Soonawala, [is streamlined] has been jettisoned.'

Mistry continued, 'It is imperative that trustees of the Tata Trusts through Tata Sons or otherwise do not receive, demand and/or procure any unpublished price-sensitive information unless such receipt of information is in accordance with the provisions of the insider trading regulations.'

When Mistry told the court that Soonawala may be breaching insider trading rules, Soonawala protested. 'I take strong objection to the statement that my conduct bordered on violating insider trading norms. There is no instance that has been pointed by Mr Cyrus Mistry where I have traded or derived any personal benefit from the knowledge of any such alleged information.'

He further said that, on all occasions, he had met Mistry or Tata Group executives only on their request, and only after the approval of Ratan Tata. He had sought additional information only on those occasions when he was unable to offer a conclusive opinion based on the data the team had shared with him. For his efforts to have been called interference was 'unfair and more exasperating', he said. 'If at any time I was provided information regarding the listed operating companies, it was only to seek my guidance and advice at the behest of the senior officials of such companies, given my long association with the Tata Group and, presumably, my experience in the relevant field.' He further added that he was contributing in his personal capacity every time Mistry called on him and not in his capacity as a trustee. Therefore Mistry's assertion that consulting him amounted to consulting the Trusts was incorrect, Soonawala said.

The Trusts were able to present email exchanges to show that initiation of meetings and request for advice in fact came from Mistry's end. Ratan Tata questioned Mistry's right to even raise the issue of maintaining confidentiality, since Mistry had 'parted with confidential and commercially sensitive information pertaining to Tata Sons and unabashedly filed such documents along with the present petition'.

Ultimately, several of the rules of engagement between the Trusts and Tata Sons were governed by the articles of association of Tata Sons – and it is to this that we now turn.

# 14

# Mistrust or Future Proof

Mistry could recall a number of occasions when he had been warned by Trust-nominated Tata Sons directors that he was flouting the articles of association of Tata Sons by not keeping the Trusts in the loop. In his complaint to the court, he said that this was a major tool through which the Trusts were undermining the management of Tata Sons.

In the two decades that Ratan Tata led Tata Sons as its chairman, he also headed the seven charitable trusts that owned majority stake in it. So there was never any conflict regarding disclosures or rules between the companies and the Trusts. As he handed over charge to Cyrus Mistry, it was assumed by some that perhaps the day would come when someone outside the Tata family would also control the Tata Trusts. It seemed logical then to build a framework that made Tata Sons more transparent to the Trusts, who were the majority shareholders. Ratan Tata had said as much in his last hours at Tata Sons.

When Ratan Tata retired in 2012 he said he would focus on the Trusts' activities and charitable work in a variety of fields, such as education, medicine and social welfare. The Trusts are estimated to have spent Rs 15,000 crore on charitable activities in the years Ratan Tata headed the Tata Group. Yet, the recall value of their work remained limited. Tata wanted to turn the Trusts into a strong, memorable institution. At the outset, that meant that the Trusts would also need rules and governance structures like the companies themselves. The first step in that process was to secure the hand that feeds the Trusts – the entire funding of the Trusts came by from dividends paid out by the Tata companies, largely Tata Sons.

By law, charitable trusts cannot hold shares in profitable companies. However, the Income Tax Act of India provided an exemption for the Tata Trusts and a few others because they had existed since pre-Independence and their work relied on money they received from company dividends. The Income Tax Act says that any shares held by the Trusts before 1973 may remain with the Trusts. But further acquisitions are not allowed, so much so that when bonus shares – free shares that are given to existing shareholders sometimes in lieu of dividend payments – are allotted, the Trusts have to sell them within a stipulated period of time. Experts suggest it would be better for the Trusts to guard against any possible dilution of their shareholding in Tata Sons which could happen if Tata Sons theoretically announces a rights issue or the allocation of bonus shares. The articles of association of Tata Sons allow the trusts to safeguard against such a dilution.

The founding principles of Tata Sons contained in its articles of association were first written in November 1917, though they have been amended over the years. These founding principles limited the entities that can own Tata Sons shares and those to which shares can be sold. At any time, the company cannot have more than fifty shareholders. They restrict the ability to issue new shares and require expressed board approvals for this.

Under the articles the board then has the right to propose a buyer for a shareholder looking to exit or being removed, within three months. If at the end of those three months the board cannot find a buyer, only then can the Tata Sons shares be offered for sale outside. And even then, as mentioned earlier, the buyer has to be approved by the board. Even an heir inheriting the shares of Tata Sons can be denied the right to hold shares. Anyone who has bought over 5 per cent stock in the company would be required to pay a board-defined royalty for the Tata brand name. This clause has helped in keeping the shareholding of the company in just a few hands.

The casting vote in case the board is divided on an issue rests with the chairman presiding over the meeting.

The articles of association also provide for Trust representatives to form a third of the board of Tata Sons. The board can nominate a member as MD. The MD would be contracted like any other employee in the company. The MD is subject to retirement and even termination as per the contract. In case the MD is removed from the executive role, he would automatically stand removed from the board, too. Or if the executive is removed from the board his executive role would also cease. Cyrus Mistry was titled chairman not MD, the interpretation of these rules in his case were therefore different and somewhat ambiguous.

It was this clause that made it possible to fire the executive head of the company. Mistry was functioning as a CEO in his capacity as chairman. However, at the board meeting he was fired, Mistry was only removed from being chairman, not from remaining on the board in a non-executive role. He had neither resigned from the Tata Sons board following the meeting in which he was removed from chairmanship nor was any resolution passed to remove him from the board. In fact, he was offered to retain that position as the minutes of the Tata Sons 24 October 2016 board meeting revealed. Cyrus Mistry would quit as member of the Tata Sons board at the same time as he resigned from the boards of the group operating companies in December 2016.

In 2012, when he retired, Ratan Tata's aim was that the Trusts' voice should be well heard in decision-making as a 65 per cent shareholder. This meant some changes in the articles of association of Tata Sons. The first change that was made during Mistry's tenure, towards that end was the creation of a selection committee for the next time a chairman would be needed. Under the amended clause 118 of the Tata Sons' articles of association, the selection committee for a new chairman would now comprise three nominees from the Trusts, one from the Tata Sons board, and one independent voice. Up to December 2012, the Trusts had only two members on the selection committee, the Tata Sons board could also nominate two members, and there was one independent representative.

Earlier, the articles did not clarify what would happen if the Trust representatives did not agree with the final selection of the candidate. After the amendment, the selection committee had to present a shortlist of approved candidates. The Trusts had the right to pick the final leader. The buck needed to stop somewhere, and the Trusts were a good place.

Paragraph 118 of the articles of association also said, 'The same process shall be followed for the removal of the incumbent chairman.' Mistry had contested his removal on the basis of this clause. There was no committee set up to remove him. He had turned the tables and said that the Tata Sons board was now in violation of the articles of association and therefore he could not be removed. He was told there was legal opinion to the contrary.

The second change made in 2012 to the articles of association concerned the manner in which the Trust-nominated members of the selection committee would vote. In case of dissent among members nominated by the Trusts, the majority vote of the trustees would hold as the final choice on behalf of all the Trust-nominated members. It was a way to ensure that, if at any point, the different Trusts came under separate managements, the Trusts would still vote as a block and retain their power. The majority decision of the Trusts would appear as the single voice of 65 per cent at Tata Sons. The same principle was applicable for appointing and removing any directors.

Mistry, in his court filings, said that these myriad principles were detrimental to a minority shareholder because the Trusts could in effect veto decisions. At the time Mistry joined the Trusts' directors had to form at least one-third of the board of Tata Sons and no board meeting could be held without at least two Trust-nominated directors being present. In 2014 the pre-existing Article 121 was modified whereby a majority of the directors appointed by the Trusts must support any decision taken by the company. Earlier, all the Trust-nominated directors had to agree. At the outset, Mistry himself saw no harm in this. Over time though, he came to see this clause as one that gave too much power in the hands of the Trust-nominated directors.

Tata Sons, in turn, had to vote on all major decisions in the operating companies of the Group. And so the Trust-nominated directors had a veto of sorts over those decisions too. 'I had to contend with vague assertions and allegations from Ratan Tata and Soonawala,' said Mistry.

To address the ambiguity over what constituted a major decision and therefore fell under the purview of the Tata Sons board the articles of association were amended in August 2014. A newly inserted clause listed out matters that must be presented for voting before the board. Among these matters was a five-year strategic plan for Tata Sons that the board must consider and approve with enumeration of immediate steps that would need to be taken to implement the plan.

The plan had to be accompanied with annual investment plans, total debt with relation to the value of shares of Tata Sons, or debt – equity ratio, as well as a projection of the company's cash flow over the course of the year. Should there be a change or deviation from the plan, it had to be explicitly presented to the board.

Any debt that any Group company incurs over two times its net worth must be brought up before the board. Any investment above Rs 100 crore must be voted upon. The board must approve any increase in the capital of a Group company. But the single most significant item was anything being voted on by the boards of other Tata companies – which included all of them, big and small – must find mention on the Tata Sons board.

In 2014 there was one more meaningful change made to the articles of association (in Article 124). It said that the board must vote before assigning blanket decision-making powers to another committee or appointee.

'The articles of association, by themselves, were well intentioned but it is their abuse in practice and how they have come to be interpreted at the instance of Ratan Tata and Soonawala that have come to their being instruments of oppression of Tata Sons,' Mistry said. Mistry continued on the alleged misuse of the Articles, saying, 'They (articles of association) were not meant to become the handmaiden of the trustees, more particularly Ratan Tata and Soonawala, in becoming a super board ... the articles of association became a device for superintendence and control of Tata Sons by Ratan Tata and Soonawala. The Trust-nominated directors became agents of Tata instead of being directors discharging fiduciary duties.'

The Trust-nominated directors did not agree. They were responsible for bringing to the discussion table the thinking of the Trusts, which would include the collective opinion of the leaders at the Trusts.

As professionals, each of the Trust-nominated directors said that they had put Tata Sons ahead of all else when taking decisions as board members. Nohria said the fact that he had spent more time with Cyrus Mistry than with Ratan Tata, since the time he joined the Tata Sons board demonstrated that.

Eventually, Mistry's arguments against the articles of association shifted to Article 75, which if invoked was the one under which Mistry could be forced to sell his shares in Tata Sons if more than 75 per cent of the shareholders present at any meeting demanded this. Mistry requested the court that this rule be deleted from the founding principles of the company; he feared that he might be forced to sell his stake once the scuffle was over in the courts.

But this particular clause had been part of the articles since the inception of Tata Sons. While the battle on this particular point was ongoing, Mistry moved on to proving how minority interest, including his own, in Tata Sons was being undermined.

# 15

# Made of Steel

Mistry narrated in detail to the court how he was constrained in tackling the loss-making hotspots he had identified. According to him the controls imposed by the Tata Trusts and trustees were hindering resolution of these losses and therefore harming the minority shareholders of Tata Sons and its operating companies. Tata Steel Europe was a case in point.

To support his drastic suggestions to fix Tata Steel Europe, Mistry demonstrated his success with the Indian arm of Tata Steel. Cost and time overruns at Kalinganagar, a greenfield project undertaken in 2005, had made the project seem like a money pit. But under Mistry, there had been a turnaround and the plant commenced operations in May 2016. Tata Sons conceded this success of Mistry's in one of its press statements. 'In all fairness, some major growth projects like the new steel plant at Kalinganagar will show results only in coming years.'

Yet, Mistry's solution for Tata Steel Europe, largely

comprising Corus, a company the Tata Group had acquired, was to axe it. Corus, Mistry said, was an overpriced and undesirable addition to the Tata trousseau. He proposed that this asset be sold or wound up – just like Tata Teleservices was given away to Airtel. They probably wouldn't even be able to find a buyer for the asset. Till 2016 the Tatas had invested $17 billion in Corus and a turnaround was still not in sight. Mistry asserted that Corus had only been bought to satisfy Ratan Tata's ego. Neverthless it was an internationally important acquisition, one that raised the profile of the Tata Group overseas, even if its financial performance was weak.

Tata Sons used the affirmation of Tata Steel's former head to defend the acquisition. 'I am surprised and very sad to see the speculative and biased views being fed in the media regarding the acquisition of Corus nearly a decade back in early 2007,' said B. Muthuraman, former vice chairman and managing director of Tata Steel, in a press statement. 'The Corus Group provided a natural fit for the [Tata Steel] portfolio.'

Tata Sons said that the new buyers to whom Mistry was proposing to sell the asset for one pound sterling had projected a dramatic turnaround in the very first year of their takeover. So why could Mistry not turn around the company himself? 'In our view, these subpar results cannot be blamed on the commodity cycle or economic conditions, but on his [Cyrus Mistry's] leadership,' said Tata Sons later.

Mistry's history within the steel business hardly suggested that he did not understand the industry. There were two steel-sector acquisitions the Shapoorji

Pallonji Group had dealt with – South India Viscose and Special Steel Co. One of these was acquired by the SP Group as early as in 2000, and Mistry was credited for its turnaround. The Tata side's point was that Mistry managed to turn those businesses around so why couldn't he do the same with Corus?

But back in the 2000s when Corus was acquired by the Tatas, the steel game was different. The Indian economy was growing fast in 2007, sales of automobiles were high, construction in the country was led by the need for infrastructure, and Tata Steel was enjoying the ride.

While consumer demand in India was increasing, in Europe it was tapering. In the UK, this led to stress in manufacturing, including in the automobile and steel sectors. Corus was one of the UK's largest steelmakers with major production centres in Port Talbot, Scunthrope and Teesside. It was in trouble and was up for sale. Unlike the Europeans, Tata Steel could see the opportunity that increasing steel consumption in emerging economies presented. Tata was not alone. In the aluminium space, the Aditya Birla Group similarly gunned for Novelis. So, Tata Steel put in a $10 billion bid for Corus. Of course, there was more than one bidder for Corus. A Brazilian company was also after it and forced Tata Steel to up its bid. After nine rounds of this, Corus arrived at a final winner. An editorial in *Business Standard* equated Tata Steel's situation to that of a frog in a boiler. The price edged up ever so slowly that identifying when it turned lethal became hard.

In the end, Tata paid around $2.7 billion more than its first bid. The bid was around $110 million higher than the next highest bid. The deal was sealed in April 2007. The Group paid a whopping $12.7 billion for it.

The debt burden on the company and the Group would have resulted in a change of credit rating for Tata Steel. So, the Tata Steel board created a special purpose vehicle, a company called Tata Steel Europe. It was this company that raised the funds. Tata Sons subscribed to a preferential issue of shares of Tata Steel Europe to provide around $670 million of capital. Tata Steel similarly funnelled $700 million into the company. Around $1 billion was funded through convertible bonds, which are debt to begin with but can be converted into shares later, resulting in lower interest rates. The rest was funded by loans raised through bonds and other instruments. Tata Steel and Tata Sons had dug deep to scrounge together every penny, to make this work.

Typically, an acquisition entails a major overhaul in staff, and changes in processes and culture. Tata's approach was very different. The Indian conglomerate allowed the existing CEO to run the operations for two years with no major layoffs. Mistry's petition said, 'The shares of Tata Steel Ltd on Indian exchanges came crashing down, clearly suggestive that the transaction was not in the best interests of Tata Group.' But the deal had been discussed threadbare with the Tata Steel board, said Ratan Tata. Every rebid was backed up by a fresh board resolution. The board had also agreed upon the structuring of the funds raised. Nusli Wadia, who was a board members of Tata Steel, claimed he was a dissenting voice, though. In his letter to shareholders of Tata Steel when he was being removed from directorship, he said: 'I differed strongly with the acquisition of Corus for sound reason. However, a decision was ultimately taken by consensus. I had a fundamental difference on the strategy as to whether Tata Steel would be best served in expanding in the UK. I was strongly of the view that Tata Steel should concentrate on the rapidly growing Indian market, and develop its new greenfield steel plant where the margins and returns would be far superior. My strategic view was that Tata Steel would become the No. 1 steel company of India. Unfortunately, that is not the case today.'

As a director of Tata Steel for nearly four decades, his words carried weight. Yet, as board meeting minutes showed, Wadia had missed a couple of the board meetings while discussions of the acquisition were on, but his final stamp of approval was there on the last meeting when the decision to buy Corus was ultimately taken.

Ratan Tata said, 'It is really not understood as to why I would deliberately want my company to enter into or to continue with loss-making projects since it is not even Mistry's case, nor can it ever be said that I made some personal gains at the cost of such decisions.'

Corus's run was good for the first year. In 2008, there was growth in the company as well as its profitability. Yet, danger was looming large. No one had predicted what was to come in September 2008 when the stress in the US financial sector erupted and one of the largest financial institutions, Lehman Brothers, went bankrupt. This precipitated the crisis across the board. The root cause of it turned out to be subprime lending, or loans that were given to people who would ordinarily not be able to secure a loan. The institutions lent these people money at a higher interest rate, in the hope that even if they were unable to repay the loan, the value of the assets – mostly houses – would still be more than the loan amount. The banks then bundled these loans as more precious than others since the interest rates were so high and sold groups of them or derivatives to each other as mortgage-backed securities. When repayment failed, this entire model collapsed, bringing down with it global prices of housing and real estate. Construction activity that relies heavily on steel was gravely affected. Construction stopped, auto sales also suffered a setback, and of course planned capacity additions by firms were put off.

The price of steel crashed nearly 50 per cent while costs increased. Tata Steel had to stop production, or mothball, its plant at Teesside. But pension obligations of Tata Steel Europe were ballooning apace and needed resolution. By 2009, while synergies between Tata Steel India and Europe from overlapping staff, work, sourcing and some other aspects reduced costs by $256 million, the company needed to let go of nearly 3,500 people, largely in the UK and the Netherlands under a special programme it called 'Fit for Future' aimed at retaining competitiveness of the acquisition in the years to come. With a projection of $450 million savings from synergies over the subsequent year, and a plan to sell the mothballed unit, there was hope for Corus yet. Finally, parts of the halted unit were sold in 2011. Still, the sale did not help turn Corus around.

It was at this point that Tata Steel fell into Mistry's lap. At the time he was fired, Mistry was in negotiations to sell the bleeding asset to the German steel company

Thyssenkrupp. Mistry said: 'Even after a decade of trying to make the Corus acquisition work, its financial condition did not show any improvement. Continuing losses in the operations of Tata Steel Europe impacts the ability of Tata Steel to pay dividend to Tata Sons, which in turn impacts the ability of Tata Sons to pay dividend to its shareholders.'

Referring to a March 2016 press statement of the company, Mistry said that Tata Steel had written off Rs 16,500 crore over five years. He further added, 'We confronted so many issues that rendered the UK operations structurally uncompetitive. Ratan Tata was completely against the decision to restructure the Tata Steel UK operations; and irrespective of its financial performance, wanted to continue with its operation, thus jeopardising the merger talks with Thyssen.'

To top it off, while Mistry was negotiating with the UK government to curb pension programmes, Ratan Tata's friend, the late Lord Kumar Bhattacharyya[1], spoke in public about how Tata Steel was there to stay and would generate jobs in the UK's steel sector in the years to come. Did he know better than Mistry himself? In his speech to the House of Lords, Bhattacharyya seemed to suggest that he was instrumental in Tata's takeover of Corus and very nearly accused Mistry and his management of running the company into the ground. It sounded like a public threat to Mistry's stance.

Mistry said outsiders, not even board members, were scuttling negotiations and acting on behalf of the Tata Group. The only reason Bhattacharyya's words had weight was because of his historical connect with Ratan Tata.

'The outsider-friends of Ratan Tata, who failed to coerce me into committing to unconditionally staying in UK, were now making such commitments quoting proximity to Ratan Tata,' said Mistry. Nusli Wadia said Ratan Tata was being heroic by saving UK jobs at the cost of Tata Steel shareholders. 'It is ironic that the founder Jamsetji Tata started Tata Steel to fight British steel and now Ratan Tata is trying to save British steel (Corus/Tata Steel Europe) by deploying huge resources at the cost of Tata Steel India.' After Mistry's departure, Tata Steel entered into a 50:50 joint venture with Thyssen and arrived at a resolution to discontinue the pension fund that had been bleeding the company dry.

The financial performance of Tata Steel's European arm is now much better. In the financial year that ended in March 2018, while Tata Steel Europe's revenue was less than a quarter of that in March 2016, the operating loss turned to profit. In the financial year ended 2018 the operating profit of Tata Steel Europe stood at Rs 1,154 crore compared with an operating loss of Rs 7,621 crore two years ago. But back when Mistry was in charge, Tata insiders did not understand his hasty attempt to sell the asset and were worried that Mistry had lined up more such sales. Tata Power, for instance, had the problematic Mundra plant on its hands, and to keep it afloat, Mistry was possibly looking at selling the historic land parcels the company held, in a way giving away the family jewels. Whether or not this was true, there was an endemic lack of trust between the management and the largest shareholder.

# 16

# Nano Car Mega Spar

Initially when people were still guessing what had gone wrong between Mistry and Tata, they speculated that Mistry wanted to axe the Nano project and Ratan Tata did not, which caused the feud. Both Tata and Mistry were looking at the venture in Tata Motors closely after the sudden demise of Karl Slym, the chief executive, in January 2014. Mistry became de facto chief executive of the company and remained in that position for two years. In his filings to the court he said that he was forced to be in this position because three candidates that he proposed for the job had been rejected, until Guenter Butschek was appointed chief executive and managing director in February 2016. As mentioned earlier, during his tenure as chairman, Mistry relied on Ratan Tata, especially on matters of design and strategy. Mistry also preferred staff at Tata Motors to directly interact with Ratan Tata and draw on his experience. This company had been Ratan Tata's baby and Mistry recognized that. After

Butschek joined, a detailed analysis of the Tata Nano's performance was presented to Ratan Tata. The numbers painted a bleak picture. It was only after his dismissal that Mistry publicly expressed that he thought this was the loss-making project that undermined the entire Indian operation. Mistry set out to prove to the court that this was another case of Ratan Tata overshadowing executive decisions. The Nano project caused Tata Motors a loss of Rs 6,400 crore over its life, but when it came to making a hard decision to stop production, Mistry said Ratan Tata held it up.

From the very outset, Ratan Tata had been emotionally invested in the project. 'My first doodle was to rebuild a car around a scooter, so that those using a scooter could be safer if it fell. Could there be a four-wheel vehicle made of scooter parts? Nobody took the idea seriously, nobody responded. So, Tata Motors had to do it alone,' said Tata.[1]

It had taken almost five years to conceptualize and make the car for the Indian masses. Keeping in mind affordability, the Rs 1 lakh car was created and launched in 2008 at an automotive exhibition with much fanfare. 'Cute' was the most frequent and apt description for the Tata Nano. For Ratan Tata it was a dream project. Even before the car came to the market, merchandise around it sold like hot cakes. Nano T-shirts and toys found their way into people's homes.

But the car was not meant to be. First, there was a huge setback in production as the factory planned in West Bengal became embroiled in local politics. The farmers of Singur, the region in West Bengal where the factory was to be built, took up arms against the project in what came to be seen as an 'evil corporate' versus 'local farmers' dispute. Eventually, Tata Motors had to relocate the manufacturing of the car to Sadanand, Gujarat, and the project was set back by nearly a year.

By that time, enthusiasm had started to wane as the Nano went from being seen as an 'affordable car' to a 'cheap car'. In Mumbai, Tata's home city, at one point, people wondered if the Nano would also be banned in the city centre, as autorickshaws had been because of noise and air pollution, and traffic congestion. Nonetheless, several chauffeurs and lower-middle-class families still dreamt of owning the car.

Then by around 2011, petrol prices had risen by so much that the viability of fuelling the car for a low-income household seemed questionable. By 2012, there were even a couple of reports of engine fires. These, combined with higher on-road costs and the tag of the cheapest car had done the Nano in. Demand was drying up, while production cost was rising.

Mistry said, '[The] Nano project is a severely loss-making project, with serious investments in land and machinery being tied down in it, causing a heavy drain on the Tata Group's financial resources. This project has consistently lost money with losses peaking at Rs 1,000 crore.

'Tata Motors, a once-profitable company, slipped into losses on account of the Nano project leaving no option for Tata Motors but to skip dividends which in years prior to the Nano project gave handsome returns to its shareholders.

'Emotional reasons involving Ratan Tata alone have prevented him from taking the crucial decision to shut down the project.'

Cyrus Mistry accused Tata of doing this for fame and adulation and to boast about giving the people a record-breaking car at the lowest possible price, but the sale of each unit was hurting Tata Motors. The Nano's cost-effective pricing was dependent on the large volumes it was anticipated to generate. It dragged down the overall performance of the company and cannibalized the profit generated by its foreign arms and commercial vehicle sales.

~

If Tata Motors had its failures, it also had a romantic turnaround to its credit. The company acquired Jaguar and Land Rover, luxury passenger car brands, from the nearly bankrupt Ford. The story began when, in 1998, under Ratan Tata, Tata Motors introduced the completely indigenously made passenger car, the Indica. The car initially failed to take off. Reports suggest that Tata had tried to sell the Indica along with the passenger vehicles unit of Tata Motors in 1999 to Ford. Having found the US car maker condescending, Tata resolved to turn things around. The Indica was resurrected and became among the top three cars in India over the next five years. As the Indica soared, Ford fell on hard times, and Tata mopped up JLR in mid-2008.

The timing of the Jaguar buy could not have been worse. Soon after Tata Motors had forked out $2.7 billion for it, the global economic crisis hit the automotive industry and Tata Motors. Commercial vehicle sales, that had been Tata Motors' very profitable mainstay, began to dry up. The time would have been ripe for Ratan Tata to put his hands up and walk away from JLR, but he held on. For nearly four years, he heard Tata Motors' dealers' complaints about JLR. He did road trips around the globe, meeting them, collecting feedback on what changes would make them better. He assuaged investor sentiment all the way up to 2012, when JLR made a complete turnaround to profitability. He then left the company under the care of the newly appointed Mistry.

~

Mistry also accused Ratan Tata of various conflicts of interest. He said Ratan Tata pushed Tata Motors towards a bulk deal for selling the Nano to the cab hailing company Ola, to keep the project alive. At the time, Tata Motors was already engaged in a similar conversation with Ola's foreign competitor, Uber. The deal with Uber was for a much larger number of cars. In fact, Madhu Kannan had even opened discussions about the Tata Group picking a stake in Uber globally, in exchange for the deal.

Ratan Tata in his personal capacity had already invested in Ola. Mistry ascribed this as the reason for Tata scuttling the Uber deal. 'Ratan Tata pushed for increasing production of Nano cars by continually pestering for a higher market share and also suggesting that the company must chase large orders for taxi ventures with Ola instead of Uber (with whom the Tata Group was pursuing an engagement). Ola was a company in which Ratan Tata had made an investment in his personal capacity,' he said.

Ratan Tata, in contrast to Mistry's version of events had favoured the Tata Group buying stake in Uber. Investment in such a company would be interesting to explore from a technology and service delivery perspective, Tata had told Mistry in an email dated 28 May 2015.

Ratan Tata now defended himself, saying, 'I brought to the management of Tata Motors an offer to enter into a bulk supply contract with cab service company Ola for 1,50,000 cars each year. This offer was not pursued by the management of Tata Motors. It is unfortunate that my concern for Tata Motors would be coloured with a taint of ulterior motives on my part.'

Mistry, also connected Ratan Tata's push for the car's sales with another personal investment – a technology-based small automotive company called Jayem Auto. Mistry said Tata insisted on keeping the Nano in production for the benefit of Jayem. Ratan Tata had thought if the petrol version was not successful, the Nano was lightweight enough and suited for alternative power such as electric. Jayem could try fitting battery and alternative fuel engines in the Nano. For this, Jayem would need Nano gliders, or the shells of the cars without the engines.

When Ratan Tata made the investment in Jayem Auto in February 2016, he sent Mistry an email disclosing the investment to Tata Sons, which soon degenerated into another acrimonious personal exchange. Mistry said he would share the disclosure with the Tata Motors board. To that, Ratan Tata replied that since his retirement agreement was with Tata Sons and not Tata Motors, he was not bound to disclose the investment to Tata Motors. Tata also emphasized that his investment was not in conflict with his involvement with the Tata Group.

Curiously Mistry himself saw value in the technology Jayem Auto had to offer. As head of Tata Motors he had formed a joint venture with Jayem in July 2016. Jayem was meant to experiment and create modified versions of other Tata Motors models with alternative fuel and technologies.

But Mistry accused Ratan Tata of conflict of interest and using the knowledge of the joint venture between Tata Motors and Jayem to his advantage. He said: 'It is clear from the correspondence available with me that Ratan Tata was privy to the dealings of Tata Motors with Jayem even while making an investment in Jayem.'

~

Tata Motors was also a means for Mistry to demonstrate how Ratan Tata was interacting directly with the management, bypassing him without any executive authority.

Ratan Tata had flagged problems with Tata Motors as early as 2013. 'It is my view that we are in crisis situation in Tata Motors and it is not caused by our product alone, but more something that has happened to our network relationship.' Over the years as the discourse around Nano's losses intensified, Ratan Tata had flagged to Mistry that Tata Motors woes extended beyond one failing model. In March 2015, Ratan Tata wrote that among the staff of Tata Motors, 'There is a huge comfort zone which needs to be challenged.' And also that 'the organization does not seem to have responded to your [Cyrus Mistry's] interventions.'

On 8 January 2014, Tata wrote to Karl Slym, managing director of Tata Motors, asking him if the company was doing all it could to offer the Indica to taxi owners. Mistry came to know of Tata's communication with Slym in the weeks after the demise of Slym. 'It was only when Ratan Tata learnt that the late Mr Karl Slym had expired on 26 January 2014, that he addressed an email dated 29 January 2014 to me on the same lines,' Mistry said to the court.

Interestingly, it was Mistry himself who invited Ratan Tata to join him on auto jaunts. From the Geneva Auto Car Show to the Shanghai Motor Show to relationship building with the Saudi Prince, Mistry wrote to Tata asking him to join, if possible.

Mistry said that in an effort to shore up sales the company was fostering losses elsewhere. He wrote to Ratan Tata that aggressive selling by lending money to buyers and push car sales had led to vehicle loan write-offs worth Rs 2,900 crore in the vehicle financing arm of Tata Motors.

But Ratan Tata was right that the losses in Tata Motors, though compounded by the Nano, were caused by a host of factors, a big one being the lack of new models. The factory, which was built to make Nano and was idle for lack of demand, could just as well have been allocated to make other models. It was only towards the end of Mistry's stint that newer car models were even announced.

In March 2016, with uptake of the Tata Tiago and other new models, the losses were turning around. The standalone revenue for the year stood at Rs 42,370 crore with a small net profit of Rs 234 crore. The loss in the previous year was Rs 4,740 crore. Of course this was not a figure that caught the public eye, because when consolidated with the Jaguar numbers, Tata Motors results always looked profitable. In the years after Mistry's exit, the performance of JLR began to flag, but the new Tata Motors entrants in the Indian market helped offset this.

Did Ratan Tata ever object to shutting down the Nano project? Ratan Tata pointed out that Mistry had in fact submitted proof that Tata had never refused the shutdown of the Nano. In September 2016, Butschek spent two hours with an unwell Ratan Tata, presenting the state of Tata Motors. A message Butschek wrote to Cyrus Mistry when he was done, read: 'Without reading between the lines, he was obviously in line with our assumptions and conclusions . . . Note: he did not address the gliders although we talked about "stop Nano" (no objections after I shared volume and contribution).'

Later, in an interview, Butschek said the firing of Cyrus Mistry had made him feel insecure and he wondered if he was going to be the next casualty. He was not. He continues as chief of Tata Motors. Nano production stopped in 2018 and the facilities have been redirected to other models.

# 17

# Up in the Air

Cyrus Mistry's father Pallonji had once flirted with an aviation venture that didn't work out. As chairman of Tata, Cyrus Mistry would be deeply involved in the sector – something he wasn't happy about.

The Tata Group had several small aviation-related businesses. At the time Cyrus Mistry took over as chairman, the Tata Group was already involved in a failing joint venture with AugustaWestland to assemble helicopters for the Indian and Asia-Pacific market. A designated facility in Hyderabad was to start assembly in 2011, but was caught amidst corruption charges pertaining to an Indian defence contract.

Then there was the relatively small corporate jet business, TajAir, and other small chartered plane service companies: B-Jets, Piaggio Aero and BAHC5.

The bigger of the Tata Group's aviation businesses were their two commercial airline ventures which were started during Mistry's tenure: AirAsia India, a budget airline formed in a joint venture with the Malaysia-based AirAsia, and Vistara, a full-service airline, also a joint venture, with Singapore Airlines.

Even though these were started during Mistry's helmsmanship, in court Mistry said he was saddled with these aviation ventures, all of which were rotten apples. He said, 'Every decision in this sector has inflicted serious damage to the Tata Group . . . these include decisions relating to TajAir, B-Jets, Piaggio Aero, BAHC5, and more recently the adventure into AirAsia India and Vistara.' Mistry said that the aviation joint ventures had been imposed on him as a done deal and he had had no say in the matter.

TajAir under IHCL operates a charter flight service under the Taj brand, but is used more as the Group's corporate jets. When Mistry became chairman, he told the court he was looking at an unaccounted $73 million liability which he needed to clear up. In an e-mail to Ratan Tata, Mistry said that he had been unable to convince TCS and JLR the group's cash rich companies from taking a stake in the company plane. In May 2015, in an e-mail to Ratan Tata, Mistry explained the chain of events.

In March 2008, the Tata Group, thorough IHCL invested in BJets, a company started by a non-resident Indian to enter the Indian chartered plane market. IHCL took 45 per cent stake in this company. Typically if a company holds less than 50 per cent in a subsidiary, its financials are not consolidated with the parent company. In this case the operations of BJets would not be included in IHCL's financial statements. This company bought a long-range aircraft to be used by the Tata Group as needed and otherwise to be deployed commercially. The deal to buyout the long-range aircraft needed to be completed faster than BJets could finance it, so a special purpose vehicle BAHC5 was created to house the plane. To complete the transaction Tata Global Beverages provided $56 million short-term financing to be repaid by BJets. However, a falling out with the partner in BJets led to the Tata Group taking over BAHC5. Once again, closure needed to come fast, so the seized entity was placed under another subsidiary in which IHCL held 46 per cent. The loan from Tata Global remained unpaid. In 2011, the partner in this arm of IHCL exit and the subsidiary became fully-owned by the Tata Group, and now BAHC5 and the loan from Tata Global Beverages became a liability that needed to be accounted for in IHCL's financial statements. Since no interest had been serviced on the loan and depreciation of the plane's value had not been factored, IHCL was staring at a hole of $73 million, which was flagged in a financial audit.

At the same time, the loan had come with a guarantee that neither IHCL nor Tata Global Beverages shareholders or financial results would be affected by the chartered flight service, so Tata Sons needed to take the hit. Mistry was proposing equity infusion from Tata Sons of Rs 200 crore into the plane and pay off the loan. This could of course affect Tata Sons cash flow and therefore dividend payout.

Then there was, Piaggio Aero was the maker of a plane called Avanti in which the Tata Group took a stake in 2008. The plane, meant primarily for charter carriers, saw tepid sales. In 2014, Abu Dhabi-based Mubadala Aerospace bought out all other shareholders including Tata. Tatas had to write off £116 million ($150 million).

Of all the Tata Group's aviation ventures, it was AirAsia that had given Cyrus Mistry the most sleepless nights, and was central in Mistry's court arguments on Ratan Tata's alleged insistence to take up aviation ventures. AirAsia India was a partnership agreed upon in one of the last Tata Sons board meetings that Ratan Tata chaired in 2012. But why was Ratan Tata so keen to enter the aviation sector?

Like many of the Tata businesses, aviation was started by J.R.D. Tata. It had always aroused curiosity because it involved spending so much effort for so little profit. This, however, was more of a passion for JRD, one that Ratan Tata shared with him in later years.

France born-JRD was India's first licensed pilot. In 1932, he flew the country's first commercial flight carrying mail from Karachi to Bombay. Karachi had an aerodrome and Mumbai a mud path between hutments for a landing strip. The enthusiasm of young JRD made a reluctant Dorab Tata, the sitting chairman of the Tata Group, shell out Rs 2,00,000 to start Tata Airlines. Initially, the operation, that consisted solely of carrying mail, barely broke even, but after Britain started the Empire Mail Service programme in which companies were paid additionally for carrying airmail in all parts of the British empire including India, Tata Airlines' revenue catapulted to more than ten times. The airline ploughed the funds back to turn the company into a passenger service.

In 1946, the Tata Group had already made the company public and had named it Air India. It handled a third of the country's air traffic.

In 1947, post-Indian Independence and Partition, JRD requested the government's permission to form an international Indian airline – Air India International. It was very successful. Passengers flew Air India over European and American peers, such as KLM and Pan Am. That Air India planes carried more foreign travellers than Indians was seen as a testament to its success.

The Tata Group lost control of its aviation business in two phases. The first was a forced nationalization of the airline in 1953. The government initially acquired 49 per cent with a right to take 2 per cent more. Slowly the government took the shares over fully. Yet, JRD remained chairman of the company.

The second and final blow came in 1978 when the government suddenly and surreptitiously removed JRD. The organization protested. JRD did get reinstated in the 1980s, but it was never quite the same. Later, in 1986, Ratan Tata was invited to chair Air India but he did not accept.

In the history of the Tatas, this was an unhappy memory. For Ratan Tata, returning to aviation was a cherished goal. When talk of privatization of Air India came up in 2000, Tata was one of the two potential winning bidders. However, the privatization process did not get completed. Tata had also explored the possibility of a partnership with Singapore Airlines to set up a carrier earlier, in 1994, soon after he became chairman. Ratan Tata at one point even said that his attempts at re-entering the aviation sector were foiled by corruption in awarding licences.

In the meantime several airlines had come and gone, such as Vijay Mallya's Kingfisher and the Sahara Group's airline by the same name. Wadia's GoAir and SpiceJet also struggled with high debt and inadequate revenue.

In 2012, norms were eased for foreign investment in aviation. This had come almost too late for Ratan Tata. Even though this was a business Ratan Tata had long hoped to bring back into the Tata fold, he was all set to retire that year. Ratan Tata grabbed the opportunity with both hands. Malaysia's AirAsia was looking to enter the Indian market. Partnering with the Tata Group and the Malaysian airline was the Delhi-based industrialist Arun Bhatia, who had a venture making precision instruments for the aviation sector. On 28 March 2012, Tata Sons and Arun Bhatia's Telestra Tradeplace formed the joint venture and called it AirAsia India. On 4 April, the finance ministry cleared Malaysian AirAsia's entry into the country after which the Malaysian partner bought a stake in AirAsia India. By 18 April, all three partners were set to start work. The deal went through at a fast pace and in less than a year the first plane was off the ground. The Tata Group agreed it would follow AirAsia Malaysia's lead in engaging management in AirAsia India.

The AirAsia deal paved the way for other airlines to come to India. Among them was Singapore Airlines, that had been eyeing the Indian market for a while. That is how Vistara, a joint venture between the Tata Group and Singapore Airlines, came about in November 2013.

AirAsia got off to a rocky start from the word go. Mistry shared with the court several emails of Bharat Vasani, group general counsel and AirAsia board member, to show that signs of mismanagement at AirAsia had been present from the beginning. Among other things, Vasani had raised concerns about related-party transactions because AirAsia India was giving contracts to AirAsia Malaysia and its sister concerns. Vasani questioned the pricing of these contracts. In a later email, Vasani objected to an agreement to lease a plane from AirAsia Malaysia, which had not been appropriately vetted. Finally, in November 2015, Bharat Vasani quit the board of AirAsia citing regulatory infractions that he could not condone.

In May 2015, AirAsia India needed more funds to operate. It made a capital call on its shareholders. Arun Bhatia did not want to subscribe to the issue, so the Tata Group's stake in the business went up. Hereafter, AirAsia Malaysia held 49 per cent in AirAsia India, Bhatia's stake reduced to 11 per cent and Tata became a 40 per cent shareholder. Ratan Tata wrote in an email to Vasani, 'The dilution of Mr Bhatia's holding to 11 per cent will, in my view, be a good development. It resolves several issues and, I believe, will make the board discussions less onerous.'

In March 2016, Arun Bhatia wanted to exit the venture. Acquiring his shares would make the Tata Group a 51 per cent shareholder. But the financial accounting of the AirAsia India investment would affect the results of Tata Sons. People involved said Mistry was reluctant for Tata to buy more than 49 per cent. AirAsia Malaysia could not increase its stake because it was bound by the foreign investment norms of India. This left 2 per cent which needed to be sold to another investor.

It was thus decided that four directors in the company would buy 0.5 per cent each. S. Ramadorai, chairman of AirAsia, former chief of TCS, bought 0.5 per cent. However, two other directors reneged. In the end director and former executive assistant to Ratan Tata, R. Venkatramanan, bought the remaining 1.5 per cent in AirAsia India, financed by his mentor.

~

After Cyrus Mistry was sacked, AirAsia found itself in his line of fire. Mistry said that the initial investment in the business had been made due to emotional reasons, not commercial ones. The Tata Group had released more funds to buy out Bhatia and even more to give to the venture after Mistry's departure. He added that continuing the business was not a rational decision.

Mistry would repeatedly say that he was saddled with an aviation sector investment, which in the beginning he did not fully understand. He had to deal with two separate partnerships. When Mistry began to understand the aviation business, he had made his displeasure on these deals known, he said explaining to the court that his original agreement to enter these partnerships was an uninformed decision.

If the tension between the Tata Group and AirAsia wasn't enough, in 2016 a serious fraud at AirAsia India would be confirmed by a Deloitte forensic audit report

– this was on Cyrus Mistry's mind when he went into the fated board meeting on 24 October 2016. It was still on his mind after being fired! As briefly mentioned in 'The Wish List', Mistry had accused R. Venkatramanan of trying to throw a lid over the fraud. Venkat, as he is often referred to, was still seen as someone close to Tata.

Ratan Tata felt anguished by the allegations flying around. When it came to decision-making, 'Mr Cyrus Mistry not only presided at several such meetings as the executive chairman [of Tata Sons] but also actively participated in these meetings of the Board of Directors of Tata Sons where it was unanimously resolved to set up Vistara, the joint venture with Singapore Airlines'. Tata Sons pointed out that there had been never an instance in the Board Meeting minutes where Mistry had voted against any decision.

Of all the accusations Mistry levelled against Ratan Tata, the one regarding AirAsia had the most dramatic repercussions. Mistry sent the relevant documents related to the fraud to the authorities and also accused Venkatramanan of corruption and lobbying to secure licences for AirAsia. The Central Bureau of Investigation (CBI) and enforcement directorate latched on to this information and opened an investigation. It was an unprecedented day in the history of the venerable Tata Trusts when on 1 June 2018 Venkatramanan's office was raided and documents taken away.

But Mistry contended that the AirAsia India issue was no ordinary fraud. It involved international criminal and terrorist elements. Mistry said, 'These dealings by Tata

Sons, at the behest of Ratan Tata, involved transactions with one Mr Hamid Reza Malakotipour, who has been classified as "Suspected and UN-Sanctioned Alleged Global Terrorist" by the Government of the US.' The Deloitte report had connected the dots of some of AirAsia India's payments to Malakotipour. In fact, Mistry would sensationally tell the court that through these aviation ventures, the Tata Group was sponsoring terror through hawala transactions!

When Mistry asked Bharat Vasani to initiate action based on Deloitte's findings, he was informed that Venkatramanan had asked him to wait for a few days. But before the next follow-up, Mistry was fired. So, Mistry asked the court to examine whether Venkatramanan benefited from the fraud and was sweeping it under the carpet.

Venkatramanan said, 'To attribute any involvement with a "Suspected and UN-Sanctioned Alleged Global Terrorist" is downright defamatory and scandalous.' Venkatramanan contended that he merely wanted time to confer with S. Ramadorai, the chairman of AirAsia, who was at the time away on personal leave. Ramadorai had already been in touch with the police authorities and Venkatramanan considered it better to check with Ramadorai before filing an FIR with the police.

But Mistry did not let up. He claimed that Venkatramanan was also personally involved in the formation of AirAsia India through an old email exchange. Vasani wrote a mail to Mistry saying Venkatramanan had approved the planned structure.

Mistry questioned the capacity in which Venkatramanan was advising.

Venkatramanan had been nominated on the board of AirAsia India in March 2013 itself, when the company had been formed. As a director of the company, he legitimately had access to details of the deal and was free to share advice on its structure, he said.

'Allegations regarding my alleged active role in influencing the structure of the deal, etc., are baseless and a figment of Mr Cyrus Mistry's imagination. It ought to be noted that AAIL [Air Asia India Limited] is a company governed by its board of directors and decisions taken reflect the collective wisdom of the board and are not attributable to any one person.'

Based on the fraud that was detected in the Deloitte report of September 2016, a complaint was filed with the police on 9 November 2016, a day after Ramadorai returned from his vacation. The Group moved court to recover a part of the Rs 22 crore by blocking two properties and one bank account of the former chief executive, Mrithyunjay (Mittu) Chandilya, who the report suggested was siphoning money from the company. A civil suit is still on in the Bangalore High Court for the full recovery of Rs 24.32 crore since June 2017.

Deloitte followed up its report with a review in May 2017 and cleared Venkatramanan of any involvement in the transaction. The chartered accountancy firm issued a letter saying that while it found a fraud in AirAsia India, it had found no link to Venkatramanan. The CBI case on Venkatramanan continues, but no irregularities have been found out yet.

Vistara on the other hand remains operationally strong with the highest capacity utilization among peers. Its losses in the financial year ended March 2018 narrowed after revenue grew by 50 per cent. The airline has ordered fifty-six new aircraft, which it expects in 2019.

# 18

# Call Drop

Of all the businesses Cyrus Mistry inherited, Tata Teleservices, the Group's telecom arm, turned out to be the most difficult to handle. It cost Tata Sons over Rs 35,000 crore when it was cauterized and practically gifted away to Bharti Airtel in 2017. Mistry called it a $5 billion write-off which, in hindsight, seems like a generous estimate.

Tata Teleservices partnered with NTT Docomo, Japan's number one telecom operator in 2008. Docomo invested in Tata Teleservices for 26 per cent stake. The brand under which their mobile services were sold was called Tata Docomo. Things went sour pretty quickly.

The problem at Tata Teleservices was not that Mistry couldn't perform, it was the headlines that the company was grabbing during a vicious court battle with NTT Docomo.

The negative publicity was dragging the Tata brand down because of the standoff with NTT Docomo. The discord became Mistry's fault. Most people believed, perhaps without reason, that it was his mishandling of the partner that led to the fall out.

At the time Mistry was sacked the tussle between NTT Docomo and Tata was bubbling like a live volcano. It was both public and in the court. In all televised interviews where Harish Salve and Abhishek Singhvi defended Ratan Tata's dismissal of Mistry, Docomo was mentioned as the final trigger. Of course, they were quick to emphasize this was only one among several reasons.

~

The Tata Group's tryst with telecom had been troublesome from the very beginning.

The Group started with telecom services in the late 1990s, with two companies. One had a licence for fixed-line services, and the other for mobile services. The mobile services company was a co-investment with the Aditya Birla Group and US telecom major AT&T in a company colloquially referred to as Batata (which means potato in Marathi). Batata later morphed into Idea Cellular.

The fixed line business, Tata Teleservices, was running into trouble. The company was not able to procure the permissions to lay cables to connect landlines at the speed and cost it had expected. This was a universal problem, not just limited to Tata. Around 2003, the government allowed the use of code division multiple access (CDMA), a mobile technology for providing short distance coverage to complete landline services where wires could not reach. Struggling with market conditions, the company

could well have wound up in 2002. Fortunately for Tata
Teleservices the policy change at the time allowed the
company to offer mobile services on CDMA technology.
Tata Teleservices, which was already offering landline
services using CDMA technology, was converted to a
mobile operator. This gave a new lease of life to Tata
Teleservices, but also made it a competitor for Tata's other
mobile-service venture, Batata. In Batata first, AT&T exit,
selling its stake to Tata and Birla equally. Eventually, the
Tata Group sold its stake in Batata in 2006, leaving Idea
Cellular, a mobile operator using GSM (Global System
for Mobile) technology, with the Birla Group. After 2006,
the Tata and Birla Groups focused on building their own
telecom businesses. But, it soon became clear that Tata
Teleservices had chosen the wrong technology. By 2008
globally the ecosystem had shifted to GSM. CDMA
handsets were not attractive and the technology was
only drawing low-end customers who could not generate
enough sales to make the company profitable.

In spite of the losses, the Tata Group had honoured
all commitments made to its vendor partners, service
providers as well as handset makers while its competitors
were defaulting. As a result, the brand value of Tata
Teleservices among partners continued to rise, but only
because of regular repayment of liabilities. The liability,
as Mistry pointed out, invariably fell on Tata Sons.

In 2006, the government permitted both technologies
– CDMA, which Tata had deployed, and GSM, which
the others were using. Tata's mobile company applied for
permission to provide GSM services. Tata Teleservices

received its first round of airwaves for its GSM venture in 2008.

Adopting a different technology meant setting up an entirely new network. This was expensive. It needed immense capital expenditure and some serious rebranding. For this, Tata partnered with NTT Docomo, which brought 3G technology to the table apart from the Rs 14,500 crore for 26 per cent stake.

Negotiations with NTT Docomo were precarious at the beginning. They were on the anvil during the global economic meltdown in 2008. Billions of dollars were being written-off on investments around the world. Many negotiations fell through during this period. The Japanese partner remained onboard only because it was the Tata Group. Even then, the deal went back and forth.

NTT Docomo offered to come into the company via a convertible bond – a financial loan instrument that turns debt into equity after a defined time period or on achieving pre-agreed business conditions. Tata Teleservices was already quite leveraged and consequently Ratan Tata insisted on an equity investment. Till the end, NTT, the parent company of Docomo, was not pleased about the investment. It agreed only after Tata offered a guarantee to cash Docomo out, in case it wanted to exit the business, in three to five years.

Therefore, the contract included a 'put option' or ability to sell stake for Docomo in three years. Tata gave a minimum guarantee to buy back the shares at half the price. Little had they imagined that the company's value would breach that floor too.

The partnership was particularly valuable for Tata and got off to a bright start with the service being launched within eight months. Tata Docomo pre-empted the policymakers by offering a per-second billing system rather than a per-minute one in mid-2009. It also offered a tariff that was half the contemporary call rate. This created a rise in its subscription base and consumption volumes, but not so much in revenue and profitability.

Ratan Tata had invested in telecom to create the next TCS. Over time he realized the sector was unsuitable for the Tata Group. He had hoped that with a partner like NTT Docomo the Group would in due course dilute its stake to a minority and allow Docomo to run the ship. That was not to be. The first time the company needed money after the alliance, Docomo was forthcoming in subscribing to a rights issue. The second time around however, Tata was alone in providing the funds. At the end of five years, Docomo's management had changed and the market conditions for Tata Teleservices had significantly worsened.

So, in April 2014, NTT asked to exit its investment. According to a NTT Docomo press statement, 'Docomo, TTSL [Tata Teleservices] and Tata Sons Limited concluded a shareholder agreement when Docomo entered into a business alliance with TTSL in March 2009 ... Docomo plans to exercise the above-mentioned right [to sell shares for half or higher value than the original $2.7 billion] in or before June 2014. Docomo expects to sell its TTSL shares in accordance with the agreement. It is uncertain how the option will be performed, however, and Docomo is not able to predict how events will unfold.'

For nearly nine months, the Japanese partner hoped to sell its shares in a deal with Vodafone India. By December 2014, it seemed clear that a deal in Tata Teleservices would be hard to come by. NTT again pressed Tata Sons to buy off its stake. By this time, the net worth of Tata Teleservices had been completely wiped out because its debt to build and maintain infrastructure was ballooning and the revenue and operating margin was not commensurate to offset costs. The Tata Group, now headed by Mistry, quoted a change in the RBI's foreign exchange policy. Tata said it could not pay the $1.3 billion for Tata Teleservices shares, because the share value had fallen and the RBI restricted a transaction involving out-bound repatriation of foreign exchange in such circumstances. As per the policy Tata could only pay 'fair value' for the shares. But the company's value as per the financial filings was below zero. NTT Docomo interpreted this as the Group's reluctance to keep its word and the RBI rule was just a fig leaf to hide behind.

The Japanese partner decided to invoke international arbitration to recover its money.

After much animosity, the two groups held a meeting in Singapore. The Tata Group offered half of the amount the Japanese investors wanted – a quarter of NTT Docomo's original investment of $2.7 billion – as permissible under the new rules regarding fair value. This again was interpreted as Cyrus Mistry's stinginess. The Japanese team believed a solution could have been chalked out had Ratan Tata been at the helm.

In the meantime Mistry had tried to course-correct at Tata Teleservices. He stopped infusing excess cash, shut loss-making operations area-wise and eventually brought operating profit up to Rs 2,500 crore from Rs 400 crore when he had taken over. This came at the cost of expansion and technology upgrades for Tata Teleservices.

In June 2016, NTT Docomo won an international arbitration award, which ruled that the Tata Group should pay up. Since India is a signatory to international arbitration rules, NTT believed that Tata could now pay irrespective of the RBI rule. To its surprise, the Tata Group challenged the enforceability of the award in the Delhi High Court, and issued a statement saying while it intended to pay NTT as per the award the Tata Group could still not do so until the RBI cleared the payment.

Mistry was constantly in contact with the Japanese team, firmly maintaining that the Tata Group intended to pay, but was strapped by regulation. At one point during this tussle the RBI recommended allowing the transaction but the finance ministry shot it down owing to its implications on other similar cases.

NTT Docomo read Tata's actions as a signal that the Group was still trying to renege on the payment.

The friction was acute. NTT Docomo filed for enforcement of the arbitration order in courts overseas, which was almost certain to be granted. Following this, the global financial daily *Financial Times* ran a story stating that assets of other Tata companies overseas ran the risk of being attached. The story listed Group assets such as European operations of Tata Steel, Tata Motors JLR and offices of TCS among others. Of course, these were companies with independent status and could not be attached to punish Tata Teleservices or Tata Sons.

The only attachable company was a small London-based subsidiary of Tata Sons, but the threat of having assets attached was enough to hurt the Tata brand.

This public litigation brought much disrepute to the Tata Group. 'Docomo debacle is a depth of dumb', declared a Bloomberg news agency headline. A *Washington Post* editorial said, 'Once again, India is in danger of sabotaging its own efforts to raise foreign investment to China-like levels.' Chief executives of many major Japanese companies, such as Honda, spoke openly of how damaging the Docomo fight was for India's image as an investment destination. These events prompted Mistry and Ratan Tata to meet the Japanese ambassador, Kenji Hiramatsu, in Mumbai to seek diplomatic intervention and reinitiate a dialogue. Political engagement in India also went to the highest levels. The Tata Group deposited Rs 8,000 crore with the Delhi High Court registrar to give comfort to Docomo that it intended to pay – a move that Vasani described as 'irrational hurry' on the part of Ratan Tata, in an email he wrote to Mistry.

With the ouster of Mistry, the optimism in the Docomo camp was evident. 'We are much more hopeful of a solution as a result of this change in guard,' a person close to Docomo had said. It took five months after Mistry's exit for the two sides to jointly present to the Delhi High Court that they agreed to settle the matter. When the RBI intervened in the matter to explain its objection to Docomo's exit at $1.3 billion, the judge decided that the RBI had no authority to oppose the arbitration order. The requisite monies were finally paid to NTT Docomo and the Japanese partner is back on good terms with the Tata Group again.

Mistry presented documents to the court to show that Ratan Tata had been looped into the legal dealings with Docomo all along. He submitted a transcript of a discussion with the law firm that was handling Tata's case against NTT Docomo to show the court that Ratan Tata had proposed suing Docomo outside India because of the damage to the Tata brand. Still, the blame for mishandling the partner fell squarely on Mistry's shoulders. Apart from the Rs 8,000 crore paid to NTT Docomo, the Tata Group paid and wrote off loans worth Rs 28,651 crore and some more to vendor partners for not completing orders.

# 19

# Siva Siva

Mistry, in his prayer to the court, had flagged certain transactions of the Tata Group in which he suspected fraud or some illegality: the Mehli Mistry matter, the Venkatramanan and AirAsia affair, and, lastly, a matter involving C. Sivasankaran, a vendor partner and shareholder in Tata Teleservices.

Mistry alleged that wrongful gains were made by Seychelles' citizen C. Sivasankaran, at the behest of Ratan Tata. In his suit Mistry said, 'dubious transactions with one Mr C. Sivasankaran, a close and deep confidant of Ratan Tata' were part of the oppressive behaviour at Tata Sons that undermined minority shareholder rights. 'Dealings with Sterling [Sivasankaran's company] and Siva have resulted in Tata Sons and other Tata Group companies such as TTSL [Tata Teleservices] incurring huge losses and/or liabilities, which are subsisting even today,' Mistry argued in court.

According to Mistry, Siva had first made a profit of

Rs 468 crore when he bought 7 per cent shares in the Tata Group's telecom venture at Rs 17 a share in 2006, while investor Temasek bought it at a rate of Rs 26 per share just ten days later. When Japan's NTT Docomo picked up a 26 per cent stake in 2008, Siva sold some shares at Rs 117 a piece taking home Rs 209 crore. Yet, when the downturn and struggle with Docomo struck Tata Teleservices, Siva, still a shareholder of the company, refused to pay his share of Rs 694 crore towards repaying NTT Docomo.

Mistry also said that one of the many benefits Siva enjoyed on account of being Ratan Tata's friend was that he was able to borrow money from Tata Capital, a Tata Group company, to pay for his shares in Tata Teleservices. Vasani wrote to Mistry that he was 'not sure how the Tata Capital board agreed to lend (to) him'.

Under Mistry's chairmanship, when trouble starting brewing between Tata Sons and Docomo, Siva asked the Tata Group to buy out his shares and refused to contribute his due as a Tata Teleservices shareholder to pay back NTT Docomo. The exchange between Mistry and Sivasankaran had degenerated just before Mistry's departure – there was even talk of legal charges. Mistry was intent on finding out whether Siva had been verbally assured an exit from Tata Teleservices without loss, and whether Tata Sons would be paying the price for it.

~

C. Sivasankaran, or Siva as he is popularly known, started his journey in Chennai in the late 1980s. He brought computers to India at a third of the prevailing domestic market price. When the telecom sector opened up in 1994, Siva was quick to jump into the fray. His first investment was to buy 10 per cent in Bharti Airtel. Siva had to exit it at a loss, selling back his share to the promoter, Sunil Mittal. He then secured mobile operating licences for Mumbai and Chennai, but sold them amid legal controversies.

Next Siva started to work on building a mobile network in Tamil Nadu. He also got licences in a few other states in eastern and northern India. During this time, he is said to have assiduously cultivated political patronage. Towards the end of 2003, he formed Aircel – a prized asset in his bouquet.

By 2004, Siva had become a consultant with the Tata Group to negotiate sweet deals on equipment for Tata Teleservices with vendors. This was the time Tata was trying to launch a CDMA service. With his vast knowledge on the products and sector and exceptional negotiation skills, Siva was a valuable resource for Tata Teleservices.

In 2004 Siva sold Aircel to Malaysia's Maxis for a whopping $880 million, in a deal that required him to stay out of telecom for five years, allowing him only a 10 per cent limit for investment in another telecom operator.

Siva then picked a small 2 per cent stake in Idea Cellular. At that time, Idea was a joint venture between Tata and the Aditya Birla Group. He bought the Idea stake from the foreign insurer, the American International Group (AIG). The transaction was completed overseas, and Tata did not seem to know about it. In fact, the quiet move strained relations between Tata and Birla. Birla believed that Siva made the move on Tata's behest, so when it came to splitting equity evenly between the groups, Birla counted Siva's shares as part of Tata's half. Ratan Tata believed both Tata and Birla should have stood evenly at 49 per cent each, notwithstanding Siva's stake. Tata ultimately decided to exit Idea in 2006. Siva helped the Tata Group get better value for its shares in Idea by securing a bid from Maxis. The Birla Group had earlier offered a lower price to buy out Tata but was now forced to match Maxis's offer. In the documents Mistry presented to the court, Siva's company was promised an unrecorded 4 per cent fee if Maxis bought Tata's stake in Idea. The Tata Group ultimately sold its shares to Birla in a transaction that ended well for them. Tata's fallout with Birla also seemed to have soured relations between Ratan Tata and Siva – though the latter still remained interested in Tata Teleservices as an investment opportunity.

In 2006, Siva bought 7 per cent stake in Tata Teleservices (at the rate of Rs 17 per share). As mentioned earlier, he reaped high returns in a very short time after Temasek bought shares at Rs 26 a piece merely days later. Such was Siva's confidence that when Mistry flagged this transaction, Siva told a TV interviewer, 'If I had not invested, the value [of Tata Teleservices] would not have gone up.'

Siva paid only Rs 100 crore from his own pocket out of the Rs 1,000 crore that he had to pay the Tata Group for his Tata Teleservices stake. The rest came from loans from, as mentioned earlier, Tata Capital and Standard Chartered Bank. The bank had loaned the money to Siva only after the Tata Group issued a guarantee that it would buy back Tata Teleservices shares, should that come to pass. However, three years later, Siva had to collateralize the loan with his own assets when the loan came up for renewal and the Tata Group revoked its guarantee.

In 2009–10, when his non-compete agreement with Aircel ended, Siva once again made a big bet on Indian telecom, buying a significant stake in the newly launched S Tel along with investment partner Bahrain Telecom (Batelco), an investment that eventually led to his bankruptcy.

Siva's bankruptcy was triggered when the telecom sector took a nosedive at the end of 2010. It affected Tata Teleservices too, but S Tel, a new licensee, was worse hit. In February 2012, the Supreme Court of India rolled back 122 telecom licences including those of S Tel. Siva, as the Indian partner responsible for permissions, was now in trouble with Batelco, which claimed $212 million from him.

Siva wanted to exit Tata Teleservices under such pressure. He asked for over Rs 2,000 crore for his shares at a time when Tata was already at loggerheads with its Japanese partner and its net worth had been completely wiped out. But Tata Teleservices had already revoked its earlier buyback guarantee.

Siva wrote a letter to Cyrus Mistry on October 3, 2013, marking a copy to Ratan Tata, formally asking that the Tata Group buy back his stake in Tata Teleservices. In continuation of this email exchange, Ratan Tata urged Mistry to meet Sivasankaran to discuss this. According to his court filings, Mistry saw this as having the 'sole purpose of attempting to influence Mistry in acceding to Siva's requests'.

Apart from the request to buy him out, Siva also owed Tata Capital money that he had borrowed to pay for the shares in the first place. When Mistry enquired about Siva's loans internally, Tata Capital told him that the write-off on loans to Siva could be as high as Rs 800 crore.

Then there was also the matter of Siva, as a shareholder, contributing for the payment to be made to NTT Docomo – something that Cyrus Mistry insisted on.

Ratan Tata told the court that Siva received a loan like anyone willing to pledge collateral – in this case shares of Tata Teleservices – and Tata Sons was not privy to this. If Tata Capital decided to take over Siva's shares and annul the loan, it would also be a business decision, one that Tata Sons would have no role to play in.

About a month before Mistry's ouster, Tata Sons mulled legal action against Siva for not contributing his share to pay off Docomo. At a board meeting held on 15 September 2016, 'Mistry apprised the board about Siva's unwillingness to contribute his proportionate share in the amount deposited in court; and accordingly obtained the approval of the board of directors to initiate legal proceedings against Siva and Sterling for recovery,' read the minutes of the meeting. It was Nitin Nohria who proposed legal action against Siva.

Four days later Mistry received a legal notice from Siva dated 15 September 2016 – the same day Tata Sons decided to take legal action against him. Siva was proposing to sue Tata Teleservices and NTT Docomo. His notice accused Tata Teleservices of oppression and mismanagement against a minority shareholder. 'The legal notice of Siva was consciously backdated so as to make it appear that any legal action by Tata Sons against Siva is only a counter-blast to Siva's legal notice on account of Siva's claims inter alia against Tata Sons,' Mistry said. He suspected information from the Tata Sons board had been leaked to Siva.

For his part, Siva was outraged at Mistry dragging him into his own battle after being fired from Tata Sons. He ventured so far as to say that Tata Teleservices would not have failed if he had been in charge. He added that he had lost Rs 3,000 crore ($462 million) on his investment in TTSL.

Ratan Tata publicly distanced himself from Siva after Mistry's exposure of the subject. He said he had little to do with how Siva's purchase of assets was funded. Tata Sons told the NCLT that there was no provable collusion among Group companies to help Siva.

With this, Cyrus Mistry's arguments to prove that Tata Sons was being mismanaged came to a close. The Tata Group thought it had adequately defended its actions and refuted Mistry's stance. The wait for the NCLT verdict seemed long. When the matter was listed in the court on 12 July 2018, there was a flutter of activity in both camps.

# 20

# The Judgement

If Mistry's retaliation to his firing and the support he garnered from independent directors of operating companies in November came as a surprise to Tata, the NCLT order left Cyrus Mistry and his team shocked. Mistry had hoped the court would be sympathetic towards his arguments on at least some counts. Instead, the final order, passed in July 2018, was disparaging and rejected Mistry's claims completely.

The judges thought the suit was motivated by personal hurt. They opined that Tata was in the clear, while Mistry was wrong to pursue court action. The order, nearly 400 pages long, said that Mistry had laid too much emphasis on having a 'free hand' in managing affairs of the Tata Group. A 'free hand' as company's management in itself was 'incongruous with corporate governance', said the order. The Indian Companies Act defines a pecking order in enterprises with the shareholders as the apex body, followed by the board of directors and to these is subservient the management. And the judges concluded that Mistry was management. He was not selected as chairman because of his shareholding in Tata Sons, but rather as a suitable candidate to run Tata Sons professionally. Mistry had not presented or produced any document that proved he was promised complete discretion to take decisions and actions at the Tata Group. So, for him to assume that he would have a 'free hand' was wrong. Mistry was an employee, and was answerable to his board and shareholders as any management would be. As such, his hiring and firing was in line with the change shareholders could effect within any company.

In order to protect the minority shareholder, the majority's viewpoint could not be overlooked, the order argued. 'Otherwise, it will become curtailment of the rights of the majority shareholders.'

Besides neither Mistry nor other minority shareholders had been wronged by Tata Sons. Mistry's oppression and mismanagement suit seemed pre-emptive. Documents he had presented did not show the majority shareholder, Tata Trusts, getting undue benefits to the detriment of any minority shareholders. The judges pointed out that Mistry was making a case for a potential infraction in the future.

Normally, oppression and mismanagement petitions will be filed in myriad situations such as allotment of shares, siphoning of funds, dilution of shareholding, insertion of new articles, depriving the rights already in existence, selling of assets, passing resolutions without putting it to the notice of the minority shareholders etc., but normally nobody will file a petition saying that since an Article is in existence in the articles of association and for now the minority having felt that it is likely to prejudice the interest of the petitioners, it has to be struck off . . . reliefs cannot be invoked just by seeing abstract arguments like this without any proof of oppression or unfairness and prejudice against the petitioners.

The bench comprised Judge B.S.V. Prakash Kumar and Technical Judge V. Nallasenapathy. Their verdict was:

🪓 On whether introducing the agenda to remove Mistry in the board meeting was legal: 'Here, personal emotions or personal egos will not have any place to attribute it as grievance under Section 241. We have not found any merit to say that inclusion of agenda item for removal would become grievance under Section 241. Henceforth, this point is decided against the petitioners.'

🪓 On barring the Trust-nominated directors from voting to remove Mistry: 'We don't find any merit in this argument saying that the Trust-nominated directors should have abstained themselves from the proposal moved by them. This issue has been decided against the petitioners and Mr Cyrus.'

This pretty much set the tone for everything else the order ruled on.

🪓 On the matter of changes in articles of association: 'Argument of the petitioners in this respect is not only far-fetching and abstract but also misconceived. We have not found any merit in the argument that . . . the articles of association [are] per se oppressive against the petitioners.'[1]

The order said that several of the articles of association Mistry was challenging, including Article 75 under which Mistry could be forced to sell his shares, had existed before the shares were bought by the Shapoorji Pallonji Group. Among those that were modified after Mistry's induction, Mistry had most vociferously argued against the one that gave veto right to the Trust-nominated directors.

The judges noted that there had been no instance in which the directors had exercised this veto right to shoot down a proposal. In fact, the directors had found a meeting ground to allow business continuity in the case of the Welspun acquisition, where they could have used the right to reject plans. While Mistry had argued that Trust-nominated directors could prevail over the chairman and the rest of the board using veto rights, the judges found no concrete examples where this was done.

The court also rejected Mistry's request to allow the SP Group to get board representation in proportion to its equity. The order said that if the court accorded the board seats in proportion of shareholding, it would achieve the same end as the articles of association, which gave the Trusts a veto. Tata Trusts would then have two-thirds representation on the board in relation to its shares and would always have majority say.

The SP Group with 18.4 per cent shares in Tata Sons have never historically had such special rights to nominate a director, the order further clarified its position.

On the matter of Corruption at AirAsia: 'We hereby dismiss this allegation against the answering respondents holding no case is made out against Mr Tata or Mr Venkat.'

For the allegations against AirAsia India and R. Venkatramanan, the judges snubbed Mistry. 'I can say that the petitioners miserably failed to at least set up a case basing on this allegation, all are abominably baseless allegations thrown at a reputed person and not knowing what consequences follow when such scurrilous allegations are not supported by any material paper.'

On the matter of meddling in company affairs at Tata Motors: 'We have not found any merit either to say it is maintainable.'

On the matter of Tata Steel: 'These petitioners as well as Mr Cyrus have come out with unfounded allegations against Mr Tata so as to settle their score for Mr Cyrus who was removed as executive chairman of the company.'

For Tata Motors and Tata Steel, the court said it was not its place to ascertain whether a business investment was correct. The court could not be sure of how Ratan Tata had felt about shutting the Nano project, but Tata had never articulated that it should not be shut down.

Even though Mistry identified Corus as a 'hotspot', he had not challenged the actual acquisition. The order said perhaps Mistry could not challenge it because he was on the board of Tata Sons when the acquisition was made. Once again, without going into the financial merits of it, even if there was a problem with Corus, Mistry failed to highlight it to the Tata Sons board. The judges said, 'We are of the view that we are not required to deal with as to whether Corus acquisition is a [good] business decision or not.'

On the matter of the Trusts seeking inside information and Ratan Tata's investment in Jayem Auto: 'We have not found any merit either to say it is maintainable or to say that there is material proving the actions of Mr Tata are prejudicial to the interest of either the company or the petitioners [Mistry's investment firms].'

The judges also concurred with the argument that Ratan Tata and Noshir Soonawala, by virtue of their long association with the Tata Group, made material contribution to business notwithstanding their age. Mistry's argument that they had acted as 'shadow groups' or were interfering was rejected. The judges pointed out that there were a number of instances when Group executives had reached out to Tata for support. 'We have also found no merit in saying that Mr Tata and Mr Soonawala giving advices and suggestions amounted to interference in administering the affairs of the company.'

The order turned the tables on the charge of insider trading and sharing of confidential information. It held that Mistry was responsible for leaking information. The order said that there was no need for Mistry to forward hoards of information to the tax department. The judge reprimanded Mistry on his move to send papers to the tax department regarding the charitable status of the Trusts.

This, along with the leaked letter to the board of directors was indicative of the untenable position Mistry was in. Mistry 'leaked the company information to media and openly came out against the board and the Trusts, which hardly augurs well for smooth functioning of the company . . . The burden lies upon Mr Cyrus to prove that it was not leaked from his side, but no such efforts has been made'.

🪓 On the matter of partisanship to Sivasankaran: Issue was decided against the petitioners.

Similar was the case with Mehli Mistry and Tata Power. The order said that Mistry's complaint of benefits accorded to Mehli did not come under any of the provisions for 'oppression and mismanagement', which the court was trying to ascertain as part of the current challenge.

🪓 On the matter of preferential treatment for Mehli Mistry: 'These allegations with respect to Mr Mehli and Tata Power are hereby dismissed against the petitioners.'

'For the reasons aforesaid, we hereby dismiss this company petition by closing applications if any remain pending. No costs.'

The case was closed.

~

The judges not only ended Mistry's bid for corrective action against Tata Sons and Ratan Tata, but also allowed Tata Sons to convert its status from a 'public limited' company to 'private' for which shares cannot be traded or offered to the public. Mistry had sought to prevent this, saying that, should this happen, it would lock his equity in Tata Sons and by implication deny him the chance to monetize it, if he so desired.

The Tata Group had responded that the company had always been private. When a change in the prevailing law restricted the size of private companies, Tata Sons was forced to become public, but continued to operate like a private entity. Now the regulations have been rolled back and Tata Sons would like to revert to its earlier position. So, Mistry would now become the billionaire locked into his fortune and even more dependent on decisions of the Tata Sons board on what he can do with it.

A portion of the judgement also praised the work of the Tata Group and Tata Trusts. This opened the order up to challenge on the grounds of bias and Mistry was prompt to seize the opportunity. He challenged the decision in the appellate court. While accepting the appeal, the National Company Law Appellate Tribunal commented on the tone of the NCLT order, but made no observation on its logic or contents.

And so the battle continues. The arguments in the appeal are ongoing.

# Epilogue

Nearly three years after Cyrus Mistry's dramatic removal as chairman of Tata Sons, business seems to have returned to normal at the Tata Group. Bombay House, the Tata Sons headquarters, was remodelled from inside while keeping the heritage stone facade intact – a metaphor for a modern conglomerate with old-world values. After nearly a year of renovations, and estimated Rs 80 crore of expenses, the building was reopened in July 2018. Near the entrance there is a small corner reserved especially for street dogs, a testament to Ratan Tata's love for dogs. The building also boasts of an 'experience centre' that tells visitors about the Tata Group's 150-year history.

In February 2017, the Tata Group appointed N. Chandrasekaran as the chairman of Tata Sons. He had been the head of TCS, considered the Tata Group's most successful company, for nearly seven years. The current chairman and his top team continue to deliberate the fate of the Group from within the walls of Bombay House.

Ratan Tata remains chairman emeritus of the Tata Group. Apart from N. Chandrasekaran, another member from the Tata Sons leadership sits on the board of most major operating Group companies. Having only one Tata Sons representative on the boards of these companies was a matter of concern, Tata Sons had said in the aftermath of Mistry's firing. Confidants suggest that Tata and Chandra meet frequently and both respect each other's views.

The Tata Group's market capitalization rose 25 per cent between March 2017 (the beginning of the first financial year since Mistry's firing) and  March 2019. Revenues of the Group hit a whopping Rs 7.2 lakh crore in March 2019, up 21 per cent since March 2017. TCS was at the head of this improvement, with its share price rising nearly 66 per cent since the beginning of Chandra's term. The first financial year after Mistry's sacking, growth at the group seemed to be stellar, with profits rising 41 per cent to Rs 46,186 crore in March 2018, and revenue to Rs 6.4 lakh crore.

Ratan Tata continues as chairman of the Tata Trusts as well but the Tata Trusts management has undergone significant change. It is no longer run by a single managing trustee but by a committee formed under the board.

Noshir Soonawala  resigned as a trustee in March 2019. His retirement came as a surprise to many even though Soonawala was eighty-four years old. A news report in the *Economic Times* said he had been considered a 'conscience keeper' at the Tata Group and at the Trusts. Before resigning he was instrumental in inducting Tata family member and brother-in-law of Cyrus Mistry, Noel Tata, to the board of the Sir Ratan Tata Trust. It is said Ratan and Noel share a much closer relation now than they did some years ago.

In February 2019, Ratan Tata's trusted lieutenant R. Venkatramanan resigned as a trustee and later from Ratan Tata's personal investment arm RNT Associates as well, in the aftermath of Mistry's complaint to the income tax department. The reason for this is not known. It was through RNT Associates that Ratan Tata made many investments, including in the cab-hailing company Ola and in the online retailer Snapdeal.

Along with Noel Tata, the philanthropist Jehangir H.C. Jehangir, chairman of the Jehangir Hospital in Pune, was also appointed as a trustee. Jehangir is also likely to represent the Parsi voice at the Tata Trusts. The apparent succession plan suggests that in the years to come, the Trusts may no longer be led by Parsis. Retired civil servant Vijay Singh and TVS Group chairman Venu Srinivasan have been appointed as vice chairmen of the Trusts.

Cyrus Mistry has taken the opportunity to become a venture capitalist. In 2018 he started a firm called Mistry Ventures LLP to invest in start-ups. The firm focuses mainly on technology and emerging business sectors, but a re-entry into real estate for Mistry is not precluded. He has not taken a position in the Shapoorji Pallonji Group, which continues to be headed by his brother.

For the moment, all the players are waiting for the result of Cyrus Mistry's legal appeal.

# Appendix

## The Plan – Presentation dated 1 June 2015

- Increase the Tata Group's market capitalization to $350 billion (Rs 22.75 lakh crore) by 2025, accompanied with portfolio holdings value $200 billion for Tata Sons (up from around $76 billion).
- Maintain cash of Rs 3,000–Rs 5,000 crore ($450–$750 million) in Tata Sons to ensure adequate liquidity for investments and contingencies at Group companies.
- Increase the dividend payout ratio, or the proportion of dividend paid from profit, to 15–25 per cent by 2025 (from 7.1 per cent in 2015).

The last goal was aimed to please the Trusts that would get more funds for their activities. It could also be interpreted as a move in which Mistry had personal motivation, since his family would get an 18 per cent slice.

Future investment for 2025 fell under four categories:
- Finance cluster – Ramp up substantially. Key steps include adding right talent, possibly infuse equity and explore consolidating auto loan arm from Jaguar Land Rover. Companies under this cluster that could

be consolidated included Tata Capital, Tata AIA, Tata AIG, Tata Asset Management.

- Consumer packaged goods – build platform and business in digital health and wellness and possibly make a major acquisition in this space directed through Tata Chemical and Tata Global Beverages. A separate Tata Health initiative was already in the process. ompanies under this cluster that could be consolidated included Titan and Trent (owner of Westside Stores).
- Global move for Tata Motors – Make a wider range of consumer and commercial vehicles and possibly acquire overseas outfits to ramp up sales.
- Real estate and infrastructure portfolio – Spend Rs 10,000 crores ($1.5 billion) to build a portfolio that would generate Rs 700–Rs 800 crore (around $115 million) rent per annum, translating into a consistent 7–10 per cent yield. This would reduce volatility seen in the current business. Companies that could be consolidated included Tata Power, Tata Realty and Infrastructure, Tata Projects, Voltas EPC, and Jamshedpur Utilities and Service Company.
- Defence and Aerospace cluster with companies that included Tata Advanced Systems, Tata Power Strategic Engineering Division, Tata Advanced Materials, TAL (heavy engineering and automation arm of Tata Motors).

Mistry hedged that the plan may change as per the performance and business environment for different verticals.

New businesses would be incubated under Tata Sons (such as online retail platforms, Tata CliQ and the big data mining company Tata IQ), and sold to the company where they fit best, once they become sizeable.

But the focus of the plan remained on the period to 2020. Goals for 2020 would include:

- Turn around hotspots
- Reduce concentration risk of depending on a few companies to generate cash and profit
- Develop a growth platform
- Selectively invest in new generation businesses
- Increase holding of Tata Sons in select Group companies

# Notes

## 1. The Suitable Boy

1. Lala, R.M. *The Creation of Wealth: The Tatas from the 19th to the 21st Century*. New Delhi: Penguin India, 2006.

## 2. The Board Meeting

1. https://nirmalyakumar.com/2017/10/21/how-cyrus-mistry-wasfi red-as-tata-chairman
2. An executive director represents the voice of the management on the board of a company.
3. https://nirmalyakumar.com/2017/10/21/how-cyrus-mistry-was-fired-as-tata-chairman

## 3. Mistry History

1. Letter sent by Pallonji Mistry in September 2003 clarifying the history of Mistry's ownership of Tata Sons to an editor at *Business World*.
2. Letters exchanged between Ratan Tata and Cyrus Mistry from 24 September 2013 to 24 October 2013.

## 5. More than Money

1. Lala, R.M. *The Creation of Wealth: The Tatas from the 19th to the 21st Century*. New Delhi: Penguin India, 2006.
2. Lala, R.M. *The Creation of Wealth: The Tatas from the 19th to the 21st Century*. New Delhi: Penguin India, 2006. As the official biographer to J.R.D. Tata and writer on the Tata Group, Lala's books are an authentic source of the Group's history. *Creation of Wealth* includes a prologue by J.R.D. Tata and epilogue by Ratan Tata which have been referenced here.
3. Lala, R.M. *The Creation of Wealth: The Tatas from the 19th to the 21st Century*. New Delhi: Penguin India, 2006.

## 6. The Chase

1. Nusli Wadia's letter to Tata Steel shareholders.

## 8. The Shareholders

1. Mistry's representation to shareholders.

## 10. Mistry Goes to Court

1. Cyrus Mistry owns one of the two firms – Cyrus Investments – that filed the lawsuit petition. In his reply to the petition, Mistry had supported the case made out by the petitioners, even though he is named as a respondent. As such statements in both the petition and Mistry's affidavit are attributable to him.
2. https://www.ft.com/content/743bf9b2-fa76-11e5-8f41-df5bda8beb40

## 15. Made of Steel

1. Lord Kumar Bhattacharyya passed away on 1 March 2019 after a brief illness.

## 16. Nano Car Mega Spar

1. Lala, R.M. *The Creation of Wealth: The Tatas from the 19th to the 21st Century*. New Delhi: Penguin India, 2006.

## 20. The Judgement

1. Judge's comments from NCLT order passed on 12 July 2018.

# References

## Books

Lala, R.M. *The Creation of Wealth: The Tatas from the 19th to the 21st Century*. New Delhi: Penguin India, 2006.

Nath, Aman. *Changing Skylines: The Shapoorji Pallonji Sesquicentennial 1865-2015*. Mumbai: Pictor Publishing, 2015.

## News Articles

Deshpande, A. 'Rs 60,000-crore Mumbai land dispute intensifies'. *The Hindu*. 4 July 2014. https://www.thehindu.com/news/cities/ mumbai/rs-60000crore-mumbai-land-dispute-intensifies/ article6178176.ece/

Deshpande, S. 'He has a very old head on young shoulders: Iqbal Chagla.' *Times of India*. 24 November 2011. https://timesofindia.indiatimes.com/business/indiabusiness/He-has-a-very-old-head-on-young-shoulders-IqbalChagla/articleshow/10851068.cms

Doshi, M. 'The Tata-Mistry Battle Is a Sideshow, the Real War Is yet to Come.' *Quint*. 7 December 2016. https://www.thequint.com/news/business/the-ratan-tata-cyrus-mistry-battle-is-a-sideshow-the-real-war-is-yet-to-come-r-venkataramanan-tata-trusts-tata-sons/

Doshi, M. 'Amit Chandra, Nitin Nohria Lead 60 Minute Play
That Brought the Curtains Down on Mistry.' *Bloomberg
Quint.* 21 December 2016. https://www.bloombergquint.com/
business/amit-chandra-nitin-nohria-heroes-of-a-60-minute-
play-that-brought-the-curtains-down-on-mistry

'Ratan Tata vs Cyrus Mistry: Why all eyes are now on
EGMs.' *Times of India.* 13 December 2016. https://
timesofindia.indiatimes.com//business/indiabusiness/Ratan-
Tata-vs-Cyrus-Mistry-Why-all-eyes-are-now-onEGMs/
articleshow/55953398.cms/

'Soonawala steps down from Tata Trusts on health grounds.' 28
March 2019. https://economictimes.indiatimes.com/news/
company/corporate-trends/soonawala-steps-down-from-
tata-trusts-on-health-grounds/articleshow/68596545.cms

'In a spot: How Supriya Sule was caught between Cyrus
Mistry and Ratan Tata, courtesy a noble cause. *ET Panache.*
https://economictimes.indiatimes.com/magazines/panache/
in-a-spot-how-supriya-sule-was-caught-between-cyrus-
mistry-and-ratan-tata-courtesy-a-noble-cause/article
show/65047517.cms

'Full Text of Cyrus Mistry Interview that Tata Group Scrapped.'
*News.* 18 October 2016. https://www.news18.com/news/
business/full- text-of-cyrus-mistry-interview-that-tata-
group-scrapped-1305311. html/

Gupta, I. 'Tata Corus – A deal from hell.' *Business Standard.*
14 April 2016. https://www.business-standard.com/
article/opinion/ indrajit-gupta-tata-corus-a-deal-from-
hell-116041400916_1.html/

John, S. 'Cyrus will go down as lame duck of Bombay House:
Mehli Mistry.' *Times of India.* 5 January 2017. https://
timesofindia.indiatimes.com/business/india-business/
cyrus-will-go-down-as-lame-duck-of-bombay-house-mehli-
mistry/articleshow/56346937.cms/

John, S. and N. Lakshman. 'Ideas differ in Tata-Birla war.' *DNA*. 9 March 2006. http://www.dnaindia.com/business/report-ideas-differ-idea-suffers-in-tata-birla-war-1017245/

Karadia, C. 'Two Air-India top men resign in protest against appointment of Air Chief Marshal P.C. Lal as chairman.' *India Today*. 28 April 2018. https://www.indiatoday.in/magazine/indiascope/story/19780228-two-air-india-top-men-resign-in-protest-against-appointment-of-air-chief-marshal-p.c.-lal-as-chairman-822903-2014-04-28/

Kumar, N. 'I Just Got Fired.' *Nirmalya Kumar Blog*. 5 November 2016. https://nirmalyakumar.com/2016/11/05/i-just-got-fired/

Kumar, N. 'How Cyrus Mistry Was Fired as Tata Chairman.' *Nirmalya Kumar Blog*. 21 October 2017. https://nirmalyakumar.com/2017/10/21/how-cyrus-mistry-was-fired-as-tata-chairman

Kurup, Rajesh. 'Cyrus Mistry makes a comeback, starts VC firm.' 24 October 2018. https://www.thehindubusinessline.com/companies/cryus-mistry-makes-a-comeback-starts-vc-firm/article25306530.ece

Kurup, R. and T. K. Thomas. 'Mehli Mistry lashes out at cousin Cyrus.' *The Hindu*. 8 January 2018. https://www.thehindubusinessline.com/companies/mehli-mistry-lashes-out-at-cousin-cyrus/article9466846.ece/

Lakshman, N. 'Tatas say bye-bye to Idea Cellular for Rs 4,406 crore'. *DNA*. 10 April 2006. http://www.dnaindia.com/business/report-tatas-say-bye-bye-to-idea-cellular-for-rs-4406-crore-1023398/

Madhavan, N. 'As a minority shareholder, I have been left in the lurch: C. Sivasankaran.' *Forbes India*. 15 December 2016. http://www.forbesindia.com/article/battle-at-bombay-house/as-a-minority-shareholder-i-have-been-left-in-the-lurch-c-sivasankaran/45109/1/

'Madras Maverick.' *Financial Express*. 20 May2006. https://www.
financialexpress.com/archive/madrasmaverick/97307/

Manghat, S. 'Details Of Cyrus Mistry's 5-Year Strategy That Ratan
Tata Rejected.' *Bloomberg Quint*. 22 December 2016. https://
www.bloombergquint.com/business/details-of-cyrus-mistrys-
5-year-strategy-that-ratan-tata-rejected#gs.6zzGX20

Manghat, S. 'The Mistrys Acquired Stake In Tata Sons From JRD
Tata's Siblings.' *Bloomberg Quint*. 17 January 2018. https://
www.bloombergquint.com/law-and-policy/the-mistrys-
acquired-stake-in-tata-sons-from-jrd-tatas-siblings#gs.
Il=g9zc

'Mistry's elephant.' *The Economist*. 24 September 2016. https://
www.economist.com/business/2016/09/24/mistrys-elephant.

'Mistry-Tata row: Brickwork Ratings downgrades Tata Steel.' *Times
of India*. 31 October 2016. https://timesofindia.indiatimes.
com/business/india-business/Mistry-Tata-row-Brickwork-
Ratings-downgrades-TataSteel/articleshow/55152576.cms?/

Mishra, L. 'We need to get on with our lives: Hussain.' *The Hindu*.
23 December 2016. https://www.thehindu.com/business/We-
need-to-get-on-with-our-lives-Hussain/article16933538.ece

Mohile, S. S. 'C Sivasankaran looks to settle DoCoMo issue with
Tata.' *Livemint*. 16 January 2017. https://www.livemint.com/
Companies/ FldSBiF8dWvBu6iJfnXGGO/C-Sivasankaran-
looks-to-settle-DoCoMo-issue-with-Tata-Sons.html/

Mohile, Shally Seth. 'Tata Trusts inducts Noel, Jehangir; Managing
Trustee Venkatramanan quits.' *Business Standard*. 14 February
2019. https://www.business-standard.com/article/companies/
tata-trusts-inducts-noel-jehangir-venkatarmanan-quits-as-
managing-trustee-119021301085_1.html

Mukherjee, R. 'Minority investors rush to be part of cos' mgmt.'
*Times of India*. 22 September 2017. https://timesofindia.
indiatimes.com/business/india-business/minority-investors-
rush-to-be-part-of-cos-mgmt/articleshow/60787117.cms/

'NTT DoCoMo Decides to Exercise Option for Sale of Stake in Tata Teleservices in India.' *NTT DoCoMo*. 25 April 2014. https://www. nttdocomo.co.jp/english/info/mediacenter/pr/2014/0425_00. html/

Panchal, S. 'Nusli Wadia removed as Tata Steel director through EGM vote.' *Forbes India*. 21 December 2016. http://www.forbesindia.com/ article/battle-at-bombay-house/tata-steel-shareholders-express- support-for-ratan-tata-at-egm/45191/1/

'FIPB clears Tata-AugustaWestland chopper facility proposal in Hyderabad.' 14 October 2015. https://economictimes. indiatimes.com/news/defence/fipb-clears-tata-agustawestland-chopper-facility-proposal-in-hyderabad/articleshow/49352943.cms

PTI. 'Tata Trusts appoints Vijay Singh, Venu Srinivasan as vice chairmen.' 13 December 2018, https://www.livemint.com/Companies/6aRNFXdfoPHDtHp8wO2mpO/Tata-Trusts-appoints-Vijay-Singh-Venu-Srinivasan-as-vice-ch.html.

Pocha, J. 'Tata Sons: Passing the Baton.' *Forbes India*. 12 December 2011. http://www.forbesindia.com/printcontent/31052

Pocha, J.S. 'Passing the Baton at Tata.' *Forbes*. 4 January 2012. https://www.forbes.com/2012/01/04/forbes-india-passing-the-baton-cyrus-mistry-appointment-ratan-tata-successor.html#348b8c286e62

'Ratan Tata personally asked Cyrus Mistry to resign before ouster.' *Livemint*. 9 January 2017. https://www.livemint.com/Companies/ZVWlxcSzsZ1fx832GlEGaM/Ratan-Tata-personally- asked-Cyrus-Mistry-to-resign-before-ou.html

'Ratan Tata: Shifting from Singur cost us heavily.' *The Hindu*. 6 August 2014, https://www.thehindubusinessline.com/companies/Ratan-Tata-Shifting-from-Singur-cost-us-heavily/article20837281.ece/

Ravi, A. B. 'Chairman Russi Mody learns a few lessons at TISCO

EGM.' *India Today*. 27 June 2013. https://www.indiatoday. in/magazine/ economy/story/19920131-chairman-russi-mody-learns-a-few- lessons-at-tisco-extraordinary-general-meeting-765735-2013-06-27/

Ray, S. and J. Dubey. 'All you wanted to know about Cyrus Mistry and his Shapoorji Pallonji Group.' *Hindustan Times*. 25 October 2016. https://www.hindustantimes. com/business-news/all-you-wanted- to-know-about-cyrus-mistry-and-his-shapoorji-pallonji-group/story-pJcwop4AesQyxVOWUcU8JJ.html/

Roy, D. 'Windfall for Ace Lawyers as Tata-Mistry Courtroom Battle Set to Prolong.' *News 18*. 26 October 2016. https://www. news18.com/news/business/windfall-for-ace-lawyers-as-tata-mistry-courtroom-battle-set-to-prolong-1305483.html/

Saxena, S. 'Tatas Get The Last Word As Their Battle With Mistry Concludes At NCLT.' *Bloomberg Quint*. 2 February 2018. https:// www.bloombergquint.com/law-and-policy/2018/02/02/tatas-get- the-last-word-as-their-battle-with-mistry-concludes-at-nclt#gs. RYceIkk/

'Shareholders voice support for Ratan Tata at Tata Motors EGM.' *Economic Times*. 23 December 2016. https:// economictimes.indiatimes.com/news/company/ corporate-trends/shareholders-voice-support-for-ratan-tata- at-tata-motors-egm/articleshow/56128828.cms/

Singh, R. 'Tata-Mistry battle: Why Cyrus's cousin Mehli evokes strong reactions from both sides.' *The Economic Times*. 21 November 2016, https://economictimes.indiatimes.com/ news/company/ corporate-trends/tata-mistry-battle-why-cyruss-cousin-mehli- evokes-strong-reactions-from-both-sides/articleshow/55531663

'Sly takeover of Air-India hurt JRD.' *Rediff.com*. 4 August 2004. http://www.rediff.com/money/2004/aug/04spec.htm/

Subramanian, N.S. 'Mehli Mistry's interests go beyond paints and

Tatas.' *Business Standard*. 21 November 2016. https://www.
business-standard.com/article/companies/mehli-mistry-s-
interests-go-beyond-paints-and-tatas-116112100830_1.
html/

'Tata-Pallonjitiesdatebackto1930.' *HindustanTimes*. 24
November 2011. https://www.hindustantimes.com/
business/tata-pallonji- ties-date-back-to-1930/story-
KWGIj7Cdxamn4vMjHSqA7L.html/

'The Tatas' flight story.' *Business Standard*. 20 February 2013.
https:// www.business-standard.com/article/companies/the-
tatas-flight- story-113022000585_1.html/

Vasudevan, N. 'Tata Group feud: Tata camp may hold the edge
in groupcompanies' EGMvote.' *Times of India*. 12 December
2016. https://timesofindia.indiatimes.com//business/india-
business/Tata-Group-feud-Tata-camp-may-hold-the-edge-
in- group-companies-EGMvote/articleshow/55934822.cms/

Vijayraghavan, Kala and Maulik Vyas. 'Trusts seek nominees to
Tata Sons board.' 31 March 2019. https://economictimes.
indiatimes.com/news/company/corporate-trends/trusts-
seeks-nominees-to-tata-sons-board/articleshow/68661043.
cms

Vyas, M. 'Who's who of the legal fraternity in the fray in Tata-
vs- Mistry battle.' *VC Circle*. 20 December 2016. https://
www.vccircle. com/who-s-who-legal-fraternity-fray-tata-
vs-mistry-battle/

## Web Links

http://www.valueabled.com/CFE/CFE Archives/A%20
Chronicle%20-%20JRD%20Tata.pdf

https://ir.airasia.com/news.html/id/646223

https://newsroom.airasia.com/news/2017/11/6/airasiagroup-
ceos-flying-high-autobiography-now-available-on-board-

all-airasia-flights?rq=autobiographyy/

https://www.outlookindia.com/website/story/air-india-the-niira-radia-tapes/278256/

https://www.rediff.com/business/report/a-year-of-renovation-later-tatas-hq-bombay-house-throws-its-doors-open/20180729.html.

https://www.youtube.com/watch?v=v16nH4cUp6M

https://www.vccircle.com/siva-redials-telecom-51-stake-s-tel-report/

http://cyrusforgovernance.com/

https://www.iiasadvisory. com/

https://www.uber.com/en-IN/blog/madhu-your-uber-is-arriving-now/

https://ir.airasia.com/newsroom/Press_Release_Indian_airline_JV.pdf/

https://www.youtube.com/watch?v= w0QpSRGa2Hc

https://www.youtube.com/watch?v=NZhz6kUIRUo

http://www.tata.com/media/ index/Media-room/

https://www.bseindia.com/xmldata/corpfiling/CorpAttachment//2016/11/4E24A052_5CE2_4173_8A0B_A8C6CCF5E692_081217.pdf

https://www.tatasteel.com/media/newsroom/press- releases/india/2007/funding-ofcorustransaction/

http://www.mca.gov.in/Ministry/pdf/ CompaniesAct2013.pdf

https://www.airvistara.com/trip/company-info/

https://www.youtube.com/watchv=dIumluXFmY

https://www.youtube.com/watchv=w0QpSRGa2Hc/

https://www.facebook.com/zeebusinessnline/videos/exclusive:-'cyrusmistry-was-asked/1293670613978106/

https://www.youtube.com/watch?v=v16nH4cUp6M

## Court Filings

Company Petition No. 82(MB)/2016. Cyrus Investments Pvt Ltd and Sterling Investment Corporation Pvt Ltd versus Tata Sons Ltd, Ratan N Tata, Amit Ranbir Chandra, Ishaat Hussain, Ajay Gopikisan Piramal, Venu Srinivasan, Nitin Nohria, Ranendra Sen, Vijay Singh, Farida Dara Khambata, Cyrus Pallonji Mistry, Ralf Speth, N. Chandrasekaran, N.A. Soonawala, J.N. Tata, K.B. Dadiseth, R.K. Krishna Kumar, S.K. Bharucha, N.M. Munjee, R. Venkatramanan, Dr Amrita Patel, V.R. Mehta, and F.N. Subedar.

Affidavit in Response to Company Petition No 82 of 2016 by Respondent 11.

Reply to The Petition On Behalf Of Tata Sons Limited- Respondent No. 1.

Affidavit of Respondent No. 14, Mr Noshir A. Soonawala in Reply to Affidavit in Reply of Respondent 11.

Affidavit of Mr Noshir A. Soonawala Respondent No.14, in Reply to the Petition.

Reply on Behalf of Tata Sons Ltd, Respondent No. 1 to The Affidavit in Reply of Mr Cyrus Mistry, Respondent No. 11

Affidavit of Mr Bharat D. Vasani.

Affidavit of Ramachandran Venkataramanan, Respondent No. 20 In Reply to the Affidavit in Reply Dated 29 December 2016 Filed by Respondent No. 11.

Affidavit of Ramachandran Venkataramanan, Respondent No. 20, in Reply to the above Petition.

Affidavit in Reply of Mr Ratan Tata, Respondent No. 2, in Response to The Affidavit in Reply of Mr Cyrus Mistry, Respondent No. 11.

Affidavit in Reply on Behalf Of Mr Ratan N. Tata, Respondent no. 2, in Response to the Petition.

Affidavit in Reply to the Petition on Behalf of Amit Ranbir Chandra, Respondent No. 3.

Affidavit in Reply to The Petition on Behalf of Mr Nitin Nohria, Respondent No. 3.

Affidavit of Cyrus P. Mistry, Respondent No. 1,1 in Response to thee Reply of Tata Sons Ltd, Respondent No. I.

Affidavit of Cyrus P. Mistry, Respondent No. 11, in Response to the Reply of Mr Ratan N. Tata, Respondent No. 2.

Affi davit of Cyrus P. Mistry, Respondent No. 11, in Response to the Reply of Noshir A. Soona Wala, Respondent No. 14.

Affidavit by the Petitioners in Rejoinder to the Reply Filed by the Respondent No. 1 to the Petition.

Affidavit in Rejoinder on Behalf of the Petitioners to the Affidavit in Reply of Respondent No. 2.

NCLT Mumbai Order, 9 July 2018.

## Correspondence and Other Documents

Memorandum and Articles of Association of Tata Sons, 2017 Ministry of Corporate Affairs. http://www.mca.gov.in/

Memorandum and Articles of Association of Tata Sons, 1917, 1954, 1958, 1993, 2014.

Term sheet of preferential share offer of Tata Teleservices to Sterling Infotech, 23 December 2005.

Minutes of meeting of board of directors of Tata Sons Ltd, 18 October 2006.

Minutes of meeting of board of directors of Tata Sons Ltd, 3 May 2007.

Minutes of meeting of board of directors of Tata Sons Ltd, 14 August 2007.

Minutes of meeting of board of directors of Tata Sons Ltd, 15 June 2010.

Minutes of meeting of board of directors of Tata Sons Ltd, 23 November 2011.

Minutes of meeting of board of directors of Tata Sons Ltd, 6 December 2012.

Minutes of meeting of board of directors of Tata Sons Ltd, 18 December 2012.

Minutes of meeting of board of directors of Tata Sons Ltd, 21 October 2013.

Minutes of third meeting of board of directors of Tata Sons Ltd for FY 20016–17, 29 June 2016.

Minutes of sixth meeting of board of directors of Tata Sons Ltd for FY 20016–17, 24 October, 2016.

Minutes of meeting of board of directors of Tata Steel Ltd, 20 October 2006, 30 October 2006, 23 November 2006, 9 May 2007.

Minutes of meeting of board of directors of Tata Global Beverages Ltd, 15 November 2016.

Draft: Decision Making at the Tata Group Apex Level, 15 May 2016.

Board meeting minutes extracts of several PIEM, IHCL meetings including 15 April 2009, 4 May 2012, 8 February 2013, 7 November 2013, 6 May 2014.

Draft minutes of the first meeting of the nomination and remuneration committee of directors of Tata Sons Ltd for FY 2016–17, 28 June 2016.

Tata Consultancy Services, ISS Proxy Analysis and Benchmark Policy Voting Recommendations Report, 2 December 2016.

Letter from Ratan Tata to Cyrus Mistry, April 12 2012, 12 February 2013 (exchange), 14 March 2013, 24 June 2013, 24 September 2013 (exchange), 29 January 2014, 1 July 2014, 19 August 2014 (series of exchanges to August 22 2014), 6 November 2014 (exchange), 30 January 2015, 3 April 2015, 28 May 2015, 18 January 2016 (exchange including between

Trusts and Tata officials), 16 September 2015 (exchange), 2 February 2016 (exchange), 5 April 2016 (exchange), 28 July 2016, 3 October 2016.

Letter from Cyrus Mistry to Ratan Tata, 20 August 2014 (series of exchanges to August 22 2014), 4 February 2015, 31 August 2015, 2 September 2015, 2 February 2016, 7 April 2016 (exchange), 17 March 2016, 5 May 2016 (exchange), 15 May 2016, 30 May 2016 (exchange), 15 June 2016 (sent also to others), 20 June 2016, 24 June 2016, 21 July 2016, 23 September 2016 (with attachments).

Letter from Cyrus Mistry to Amit Chandra, Ajay Piramal, Venu Srinivasan, 20 September 2016.

Letter from Cyrus Mistry to Tata Sons board of directors, 25 October 2016.

Letter from Cyrus Mistry to selection committee, 4 October 2010.

Letter from Noshir Soonawala to Cyrus Mistry, 16 February 2015 (exchanges till February 18), 4 December 2015, 15 January 2016, 20 July 2016, 25 July 2016 (exchange),14 October 2016.

Letter from Cyrus Mistry to Noshir Soonawala, 4 January 2016.

Letter from Noshir Soonawala to Bharat Vasani, 18 May 2015.

Letter from F.N. Subedar to Cyrus Mistry 8 November 2013, 30 April 2014 (exchange), 12 February 2015, 17 November 2015, 24 January 2016, 28 September 2016.

Letter from Bharat Vasani to Cyrus Mistry 9 September 2013, 1 February 2015, 5 May 2015, 16 May 2015 (sent along with S. Ramadorai, also marked to Ratan Tata), 20 September 2016, 5 October 2016.

Letter from Bharat Vasani to F.N. Subedar, 27 June 2015, 23 January 2016, 24 January 2016.

Cyrus Mistry's Representation to shareholders, 20 December 2016.

Cyrus Mistry's Representation to IHCL shareholders, 13 November 2016.

Nusli Wadia's Representation to shareholders of Tata Steel, 12 December 2016.

Nusli Wadia's Representation to shareholders of Tata Motors, 12 December 2016.

Sundaresan, Somasekhar, Tata Sons – Opinion on governance aspects, 26 September 2016.

Letter from C. Sivasankaran to Cyrus Mistry, 3 October 2013 (exchange), 24 November 2014.

Aide-memoire: Siva group investment in TTSL, 3 October 2013.

Aide Memoire of discussions held on 13 July 2016 regarding Tata Power's proposed Investment Platform.

Circular No 19: Removal of chairman of the board of directors of Tata Steel Ltd, 25 November 2016.

Letter from Tata Sons to ILFS Trust Company Ltd. 24 February 2006.

Letter from Mehli Mistry to S Padmanabhan, 4 May 2013.

Ratan Tata's Representation to shareholders, 7 December 2016.

Tata Strategy 2025, 1 April 2015.

Tata Sons press release, 24 October 2016, 25 October 2016, 27 October 2016, 4 November 2016, 10 November 2016, 13 November 2016, 5 December 2016, 19 December 2016, 20 December 2016.

Tata Steel press release, 23 November 2012, 29 March 2016, 12 July 2016.

Stock Exchange Announcements: Tata Steel, 20 October 2006, Tata Steel, 11 December 2006, Tata Steel, 31 January 2007, Tata Steel, 8 March 2007. Tata Steel, 2 April 2007. Tata Chemical, 10 November 2016. Tata Motors 14 November 2016.

juggernaut

# THE APP FOR INDIAN READERS

*Fresh, original books tailored for mobile and for India. Starting at ₹10.*

**juggernaut.in**

# CRAFTED
# FOR MOBILE
# READING

*Thought you would never read a book
on mobile? Let us prove you wrong.*

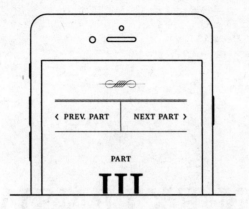

## Beautiful Typography

The quality of print transferred
to your mobile. Forget ugly PDFs.

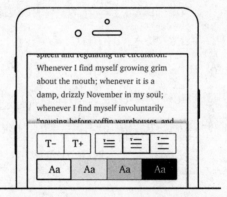

## Customizable Reading

Read in the font size, spacing
and background of your liking.

# AN EXTENSIVE LIBRARY

*Including fresh, new, original Juggernaut books from the likes of Sunny Leone, Praveen Swami, Husain Haqqani, Umera Ahmed, Rujuta Diwekar and lots more. Plus, books from partner publishers and loads of free classics. Whichever genre you like, there's a book waiting for you.*

# DON'T JUST READ; INTERACT

*We're changing the reading experience from passive to active.*

# Ask authors questions

Get all your answers from the horse's mouth.
Juggernaut authors actually reply to every
question they can.

---

# Rate and review

Let everyone know of your favourite reads or
critique the finer points of a book – you will be
heard in a community of like-minded readers.

---

# Gift books to friends

For a book-lover, there's no nicer gift than
a book personally picked. You can even
do it anonymously if you like.

---

# Enjoy new book formats

Discover serials released in parts over
time, picture books including comics,
and story-bundles at discounted rates.
And coming soon, audiobooks.

# 4

# LOWEST PRICES & ONE-TAP BUYING

*Books start at ₹10 with regular discounts and free previews.*

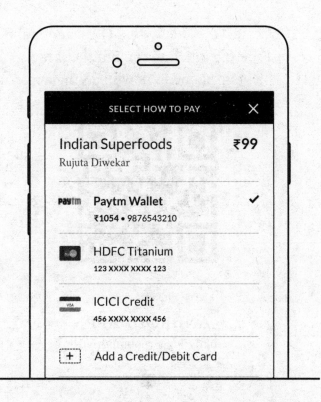

# Paytm Wallet, Cards & Apple Payments

On Android, just add a Paytm Wallet once and
buy any book with one tap. On iOS, pay with one
tap with your iTunes-linked debit/credit card.

Click the QR Code with a QR scanner app
or type the link into the Internet browser
on your phone to download the app.

## ANDROID APP
bit.ly/juggernautandroid

## iOS APP
bit.ly/juggernautios

For our complete catalogue, visit www.juggernaut.in
To submit your book, send a synopsis and two
sample chapters to books@juggernaut.in
For all other queries, write to contact@juggernaut.in